The Greatest Minor League

The Greatest Minor League

A History of the Pacific Coast League,
1903–1957

DENNIS SNELLING

McFarland & Company, Inc., Publishers
Jefferson, North Carolina, and London

LIBRARY OF CONGRESS CATALOGUING-IN-PUBLICATION DATA

Snelling, Dennis, 1958–
The greatest minor league : a history of the Pacific
Coast League, 1903–1957 / Dennis Snelling.
p.   cm.
Includes bibliographical references and index.

ISBN 978-0-7864-6524-8
illustrated case : 50# alkaline paper ∞

1. Pacific Coast League — History — 20th century.
2. Minor league baseball — West (U.S.) — History — 20th century.
3. Baseball — Pacific States — History — 20th century.
I. Title.
GV875.P33S52   2012   796.357′640979 — dc23   2011035280

BRITISH LIBRARY CATALOGUING DATA ARE AVAILABLE

Front cover: 1904 Pacific Coast League Champion Tacoma Tigers
(photograph courtesy of Marc H. Blau); design by
David K. Landis (Shake It Loose Graphics)

Manufactured in the United States of America

*McFarland & Company, Inc., Publishers
Box 611, Jefferson, North Carolina 28640
www.mcfarlandpub.com*

To all those who played in the Pacific Coast League,
who supported those chasing their dreams,
and those who watched, rooted, reported and
worked for the league.

And to my son, Connor, whom I love very much

Table of Contents

Preface

In 1903, a small baseball league in California defied Organized Baseball and added teams in Portland and Seattle to become, as the American League had three years earlier, an outlaw organization. Calling itself the Pacific Coast League, its expansion at the expense of the existing Pacific Northwest League created the strongest minor league of the twentieth century; it would challenge the authority of Organized Baseball for more than five decades. This new league, operating in cities that hugged the Pacific Ocean, with two mountain ranges and the Great Plains separating it from the National and American leagues, would reflect the rigid independence of those that had originally settled the region.

By the time the Pacific Coast League was established, big league teams had already recognized the money to be made in California, having regularly barnstormed the region since the 1880s. Many teams spent spring training there each winter. The Pacific Coast League grew in wealth and influence in the 1920s and 1930s — its franchises signed most of their own players and the quality of play was the best outside of the majors.

Indeed, prior to 1958, baseball fans living on the West Coast considered the Pacific Coast League to be *their* major league. Instead of the Yankees, Dodgers and Cardinals, youngsters rooted for the San Francisco Seals, the Los Angeles Angels and the Oakland Oaks. Thanks to geography, the league remained outside the direct sphere of influence of the major leagues. Franchises in the other top minor leagues, the American Association and the International League, operated in the shadows of major league cities and could not even pretend to have the aspirations of the teams on the West Coast.

The Pacific Coast League shattered all minor league attendance records. Its teams frequently outdrew major league franchises year after year, especially in relation to the population of its represented cities. Players repeatedly spurned offers to play in the major leagues because they wanted to remain in the PCL. For a time, it appeared that the Pacific Coast League might become baseball's third major league.

Before it was relegated in the 1960s to the role of farm system for the established major leagues, the Pacific Coast League was unlike any other minor league in the history of the game. The schedule was longer — many seasons stretched for more than two hundred games. The players were older — many were major league veterans who knew how to play the game. And they cared about winning — the rivalry between the Los Angeles Angels and Hollywood Stars was without equal anywhere. No college or professional sports rivals played with more fire and intensity than those two minor league baseball teams did during the 1940s and 1950s.

And there were the players. The Pacific Coast League introduced the world to Joe, Vince and Dom DiMaggio, Paul and Lloyd Waner, Ted Williams, Tony Lazzeri, Lefty O'Doul, Mickey Cochrane, Bobby Doerr, Gavvy Cravath, Larry Jansen, Ferris Fain, Hal

Chase, Frank Crosetti, Jackie Jensen, Harry Heilmann, Billy Martin, Dolph Camilli, Cookie Lavagetto, Joe Gordon, Ernie Lombardi, Lefty Gomez, Earl Averill, Babe Herman and numerous other baseball stars, all of whom were signed originally by PCL teams.

The PCL was a league that early on recognized the value of entertainment, from Jim Morley's marriage of a ballpark with an amusement park to the antics of Happy Hogan, who always wanted to give the fans a show, and on through various "clowns," such as Carl Sawyer, Billy Schuster, Chet Johnson, Bud Beasley, Walter Mails and Jackie Price. The league also had, and has, an unusual attachment among its fans and its players. Those who appeared in the league invariably enjoyed it thanks to the easy travel, great weather and week-long series that allowed a player to unpack his bags and enjoy some beautiful and hospitable cities. Of course, if the opposing team was on a hot streak, it could be a long week — and a dispute on Tuesday could develop into a full-fledged war by Sunday.

This book aims to tell the story of the Pacific Coast League, its major personalities and relationships, the governance of the league, and the interrelationship between the minor and major leagues. It is a story of a constant battle — the majors desirous of keeping the Pacific Coast League subservient, plucking its best talent and siphoning customers through an invasion of territory via radio, tryout schools, exhibition games, televised regular-season games, and then finally the relocation of existing franchises into the league's two largest cities.

The history of baseball involves far more than what happened in the American and National leagues. The growth and development of the game as a business, the evolution of scouting, the emergence of the international game, the Black Sox scandal — these are topics that cannot be understood completely without including the perspective of the minor leagues, and particularly that of the Pacific Coast League, the most important and charismatic of those "minors."

When I completed my first book on the league, *The Pacific Coast League: A Statistical History, 1903–1957*, I thought it would serve as a companion to this book. Little did I realize it would take more than fifteen years for this second book to be completed.

No book on a subject of this magnitude, covering half a century of baseball on the West Coast, is accomplished without plenty of assistance. This help came over the course of nearly two decades.

I conducted more than sixty interviews, most occurring between 1991 and 1995 and between 2009 and 2010. Unfortunately, many of these individuals are no longer with us. In addition to former Pacific Coast League players, interview subjects included sportswriters Bob Hunter and Bill Conlin, legendary *Oakland Tribune* cartoonist Lee Susman and San Francisco Seals broadcaster and "Little Corporation" member Don Klein. A complete list of interview subjects can be found in the back of the book. I sincerely want to thank everyone who took the time to talk to me.

The staff of the History Room of the San Francisco Library, especially Christina Moretta, was particularly helpful in locating photographs. So was Frank Kern of the Hall of Champions in San Diego; Brandon Standafer was helpful in gaining permissions from that same collection. Cathy Brovia generously allowed me to use a photograph of her husband, Joe, for this book. She has always been gracious, as was Joe before his passing in 1994.

Joe Hoppel of *The Sporting News* generously provided access to the contents of that publication's clip files for dozens of players. The staff at the library of the National Baseball Hall of Fame was always responsive to requests, providing an entire run of league statistics from the *Reach* and *Spalding Guides* as well as photographs and articles from their player files. John Horne was always quick to respond to my queries.

Although the Internet provides access to a number of newspapers, most remain available only through more laborious means. I made numerous visits to microform rooms of the San Francisco Library, the Bancroft Library at the University of California, Berkeley, the Stanislaus County Library in Modesto, California, the California State Library at both Sacramento and West Sacramento, the San Diego State University Library, and the Lied Library at the University of Nevada, Las Vegas. I want to make a special note of the tremendous courtesy and professionalism of the staff in the Microform Room at the San Diego Public Library, who were always especially helpful during my visits there.

Frank Dasso generously provided me his newspaper clippings and an unpublished autobiographical sketch. Don Klein provided copies of pages from San Francisco Seals yearbooks. Joe and Cathy Brovia also provided newspaper clippings and photographs from Joe's career. Bernice Hittle was very helpful in my interview with her husband and shared some insightful recollections of life as a baseball wife. Jim Zinn, Jr., shared memories of his father and sent along a photograph of several of the San Francisco Seals.

The staff at the Utah History Resource Center provided information on the ballparks in Salt Lake City, including diagrams and an explanatory history of the sports facilities located there. Joy Werlink of the Washington State Historical Society was extremely helpful in providing material from their files on the Seattle Rainiers, which included correspondence and meeting minutes of that team's board of directors. The staff at the North Hayes Research Library of the California Historical Society in San Francisco was of great assistance during my visit to review the league president records and other correspondence from the Dick Dobbins Collection on the Pacific Coast League. I had the pleasure of briefly meeting Mr. Dobbins on a couple of occasions and he was always a positive and supportive individual. His collection and research on the Pacific Coast League are invaluable resources. He passed away far too soon.

Several people helped review the manuscript. Jim Norby deserves special mention for reading the entire book and providing invaluable feedback and insights. Jim Enochs assisted in the early stages and helped me develop my ultimate approach to this subject. John Spalding, noted baseball historian and author of *Always on Sunday* and *Senators and Solons*, among other books, reviewed the first three chapters of the book and provided guidance and corrections.

David Eskenazi of Seattle, Washington, deserves special mention for allowing me access to his amazing collection of photographs and ephemera. He also provided some insight into the early history of the game in Seattle. Ray Saraceni also provided photographs from his extensive collection; I cannot adequately express my thanks to both David and Ray for their invaluable assistance to this project. They are doing an incredible job of preserving the league's history. Marc Blau of the State of Washington Sports Hall of Fame in Puyallup provided a great photo of the 1904 Tacoma Tigers.

Of course, I would be remiss without thanking my wife, who helped track down photographs and set up some of the interviews, and my children, who allowed me the time and opportunity to pursue this project. It would have been impossible to complete this book without their help and support.

It is difficult to cover a subject of this size within a reasonable length. There are many details and stories I wish had made the final cut — but I guess those are for another book.

CHAPTER ONE

Before the PCL:
From the Gold Rush to 1900

The crowd began congregating on a gray, drizzly December morning in 1890 at San Francisco's Clay Street Wharf. Bracing themselves against the cold wind and brisk dampness of the seafront, people from all walks of society had assembled in response to the arrival of the U.S. Navy flagship *Charleston,* which sat anchored in the bay. Undaunted by the dreary weather, the throng waited patiently in the hope of catching a glimpse of the *Charleston* and its famous passenger, David Kalakaua, the King of Hawaii. The King disembarked at fifteen minutes to four o'clock in the afternoon and, accompanied by Admiral George Brown, boarded a twelve-oar barge that rowed him ashore. Shouts went up as royal salutes were fired from other ships in the harbor, and smoke enveloped the entire scene. Emerging from the smokescreen, the barge reached the gangplank and the coxswain shouted, "Way enough! Toss oars!" King Kalakaua, cutting an impressive figure in his Prince Albert coat and a black, chimney pot hat, stepped onto the wharf and was greeted warmly by General John Gibbon and the Fourth United States Cavalry. The King acknowledged his crowd of admirers and was escorted to one of twelve carriages waiting to transport the dignitaries up Market Street to the Palace Hotel.[1]

Numerous events were held in the King's honor, including an all-star baseball game staged five days before Christmas at Haight Street Grounds between a team of native Californians who played in the eastern professional leagues and a group of locals from the California State League.[2] The King, whose attendance made him the first monarch to attend a baseball game on American soil, was quite familiar with the sport thanks to his financial advisor, Alexander Cartwright — the same Alexander Cartwright often credited with creating the modern game. The King's presence was a measure of how far Cartwright's favorite game had progressed.

The story goes that baseball was introduced in the West during Cartwright's journey to California via wagon train during the Gold Rush. Whether true or not, it is almost certain that he or some other veteran of East Coast "base ball" planted the seed, and by the early 1850s there were accounts of people playing "town ball" in the streets of San Francisco.[3] Cartwright did not linger, instead sailing on to Hawaii where he sent for his family and became a prominent citizen. By the time of his death in 1892, Cartwright's connection to baseball was forgotten, even in his native New York. Nearly a half-century would pass before the ex-bank clerk/volunteer fireman and his Knickerbockers teammates received credit for their contributions to the game. By that point, the Abner Doubleday myth was entrenched and Cooperstown had the Baseball Hall of Fame.

Although Cartwright may have been forgotten, the game he promoted was not. It developed, thrived and spread everywhere, including the West. Teams were soon being established all over California, although they initially functioned as social clubs requiring little physical activity beyond drinking and exaggerated storytelling. That began to change by 1860 when players from Sacramento and San Francisco met in a state championship series. The San Francisco team, the Eagles, captured the prize — a silver ball engraved "For The Best Base Ball Playing, September 25, 1860."[4]

The region's interest in baseball accelerated during the next decade and an enclosed park, Recreation Grounds, was built in San Francisco at 25th and Folsom. Umpire De Witt Van Court, reminiscing more than four decades later, stated that the ballpark, which opened in 1868, had an excellent adobe soil infield he remembered being "level as a billiard table."[5] The year after it opened, Recreation Grounds hosted the first all-professional baseball team, the Cincinnati Red Stockings, who were taking on all comers while touring the nation thanks to the opening of the Transcontinental Railroad.

It was not long before the best teams in the area wanted to play against each other on a regular basis. The Pacific League, consisting entirely of teams in San Francisco, was formed in 1878, followed by the California League a year later. Players were semi-professional, taking the field on weekends while maintaining regular jobs. There was no set schedule; teams often challenged each other to match play throughout the year based on mutual interest and the potential for selling tickets. Both scoring and errors were plentiful since players did not wear gloves.

The leagues became more organized and other ballparks were built, with the two most substantial facilities located in San Francisco. Central Park at Eighth and Market streets was an intimate venue that seated several thousand. Small shops on the Market Street side of the property buffered the park from the busy thoroughfare.

Haight Street Grounds, the site of the contest attended by King Kalakaua, was at Waller and Stanyan streets, across from Golden Gate Park.[6] The Southern Pacific Railroad leased the field, and company president Charles Crocker had a private box. It was a popular ballpark capable of handling large crowds, which were not at all unusual. Despite cold weather and the threat of rain, twenty thousand people attended a game in November 1887 that featured the New York Giants versus Greenhood & Moran, a talented Oakland-based team operated by a pair of clothiers.[7]

As players started to reap adulation and notoriety because of those crowds, egos and prima donna attitudes began to manifest themselves.

At one point, Pioneers outfielder Hen

In December 1890, King David Kalakaua of Hawaii became the first monarch to witness a baseball game on American soil when he attended a game at Haight Street Grounds in San Francisco (courtesy of KJR).

One of the first great teams in Northern California, Greenhood & Moran, held its own against major league teams that barnstormed each winter and sent several players to the major leagues. Pictured left to right are (back row) Tom McCord, Fred Lange and George Fisher; (middle row) George Van Haltren (who starred many years for the New York Giants), George Borchers (a talented but notoriously troubled pitcher who played for the Chicago Colts in 1888), manager Tom Robinson, Billy Smalley (who played for Cleveland and Washington before dying from stomach cancer at age 20) and Jack Ryan; (front row) James A. McDonald and Danny Long (who briefly played for Baltimore in the major league American Association and would manage the San Francisco Seals for Cal Ewing from 1907 to 1914) (Oakland History Room, Oakland Public Library).

Moore became angry at a teammate and refused to catch fly balls. California League president John Mone witnessed the spectacle of Moore crossing his arms, standing as if awaiting a subway car while a ball struck the ground and bounced away. Mone immediately suspended him.[8]

One of the more controversial incidents in California professional baseball during the 1880s involved pitcher Jimmy Mullee. A member of the Stars in the California League, Mullee was valued for his ability to defeat the powerful Haverly team. The Stars were playing against Haverly at the Alameda Grounds on May 2, 1886, and Mullee seemed to give almost no effort in a 13–0 loss.[9] Many believed Mullee had thrown the game. He responded to the accusation by writing to several San Francisco newspapers, apologizing for his actions and offering the interesting explanation that he had become disgusted with the lack of effort made by his teammates, who committed fourteen errors in the game (compared to two by Haverly) and collected only two base hits. He decided if they would not try, neither would he. Mullee also claimed the reason for the poor play of his teammates was because unnamed individuals were trying to ruin the Stars so the team could be reorganized. The Stars *were* disbanded in the wake of the scandal and the California League blacklisted Mullee. Greenhood & Moran was enlisted to replace the Stars.[10] Despite the threat of legal action, Mullee joined the rival California State League to pitch for the Californias.

In the second inning of Mullee's first game with his new team, the umpire called time and handed him a gold medallion featuring the likeness of a pitcher on the front and "a big, sparkling diamond" on the reverse, surrounded by the inscription "Presented to James Mullee by his many friends as a recognition of his faithful service as a pitcher."[11] Whether Mullee was being rewarded for foiling a scandal, jumping leagues or simply throwing a game was a matter of debate for a long time.

For their part, fans often displayed boorish behavior bordering on criminal. The same day Mone banished Hen Moore, a team called the Altas was hosting Haverly in Sacramento and umpire Al Foreman made several calls detrimental to the home team. After the game a group of disgruntled rooters chased Foreman, who retreated to a trolley car full of Haverly players. The car was pelted with stones, one hitting the driver and another striking Haverly catcher Lou Hardie below his right eye. The *Sacramento Bee* pointed out that the umpire's calls had no effect on the outcome of the game and called the episode "a cowardly, disgraceful proceeding."[12] The incident was not unique.

* * *

As players became more accomplished and the fan base increased, opportunities for athletes to become full-time professionals increased as well. Local stars began to develop, such as Andy Piercy, the first native-born Californian to play in the eastern major leagues, and Billy Incell, star pitcher for Haverly of San Francisco, winner of four straight California League championships in the 1880s.[13]

Occasionally, holdout and/or disgraced players from the eastern leagues ventured to California to play, far from the clutches of Organized Baseball. This group included Edward "The Only" Nolan, the first curveball pitcher seen on the Coast, as well as James "Pud" Galvin, who would win more than 360 games in the major leagues and earn induction into the Baseball Hall of Fame. Galvin pitched a month for San Francisco's Athletics in 1880 during a contract dispute with Buffalo of the National League. He finally agreed to terms in June and returned east.

The Athletics replaced Galvin with Jim Devlin, the disgraced Louisville pitcher who had been kicked out of the major leagues in 1877, along with three teammates, for throwing baseball games in the National League's first major scandal. The San Francisco press ignored Devlin's past, characterizing it as a "misunderstanding" while noting that he had not pitched in two years. Devlin made his debut with the Athletics on July 4, defeating the Knickerbockers, 2–1, before a large crowd.[14]

As the quality of play improved, local stars began attracting offers from eastern teams. Among the most prominent early West Coast players to appear in the major leagues were third baseman Jerry Denny, outfielders George Van Haltren, Jimmy Fogarty and Bill Lange, pitchers "Grasshopper" Whitney and Charles Sweeney, and the Pittsburgh battery of Edward "Cannonball" Morris and Fred Carroll.

Van Haltren starred for the New York Giants for many years and retired with more than 2,500 hits as a major leaguer. Fogarty, a native San Franciscan and Haverly star, was an excellent center fielder for Philadelphia and toured with Albert Spalding's all-star team that circled the globe in the winter of 1888, a group that dined with King Kalakaua during a stop in Hawaii. (It is not known whether Albert Spalding and Alexander Cartwright met

George Van Haltren was a star center fielder for the New York Giants during the 1890s. He left the major leagues after the 1903 season with a lifetime batting average of .316, a total of 2,544 career base hits and 583 stolen bases. He then played in the Pacific Coast League from 1904 to 1909 before retiring at age 43 (National Baseball Hall of Fame Library, Cooperstown, New York).

on that occasion, but it is interesting to speculate.)[15] The best of the players to come out of California were Charles Sweeney and Bill Lange. Hall of Famer Tim Keefe rated Sweeney as the best pitcher he had ever seen.[16] He was also certainly among the most troubled. In the 1880s no one threw harder or a more wicked curveball — or displayed a more wicked temper. In 1883, the twenty-year-old Sweeney quit his California League team ... in the middle of a game.[17] Immediately jumping to the Providence Grays in the National League, Sweeney was united with West Coast veterans Sandy Nava and Jerry Denny, with Nava becoming Sweeney's favorite catcher.[18] The brash Californian soon became the second pitcher for the Grays, behind "Old Hoss" Radbourn, winner of a league-leading forty-eight games.

The next season, Sweeney used his baffling curveball to set a record with nineteen strikeouts against Boston.[19] Six weeks later he baffled his own team, stalking off the field when asked to move to the outfield for the last two innings of a game — a repeat of his tantrum in California the year before.[20] Sweeney immediately abandoned Providence for St. Louis of the Union Association and finished out the year.[21] Despite a great season, batting .307 in addition to winning a total of forty-one games, Sweeney's career began a downward spiral due to his temper, alcoholism and arm problems that continually plagued him. Sweeney's combustible nature eventually led to an off-field incident during which he killed a man and received an eight-year prison sentence at San Quentin.[22]

Bill Lange was at the other end of the personality spectrum from Sweeney. A native San Franciscan whose father was sergeant of the commissary at the Presidio, Lange ran away from home as a teenager to live with his brother in Port Townsend, Washington. He played amateur ball there before turning professional in 1892, first with Seattle until that team folded and then with Oakland in the California League. Along the way he grew to a height of 6′2″ and, despite weighing two hundred pounds, was one of the fastest men in the game. Lange attracted attention from eastern teams and was signed by Chicago for the 1893 season, quickly emerging as a fan favorite. An excellent defensive center fielder — considered by those that had seen him play as the equal of Ty Cobb and Tris Speaker — Lange hit .330 in his major league career, including a mark of .389 in 1895. He was described as "a bundle of springs in activity, with the power of a steam engine and the speed of a greyhound. He makes every play as if his life depended on it, and the next moment, when the play is accomplished and the crowd is cheering, he is again the careless, laughing, overgrown boy."[23] When John McGraw took his National League champion Baltimore Orioles on a tour of Europe in 1896, he invited Lange to participate, the only non–Oriole so honored. Lange would play only three more years, retiring at age twenty-eight in order to marry San Francisco socialite Grace Giselman and pursue real estate and insurance ventures in California with her father.[24]

At the dawn of the 1890s, the professional rather than the amateur was becoming dominant in baseball. Players traded on their celebrity as the game increased in popularity, supplementing their income through product endorsements or appearances on the vaudeville circuit, re-enacting famous feats or taking part in short stage sketches revolving around the game or their notoriety. Al Reach and Albert Spalding, who were among the first professional baseball players, entered the sporting goods business; Spalding in 1876, Reach a year later. Both were extremely successful, first selling baseballs and later branching into all manner of sports equipment. Spalding bought Reach's retail business in 1889 but the latter company continued manufacturing baseballs for decades.[25]

* * *

Ironically, one of the most famous West Coast baseball figures was entirely fictional. De Wolf Hopper, a featured actor in a theatrical troupe in New York City, was a rabid baseball fan. In the summer of 1888, Hopper and the rest of the company were performing the comic opera *Prince Methusalem* at the Wallack Theatre on Thirtieth Street and Broadway in New York, only a quarter-mile from the spot where Alexander Cartwright and the Knickerbockers played a version of baseball prior to their formulating the rules for the modern game. Aware that company manager John McCaull hated the sport, Hopper began regularly altering verses in songs to include references to baseball as a way of needling his boss, especially when Hopper knew McCaull would be at a performance. Audiences were in on the joke and always laughed.[26]

On August 14, *Prince Methusalem* was staged before an audience that included members of the New York Giants and Chicago White Stockings. The theatre company had attended a game between the teams at the invitation of Giants manager Jim Mutrie. As a tribute, Hopper decided to recite a comic poem given to him by novelist Archie Gunter, who had clipped it from the *San Francisco Examiner*.[27] Entitled "Casey at the Bat," it was an instant smash.[28] Hopper became forever identified with the fictional slugger, and it made him world famous. By the time of his death in 1935, Hopper had performed the act more than ten thousand times, even playing the title role in a 1916 silent film.[29]

Ernest Thayer was the unlikely creator of "The Mighty Casey" and would not be identified as author of the piece until several years after Hopper's first performance of it. A graduate of Harvard who excelled at the university despite problems with his hearing, Thayer was editor of the *Harvard Lampoon* and wrote the Hasty Pudding Play in his senior year. One of his friends and classmates was William Randolph Hearst. Following graduation, Thayer went to work for one of Hearst's newspapers, the *San Francisco Examiner,* writing a number of comic ballads under the name "Phin" (short for Phineas, his nickname at the university). One of the last he submitted was "Casey." A student of classical literature, Thayer did not exactly consider his poem in the class of the *Iliad* and was in fact a little embarrassed by it. Despite its instant success, he did not embrace "Casey" until late in life and refused to take any royalties.

Questions remain about the poem's inspiration. Although Thayer insisted there was no real-life basis for the story, many have noted that Stockton had a team in the California League and was often called "Mudville" because of the swampy conditions around the inland seaport. Several Stockton players had names very similar to those in the poem and Thayer saw the team play when he was in California.

Hopper and Thayer met once, after one of Hopper's performances in Thayer's hometown, Worcester, Massachusetts. Of meeting the author and asking him to recite the poem, Hopper recalled, "He was the most charming of men, but ... inclined to deafness and, like most persons so afflicted, very soft spoken. He had, too, at that time a decided Harvard accent. I have heard many another give *Casey* ... but Thayer's was the worst of all. In a sweet, dulcet Harvard whisper he implored *Casey* to murder the umpire, and gave this cry of mass animal rage all the emphasis of a caterpillar wearing rubbers crawling on a velvet carpet. He was rotten."[30]

* * *

The California League continued through the 1880s as a weekend league based exclusively in Northern California, with teams in San Francisco, Oakland, Sacramento and Stockton, before lengthening its schedule in 1890.

It was not long before dreams of incorporating teams from the Pacific Northwest to create a strong regional league took hold. Henry Harris, California League secretary and owner of the San Francisco team, was the first to propose a "Pacific Coast League" by adding Los Angeles and consolidating other California League cities with those in the two-year-old Pacific Northwest League.[31] Although Los Angeles remained in the league, Harris's scheme to add teams in Washington and Oregon fell through, largely because special fares could not be negotiated with the Southern Pacific Railroad.

Even though the proposal died, talk of expansion was evidence that, as in California, baseball in the Northwest was beginning to thrive. Portland had a long history with the game; the first organized baseball team, the Pioneers, started playing at a vacant lot on Washington Street in 1866. That team eventually morphed into one of the great Portland baseball squads, the Willamettes, which in turn begat the Portland Gladiators, briefly operated by Henry Harris as one of the founding members of the Pacific Northwest League. The Gladiators competed against several California League teams in the 1890s and sent brothers Tom and Jiggs Parrott to the majors.[32]

Seattle developed as a city later than its Oregon neighbor, so the game likewise became established later than in Portland. Baseball entrepreneur William Lucas was among a number of midwestern baseball veterans who organized the Pacific Northwest League in 1890, which would last two-and-a-half years and include a team in Seattle that played at Madison Park on a field completed only one day before its first game, against Spokane on May 24.[33] Lucas was kicked out of the league following its first year and left the area to manage Kansas City in the American Association.

The California League briefly reaped the benefits of the Pacific Northwest League's failure, but by the end of 1893 it had also disappeared amidst backstabbing among owners, widespread gambling, and a severe recession that resulted in tough economic conditions throughout the country. Several years would pass before another serious attempt was made to form a true Pacific Coast League.[34]

* * *

The year before the California League collapsed, it served as the backdrop for one of the most shocking nineteenth-century scandals involving a baseball player. The story began on a "Ladies Day" during a beautiful autumn afternoon in 1892 at Athletic Park in Los Angeles. Edgar "Pete" McNabb, the Angels pitcher, was methodically retiring Oakland batters, all the while flashing the brilliant smile he always wore on the diamond. McNabb was a happy-go-lucky type when things went his way. He would frequently yell to the batter, "What can you hit best, a high one or a low one?" After retiring his opponent he would laugh and doff his cap to the crowd, which roared its approval.[35]

Angels owner George Van Derbeck signed McNabb after the Pacific Northwest League failed in August 1892, and he became a favorite of team captain Bob Glenalvin, who could always be heard yelling from his position at second base, "Now pitch some ball for them, Peternab!"[36]

On that "Ladies Day," McNabb's smile was more prominent than usual because he had a secret. The reason for his immense grin was Louise Rockwell — better known as Mrs. William Rockwell, wife of the Pacific Northwest League president — whom McNabb first met in 1891 when pitching for Portland.[37] Now that the popular ballplayer was in Los Angeles, Mrs. Rockwell had abandoned her husband and young child to live in California with her favorite pitcher.

McNabb's success in Portland and Los Angeles in 1892 led to a contract with the Baltimore Orioles of the National League for the following season, and Louise Rockwell joined the twenty-seven-year-old pitcher as he went east. The pitching rules were changed over the winter, including an increase in distance of ten feet from the mound to home plate, to the current sixty feet six inches. As a result, McNabb experienced arm problems and was released by Baltimore in August.[38] He and Mrs. Rockwell returned to Los Angeles, posing as husband and wife. Money began running low and to make ends meet, Louise, now going by the last name of Kellogg, secured a job as a "skirt dancer," first in a vaudeville show in Los Angeles and then for a weeklong engagement at The Wigwam, a theatre in San Francisco. McNabb decided to join her in the north when William Rockwell arrived in Los Angeles on business.[39]

Following the San Francisco engagement, Louise Rockwell was hired by the Alvin Joslyn theatrical troupe for a national tour and McNabb signed to pitch for Grand Rapids in 1894 in the Western League. Unfortunately, McNabb would never stand on the mound and flash his smile for Grand Rapids.

On February 28, 1894, McNabb and Rockwell checked into the Hotel Eiffel in Pittsburgh. That afternoon, Mrs. Rockwell visited her parents, who lived nearby, and she returned around eight o'clock that evening. About a half-hour later, Lou Gilliland, a former teammate of McNabb's and a friend of the couple, arrived for a visit. When Gilliland knocked on the door, he heard a woman groan. He immediately called police, who burst in and discovered the ill-fated lovers lying next to each other on the floor. McNabb had apparently killed himself with a gunshot to his mouth. Louise Rockwell had bullet wounds in her head and neck but was still conscious.

Visited in the hospital by her mother and brother-in-law, Mrs. Rockwell lay partially paralyzed by a bullet lodged in her spine, its location making a life-saving operation impossible. Doctors informed the young woman that her time was short. She called for her estranged husband but died before he was able to arrive.[40]

There were differing theories about the cause for McNabb's drastic action. Some acquaintances of the couple thought it an act of jealousy. Some wondered whether Mrs. Rockwell had threatened a return to her husband. Still others speculated about financial problems. The entire episode has retained an air of mystery to this day even while consistently being characterized as a murder-suicide.[41]

One thing was clear. The details of this sordid affair were reported nationwide and served as sad evidence that ballplayers had become celebrities who could make headlines with scandal just as easily as with on-field accomplishments.

* * *

With two prominent leagues failing within a year of each other, professional baseball struggled in the West. The Pacific Northwest League tried again in 1896 with two teams each in Seattle and Tacoma, plus single franchises in Portland and Victoria, British Columbia, but was unable to finish the year. There was no successful professional league in California between 1894 and 1897.

At one point Charles Comiskey, who owned the St. Paul franchise in the Western League, tried backing a four-team winter league of major league players but pulled the plug when profits failed to materialize as hoped. The idea had been to form a new California League run by men from the East — if business was good enough. It was not, and Comiskey headed home, abandoning the winter league before the season was over.[42]

During the mid–1890s, baseball in California was once again the province of the amateur and the semi-pro. There were a number of top-flight teams, such as Tufts-Lyon in Los Angeles, Gilt Edge in Sacramento, the Alameda Alerts, and Reliance in San Francisco. The *San Francisco Examiner* staged a major statewide tournament. College baseball was popular, with excellent teams at St. Mary's and Santa Clara that often included professional "ringers." There was also the winter game, featuring teams that included top amateurs and professionals returning from the East after their seasons ended.

The Examiner tournament was amateur only in 1896 but expanded to include professionals the next year. In that tournament, future Hall of Famer Frank Chance was signed by Chicago of the National League while playing for a team from Fresno. Bill Lange accompanied Chance for the youngster's first trip east, taking the rookie under his wing, and he eventually became a vital cog in the next great Cubs team.[43]

The California Markets, who eventually were crowned champions, met Santa Cruz and Santa Clara in a three-way final for the tournament title, and attendance for the series at the new Recreation Park in San Francisco was impressive.[44] The popularity of the Examiner tournament rekindled public interest and led to a return of professional baseball in the Golden State. Two leagues were formed in 1898: the Pacific States and the California, again with teams only in Northern California. By the end of April, it was apparent public support would not sustain both and the two organizations consolidated into what was briefly called the Pacific Coast League before reverting to the traditional California League designation.[45]

The league grew more successful each year and the schedule expanded. During the 1899 season, Henry Harris pushed again for the California League to increase to eight teams, with four in California and four in the Northwest. At first the idea seemed to gather some momentum, but by October it was reported the plan had run into intractable opposition thanks to the usual impediments — increased travel time and costs associated with the longer trips that expansion required.[46]

Meanwhile, a portly ex-big league catcher named Dan Dugdale arrived in Seattle, planning to take part in the Klondike gold rush. He worked for the Seattle cable car system to earn money for his trip to the gold fields before switching his focus to local real estate.[47] Still infected by the baseball bug, Dugdale founded a team in his new hometown as part of a revitalized Pacific Northwest League. Even though it took a couple of seasons for the circuit to stabilize, Dugdale survived to battle California baseball team owners on many occasions, act as a fervent booster of baseball in the Northwest, and relish his emergence as the most powerful baseball figure in the region. Dan Dugdale would spend the rest of his life in Seattle.

William Lucas, an old friend of Dugdale, returned in 1900 to take another shot at baseball in the West with the formation of the Montana State League.[48] He quickly began raiding the outlaw California teams — a total of eight California League players, four from Oakland alone, jumped to Big Sky country that season. Other California-based leagues were hit as well. By the end of July it was estimated that one-fourth of the players in the Montana League were from California.[49]

Lucas left the Montana State League in 1901 to join forces with Dan Dugdale and expand the Pacific Northwest League, thereby offering a direct challenge to Henry Harris and his dream of baseball dominance on the coast. And Harris was at a disadvantage. With only one major market, San Francisco, he would need to look south once again to increase his league's population base. Los Angeles would return to the California League. The stage was set to determine control over baseball on the West Coast.

Chapter Two

1901 to 1905:
The Pacific Coast League Is Born

Stockton is out. Los Angeles is in. With that January 1901 announcement, the California League took a significant step toward realizing Henry Harris' goal of becoming a true Pacific Coast League.[1] The owner of the new Los Angeles franchise was Jim Morley, a thirty-one-year-old billiard expert, pool hall owner and former amateur baseball player whose father had opened the first shoe store in Los Angeles.[2]

The product of an English father and an Irish mother, James Furlong Morley was a tall, thin, jug-eared man whose appearance resembled a strange cross between Abraham Lincoln and fictional *Mad Magazine* mascot Alfred E. Neuman. Constantly indulging his entrepreneurial streak, Morley invested heavily over the years in myriad endeavors, including bowling, prize fighting, billiards and gemstones. He promoted the first automobile show in Southern California. At one time he owned a café, managed a hotel and operated perhaps the finest pool hall on the West Coast, staging tournaments that involved the top players in the world.[3] He was no slouch with a pool cue himself, talented enough to take on the likes of Bennie Allen and Willie Hoppe even after a laundry accident in 1896 cost him portions of three fingers.[4]

The quixotic promoter's variety of interests encroached on his personal life; he eventually had three marriages and an equal number of divorces. He was also prone to the silly, petulant outbursts that seem a hallmark of Pacific Coast League team owners. But Morley's role in establishing baseball in Los Angeles, beginning with his pitching and playing first base as an amateur for Tufts-Lyons, was acknowledged during his lifetime. In his old age the *Los Angeles Times* anointed Jim Morley "the real father of baseball in Los Angeles."[5]

When Morley secured the franchise, it was far from certain he would be successful, largely because of travel costs to a city still geographically isolated. But there was reason for optimism. Although Los Angeles was only one-fourth the size of San Francisco at the turn of the century, the discovery of oil coupled with the extension of rail lines from the north and east had drawn attention to the City of Angels. The community, founded in 1781, had grown from a nondescript village of eleven thousand people at its 1881 centennial, with its main reputation stemming from lawlessness, to a booming potential metropolis of more than one hundred thousand in 1900.[6]

Jim Morley's immediate goal was for Los Angeles to become "winter headquarters for eastern players" and to that end he announced that his new baseball park, to be constructed at Nineteenth and Main streets on a parcel popularly known as Washington Gardens, would be a "first class accommodation for baseball."[7] The twelve-acre site occupied a portion of a rundown vacant lot that was formerly the location of a seedy beer garden, land that had fallen into disuse, inhabited only by a small bicycle shop and the occasional traveling circus.

The ballpark was to be part of an entertainment complex funded by the Los Angeles Improvement Company, an urban development corporation formed in the 1880s by venture capitalists from San Francisco and Los Angeles. The company obtained a ten-year lease on the property and invested one hundred thousand dollars to create an amusement park and Morley's baseball diamond. The stadium was to be designed in such a way that the center field fence divided it from the rest of the complex. At game's end fans would pass through that fence via a big gate and amble past the animal cages into the amusement park, where they could spend the rest of the day for free.[8]

The new Washington Gardens was also to feature zoological exhibitions, a Japanese village and tea garden, a theatre with four thousand seats, restaurants and concession stands, a railway and a "Shoot the Chutes" water ride, which led to both the park and the baseball stadium being commonly known as Chutes Park. Jim Morley's baseball diamond would be in the middle of all this, and he wanted a team that would be the center of attention.

The California League that Morley had joined consisted of four teams; in addition to Los Angeles, there were franchises in San Francisco, Oakland, and Sacramento. The circuit was coming off a season that included team owners blacklisting several players who in 1900 had jumped California League contracts to play in William Lucas' league in Montana, a decidedly hypocritical stance that ignored their own refusal to honor other league's player contracts.[9]

The California League opened its 1901 season in San Francisco and Los Angeles and was successful from the outset. Five thousand fans attended the opening game in Los Angeles, including several hundred who stood in the outfield.[10] San Francisco hosted Sacramento in its home opener the same day and had to turn away a large number of people, some of whom then gathered on rooftops to watch from across the street.[11]

Morley wasted no time devising ways to promote his team, which was being called the "Looloos" in the press. During the season's first week he staged a souvenir day, with every woman in the ballpark receiving a lithograph depicting a black, curly-haired cocker spaniel — Morley's beloved pet, Chum, which he was promoting as team mascot.[12] Morley also had a decided view that a big league city needed a team with big league names. He began signing stars possessing marquee value, albeit with mixed results. One of the first was ex–Baltimore Orioles second baseman Heine Reitz, still considered one of the best infielders in the country and a figure familiar to California League fans. Quite a showman, Reitz was one of the game's best bunters, using a unique approach in which he held the bat straight out with only one hand. He was quite adept at putting tremendous topspin on the ball and on occasion would even flip his bat around during the pitch and bunt with the handle.[13]

Reitz also was a notorious drinker, and it did not take long for him to demonstrate why he had fallen from his glory days with John McGraw and the legendary Orioles. He disappeared in San Francisco during a drinking binge and upon reappearing performed so poorly everyone wished he had stayed away. Reitz was in and out of the lineup for much of the 1901 season.[14]

The next spring, Morley signed the great eccentric pitcher, George "Rube" Waddell, who had traveled to Southern California as part of Napoleon Lajoie's all-star team of major league players on a barnstorming tour. Waddell was on the suspended list of the Chicago National League team after jumping his contract over a disputed fine.[15]

From a perspective more than a century removed, Rube Waddell seems more folk legend than living, breathing human being. Waddell would set a major league strikeout record that stood for more than sixty years, help the Philadelphia Athletics win two American League pennants, and eventually earn enshrinement in the Baseball Hall of Fame.[16] At the same time, he often acted impulsively, like a child who upon discovering an interest jumped into it with abandon. He drank like a fish, fished like he drank (all the time), loved to wrestle alligators and bears, repeatedly disappeared for days on end, married four times within six years — once having forgotten to divorce his previous wife — and was so fascinated with fire engines he was known to leave the mound to give chase if one passed the ballpark with its sirens wailing.[17] Waddell reportedly helped save a life in a fire and became engrossed in the idea of performing heroic deeds.[18] Despite his considerable physical gifts, to this day Waddell's reputation is based on equal measures of eccentricity and talent, forever intertwined and impossible to separate.

Waddell got into mischief shortly before Opening Day, landing in jail for accosting a man who was spending time in the company of a woman with whom Rube had become infatuated.[19] Waddell began the season in a love-struck funk but showed flashes of brilliance when he had a mind to. He even played first base and outfield on a semi-regular basis when not pitching, all the while denying rumors he would quit Los Angeles for the major leagues.[20] Waddell was most effective when not distracted by his love life, fire engines, fishing — or the new hot air balloon ride at Chutes Park that rose above the outfield fence during ballgames.[21]

Despite repeatedly insisting he would not abandon Los Angeles, Rube Waddell jumped to the Philadelphia Athletics during the summer. The pitcher was still on the Cubs' suspended list in early June when Athletics owner and manager Connie Mack bought from Chicago the rights to the eccentric man-child. Mack sent a first-class train ticket to Waddell who in turn, feeling guilty, immediately handed it over to Jim Morley. Mack was persistent and sent another ticket and two hundred dollars advance money, along with a couple of Pinkerton agents to ensure Waddell boarded the train. He did so, leaving his luggage behind. Years later Morley still had Waddell's steamer trunk. The pitcher never reclaimed it.[22]

Waddell went on an incredible tear for the Athletics. After his modest record of 12–7 for Los Angeles, the big left-hander joined Philadelphia for the last eighty-seven games of the 1902 American League season and won twenty-four in what amounted to less than two-thirds of the schedule. Two weeks after his arrival in the City of Brotherly Love, Waddell became the first big league pitcher to strike out the side on just nine pitches. Those accomplishments demonstrated why many had felt him "too fast" for the California League.[23] Indeed, there were many who believed that had the colorful pitcher set aside his many distractions he might never have lost a game with Los Angeles.

Jim Morley endeavored to replace his star pitcher with another. He tried to lure Win Mercer of the Detroit Tigers, offering him the opportunity to also serve as team captain, but was turned down.[24] It was just as well. Mercer had issues of his own and died in a San Francisco hotel room the following January under mysterious circumstances.[25]

* * *

Despite big names and big ideas, Jim Morley was unable to capture the California League pennant in either of his first two years in the league. Honors in 1901 went to Henry Harris and his San Francisco "Wasps," which were led by the best one-two pitching combination in the California League — Herman "Ham" Iburg and Jimmy "The Whale" Whalen. Between them they won seventy-three games. Both were San Francisco natives; Iburg, who was hearing impaired and of a rather slight build, was best known for his "slow ball," which he used almost exclusively. He went to the National League in 1902 with Philadelphia before returning to the Coast a year later. The red-haired, freckle-faced Whalen was a workhorse and career minor leaguer who had grown up playing ball in the streets in the Mission district.[26] The Wasps also featured four of the league's top ten hitters. Of note was the catching duo of Parke Wilson, a veteran formerly with New York of the National League, and Charlie Graham, who would eventually own the team and become one of the giant figures of the Pacific Coast League. San Francisco easily captured the 1901 California League pennant with a record of 95–66, winning fourteen more games than second-place Los Angeles.

But Henry Harris would quickly become frustrated with his 1902 team once he realized it was not going to repeat as league champion. He had had high hopes for team captain Frank Shugart, an eight-year major league veteran signed in the spring after being released by the Chicago White Sox.[27] Shugart failed to hit or take his role with the club seriously, and Harris complained that the ex–big leaguer "had not taken good care of himself." He relieved Shugart of his captaincy in August and gave the job to shortstop Danny Shay.[28]

The 1902 championship would instead reside across San Francisco Bay, in the hands of Oakland owner Cal Ewing and his popular catcher/manager Pete Lohman, who had once played briefly in the major league American Association. The championship would prove to be the highlight of a long career for the thirty-nine-year-old Lohman.[29]

The Oaks featured the league's leading pitcher, Henry Schmidt (who had jumped from Mobile of the Southern Association), and its leading hitter, Walter McCredie. Veteran second baseman Kid Mohler, on Denver's suspended list for jumping his contract to sign with Oakland, was one of the league's great defensive middle infielders despite being a left-handed thrower. Pitcher Billy Cristall, who had jumped from the New York State League, also had a memorable season. He pitched a no-hitter on June 1, and then was released by Oakland and signed by Los Angeles, whereupon he threw out three runners at home plate while playing a rare game in the outfield in early November. He ended the season by wading into the stands during a game and punching a fan.[30]

The 1902 California League season was also noteworthy for the introduction of one of baseball's more interesting innovations. Outfielder George Hildebrand began the season in Brooklyn before moving on to Providence of the Eastern League, where he discovered wetting a baseball with saliva caused it to curve dramatically when thrown in a particular manner. He jumped to Sacramento during the summer and was talking to one of his new teammates, pitcher Elmer Stricklett, who was in danger of being released. Hildebrand took Stricklett aside and said, "Let me show you something."[31]

Stricklett immediately mastered the pitch and began a winning streak, eventually compiling a 20–16 record for a Sacramento team that finished in last place, thirty-two games below .500. He rode the pitch to the major leagues for Chicago and Brooklyn and taught the delivery, commonly called a spitball, to Jack Chesbro, who used it to win forty-one games for the New York Highlanders (now the Yankees) in 1904. Even though New York lost the pennant when one of Chesbro's wet ones got away for a wild pitch, use of the delivery became widespread before it was eventually banned in an effort to increase offense.

* * *

Los Angeles was an emerging lynchpin in the financial stability of the California League, boasting attendance figures that rivaled the circuit's bellwether franchise in San Francisco. Additionally, the fact that Jim Morley, Henry Harris and Cal Ewing could make competitive financial offers to established major league stars was evidence of the profits to be made in California baseball. The transition of the pastime from hobby to business was underway.

The *Los Angeles Times* reported locals were spending a quarter-million dollars each year on tickets to sporting events; baseball led the way, followed by horse racing, bowling, billiards and pool, then prize fighting, golf, tennis, and other minor sports.[32]

The financial success of the Los Angeles franchise also provided the California League with two strong anchors, same as the Pacific Northwest League had with Seattle and Portland. This made it possible for the league to conquer obstacles of geography; teams could be located farther apart without necessarily sacrificing financial viability.

Henry Harris remained interested in annexing Portland and Seattle, cities of sufficient size to fulfill his vision of a true Pacific Coast League. Although most accounts of PCL history indicate defection of the two major Northwest cities from the Pacific Northwest League was a secret until December 1902, there had been reports printed five months earlier in several major West Coast newspapers that groups representing Portland and Seattle had applied for admission to the California League in the middle of the 1902 season. Those reports stated that allowing the two teams to join the league at that stage of the year was deemed impractical but that they would be added in 1903. The article in the *Los Angeles Times*, under the headline "A New League," said that it had been "definitely determined to make the consolidation during the coming winter."[33] Harris, ready to take advantage of the situation, began working feverishly on the details to bring Portland and Seattle into an expanded California League.

Just as the 1902 season was ending, Henry Harris publicly revealed that all was in place to bring Portland and Seattle into a new Pacific Coast League, hopefully one that would include Dan Dugdale. However, Dugdale was staunchly committed to the Pacific Northwest League and president William Lucas, and was unwilling to abandon his power base for an organization with an uncertain future. He demanded that Harris and the other California teams post a ten-thousand-dollar guarantee for the Northwest franchises.[34]

Harris flatly rejected Dugdale's demand. In a statement to the press, he declared, "I want the people to understand that the overtures for expansion came from Portland and Seattle, and they have no right to ask us for any guarantee."[35]

For his part, Dugdale vowed to crush the upstart Pacific Coast League, maintaining that he had made a profit of twenty-three thousand dollars in 1902 and would "spend it all, if necessary, in fighting these invaders. We have organized baseball back of us, while this new league is an outlaw of the worst type. I will not be swiped off the map."[36]

Immediately before Christmas, the directors of the Portland franchise announced the team was resigning from the PNL and joining Harris' new league.[37] A new ballclub was organized in Seattle without Dan Dugdale, and within a week the Pacific Coast League was officially in business.[38] The *Seattle Times* asserted that if the Pacific Coast League wanted, it could get Tacoma and Spokane to jump as well.[39]

Since the Pacific Coast League was locating two of its franchises within another league's territory, it would operate as an outlaw in 1903, as the California League had often done. James T. Moran and Eugene Bert were named president and vice president of the new league. PCL owners declared there would be no salary limit and every available player would be pursued. Forgiveness was offered to those that had jumped contracts.[40] Henry Harris stated, "We are in baseball to stay. We are not seeking trouble nor a fight, but we are ready for one or both, if the Pacific Northwest League so wishes."[41]

* * *

Dissatisfied with consecutive second-place finishes, Jim Morley tried to take advantage of the continuing war between the American and National leagues by offering a contract to

Wild Bill Donovan, pitching ace of Brooklyn. When Donovan expressed reluctance to play so far from his family, Morley offered to cover the cost of moving them to Los Angeles.[42] Donovan opted instead to jump to the American League and pitch for Detroit, where he replaced the late Win Mercer and was a mainstay of the Tigers rotation for much of the next decade.

Having lost his bid for Brooklyn's ace, Morley turned his attention to Eustice "Doc" Newton, a teammate of Donovan's before his recent jump to New York of the American League.[43] The hard-drinking, left-handed curveball pitcher had a peculiar pitching motion, taking almost no windup and stepping toward first base while slinging the ball with a cross-fire delivery that made the baseball appear as if it were headed directly at a left-handed hitter.[44] This left Newton in a bad defensive position and, indeed, he was a poor fielder. But he would lead a very strong pitching staff during his two years in Los Angeles, winning seventy-four games and more than ably replacing Morley's ace pitcher, Oscar Jones, who coincidentally replaced Newton in Brooklyn.[45] Morley signed another ex–major league pitcher, San Francisco native Joe Corbett, brother of heavyweight boxing champion "Gentleman" Jim Corbett. Making a comeback at age twenty-seven, Corbett had not pitched professionally since 1897, when he had a record of 24–8 for the Baltimore Orioles of the National League. He left after that season to become a sports reporter for the *San Francisco Call* because he did not like playing in the East.

Morley was not done. He signed a young player out of Escondido, California, named Clifford Cravath.[46] Better known as "Gavvy" or "Cactus" (the latter a tribute to his "prickly" personality), Cravath was an outfielder and back-up catcher who would become one of the great sluggers of the Dead Ball era, winning six National League home run titles for the Philadelphia Phillies between 1913 and 1919. Morley also re-signed Frank "Cap" Dillon, a first baseman who joined Los Angeles from the American League during the 1902 season. A cousin of star major league pitcher Clark Griffith, Dillon would be a mainstay of the franchise for a dozen years.

The most recognizable player signed by Morley was William Ellsworth "Dummy" Hoy. A victim of meningitis as a child, the forty-one-year-old deaf-mute center fielder would play in all 211 games of the 1903 schedule. At 5'4" and weighing less than one hundred fifty pounds, Hoy made his living slapping down on the ball and beating out high choppers on the infield. A big leaguer for fifteen seasons, Hoy devised a system to avoid collisions on fly balls by yelling when about to make a catch. His yell was better described as a squeak.[47]

While Morley was building a powerhouse in Los Angeles that would win its first fifteen games and run away with the 1903 Pacific Coast League pennant, the Pacific Northwest League prepared to wage open warfare. William Lucas announced that the National Association of Minor Leagues would enforce his league's blacklist against anyone playing in the outlaw Pacific Coast League after April 1. To be reinstated, a player would have to pay a six-hundred-dollar fine.[48] Lucas also announced that the Pacific Northwest League was changing its name to the Pacific National League and would compete directly with the PCL in California by placing teams in both San Francisco and Los Angeles.

Responding to the threat of war, the presidents of the American Association and the Western League traveled to California for a meeting with Henry Harris and other Pacific Coast League officials in a bid to avoid hostilities and persuade the PCL to come under the umbrella of Organized Baseball.[49]

It was too late. Secure in their foothold in Seattle and Portland — where Harris had reached agreement with streetcar companies to ensure they served only Pacific Coast League teams — the league owners' attitudes mirrored Jim Morley's bold assertion that "The Pacific Coast League, as now constituted, is not only stronger than the Pacific Northwest League, but stronger than any minor league in the country, and is really a major league in itself. We have these two cities [Seattle and Portland] now, and we will meet any fight or blacklist more than halfway." As far as threats from Organized Baseball, Morley went on to say in his usual understated way "before we get through with them, we will make them come to us on their knees and ask for peace."[50]

With no settlement in sight, the Pacific National League broke ground in March on new ballparks located across the street from their California rivals.[51] Butte owner John McCloskey, a well-known organizer of baseball leagues, traveled throughout California looking for financial backers. Battles erupted everywhere. Portland management took the Northwest League to court, claiming the league excluded its representative to official meetings and had conspired to throw the 1902 pennant to Butte. The team also sought an injunction to prevent the PNL from operating another franchise within five miles of the city of Portland.[52] The Pacific Coast League franchise in Seattle faced enormous difficulty in securing and keeping players and was forced to build from scratch after Dugdale's refusal to join the PCL.[53] The team was saddled with the additional burden of having to construct a ballpark at the same time.[54]

Elmer Stricklett, who had signed with the opposition in Los Angeles, visited Sacramento and stole three of that team's players. Owner Mike Fisher had two of the three arrested, and they were forced to post two hundred-fifty dollars bail. All three eventually remained in the Pacific Coast League.[55] Ex-Oakland pitcher George Borchers tried to raid his former boss, Cal Ewing, but the four Oakland players Borchers recruited demanded cash guarantees in order to jump and ultimately stayed put.[56]

Although the Pacific National League did successfully skim players from PCL rosters, there were many jumping the other way as well. The war fizzled and by August the PNL's California teams folded and William Lucas and Dan Dugdale accepted defeat.

Outside of Los Angeles, teams in the Pacific Coast League scrambled in 1903 to find a winning combination. Ham Iburg was back in San Francisco after his one-year sojourn to Philadelphia and Henry Harris tried teaming him again with Jimmy Whalen to repeat the magic that brought Harris the 1901 pennant. But the longer schedule and various ailments suffered by the two pitching aces prevented his team, now called the Stars, from contending.[57]

Defending champion Oakland tried to compete without spending money while at the same time losing Henry Schmidt and Walter McCredie to Brooklyn — as well as much of their starting lineup from the previous year — and returned to the cellar. A game in May, during which the team committed fifteen errors in a 17–3 loss to Seattle, provided a clear indication of the direction in which Pete Lohman's team was headed.[58]

Portland and Seattle were in a state of flux all season, especially the team from Puget Sound, which unexpectedly rocketed to third place by winning twenty-four of twenty-five games during October, including an incredible streak of nineteen straight victories.[59] The surge was attributable in part to the hitting of the Pacific Coast League's first batting champion, Harry Lumley, who joined the team about halfway through the schedule, and the pitching of former major league star Jay Hughes.[60]

Sacramento, operating in the league's smallest market and employing a largely rookie pitching staff, finished in second place. Late in the year, Mike Fisher added Phil Knell, a long-time California League pitcher eight years past his final major league appearance. The popular veteran with the sunny disposition won ten games.

But Los Angeles proved unstoppable as the dominance of Morley's pitching staff, led by Doc Newton, Warren Hall, Dolly Gray and Joe Corbett, provided the final margin of twenty-seven-and-a-half games. Placing an exclamation point on that superiority, thirty-five-game winner Newton threw a no-hitter against Oakland on November 8 while facing the minimum twenty-seven batters. The left-hander allowed only two base runners, both on errors. Each was erased by a double play.[61]

Unlike the Pacific National League, every team in the Pacific Coast League survived to the end of the 1903 season — but there was a cost. Owners were forced to pay higher than normal salaries to keep players in the league, and the one-sided pennant race did not help matters. Every team suffered financially; even Los Angeles was estimated to have broken even at best.[62] Mike Fisher, in the weakest financial position to begin with, had not fared well in Sacramento and quickly announced his intention to move the franchise to Tacoma, Washington, a city abandoned by the Pacific National League. Literally seeking greener pastures, Fisher wanted to escape the small Sacramento market's meager fan support as well as the blistering summer heat and frequent dust storms that whipped off the dirt skin of the infield at Oak Park. At one point he offered to sell the team to the city of Sacramento, but the offer was refused and Fisher left the California capital.[63]

After Fisher's first trip to Tacoma, during which he oversaw the renovation of the ballpark at South Eleventh and L streets, he returned to California more enthusiastic than ever. Having signed most of his players for the upcoming season, Fisher proclaimed, "I am going to have the strongest team in the whole league. Why, we could draw rings around Ringling's circus."[64] Although many chuckled at Fisher's exuberance, his would not prove to be an idle boast.

* * *

To counter the lack of interest accompanying lopsided pennant races such as that in 1903, the Pacific Coast League adopted a "split schedule" for 1904 that would result in crowning first- and second-half champions that would subsequently meet in a playoff to determine the league's overall pennant-winner. Owners also agreed there would be no salary limit, ticket prices would remain the same, and players that had forsaken league contracts would be banned.[65] A delegation headed by owners Harris and Morley, accompanied by Eugene Bert (who had succeeded James T. Moran as league president), met with Cubs owner James Hart, American League president Ban Johnson and Brooklyn manager Ned Hanlon (who also owned Baltimore in the Eastern League and therefore represented minor league interests) to arrange for an end to the Pacific Coast League's outlaw status.[66]

An agreement was finally reached in early February 1904 for the Pacific Coast League to come under the umbrella of the National Commission and receive a higher classification than any other minor league. As part of the deal, the PCL agreed to allow the major leagues to draft its players every November 1 for $750 each. A maximum of two players could be secured from each PCL team. In turn, Pacific Coast League teams could draft players from leagues in lower classifications.[67]

But there remained a major sticking point before the final settlement could be reached. Ned Hanlon claimed that three Pacific Coast League players, Cap Dillon of Los Angeles and Ed Heydon and Louis Castro of Portland, belonged to him. Heydon returned willingly but the other two men balked. Hanlon notified Harris and Bert that the deal between the PCL and Organized Baseball was not complete until the matter was settled.

Morley's team had already lost one of its best drawing cards in the offseason when Joe Corbett accepted an offer from the St. Louis Cardinals. Corbett had been valuable to Los

Angeles, winning twenty-four games and hitting .336 while filling in at second base when he was not pitching. Morley wanted to keep Corbett but could not afford to continue paying him five hundred dollars a month. The extremely popular and personable pitcher, whose comeback in 1903 was one of the league's great stories, became the object of a bidding war that subsequently priced him out of Morley's reach.[68]

Upon learning he might also lose Dillon, an angry Morley defiantly hissed, "Say for me that if Dillon is to be the price of peace ... there will be no peace in baseball."[69]

The Looloos owner continued to count on having Cap Dillon at first base, the demands of Ned Hanlon notwithstanding. Hanlon continued to insist the big first baseman report to Brooklyn or the deal to bring the PCL into Organized Baseball was off. Over Morley's strident objection, the Pacific Coast League owners finally capitulated to Hanlon's demand, without debate, on a 5–1 vote taken by wire, and awarded Dillon and Louis Castro to Hanlon as part of the settlement. Morley hit the roof.

Complaining that he was now without a first baseman or team captain, Morley resigned as president and manager of Los Angeles. "I positively refuse to surrender Dillon.... I spent enough money last year for the benefit of the league," he fumed. "If you wish to furnish them further concessions do so at your own expense. The Los Angeles franchise is behind Dillon in this matter. This is final."[70]

The team's board of directors refused to accept Morley's resignation and Morley continued his refusal to relinquish Dillon in a battle that raged all spring. Morley also railed against Harris and Bert, saying, "I contend the Pacific Coast League has no authority whatsoever to take a player belonging to any one of the clubs, or give him away for some benefit that may accrue

Cap Dillon. "Say for me that if Dillon is to be the price of peace ... there will be no peace in baseball"—Jim Morley (David Eskenazi Collection).

to the league. Our ultimatum was the player list in toto or no affiliation. Now I call for living up to that ultimatum."[71]

Dillon remained in Los Angeles. Hanlon enlisted Oscar Jones to bring Dillon with him to the Superbas' spring training camp. Dillon told Jones to go "chase himself" (or words to that effect).[72] At Portland's spring training camp in Bakersfield, Browns owner Fred Ely vowed to "hold on to Louis Castro as long as Morley held on to Dillon."[73]

Ely finally relented two days before the start of the 1904 season, paying Ned Hanlon $1,250 to keep Louis Castro.[74] Morley remained uninterested in compromise.

The day before the Looloos opener, National League president Harry Pulliam announced that Morley had failed to produce a contract with Dillon's signature. He went on to say he was confident the Pacific Coast League would not allow Dillon to play. President Bert wired umpire Jack O'Connell that night with instructions to prevent Dillon from taking the field. Bert also sent a telegram to Pete Lohman ordering Oakland not to play if Dillon was in the lineup.[75] Morley responded by filing an appeal with a superior court judge to stay any order preventing Dillon from suiting up for Los Angeles.

The Opening Day showdown took place in a steady drizzle. Morley's annual automobile parade was delayed about half an hour because of the wet conditions. After the throng arrived at Chutes Park, the teams marched to the flagpole in center field and ceremoniously hoisted the pennant — a twelve-foot-long dark blue flag with stars in the background, emblazoned "Champions 1904." (It was customary at the time for teams to declare themselves champions of the year they defended their title rather than the year they won.)[76] Los Angeles mayor Meredith Snyder threw the first pitch as the drizzle continued. Dillon then stationed himself at first base and tossed the ball around the infield as the crowd murmured in anticipation.

Warm-ups complete, Oakland leadoff batter Bob Ganley stepped to the plate. Dillon remained at his position. Umpire O'Connell immediately called time and walked over to the first baseman. Extracting a piece of paper from his pocket, he read aloud the order from Bert that Dillon was not to play. Dillon left the field and Heine Spies took his place. The confrontation was over and the game began.[77]

Morley maintained that Dillon would play the next day, but he did not. Threats were tossed back and forth, but Dillon ultimately reported to Brooklyn.[78] The episode created a rift in the relationship between Morley and the rest of the league, particularly with Eugene Bert and Henry Harris, which would never heal.

Not that losing Dillon left Morley high and dry; he was too smart for that. Dillon's replacement was a charismatic athlete from Santa Clara College named Hal Chase, who would later become synonymous with scandal, appearing at the periphery of both the Black Sox debacle and its sister disgrace in the Pacific Coast League.[79] Along the way he became unwelcome in just about every ballpark in America. But in 1904, he was a unique and spectacular talent who would revolutionize infield defense.

Although Dillon was an excellent first baseman, no one played the position like Chase, a right-handed batter and left-handed thrower. At a time when bunting was a major offensive tactic, infielders rarely charged the plate to take away the play. Chase did so incessantly, with amazing reflexes and a fearless nature second to none. He would begin creeping in on the batter at the start of the pitcher's delivery, then sprint in almost on top of the hitter, daring him to bunt or hit the ball through him. It was not unusual for Chase to end up all the way over on the third base line and throw out a base runner. He was a gambler to his core and it showed with an aggressive style that resulted in a lot of spectacular plays and a lot of errors. No one had ever seen anyone play like Hal Chase, and fans loved it. So did Jim Morley, who especially delighted in having signed his new star out from under Henry Harris's nose — especially in light of Harris's lack of help in the Dillon affair.

* * *

Mike Fisher's forecast of success for his 1904 Tacoma Tigers proved most accurate. His continued practice of employing "incubator" pitchers — youngsters he recruited from semi-pro teams or college campuses — paid off. Bobby Keefe, a pitcher who arrived in 1903 from Santa Clara College, was teamed with Orval Overall, a hurler from the University of California, to form the league's best one-two punch. Originally from Visalia, California, Overall, who had also starred on the gridiron for the Golden Bears, was a talented athlete who would later pitch several years for the Cincinnati Reds and Chicago Cubs until injuries cut short his career.

Fisher also had one of the league's great offensive stars in slugging shortstop Truck Eagan. Slow of foot and a so-so defensive player (sportswriter Bill Henry joked that when Eagan charged short grounders, the ball would either go through his legs or he would make a spectacular stop and throw the ball into the stands), Eagan was discovered by Henry Harris on the San Francisco sandlots.[80] From there, he became a star for the Sacramento Gilt Edge championship teams in the late 1890s. Fisher acquired Eagan in 1902 and he led the league in home runs three straight years, often with long, majestic shots, including one in Portland that landed on a schoolhouse roof and another in San Francisco that cleared not only the right-field fence but a house beyond it. Unlike most heavy hitters of the era, Eagan generally used a light bat, although he was also known for grabbing whatever was handy. "Bats all look alike to me," he said.[81]

Fisher's Tigers easily took the first-half crown, led by Eagan, the "incubator" pitchers and solid veterans, including George McLaughlin, Tommy Sheehan and Mike Lynch, whose constant chatter and booming voice from his left-field position could be heard to the top of the grandstand. In honor of Fisher's new team, *Tacoma Ledger* cartoonist Ernest Reynolds began inserting a tiny tiger into his drawing each day in the newspaper. The tiger would smile after a Tacoma win and carry a sad expression and droopy tail following a loss. It smiled a lot in 1904.[82]

Tacoma's success surprised everyone because Fisher was considered neither knowledge-able nor an especially keen judge of talent. But he had a secret weapon in his captain, catcher Charlie Graham, who Fisher had acquired from San Francisco in 1903. Over the next forty years, no one in the Pacific Coast League would be more respected than Graham for the ability to spot and develop young talent. Fisher believed in the young man's judgment and it paid off.[83]

A mid-season controversy erupted that threatened the agreement between the PCL and the major leagues, and once again Ned Hanlon was involved. Joe Corbett, who had been a disappointment in St. Louis, requested and was granted his release in July. San Francisco promptly signed him without any objection from Hanlon, who had claimed the rights to Corbett every year since the pitcher jumped Baltimore after the 1897 season, except when he allowed him to sign with St. Louis. Corbett proceeded to win three games for the Seals (as Harris was now calling his ball club), showing that perhaps he was not washed up after all.[84]

Hanlon reinstated his claim and the National Commission ruled Corbett ineligible to play anywhere until the dispute was resolved.[85] Henry Harris ignored the edict and pitched Corbett against Orval Overall and Tacoma on August 20.[86] Following a week and a half of screaming between the parties, Brooklyn team president Charles Ebbets overruled his manager and announced that he was renouncing rights to Corbett for the year; the pitcher could stay in San Francisco.[87] Of course, it was not lost on Jim Morley that when a player belonging to Henry Harris was at stake, the league fought more forcefully than it had for Morley in the Dillon case. Aware that Harris preferred to sign local talent from the Bay Area, Morley let it be known he would give an automatic tryout to anyone from San Francisco.[88]

The Los Angeles owner's attitude further soured after he learned which of his players had been drafted, especially after discovering that Eugene Bert had agreed to a request by the major leagues to move the draft date six weeks earlier, to September 15.[89]

He lost Doc Newton, winner of a league-leading thirty-nine games, and his new star, Hal Chase; both went to the New York Highlanders. Morley replaced Chase by gritting his teeth and re-acquiring Cap Dillon from Ned Hanlon.[90]

Other teams also lost star players. The Philadelphia Athletics snapped up the league's top hitter, Seattle's Emil Frisk. His teammate, catcher Cliff Blankenship, was taken by Cincinnati. Orval Overall was also drafted by Cincinnati and Oakland pitcher James Buchanan was taken by the St. Louis Americans.[91]

Although those drafted would not report to the major leagues until the beginning of the 1905 season, the change in the draft date meant these players would spend the last ten weeks of the PCL season aware they were not returning, leaving little motivation for them to perform. Pacific Coast League owners began making noises about abandoning the agreement with the National Commission, openly questioning the wisdom in joining Organized Baseball since it seemed all the benefits flowed in one direction. Bert headed off some of the rancor by announcing at the beginning of October that the major leagues had agreed no further drafting would take place prior to the original November 1 deadline. Of course, anyone taken up to that time belonged to the major league team drafting him.[92]

* * *

Tacoma was again leading the league in the second half of the 1904 season and Jim Morley decided the only way to make a run at the Tigers was by signing several major league stars whose seasons had already ended. A month remained in the PCL schedule when Morley announced he was making lucrative offers to Christy Mathewson, Honus Wagner, Joe McGinnity and Frank Chance to finish the season in Los Angeles in the hope of denying Tacoma a sweep of both halves.[93]

Mathewson and Wagner backed out, although it is not clear if they ever seriously considered coming west. McGinnity was another matter. Offered $2,500 to play a month for Los Angeles, he was angered when New York Giants owner John Brush refused to grant him permission to play. (Morley insisted he would not sign the great right-handed pitcher without Brush's okay.)[94] Morley did sign Frank Chance, who split time between catcher and first base with Los Angeles. Brooklyn's Oscar Jones also agreed to an end-of-the-year contract, as did Del Mason, a pitcher for Ned Hanlon's Baltimore Orioles of the Eastern League.[95] The newcomers played hard; Chance was slapped with an ejection in Los Angeles for punching an umpire following a disputed tag play.[96]

Despite Morley's inability to procure his full "dream team," the Looloos did close the gap with Tacoma, coming within one loss of tying Fisher's team for the second-half pennant. To the rescue rode Eugene Bert — normally not one to bail out Jim Morley — who ruled in favor of the Looloos on a pending protest of an August 22 game against Portland. The loss was thrown out, leaving Tacoma and Los Angeles tied for the second-half crown.[97] According to league rules Tacoma was the champion, having finished first both halves, but Morley

1904 Pacific Coast League Champion Tacoma Tigers. Pictured left to right are (back row) Pearl Casey, Truck Eagan, David W. Evans, Dean B. Worley, George Schreeder, Bobby Keefe, George McLaughlin; (middle row) Bill Thomas, Orval Overall, Charlie Graham, Mike Fisher, Lou Nordyke, Mike Lynch, Charlie Doyle; (front row) John Fitzgerald, Jimmy St. Vrain, Tommy Sheehan, Happy Hogan (courtesy of Marc H. Blau).

argued that the pennant remained up for grabs. Since there was no provision for a playoff of the second half in the event of a tie, Bert declared the season was over. He said he would like to see a series between the teams but that he had no authority to sanction it as an official league event.[98]

Morley and Fisher decided to capitalize on the controversy and announced a ten-game playoff series. Since early December weather made a series in Washington impossible, Tacoma's five home playoff games were to be played in San Francisco. Although the two sides differed on what the series meant — Morley claimed it would determine the league champion while Mike Fisher stated his team had already won the pennant — it was agreed that players would share in the gate receipts in order to encourage their participation. Tacoma eventually won the series five games to four, with one game ending in a tie, although Morley claimed the tie did not count. When Fisher refused to continue the series, the Angels owner sent his team onto an empty diamond on consecutive days, claiming forfeit victories and therefore, at least in his mind, the PCL title. The rest of the league ignored Morley's theatrics.[99]

The league directors toyed in the offseason with expansion to eight teams by adding one in the north — in Spokane — and another in the south, but nothing came of the plan. Travel costs remained a concern, and despite Tacoma's enormous success on the field, the community had not supported the team. Attendance league-wide had dropped as the 1904 season wore on, and though the Pacific Coast League generated a half million dollars in revenue, the circuit had only broken even at best.[100] Expansion did not seem to be the best strategy for a league with existing franchises teetering on the edge of viability.

* * *

It was vital that the PCL's northern teams attract a consistent following in order to maintain dominance in the West and make traveling the great distance from California worthwhile. Portland had employed four managers in two years, even hiring Dan Dugdale at one point. An important step to solidify a Portland franchise that had lost more than twenty thousand dollars occurred at the league meeting in December 1904 when Judge William Wallace McCredie purchased the team. He immediately named his nephew, Walter, as player-manager.[101]

Walter McCredie, already a star outfielder on the team, immediately set out to remake the roster. Other than McCredie himself, infielder Louis Runkel was the only holdover from 1904 and he would be sent to Seattle before the end of the season.

The battling nature of the replacements recruited by McCredie was striking. The tall Scot was clearly after men who would fight to win. Although the initial on-field results were mixed — Portland would finish fifth in 1905 — the team was competitive. More importantly, the community supported it. The franchise turned a profit for the first time, aided by a popular exposition celebrating the one hundredth anniversary of the Lewis and Clark expedition. Along the way, McCredie put together one of the most volatile batteries in the history of the game: catcher Larry McLean and pitcher Virgil "Ned" Garvin, men who were extremely talented but whose lives would be marked by violent episodes and premature ends due to alcoholism.[102]

Although the pennant race again lacked suspense, the 1905 season featured a number of memorable performances. Los Angeles and Oakland marked the end of the first half of the schedule with an unusual doubleheader that was completed in a total of one hour and forty minutes. Because both teams needed to catch a train to San Francisco and neither could advance in the standings, an agreement was made to play the games as quickly as possible. Players ran on and off the field once each side was retired, batters swung at almost every pitch, and only three minutes elapsed between contests. Los Angeles won both games.[103]

Seattle's Charlie Shields set a record by striking out nineteen Portland batters on July 8, including Larry Schlafly, Deacon Van Buren and Eddie Householder three times apiece.[104] Schlafly, a second baseman, had earlier completed an unassisted triple play against Seattle on June 21.[105] Jim Whalen had ended the 1904 season by allowing only one run in his last four starts. He was even better at the beginning of the 1905 season, opening the year with four straight shutouts while stretching his scoreless streak to forty-seven innings over two years.[106] Bill Tozer, a young pitcher Jim Morley had acquired from Salt Lake City, set a single-season Pacific Coast League mark with forty-six consecutive shutout innings, including a fourteen-inning, 1–0 win against Shields on November 9.[107] Another find, Walter Nagle, made his debut for the Angels on September 30 and won eleven games without a defeat, playing a key role in Jim Morley's second league championship in three years.[108]

* * *

The most shocking incident in the PCL in 1905 came off the field. In mid–July it was reported that an armed intruder had entered league president Eugene Bert's home and wounded him. The Bert family remained strangely tightlipped about the entire incident and little about the story made sense. It soon became apparent that Bert had actually shot himself in a suicide attempt.

Said to be despondent over health issues, Bert survived and amazingly was back at work before the end of the season. Although he remained at risk of hemorrhage or infection for a time, he was fortunate the bullet passed through a lung and broke a rib but hit no other major organs.[109] Bert was reconfirmed as president during the league meeting in August. At that same meeting, the league decided it was time to rein in Jim Morley.

Weary of the Los Angeles owner's free-spending ways, his habit of speaking to them through the newspapers, and a growing tendency to look after his own best interests rather than the league's (although he was hardly alone in having that attitude), Henry Harris and the other owners announced Morley's franchise had been taken from him because of his failure to attend the meeting.[110] Harris, clearly calling the shots, stated that Morley had made a big mistake in missing the meeting. Obviously annoyed, Harris sneered that Morley had finally sent a proxy only after reading in the press that he was in danger of losing his team.

"At the close of the present year the Los Angeles franchise will be at the disposal of the league," said Harris. "It is decidedly an open question as to whether Jim Morley will get it. There is considerable opposition to the southern magnate in the league at the present time, and the chances are that someone else besides Morley will be awarded the Los Angeles franchise."[111] But if the directors had intended to send a message to the renegade Los Angeles owner, it was not acknowledged.

Morley retorted, "They can't take my franchise away legally, and they know it, and I could enjoin them from forfeiting it if the case was serious." He went on to proclaim, "The franchise really belongs to the city of Los Angeles and if the fans want me to keep it here I'll fight the case to the finish, or if they want some other manager I'll quit."[112]

Nothing happened and Morley continued to entertain Los Angeles fans, including a game in September against San Francisco that featured a circus and the ascension of an airship in the price of admission. The game drew more than four thousand spectators.[113]

Elsewhere league attendance was dwindling to a disappointing level. The marathon 1905 season, including playoffs, extended nearly to Christmas and was too long to sustain interest. The league had continued the split-season format but it was apparent Los Angeles and Tacoma would meet again in a post-season playoff—a prospect that generated little excitement, especially since the Tigers had collapsed and sat in last place for the second half.[114]

Portland, Seattle and Tacoma were supposed to play the final six weeks of the season in California because of the potential for inclement weather in Oregon and Washington, but Mike Fisher could not wait that long because of the absence of support for his Tigers. In late September, Fisher moved a series against Oakland from Tacoma to Spokane. He also switched the homestand for the week of October 10 to Los Angeles.[115]

After playing a series in Portland the first week of October, the Tacoma Tigers boarded a train to California. Hoping to capitalize on the number of former Santa Clara College players on his roster, Fisher scheduled the last two days of a series versus Oakland at Cycler's Park in San Jose.[116] Tigers pitcher Bobby Keefe obviously enjoyed performing before his friends and family, throwing a no-hitter on November 18 in which only one runner reached base, on an error by Truck Eagan.[117]

Frustrated by the necessity for alternate venues and ready to abandon Tacoma after only two years, Mike Fisher cast about for a place to play in 1906, looking first at Fresno or Spokane and then Pasadena. Walter McCredie floated a plan that would have Fisher remaining in Tacoma but playing most of his home games in Portland.[118] As the year ended it was far from certain where Fisher would go, but Tacoma was not on his list.[119]

Oakland also moved home games, playing a series in Sacramento against Seattle in late November and then immediately traveling to Bakersfield to take on Portland. The latter site was chosen probably because that city was trying to acquire a PCL franchise and had served for the past two years as Portland's spring training camp.[120]

As the 1905 season ended, it was clear that the league faced serious problems. And there were major challenges ahead, including a catastrophe for the city of San Francisco. Even so, the previous five years had been significant for baseball on the West Coast. The stops and starts that had plagued baseball leagues in the West over the previous twenty-five years would not be an issue for the Pacific Coast League; the organization had the financial wherewithal to survive the lean times.

Thanks to the McCredies, the PCL had established a solid foothold in the Pacific Northwest, notwithstanding the problems in Tacoma. Los Angeles had developed into a strong market vital to the league's ability to attract talent and maintain a solid financial base. San Francisco remained the cornerstone of the league and its center of power, but the indomitable Jim Morley, as controversial as he was, had been a major contributor to the success of the PCL. He had advanced the idea that the league could challenge the majors on its own terms. He also had prevented the Pacific National League from gaining a foothold in Los Angeles. At the same time, he seemed incapable of seeing his franchise as part of a larger organization — envisioning it instead as a stand-alone business he could handle as he pleased, regardless of whether or not it was good for the Pacific Coast League.

Major changes were coming. Mike Fisher and Eugene Bert would be gone from the scene in a little over a year. Morley's remaining time in the league was short as well. By the next summer, he would essentially be out of the picture. Amazingly enough, he would outlast Henry Harris.

CHAPTER THREE

1906 to 1909: Things Get Shaken Up

The Pacific Coast League owners, coming off a disastrous season both artistically and financially, attempted to remedy the league's attendance problems by shortening the 1906 schedule by three weeks and reducing ticket prices from thirty-five cents to a quarter. They also tackled the issue of Mike Fisher's desperate need to relocate his financially moribund Tacoma Tigers.

Fisher's first choice for a new home had been Pasadena, which would have given greater Los Angeles two PCL teams, one of which would always be at home, the same as the San Francisco Bay Area.[1] Many viewed continuous baseball as a positive arrangement; when a city had only one team, it was a continual struggle to maintain interest in the ball club during road trips that could last several weeks. Most owners worried about fans finding other things to do with their spare time, but Jim Morley was not of that mindset. Feeling it more important to keep the Los Angeles market to himself, Morley vetoed Fisher's proposed move to Southern California.[2]

Fisher then announced he would move his team to Fresno. Echoing his excitement about Tacoma two years earlier, he proclaimed to be "enthusiastic over the outlook for the Raisin City."[3]

As the Pacific Coast League entered its fourth season, its center of power remained in San Francisco — specifically in the hands of Henry Harris and league treasurer Theodore Goodman, a business partner of Harris who owned a large block of stock in the San Francisco franchise. But things were about to change, thanks to another partner, Andrew Clunie, who was upset about the proliferation of gambling at Recreation Park and the fact that his two partners were profiting from it.[4] Clunie purchased Goodwin's share of the team in January 1906, giving him majority ownership. Henry Harris instantly recognized the shift in power, remarking, "You can say I won't be as prominent in baseball as I have been." He too sold out to Clunie and resigned as manager.[5]

But Clunie would quickly become disillusioned by the politics of the league. Within two months of buying out Harris and Goodman, he sold his ninety percent ownership stake to Oakland owner Cal Ewing and boxing promoter James Gleason. Ewing announced he would dispose of his interest in Oakland and act as a silent partner at San Francisco while Gleason ran the Seals on a daily basis.[6] A few weeks later, Andrew Clunie would realize how lucky he was to get out when he did.

* * *

At 5:12 on the morning of April 18, 1906, a jolt awakened San Francisco Seals teammates Kid Mohler and John Gochnaur in their room at the National Hotel. Seconds later, the entire building began shuddering as the ground underneath was ruptured by an earthquake of incredible force. The quake, which a University of California professor likened to a terrier violently shaking a rat, lasted nearly a full minute and left San Francisco in ruins.[7] There was major destruction north and south of the city as well; the entire business district of Santa Rosa was reduced to rubble and San Jose suffered serious damage. Telegraph lines from San Francisco were immediately knocked out and for more than three hours the city was cut off from the rest of the world.[8]

The San Andreas Fault split the earth along a 290-mile line.[9] A twenty-foot-wide crack opened up on Point Reyes. A fence on a farm in Marin County offset eight and a half feet. The quake was felt in Oregon and Nevada, and significant damage was reported into central California.

Daylight was only a suggestion on the eastern horizon as Mohler and Gochnaur witnessed a mind-numbing scene of total devastation. Dazed, people staggered into the dark streets, trying to comprehend what was happening while clutching onto each other as aftershocks threatened to bring buildings down around them. Some made attempts to continue life as usual, cooking breakfast while assessing the destruction. Unfortunately, the chimneys in many homes were damaged and these efforts at making the situation somewhat normal resulted in fires, the largest of which — the Hayes Valley inferno — destroyed most of the business district of San Francisco.

A number of water mains were rendered useless in the quake and many of the fires proved too intense to battle, spreading unchecked before devouring portions of the city previously left standing. As Mohler and Gochnaur watched flames race toward their hotel, they recognized the urgency of their situation. Taking notice of a recently dug trench for a sewer line running in front of the hotel, the two ballplayers dragged their trunks downstairs and tossed them into the ditch, burying them and rushing to safety. They returned ten days later and retrieved their belongings intact.[10]

There were only minimal casualties among ballplayers. Portland was in town to play the Seals and two of that team's members suffered minor injuries from broken glass when they jumped from a second-story window at their hotel.[11] Amazingly no other players were injured in the disaster, although umpire Phil Knell lost everything he owned, as did his parents.[12] The Pacific Coast League offices were destroyed and flames consumed Recreation Park on the second day of the disaster when a firebreak across the street proved ineffective.[13] Eugene Bert lost his home and his office. With communication to the area cut off, Los Angeles pitcher Walter Nagle jumped on a special northbound train to his home in Santa Rosa and was enormously relieved to find his parents safe and sound.[14]

* * *

Eugene Bert was still league president despite his suicide attempt the year before, and in the wake of the disaster he had a real battle on his hands. With telegraph lines on the West Coast either inoperative or in control of the military, communication between Bert and team officials was sporadic. There was open debate whether the league would, or should, continue, especially in San Francisco and Oakland, which were besieged with homeless refugees preoccupied with survival. The other PCL teams continued to play but it was clear something would have to be done to maintain the semblance of a regular season.

On April 27, Bert announced that San Francisco and Oakland would travel to Portland and Seattle while Fresno and Los Angeles would play each other, alternating cities. When the Seals returned to California, they would play the remainder of their home schedule at Idora Park, the Oaks' home stadium.[15] It was also decided that league offices would be relocated to Oakland.

A view of the devastation at Harrison and Sixth in San Francisco. This is two blocks from Recreation Park, which was destroyed by the fires that resulted from the quake (United States Geological Survey).

There were mixed feelings about continuing play. It went without saying that the loss of Recreation Park, located in the league's largest market, was a major blow to the fortunes of the PCL. Cal Ewing, Judge McCredie and Mike Fisher were all solidly in favor of completing the 1906 schedule. On the other hand, Jim Morley and Seattle's Jim Agnew were less certain. Morley claimed the league had suffered a forty-thousand-dollar deficit in 1905 and that he had personally lost another seventy-eight thousand dollars in the San Francisco disaster when several bowling alleys he had recently opened there were destroyed.[16] Unwilling to assume further financial risk, Morley vowed to suspend operations and allow players he had under contract to perform elsewhere for the remainder of the year.

At the same time he was publicly moaning about his problems in the Pacific Coast League, Morley was accused of secretly conspiring with Jim Agnew to take their two teams and join the Pacific Northwest League, a maneuver that could have destroyed the PCL.[17] Agnew opted to stay in the league, but his commitment to do so was tenuous.

Eugene Bert convened an emergency meeting on May 14, at which Morley announced he wanted out, albeit temporarily. His fellow owners were only too willing to oblige, although they were not interested in ridding themselves of Morley on anything less than a permanent basis.

Morley was willing to return his franchise to the league, but only if the $1,500 guarantee posted at the beginning of the season was returned. Judge McCredie, Cal Ewing and Fresno team president A.B. Evans wasted no time reaching for their checkbooks to contribute $500 each to be rid of him, but Morley failed to appear at the bank the next day. Instead, he demanded the PCL post a ten-thousand-dollar bond subject to forfeiture should the league drop the city in less than two years. Bert and Ewing replied that it was too late to be making demands; Morley had already lost his team.[18]

Morley responded by asking that every Angels player sign an agreement releasing them on the condition they return in 1907.[19] On May 18 he wired J.H. Farrell, secretary of the National Association, stating that he had disbanded his roster and was requesting guidance on what he should tell the players. Farrell told Morley that the Pacific Coast League was remaining intact and that the players must remain in Los Angeles.[20]

After learning of Morley's telegram to Farrell, an apoplectic Eugene Bert reacted by wiring instructions to Cap Dillon to take the Los Angeles team to Portland and play against the Beavers. Dillon said he would do so, adding, "Morley has nothing further to do with the team."

But only six players, including Dillon, boarded the train north; none of them had uniforms and only one possessed a bat. Seven stayed behind and the remainder left to play in other leagues.[21] When the train stopped briefly in Oakland, Bert had players from Oakland, Fresno and San Francisco available in order for Dillon to field a squad. Cal Ewing also met with the group, handing each player a five-dollar gold piece as a gesture of good faith.[22]

Bert announced he had secured pledges totaling nearly fifteen thousand dollars from the eastern leagues to keep the PCL operating. Even though his Oakland and San Francisco teams had been the most affected, Cal Ewing urged that the funds be divided equally among the six teams since all were suffering.[23] Both Ewing and Judge McCredie indicated they were willing to spend whatever it took to keep the league going.

Cal Ewing wrote a $1,500 check to meet the Angels' payroll as well as the cost of purchasing team uniforms and replacing home plate and the bases, which Morley had taken with him when his team was confiscated. Ewing also pledged twenty thousand dollars as protection should Morley file a lawsuit that proved successful.[24] The Angels were eventually purchased by a syndicate of Los Angeles businessmen, who chose mining tycoon Henry Berry to run the franchise.[25]

A short, stout, round-faced man, with his baldness usually obscured by a colored beaver hat, Henry Berry was comfortable being the center of attention. He loved to tell stories and spend money in equal measure. Berry did not look the part of an adventurer or millionaire but was indeed both. At one time, he and his brothers controlled one-half of the gold-producing property in the Klondike, pulling out as much as $53,000 from the ground in a single day. A trained mining engineer, Berry had been no neophyte striking out across Chilkoot Pass in the blind hope of falling into a fortune. He and his brothers knew what they were doing.

In October 1900, Henry Berry married Edna Bush in Selma, California, and they honeymooned down the rapids of the Yukon River and into Dawson. Berry had so expanded his wealth through investments in oil fields and fruit orchards that a year later, when he and his new bride moved to Southern California, he was instantly one of the richest men in Los Angeles. Henry Berry was a great fan of baseball, billiards and boxing. The league could not have found a better man to take over in Los Angeles.[26]

* * *

The league was cursed with another runaway pennant-winner in 1906, this time fielded by the McCredies in Portland. There had been suggestions about restarting the season because of the disruption caused by the earthquake, but it was doubtful anyone would have caught the Beavers anyway. Walter McCredie's charges won by nineteen and a half games despite selling catcher Larry McLean (batting .355) and pitcher Bill Essick (with a record of 19–6) to Cincinnati for immediate delivery in early September.[27]

As a result, the season proved to be a second straight year of financial disaster for the PCL. Seattle remained on the verge of financial collapse, although the team's ace pitcher, Rube Vickers, compiled one of the greatest seasons in minor league history by winning thirty-nine games and striking out 409 batters in 517 innings.

San Francisco and Oakland were struggling with the lingering effects of the earthquake. Los Angeles, which had been hit hard by defections thanks to Morley's shenanigans, suffered a scare when Cap Dillon barely escaped catastrophic injury in a collision between a streetcar and a commuter train in Oakland on August 12.[28]

The league's sixth franchise, Fresno, was simply awful. Ten thousand dollars had been pledged by local businessmen at the beginning of the year to land the franchise for the city, but less than half that amount actually materialized. Charlie Graham had been drafted by the Boston Red Sox, which meant he was not around to help Mike Fisher find talent.

Before the season had started, Fisher traded Elmer Emerson to Oakland for notoriously troubled star pitcher Henry Schmidt, who failed to win a single game for the Raisin Eaters and was loaned to Los Angeles to replenish the Angels roster following Morley's release of his players.[29] Fisher had to compete for most of the season with a roster of only eleven players. The situation grew so desperate that player-strapped Los Angeles donated Warren Hall to Fresno when the Raisin Eaters ran out of pitchers.[30]

Fisher was replaced as Fresno's manager before the season ended, resigning under pressure on November 1. He then argued with Raisin Eaters directors about five hundred dollars he said was owed to him because the resignation had not been voluntary.[31] The colorful Fisher would never again play an active role in the Pacific Coast League but would leave his mark on baseball two years later by organizing the first exhibition tour of professional players to Japan.[32]

* * *

Despite his successful efforts to keep the league functioning, Eugene Bert had his detractors. Seen as weak and unable to stand up to the major league owners and plagued by drinking problems, Bert resigned prior to the start of the 1907 season. Cal Ewing, who controlled two of the six PCL franchises, replaced Bert as president.[33] Rumors circulated that Jim Morley had traveled to San Francisco to lure old foe Henry Harris into forming an opposition league. Harris was reportedly uninterested; he was focused on running the three cigar stores he had opened since the earthquake.[34]

Although Morley would disappear as a problem, Cal Ewing would face other obstacles. The Seattle franchise could not secure financial backing and the team was sold to Dan Dugdale, who pulled it out of the PCL and into the Pacific Northwest League. "We want this territory," Dugdale declared, "and we are going to get it."[35]

Ewing cried foul but there was little he could do. Dugdale's maneuvering also meant that little could be done with moribund Fresno. There was no time to establish a sixth franchise, and a five-team league was clearly not feasible. The Raisin Eaters folded and the Pacific Coast League became a four-team aggregation.[36]

Dan Dugdale had scrambled the plans of the Pacific Coast League, but he had miscalculated on one count; he had thought the McCredies would abandon the PCL. But the McCredies remained in the Pacific Coast League, maintaining the circuit as an interstate entity rather than simply a California aggregation — albeit in a weakened state.

* * *

James Carroll "Cal" Ewing was born in Solano County, California, in 1866. His father, a native of Ohio, was employed as a clerk and moved the family to Oakland when Cal was six. Young Cal was always interested in organizing activities, especially sports. At eight years of age he helped form his first ballclub, the Twenty-First Street team.[37] As an adult he worked for Alameda County, first as a clerk and later as the county auditor, and was credited with introducing modern bookkeeping and auditing methods to the county. He was also very active in community affairs: organizing the community chest, reorganizing the chamber of commerce, and receiving an appointment as secretary of the California Bank Commission. Ewing was an expert parliamentarian, and baseball's National Commission frequently consulted him on procedural issues. He even appeared on stage in local theatrical productions in his spare time.[38]

But Cal Ewing's first love was sports. He had played amateur baseball, taking over management of the Reliance Club in Oakland in the late 1880s and organizing the club's sports teams. In 1898, Ewing purchased the Oakland franchise in the revived California League and had owned it ever since.[39] Never one to back away from a fight, Ewing had little time or patience for reporters or any other outsider who questioned his decisions. He was also one of those men who could engage in a heated debate all day with someone and have a drink with the same person that night. Although tough, he had a twinkle in his eye and enjoyed practical jokes. He was honest and kept both friends and enemies for a long time. Ewing also came to be considered as the man who saved the Pacific Coast League.

The future of baseball in the post-earthquake Bay Area was far from certain. There was particular doubt regarding the viability of the Oakland franchise; a proposal had surfaced that involved the Oaks becoming a traveling squad. Ed Walter, in charge of day-to-day operations at Oakland on behalf of Ewing, managed to whip up enough support from local businessmen and boosters to keep the team in the East Bay. He moved the Oaks from Idora Park, where they had played for three years, back to Freeman's Park at Fifty-Ninth and San

Pablo for the beginning of the 1907 season and arranged to have Idora Park's bleachers moved to the old stadium. Walter also acquired additional land so that the left-field fence could be moved back to a respectable distance.[40]

Meanwhile, Cal Ewing knew he had to replace burned-down Recreation Park in San Francisco. He quickly constructed a new facility farther west from the old site, at Fourteenth and Valencia streets. According to Angels owner Henry Berry, Ewing spent one hundred thousand dollars on the new baseball plant, including an expansive clubhouse and team offices located in a two-story building tucked away in deep center field.[41] March rains rendered the new playing surface a sea of mud, so the league delayed the schedule a week in order for the field to be ready for Opening Day. There were no special ceremonies marking the return of baseball to San Francisco outside of the traditional parade of the teams through the streets, yet the bleachers were completely filled by eight o'clock in the morning.[42] Baseball was back in San Francisco.

The new Recreation Park was an oddity. Because of the shape of the lot on which it was constructed, the distance to the right-field fence was extremely short, only 235 feet from home plate. A fifty-foot-high wall with wire mesh at the top was erected in an attempt to reduce the number of cheap home runs; its limited effectiveness was demonstrated in August when Los Angeles outfielder Walter Carlisle took advantage of the wall to become the first Pacific Coast League player to hit three home runs in a game.[43]

Along the first base side of the diamond, a few rows of bleachers at ground level were enclosed with chicken wire along the front. This early luxury box allowed fans proximity to the action while grabbing a sandwich or a shot of whiskey, the choice of which was included in the ticket price. Over time, the section would become known as the "Booze Cage," where liquor flowed freely, even during Prohibition, and players could hear insults as well as wagering—the latter of which often flowed more freely than the alcohol. The team was hurt financially in 1907 by several major strikes in San Francisco, including a bloody streetcar dispute, but overall the Seals were in better shape than the year before; by extension, so was the rest of the league.[44]

* * *

The Angels' Frank "Cap" Dillon projected the most businesslike image among the Pacific Coast League managers. His prematurely gray hair and ramrod straight posture gave him an air of distinction. Dillon enjoyed automobiles; his wife would always recall his first, a Ford purchased in 1914 from Christy Mathewson. Before that, the Angels manager and his wife took a streetcar to the game each day.[45] A man of few words, some described Dillon as "chilly" and no one wanted to incur the icy stare of contempt he employed when perturbed. When Dillon grew impatient, his sarcasm could cut to the bone. An excellent judge of talent, he had little patience for those lacking it.[46]

A native of Illinois, Dillon began his career as a pitcher before moving to the outfield and finally first base with Buffalo in the Western League in 1899. He then played for Pittsburgh and Detroit, plus two games for Baltimore in the American League, before signing with the Angels in August 1902. Dillon married during the 1903 season, and though his wife had never seen a baseball game, she became a rabid fan. Other than the 1904 season, which he was forced to spend with Brooklyn, Dillon remained in Los Angeles for the rest of his career. A good clutch hitter and an excellent first baseman, Dillon was known for quick footwork that allowed him to play off the bag. Some felt his footwork a little too quick; he had a reputation for pulling his foot off the base just before the throw got to him, affording him a split-second advantage against a base runner.[47]

Dillon's 1907 and 1908 Angels were smart, veteran teams. Many of the players had been with Los Angeles for at least a couple of years. Pitcher Dolly Gray won sixty games in those two years while veterans Jud Smith, Rube Ellis and Dillon led the offense. When the Boston Red Sox acquired outfielders Walter Carlisle and Gavvy Cravath from Los Angeles after the 1907 season, Dillon moved second baseman Kitty Brashear to the outfield and drafted Ennis "Rebel" Oakes from Cedar Rapids. The Angels did not miss a beat. Los Angeles captured the 1907 pennant by fifteen games over San Francisco and by thirteen and a half games the next year over Portland, with Ewing's Bay Area teams bringing up the rear of the four-team league.

During this period, Henry Berry and Cal Ewing remained focused on expansion, trekking numerous times to consult with Judge McCredie on the best strategy to do so. There were proposals for a six- or even an eight-team league, but Dan Dugdale, as usual, was one of the impediments. The Pacific Coast League desperately wanted Seattle, but Dugdale held rights to the territory and was unwilling to leave the Northwest League without some guarantee of power. Judge McCredie hoped to see three northern cities admitted to the league and thought Dugdale should be part of the mix. Ewing, who was wary about making any concessions to the fat man up north, nevertheless signaled that he was willing to entertain the notion, saying, "If we can get that territory [Seattle] and Tacoma wants to come with us, I will favor an eight-team league. If we should not get Seattle, we would have to be satisfied with a six-team league, five cities in California and one in the north."[48]

* * *

As the Pacific Coast League looked to grow it faced another challenger, an outlaw circuit called California State League. After two years of operation with four teams, expansion by at least two franchises was a necessity for the PCL to maintain its classification as a top minor league. The California State League had operated in Northern California since the formation of the Pacific Coast League and had gained momentum — and ambition — since the San Francisco earthquake. The CSL's strength was such that it was in a position to obstruct the PCL's goals to grow in both territory and talent.[49]

The Pacific Coast League owners tried coaxing the outlaws into the fold during a meeting held at the St. Francis Hotel in San Francisco on December 1, 1908. Cal Ewing and Henry Berry huddled with the directors of the California State League, including its most influential figure, Stockton owner Cy Moreing, but broke off talks when the CSL demanded to retain Hal Chase and others they had illegally signed.[50] Berry was particularly upset about the attitude of CSL owners, declaring, "They didn't talk reason when we met with them and I will not attend any more conferences."[51]

The rhetoric continued for weeks. The *Stockton Evening Mail* branded Ewing and Berry as liars and backed Moreing in his fight against what the newspaper called "The Baseball Trust." The gravity of the situation was such that National and American league presidents Harry Pulliam and Ban Johnson traveled to the Coast and attended meetings aimed at ending the impasse. It was quite a turn of events for a league that six years earlier had been the outlaw fighting the establishment.[52]

Mike Fisher's old catcher, Charlie Graham, owned the Sacramento franchise in the CSL and suggested a compromise that would have allowed the California State League to keep disputed players but split any money with the PCL should those players be sold or drafted. In late December, PCL owners agreed to accept Graham's proposal, and the plan was presented to Cy Moreing. He flatly dismissed it.[53]

Following a five-hour meeting between the two sides a few days later, the California

State League rejected all offers from Organized Baseball and vowed to remain an outlaw.[54] Graham, thinking his fellow State League directors suicidal in rejecting the PCL's overture, announced he would transfer his team to the PCL and that it would play at the grounds used by the California State League.[55]

Abandoning any hope of peace with the CSL, Pacific Coast League directors turned south to locate the league's sixth franchise. Unlike Jim Morley, Henry Berry had no qualms about continuous baseball in Los Angeles and welcomed the league's decision to place a team in Vernon, a small industrial city just outside the Los Angeles city limits. Not coincidentally, it was also one of the few areas in Los Angeles County where liquor could be openly sold on Sundays. The franchise was awarded to brewery owner Fred Maier for the token sum of one dollar. He announced that the field at Vernon, which was used by amateur players, would be enlarged and improved for league play. Although the ballpark was not in the most desirable location, it was within the five-cent fare limit on the Santa Fe Avenue car line. A fight promoter named Jack Doyle owned the ballpark, as well as the saloon adjoining it, and permitted free use of the facility, provided the team played there twice a week during homestands.[56] Vernon's other home games would be staged at Chutes Park.[57] With a six-team league assured, Cal Ewing traveled to Cincinnati for the National Commission meetings and on January 6, 1909, it was announced that the Pacific Coast League, along with the American Association and the Eastern League, would be awarded "AA" status, the highest ranking among minor leagues.[58]

Determined to take the fight directly to the Pacific Coast League, Cy Moreing responded by taking charge of the CSL franchise in Oakland and announcing he would boost the fortunes of the two CSL teams in the Bay Area by building new ballparks near Idora Park and at the Seals' old grounds at Harrison and Eighth. (Both teams eventually shared the new Oakland ballpark at Fifty-Seventh and Grove.)[59]

But Charlie Graham had been accurate in his assessment that the smaller outlaw was not equipped to survive open warfare against its bigger rival. In fact, Graham would prove to be a part of the CSL's problem as he began raiding his old State League partners even before the 1909 season began. He signed first baseman Arnold "Chick" Gandil (one of a parade of several future "Black Sox" figures to appear in the PCL) and also persuaded Jack Fitzgerald, a talented but troubled pitcher, to jump from Stockton.[60] Graham's roster was soon filled with old PCL names, including Spider Baum, Jimmy Whalen, Jimmy Byrnes and Charlie Doyle.

The CSL tried to counter Graham's moves with an offer of five thousand dollars to Mike Donlin if he played for the outlaws in Stockton. (The star outfielder of the New York Giants was taking the year off to travel the Orpheum Circuit with his wife.) Donlin, who had played in Stockton before and was very popular there, turned down the deal.[61]

When all was said and done, it was obvious the CSL had undertaken a battle that only resulted in its undoing. It was a war that was essentially over before it started—a repeat of what had occurred six years earlier with the Pacific National League. With no presence outside of Northern California, the CSL lacked the resources to compete. By mid–July, the California State League was down to four teams. The league would struggle on until October before shutting down for the year. A few weeks after that, the California State League agreed to become part of Organized Baseball.[62]

* * *

In yet another runaway, the San Francisco Seals captured the 1909 PCL pennant, taking the lead for good in mid–May and posting twenty more victories than second-place Portland.

The team's first title since the days of Henry Harris was attributable in part to a deep pitching staff led by two aces. One was Frank Browning, a diminutive right-hander from Kentucky who won thirty-two games, including a PCL record sixteen in a row. The other was a lanky bricklayer named Clarence "Cack" Henley, who won thirty-one games, including a magnificent twenty-four-inning complete-game shutout in June against Oakland.[63] From July 1 through July 6, Seals pitchers held Sacramento scoreless for forty-eight consecutive innings, including five shutouts in a row.[64]

The other strength of the Seals was their infield, which included slick-fielding first baseman Tom Tennant and defensive whiz Kid Mohler, the last of the left-handed second basemen. Shortstop Harry McArdle and third baseman Rollie Zeider had switched positions from the year before to take better advantage of their defensive skills; Zeider also led the PCL with ninety-three stolen bases. Catcher Claude Berry, who had brief trials with the Chicago White Sox and the Philadelphia Athletics, played on the fifth pennant-winning team of his pro career.[65] Thanks to pitching and defense, the Seals had emerged from the rubble of the 1906 earthquake to claim their first PCL championship.

* * *

Cal Ewing's running the league at the same time he owned two of its franchises had led to friction among the other owners. Ewing publicly proclaimed his desire to relinquish the job of league president and Judge McCredie planned to hold Ewing to that pledge.[66] The two had openly feuded since summer, when McCredie charged Ewing with pulling a fast one in signing California League outfielder Jimmy Smith when Smith had already agreed to a contract with Portland.[67]

There were other reasons for McCredie's crankiness. Weary of defending his territory against the Pacific Northwest League by himself, the Judge had wanted an eight-team PCL in 1909 with four teams in the Northwest and four in California.[68] The Judge had been trying to entice Dan Dugdale to join the league and insisted that Spokane, Seattle and Tacoma had been ready to enlist, but that Ewing had failed to respond to the opportunity. McCredie claimed that Ewing turned down the proposal so he would be assured of the votes for the league presidency.[69]

At the end of the 1909 season there were rumors fueled by harsh comments attributed to the Judge that the McCredies were taking the Beavers to the Pacific Northwest League.[70] "I have carried out every obligation I had on the Pacific Coast League," the Judge said. "I am through with the Coast League as far as sentiment goes because I think it is ruled by a lot of selfish pikers. I could sit back and laugh if an earthquake hit the league as hard as it did in 1906, provided it did no other damage."[71]

Cal Ewing kept his promise not to run for re-election as league president. Bill Lange was suggested as a possible candidate, but it was a surprise compromise choice, San Francisco Superior Court Judge Thomas Graham, who was named the new head of the league in November 1909.[72] As a result, Judge McCredie announced he was satisfied with the selection and would remain in the PCL.

As a new decade dawned, the league had suffered through an earthquake, both literally and figuratively, and other than Cal Ewing, all of the major players at the founding of the league were gone. The landscape of the PCL had shifted dramatically since that disastrous April morning in San Francisco, with the league surviving raids by the Pacific Northwest League and the California State League, players jumping contracts, and the loss of two of its franchises. With Judge McCredie mollified, it was hoped the Pacific Coast League was heading into a period of relative stability.

CHAPTER FOUR

1910 to 1914: The McCredie Era

A tall, angular Scotsman with a jutting jaw line and the intimidating presence of a military commander, Portland player-manager Walter McCredie was often branded a cynic, but when it came to his team he had little to be cynical about. The Beavers had come a long way since he and his uncle had purchased the team in 1905 and the franchise was about to hit its peak, taking four of the first five Pacific Coast League pennants in the new decade. Walter McCredie deserved a lot of credit for that success.

At age thirty-three, McCredie was winding down as a player but still appeared in right field occasionally, striking his familiar pose — hands on hips while pacing back and forth, literally wearing a path in the ground and muttering profanities to himself about a play or an umpire's call. He was supremely superstitious, especially about scraps of paper lying on the ground, and those knowing of his compulsion to pick them up would try to drive him crazy at times with a rain of confetti near the Portland dugout.

McCredie was unconventional in his use of pitchers: instead of following a standard rotation, he matched pitchers against particular opponents and used them whenever he felt they were ready and the situation dictated. "Pitchers on my team don't pitch in turns," he said. "When I think they are right and have had their rest, they pitch."[1] His credo for his players was: don't drink, don't overeat, and don't gamble.

While capable of giving a pat on the back or a word of encouragement, McCredie's usual manner in the dugout included non-stop chatter about everything, much of it caustic and/or profane. Harry Williams called him "a sarcastic cuss." McCredie seemed alternately bored or annoyed, grousing at anyone within earshot, among them umpires, players both on the field and the bench, and even himself. He would grow impatient at times, sometimes cupping his hands and yelling disgustedly, "Not yet, not yet!" at players failing to follow instructions. Walter McCredie's players were unlikely to consider him a great human being, but they respected his track record for sending players to the major leagues, adding to the PCL's burgeoning reputation as a talent goldmine.

Early to recognize the competitive benefit in aligning themselves with a major league franchise, the McCredies entered into a gentleman's agreement of sorts with Cleveland of the American League. (Open "farming" of players was illegal under the rules set down by the National Commission.) Operating the most geographically remote franchise in the PCL, the arrangement with Cleveland was the business model that made the most economic sense for the McCredies. The arrangement was so successful that for much of the second decade of the 1900s the Cleveland roster regularly included at least a half-dozen players that had worn a Portland uniform.

The McCredies' new sensation in 1910, Sylveanus "Vean" Gregg, was a tall, twenty-

five-year-old left-handed pitcher fresh from the Pacific Northwest League. Purchased from Spokane during the 1909 season by Cleveland, Gregg refused to report so the Naps allowed him to play for Portland in 1910.[2] Gregg started the season slowly, but once the weather warmed up he was practically unhittable. On the Fourth of July, the left-hander combined with teammate Bill Steen to sweep a double-header against Vernon; both men pitched one-hitters.[3]

On July 9 Gregg had a scare, forced to leave a game with a sore arm after two innings. The next day he felt better and shut out Vernon on three hits.[4] Three days after that, Gregg relieved Tom Seaton to get the last out of a 1–0 victory over Oakland that moved the Beavers into first place.[5]

* * *

Each Pacific Coast League season brought new characters that captured the public's attention and 1910 proved no different. Besides Vean Gregg, two San Francisco players made the biggest impression.

The first was not a newcomer to the league — slugging outfielder Ping Bodie was in his third season with the Seals — but in 1910 he went on a home run tear that captivated fans. A likable braggart prone to odd but vaguely colorful statements, such as "I rammy-cackled the old persimmon," "I can really hemstitch the spheroid," and "I walloped the old onion," Bodie loved playing to the crowd and celebrating his home runs.

Born Francesco Pezzolo to a vegetable dealer in the Cow Hollow section of San Francisco, the Seals star did not look the part of a great athlete, being somewhat short and stumpy with broad, sloping shoulders. However, his popularity and ability to hit a baseball paved the way for a string of outstanding Italian American ballplayers from the Bay Area; the DiMaggio, Lazzeri, Lombardi and Crosetti families would each grudgingly see baseball as an acceptable profession in America and allow their sons to play. During the 1910 season Ping Bodie wielded his fifty-two-ounce bat to twice blast a pair of home runs in a game, an amazing feat in the Dead Ball era.

After Bodie broke Truck Eagan's league record with his twenty-sixth home run, a group of fans journeyed from Vallejo to Recreation Park to honor the slugger during a double-header. To their delight, Bodie responded with three hits on the day, including his twenty-seventh home run.[6] He added three more before season's end, giving him an impressive thirty for the year — twelve more than Vernon's Roy Brashear, the runner-up in that category. The Chicago White Sox purchased Bodie's services for 1911 and he went on to become a colorful baseball legend.[7]

Meanwhile, Bodie's new teammate, Fred Mitchell, was attracting attention precisely because he did not want it. A right-handed spitball pitcher signed by the Seals at the end of August, Mitchell refused to reveal anything about his background and was a mystery even to his teammates, having come from nowhere and seeming to have no past — at least not one he was willing to share. Before long he was dubbed "Mysterious" Mitchell and became the subject of countless rumors.

When San Francisco and Los Angeles played at Chutes Park on September 9, a *Los Angeles Times* photographer managed to snap a photograph of the reluctant celebrity as he sat watching the game. Realizing what had happened, Mitchell leaped to his feet and grabbed

Opposite: **Portland player/manager Walter McCredie, giving instruction to Beavers captain Otis Johnson. He would lead his Portland Beavers to four pennants in five years, between 1910 and 1914 (Ray Saraceni Collection).**

a rock, threatening to smash the camera and yelling to Seals captain Kid Mohler to keep photographers out of his face or he would refuse to appear in uniform.[8]

Mitchell took his anger out on the Angels the next day, winning both games of a doubleheader and adding to everyone's determination to discover whether Mitchell was crazy, hiding something or merely eccentric.[9]

When the Seals returned to San Francisco, Mitchell was scheduled to pitch for the first time at Recreation Park but refused to take the field until photographers were removed. After several minutes delay, the umpire ordered the cameras away and Mitchell finally walked out to the mound.[10] In spite of these antics, an action shot of the reclusive pitcher appeared the next day in the *San Francisco Chronicle* thanks to a new telescopic lens utilized by a *Chronicle* photographer.[11]

By the time he made his next start, on September 17 before eight thousand raucous Seals fans, Mitchell had mastered the art of manipulating the home crowd. Working into the eighth inning that day, Mitchell was on the short end of the score largely because of four errors by shortstop Hunky Shaw. Manager Danny Long decided to remove Mitchell from the game and the pitcher responded by angrily throwing his glove to the ground and stalking off to the clubhouse in center field, making sure to pass slowly in front of the left-field bleachers. Seals fans began booing loudly, aiming most of their frustration at Shaw, whom they held most responsible for their favorite player's departure. Reaching the clubhouse door, Mitchell huffed and puffed and slammed it as hard as he could, which the crowd took as a cue to boo even louder. After changing out of his uniform, Mitchell emerged in an expensive suit, a gray cap and a pair of black kid gloves. He bowed as he strolled along the right-field bleachers and the crowd reacted in an absolute frenzy. He then entered the grandstand and sat there for the rest of the game, the very picture of a hero among his people. Even though the Seals rallied to win, Mitchell's early exit remained a sore point for his fans.[12]

After the game several hundred of them followed Mitchell to the street, where they managed to clog traffic and create a spectacle. Mitchell then turned and headed to the team offices where the mob stopped and begged that he favor them with a speech. The pitcher held up his left hand to ask for silence. He then announced, "I thank you for your appreciation of my services with the club. I am doing the best I can. You shouldn't blame the management, for they thought they were doing the best thing when they took me out. After all, San Francisco won and that is what we were all hoping for." His speech concluded, Mitchell headed back out to the street, fan club in tow.[13]

A few days later, Mysterious Mitchell was identified through the photographs published in the *Los Angeles Times* and the *San Francisco Chronicle* as Fred Walker, a former star athlete at the University of Chicago who had briefly pitched for the Cincinnati Reds earlier in the year before being released. Walker had signed with the New York Giants in July but disappeared after being accused of assaulting a young woman in the hotel in which he was living.[14]

Walker's cover was blown and his act quickly grew stale; he lost a couple of games and fans became less enamored of him. Teammates had tired of his pomposity, his refusal to interact with them and his insistence on special treatment. On October 8 he was arrested for being drunk and disorderly during a joyride to the beach.[15] It was decided to drop him when he refused to carry his bags and announced he would send a boy from the hotel to pick them up. Danny Long released Mitchell/Walker on October 11.[16]

* * *

While Mysterious Mitchell had been making a name for himself, Portland was fighting for first place and Vean Gregg was virtually unstoppable. He struck out sixteen men on August 16 in a twelve-inning one-hitter against Oakland.[17] Shaking off a bad cold, Gregg pitched a no-hitter on September 2 against Los Angeles, striking out fourteen batters, including eight in succession. Of the eight only George Wheeler managed to even foul off a pitch.[18] Gregg shut out Oakland, the Beavers' closest pursuer, again on a one-hitter on September 7.[19] He finally lost to Oakland five days later despite his fourth one-hitter of the season largely because he allowed eight walks.[20] During an eleven-day stretch in October, Gregg combined with Gene Krapp, Bill Steen and Jess "Red" Garrett to pitch eighty-eight consecutive shutout innings against Sacramento and Los Angeles.[21] For the season, Vean Gregg threw fourteen shutouts, four one-hitters and a no-hitter, and won thirty-two games while striking out 376 batters in 387 innings.

Oakland kept pace, thanks in part to a successful protest lodged against Portland when the Beavers used infielder Gus Hetling in three late–September games against them. The McCredies had illegally loaned Hetling to Spokane of the Pacific Northwest League early that month for three weeks, apparently to help Vean Gregg's old team in its pennant race. To cover up what was being done, the McCredies cast Hetling as a contract jumper who had signed with Spokane and then returned due to a change of heart.[22] League President Graham did not buy it and ruled that the Beavers had to forfeit the three games to Oakland, bringing

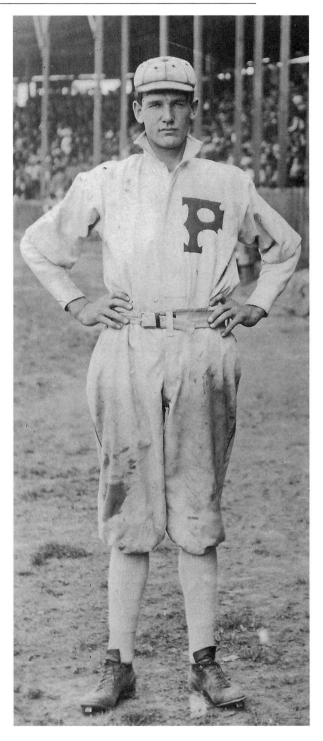

Vean Gregg threw a no-hitter and four one-hitters for Portland in 1910. He began his major league career with three straight twenty-win seasons for Cleveland, from 1911 to 1913 (David Eskenazi Collection).

about a dramatic six-game swing in the standings that put the Oaks in first place by percentage points.[23]

Claiming the decision was made to "satisfy the peanut politicians" of San Francisco, Walter McCredie growled, "You can quote me as saying ... that I think the whole thing is a frame-up to beat Portland out of the pennant in favor of Oakland, and also think the Coast League is crooked all the way through."[24]

In the end it made no difference as the Beavers recovered to win the 1910 pennant despite the forfeits. The National Commission eventually overturned Judge Graham's ruling, although they fined Portland and Spokane one hundred dollars each for their role in the conspiracy.[25] Ironically, by that time Hetling was a member of the Oaks after he was acquired from Portland to back up Harry Wolverton at third base in 1911.[26]

* * *

The stadium at Chutes Park was undergoing changes. The Los Angeles Angels and Vernon Tigers invested nearly twenty thousand dollars to remodel the facility in time for the 1911 season.[27] By mid–January Jim Morley's old stadium was a pile of lumber as workers, including several Pacific Coast League ballplayers, were setting new concrete foundations.[28] Six weeks later, five thousand fans were on hand as the ballyard, now called Washington Park, opened with an exhibition between the Angels and the Boston Red Sox. The grandstand was double the size of the old one and the right-field fence was higher, both to eliminate cheap home runs and prevent non-paying customers from watching the game. An underground sprinkler system was installed, allowing the Angels to play on a grass infield for the first time in several years.[29] The grandstand was accessed by walking through ornamental iron gates and up an inclined ramp through the middle of the facility, eliminating the need for stairs. Brand new features included a parking area set aside for those driving to the ballpark in their automobiles.[30]

After christening Washington Park with the exhibition versus Boston, Cap Dillon took his team to Murrieta to complete spring training, putting his charges on a strict diet and having them play soccer and water polo every day to improve endurance and speed.[31] But it soon became apparent that 1911 was not to be the Angels' year. Catcher Fred Abbott was taking batting practice one morning and the bat flew out of his hands, striking first baseman Howard Deal on the side of the head. It took six stitches to close the wound.[32] Pitcher Lee "Flame" Delhi narrowly escaped serious injury while diving into a pool and striking his face on the bottom.[33] Then Ed Klein fell into a cactus bed and suffered a dozen or so serious puncture wounds.[34] Finally, a group of obviously drunken ballplayers, newspapermen and hangers-on were involved in a wild episode that ended with star pitcher Bill Tozer suffering gunshot wounds to both shoulders.[35]

* * *

The lack of scoring was sapping fan interest, and while shooting pitchers was definitely not the solution, something needed to be done. Pitchers kept inventing new tricks to frustrate batters. The problem was acute everywhere, including the Pacific Coast League, which had not produced a .300 hitter for three straight seasons. (San Francisco's Hunky Shaw won the batting title in 1910 with an embarrassingly low .281 average.) The distance from the mound to home plate had been increased almost two decades before; now it was time to look at the ball.

For more than a quarter-century the inside of a baseball had basically remained the same — a rubber core, wrapped in yarn that was covered with rubber cement to hold the core in place. Baseballs became mushy long before the game was over.

Experiments with a cork core began in 1910. Placed inside a layer of vulcanized rubber and wound in three layers of yarn before being covered with horsehide, the ball lasted longer and offense increased.[36] In 1911, teams averaged 4.6 runs per game in the American League, an increase of a full run over the previous year. The league batting average jumped thirty points. While the impact on National League scoring and batting averages was less significant, the number of home runs doubled between 1909 and 1911. Results were just as dramatic in the PCL: in 1910 no team had hit higher than .226, with Sacramento batting only .203. After the introduction of the new ball, every team in the PCL had a batting average of at least .251, with Vernon leading the league at .266.

Not that modifying the ball exactly crippled pitchers. On April 6, 1911, the same day Flame Delhi engaged in an eighteen-inning pitcher's duel with Oakland's Kitty Knight, Harry "Rube" Suter of San Francisco struck out seventeen Sacramento batters in eight innings.[37] Six months later Jack Fitzgerald of Sacramento and Elmer Koestner of Portland pitched twenty-four innings to a 1–1 tie that was called because of darkness.[38] Five days after that, Sacramento and Los Angeles played twenty-one innings to a 4–4 tie, with Spider Baum pitching for the Senators and John Halla for the Angels.[39]

Pitching remained a major reason Portland repeated as PCL champion in 1911 despite the loss of Vean Gregg, who had joined the parade of former Beavers to Cleveland where he would win twenty games in each of his first three major league seasons. The Beavers staff included thirty-game winner Bill Steen, a cool customer Walter McCredie considered his smartest pitcher. Elmer Koestner used his fastball to add twenty-five wins while Tom Seaton, a knuckleballer and breaking ball specialist who was probably the most talented pitcher on the roster, won twenty-four.[40] Troubled Ben Henderson was a fourth twenty-game winner even though he began drinking heavily and then disappeared from a Stockton hospital in the middle of the season.[41]

During Henderson's absence, McCredie turned to Ferdinand Henkle, a left-hander one year removed from the University of Oregon. The youngster responded with a no-hitter against Sacramento in only his fifth game for the Beavers.[42]

Changing the baseball was not bringing about an end to the pitchers' livelihoods.

* * *

The defensive play of 1911, or indeed any other year, was made by twenty-eight-year-old Vernon Tigers center fielder Walter Carlisle, whose name should be synonymous with the term "circus catch." One of the fastest players in the league, he was known for his peculiar method of diving for fly balls. After making the catch, he rolled into a forward somersault before popping back to his feet to execute the return throw to the infield.[43]

Carlisle's unmatched feat occurred in the sixth inning of a July 19 game between the Tigers and Angels. With the scored tied, 3–3, and Angels base runners George Metzger and Charlie Moore at first and second with no one out, Tigers manager Happy Hogan brought Harry Stewart in to relieve starting pitcher Alex "Soldier" Carson.[44]

The Angels' next batter, Roy Akin, hit a low line drive just beyond the reach of the infielders. Certain the ball would drop, Metzger and Moore took off immediately. Playing in center field, Carlisle had positioned himself extremely shallow, directly behind second base, and got a terrific jump. At the last moment he dove, snagging the ball before it touched the ground and tumbling into a double somersault. Neither Angels base runner realized Carlisle had made the catch. When he popped back to his feet, Carlisle saw that Moore had already rounded third, so he ran in and touched second base for another out. Realizing the other runner, Metzger, had passed second base and could be easily beaten back to first,

Carlisle calmly trotted over to complete what remains the only unassisted triple play by an outfielder in the history of professional baseball.[45]

It took a moment for the crowd to realize what had happened. After absorbing Carlisle's feat, the fans exploded with a sudden shriek, throwing into the air everything they could find. According to the *Los Angeles Times*, one man in the crowd simply could not contain himself:

> Down in the boxes, one excitable fan seemed to get a sudden attack of insanity. He jumped up and down and yelled, "It's the greatest play ever made in the world; it's the greatest play ever made in the world!" He began grabbing the men in the box with him and shaking them as a rat terrier does a rag doll. "It's the greatest play ever made in the world!" he yelled into their ears. He flung himself almost head first into the next box and thumped the nearest man over the head, "It's the greatest play ever made in the world; it's the greatest play ever made in the world!" he shrieked.
>
> After a while he quieted down and smoothed out his clothes. Straightening his hat and his tie, he sat back in his chair and remarked in a serious, earnest, confidential tone to his next neighbor, "We have just seen the greatest play ever made in the world."[46]

* * *

The Oakland Oaks had a new manager for 1912. Former Boston and Pittsburgh first baseman Bud Sharpe replaced Harry Wolverton, who had been hired by the New York Highlanders. Sharpe, who for years had suffered from severe health problems, thought to be malaria, faced several challenges with Oakland in 1912. Like Sharpe, Wolverton had been a player-manager but at a different position. Although Sharpe could fill Wolverton's seat in the dugout, he had to find an on-field replacement at third base. Unenthusiastic about promoting back-up Gus Hetling, Sharpe waited until the end of training camp before finally awarding the job to Jimmy Frick, a thirty-year-old infielder acquired during the offseason from the New York State League.[47]

There was an interesting article next to Frick's photo in the *Oakland Tribune* on the day it was announced he had beaten out Hetling for the third base job. The story carried Chalmers Automobile Company representative E.P. Brinegar's announcement that a Chalmers "36" would be awarded to the player voted the most valuable in the Pacific Coast League for 1912. It was the same automobile that Hugh Chalmers, founder and president of the company, was offering to players deemed the "most valuable" in the American and National leagues.[48]

The Oaks started the 1912 season sensationally; after dropping the season-opener to San Francisco, they reeled off twelve straight wins. Frick started the first two games of the season at third base but was then forced out of the lineup for a few days after injuring his toe. Hetling took his place and the team kept winning, so Sharpe decided to keep Frick on the bench.[49]

As with every team in the Pacific Coast League in 1912, Oakland players sported a numbered patch sewn on their sleeve — the first league-wide adopted uniform number.[50] It was a sequential system, with the number thirteen skipped by most teams out of superstition. Oakland was the exception, with ace left-hander Harry Ables insisting on wearing it.[51] On April 17, Ables confidently took the mound against Los Angeles and shut out the Angels while striking out ten, improving the Oaks' record to 13–1.[52]

* * *

Los Angeles was to be Oakland's main competition during the first half of the 1912 season and the Angels were loaded with talent. Star outfielders Heine Heitmuller and Pete

Daley, who loved to jaw good-naturedly at each other during games, fought for the league lead in batting average. Shortstop Joe Berger was having a great year as well, mentioned along with Vernon outfielder Johnny Kane as a front-runner for the Chalmers automobile. But the Angels began to unravel in late August. Bill Tozer, having recovered from his wounds of the previous year, had his left arm broken by a vicious line drive in a game against Oakland.[53] Catcher Hughie Smith was shelved by illness. Pitcher Walter Nagle was struck in the chest by a liner off the bat of San Francisco's Joe Gedeon. After staggering to the ball and throwing Gedeon out, Nagle collapsed and was carried off the field with two broken ribs.[54] Outfielder Heitmuller, the team's best player, fell into a mysterious slump in September that proved to be a particularly serious blow to the Angels' pennant hopes.

Heitmuller was a four-year baseball and football star at the University of California, playing alongside Orval Overall on the California football team's offensive and defensive lines and blocking a punt in the final minutes of the Big Game against Stanford in 1903, recovering it in the end zone for a touchdown that tied the contest. The play left him with a scar over his left eye that he bore proudly for the rest of his life.[55]

Heitmuller first played professionally in 1905 at Everett, Washington, under an assumed name — he was still in college — then spent three years in the PCL, first with Seattle and then Oakland. He played for Mike Fisher's Reach All-Stars in Japan and then was sold to the Philadelphia Athletics in 1909, beating out a young outfielder named "Shoeless" Joe Jackson for a roster spot.[56] Somewhat clumsy in the outfield and slow on the base paths, Heitmuller spent two years with Philadelphia as a reserve outfielder and then returned to the PCL with the Los Angeles Angels during the 1911 season, hitting .343 over the last half of the schedule. He was having another great year in 1912 even while seriously considering retirement after the season to start his own business.[57]

Angels outfielder Heine Heitmuller taking batting practice at Recreation Park in San Francisco (San Francisco History Center, San Francisco Public Library).

Holding his forty-two-ounce, thin-handled Frank Schulte model bat at the end of the knob, Heitmuller was never cheated at the plate, usually deciding whether or not to swing before the pitch was thrown.[58] A ball up and in to Heitmuller was frequently belted off of or over the left-field fence. He always tried to hit the ball as hard as he could, reasoning that if it did not clear the fence he would still hit it hard enough to get it past the fielders.[59] On August 24, Heitmuller hit his fifteenth home run of the 1912 season — a walk-off shot against Oakland that rattled the shingles of a building beyond the fence.[60] He then went into a long slump that shook his confidence. Admitting to feeling less than at his physical peak, and discouraged by his corresponding drop in production, Heitmuller spoke of abandoning his free-swinging ways to start choking up on the bat.[61] Suffering from a lingering case of the flu, Heitmuller refused to leave the lineup even as Hughie Smith, his roommate, was hospitalized with similar symptoms.

Heitmuller seemed to break out of his slump in a doubleheader on September 27, collecting six hits in six at-bats, including two doubles and a walk.[62] The next day he failed to produce a hit but contributed to a win with a sacrifice fly.[63] On September 29, Los Angeles and Vernon were playing a doubleheader that marked the return of Bill Tozer from his broken arm; Heitmuller did not show up for the morning game.[64] When he finally arrived for the afternoon contest, visibly quite ill, he was promptly sent home. Team trainer Doc Finlay visited the outfielder that evening and, instantly recognizing the symptoms as those of typhoid fever, called a physician. Heitmuller was immediately admitted to Good Samaritan Hospital.[65] Hughie Smith, hospitalized in Riverside, was re-examined. It was determined he also had typhoid and that Heitmuller had probably caught it from him.

At first it was thought Heitmuller would recover, but his condition worsened dramatically on October 7. Henry Berry visited the hospital that evening and discovered a delirious Heitmuller, who was unable to recognize anyone. Within a few hours he was dead.[66]

Black crepe covered the doorway to the Angels offices and the stadium flag flew at half-staff. Heitmuller's body was accompanied by his brother, Henry, aboard the Lark, the passenger train normally used by the Angels on trips north. Harry Williams wrote of the send-off as Heitmuller's last trip: "But it was not the 'Heine' at whose shrine the fans from Los Angeles to Portland had worshiped for nearly two seasons. It was merely the husk of the great home run king. The powerful muscles were no longer pliant, the keen eye was unseeing, and the ears which had heard cheers of applauding thousands were deaf to the farewells of his baseball mates, who were gathered in a mournful group."[67]

Cap Dillon spoke for the team, saying, "The entire team is depressed in the loss of Heitmuller. We have lost one of the best-liked members of our baseball 'family' and that, you know, is coming pretty close to home."[68]

The Angels paused for ten minutes at the end of the third inning of their game on October 11, marking the exact time of Heitmuller's funeral in San Francisco. The players vacated the diamond as the stadium fell silent, save for the occasional clearing of a throat or a cough, the wide expanse of grass empty in tribute to a fallen hero.[69]

Already weakened by the injuries to their pitching staff, the Angels fell to third place. Hughie Smith eventually recovered after a long ordeal. Meanwhile, as if something out of *Ripley's Believe It or Not*, Heine Heitmuller won the Pacific Coast League batting title in 1912. When hospitalized, he trailed teammate Pete Daley, but Daley slumped and Heitmuller took the title by three points, .335 to .332. To this day, he is the only man in the history of professional baseball to win a batting title after his death.

* * *

Prior to losing Heitmuller, Los Angeles had essentially been in lockstep with Oakland and Vernon. On Labor Day, the two teams shared the top of the standings, with the Oaks sitting four games behind. But then Oakland caught fire. While Los Angeles played break-even in September and Vernon had a losing record, Oakland won twenty-five of thirty-three games to overtake both and grab first place.

The move to the front of the pack was accompanied by a minor controversy that erupted during a time when Honus Mitze subbed as manager for an ailing Bud Sharpe, whose malaria had flared up. The *Oakland Tribune* noted that the Oaks had played well under Mitze and editorialized that the veteran catcher should be made manager on a permanent basis. Appalled by the editorial, every player on the team emphasized their full support for Sharpe by signing a letter that was published in the *Tribune*.[70] Then Oakland's lead shrunk as injuries and other health problems began taking their toll.

Sharpe's ill health kept him out of the lineup for the final two months. Mitze was put out of action when his finger was split by a foul tip. Pitcher Bill Malarkey injured his back in a game against the Angels and needed additional rest between starts. Jimmy Frick, apparently battling severe depression, suffered a mental breakdown of sorts and disappeared in late September, never to return.[71] This was followed by star outfielder Claire Patterson coming down with typhoid, which knocked him out for the season. In addition, Al Cook had a 103-degree fever and outfielder Elmer Zacher was nursing a strained shoulder he suffered in a collision with teammate Ody Abbott.[72] Happy Hogan's Vernon Tigers moved closer but still needed help to overtake Oakland.

After Harry Ables completed the ironman stunt of shutting out Los Angeles in both games of a doubleheader on the next-to-last day of the season, the Oaks had a one-game lead with only the final-day doubleheaders remaining.[73] Both teams won their morning games, leaving Oakland one game ahead of Vernon with one game left as the Oaks boarded a ferry to sail across the bay and play the nightcap in San Francisco.

The Tigers had to defeat Portland in the afternoon to stay alive, and they jumped to a 5–0 lead. But Happy Hogan and his men could only watch helplessly as the scoreboard revealed the Oaks had put three runs across the plate in the top of the first against the Angels. Throughout the contest, Tigers fans continued to eye the scoreboard as Oakland's Bill Malarkey shut out the Angels through eight innings.

Malarkey stood atop the mound at Recreation Park, with eighteen thousand fans imploring him to finish off the Angels. Bud Sharpe, so nervous he could not bring himself to sit on the bench, watched events unfold from the clubhouse in center field. With two out in the ninth, Charlie Moore of the Angels lifted a soft fly ball to Ody Abbott in left field; Abbott dropped it, eliciting an audible groan from the crowd.

Malarkey was unflustered. Babe Driscoll was the next batter and he hit a ground ball to Gus Hetling at third base. Hetling fielded the ball cleanly, threw out Driscoll, and the Oaks were PCL champions. The fans reacted wildly to Oakland's first championship since 1902, running onto the field to celebrate amid an explosion of cushions, hats and umbrellas catapulted into the air.[74] A beaming Bud Sharpe corralled Malarkey in the clubhouse, hugging the pitcher and pressing a twenty-dollar gold piece into his hand.[75]

Oakland owed its pennant to a number of outstanding performances, all of which were worthy of capturing the coveted Chalmers automobile. Jack Killilay won fifteen of nineteen decisions after being released by the Boston Red Sox to the Oaks in June. Outfielder Bert Coy led the league in home runs. Honus Mitze was probably the best all-around catcher in the PCL, and manager Bud Sharpe batted .300 while holding down first base despite poor health that kept him out of the lineup for long stretches. Claire Patterson batted .305 before being sidelined by illness, and Harry Ables won twenty-five games while striking out more than three hundred batters. But it was Gus Hetling, the man whose demotion had been published in the *Oakland Tribune* in April alongside the announcement of the Chalmers award, who was named MVP.[76]

Bud Sharpe decided to retire because of his health, but it still appeared as if great times were ahead for Oakland.[77] Immediately after the season, the Oaks announced that a new playing field would replace Freeman's Park. Ground was broken in December on the new stadium — Oaks Park — which would seat ten thousand when completed the following March and serve as the team's home for more than four decades.

But disharmony suddenly surfaced. Cal Ewing had been majority owner of the Oaks since the 1906 earthquake while remaining a silent partner, allowing team president Ed Walter to run the ballclub. It was an arrangement that had seemingly worked well, but Walter wanted to be recognized in a tangible way for his efforts in saving the team after the earthquake and helping it prosper. Ewing was disinclined to do so.

On December 8, 1912, Walter announced he was resigning and accused Cal Ewing of engaging in "syndicate" baseball since he owned both Bay Area teams. Walter added that he saw no way the new stadium could be financed and asserted that Ewing's actions were detrimental to the Oakland franchise — a strange accusation coming as it did on the heels of the team's greatest success. Ewing countered Walter's charge with his own, claiming the dispute arose only after the Oaks president attempted unsuccessfully to take advantage of him.[78]

Ewing had confided to Walter about his difficulties in gaining approval to build a new ballpark for the Seals in San Francisco, between Twenty-Sixth and Army streets. Ewing's obstacle was St. Luke's Hospital, located across the street from the proposed site. The hospital objected to the plan on the basis of potential increases in traffic and noise.

Armed with that information, Walter immediately purchased the lease for Recreation Park out from under Ewing, securing the ballpark for twenty years, beginning with the 1916 season. Walter then offered Ewing an extension of his current lease at the same annual payment but added a demand for six thousand dollars cash and ten thousand shares of Oakland stock, which would give Walter majority ownership of the Oaks. Ewing refused and Walter went public with the syndicate charge.[79]

Ewing's fellow PCL owners sided with him and he was allowed to keep his investments in both the Oakland and San Francisco franchises for the time being.[80] But stung by Walter's criticism, Ewing decided to sell most of his interest in the Oaks to former California Senator Frank Leavitt, who had been named president of the team after Walter's resignation.[81] None of this altered the reality that Ed Walter still held a twenty-year lease on Recreation Park effective at the conclusion of the 1915 season. Cal Ewing would be forced to find a new site or face the prospect of not having a stadium in San Francisco for the Seals.

* * *

Oaks Park was completed in time for the opening of the new season, but events continued to unfold that made it seem as if someone connected with the Oakland franchise had made a Faustian bargain in exchange for the 1912 championship. During spring training, Harry Ables was pitching batting practice and instinctively reached out with his pitching hand to grab a line drive off Gus Hetling's bat, resulting in a badly broken finger. Ables was out of action until June and was never again as effective.[82]

In late March, the flag at the newly opened ballpark hung at half-staff because of the death of Claire Patterson, whose typhoid had proven fatal.[83]

Pitcher Cy Parkin, a thirteen-game winner for the 1912 champions, proved less effective in 1913 and was cut in July. The day after his release he came down with typhoid fever and nearly died. A week later, Oaks pitcher Tyler Christian also came down with the illness. He and Parkin spent two months together in the same hospital.[84]

Bud Sharpe never recovered his health. After a couple of years supervising the Atlanta plantation of his close friend, Boston Braves manager George Stallings, Sharpe became bedridden and died on June 1, 1916. He was only thirty-four years old.[85]

While Gus Hetling was never again as successful as he had been in 1912, reality proved most stark for Jimmy Frick. It had been his photo next to the *Oakland Tribune* article announcing the establishment of the Chalmers award but it was Hetling, the man he originally beat out for the starting position, who won the automobile.

Following his mental breakdown and desertion of the team, Frick surfaced in Portland, remaining there while his teammates won the pennant. A few weeks after the season ended, Frick was left alone by his wife while she went to purchase tickets for both of them to go to Oklahoma, where the couple had a ranch. Before she was able to return, Frick killed himself by drinking carbolic acid.[86]

The Oaks were obviously unsettled by the tragedy and turmoil. Even though Bill Malarkey won twenty-five games and Bert Coy took his second straight PCL home run title, the team fell to last place in 1913 — just as it had after its first title in 1902. Oakland would not win another pennant for fifteen years.

* * *

Vernon owner Eddie Maier, tired of having his Tigers play their lucrative Sunday home schedule in a rough and tumble neighborhood dominated by saloons, was looking to move the team out of the area. Pasadena, which had occasionally hosted Angels home games, made a pitch for the team, but the popular seaside resort town of Venice had a clear advantage because Maier had property interests there. Also, Venice allowed Sunday baseball while Pasadena did not.[87]

Maier, who had once pitched for Los Angeles High, was attending the University of California at Berkeley when his brother, Fred, died a few weeks after founding the Tigers in 1909. Maier had assumed leadership of the franchise and was in the process of building an amusement pier near Venice, leading to rumors he was planning to construct a spectacular ballpark on a concrete pad jutting into the ocean. Maier refused comment, but it was clear he wanted to link the Tigers to other attractions that could draw crowds on Sundays, just as Jim Morley had with the Angels and Chutes Park a decade earlier.[88]

In late 1912, Eddie Maier and Happy Hogan met with the Venice Exploitation Committee — a group dedicated to attracting hotels, restaurants and amusements to the area — and reached agreement to bring the PCL to Venice. It was decided to locate the new stadium on the site of the Los Angeles Gun Club, on a five-acre parcel about a half-mile from the beach.[89] The city pledged six thousand dollars to fix up the grounds, and Maier expended fifty thousand dollars to construct a ballpark. Lacking enough time to grow grass on the diamond, part of the lawn at Venice City Hall was dug up to provide a proper playing surface.[90]

A depot for the Pacific Electric Line was erected about twenty feet from the stadium entrance. The new ballpark, which would be used for Sunday morning home games only, seated about five thousand. (The Tigers would play their other home games at Washington Park.) The stadium was outfitted with a telephone system, including a megaphone for announcing the starting batteries. Plywood cutouts of snarling tigers were posted at the fence near the entrance as well as on every flagpole. The playing field featured an unusual layout, with outfield fences located an equidistant 325 feet from home plate. A huge scoreboard rose above the center-field fence and the grandstand featured flags representing each of the Pacific Coast League teams. The words "Visitors" and "Venice" were outlined in the grass in front of the dugouts. On a clear day, Catalina Island could be spied from the bleachers.[91]

Parking spaces for one hundred and fifty automobiles were installed beyond the outfield fences, which consisted of three feet of plywood topped with six feet of wire mesh. The area had its own entrance and fans could sit in their vehicles to watch the game.[92] The park, and especially its playing surface, opened to rave reviews, with much of the credit going to Howard Lorenz, Maier's business manager. The day of the Tigers' first exhibition game, against the Chicago White Sox, was declared a local holiday. A parade wound its way to the ballpark and Venice schools were closed, with students attending the game as Maier's guests.[93] The White Sox won but few Venice fans were disappointed, mesmerized as they were by festivities that included daylight fireworks, the mayor throwing out the first pitch, and the presence of sports dignitaries, including Cap Anson and Jim Jeffries. To celebrate their new identity, the Tigers donned fresh white uniforms adorned with black pinstripes and a tiger-head emblem decorating each player's chest. Dark red mackinaw coats served as warm-up jackets.[94] Henry Berry and Eddie Maier toasted each other with mineral water and motion pictures of the game and surrounding festivities were recorded.[95]

The manager of the Tigers was as colorful as the canal city his team represented. Happy Hogan's real name was Wallace Louis Bray, but his devoutly religious father frowned on baseball and forbade use of the family name in such a lowly endeavor.[96]

Hogan's baseball career began at Santa Clara College thanks to the persuasion of Win Cutter, later a teammate of Hogan's in the Pacific Coast League. In a time when some college teams did not require their players to attend classes, Hogan was asked what he planned to study. He replied, "Eloquence and shower baths."[97] Hogan later captained and caught for the University of Southern California, leading the Trojans to a championship.

Rumored to be blind in one eye, Hogan was probably one of the worst hitters in professional baseball — and one of the game's best bunters.[98] What he lacked in natural ability he compensated for in gamesmanship; he might distract opponents by pointing his bat at the opposing pitcher as if it were a rifle or by dancing a jig in the batter's box. His ability as a bench jockey was legendary. Hogan loved needling his adversaries, especially younger players, until they became so angry they would rather fight than play. The league admonished him on more than one occasion because of the practice.[99]

By 1913 Hogan was the senior player in the PCL in terms of continuous service, having been originally signed for sixty dollars a month in 1901 by Charlie Graham to play for Mike Fisher's Sacramento team. (Graham later served as Hogan's best man at his wedding.)[100] An excellent defensive catcher, Hogan remained with Fisher through his moves to Tacoma and Fresno and had just signed to manage the latter team when it folded. He was drafted by the Los Angeles Angels and played on their pennant-winning teams in 1907 and 1908. The next year, Hogan was hired to manage Vernon.

As a manager, no one in the PCL had more "ginger" than Hap. He was always inventing ingenious plays he could use to produce a run in a pinch. Hogan favored those who studied the game and could think quickly on their feet. He even held classes, quizzing players on what to do in certain game situations. Hogan still caught on occasion, usually in an emergency; he was behind the plate for veteran Roy Hitt's no-hitter in 1914 and even banged out a couple of hits.[101]

Thanks to his personality and antics in the coach's box, Hogan was the most popular figure in the league. "The fans come out here to have a good time and they pay good money for it," he said. "I feel that it is as much my duty to see that they enjoy the game as it is to win the game."[102]

Although Hogan loved the fans, he was disturbed by reports that some were praying in church each Sunday for the Tigers to win. He said, "I am a good sport, and I think I am about as anxious to win as ever a baseball captain was, but it seems to me that it's going pretty strong when they ask God to help win a baseball game."[103]

Hogan's teams reflected his personality: scrappy and always fighting for an advantage. His strength was in handling players: some he chewed out openly and let them give back as good as they got. Others he never directly criticized, among them Walter Carlisle, who was too sensitive to respond to that kind of treatment. Hogan specialized in coaxing the most from players, especially veterans everyone else thought had nothing left. He bristled at any suggestion such players were "cast-offs."

Hogan would sit cross-legged on the bench during games, energetically chewing on a stick of gum he had conned out of Ed Maier. When sensing his players needed more energy, he would jump from his seat and insist that a big rally was imminent. Hogan was famous for his ninth-inning cry to fans, "Don't go home yet! The game isn't over!" and if the Tigers got a big hit, he would march up and down the dugout, proclaiming to his team, "I told you so! This is the inning I told you about. Play hard boys!" When a run scored he would shout, "That run is a big one, boys. We have 'em now!"

As much as he constantly spoke of retiring to his family's ranch in Santa Clara, they would have had to tear the uniform off Happy Hogan before he would leave baseball. He loved every minute he was part of the game. So did everyone else.

* * *

Shed of the Oakland Oaks, Cal Ewing turned his attention to the San Francisco Seals, opening his wallet to procure talent he hoped would result in a pennant. Young players Jimmy Johnston and Phil Douglas were acquired from the Chicago White Sox. Johnston would steal a professional baseball–record 124 bases for the Seals in 1913 while Douglas, who later starred for the New York Giants before scandal ended his career, won only six of fourteen decisions.

After the season started, Ewing acquired two expensive veteran pitchers from the Chicago Cubs—former twenty-game winners Lefty Leifield and Orval Overall, the latter making a comeback after being out of baseball for two years because of a sore arm. Both pitched well and were solid gate attractions, but the influx of high profile talent netted Ewing no better than fourth place.

In an effort to rebound from a dismal 1912 campaign, made somewhat embarrassing after the McCredies had financed a major renovation of Vaughn Street Park, Portland brought pitcher Gene Krapp back from Cleveland and acquired veteran left-hander Harry Krause from Buffalo. Another young Cleveland pitcher, "Big" Bill James, also joined the Portland staff. Shortstop Dave Bancroft had proven too green for the PCL so he was sent back to the Northwest League for more seasoning and replaced by Art Kores.

Getting back to the top was not as easy as McCredie had hoped. On June 22 the Beavers sat in last place, eleven games behind Los Angeles. Yet his confidence in his players remained unshaken as he proclaimed, "If I can't win with this club, then I had better retire to private life."[104] McCredie stuck with his lineup, making only a couple of moves. He replaced Fred Derrick at first base with Bill Speas and swapped veteran outfielder Art Kruger to the Angels for Ty Lober. The players responded, taking seven of eight from Oakland during the last week of June.[105] Portland was in first place by July 17 and on its way to winning the 1913 pennant by seven games over Sacramento.

In October 1913, another outlaw, calling itself the Federal League, announced its intention to compete directly with the major leagues, a decision that would have implications for the Pacific Coast League as well. The new league announced it would not pursue players who were under contract but would target unsigned players bound to teams only by the reserve clause. The Federal League had an agent aggressively recruiting players on the West Coast — George Stovall, manager of the Fed team in Kansas City and the first big leaguer signed by the new outlaws. Temperamental but popular, Stovall set up shop in Happy Hogan's poolroom in January 1914 and began recruiting PCL players as well as major leaguers wintering in Southern California. Soon there were rumors that four Seals players were in contact with the Federal League, causing Cal Ewing to criticize Hogan for allowing Stovall to establish headquarters.

Hogan replied that he was not going to do anything about Stovall. If the former big leaguer wanted to visit his poolroom and happened to talk to players who were there, he was not going to stop him.[106]

Stovall's first PCL signing was Angels outfielder Art Kruger, followed quickly by Kruger's teammate, second baseman Claire Goodwin. Henry Berry had enough. He negotiated to steal Goodwin back from the Feds and declared a war of his own, threatening to take the Pacific Coast League outlaw if Organized Baseball did not back him.[107] Berry received sympathy but little else as Goodwin jumped to the Feds anyway.

Other players left the PCL for the Federal League. Sacramento's Duke Kenworthy signed with Stovall's Kansas City team.[108] So did Chet Chadbourne, Portland's star center fielder.[109] Of all the PCL owners, the McCredies were hit hardest by the Federal League; besides losing Chadbourne, they also lost pitcher Gene Krapp to the upstart league. Then three players acquired from Cleveland in exchange for Beavers pitcher Rip Hagerman jumped to the Federal League instead of coming to Portland, leaving the McCredies with nothing after trading one of their most valuable prospects. Walter McCredie estimated losing those players cost him seven thousand dollars.[110]

Player salaries would nearly double over the next two years as teams scrambled to keep their best talent. In all, the Feds grabbed more than two hundred players, with not quite two-thirds of them coming from the minor leagues. Although the Federals would not hurt the PCL as much as the eastern minor leagues, there was a definite impact.

* * *

Determined to leave Recreation Park and end his standoff with Ed Walter, Cal Ewing acquired a location for a grand new ballpark at the base of Lone Mountain, west of downtown San Francisco near Golden Gate Park. Built at a cost of more than one hundred thousand dollars, the stadium was promoted as the finest west of Chicago. Featuring a seating capacity of twenty thousand, Ewing Field opened on May 16, 1914, with cross-bay rival Oakland as the Seals' opponent. The day began with a luncheon for six hundred dignitaries at the Palace Hotel, followed by a procession of one hundred automobiles to the new ballpark. Thomas Graham dedicated home plate and praised the stadium, noting its location at a "magnificent site at the base of Lone Mountain." A time capsule was buried under home plate and the game began under sunny and windy skies.[111]

By the seventh inning the field was shrouded in fog. Ewing Field was much closer to the Pacific Ocean, giving it a greater influence on the weather at the new stadium than downtown at Recreation Park. Additionally, Lone Mountain served as a natural funnel for freezing winds whipping off the ocean. L.B. Gross of the *Oakland Tribune* remarked that the park should be called "Icicle Field."[112]

Earlier starting times were introduced in an unsuccessful effort to complete contests before fog and cold descended each afternoon.[113] Nearly every game was played in bitter cold, with conditions deteriorating sometimes as early as the second inning. The wind blasted into the faces of those sitting in the grandstand; the center-field bleachers were often the most populated because the high fence rising above and behind the stands provided at least some protection. Attendance dropped dramatically, and visiting teams experienced a corresponding decrease in their share of gate receipts in the league's most lucrative market.[114] It was becoming obvious that the Seals could not remain in their new home, and league directors began private but serious discussions about the problem. Harry Williams wrote in the *Los Angeles Times*, "Ewing Field has developed into a white elephant of exceptional dimensions, and the league will not stand for it another year."[115]

But returning to Recreation Park was not an option. Not only was Ed Walter uninterested in helping Ewing, the stadium had a new tenant. Cal Ewing was out in the cold — figuratively *and* literally.

* * *

The Sacramento Senators had experienced uneven success since bolting the California State League in 1909 and by the summer of 1914 the franchise was in serious trouble. Former Oakland manager Harry Wolverton, back in the PCL after a disastrous one-year stint managing in New York, had assumed control of the team and piloted it to a surprising second-place finish in 1913. However, the team lacked solid financial backing.

After nearly six seasons, three different owners, and diminishing fan support in the league's smallest market, the franchise was temporarily assigned by the league in late September 1914 to the Bay Area and re-christened the Missions. The team was to use Ewing Field and Oaks Park as its home fields. At the same time, Ed Walter was representing those wanting to establish a minor circuit for the Federal League on the West Coast and was searching for a new tenant for Recreation Park. Within a few days he convinced his friend Wolverton — the two having become close during their days together in Oakland — to exercise an option on his twenty-year lease of the stadium.[116]

Not every team was struggling financially. Happy Hogan had ample backing from Eddie Maier and both men were determined to see the Venice Tigers end Portland's run of pennants. The Tigers had signed several ex–big league pitchers at the beginning of the year, including Doc White, a star left-hander from the White Sox, and veteran side-armer Jack Powell, who had won nearly two hundred and fifty games during sixteen seasons in the majors. White had proved to be worth the money he was being paid, but Powell reported overweight and was released in July after compiling a record of 5–5.[117]

The Tigers were hampered by injuries much of the season. Hogan was so desperate for catching help in July that he handed a uniform to old friend Jess Orndorff and asked him to be ready at a moment's notice in case of emergency.[118]

Hogan also signed forty-three-year-old Joe McGinnity for the stretch run. Walter McCredie immediately objected, protesting that the move violated league rules and smacked of the days when Jim Morley tried to stack his roster with established major league stars, including McGinnity, after the big league season ended. McCredie threatened to protest any games McGinnity pitched, pointing out the hurler owned the Tacoma franchise in the Northwest League and that Hogan had no intention of bringing him back in 1915.[119] McGinnity was allowed to remain with the Tigers but he had no impact on the pennant race, winning only one game while losing four.[120] Venice faded from contention and the Beavers captured their fourth pennant in five years.

* * *

The talent level of the Pacific Coast League was improving dramatically, especially as arrangements with major league teams became more common. It was increasingly difficult for a "green busher" to make it in the Pacific Coast League. According to an informal survey by the *Los Angeles Times* in June 1913, seventy-five players on the six PCL teams had major league experience.[121] Turnover was increasing as well. By 1914, only twenty-eight of 131 men who had been on PCL rosters in 1910 remained in the league, and six of those were managers.[122]

While unquestionably fielding a quality product, the Pacific Coast League had a terrible season in 1914 from a business standpoint — the gains of the previous four years largely evaporating. The California League, in which several Pacific Coast League owners were heavily invested, had failed. The Federal League was driving up salaries, stealing talent, and even worse for the Pacific Coast League, wreaking havoc with optioned players from the major leagues. Big league teams cut back on the practice, worried that players unhappy about reporting to the minors might instead jump to the Feds. Teams in the PCL were above the league limits on roster size and salary past the May deadline — further hurting the league financially — because of the same fear players would bolt for the outlaws or that an outlaw league would spring up on the West Coast.[123] The downturn in fortune from the previous year was startling; it was estimated the PCL lost two hundred thousand dollars in 1914.[124]

Then Cal Ewing dropped a real bombshell. With his new stadium untenable and the path of return to Recreation Park blocked by Ed Walter, the Seals owner announced in late October that he was leaving baseball.[125] Judge McCredie almost immediately submitted a bid for the franchise, but Ewing asked Henry Berry to conduct an open search for the best buyer for the team. Berry accepted the task, declaring, "The San Francisco franchise is the most valuable minor league property in the country.... The main thing will be to select the most desirable purchaser. The men who buy it will be high-class people, whose very names will be a guarantee of clean sport, and who will be popular with the fans of San Francisco."[126]

It appeared that the survival of the league's flagship franchise was at stake.

CHAPTER FIVE

1915 to 1916: An Oasis in the Desert

With the Federal League standing defiant and Cal Ewing's decision to sell the San Francisco Seals coming literally at the same moment league directors were struggling to determine the fate of the Sacramento/Mission franchise, it was clear PCL owners had a massive problem on their hands.

Sacramento/Mission was the most immediate concern. Harry Wolverton had been dependent on the largesse of the other PCL owners during the 1914 season, but after being provided more than ten thousand dollars to pay his players in the middle of the year, it was discovered that he had once again failed to meet payroll in October.[1] The league finally assumed control of the franchise and appointed a committee of Ewing, Allan Baum and Frank Leavitt to find a new owner and location for it.[2]

Although Wolverton maintained he would not bow out without a fight, the league was committed to moving the Missions out of the Bay Area, and other cities began lining up for the chance to land the franchise.[3] Jim Morley spearheaded a dark-horse effort, angling for a return to the PCL with a group from San Diego — a city that had experienced enormous growth over the previous five years, more than doubling its population to more than one hundred thousand. The former Angels owner hoped the city's staging of the Panama-California Exposition would prove a strong selling point, but the smart money was on the Missions either moving back to Sacramento or to Salt Lake City.[4]

The Utah capital took the early lead over Sacramento through the efforts of local businessmen, who pledged fifty thousand dollars to purchase the franchise, pay off its debt, and invest in a downtown stadium. During their presentation to league directors in Los Angeles, the Salt Lake delegation displayed thirty-three years of weather information to prove the area had fewer rainy days in April and October than did San Francisco. In response to complaints about the distance to Utah, it was pointed out that Salt Lake City was a railroad hub and with three competing rail lines serving the community, league directors were assured that reasonable rates could be secured for travel from Oregon and California. As a show of confidence, the Salt Lake contingent said it would provide visiting teams a two-thousand-dollar guarantee for each homestand.[5]

A key vote swung in Salt Lake City's direction in mid–December when Judge McCredie signaled his intention to vote in favor of the group from Utah.[6] At the league meeting later that month, Pacific Coast League directors awarded the franchise to the Salt Lake syndicate for fifteen thousand dollars.[7]

By that time, the fate of the league's other troubled franchise had been settled. It turned out Henry Berry was describing himself when he called for "the most desirable purchaser" for the San Francisco Seals. Johnny Powers, a Chicago native who had owned a Three-I

League team in Davenport, Iowa, and whose father was a famous alderman in the Windy City, assumed majority ownership of the Angels. Tom Darmody remained as Los Angeles team president.[8]

Berry officially took over in San Francisco on December 1, 1914, ending Cal Ewing's involvement with the league he had rescued from the ashes of the 1906 disaster.[9] "I have been in the game many years and stand on my record, which is honest and clean," said Ewing. "I am retiring to private life but I will always be a booster for baseball and Henry Berry can count on my support at any time and any place."[10]

Having consummated one of the biggest minor league purchases in history, Berry made no promises. "Naturally I am going to try and land a winning ball club.... I will immediately move my residence to San Francisco and attend to the business of the club. For the present, this is all I care to say, but I am confident of winning the support and confidence of the people of San Francisco."[11]

The moves to stabilize the San Francisco and Mission franchises seemed to have left Harry Wolverton out of the mix, but the "Gray Wolf" had one last card to play — a twenty-year lease on the only viable ballpark in San Francisco. Wolverton had an option to purchase the lease from Ed Walter, provided he exercised it by January 1, 1915.[12] Wolverton even added a hollow threat to form an independent league.[13] Berry retorted that he would play one season in Recreation Park and made a similarly hollow boast of having another site in mind for a ballpark for the 1916 season. Actually, both men were more than ready to strike a deal.[14]

On December 30, Berry ended the showdown by naming Wolverton manager of the Seals and handing him total control of the team. Wolverton had parlayed his bargaining position into a three-year contract that made him the highest paid manager on the West Coast.[15] Berry's decision would lead to friction down the road, but it also meant the Seals were returning to Recreation Park, and as far as the Pacific Coast League was concerned, Ewing Field was history.[16]

* * *

Harry Wolverton's connections with Detroit Tigers owner Frank Navin opened a talent pipeline for the Seals, and the first benefit from the relationship was twenty-year-old first baseman/outfielder Harry Heilmann, who had played for Detroit as a reserve in 1914.[17] Heilmann was talented but awkward and seemed unlikely to become one of the greatest hitters in baseball history. A native San Franciscan, he was originally signed by the McCredies in 1913, when they tried him out for two games at shortstop with the Beavers before sending him to their team in the Northwest League.[18] Detroit drafted Heilmann and he played for the Tigers in 1914, but he was still too green and was optioned to San Francisco. Wolverton openly predicted that Heilmann would become one of the best first basemen in the game despite skepticism about the youngster's defensive deficiencies. The Seals manager preached patience.

"He is a terrific hitter and a sensational fielder. All that he needs is experience.... Why, he is only a kid. He is just learning baseball. You know how awkward a thoroughbred colt looks at a certain age. Heilmann is nothing more than a colt. He doesn't even know his own stride. Just watch him — that's all."[19]

Wolverton could not have been more correct in his assessment, at least in regard to the young player's hitting ability. By late July, Heilmann had already hit twelve home runs with a batting average hovering around .360.

Wolverton made other changes. Veteran third baseman Charley O'Leary held out for more money, so youngster Bobby Jones was brought in to replace him.[20] Ping Bodie was signed after his release by the Chicago White Sox, joining left-handed hitters Biff Schaller and Justin Fitzgerald in the Seals outfield.[21] Shortstop Roy Corhan and catcher Walter Schmidt flirted with the Federal League but decided to stay in San Francisco.[22] Wolverton realized that if he could put together a serviceable pitching staff to complement his everyday lineup, the Seals would be a force to be reckoned with.

* * *

There had been a third franchise move proposed for 1915. Although attendance was respectable for the Venice Tigers at Washington Park, the team averaged only five to six hundred fans for Sunday games at the beach, causing it to suffer financially.[23] Ed Maier realized he needed to move the Sunday games away from Venice and closer to his fan base in Los Angeles. Prior to the 1915 season, he announced the Tigers would return to Vernon. However, the plan stalled when that city's officials balked; apparently Maier had insulted the community two years earlier when he left Vernon for Venice. City officials demanded an apology before allowing the Tigers to return. Maier refused.[24]

The Tigers opened the season in Salt Lake City and were easily defeated by Bees ace Claude "Lefty" Williams. Nevertheless, Happy Hogan was in top form; later that week, Venice was trailing Williams again, 5–0, after six innings when Hogan suddenly pulled a wad of cash from his pocket with a flourish, held it aloft, and offered to bet everyone in the ballpark that Williams would fall apart the next inning. The Tigers promptly scored five runs to tie the score. Although Salt Lake eventually won the game, Hogan's antics had once again proved effective.[25]

With the Tigers on the road to open the season, Ed Maier and team secretary Howard Lorenz completed plans for Opening Day in Venice. They adopted new home uniforms, unusual in that they were completely white, with no color, lettering or insignia of any kind.[26] They also trained a pair of elephants—one to throw a baseball and the other to swing a bat—and hired aviation pioneer Glenn Martin to drop a baseball on home plate from five thousand feet. Film star Charlie Chaplin was recruited to lead the traditional parade to the ballpark.[27]

The Tigers' home opener against San Francisco was delayed a day by rain. The schedule change made Chaplin unavailable but the pachyderms were ready, appearing resplendent in hideous painted-on tiger stripes of rainbow colors. One of the animals carried opposing managers Hogan and Wolverton. The elephants failed miserably in their attempt to play baseball; Harry Williams charitably said of the "pitcher," "like most southpaws he had bad control." But the spectators did not mind, appreciating the effort. The crowd then stood at attention as a band marched across the field and played "The Star-Spangled Banner." The game featured a spectacular collision at home plate between Ping Bodie and Venice catcher Tub Spencer, with the resulting crash felt all the way into the stands. The only blemish on the day was the Tigers losing, 5–3.[28] Happy Hogan's team had enjoyed a very successful and entertaining start to the season.

* * *

Baseball was booming in Salt Lake City. There had been skepticism over awarding the franchise to the Mormon city but the community had embraced the team and supported it beyond everyone's expectations.

The team's directors had worked quickly to get the ballclub up and running, hiring fiery Cliff Blankenship as manager. A number of Missions players were retained, including star pitcher Lefty Williams, who had been much more impressive in 1914 than his 13–20

Home of the Salt Lake City Bees from 1915 to 1925. Originally named Majestic Park, it was renamed Bonneville Park in 1917 (used by permission, Utah State Historical Society, all rights reserved).

record indicated. Despite not joining Harry Wolverton's team until June, he had pitched nearly 280 innings and finished fourth in the PCL in strikeouts.[29]

A group of local speculators built a new stadium, called Majestic Park, on the site of the old Salt Palace, an amusement park that had been a major venue for bicycle racing. The Rotary Club handled the opening festivities and encouraged businesses to close for the day, or at least allow some of their employees to have the day off. Ten thousand fans attended the Pacific Coast League's debut in Salt Lake City as the local citizenry celebrated "the transformation of a low swampy field covered with mud, snow and stones into one of the finest baseball fields in the United States."[30]

By the end of May the Bees were averaging three thousand fans per game. When the team was on the road, hundreds of people, including scores of enthusiastic children, gathered around an electronic scoreboard at the ballpark to watch results being posted. In other parts of the city, men with megaphones shouted out the scores.[31] Although many considered it doubtful the level of interest would be maintained through the hot summer, Pacific Coast League owners were nonetheless delighted. Henry Berry said, "Salt Lake City is the salvation of the league."[32]

* * *

On May 8, the Venice Tigers were playing against Los Angeles at Washington Park. The game was a close one, tied at 2–2 after thirteen innings. In the top of the fourteenth the Tigers loaded the bases with no one out. With the pitcher due to bat, thirty-eight-year-old Happy Hogan inserted himself as a pinch-hitter — his first appearance in a game that year.

After working the count to three-and-two, Hogan signaled for all three runners to take off with the pitcher's wind-up. He chopped down on the pitch perfectly, causing the ball to bounce high in the air in the hard dirt in front of the plate and then bound slowly past the pitcher's mound. By the time Los Angeles shortstop Zeb Terry fielded the ball, the first Tigers base runner was already across home plate with his teammate close behind. Terry's only play was to first base as two runs scored.[33] Hogan marched back to the bench with cheers ringing in his ears. Neither he nor the crowd realized how dramatic an exit he was making.

The day after his successful "double" squeeze play, Hogan was playing catch at the ballpark with Orval Overall, his friend and old Tacoma Tigers teammate, and mentioned his inability to shake a nagging fever. The next day, Hogan decided to swim in the ocean as a cure. By Tuesday he was gravely ill with double pneumonia.[34]

Doctors nearly gave up hope on Thursday even as Hogan repeatedly insisted, "I'll beat it, I'll beat it," with the same conviction he summoned when rallying his players in a big game. Hogan seemed to gain ground on Friday, improving to the point that doctors felt he might recover. Calling to his wife, Hogan put his arm around her and said, "Well, little girl, I've beaten it," and fell asleep.[35] But the rally was temporary.

Hogan took a turn for the worse on Sunday evening. Ed Maier, who had survived a recent bout with pneumonia, rushed to his manager's side, speaking to Hogan only ten minutes before he died, at two-thirty in the morning on May 17.[36] One of baseball's most unique and popular personalities was gone.

For several days a grieving Ed Maier could not bring himself to go to the ballpark. Outfielder Dick Bayless took charge amid speculation about Hogan's successor. Maier finally addressed the team four days after the funeral, gathering the players to announce that Doc White was being given the task of completing Hogan's unrealized dream — a Pacific Coast League pennant.[37]

Hogan was heavily in debt when he died, and on June 25 all three Pacific Coast League games were designated as benefits for his widow.[38] The Angels and Tigers participated in a program at Washington Park planned by Orval Overall. Ten thousand attended a game preceded by a comic baseball contest between teams captained by Charlie Chaplin and Roscoe "Fatty" Arbuckle. Every penny collected through ticket sales and concessions was donated to Hogan's wife. Fatty Arbuckle rushed through the stands offering five-cent bags of peanuts for a quarter and had no trouble selling all of them.

The Tigers won the game with an old-fashioned rally that would have done old Hap proud. After falling behind, 2–0, Venice tied the score in the eighth inning when Joe Wilhoit drove in Walter Carlisle with a triple. The Tigers won the game in the tenth inning when Carlisle scored on a hit-and-run double by Joe Berger. Nearly five thousand dollars was raised. Angels pitcher Jack Ryan remarked, "No man, however great, could have been paid a finer tribute."[39]

The Venice Tigers were about to pass into memory as well. Less than two months after Hogan's death they ceased to exist. Eddie Maier and the Vernon city fathers put aside their differences and the Tigers returned to their original home on July 11, sweeping a doubleheader from Salt Lake. Jack Doyle patched up the old ballpark on a temporary basis for the rest of the season, sans right-field bleachers.[40] Meanwhile, the ballpark in Venice was cut into sections, which were numbered in preparation for shipment and reassembly in Vernon for the 1916 season.[41]

* * *

Oakland was not a serious contender in 1915, but Oaks field captain Jack Ness created a stir during June and July. Outside of a dozen games with the Detroit Tigers in 1911, the lanky, easy-going thirty-year-old first baseman with big hands and a nose that would have made Jimmy Durante envious had been a career minor leaguer. During a doubleheader on May 31, Ness began a record-setting hitting streak that lasted almost two months. On June 26 he lined a single to center to tie Chet Chadbourne's PCL record of twenty-eight straight games. As the streak continued, the *Oakland Tribune* invited fans to call the newspaper each day for updates on Ness's progress.[42]

And continue it did, with anticipation peaking as Ness neared, and then matched, the "world record" of forty straight games set by Ty Cobb.[43] On July 13, Ness singled up the middle against Salt Lake City's Lefty Williams to extend his streak to forty-one. He later won the game by leading off the tenth inning with a home run.[44] Two days later the Oaks held a day in Ness's honor with a motion picture camera recording the presentation of a loving cup and a diamond ring. Ness then delighted the crowd by slamming a double, giving him a forty-three-game hitting streak.[45]

Vernon's Art Fromme finally stopped Ness on July 22, ending the first baseman's run at forty-nine games, a PCL record that would stand for nearly two decades. Ness hit for a .440 average during the streak, with thirteen doubles, three triples and six home runs. Although disappointed he fell one game short of fifty, Ness was relieved the ordeal was over. Suffering from night sweats, insomnia and a painfully abscessed molar, he had lost his appetite and begun losing his hair.[46]

* * *

While Ness was making headlines, the San Francisco Seals were leading the league yet struggling financially. It had been thought the Pan-American Exposition would be a boon to the Seals, but it instead became a rival attraction. Berry's vision of out-of-town patrons flocking to the ballpark not only failed to materialize, locals abandoned the ballpark for the Exposition on weekends when special exhibitions and performances were featured.[47]

Noting Salt Lake City's success in selling shares to raise capital, Berry decided to copy the approach, offering twenty thousand shares of stock to the public at five dollars each. He hoped the infusion of cash would boost local loyalty and finance a new stadium in time for the 1916 season.[48]

Finances aside, manager Harry Wolverton had confidence in his team. In mid–June, San Francisco had four men hitting .300 or better: Harry Heilmann, Justin Fitzgerald, Ping Bodie and Jerry "Red" Downs. But Wolverton had concerns about his pitching. His best returning starters, Skeeter Fanning and Spider Baum, were good pitchers, but thirty-one and thirty-three years old, respectively. Even older was curveball specialist Charlie "Hook'em" Smith, a thirty-five-year-old, ten-year big league veteran picked up during spring training from the Chicago Cubs.[49] Although the veteran pitchers proved advantageous with their ability to cope with the unusual layout of the ballpark (The Seals were tough to beat at home, with opponents crediting the short right field fence at Recreation Park for their success.), Wolverton continued to worry about the age and depth of his pitching staff and how well it would hold up during the long PCL season. Shortstop Roy Corhan's dead arm was also a major concern. Then Wolverton managed to run himself over with his own automobile and break both collarbones.[50]

The Seals remained comfortably atop the standings in late July but were dealt another serious blow when Harry Heilmann developed vertigo as a result of an inner ear problem. After spending a month out of the lineup, Heilmann thought he was on the mend but discovered otherwise when he collapsed while making a quick dash for a train.[51]

With an aging pitching staff and the loss of Heilmann for an extended period, Henry Berry felt he could not risk standing pat if he wanted to retain whatever following he had in San Francisco. Shortly after Heilmann's ill-fated dash for the train, Berry sent a telegram to Wolverton that said, "Go as far as you like, regardless of cost, to get players to win the pennant."[52]

Wolverton took Berry at his word and two days later signed veteran Bill Steen, who had been given his ten-day notice of release by Detroit.[53] The former Portland star became the Seals' most effective pitcher down the stretch. Once it was clear Heilmann was out for the year, Wolverton signed Minneapolis first baseman Chick Autry, who had already finished his season. Other owners raised objections, including Judge McCredie, who noted that Oakland, Los Angeles, Portland and Salt Lake City had remained within the five thousand dollar-per-month league salary limit. McCredie added, "For this reason, I would much rather see Los Angeles win, for its owner and manager are true sports and deserve to win.... The padding of the San Francisco payroll has been done in order to win at any cost, which I don't call good sportsmanship."[54]

Much to the judge's chagrin, San Francisco continued to hold onto first place. At the same time, Salt Lake City made a dramatic move in the standings, surprising everyone thanks to the incredible slugging of Bunny Brief—who hovered above the .400 mark for several weeks—and the best pitcher in the league, Lefty Williams, who won thirty-two games and led the league in almost every pitching category.

Salt Lake fans held a day in Williams' honor on October 6. The event also served as a farewell of sorts since he would be returning to the major leagues after the season. Before a large, appreciative crowd, the pitcher was presented with a one-karat blue diamond ring by the team's directors. Teammates gave him a gold watch. Williams also received a suit from manager Cliff Blankenship, a silver-handled umbrella and walking stick, a check from the team and additional cash collected by fans. After the ceremony, Williams defeated Portland, 9–2, aiding his cause by hitting a double and scoring a run as the Bees moved to within a game and a half of second place. The day ended with both teams heading to the Majestic Park skating rink for a party in Williams' honor. It was a wonderful event the pitcher could look back on with pride.[55]

Four years later to the day, Claude "Lefty" Williams was losing the fifth game of the 1919 World Series on purpose as a member of the infamous Black Sox.[56]

* * *

The San Francisco Seals won the 1915 Pacific Coast League pennant—the team's first title since 1909—as Harry Wolverton's worries about his pitching staff proved to be unfounded. Spider Baum used his licorice and tobacco spitball to fashion the best season of his career, his thirty wins second only to Lefty Williams. Skeeter Fanning effectively scuffed the ball to add twenty-five victories and "Hook'em" Smith had a 15–4 record at the end of July before stomach problems caused him to fade a bit. Bill Steen then picked up the slack, with a record of 10–5 and a sparkling 1.55 earned run average during the final two months of the season. The offense was as good as advertised; Biff Schaller and Ping Bodie combined for thirty-nine home runs and, along with Justin Fitzgerald, formed an all-.300-hitting outfield.

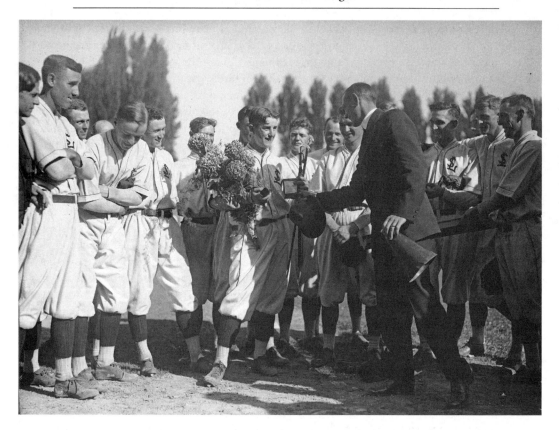

Claude "Lefty" Williams during ceremonies in his honor in Salt Lake City on October 6, 1915. Four years later to the day, he and his Chicago teammates would throw Game Five of the 1919 World Series as members of the infamous "Black Sox" (used by permission, Utah State Historical Society, all rights reserved).

The champions were honored at San Francisco's Pan-American Exposition in November, ironically one of the major factors in the Seals financial distress in 1915. Henry Berry declared bankruptcy about that time, claiming debts in excess of $116,000. His assets, consisting of only the clothes on his back, were valued at $150. He owed most of the money to his brothers. Cal Ewing was listed as a creditor for $500.[57]

Meanwhile, the surprising Salt Lake City Bees, which had charged from last place in late July to finish second, reaped the financial rewards Henry Berry must have thought rightfully belonged to him as league champion. The week prior to Berry's bankruptcy court date, the directors of the Bees declared a ten percent dividend for their stockholders. The team was so successful it had not been necessary to issue all of the authorized stock. The Bees drew more than two hundred thousand fans with total gate receipts of $105,000; even after paying out the dividend and purchasing Majestic Park, the team still had $14,000 cash on hand and was debt-free.[58]

It had been another rough season financially for the Pacific Coast League, but the team in the Great Salt Desert had been invaluable in helping the circuit survive another year. Henry Berry had been absolutely correct when he hailed Salt Lake City as the league's savior, especially following the disaster of 1914. Walter McCredie called Salt Lake "a godsend to the Pacific Coast League," while league President Baum declared that Salt Lake City ranked with any minor league city in the country.[59] It was impossible to over-emphasize the city's role in the league's survival.

* * *

The Federal League finally capitulated in the baseball war in December 1915, with the major leagues declaring victory and Federal League owners taking over teams in Chicago and St. Louis. The toll on the minor leagues had been substantial. According to the *Oakland Tribune*, only twenty-two of the forty-seven leagues operating in 1915 would return in 1916.[60]

But the Pacific Coast League was in a better position than most. The city of Los Angeles was about to experience explosive population growth, enhancing the league's profile. Despite having eight times more water than it needed, the city refused to sell any to surrounding communities; if another city wanted Los Angeles water, it would have to agree to be annexed. The San Fernando Valley did just that in 1915, instantly doubling the size of Los Angeles to more than two hundred and eighty square miles. By the end of the decade, the City of Angels would be home to a half-million people and on its way to becoming a major world city.

The owner of the Los Angeles Angels, Johnny Powers, wanted his team to project a major league image to match the ambitions of the city it represented. Cap Dillon had worn the Angels uniform for thirteen years, serving as manager eleven of those seasons, long enough for his hair to turn completely white and earn him the new nickname "Pop."

Powers had been persuaded to keep Dillon in 1915, after attempting unsuccessfully to talk former Giants third baseman Art "Tillie" Schafer into taking the job. But Powers was no longer satisfied with standing pat — the Angels had not won a pennant in seven years. Convinced he needed a new manager, Powers told Dillon he was fired. "To release Dillon was the hardest act of my life," Powers said. "He is clean, conscientious, sincere and a credit to baseball."[61]

However, those were not the attributes Powers was seeking. The other managers in the Pacific Coast League — Harry Wolverton at San Francisco, Rowdy Elliott at Oakland, Walter McCredie at Portland, Ham Patterson at Vernon and Cliff Blankenship at Salt Lake — were popular. While Dillon could scream at umpires with the best of them, he was not close to his players or the fans. Plus, Powers wanted a big league name.

He reached back to his Chicago roots to hire Jimmy Callahan, late of the White Sox.[62] Callahan began his career as a pitcher with the Chicago Colts, twice winning twenty games. After injuring his arm he switched to the outfield and became a top hitter for the crosstown Chicago White Sox. Callahan had the credentials Powers required; he was well known, fiery, and possessed big league experience.

Callahan's conditions for taking the job included becoming part-owner of the Angels. Powers arranged for his new manager to purchase one-fourth of the team from Tom Darmody's holdings. However, no one had asked Darmody. Furthermore, Darmody was not interested in selling. If Powers wanted Callahan, he would have to cough up a portion of *his* ownership stake in the Angels, leaving Darmody and Callahan as majority stockholders. Powers was not willing to sell his stake in the team any more than Darmody was. A stalemate developed.

Luckily, a way out presented itself. The Pittsburgh Pirates were interested in having Callahan succeed Fred Clarke as their manager and made him an offer that included his becoming part-owner in Pittsburgh. Powers released Callahan from his contract and immediately began pursuit of one of the most respected figures in baseball.[63]

Frank "Cap" Dillon in a rare in-game photograph of the Los Angeles Angels dugout. By the end of the 1915 season, Angels owner Johnny Powers was ready to make a managerial change (David Eskenazi Collection).

The man Powers set his sights on was Frank Chance, generally thought to be one of the top three managers in the game at that time, John McGraw and Connie Mack being the others. Chance began his managerial career with the Chicago Cubs during the 1905 season after Frank Selee, manager of five pennant-winning Boston teams in the 1890s, was sidelined by illness. Selee built the foundation for a powerful Cubs team by moving Chance from catcher to first base and Joe Tinker from third to short, establishing baseball's most famous double-play combination: Tinker to Evers to Chance. But before he could lead Chicago to a pennant, Selee was diagnosed with tuberculosis. Chance took over and led a franchise that had not won a title in twenty years to the National League championship in 1906, setting an all-time mark for winning percentage with a record of 116–36. He followed that with pennants in 1907, 1908 and 1910, twice winning the World Series and earning the nickname "The Peerless Leader."

After a falling out with Cubs owner Charles Murphy, Chance managed the New York Highlanders for two unsuccessful seasons before retiring to his orange grove in Glendora, California, in an attempt to regain his health. He had suffered head injuries going back to his early playing days, including a 1901 incident in the California winter league when he was hit in the head by a pitched ball and it was feared a blood clot had developed on his brain.[64] Over the years it was estimated Chance had been hit in the head by pitches more than two dozen times, and at one point he underwent a delicate brain operation to relieve headaches.[65]

One of Chance's close friends, racer Barney Oldfield, had been negotiating to purchase a large block of stock in the Angels and hoped to persuade Chance to manage the team.

Although Oldfield ultimately did not go forward with his plan to become part-owner, the idea of hiring Chance appealed to Johnny Powers. On New Year's Day, Powers took Chance, Chance's wife and Oldfield to the horse track in Tijuana. While there, Powers offered Chance the opportunity to manage the Angels in 1916. After asking for time to think about it — largely because he had to win his wife over to the idea — Chance agreed and Powers had his big-name manager.[66]

* * *

Harry Wolverton was optimistic as the San Francisco Seals began preparations to defend their 1915 pennant. Most of the team would return, outside of Harry Heilmann, Roy Corhan and Walter Schmidt, each of whom had become major league property. At one point, it appeared that Hal Chase, who was a free agent in the wake of the Federal League's collapse, might be Heilmann's replacement at first base. Chase expressed interest in playing for the Seals and met with Harry Wolverton, who was also keenly interested. But the flashy first baseman's $8,000 contract was too rich for Henry Berry and Chase signed with the Cincinnati Reds.[67]

Having succeeded the previous season despite employing a decidedly veteran (most would say old) pitching staff, Wolverton seemed to make an about-face and embrace the concept rather than fight it, even welcoming the ancient but still popular Joe Corbett for yet another comeback. The forty-year-old had last appeared in the PCL seven years before but insisted he felt good and wanted to see if he could still pitch.[68]

The Corbett story was an interesting sidelight throughout the spring and that interest carried over into the season opener. League attendance was the best it had been in years. The Seals drew more than thirteen thousand for Opening Day and set a record with sixty-two thousand admissions for their opening series against Portland, a fifty percent increase compared to the year before.[69] Crowds were even better in Los Angeles as the hiring of Frank Chance began paying immediate dividends.

In honor of the opponents from Vernon, the traditional Opening Day parade in Los Angeles included a live tiger as part of the procession, while the Angels float featured a large baseball cut into halves with a child dressed as a cherub seated in the middle.[70] A total of 16,212 people plus another five hundred with passes waited at Washington Park for the teams. Johnny Powers employed his young son, Kelly, as the team's official mascot. When an Angels player hit a home run, the boy would rummage through his pockets and hand him a five-dollar bill.[71]

Los Angeles won the opener, 5–2, with Jack Ryan pitching a complete game. Chance showed he was indeed a battler, earning an ejection after outfielder Harl Maggert was called out on a close play at home plate.[72] Johnny Powers could not have asked for a better start to the season.

Frank Chance was not the league's only new drawing card. Twenty-one-year-old Portland first baseman Louie Guisto slammed four home runs on the road during the first week of the season, generating interest in a Beavers franchise that had finished last in 1915. The barrel-chested slugger, who had been discovered by Walter McCredie while playing football at St. Mary's College, could also be somewhat barrel-headed. During a series in Los Angeles he went into a slump and blamed it on a lack of fresh air in his hotel room. Guisto had a tent erected on the hotel roof and stayed there until the wind blew it over, forcing him to make a hasty retreat.[73]

Eager to see their new hero, ten thousand Beavers fans jammed into Vaughn Street Park for Portland's home opener on April 19 against Salt Lake City, braving dreary weather that persisted during the long parade through the streets of the city. The big first baseman was overshadowed by Salt Lake's Bunny Brief, who had five hits, including two home runs.[74] But Guisto would provide Beavers fans with plenty to cheer about, including his winning a game against Vernon at Vaughn Street Park on April 29 with a home run that smashed into the last row of bleachers and bounced out of the stadium.[75]

Despite Guisto's heroics, Portland failed to win. Short on money, the McCredies sold their new star to Cleveland in August, ensuring that 1916 would be another bleak season for Beavers fans. Allan Sothoron led the league with thirty wins, including fifteen in a row, and second baseman Bill Rodgers, who joined the team in mid–April after his release by the Cincinnati Reds, pulled off an unassisted triple play in July. But other highlights were few and far between, and Portland finished fifth.[76]

* * *

The San Francisco Seals' attempt to repeat suffered a blow when the pitching staff began to break down — exactly as Wolverton had feared the year before. Joe Corbett's comeback lasted only until May 1.[77] Skeeter Fanning, after three straight twenty-win seasons, was hampered by arm problems that kept him on the sidelines most of the time. The veteran pitcher visited a doctor in Los Angeles in June and the initial results were very encouraging; on June 23, Fanning threw a no-hitter against Vernon and struck out eleven batters.[78] Unfortunately, Fanning would win only one other game and the Seals released him.[79] The pitchers that remained healthy, veterans Spider Baum, Bill Steen and Curly Brown, were steady but unremarkable, losing as many games as they won.

The Seals also lost speedy outfielder Justin Fitzgerald for a couple of months after he injured his knee in a collision at second base following a pick-off attempt by Los Angeles pitcher Brad Hogg. The fact that Hogg's move was ruled a balk was of little consolation to Fitzgerald, who had to be helped off the field by teammates.[80] The Seals slipped to fourth place in a disappointing season.

The month of July featured one of the season's more intriguing developments with the announcement that Del Howard had purchased Frank Leavitt's share of the Oakland Oaks, putting control of the team in the hands of Howard, who became manager, and Leavitt's former partner, Jack Cook. A week later, the man financing Howard was revealed to be Cal Ewing, reversing his dramatic exit of nineteen months earlier.[81] Cook then sold his share of the team and left for Salt Lake City to become the Bees' business manager, leaving Ewing in total control of Oakland.[82]

Jack Cook was en route to a franchise in turmoil. Salt Lake City's second season had not been as successful as its first. Manager Cliff Blankenship argued with team president Frank Murphy all summer about acquiring players he felt were needed. With the Bees in fourth place on August 31, Blankenship announced he was resigning as manager unless the directors gave him more authority. He said of Murphy, "I am tired of acting as assistant to a business manager and I am through if they want my job."[83]

The directors were not inclined to give in to Blankenship. They named Bud Ryan interim manager and began seeking a permanent successor. Detroit Tigers star Sam Crawford was rumored for the job and at one point Napoleon Lajoie expressed interest, but nothing came of either man's inquiries.[84]

The 1916 pennant race ultimately came down to a Southern California battle for supremacy between Los Angeles and Vernon. In September, Frank Chance made a key acquisition by exchanging light-hitting Johnny Butler for Bobby Davis, an Oakland infielder. Davis, who was far more talented than Butler, was available only because of a nagging leg injury that caused him to be in and out of the lineup.[85] Understanding the asset Davis could be if healthy, Chance sent the infielder to a specialist who fitted him with an elastic bandage. The added support gave Davis confidence that his leg would not give out, and he played a vital role in the Angels' drive for the pennant.

Chance was not finished making deals with Oakland. Shortly after roster limits were lifted on September 15, he picked up pitcher Doc Crandall, the former New York Giants star who had been optioned to the Oaks by the St. Louis Browns.[86] The acquisition of Crandall, along with that of Davis, elicited howls of protest from Vernon owner Ed Maier. Charging that the deals smacked of collusion, Maier pointed out that Chance and Oakland manager Del Howard were former Cubs teammates and long-time friends.[87]

Vernon managed to hang close, actually grabbing first place for a time in September. But last-place Oakland would not only doom the Tigers' chances by trading Davis and Crandall to the Angels, the Oaks also would hurt them on the field. Although Oakland would tie a PCL record for losses in a season, the Oaks beat the Tigers five straight times in a late–October series, with Bill Prough defeating Vernon twice.[88]

The Angels staged "Frank Chance Day" to honor the man that had led the Angels to their first pennant in eight years. The Keystone Cops staged a one-inning farce that featured Edgar Kennedy, Slim Summerville and Fatty Arbuckle. The skit ended with the Cops chasing the umpires over the fence. Kelly Powers raced Barney Oldfield twice around the ballpark in a cycle car — a cross between a motorcycle and an automobile — while Oldfield drove a primitive circa 1900 motor vehicle. Washington Senators infielder Carl Sawyer entertained spectators with some baseball comedy and Chance manned first base for the Angels against a team of all-stars consisting of major leaguers from California. Four thousand dollars was collected and split twenty ways among the players as a reward for winning the championship.[89] A justifiably proud Johnny Powers watched the celebration; Frank Chance had delivered a pennant, just as Powers had envisioned back on New Year's Day in Tijuana.

* * *

For Eddie Maier, it was another disappointing end to a season marked by conflicts with other league directors. The Tigers owner had been at odds with the rest of the league for some time over accusations he had "side agreements" that provided additional, secret compensation to several players beyond that called for in their contracts. This allowed Maier to appear as if he was within league roster and salary limits. Players on other teams inevitably discovered these agreements and demanded similar terms, putting Maier's competitors in an uncomfortable situation.

Maier finally had enough and reached agreement to sell the Tigers to Tom Darmody, who had recently acquired a minority partnership in the Vernon franchise after selling his share of the Angels to Frank Chance (only a few months after refusing to do the same for Jimmy Callahan).[90] Maier then wrote an open letter to fans that was published in the *Los Angeles Times*. In it, he bitterly referred to the Butler and Crandall deals he felt had cost his team in yet another close pennant race. He credited Cal Ewing with being fair to him, and also praised Judge McCredie, before leveling his parting shot.

> I assure you that I have not relished this 10-cent notoriety and only stayed in the game until the brick house fell on me, because I was a true lover of the game, but when the edifice fell on me I finally got it through my head that I was spending money for naught. It had at last dawned upon me that my dream of a pennant, instead of being a sweet dream, was a weird nightmare and could never come true as long as I remained in the Pacific Coast League, as everything was framed against the Vernon club.

Maier added, "I have sold to a mighty fine fellow and I wish him the best in the world both for himself and the old Tigers, and I shall always be ready to do anything in my power to help him. I am and ever will be a true friend of baseball. Farewell."

Predictably, Maier's charge of collusion did not sit well with the powers of the Pacific Coast League. President Baum replied, "Such false and unfounded statements and accusations are not worthy of comment." Henry Berry was far more blunt. He snorted, "Ed Maier is either a crook himself or he is ignorant."[91]

Maier, seemingly unconcerned about whether he had burned his bridges behind him, decided against issuing further statements. He busied himself by getting married and running his brewery, certain his days in baseball were over.[92]

Henry Berry had his wish; the Vernon Tigers had finally been sold and Ed Maier was out of the league. The real challenge would be keeping it that way.

CHAPTER SIX

1917 to 1919:
A Southern California Rivalry

There were two men named Bill Lane connected with the Pacific Coast League in 1917. One was a speedy outfielder for the Oakland Oaks and the other was part-owner of the Salt Lake City Bees. But there was a third Bill Lane who should have been part of the league, an unquestioned talent that John McGraw had wanted to sign to a contract the first time he saw him play. This Bill Lane had grown up in Los Angeles, playing infield at Polytechnic High School alongside Zeb Terry, who later played shortstop for the Angels, the Chicago Cubs and three other big league teams. Although as talented as Terry, everyone knew this Bill Lane would never play for the New York Giants. As John McGraw bluntly put it, "I'd give fifty thousand dollars if that boy had been born white instead of black."[1]

The game of baseball remained largely segregated at all levels, especially when it came to dark-skinned athletes. Blacks sometimes played on high school or college teams in the early twentieth century, but only if they were stars. Even then, schools playing African American athletes in their lineups faced objections from opponents. Although blacks and whites sometimes played together in semi-pro and winter leagues, Organized Baseball had maintained a "separate and unequal" stance since the late 1880s. Prior to that, there had been occasional black players on white teams — and once in a while an all-black team in otherwise white leagues — but by 1900 the practice was long since past.

Other minority groups faced various levels of discrimination, including Asians on the Pacific Coast. Walter McCredie tried openly challenging barriers in the winter of 1914 by signing a half–Chinese, half–Hawaiian player named Wan Tee Teha Akana, who captained a team of Chinese university students from Hawaii that had barnstormed across the United States in 1912, 1913 and 1914.[2] Playing under the name Lang Akana, he helped turn a triple play at Comiskey Park against a group of all-star semi-pro players during the team's first tour.[3] He also attended the World Series and met Christy Mathewson and Ed Walsh; both shared their pet deliveries with him.[4]

Outfielder Johnny Kane saw the Chinese star play in Honolulu: "Akana appeared in two games against us," said Kane, "and in each of these he acted like a real ballplayer. He is a left-hander, who throws and fields well. He also showed considerable speed. The islands have contributed a number of good players and Akana may prove to be another."[5] But Akana was dark-skinned, and his prospective Beavers teammates refused to play alongside him. Walter McCredie reluctantly released his find and, clearly disgusted by the attitude of his players, explained, "His skin's too dark. I have received a couple of letters from players telling me Akana is as dark as Jack Johnson."[6]

Lang Akana. "I have received a couple of letters from players telling me Akana is as dark as Jack Johnson" — Walter McCredie (courtesy of KJR).

Although Asians were not welcome to play with or against whites on the Pacific Coast, mixed-blood Hawaiians could, provided they were of the right mix, unlike Lang Akana. Pitcher Barney Joy had been the first, joining the San Francisco Seals in 1907.[7] "Honolulu" Johnnie Williams was a pitching sensation for Sacramento in 1913; the Detroit Tigers offered eleven thousand dollars for his contract and he played briefly for them the following year. Williams then returned to the Pacific Coast League until arm problems led to his release by Los Angeles during the first week of the 1916 season.[8]

Latins had never been represented in numbers reflecting their interest in the game, although a few had been allowed to make their mark. Esteban Bellan, a native of Cuba, played in the National Association — a forerunner of the National League — from 1871 to 1873. Sandy Nava caught Charlie Sweeney in the major leagues. Cuban Armando Marsans played in the majors even though he was fairly dark-skinned. Fellow countrymen Dolf Luque and Mike Gonzales had long careers in the major leagues. Pitchers Jose Acosta and Ignacio Rojas, outfielder Jacinto Calvo (whose father was a rich sugar planter in Havana) and infielder Louis Castro were among the few Latin-born players to appear in the Pacific Coast League during its first couple of decades.[9] Pitchers Frank Arellanes and Sea Lion Hall (born Carlos Clolo), also pitched in the PCL and were of Mexican heritage but born in the United States. Hall gained notoriety as one of the first relief pitchers in the major leagues and threw four no-hitters in the minors. He earned his nickname because of his loud, barking voice. He was also called "The Greaser" by those less genteel, who quickly learned those were fighting words.[10]

Consistently derided about their racial heritage, Native Americans were nevertheless considered valuable drawing cards. Louis Sockalexis was one of the first, starring at both Holy Cross and Notre Dame and then with Cleveland in the National League in the late 1890s. The New York Giants employed catcher John "Chief" Meyers. Brooklyn's star outfielder Zack Wheat was half–Cherokee, although he did not advertise that fact. Albert "Chief" Bender of the Philadelphia Athletics was one of the game's best pitchers. The great Jim Thorpe was playing in the major leagues of both baseball and football. There had been several Indians in the PCL, most commonly pitchers, including Casey Smith, Ed Pinnance, Sammy Morris, Louis LeRoy and George "Chief" Johnson.

Because Indians enjoyed relative acceptance among the public and their teammates, there were occasional but almost universally unsuccessful attempts to masquerade black players as Native Americans.

The tactic was successfully employed once in the PCL, albeit very briefly. The Oakland Oaks, desperate for pitching help, announced in late May 1916 that they had signed twenty-three-year-old left-handed pitcher James "Minnehaha" Claxton, an Indian who had been a sensation in the Bay Area semi-pro leagues that spring.[11] Claxton pitched briefly in both games of a May 28 doubleheader for Oakland against Los Angeles, but his debut also proved to be his finale. He was released a few days later when the Oaks were tipped off that he was a mulatto instead of a full-blooded Indian.[12]

Despite his brief period of service, Claxton's stint as a member of the 1916 Oaks was immortalized by the Zeenut candy company, which took photographs of players for baseball cards to be inserted into packages of the company's candy bars. It served as proof that the color-line had been breached in the PCL, if only for a week.

Although white players seemed adamant about not sharing the diamond during the regular season, white fans showed they would pay to see exhibitions of integrated baseball. In February 1917, John Donaldson, often dubbed the "Colored Rube Waddell" (because he was left-handed and threw hard, not because of any erratic behavior), joined the all-black Los Angeles White Sox to pitch in a series of games against teams that included minor and major league players wintering in Los Angeles. The contests attracted the interest of fans and players alike and everyone agreed Donaldson was one of the best pitchers in the country. But even with his unquestioned talent, Donaldson was barred from pitching against these same players once the regular season started.[13]

The inability to use the best players, regardless of ethnicity, always bothered Walter McCredie, who had faced criticism in some quarters simply because his team played against the Chicago Black Giants during spring training in 1914 and 1915. He argued, "I don't think the color of the skin ought to be a barrier in baseball. They have Jim Thorpe, an Indian, in the big leagues; there are Cubans on the rosters of the various clubs. Here in the Pacific Coast League we have a Mexican and a Hawaiian, and yet the laws of baseball bar Negroes from organized diamonds.

"If I had my say, the Negro would be welcome inside the fold. I would like to have two such ball players as Petway and Lloyd of the Chicago Colored Giants, who play out here every spring. I think Lloyd is another Hans Wagner around shortstop and Petway is one of the greatest catchers in the world."[14]

Several years earlier, the *Los Angeles Times* had proudly published an article entitled, "Negroes Who Have Won Place or Fortune in Los Angeles," touting the advances made by African Americans in the city.[15] But the fact remained they were unwelcome at most area beaches and bars, or on the rosters of the Angels or Tigers. That applied to Bill Lane, who despite the endorsement of John McGraw was not allowed to play in the major leagues, or even the Pacific Coast League, simply because of the color of his skin. As the *Los Angeles Times* put it, "Bill was handicapped because he was the offspring of brunette parents. The color line is one of very distinct demarcation in organized baseball, and that alone prevented Lane from going straight from high school to the majors."[16]

Instead of starring in professional baseball, twenty-eight-year-old Bill Lane was working as a Los Angeles postman, supporting his pregnant wife and their two-year-old son while earning perhaps one-tenth what he would have been paid in the major leagues.

* * *

The 1917 San Francisco Seals, playing in a completely rebuilt Recreation Park, were in first place in mid–June, four-and-a-half games ahead of Salt Lake City. It seemed that Harry Wolverton had his team on the rebound from its disappointing 1916 season.[17] But the economy was weak, and with the country gearing up for the war in Europe, a new war tax was cutting into receipts. As a result, owners announced the imposition of salary cuts. In response, thirteen Seals players signed a letter of protest. Wolverton met with his players and told them that while he did not agree with the owners' action, he felt they were doing what they thought best under the circumstances. That only served to stiffen the players' resolve to refuse the pay cuts.

Henry Berry then met with the team and took a hard line, insisting that he would padlock the gates at Recreation Park if the players refused to yield. They finally acquiesced, realizing that minor leagues throughout the country were in financial distress and cutting roster sizes. Unless they had contacts to play for teams sponsored by defense contractors, there were no baseball jobs to be had.[18]

The Seals turned their attention back to the playing field. On Sunday, June 18, San Francisco pitcher Casey "Indian" Smith was at bat against Oakland when Oaks catcher Dan Murray started making derogatory remarks about Smith's racial background. Taking exception, Smith twice warned Murray to stop before smashing his bat over Murray's head, "tomahawking" him as it were. Murray managed to duck at the last instant, taking the force of the blow on his shoulder and behind his ear as he scurried away. Smith's attack ignited a free-for-all that took several minutes to quell.[19]

Wolverton sat in his office after the game, reviewing the events of the day and speculating about the length of suspension Smith would receive. Suddenly, he was handed a letter. Recognizing that the note was from Henry Berry, Wolverton opened it and quickly scanned the message. He was being fired.[20]

It was an unprecedented move; managers of first-place teams were never released in the middle of a season, especially without warning. Wolverton was stunned, and so were Seals players and fans. Henry Berry offered no specifics, saying only that it was a number of things and not any one issue that had cost Wolverton his job. There was speculation that Berry was upset by Wolverton's handling of the threatened strike by Seals players earlier in the week, but the action was evidently not as surprising to other league owners, who claimed the move had been coming for some time.

Tom Darmody insisted he was aware of Berry's desire to drop Wolverton and stated it was because of the San Francisco manager's high salary. Walter McCredie, who had always complained about Wolverton being an "expensive manager," felt the dismissal to be the inevitable result of Berry waking up to that fact. Others believed Wolverton acted like *he* was the owner and noted that Berry, who enjoyed making decisions and being the center of attention, was left out in the cold regarding his own team; if he wanted to know what was going on, he had to ask Wolverton.[21]

The shock of Wolverton's sudden dismissal was nearly equaled two weeks later when Frank Chance announced his resignation as Angels manager. There had been rumors before the season that Chance would return to Chicago as manager of the Cubs, but instead he had signed for another year with the Angels.[22] As the Fourth of July neared, Los Angeles was struggling with a record of 43–44, nine-and-a-half games behind San Francisco. The Peerless Leader was sick, exhausted and finally ready to heed the desires of his wife to retire. He simply no longer wanted the job and announced, "I am through with baseball for all time." Edith Chance quickly added, "And that's the truth."[23]

Wade "Red" Killefer was named Chance's replacement and the Angels responded, reeling off eleven wins in twelve games in early July and climbing into contention — even briefly knocking San Francisco from first place for the first time in five months — before falling short on the final day of the season. The Seals clinched the pennant with a 5–1 victory over Oakland, with the Oaks' only run resulting from a collision between Seals shortstop Roy Corhan and center fielder George Maisel on a short fly ball.[24] Although San Francisco had not played as well under new player/manager Red Downs as the Angels had under Killefer, the Seals finished with a final record of 119–93, enough to secure Henry Berry his second PCL championship in San Francisco.[25]

* * *

The ownership carousel swung round prior to the 1918 season. With the United States ready to enter the war in Europe, Portland was dropped because of the increased expense of war-time rail travel. Charlie Graham seized the opportunity to return to the game, acquiring Judge McCredie's rights and transferring the franchise to Sacramento and Buffalo Park, built in 1910 by former Gilt Edge owner Ed Kripp.[26] Although Graham brought many of the Beavers to California, Walter McCredie elected to manage Salt Lake City, where Bees director Bill Lane had recently become majority owner.

Meanwhile, Henry Berry, who had never really gained acceptance from San Francisco baseball fans, had come to realize his enthusiasm for the game had waned and he could not pour any more money into the franchise. Charlie Graham immediately stepped into the breach, abandoning Sacramento and assuming control of the Seals, leaving the Senators in the hands of Charles Heeseman, his partner in bringing baseball back to the California capital.[27]

Changes also were afoot in Southern California. Tom Darmody's Vernon Tigers were coming off a disappointing 1917 season and Bill Essick was hired to replace George Stovall as manager. At the same time, Darmody's Los Angeles rivals landed a big name in major league star Sam Crawford. The thirty-eight-year-old ex–Detroit Tigers outfielder did not join the Angels until three days before the Pacific Coast League season opener, having hoped to catch on with a major league team and continue his quest for three thousand hits (he was thirty-nine short).[28]

After spending the 1917 season mostly as a pinch-hitter for Detroit, Crawford quickly showed he had plenty of baseball life left, swatting a couple of hits and throwing out two Salt Lake City base runners on Opening Day.[29] Meanwhile, there were other signs that 1918 was going to be a memorable but odd year for the Pacific Coast League.

On April 7, Angels pitcher Doc Crandall was only one out from a no-hitter against Salt Lake City in a 14–0 blowout. Up to the plate stepped Crandall's brother, Karl, an infielder for the Bees. Proving that blood was not thicker than water, Karl Crandall calmly stroked a single to deny his brother's bid for immortality.[30]

Two weeks later, the San Francisco Seals and Vernon Tigers were playing a doubleheader at Washington Park. The Seals led, 1–0, in the first inning of the second game with one out and runners at first and third. Red Downs hit a grounder to Tigers second baseman Joe Mathes, who quickly fired the ball to home plate in an attempt to throw out the Seals runner trying to score from third. Just as Mathes released the ball, a magnitude 6.8 earthquake, centered seventy miles east of Los Angeles, shook the stadium and sent catcher Al DeVormer lurching a good five feet to his right. The throw by Mathes caromed off the screen in front of the grandstand. Two runners scored for San Francisco while Downs staggered into second base. Mathes was charged with an error.[31]

The excitement caused by natural disasters, the play of Sam Crawford, and other new faces brought in to replace those drafted into the war effort could not forestall the obvious; world events were wreaking havoc on the league in several ways. The federal tax continued eating into disposable income. The war distracted the public from baseball and attendance was even worse than it had been the year before. Then in May 1918, Provost Marshal General Enoch Crowder announced his "Work or Fight" order. Although it was not immediately clear how baseball would be affected, the general consensus was a test case would determine whether baseball was a "nonuseful" occupation and its players subject to mandatory support of the war.[32]

* * *

Charlie Graham was growing impatient with his San Francisco Seals, and at the beginning of July he released Red Downs as both the team's manager and as a player. Graham put on a uniform and manned the third base coach's box himself.[33] Although it was said that Downs was tired of Graham usurping his authority and had wanted to leave, Downs actually had no choice in the matter, and the Seals organization was not sorry to see him go. Years later, Downs admitted he had begun a downhill slide due to alcohol, which he would blame not only for the end of his baseball career but also for several post-career scrapes with the law.[34] He signed a few days later with the Los Angeles Angels to play what would prove to be the final week of the 1918 PCL season and the end of his Pacific Coast League career.[35]

With the country officially at war, in early July the draft boards in California and Utah formally declared that ballplayers were not exempt from conscription.[36] As a result, PCL directors met on July 12 and decided there was no point to continue with the season. They announced the schedule would end with games played that weekend and that Vernon and Los Angeles, which were in first and second place, would meet in a best five-of-nine playoff to determine the league champion for 1918.[37]

Despite the abrupt end to the regular season, there was considerable interest in Los Angeles for the Tigers-Angels series. Vernon seemed to have the upper hand, having won fifteen of the twenty-two games played between the teams, but the Tigers would have to play without first baseman Babe Borton, who was sidelined by a leg injury. Bob Meusel, who had obtained a ten-day furlough from the submarine base where he was stationed, replaced him.[38] The championship series began on July 17. The Angels won the first two games, holding off a furious Tigers rally to take the opener, 7–5, and then winning, 3–1, behind the pitching of Doc Crandall and the bat of Sam Crawford, who drove in two runs.[39]

The Angels and Tigers split the next four games, the last two in a morning/afternoon doubleheader, putting the Angels up four games to two and just one win from the championship. Vernon was ahead, 2–0, in the second game behind right-hander Wheezer Dell, but Dell fell apart in the bottom of the eighth, surrendering four runs to Los Angeles. Teenager Ralph Valencia, a local product who had been released by Vernon the year before, exacted a measure of revenge by retiring the Tigers in the ninth to save the win. The Angels were league champions and Vernon, although winning the abbreviated regular season, had once more fallen short of the pennant.[40]

* * *

The National and American leagues had decided to continue play through Labor Day and many PCL players beyond draft age temporarily joined the depleted major league rosters. Doc Crandall, Chet Chadbourne and Zeb Terry went to the Boston Braves. The PCL batting champ, Sacramento first baseman Art Griggs, signed with the Detroit Tigers. Rowdy Elliott and Speed Martin played for the Chicago Cubs while Jack Quinn and Al DeVormer joined the White Sox. The Yankees signed Jack Fournier. Hack Miller, Jean Dubuc, Dick McCabe and Bill Pertica joined the Red Sox; Miller and Dubuc played in the World Series against the Chicago Cubs. All of the players remained property of the Pacific Coast League and were to return to the circuit in 1919 unless purchased by a major league team.

Players subject to the military draft entered the service or worked in support of the war effort. Wheezer Dell was an electrician in the Los Angeles shipyards, where teammates Bill Essick, Franz Hosp and Elmer Rieger also reported, providing the shipyard a crack baseball team.[41] Shipyard baseball leagues were organized in both San Francisco and Los Angeles, featuring teams loaded with PCL players. Johnny Powers organized a weekend league for service teams in Southern California, and there were rumors that big league players, including Babe Ruth, would travel to the Pacific Coast to play — and supposedly work — after the World Series.[42]

But public sentiment was squarely against the notion of able-bodied men cavorting on a baseball diamond. Attendance dropped and the shipyard leagues stopped play. Two months later, in November, Armistice was declared and hostilities ceased.

In the aftermath of what had passed for a baseball season in 1918, the minor leagues were a shambles. A mere nine circuits had been able to start the year and only the International League was able to complete its schedule. The Pacific Coast League would return in 1919 and, filling the void created by the failure of other minor leagues, once again embraced Seattle and Portland, an expansion to eight teams that meant Dan Dugdale had to abandon his two-decade stranglehold on the Pacific Northwest.

Dugdale took it well, magnanimously declaring, "A league extending from Los Angeles to Seattle is ideal for the Coast.... If there ever was a time for a real Coast League it is now."[43] He sold most of his Seattle interest in late January to tobacco wholesaler James Brewster and moved into the team's front office as vice president.[44]

It seemed fitting that when Dan Dugdale finally joined the league he had fought so many years, one of his old nemeses, Jim Morley, returned to the PCL as well. Johnny Powers hired Morley as the Angels business manager and it seemed that the former owner's antics were forgiven. The *Los Angeles Times* credited Morley for having revived baseball when he brought the city into the California League in 1901. "It is true that Morley has his critics," said the *Times*, "but he always has been an ardent devotee and enthusiastic booster for the game."[45]

Another old face returned to familiar surroundings when Walter McCredie left Salt Lake City and returned to Portland to head the revived Beavers franchise. The league now had established a beachhead in four states, and the PCL would never again field fewer than eight teams. Feeling flush with the realization that big league names like Doc Crandall, Sam Crawford, Frank Chance, Tom Hughes, Doc White, Art Fromme and Jack Quinn were willing to extend their careers on the Coast — and that they could afford to pay them — Pacific Coast League owners increasingly insisted on competing with the major leagues on their own terms. During the winter the Pacific Coast League broke from the major league agreement regarding the drafting of players. If a major league team wanted a PCL player, he would have to be acquired through sale or trade.[46]

In the wake of the spirited playoff series for the 1918 pennant, the rivalry between the Angels and Tigers was booming and boosters of the two Southern California teams held a meeting for the purpose of establishing a prize fund of ten thousand dollars. The money would go to the players of the team winning the pennant.[47]

The Angels again had a veteran roster in 1919. Doc Crandall and Curly Brown headed the starting rotation while Sam Crawford agreed to return and anchor an outfield that included thirty-four-year-old Rube Ellis — in his eleventh season with the Angels — and thirty-five-year-old player-manager Red Killefer. Former White Sox first baseman Jack Fournier would have his best season with Los Angeles before going to the National League to play eight more years.

The Vernon Tigers featured veterans Wheezer Dell and Art Fromme in their pitching rotation. Byron Houck replaced Jack Quinn, who had taken his spitball to the major leagues and would pitch until age fifty. Outfielder Pete Daley retired in favor of the grocery business, but Chet Chadbourne was back, as was first baseman Babe Borton, shortstop Johnny Mitchell, catcher Al DeVormer, and manager Bill Essick.

The Tigers also had a new owner in 1919. After two frustrating years, Tom Darmody had been unable to raise the funds to complete the purchase of the team from Ed Maier. Business agent Lou Anger, brother-in-law of Byron Houck, talked one of his clients, film star Roscoe "Fatty" Arbuckle, into assuming Darmody's option. Arbuckle vowed to "show them how fast a fat man can travel in the direction of the pennant." On May 5 he signed the papers to complete what Tom Darmody had failed to do.[48]

The war over, baseball fans were hungry for the game and flocked to the PCL in record numbers. Jim Morley paced the grandstand at Washington Park while wearing his trademark straw hat, blue serge blazer and ice cream pants and reviewing the impressive attendance figures of other PCL teams. He was sure the Angels could do even better.

Washington Park featured one of the largest playing fields in baseball, with its left-field fence 395 feet from home plate. It was 425 feet to center. Morley studied the park's dimensions and reasoned that an increase in home run hitting would translate into increased fan interest.[49] He installed an inner fence of chicken wire ten feet high that shortened the distance to left field by seventy feet.[50]

It lasted about two weeks.

Critics called it tacky and asked why a permanent fence was not built instead of something that looked more at home on a farm. Players did not like it, unhappy about losing extra-base hits, especially triples, because the fences were so shallow. Vernon officials, who shared the ballpark with the Angels, did not care one way or another, but Los Angeles manager Red Killefer pointed out that he had manufactured the Angels roster based on having deep fences that negated other team's sluggers. Morley had given away his team's advantage.[51] Enraged Angels players threatened to tear down the new fence in the middle of the night, but Johnny Powers beat them to it. He ordered it dismantled on July 28, an action taken even though the controversy had increased attendance, just as Morley had predicted.[52]

* * *

By September it was apparent the 1919 pennant race would come down to a battle between Los Angeles and Vernon—exactly as boosters of the two teams had hoped when they established the ten-thousand-dollar prize pool for the players. With twelve games left to play, the Tigers fell three behind the Angels in the loss column after being defeated by Salt Lake City amid smoke and ash from a forest fire that clogged the air in Los Angeles. One bright spot for the Tigers was that the final series of the year would be played against the Angels, but that meant nothing if they were unable to defeat Salt Lake City.

The Tigers *did* start winning. Smoke apparently did not agree with the Bees, who stumbled about as if they had forgotten how to play baseball. Bill Essick's team took advantage, clubbing both Gene Dale and Pudgy Gould in consecutive games. On September 26, Vernon blasted Salt Lake, 16–1, making quick work of Spider Baum as fans started leaving in the seventh inning.[53] After a rainout (welcomed because it extinguished the forest fire), the Tigers swept a doubleheader from the Bees and moved within two games of first place.[54] Vernon's crushing of Salt Lake set the stage for an exciting, season-ending seven-game series against Los Angeles to decide the pennant.

The Tigers continued to roll, taking four of the first five games against the Angels to cap their thrilling rush to the front of the pack. All that remained was the season-ending doubleheader. One win and Vernon would capture its first outright Pacific Coast League pennant.

Bill Essick chose Wheezer Dell to pitch the early game against Curly Brown. For Dell, it was a chance for redemption after his playoff loss the year before. Fans began lining up to buy tickets at nine o'clock; by noon the bleachers were nearly full. Standing-room tickets were sold until twenty-two thousand people had been crammed into the park. Several thousand more were turned away.[55]

The Tigers struck in the bottom of the first. Johnny Mitchell smacked the first pitch of the game into the crowd in left field for a ground-rule double and Bob Meusel promptly singled him home. Vernon extended the lead to 3–0 on Bob Fisher's sixth-inning single; one female fan reacted by bounding onto the field and doing a celebratory dance. She was quickly escorted back to her seat and the game resumed.

Wheezer Dell seemed to have things well in hand, even after Red Killefer lined a run-scoring single in the eighth inning to cut the Tigers' lead to 3–1. Mindful of his collapse against Los Angeles the year before, Dell was determined to close out the ninth. He easily retired Jack Fournier and Sam Crawford, the first two Angels batters in the inning. With Los Angeles down to its last out, Killefer sent Doc Crandall to pinch-hit, and Crandall immediately smashed a ball into the standing-room-only crowd in left field for a ground-rule double. Twenty-one-year-old Fred Haney was sent in to pinch-run.

The next batter, Rube Ellis, singled to center and Haney, displaying the recklessness and daring that would be his trademark both as a player and manager, sprinted all the way home from second base, beating the tag at the plate by an eyelash to keep the Angels season alive. But Haney's mad dash had so surprised Ellis that he did not take second on the throw to home plate.

There were still two out and Los Angeles trailed, 3–2, as Angels second baseman Bert Niehoff came to the plate. Niehoff did his best imitation of Happy Hogan and chopped down on Dell's pitch, sending it bouncing high into the air between third base and the pitcher's mound. Dell fielded the ball and fired it to first baseman Stump Edington, but the throw was late and Niehoff was safe.

Rube Ellis, still angry at himself for not taking second base on Haney's play, decided to make up for his lack of aggressiveness. As Dell's throw arrived too late to first, Ellis gathered speed rather than slowing down as he reached second and rocketed toward third as everyone in the stadium roared and jumped to their feet. Edington saw Ellis make his move and rifled the ball across the diamond but Tigers third baseman Zinn Beck was out of position; he had abandoned the bag when Niehoff chopped the ball in his direction and was slow to recover. Edington's throw was high and wide and flew over Beck's head. Ellis, who had ignored third-base coach Paul Fittery's plea to slide, saw that the throw was off target and turned for home.

What Fittery had seen, and Ellis had not, was that Tigers shortstop Johnny Mitchell had anticipated what was about to happen and had dashed over to back up Beck. Mitchell made a leaping catch of Edington's overthrow. Ellis suddenly realized his mistake and attempted to reverse his momentum in an effort to get back to third. He stumbled and began clawing for the base, producing a cloud of dust as Mitchell hurled himself full-length at the bag, slamming the ball against Ellis' fingers. Umpire Bill Phyle, crouched over the play, immediately signaled that Ellis was out. The 1919 season was over. Wheezer Dell breathed a sigh of relief as the crowd exploded with a roar. The Vernon Tigers had finally won a Pacific Coast League pennant, clinched on the most exciting play of the season.[56]

Johnny Powers congratulated the Tigers and wished them luck in the long-awaited Western World Series against St. Paul, champions of the American Association. Powers also praised Red Killefer, putting a hand on the manager's shoulder and saying, "I want to tell you that here is the man who can manage the Los Angeles ball team as long as he cares to. A better and gamer manager never stepped on a ball field."

Fatty Arbuckle, flush with victory in his first season as owner of the Tigers, told reporters, "My sole regret is that Happy Hogan could not have lived to see this day."[57]

The Vernon Tigers had reason to celebrate. They had won their first undisputed Pacific Coast League pennant, which they then topped off with a hard-fought victory over St. Paul in a nine-game minor league "World Series" that ended with Wheezer Dell smashing the game-winning hit and being carried off the field in celebration.[58] It was a year to remember for the Tigers — or at least it should have been.

In December, noting the whispers about gamblers and the just-completed 1919 World Series between the Chicago White Sox and the Cincinnati Reds, *San Francisco Chronicle* sportswriter Ed Hughes wrote a column warning about the prevalence of gambling in Pacific Coast League parks. Hughes said that while no scandal had yet occurred, the situation could lead to one. He urged the league to act.[59]

Unfortunately, it was too late. In a few months it would be discovered that the 1919 Pacific Coast League pennant race had been fixed.

CHAPTER SEVEN

1920 to 1921:
Lying Tigers and Bees, Oh My!

Gambling was a great danger to sports, as paying fans demanded to know that contests were on the up and up. Horseracing and prize fighting had lost most of their credibility because of crookedness. The integrity of baseball in the West had been challenged several times during the nineteenth century. The California League collapsed in 1893 in part because fans did not feel the game was being played on the level.

Scandals inevitably ensnared players, including those in the PCL. In 1905, Oakland Oaks president Clay Hawbacker accused pitcher Henry Schmidt of trying to throw a game against Seattle. He released the ex–major leaguer, who quickly signed with the outlaw California State League, demonstrating that enforcing a sanction against bad behavior was not easy.[1]

In 1910, Oakland pitcher Ralph Willis was accused of entertaining a proposal to throw a game against Portland. Manager Harry Wolverton supposedly got wind of the plot and replaced Willis with another pitcher, although Wolverton later denied he had harbored any suspicion about Willis. League president Thomas Graham investigated the matter, and although Willis was not punished, the Oaks sent him to the Northwest League the next season and he never again pitched in the PCL.[2]

Two years later, league president Allan Baum enlisted law enforcement to assist in a crackdown on betting at Pacific Coast League ballparks. Gamblers were arrested in Los Angeles and police raided cigar stores in Oakland.[3] Nevertheless, it was not long before a group of men calling themselves the "Score Card Company" were printing numbered lottery cards for baseball betting "within a stone's throw" of Baum's office in San Francisco. They boasted of expanding to locations in each PCL city.[4]

San Francisco attorney William McCarthy, who succeeded Baum as PCL president in late October 1919, made many of the same pronouncements against gambling as previous heads of the league.[5] At the Pacific Coast League's annual meeting in January 1920, a resolution was adopted "declaring war on the baseball gamblers."[6] Baseball's National Commission signaled that it too was targeting gamblers, in response to rumors, unfortunately true, about crookedness related to the 1919 World Series.[7] This tough talk had been heard before, and cynics were of the opinion that driving the problem underground was about the most that could be done. But there was a difference this time. William McCarthy was willing to put some bite behind his bark.

His cause was aided in February 1920, when three major league players were banned from baseball for gambling.[8] Although not officially identified, it was common knowledge that the three were Chicago Cubs utility player Lee Magee, New York Giants third baseman Heine Zimmerman, and Zimmerman's teammate, Hal Chase, a talented but shady character quite familiar to West Coast baseball fans.[9]

Three months later, McCarthy had an opportunity to prove his boast to clean house in the PCL. On May 7, San Francisco owner Charlie Graham announced he was releasing two of his best pitchers, Tom Seaton and Casey Smith, because of gambling on games. Graham refused to elaborate on the specific allegations but issued a press release:

> From time to time rumors of the most serious nature have reached me regarding these ballplayers, their practices and their associates. At first I refused to listen to them, but their persistency and their growth have persuaded me that, whether true or untrue, for the best interests of baseball Seaton and Smith should be released. Unfortunately their loss to the club is most serious. They are both classed as among the best, if not the best, pitchers in the league. At this time, when we are making a winning fight for the pennant, it is to be regretted that this sacrifice must be made. But, much as I covet the pennant and anxious as I naturally am to remain in first place I would rather sacrifice the club in every way than continue with players who by their actions and associates, either on or off the field leave themselves, their club and the game open to suspicion of any kind.[10]

William McCarthy praised Graham in a statement that said, "I heartily approve of the action of Manager Graham of the Seals. So long as I am president of the Coast League no man upon whom there is even a shadow of suspicion can play in the league.

"The action of Graham should be commended by all lovers of clean sport, for he has discharged two of the best pitchers in the league, who were worth easily $10,000 to his club, showing that he is willing to sacrifice his own interest for the good of baseball."[11] McCarthy declared he was going to clean up the league, starting with San Francisco. He began by banning several well-known gamblers from Pacific Coast League ballparks. One of them, Roy Hurlburt, reacted by stalking the PCL president and sucker-punching him on a San Francisco sidewalk.[12]

The Sunday following Graham's dramatic announcement, Tom Seaton pitched for Hanford in the semi-pro San Joaquin Valley League and Casey Smith joined Hollister in the Mission League, the same circuit where Hal Chase was playing after his banishment by major league baseball. In the aftermath of the bad publicity that resulted from the employment of Seaton and Smith, the directors of the two leagues reconsidered and ruled that any player banned from the Pacific Coast League would also be banned from playing in their leagues.[13] Seaton and Smith were asked to move on.

Smith joined Logan of the outlaw Utah-Idaho League for $450 per month but was run out of there as well. He and Seaton then headed south, signing with Little Rock in the Southern Association and creating an instant firestorm.[14] Unfortunately, the episode involving Tom Seaton and Casey Smith was merely a prelude for what was to come.

* * *

Babe Ruth's slugging feats had captured the imagination of baseball fans in a way "inside baseball" never could. Suddenly the home run was in vogue and customers clamored for more, as Jim Morley had noted in his ill-fated attempt to move the fences closer at Washington Park. Professional baseball seemed obliged to give the public what it wanted — more offense — and targeted pitchers as a way of doing so.

In late October 1919, American League president Ban Johnson proposed that "trick" deliveries, such as the spitball and shine ball, be declared illegal.[15] At the major league meetings in February 1920, both the American and National leagues adopted the proposal, allowing a one-year grace period to pitchers identified by their teams as those relying on the spitter for their livelihood.[16] The Pacific Coast League followed suit, ruling that players currently in the league could continue to throw the spitter, but that pitchers new to the PCL could not.[17] At the end of that first year, St. Louis Cardinals spitballer Bill Doak was among those asserting that banning himself and fellow spitballers from using their best pitch would likely end their careers.[18]

Doak's argument carried the day and the spitball remained a legal pitch for seventeen men during the remainder of their careers, including Ray Fisher, who did not play after 1920. This group continued as an endangered species of sorts until 1934, when Burleigh Grimes threw the last legal spitter in the major leagues.

The PCL continued to mirror major league policy regarding spitball pitchers, allowing a select few to continue throwing it. Some of the Pacific Coast League's biggest pitching stars found they could continue only in the PCL. By the middle of the 1920s, the list of registered spitball pitchers in the Pacific Coast League would be a short one: Frank Shellenback, Doc Crandall, Harry Krause, Ray Keating and Pudgy Gould. All were very successful in the PCL, with Shellenback setting the all-time league record for victories by a pitcher before his retirement in 1938.[19]

There were additional suggestions to clean up the game and make it more fan and family friendly. The American Association, which had led the way in banning trick pitches prior to the 1918 season, proposed that players receive an automatic ejection for using profanity. It was common knowledge that bad language was a constant on the field and the bench; the cursing could easily be heard in the stands. Some were firmly against the plan, arguing with an apparently straight face that profanity was a safety valve of sorts that kept players from engaging in fisticuffs with umpires — a theory hardly borne out in the rough and tumble PCL.

When told of the American Association ban on cursing, one anonymous Pacific Coast League manager remarked, "That's a helluva funny idea."[20]

* * *

Since their inception, the Salt Lake City Bees had made a habit of fielding good teams but never winning. After a second-place finish in 1915, the Bees came in third in 1916 and 1917, finished a half-game out of third place in 1918 — when the schedule was aborted in July because of the war — and came in third again in 1919.

The Bees were certainly not lacking in great individual performances. Lefty Williams dominated the league's pitching statistics in 1915 and Paul Fittery won twenty-nine games with a 2.97 earned run average the following year. Bunny Brief broke Ping Bodie's PCL record with thirty-three home runs in 1916. Morrie Rath led the PCL in batting average in 1917 while teammate Jack Tobin hit .331 before returning to the major leagues to continue a thirteen-year big league career.

Individual greatness had not translated into pennants for the Bees, but the 1920 season appeared as if it might signal the team's breakthrough — if the players could pull together rather than looking out only for themselves, which had been a long-time problem for the franchise. Salt Lake City was undeniably loaded with talent.

The pitching staff was led by Walter Leverenz, thirty-two years old and in his fourth season with the team. He had an off-year in 1919 but had won twenty-two games in 1917, followed by a 16–5 record in the war-shortened 1918 season. The left-hander had a deceptive motion, making it appear as if he were tying himself into a knot. Leverenz's delivery made him both hard to hit against and susceptible to fits of erratic control.

The oldest men on the staff were thirty-eight-year-old Spider Baum and thirty-five-year-old Ralph "Sailor" Stroud. Baum, whose PCL career began in 1903, almost never threw anything other than a spitball and had the most wins of any pitcher in league history to that time — a total of 255 at the beginning of the 1920 season.

The infield was anchored by slugging first baseman Earl Sheely. In his fourth season with the Bees, Sheely had little range or speed because of a broken ankle suffered as a child that had never healed properly and would hobble him all his life.[21] But the strapping first baseman was one of the top sluggers in the Pacific Coast League and a great defensive player with soft hands who caught everything he could reach. Sheely led the Pacific Coast League in home runs in 1919 with twenty-eight, a year after tying Sacramento's Art Griggs for the title in that category. The rest of the Bees infield consisted of their new manager, Ernie Johnson, at shortstop, veteran Marty Krug at second, and Eddie Mulligan, a former Chicago Cubs infielder and high school soccer star, at third. It was a group that could match any on the Coast.

Twenty-nine-year-old Bill Rumler was in his second season with the Bees, having taken over right field following the death of former big leaguer Larry Chappell in the Spanish Flu epidemic. A pinch-hitting specialist for the St. Louis Browns prior to entering the Army in 1918, Rumler broke his leg during his stint in the military but made a comeback with Salt Lake City in 1919, winning the batting title with a .362 average.

Harl Maggert was also in his second season with Salt Lake City. At age thirty-seven, the outfielder was slowed by age and injuries. Prior to spring training in 1918, Maggert tore two ligaments in his right knee, which later gave out on him during a practice game when he rounded second base and made a quick stop.[22] Maggert had not been the same player in either 1918 or 1919 and was of little value when it came to a possible sale to the major leagues. Many considered him to be at the end of his career. Maggert also had a well-deserved reputation for being moody and resistant to authority; Harry Wolverton suspended Maggert several times during the 1911 season, the last time after he got into a fistfight with Oaks teammate Gus Hetling and then failed to appear for a game the next day.[23] When Maggert was with the Angels in 1917, he engaged in a two-part brawl with trainer Doc Finlay. The second phase of the battle took place at the team's hotel in San Francisco and culminated in Maggert holding Finlay out of a fifth-floor window and threatening to drop him to the pavement below. Teammates intervened to avert tragedy, and there was talk that Maggert would be traded. Frank Chance resigned as manager two days later.[24]

In July 1920, Maggert's attitude was great and he was surprising everybody, playing the best ball of his life and hitting higher than .370. The Bees were in second place with a 64–48 record, only a game and a half behind defending champ Vernon.

But the Bees' hopes for a pennant were about to suffer a mortal blow.

* * *

Hal Chase was sitting in the stands at Washington Park on July 27, taking in a game between Vernon and Salt Lake City.[25] That same day, a detective assigned to investigate allegations of gambling in the Pacific Coast League witnessed Tigers first baseman Babe Borton hand a check to Harl Maggert.

Unaware of the league's investigation, Chase approached Bees pitcher Spider Baum the next day and asked him if he wanted to make some "easy money." Chase told Baum he was representing someone with large amounts of cash to bet if he had an "edge" and would cut the pitcher in for a piece of the action if he played along. Baum was in on the investigation and had been instructed to tell Chase that he was not pitching in the series and to talk to another pitcher.[26]

Vernon first baseman Babe Borton then approached Baum's teammate, Sailor Stroud, with an offer of three hundred dollars to throw a game.[27] Although he later said that he had refused Borton's bribe, Stroud's performance that day aroused suspicion. After Stroud

retired the first batter, Vernon's Chet Chadbourne beat out a bunt in front of the plate that Stroud was unable to field in time. Stroud hit the next batter on the wrist and then walked Babe Borton to load the bases. Two batters later, four runs had scored and Stroud was removed from the game.[28] Stroud later testified that when Borton approached him after the game to offer him the three hundred dollars, he told Borton he had pitched his best and had refused the money.[29]

Babe Borton, pictured during his stint with the New York Yankees, was the ringleader of the 1919 scandal in the Pacific Coast League (courtesy of KJR).

The next day, Harl Maggert was ejected in the first inning after arguing a called strike.[30] Bees president Bill Lane later claimed Maggert had done so in order to receive a suspension from the league, which he would use as an excuse to jump his contract.[31] Maggert was fined twenty-five dollars by the Bees and, as predicted, threatened to quit.[32]

On August 3, McCarthy reviewed evidence gathered by his detective and decided to bar Hal Chase from all Pacific Coast League ballparks, saying, "I have today notified all clubs in the Pacific Coast League that admission to our parks shall hereafter be refused to Hal Chase. If reports are true, Chase has done more to discredit baseball than any other single individual. It was hoped that his activities would be ended with his elimination from the major leagues and would not extend further." McCarthy also suspended Babe Borton indefinitely and Salt Lake City released Maggert.[33]

Chase was then kicked out of the Mission League, where he was playing on Sundays for a team in San Jose. Chase denied McCarthy's accusations in a telephone interview, calling talk of bribery "foolish," and said he would demand that the PCL president retract his statements and rescind the order banning him from league stadiums.[34] Meanwhile, Maggert admitted receiving a check from Borton but claimed it was from a bet the two made the year before.[35] For his part, Borton claimed the whole affair involved a craps game from the previous fall. McCarthy countered that if Borton's claim was true, he must reveal the names of those involved in the game.[36]

McCarthy continued his investigation and uncovered the man bankrolling the bribery — Nate Raymond, a well-known gambler with ties to Arnold Rothstein, the man later said to have funded the Black Sox. Raymond had offered Seattle first baseman Rod

Murphy three thousand dollars, boasting, "Remember last year when some of the boys on Salt Lake sold out to Vernon. Rod, I was the man who put the deal through. It cost me $10,000 and I cleaned up about $50,000." Murphy answered that he had heard the rumors about the pennant race being fixed. He asked Raymond who else had been involved.

Raymond replied, "Rod, to prove my truthfulness to you I will mention two players. Ask Maggert and Borton how I treated them in our agreement."[37]

The exchange between Raymond and Murphy shed new light on the key series Vernon had played against Salt Lake City under smoky skies during the next-to-last week of the 1919 season, when the Bees began acting as if they had forgotten how to play the game. That series put the Tigers back in the pennant race and helped generate the momentum they needed to overtake the Angels during the final week of the season.

As the greatest scandal in Pacific Coast League history unfolded, it would prove to have connections to an even bigger scandal in Chicago that threatened to bring down the entire structure of baseball.

* * *

Babe Borton was soon implicating scores of players in the conspiracy. He claimed that everyone on the Vernon team, including manager Bill Essick, contributed to a fund to bribe opposing players. The only teammate Borton said had refused the offer was Al DeVormer. Borton also named Salt Lake City outfielder Bill Rumler and Rumler's former teammate, pitcher Gene Dale, as having received bribes. Borton claimed that the day after the Vernon–St. Paul "World Series" ended, he gave $250 to Rumler and $500 to Dale from money held out of each Vernon player's share for the series. William McCarthy was able to verify that bank drafts were sent from the Los Angeles Trust & Savings Bank to Rumler and Dale at their homes on the date in question, October 18, 1919.[38] Bill Essick and all of the Vernon players denied Borton's accusation, as did Gene Dale from Dallas, where he was playing in the Texas League.

Harl Maggert finally met with William McCarthy on August 12 to give his side of the story.[39] Bill Rumler remained in the Salt Lake lineup and the Bees, already smarting from the loss of Maggert and the revelation of his dishonesty, rushed to investigate and clear their star before McCarthy punished him as well. The Salt Lake City directors met on the same day McCarthy interviewed Maggert and unsurprisingly exonerated Rumler, announcing that the money Borton had sent to Rumler was part of a "safety bet" made by the two men. At that time, players received bonuses from a league fund based on where their teams finished in the standings; the higher in the standings a team finished, the greater the bonus for the team's players. The Bees reported that Borton and Rumler had agreed to split whatever their combined shares would be, a technically illegal but not entirely unusual practice at the time.[40]

As if not wanting to be left out of the spotlight, Hal Chase announced he was suing William McCarthy for defamation of character. Upon learning of the potential lawsuit, McCarthy seemed less than threatened: "So Hal Chase is suing me for defamation of character, I never knew he possessed such a thing."[41]

The day after meeting with Maggert, McCarthy announced the ballplayer's "confession" was anything but. Maggert insisted he had never thrown any games and had only received five hundred dollars from Borton, with two hundred dollars being paid early in the 1920 season and the other three hundred dollars given to him on July 27, two days before his meltdown in the first inning of the game against Vernon. Maggert said that was when Borton handed him the three hundred dollars and said, "Now we're even." He claimed to have no idea why Borton was giving him money.[42]

McCarthy contacted Ed Maier and insisted that the Vernon club press charges against Babe Borton for "criminal libel." He offered a five-thousand-dollar reward to anyone providing proof of the charges Borton had made against other Pacific Coast League players.[43] McCarthy also announced the indefinite suspension of Bill Rumler based on the "safety bet" he made with Borton during the 1919 pennant race.[44] Eddie Mulligan, who Harl Maggert had implicated during his meeting with McCarthy, was cleared of all charges.

Salt Lake City president Bill Lane reacted angrily to McCarthy's suspension of Rumler, while Rumler expressed surprise, pleading, "I insist that I did not enter into any proposition to throw or attempt to throw any game. My record shows that I played my hardest to win at all times."[45] In a telegram to McCarthy, Lane argued, "There is not the slightest evidence of gambling in the Rumler case. I most certainly shall not ruin the career of such an upright, straight-forward young athlete as Rumler on any such evidence as has been presented."[46]

The baseball world continued to close in on those involved in the scandal. The president of the San Joaquin Valley Baseball League, an independent weekend league, announced the banning of Maggert and Chase, who had been playing for Madera. Furthermore, records of any game in which they had played were thrown out.[47] On August 20, McCarthy handed Bill Rumler a lifetime ban, saying, "As long as I am head of the Pacific Coast League, Bill Rumler shall not play in the organization." McCarthy explained that Rumler was free to play in any other league as long as he received his release from Salt Lake City.[48]

Sacrificing Harl Maggert was one thing; he was an older player of little value. Rumler was another matter entirely. The league's defending batting champion still had the potential to bring significant value in trade or sale to a major league team—now the Bees faced the prospect of losing him and receiving nothing in return. Bill Lane and Jack Cook vowed to fight McCarthy's edict and argued that the league president lacked the authority to ban anyone from the PCL. After several days, McCarthy relented and shortened the suspension to five years, conceding that the league constitution allowed the league president to suspend players only for a defined period.[49] This failed to satisfy either the Salt Lake directors or Rumler. Lane and Cook made plans to challenge McCarthy at a special league meeting in late September.[50]

Maggert was embittered by what he saw as preferential treatment of his former teammate and insisted Rumler was as guilty as he was. He claimed that everyone involved knew money was raised to help Vernon win the pennant and threatened new revelations if Rumler's appeal of his suspension proved successful. "I got the dough from Borton and so did Rumler," complained Maggert. "You didn't see anybody breaking their necks trying to get me a hearing when

"I got the dough from Borton and so did Rumler. You didn't see anybody breaking their necks to get me a hearing when the thing broke."—Harl Maggert (National Baseball Hall of Fame Library, Cooperstown, N.Y.).

the thing broke. They just canned me and let it go at that. With Rumler it is different. He is worth a lot of dough to the Salt Lake club, so they are bringing a big delegation of prominent businessmen and orators to speak on his behalf. In the meantime I'm working in the old coal yard in Berkeley."

Maggert reasserted Borton's contention that the entire Vernon team was in on the fix and that Al DeVormer, Johnny Mitchell and Stump Edington had confessed to William McCarthy about the slush fund while he had kept quiet about the truth. "I never squealed in my life but if the directors are going to clear Rumler I am willing to go before the board and tell a few things. They are not going to make me the fall guy."[51]

Events quickly overran the entire Pacific Coast League scandal and rendered Maggert's threats moot. Rumors had swirled throughout both the 1918 and 1919 World Series, and other instances of dishonest play in the major leagues were coming to light. Buck Herzog of the Chicago Cubs was openly accused of conspiring to throw a game on August 31, 1920, along with his teammate, pitcher Claude Hendrix. During questioning about that incident, Herzog revealed his knowledge of the 1919 World Series fix, which was being investigated by a Chicago grand jury.[52]

On September 28, 1920, Joe Jackson, star outfielder of the Chicago White Sox, left the Criminal Courts Building after confessing before the Chicago grand jury to the conspiracy to throw the 1919 World Series. There were several hundred children outside waiting for a glimpse of the great player and one of the youngsters approached Jackson and grabbed his coat sleeve.

The kid looked up at Jackson and mournfully asked, "It ain't true, is it Joe?"

"Yes kid, I'm afraid it is," was Jackson's famous reply.

As the star walked away the youngster remarked out loud, "Well, I'd never have thought it."[53]

Eight White Sox players in all — including former Coast Leaguers Chick Gandil, Swede Risberg, Buck Weaver, Fred McMullin and Lefty Williams — were indicted by the Cook County, Illinois, Grand Jury. It did not escape the notice of the grand jury that Williams had played for Salt Lake City, which was gaining a national reputation for being the team most responsible for crooked play in the Pacific Coast League. Others with PCL backgrounds eventually tied to the Black Sox fix included Hal Chase, Sleepy Bill Burns, Joe Gedeon and Jean Dubuc.[54]

The timing of these revelations could not have been worse for Rumler, breaking as they did just before the meeting at which he planned to plead his case. The PCL unanimously adopted a resolution upholding McCarthy's five-year suspension of Rumler. Even Bill Lane had no choice but to vote in favor of it. In an obvious swipe at Lane and Jack Cook, the directors also adopted a resolution commending Charles Comiskey for his actions in releasing the dishonest White Sox.[55]

In mid–October, the Los Angeles Grand Jury investigated the matter of dishonesty in the Pacific Coast League during the 1919 season, with league officials and Babe Borton's attorney, Griffith Jones, each supporting it. A number of players were asked to testify and Deputy District Attorney W.C. Doran announced his intention to charge the players and gamblers under a California law making it a felony to conspire to commit a felony. Doran announced that players on five PCL teams were under the control of gamblers and that "scores" of games had been thrown during the 1919 season.[56]

Harl Maggert testified that McCarthy had first learned about the gambling scandal from Vernon catcher Al DeVormer, who had blown the whistle because of dissatisfaction with his share for winning the 1919 pennant.[57] DeVormer issued a written statement affirming that his check from the $10,000 pennant fund established by the Angels and Tigers boosters in the spring of 1919 was less than he had anticipated and that he suspected that some of the money had gone for bribes. He went on to say he understood that $700 of the fund went to one Salt Lake City player and four Portland players and $1,100 eventually went to the Salt Lake City team. Borton's attorney claimed the fan fund was short two thousand dollars.[58] (The initial investigation by the district attorney's office indicated the fund might have been the source of the bribery money.)[59]

In November, the grand jury questioned Borton about his purchasing a $425 ring in Seattle and also began focusing on the movements of Nate Raymond.[60] It was discovered that during the 1920 season, Raymond had followed Borton and the Tigers for almost an entire month, beginning on July 5 when he told friends he was taking a trip to New York but instead registered at a hotel in Portland while the Tigers played a series there. A week later, the Tigers moved on to San Francisco to play a series and Raymond followed them, checking into the St. Francis Hotel. Babe Borton was seen making visits to the St. Francis each morning the Tigers were in town. Raymond then shadowed the Tigers to Los Angeles, remaining there when they hosted the Angels and then the Bees. He was still in Los Angeles when Hal Chase made the offer to Baum, during which Chase mentioned he was "representing someone."[61]

On December 10 the grand jury returned indictments against Borton, Maggert, Rumler and Raymond, charges that carried a potential punishment of two years in prison and a fine of five thousand dollars. Bail was set at one thousand dollars. The specific complaint was conspiracy to throw games in the series played between Salt Lake City and Vernon in September 1919. The grand jury stated that Borton was the only member of the Tigers guilty of any involvement. It was also determined that the fan fund was not the source of the bribery money.[62]

McCarthy wrote to Ed Maier and Bill Essick, praising them for their handling of the situation. He also congratulated them that their players, other than Borton, had been cleared of wrongdoing.[63] Bill Lane and Jack Cook failed to receive a similar missive from the league president.

Borton surrendered to authorities on December 13 and his bail was reduced to five hundred dollars. It was announced that Maggert would surrender as well. Borton's attorney stated that he planned to ask for a postponement of the case in order to file a demurrer.[64] Maggert showed up the next day with his attorney and was released on his own recognizance.[65] In the meantime, the Pacific Coast League held its winter meeting; it was a raucous affair, even by historical standards.

First, Jack Cook and Johnny Powers, long at odds over many issues, got into an early morning confrontation that ended in a fistfight. Afterward, Powers said he would never sit in a meeting with Cook again.

Then there was controversy over re-electing McCarthy, who wanted to stay on as head of the league but felt he could not continue at a salary of only five thousand dollars a year because the duties interfered with his law practice. Before the meeting, McCarthy learned that Bill Lane, Judge McCredie and Cal Ewing had agreed to vote against increasing his salary and that Seattle's directors were leaning toward joining them. McCarthy was also likely aware that Lane had approached *Los Angeles Times* sports reporter Harry Williams about taking McCarthy's job.

Getting the drop on Lane and his group, McCarthy addressed the meeting and declared he cared nothing about his salary. Although he was willing to continue battling, even if he was paid nothing, he said, "(I) could not retain my self-respect and continue as president with men working against me as they are now." Looking directly at Jack Cook, McCarthy went on to say, "This league needs a housecleaning among club owners as well as the ballplayers. Jack Cook is the bottom of most of the trouble."

McCarthy strode out of the room and the directors chased after, trying to persuade him to return. When he refused their entreaties, the directors reconvened the meeting and re-elected McCarthy for three years at double his previous salary. McCarthy responded that he would only serve as president until January.[66] He eventually cooled down and accepted his reappointment.[67]

On December 23, attorneys for Borton, Maggert, Rumler and Raymond filed a motion in court, arguing that even if true, the allegations against the defendants did not amount to criminal actions, but were instead a civil matter.[68] The judge agreed, ruling that he had no choice but to dismiss the charges because it was not a crime to throw a baseball game in the state of California. Borton and Maggert were in the courtroom when the decision was announced and were obviously pleased.[69]

William McCarthy said he had not been entirely surprised by the ruling but added, "Even if these players may not be punished criminally, Rumler and Maggert stand indicted and convicted in the eyes of the Coast League baseball public. If the law cannot punish them it remains for baseball to do its share, anyway, and at least to keep them from participating in professional ranks."[70]

Three weeks later, the National Association of Professional Baseball Leagues, representing all minor league organizations, expelled Borton, Maggert, Rumler and Gene Dale from Organized Baseball.[71] That action would serve as a precedent for the Black Sox conspirators later that year.

At the same time, a schism developed in the American League. Three franchises — the Yankees, Red Sox and White Sox — threatened to join the National League to form a new twelve-team circuit. There had been much dissatisfaction surrounding rulings made by the National Commission over the years, and the Black Sox scandal brought those feelings to a head. A number of owners supported the revival of an old proposal by Alfred Lasker, a minority owner of the Chicago Cubs, for an independent three-man committee that would rule the game. American League president Ban Johnson advocated reform but would not even talk about the Lasker Plan. Finally, in early November, the three American League teams followed through on their threat to secede. The new larger league also threatened to invade one of the territories of the five remaining American League clubs, most likely Detroit or Cleveland. The reluctant American League owners finally agreed to adopt the Lasker Plan and the rebel teams returned to the fold, keeping the league intact. Federal judge Kenesaw Mountain Landis was asked to chair the committee, largely because the baseball hierarchy had been pleased with his handling of the Federal League lawsuit. Landis eventually discarded the idea of a three-man committee and was named commissioner. Several months later he was exercising almost unlimited power.[72] In January 1921, the minor leagues voted to subject themselves to Landis' authority and he became the final arbiter for all of Organized Baseball. It was a decision that would carry serious repercussions, both good and bad, for the PCL and the rest of the minor leagues.[73]

The Black Sox case rolled on into 1921 to the embarrassment of everyone involved, but one of the indicted and suspended ballplayers involved in the spectacle did not seem to realize the seriousness of his crime. Former Angels infielder Fred McMullin returned to play winter ball in Southern California and as a result, professional players under contract who participated in games with him were fined. One of them was Irish Meusel, who played a game against a team representing Universal Film that included McMullin. The next day McMullin quit, apparently getting the message.[74]

* * *

Lost in the turmoil surrounding the gambling scandal was that Ed Maier could finally claim an undisputed Pacific Coast League pennant. Maier had returned to the PCL quite unexpectedly when Fatty Arbuckle, who was never that excited about being an owner, announced during the 1919 Little World Series against St. Paul that he could not raise the money to exercise his option.[75] With that, Ed Maier was back. He was the beneficiary of one of the great feats of managing in PCL history, as Bill Essick had brought the Tigers home in first place in the regular season for the third year in a row despite the upheaval surrounding Babe Borton. After losing Borton, one of the team's two .300 hitters, the Tigers rode their pitching to the front of the pack; Wheezer Dell and Willie Mitchell had combined for fifty-two wins and spitballer Frank Shellenback added eighteen.

Things were not going nearly so well in Portland. The McCredies, without their friendly connections to Cleveland, were foundering and finished last in 1920. They had continued developing top players since the team's last pennant in 1914; among them were pitcher Stan Coveleski, outfielders Billy Southworth and Ken Williams (major league baseball's first 30–30 man), and shortstop Charlie Hollocher, a player not well known today because of a career cut short by hypochondria but quite possibly the best infielder the McCredies ever produced.

Even in 1920, the Beavers roster included some talented individuals. Art Koehler would be one of the PCL's best catchers over the next decade. Del Baker became a prominent major league manager. Switch-hitting first baseman Lu Blue was an excellent fielder who would hit .308 as a rookie the next year for the Detroit Tigers.[76] Colorful slugger Biff Schaller was closing out his career but was still dangerous with a bat in his hands. Nineteen-year-old future Hall of Famer Heine Manush played a handful of games in midseason when outfielder Dick Cox briefly walked out on the team in a dispute with teammate George Maisel.[77]

However, in the two years since the re-establishment of the franchise, the team had continually worsened, resulting in a predictable toll on fan support. There was open grumbling that the McCredies should sell, but the Judge and his nephew insisted they could turn things around in 1921.

The other teams most touched by the scandal did not fare well either. Injuries took their toll in San Francisco, where Roy Corhan and Phil Koerner both hurt their arms. Koerner then quit in midseason over criticism from fans and the press that he was not hitting well enough.[78] Charlie Graham could do little more than watch as the Seals, unable to overcome the injuries to the two key infielders and the loss of Tom Seaton and Casey Smith, slid from first to fourth place.

In Salt Lake City the impact was even more pronounced. The Bees battled Vernon for the league lead through much of August before sliding to fifth. One bright spot was Earl Sheely, who tied Bunny Brief's PCL record of thirty-three home runs with a blast off Oakland's Carl Holling in the last game of the season.[79] Sheely also won the league batting title with a .371 average, one point higher than ex-teammate Harl Maggert, whose average was stricken from official league records because of his banishment.

In the offseason, Bill Lane decided to break up what was left of the Bees. He traded disgruntled Marty Krug to Portland for Paddy Siglin in a straight-up swap of second base-men.[80] Spider Baum retired and twenty-six-game winner Sailor Stroud left to pitch for Hanford in the independent San Joaquin Valley League.[81] Lane also made three separate deals that sent the rest of his infield, Earl Sheely, Ernie Johnson and Eddie Mulligan, to the Chicago White Sox, where, ironically, Charlie Comiskey was replenishing a team hit even harder by gambling scandals than Salt Lake City.[82]

* * *

The Los Angeles Angels were forced to scramble following the 1920 season after learning the city planned to extend Main Street, bisecting Washington Park. With few options and short notice, Johnny Powers decided to move the stadium a block east, to the site of the old Chutes Park menagerie.[83]

But the biggest change came in August 1921 when Johnny Powers sold the Angels for $150,000 to chewing gum millionaire William Wrigley, owner of Catalina Island and the Chicago Cubs, setting in motion a seismic shift in the league's power structure.[84] When William Wrigley purchased the Angels they sat in fourth place with a record of 80–64, seven and a half games behind the San Francisco Seals, who had led almost the entire season and seemed a shoo-in for their first pennant since 1917, vindicating Charlie Graham's harsh stance against gambling.

But Red Killefer's crew won twenty-eight of their last forty-four games, while the Seals went 15–23 down the stretch and saw their six-and-a-half-game lead at the end of August completely evaporate. The Angels passed San Francisco, as did Sacramento, with Los Angeles capturing one of the closest races in PCL history. Sam Crawford was again the Angels' best hitter, with a .318 average and 103 runs batted in. Doc Crandall and Vic Aldridge led a deep pitching staff; Crandall finished with a record of 24–13 while Aldridge was 20–10 with an earned run average of 2.16.

The Salt Lake City Bees struggled all year, finishing seventh in 1921 with a record of 73–110. Shortstop Heine Sand turned an unassisted triple play during the July 4 holiday doubleheader, and Bill Lane added some star power in June when he signed former Red Sox star outfielder Duffy Lewis, who had just been released by the Washington Senators.[85] Lewis hit safely in his first thirty-two games for the Bees and batted .403 in a little more than half a season, becoming one of nine .300 hitters on the team. But Salt Lake City could not find a winning combination as the pitching staff was constantly battered.[86]

Meanwhile, the McCredies failed to turn things around in Portland, fielding their worst team ever, with a record of 51–134. Walter McCredie accepted the criticism and rec-ognized that after seventeen years, fans wanted a change.[87]

There was something else that needed to change in the PCL; despite the scandals and the resulting wariness of players to seek trouble, William McCarthy was still fighting gam-blers. A raid in Sacramento during the summer revealed evidence of widespread organized gambling on PCL games.[88] In early September 1921, McCarthy banned seven men from Washington Park for gambling. Players were also being watched closely.[89]

But the biggest challenge for William McCarthy would come from within his own ranks. The power center of the league had always been in the San Francisco Bay Area. But William Wrigley's entry into the league and McCarthy's alienation of Bill Lane over his sus-pension of Bill Rumler was about to change all that. William McCarthy was in for a winner-take-all battle to retain his power.

CHAPTER EIGHT

1922 to 1924: The Battle of Avalon

In the wake of Portland's ghastly 1921 campaign, Judge McCredie was ready to bid farewell to the PCL. Beavers fans were equally ready to see him go. The opportunity to fulfill that mutual desire materialized when Bill Klepper was forced out as Seattle Indians president by restaurateur James Boldt, the team's new majority stockholder. Klepper promptly sold his holdings in Seattle and purchased the Portland Beavers.[1]

Once in Portland, the bald, pudgy, bespectacled Klepper cast aside the Judge's nephew, long-time Beavers manager Walter McCredie, in favor of Tom Turner, a white-haired, baby-faced, thirty-four-year-old protégé of Connie Mack who McCredie dismissively called "a schoolboy."[2] McCredie's opinion aside, Klepper considered Turner's connection to the Philadelphia Athletics vital to his effort to turn around the franchise. However, Klepper's intention was to post the loquacious and micro-managing Turner in the Portland front office rather than in the dugout. That suited Turner, who considered himself executive material and harbored no ambitions to be a field manager.

It turned out that Klepper wanted Duke Kenworthy, the player/manager he had left behind in Seattle, to act in the same role for the Beavers. James Boldt, who in turn wanted Walter McCredie, did not know that Kenworthy had a secret side agreement that made him a free agent if he could not come to terms with Seattle, a fact that first surfaced after Boldt announced he was hiring McCredie.[3] Kenworthy immediately demanded that the National Board of Arbitration rule he was a free agent. Since the side deal he had negotiated with Klepper was illegal, the request was denied.[4]

Neither Walter McCredie nor James Boldt relished the idea of McCredie's predecessor sitting unhappily in the Seattle dugout all season, and McCredie proposed a swap of second basemen to resolve the stalemate. Kenworthy, who had been Seattle's best offensive player in 1921, was sent to Portland in exchange for Marty Krug. Tom Turner's title was changed to assistant manager, and everyone seemed happy.

Everyone that is, except Kenesaw Mountain Landis, who temporarily suspended Kenworthy pending a review of the matter.[5] The situation was a hot topic of conversation among league officials. While attending a game in late April, Jack Cook told Ed Maier that he could not understand what the fuss was about. "Tampering with players is nothing new; it always has been done," said Cook. Maier laughed and, probably reflecting on his own past history with side agreements, replied, "Yes, but they didn't put it in writing."[6]

In May, Landis ruled that Kenworthy was suspended until August 1, at which point he would be taken away from Portland and become property of the Pacific Coast League. Kenworthy would then be sold to a team in another league and the proceeds of the sale would go to the PCL. The commissioner also barred Bill Klepper from involvement with the Beavers for three years and vice president James Brewster for two.[7] Klepper appealed his suspension but Landis refused to reconsider, declaring he had the authority to deem the Kenworthy incident detrimental to baseball.[8]

Tom Turner reluctantly took over as field manager and the results were disastrous, including a sixteen-game losing streak in July. After the sixteenth loss, Turner walked into the clubhouse and exclaimed, "Well, boys, we can't win them all!" They were victorious the next day, 7–1, with Rube Walberg pitching a four-hitter against Salt Lake City and ending Paul Strand's thirty-three-game hitting streak in the process.[9]

Meanwhile, Bill Klepper continued to press Landis on the legal front until the commissioner finally recognized he had indeed overstepped his authority. Klepper won a concession from Landis that barred him from "baseball matters," but allowed him to handle purely "administrative" duties.[10] Klepper could run the team in every way except for signing off on trades and representing the team at league meetings. He remained in charge of the Portland Beavers and was one of the few baseball men to ever get the best of Kenesaw Mountain Landis.[11]

* * *

Feeling somewhat out of place in a Seattle uniform, Walter McCredie welcomed his new team to its 1922 training camp in Stockton, California. McCredie was happy to see one familiar face — Vean Gregg, star pitcher of his 1910 Portland PCL champions. Gregg was making a comeback attempt after retiring in 1918 because of persistent arm problems. After leaving baseball Gregg had purchased a four-hundred-eighty-acre ranch in Canada, but that enterprise was not nearly as lucrative as he hoped, and the thirty-seven-year-old pitcher returned to the game after being away for three seasons.[12] Gregg could still make the bottom drop out of his magnificent curveball, although he used it less often, choosing to mix in submarine and crossfire deliveries to keep hitters off balance.

While Seattle and Portland seemed to be starting over, Vernon Tigers owner Ed Maier brought back a couple of familiar, wizened faces to the Pacific Coast League in his effort to regain the title. Outfielder Ping Bodie and pitcher Big Bill James joined thirty-eight-year-old infielder Rollie Zeider and thirty-seven-year-old center fielder Chet Chadbourne on the Tigers roster. But the 1922 Pacific Coast League season was less about homecoming than it was about injuries, and the Tigers had more than their share, especially among those on the pitching staff.

Frank Shellenback had been counted on as one of the team's aces but pitched only nine innings before undergoing surgery for bone chips in his elbow. Slim Love likewise had arm problems. Left-hander Jakie May cut a finger on his pitching hand and missed three weeks, finally returning to action three days after teammate Roy Gilder broke his hand while attempting to snare a line drive. The Vernon mound staff was so thin that Byron Houck was asked to temporarily put aside his cinematography career for Buster Keaton and return to the mound. Manager Bill Essick also resorted to using outfielder Pete Schneider, whose career as a pitcher in the major leagues had ended prematurely because of arm and shoulder problems.[13]

Oakland had injury problems, as well. The Oaks had three good pitchers in Buzz Arlett, Harry Krause and Ray Kremer, but there was a severe drop in quality after that. Cal Ewing traded promising infielder Babe Pinelli to Cincinnati for Hod Eller, ace of the 1919 Reds, whose effectiveness had waned because his shine ball was no longer legal. Eller suffered a broken finger in May, missed five weeks, and was ineffective following his recovery. In August, he was sold to Mobile in the Southern Association.[14]

The Oaks suffered further misfortune. Third baseman Bill Marriott broke his leg in a game against Seattle in April and was sidelined for six weeks.[15] Second baseman Jack Knight hurt his left hand so badly in an 11–0 loss to the Seals on April 14 that he had to have part of the ring finger amputated.[16] During the summer, catcher Honus Mitze fractured his finger and outfielder Claude Cooper broke his hand.[17]

The relationship between the Oaks and the Seals was similarly fractured. Before the season started, Charlie Graham and his partners increased the rent for Recreation Park. Cal Ewing reacted by announcing that for the first time, Oakland would play all of its home games in the East Bay—for the second time abandoning the stadium he had built in 1907. The Seals retaliated by renting Recreation Park to a semi-pro league when the Oaks were home, putting a dent in Oakland's attendance. Ewing complained to William McCarthy that the Seals were violating Oakland's territorial rights, but McCarthy ignored Ewing. The Oaks owner finally appealed to Commissioner Landis, who ruled in Ewing's favor.[18]

Misfortune visited other teams in 1922. Los Angeles star Sam Crawford retired rather than accept a cut in pay that made him suspicious that the Angels also planned to slash his playing time.[19] The Angels also bid a temporary goodbye to outfielder Jigger Statz, who was sent to the Chicago Cubs along with pitcher Vic Aldridge for several players, including outfielder Babe Twombly and pitcher Elmer Ponder.[20] Ponder was brilliant early in the year, winning his first nine decisions before the Seals defeated him on June 8.[21] Two weeks later, the pitcher's season ended when he dislocated his shoulder while trying to catch a fly ball during batting practice.[22]

Sacramento celebrated the opening of Moreing Field, the Senators' beautiful new $100,000 baseball stadium that seated ten thousand and featured a league first—a woman's restroom. But they lost outfielder Merlin Kopp for two and a half months when he fractured his tibia on a slide into home plate during a Sunday home game in Stockton.[23] Three weeks later, player-manager Charlie Pick badly broke his ankle while sliding into second base and was lost for most of the season.[24] Sacramento finished in last place.

However, even if everyone in the PCL had remained healthy, only Vernon had the talent to challenge San Francisco in 1922. After the Seals faded down the stretch in 1921, Charlie Graham retired from managing and turned his energies to the front office. He hired the outgoing and popular Jack "Dots" Miller to succeed him and did not leave the former Pittsburgh infielder high and dry as far as talent was concerned. The Seals, already flush with cash after the sale of outfielder Jimmy O'Connell to the New York Giants for seventy-five thousand dollars, also got to keep O'Connell for a year.[25]

Graham and his partners, George Putnam and Doc Strub, were further enriched in late May when they dealt star third baseman Willie Kamm to the Chicago White Sox in return for one hundred thousand dollars and three pitchers: Clarence "Shovel" Hodge, Harry Courtney and Doug McWeeny. Kamm, born on Post Street in San Francisco, was a product of the sandlots of Golden Gate Park. As with O'Connell, the Seals were able to keep Kamm until the end of the year while also having use of the three new pitchers.[26]

Hodge had been a spot starter for Chicago the previous two seasons while Courtney, who at one time was thought to be finished as a player after taking a bullet through his stomach while seeing action in World War I, had been recently acquired by the White Sox from the Washington Senators. McWeeny was a twenty-three-year-old who had earned his spikes in the fast Chicago amateur leagues.[27]

Not only did the Seals boast a deep and veteran pitching staff of major league caliber, they also featured the league's best offense with a team batting average greater than even

Salt Lake City, despite the Bees boasting the PCL's top two hitters in Paul Strand and Duffy Lewis. The San Francisco lineup featured five regulars hitting better than .330, led by Kamm, who batted .342 with 124 runs batted in.

Despite their injuries, the Vernon Tigers made a serious run at the Seals in what quickly settled into a two-team pennant race, the teams separating themselves from the rest of the league thanks to pitching. Tigers left-hander Jakie May had one of the great seasons in PCL history, even while missing those three weeks after cutting his finger. The hard-throwing southpaw, who liked to mix in submarine deliveries among his conventional pitches, won thirty-five games and also led the league in strikeouts and earned run average. Jess Doyle, Big Bill James and Wheezer Dell all won twenty games for the Tigers.

San Francisco was led by Jim "Death Valley" Scott, an ex–White Sox star who won twenty-five games. Oliver Mitchell added twenty-four victories and Speed Geary twenty. Doug McWeeny, despite his late arrival as part of the Willie Kamm deal, won fifteen games to round out one of the best pitching staffs in minor league history.

With three weeks remaining in the 1922 season, San Francisco and Vernon were tied for first place with identical records of 115–64. The teams remained virtually deadlocked over the next two weeks until Vernon was swept by Oakland in a doubleheader and fell two games behind, setting the stage for the season's final week that featured San Francisco playing Oakland and the Tigers against Los Angeles.

On Tuesday it seemed momentum might be moving in the Tigers' direction, thanks to a two-run ninth-inning rally against the Angels' Tom Hughes. At the same time, Oakland's Harry Krause was shutting out on the Seals, 1–0, with San Francisco losing when Doug McWeeny issued a bases-loaded walk in the ninth inning.[28] But the next day the Tigers lost to the Angels in fourteen innings while the Seals defeated Oakland.

Two days later, the Seals clinched their first pennant since 1917. Seals players split a $6,000 share for finishing first while the second-place Tigers divided $4,000.[29]

* * *

After all the controversy, suspensions and hard feelings surrounding the switching of managers between Portland and Seattle in 1922, it turned out that neither Duke Kenworthy nor Walter McCredie was in the PCL at the end of the season. Kenworthy had been suspended and then sold by the league to Columbus of the American Association. Tom Turner was forced to take over the Beavers' managerial duties for a time, during which he suffered through a sixteen-game losing streak. Meanwhile, in late June, James Boldt fired McCredie and replaced him with catcher Jack Adams.[30]

The fight between the Portland and Seattle franchises, beyond its obvious pettiness — the teams even stole each other's trainers at one point — changed the balance of power in the Pacific Coast League and impacted William McCarthy's ability to lead it. Frustrated by Commissioner Landis' lack of success in punishing Bill Klepper, McCarthy tried to convince league directors to kick the Portland owner out of the league anyway. The effort proved unsuccessful largely because of Cal Ewing, who declared he would not support it out of principle. While not condoning Klepper's actions in the Kenworthy matter, Ewing insisted he could not vote to take a man's property because he violated a rule. Bill Lane and William Wrigley agreed with Ewing, creating a deadlock of four votes on each side of the issue. Klepper survived once again, and Ewing emerged with renewed power.[31] In addition, McCarthy's political maneuvering made Klepper all the more suspicious that the league president had been the original source of his battle with Commissioner Landis. As a result, Klepper joined Ewing, Lane and Wrigley as a permanent voting bloc aligned against

McCarthy, who was viewed by the group as increasingly arrogant and overstepping his authority.

McCarthy realized that many votes on important league matters would be deadlocked. As a result, he unilaterally assumed the right to cast the deciding ballot in all such future instances, fomenting further discord among the owners allied against him.[32] Heading into the final year of his contract, William McCarthy had made three steadfast enemies: Bill Lane because of the Rumler episode in 1920; Cal Ewing because of disagreements over the draft and McCarthy's indifference during the Recreation Park dust-up; and Bill Klepper over the league president trying to take away his franchise.

Although William Wrigley had not previously carried a grudge against McCarthy, the PCL president gave the Angels owner reason to at the January 1923 league meeting by casting the tie-breaking vote to eliminate Wrigley's exclusive territorial rights to Los Angeles. McCarthy's maneuver especially angered Wrigley since Ed Maier's Tigers had not played in Vernon in several years, instead playing all their home games at Washington Park.[33] Not long after, Wrigley began plotting McCarthy's downfall, a plan that gained momentum thanks to James Boldt's decision to sell the Seattle Indians after losing twenty-five thousand dollars in his only season as team owner.

The Indians were purchased by Los Angeles manager Red Killefer and Angels business manager Charley Lockard, fulfilling a long-time desire of both men; Killefer announced he was going to sell his orange and walnut ranch to finance the deal.[34] William McCarthy instantly understood the significance of two close Wrigley associates taking over in Seattle; the tie vote among league directors was broken and Wrigley's faction had a 5–3 advantage in all league matters.

Ed Maier was suspicious. Convinced that Wrigley was behind the purchase, Maier suggested to McCarthy that Wrigley was making a power play. McCarthy agreed that it all seemed a little too convenient. He fired off a letter to Wrigley, demanding to know whether the Angels owner had "directly or indirectly aided or assisted or extended credit to Charles L. Lockard or Wade Killefer or any other person to purchase stock in the Seattle Baseball Club."[35] McCarthy did not receive a satisfactory reply.

As a result, McCarthy refused to recognize Lockard as a voting member at the May 1923 league meeting, thus denying Wrigley's block its tie-breaking vote. Lockard filed suit in federal court to force McCarthy to honor his right to cast ballots on behalf of the Seattle franchise. McCarthy countered with a petition to have the suit thrown out of court on the grounds that the Indians were a "syndicate club." McCarthy further argued, "Because of the alleged action of Wrigley, the Seattle club has forfeited its membership in the league and is not entitled to any representation on the board of directors."[36]

The month of June featured a flurry of depositions, with Killefer and Lockard insisting that William Wrigley had no financial interest in the Seattle franchise.[37] Wrigley pointed out that he was not even a majority stockholder in the Angels, only owning about a one-fourth share of the team. Joe Patrick subsequently assumed control of the team after buying three thousand shares from Chicago Cubs president William Veeck.[38]

But Wrigley *had* underwritten the original loan to Killefer and Lockard to satisfy Jim Boldt's requirement of immediate cash payment. The Angels owner signed a note for $125,000 on March 16 with the understanding it would be replaced within thirty days. On April 11, a new note, endorsed by Red Killefer's uncle and W.D. Hubbard, a friend of Lockard, replaced the one backed by Wrigley.[39] Killefer and Lockard retired much of the debt by selling property to William Banning, director of the Catalina Island Company, an

The richest and most influential owner in the Pacific Coast League, William Wrigley was soon at odds with league president William McCarthy and began plotting his downfall (Chicago Daily News Collection, Chicago History Museum).

entity owned almost entirely by William Wrigley.[40] United States District Judge John S. Partridge took the various filings under advisement on June 26 and the next day announced he was ruling in McCarthy's favor.[41]

Meanwhile, there was baseball to be played. Seattle struggled, and with the team in sixth place, Killefer and Lockard decided to shake things up by letting four players go and having Killefer take over as manager from Harry Wolverton, who the obviously impatient James Boldt had hired as his third manager in only a year.[42]

* * *

Concerned about the April weather in Salt Lake City, Bill Lane received permission to play the Bees' opening series of 1923 in Fresno, leading to speculation that Lane was contemplating a permanent move to California — a development that would have pleased the other PCL owners who constantly complained about the long trek to Utah.[43] The novelty of having a Pacific Coast League team had worn off in Salt Lake City and the days of the franchise being the league's savior were long past. (Years later, *Los Angeles Times* reporter Bob Ray remembered that local boys had taken to selling rocks at the ballpark for use against umpires that had fallen into disfavor among the locals.)[44] There were constant rumors of various California cities acquiring the team; Fresno officials hoped the Bees' agreement to play an exhibition series against the Chicago Cubs and open the season there would lead to that city's return to the league.[45]

Lane shot down any such speculation, defiantly proclaiming, "We will be playing ball up there [in Salt Lake City] as a member of the Coast League long after those who are yelling the loudest will have passed out [of the league]."[46]

Another team rumored to have a shaky future, the Vernon Tigers, appeared to be a contender once again. Having fallen just shy of beating the Seals in 1922, Maier was certain the Tigers were ready for a return to the top. San Francisco had lost stars O'Connell and Kamm while Maier chose to keep thirty-five-game winner Jakie May rather than sell him for fifty thousand dollars to the New York Yankees. Maier felt May's value to the team was greater than what the Yankees had offered.[47] In addition, the Tigers were counting on the return of Frank Shellenback from his elbow injury.

But Jakie May was nowhere near the pitcher he had been in 1922, and Frank Shellenback had an uneven year in his comeback from surgery. Long-time ace Wheezer Dell was also less effective than in the past and at age thirty-seven openly spoke of retiring to become an actor in motion pictures.[48] Instead, he was sold to Seattle in mid–July.[49] The Tigers also lost Ray French and Jess Doyle when Commissioner Landis ruled they had been illegally farmed out to Vernon by the New York Yankees.[50] One bright spot was outfielder Pete Schneider, who had arguably the greatest offensive day in baseball history on May 11 against Salt Lake City when he slugged an incredible five home runs and a double in one game.[51] The Tigers, however, dropped to last place in 1923.

San Francisco had obstacles to overcome as well, including the serious illness of manager Dots Miller, who was diagnosed with tuberculosis. He left the team at the end of July for a sanitarium in Saranac Lake, New York, where it was hoped treatment would prove as successful for him as it had been for the great Christy Mathewson.[52] It was not and Miller died six weeks later with his wife, mother and brother at his bedside.[53] He was buried in New Jersey and both John McGraw and Miller Huggins attended the funeral.[54]

First baseman Bert Ellison took over as manager. In late September, the Seals began a crucial road series against second-place Sacramento, which had just swept a seven-game series from Vernon. The Seals were struggling with injuries — middle infielders Pete Kilduff and Hal Rhyne were both out of action and third baseman Eddie Mulligan was hobbled by a charley horse. Ellison told his players, "Fellows, we're badly crippled. The pennant is at stake and then some. Remember our late manager, Jack Miller. Jack's biggest wish was to win another pennant. Every one of you fellows loved him. Now I'm going to ask you to give everything this week, but do it for Jack Miller."[55]

A wild series ensued, punctuated by a riot initiated by Sacramento fans over incompetent umpiring by the notorious and egotistical William "Lord" Byron, a long-time nemesis of the Senators.[56] The Seals had a great week, winning six of the seven games, and used the series as a springboard to easily repeat as league champions.

Once again, the Seals possessed a talented roster that was the envy of any minor league team in the country. Five pitchers worked at least two hundred fifty innings; the three obtained from the White Sox the previous year in exchange for Willie Kamm — McWeeny, Courtney and Hodge — combined for fifty-seven wins while former New York Giants right-hander Red Shea won twenty-one. Eddie Mulligan hit .329 as Kamm's replacement, and every starter except shortstop Hal Rhyne (.296) batted higher than .300. The bench was productive as well, led by a young Oklahoman named Paul Waner, who had been converted from pitcher to outfielder and hit .369.

Another successful Pacific Coast League season was over, as was William McCarthy's contract as league president. McCarthy knew it was unlikely the owners would chase him down the hall and beg him to stay as they had three years earlier. He was about to face the biggest challenge yet to his authority. The fight ahead would be dramatic — an episode remembered for years after as "the Battle of Avalon."

* * *

William Wrigley spent a little over three million dollars in 1919 to buy Catalina, an island resort located roughly twenty miles off the coast of Southern California.[57] Four years after Wrigley's purchase, the island was the location of an epic showdown between warring factions of Pacific Coast League owners.

The league's annual meeting was set for Monday, November 12, 1923, on the island, in the small community of Avalon. William McCarthy and William Wrigley had been fighting all year, with McCarthy threatening to take Wrigley before the National Board of Arbitration in the belief that the Angels owner secretly owned the Seattle franchise.[58] Although McCarthy was far from being an astute politician — his relationships, or lack thereof, with Bill Lane, Cal Ewing and Bill Klepper were proof of that — he understood the league's balance of power would be decided in Avalon.

Besides selecting a president, the meeting's other major issue revolved around the draft. Wrigley and his group of five, which included Ewing, Lane, Lockard and Klepper, favored a modified draft and peace with the major leagues. McCarthy, Ed Maier, Charlie Graham and Sacramento owner Lew Moreing were opposed to a draft in any form.

But the draft was not of paramount importance to William Wrigley. He was focused on the coup attempt he was leading. *Los Angeles Times* sportswriter Harry Williams was enlisted to take over as league president, with an offer of a five-year contract at $10,000 per year if the plot was successful and an immediate payment of $7,500 should the plan fail.[59] Months in the making, the scheme resulted in a meeting the *Times* said lacked only a chorus to resemble a Gilbert and Sullivan operetta.[60]

When McCarthy gaveled the league meeting to order on Monday morning, he and Williams quickly received nominations for the league presidency. It was clear Williams had the necessary support to win election but McCarthy refused to recognize Seattle's vote, leaving the balloting in favor of Williams, 4–3, one short of the necessary majority. McCarthy asked whether the owners wanted to ballot again.

Salt Lake City owner Bill Lane jumped to his feet and bellowed, "We recognize the right of Seattle to vote and Harry Williams is elected by a vote of five to three. Mr. Williams, where is he?"[61] Williams, who had remained out of sight at the beginning of the meeting, shouldered his way through the crowd as both McCarthy and Seals owner Charlie Graham called him an interloper and shouted for him to get out. Williams replied that McCarthy was the interloper and began a roll call.

McCarthy shouted at Williams, "You can't do that!" Williams replied, "But I am doing it!" He ruled McCarthy out of order and continued the meeting.

McCarthy attempted to drown out Williams and carry on. The audience watched in stunned silence while the two sides held simultaneous meetings in the same room. Finally, McCarthy's group, realizing they had only three votes and could not conduct any business, fell mute. Williams' faction voted to move the league offices to Los Angeles and hold the next meeting in Oakland. At that gathering, to be held in January, William Wrigley would have his exclusive territorial rights to Los Angeles returned, an obvious slap at McCarthy ally Ed Maier.[62]

McCarthy's group decided to continue the fight, making for competing league offices in San Francisco and Los Angeles as the dispute continued, neither side recognizing the authority of the other. The matter was finally submitted to the National Board of Arbitration, which in December ruled in Williams' favor.[63] The power shift was complete and the league's center of authority rested for the first time in Los Angeles instead of San Francisco.

The morning after the board's decision, National League president John Heydler and Association president Mike Sexton congratulated the forty-four-year-old Williams. At the same time, they warned him that his strongest backers would quite likely become serious adversaries someday. Williams would discover the warning most prophetic.[64]

* * *

Harry Williams was an interesting choice to lead the league at a fractious time. An engaging person who loved storytelling, Williams was born into an Iowa Quaker family. His father published a newspaper in Des Moines and young Harry lived a Norman Rockwell stereotype, watching Western League baseball games through a knothole in the outfield fence. He never forgot the day Cap Anson brought his famous Chicago Colts to his elementary school.

Seven years old when his family moved to Whittier, California, Williams dropped out of school in the eighth grade to work as a printer's devil — basically a go-fer. He eventually started writing for a small newspaper and from there was recruited by the *Los Angeles Express* to cover a variety of beats, from the produce market to the court system. Williams quickly learned how to organize information he gathered, or as he put it, "sifting out of nonessentials [and identifying] the shortest distance between two points."

Through that experience, Williams learned the importance of weighing facts accurately and dealing with individuals impartially and fairly, attributes he deemed indispensable to his profession.[65] Accepting a job as a sportswriter for the *Los Angeles Times*, Williams was soon assigned as official scorer at Washington Park and reported on baseball, boxing, racing and other sports until the fall of 1917, when *Times* managing editor Harry Andrews offered him the chance to go to Europe as a war correspondent.

In 1920, Williams accepted an offer from the *New York Globe* to cover the New York Giants but decided at the end of the year he wanted to come home, passing on the opportunity to cover the World Series between Brooklyn and Cleveland.[66] Returning to his old job at the *Los Angeles Times*, Williams remained there until his election as president of the Pacific Coast League. He accurately forecast the future of baseball on the Coast, declaring it inevitable that Los Angeles would grow to a population of three to four million and that San Francisco would join the City of Angels in the major leagues in about twenty-five years. (It actually turned out to be thirty-five.) He also predicted that teams would travel exclusively by airplane, something that

Harry Williams succeeded William McCarthy as league president after "the Battle of Avalon" in November 1923. He was warned that his strongest allies would someday become his biggest enemies — a warning that proved most prophetic (Ray Saraceni Collection).

would happen in the Pacific Coast League long before it became the standard practice in the major leagues.[67]

One of the first changes under the Williams regime was the acceptance by the Pacific Coast League of the "modified" draft. After several years of the no-draft rule, during which major league teams retaliated by curtailing the practice of optioning players to the PCL, it was agreed that players acquired from the National and American leagues would be subject to the draft each winter at a set price of five thousand dollars. However, any player without major league experience, or a veteran who was not on a major league reserve list, would not be subject to selection.[68]

The theory was that the high prices for the Kamms and O'Connells would continue. At the same time, major league teams could send young players for more seasoning without having to pay a king's ransom to retrieve them. It was a change the Wrigley block wanted and Williams delivered. The quality of talent in the Pacific Coast League would never be better and professional baseball on the West Coast would reach new heights in popularity. In 1924, the eight PCL teams would draw a combined two million fans for the first time.

Williams' congenial personality and foresight would come in handy over the rest of the decade. He would shepherd the league through one of its most prosperous eras, while at the same time learning there was no way he could keep everybody happy. Especially, it seemed, those he had counted on as allies.

* * *

In late September, Pacific Coast League baseball fans were shocked to read the news of the sudden death of forty-eight-year-old Los Angeles baseball icon Frank Chance. Following an unsuccessful stint as manager of the Boston Red Sox in 1923 — Chance's first such duty since leaving the Angels during the 1917 season — Charles Comiskey had hired "the Peerless Leader" to return to Chicago as manager of the White Sox in 1924. Ill health kept Chance from assuming the position, but Comiskey thought so much of the legendary Cubs star that he held the job open, insisting on doing so even after Chance tried to resign before the season started.[69]

A tragic event of another kind unfolded a few weeks later that impacted another former PCL star. Jimmy O'Connell, the great talent George Putnam had discovered as a seventeen-year-old and sold to John McGraw and the New York Giants for seventy-five-thousand dollars, was accused of bribing another player to throw a game.

O'Connell was in his second year as a reserve outfielder for the Giants and New York was close to winning the 1924 National League pennant; a victory over the Philadelphia Phillies on September 27 would clinch it. Before the game, O'Connell approached Phillies shortstop Heine Sand, an acquaintance from the Pacific Coast League, and offered him a five-hundred-dollar bribe. Sand refused and reported the incident. Commissioner Landis immediately suspended O'Connell, who confessed, and Giants coach Cozy Dolan, who O'Connell claimed had put him up to it.[70] Dolan denied the accusation, but Commissioner Landis claimed that during questioning, Dolan repeatedly demonstrated an inability to remember even simple details.[71] O'Connell implicated others, including Giants star Frankie Frisch, but only O'Connell and Dolan were punished by Landis.

When O'Connell met with John McGraw after the news broke, the Giants manager asked, "Well, what have you to say, Jimmy?"

"I don't know what to say," replied O'Connell.

"How did you ever get yourself into a thing like this?" said McGraw. "I don't know," said O'Connell, who started sobbing. "I can't go home, I can't go home."[72]

George Putnam suggested that the World Series shares due O'Connell and Dolan be given to Sand for reporting the bribery offer.[73] O'Connell and Earl McNeely, a Sacramento native playing for the Washington Senators, were to be honored by the Sacramento Chamber of Commerce, which was recognizing them as local players appearing in the World Series. The honor was reserved for McNeely alone.[74]

O'Connell and Dolan were handed lifetime bans by Commissioner Landis. The next spring, O'Connell was in San Francisco and appeared at Recreation Park, asking permission to put on a uniform and work out. George Putnam turned away the former Bay Area hero, explaining that he "did not think it would look right."[75] It was quite a turn of events for a player who only two years before had been the toast of San Francisco. Now, he was no longer welcome in his old ballpark.

* * *

Harry Williams faced a number of challenges as the new league president, and O'Connell's misstep provided evidence to those looking for it that gambling remained a problem in the PCL. The league was seen by critics as nothing less than baseball's den of iniquity. It had not been forgotten that a number of West Coast players had been connected to the Black Sox scandal. These same critics pointed to O'Connell as proof that the problem had not been properly addressed. Although Williams vehemently disagreed with that characterization, he knew there remained too many unsavory characters hanging around the league's ballparks.

Recognizing that he had to crack down, Williams arranged for Los Angeles vice squad officers to monitor the crowd at a game between Vernon and Portland at Washington Park. Several men were seen placing bets with such well-known gambling figures as Nick "the Greek" Dandolos and Walter Boyle. It was because of Dandolos, a Chicago bookmaker who later became a charter inductee into the Poker Hall of Fame, that PCL teams had been banned from using Jack Dempsey's hotel in Los Angeles.[76]

Dandolos admitted to Williams that he had placed bets but denied approaching players. Williams wanted no part of the explanation and barred Dandolos from all league parks, saying, "This is just a starter of the war we intend to make on gamblers and we will ask major league clubs to work with us in our fight to keep baseball clean."[77]

Fighting was another problem that did not seem to be going away. Early in the season, Williams suspended three players: Duke Kenworthy of Portland (who had returned to the league following the expiration of Landis's order against him) and Eddie Mulligan and Dee Walsh of San Francisco. Kenworthy became angry when he thought Mulligan tried to spike him and he swung at the Seals infielder, who responded by knocking Kenworthy out cold. Walsh joined in the fight and earned a two-day suspension while the instigators each received a day off without pay.[78]

A week later, with Williams in attendance, umpire Bill Guthrie ejected eleven Los Angeles Angels from a game against Oakland. The trouble started when Babe Twombly of the Angels objected to a called third strike. Los Angeles manager Marty Krug, who was on the coaching lines that day, harassed Guthrie until he was kicked out of the game. The entire Angels bench began riding the umpire, who responded by walking to the dugout, shedding his mask, and ordering the bench emptied. Guthrie remained rooted in place, mask in hand, until every last Angel not in the game had exited to the clubhouse.[79]

Just as all those who came before him, Harry Williams faced an uphill fight to change the Pacific Coast League's rough and rowdy image.

* * *

The fans may not have been coming out at Salt Lake City as they used to, but it was not because the Bees were boring. Bill Lane's team boasted one of the greatest offensive lineups in baseball history, even without Paul Strand, who had been traded to the Philadelphia Athletics after winning consecutive Pacific Coast League Triple Crowns.[80] To replace Strand in the batting order, Lane acquired Boston Red Sox pitcher Lefty O'Doul, who manager Duffy Lewis was determined to finally move full-time to the outfield in spite of the ballplayer's wariness of the idea.[81] Tracked down on a golf course, O'Doul said he wanted to keep pitching despite a sore arm and "the opinion of some of his well-wishers that he would make an excellent outfielder."[82]

The Bees hitters got off to a roaring start in 1924. At the end of May, Duffy Lewis had already hit seventeen home runs and the Bees boasted four of the league's top five home run hitters.[83] Although pleased with his team's potent offense, Bill Lane was concerned about the home run barrage at his ballpark, which he felt was having a negative impact on attendance. He proposed that all balls hit over the fence be ground-rule doubles, but Harry Williams quickly nixed the idea.[84] Lane erected a twenty-foot-tall screen on top of the outfield fence; it made no difference. On May 24, the Seals defeated Salt Lake City, 30–14, with San Francisco collecting thirty-seven hits. Seals player-manager Bert Ellison swatted three home runs as he and Paul Waner each had six hits. Joe Kelly, Pete Kilduff and Sam Agnew collected five hits apiece, with Agnew clubbing three doubles and two triples.[85] Ellison had twenty-five hits in thirty-seven at-bats during the series, setting a league record with eight home runs over three games and ten that week.

It soon became public that Lewis was having trouble with his players — one of them gave him a black eye — and there were rumors all summer that Lane would either move the Bees to Vancouver, British Columbia, or purchase the Vernon Tigers from Ed Maier and sell the Bees to local investors.[86] Ultimately, he did neither.

Salt Lake City may have struggled, but the 1924 pennant race was one of the closest in Pacific Coast League history. The Los Angeles Angels were in last place on August 29 but roared back into contention, winning forty of fifty-three games to move within a half-game of first-place Seattle with a week left in the season. San Francisco, which had led much of the year in its quest for a third straight championship, was also a half-game back but percentage points behind Los Angeles. Oakland sat in fourth place, only three games off the pace.[87]

Inspired by his team's rush to the front of the pack, Angels president Joe Patrick offered his players five thousand dollars to split if they won the pennant.[88] Clinging to its slim lead, Seattle was in Portland to play the bottom-feeding Beavers, but with heavy rains forecast, plans were made with the consent of the other teams in the league to move the series to Seattle. (Rainouts in the final series between teams were not made up, resulting in the possibility of weather ultimately determining the pennant.) The skies cleared and the teams played in Portland anyway.

While the Indians were trying to clinch in Portland, Seattle baseball fans were distracted by the appearance of the great Babe Ruth, who arrived in town to play with a team of semi-pros in an exhibition against an all-star team from the Southwest Timber League. Ruth visited the children's orthopedic hospital and invited every boy in Seattle to attend the game for free. During warm-ups, Ruth swatted autographed baseballs into the bleachers. The exhibition drew nine thousand fans, who gasped in amazement as Ruth hit three home runs. That night, Ruth visited sportswriter Royal Brougham at the *Seattle Post-Intelligencer*. Seeing a crowd gathering below, he and Brougham tossed baseballs out of the office window to the people standing on the street.[89]

Los Angeles extended the pennant race to the final day by taking a doubleheader from Vernon on October 18 in front of ten thousand fans at Washington Park, with the second game featuring an Angels rally from a four-run deficit to save them from the brink of elimination.[90] At the same time, Seattle won its tenth game in a row, defeating Portland in Vaughn Street Park, which was nearly empty because of a 10:30 A.M. start time so the University of Southern California–Oregon Aggie football game could be played at the stadium later in the day.[91]

Seattle finally clinched on the season's final day with a 12–4 win over Portland, thanks to a three-run second inning and a four-run fourth.[92] Having finally received official recognition as heads of the franchise, Seattle's first league title was a satisfying closure to the season for Charley Lockard and Red Killefer. The pennant was also satisfying for the ace pitcher of the Indians, thirty-nine-year-old Vean Gregg, completing his third season of one of the more unlikely comebacks in baseball history. Gregg utilized his still-outstanding curveball to win twenty-five games for Seattle in 1924—including twelve victories in a row at one point—against only eleven losses. He pitched 326 innings, striking out 175 batters and walking only 75, and his 2.90 earned run average was more than a run and a half better per game than any of his teammates who pitched at least two hundred innings. It was a performance that earned Gregg a spot with the Washington Senators in 1925.[93]

The Indians rotation also included thirty-four-year-old Jim Bagby, a former thirty-one game winner for the Cleveland Indians and the first pitcher to hit a home run in the World Series, against Brooklyn in 1920. Other veterans included thirty-year-old Suds Sutherland and thirty-eight-year-old Wheezer Dell. The only young pitcher on the staff was twenty-five-year-old ex–Chicago Cub George Stueland, whose eighteen wins despite missing some time with blood poisoning ranked second on the staff to Gregg.

Third baseman Henry Baldwin drove in 140 runs and outfielder Bill Lane won his fourth PCL stolen base title despite missing much of August and September with a fractured skull after Vernon's Fred Groat hit him in the head with a pitch.[94] The Indians also boasted the lefty-righty slugging combination of Ray Rohwer and Brick Eldred. Rohwer had been a baseball star at the University of California when his college career was interrupted by a stint as an army officer in France during World War I. Small in stature, he nevertheless packed a punch, hitting thirty-three home runs with 155 runs batted in.

Eldred was a fleet runner and an excellent fielder, instantly recognizable by his small stature and reddish-brown hair that inspired his nickname. He specialized in hitting doubles, averaging sixty-three a year in the PCL over six seasons between 1920 and 1925. Although Eldred had a poor throwing arm, he made up for it with his speed and spent much of his career as a center fielder.

The team's fourth outfielder was twenty-one-year-old Jimmy Welsh, who used one of the heavier bats in the league, preferring to crowd the plate and reach for pitches away. He also played first base while hitting .342 with sixteen home runs in 599 at-bats.

The pennant secured, the Indians agreed to a post-season series against American Association champion St. Paul, to be played in Seattle. Unfortunately, rain interfered and only one game was played, a 12–4 victory for the Saints.[95]

* * *

Thanks to Tom Turner, Philadelphia and Portland had maintained a cozy relationship that benefited both teams; the Athletics had recently received infielder Sammy Hale and pitcher Rube Walberg while the Beavers had obtained infielder Frank Brazill, infielder Emmett McCann and pitcher Rube Yarrison from the Athletics, among others. During the

1924 season, Connie Mack showed interest in a young Beavers catcher, an ex–Boston University star named Mickey Cochrane. Tom Turner traveled across the country at the behest of Bill Klepper to try to close a deal with Mack but was unable to persuade the Athletics manager that the time was right to acquire Cochrane. He returned to Portland empty-handed.

Turner's lack of success intensified a desire on Bill Klepper's part to dispose of the entire franchise. After three years of turmoil, he decided if he could not sell his star catcher, maybe he could sell the entire team instead. Klepper dragged Turner back to Philadelphia and offered the Portland franchise to John Shibe, part-owner of the Athletics. Turner and Shibe attended the first two World Series games in Washington and then caught a train back to Portland, where the sale was completed, with Turner becoming Shibe's partner.[96] The deal ensured that Cochrane, a future Hall of Fame catcher, would play for Philadelphia. The Beavers became the second PCL franchise, after the Angels, to fall under the direct control of an owner of a major league franchise.

CHAPTER NINE

1925 to 1928: Murder, Mayhem and Manslaughter, Inc.

On Halloween afternoon 1924, five thousand people made their way to the Brea Bowl outside Fullerton, California, and saw Babe Ruth smash two home runs and pitch his all-stars to a 12–1 victory over another team of all-stars in a game played as a benefit for the Anaheim Elks Club.[1] Those participating included Ruth, Bob Meusel, Sam Crawford, Ken Williams of the St. Louis Browns, and the great Walter Johnson.

The game was the last of a barnstorming tour; for Johnson, it was a homecoming. The Orange County native was coming off a World Series victory against the New York Giants, the highlight of his eighteen years with the perennial doormat Washington Senators. Nearly two decades after Cap Dillon had rejected Johnson because he telegraphed everything he threw (ignoring the old adage that hitters can't hit what they can't see), the greatest player ever to come out of the Los Angeles area was returning as a conquering hero. And what's more, he wanted to stay on the West Coast.

On November 6, Johnson's thirty-seventh birthday, the legendary pitcher attended a meeting of the Optimist Club at the Biltmore Hotel in Los Angeles, where he begged off making a speech with the excuse he could pitch better than he could talk.[2]

The only speech Johnson wanted to make was one in which he would announce that he had become an owner in the Pacific Coast League. Johnson had been told that the Oakland Oaks might be available for the right price, so he and George Weiss, who owned the New Haven franchise in the Eastern League, decided to make an offer to Cal Ewing.[3] Excitement spread throughout the East Bay and a group of local realtors announced their willingness to assist the men in their attempt to acquire the Oaks.[4]

Throughout early November there were rumors and denials of rumors that Ewing had sold the Oaks to Johnson.[5] Washington Senators owner Clark Griffith confirmed he would not block Johnson's buying of the Oaks, out of respect for the pitcher's long and distinguished service.[6] Finally, on November 17, Cal Ewing told reporters that he had agreed to sell the franchise to Johnson and Weiss for $350,000. Johnson, winner of twenty-three games for Washington in 1924, promised to pitch for Oakland, an announcement that had the other PCL owners anticipating the sound of furiously clicking turnstiles. Johnson and Weiss began making arrangements to acquire players and announced the pitching great would take the mound at league openers in Sacramento, San Francisco and Portland. Oaks Park was to be renamed Walter Johnson Field.[7]

Unfortunately, Ewing's announcement proved premature; the financing Johnson and Weiss anticipated did not materialize and they could not raise the cash to close the deal.

On November 23, Ewing declared the proposed sale was dead.[8] Johnson returned to his home in Reno amid rumors he might sign on as player-manager for the Oaks in exchange for a minority interest in the team. Cal Ewing allowed that the prospect of Johnson wearing an Oakland uniform was enticing but could not see that it made sense, nor did he see Clark Griffith allowing it to happen.[9]

Johnson then joined forces with Bill Lane to pursue the Vernon Tigers. Ed Maier's asking price was $250,000 and he wanted cash up front — understandable after his experience during previous attempts at unloading the franchise to Tom Darmody and Fatty Arbuckle. Lane met with Joe Patrick and William Wrigley for the purpose of negotiating an agreement for joint use of the new state-of-the-art baseball stadium Wrigley was building to replace Washington Park.[10] Johnson checked into the Biltmore Hotel on January 7, hopeful of success but unwilling to comment to the Los Angeles press about the rumors of his purchasing the Tigers.[11]

In the end, Wrigley refused to allow Vernon to use his new stadium as its home field, largely because it would interfere with his grand strategy to relocate the Tigers as a second team in San Francisco and shift the Bees from Salt Lake City to Southern California, thereby ridding the league of unprofitable junkets to Utah. On January 29, Johnson abandoned his dream of becoming an owner and returned to Reno. He thanked Ed Maier and expressed disappointment that Wrigley had blocked the deal.[12]

Widely criticized for his actions, Wrigley reacted angrily to being cast as a villain. Obviously not about to let one of baseball's greatest stars upstage him in his new stadium, Wrigley declared, "It would be very nice for Johnson, or any other proposed buyer of the Vernon club, to pay Mr. Maier the $250,000 he asked for the franchise and then step right in and play at the Angels' park at our expense."[13]

Wrigley went on to add that Christmas was over and he did not intend on playing Santa Claus, insisting the deal had fallen through because of Johnson's failure to demonstrate he had the means to buy the franchise and help finance the new stadium.

Walter Johnson returned to the Washington Senators and won twenty games in 1925, pitching them to another American League pennant and World Series appearance. He remained with Washington until he retired after the 1927 season.

One of California's most famous native sons had again missed out on the chance to play in his backyard.

* * *

William Wrigley Jr. was sixty-three years old but had the look and energy of a man two decades younger. There was not even a hint of gray in Wrigley's dark-brown hair and he was said to have never been sick a single day in his life. An avid swimmer — he sponsored swim races from the mainland to Catalina — Wrigley also enjoyed boxing, riding horses and playing tennis. His mind was always brimming with ideas, especially when it came to his business empire and Catalina Island. The words that came to mind when one thought of William Wrigley were confidence, energy and enthusiasm. Fellow Pacific Coast League owners had also discovered his fierce determination.

Wrigley was born in Philadelphia on September 30, 1861, the eldest of William and Mary Wrigley's nine children. At age thirteen, William Jr. was working in his father's soap factory, earning $1.50 a week. As he grew into manhood, he attempted a number of business ventures on his own until migrating to Chicago not long before his thirtieth birthday.[14]

The young Wrigley established his business in the Windy City, at first selling his father's soap and offering a package of baking powder as a premium. Soon, the premium became more popular than the soap. Turning his attention to selling the baking powder, Wrigley continued offering a premium, this time a stick of gum, which once again proved to be more in demand than the product it was designed to promote. Recognizing the huge profit margin in chewing gum, Wrigley committed himself to the gum business exclusively in 1893, conducting most of the company's sales calls personally. Although the journey to success was not without setbacks, the business survived and then thrived with the introduction of two hallmark brands, Juicy Fruit and Spearmint. Soon Wrigley was dominating the market. Never afraid to take a calculated risk, Wrigley summed up his philosophy by saying, "A man's doubts and his fears are his worst enemy. He can go ahead and do anything as long as he doesn't know he can't do it." A strong believer in advertising, by 1920 he was spending more than one hundred thousand dollars a week promoting his products.

Shortly after purchasing the Los Angeles Angels in 1921, Wrigley vowed to replace ramshackle Washington Park with a beautiful stadium that would fit his image and make the city proud. Recognizing that ballparks in the Pacific Coast League were generally thrown up in a few weeks by nailing some boards together and securing the structure with wire mesh, Wrigley wanted to initiate a new era in the PCL. He enlisted architect Zachary Taylor Davis, creator of ballparks in Chicago and Cincinnati, to design a facility that would resemble Wrigley's fine ballpark in Chicago.

Wrigley's vision included a double-decker concrete grandstand constructed without posts so a good view could be had from every seat. Bleachers in center field would accommodate nearly three thousand people who would sit in front of an enormous scoreboard. There would be three thousand box seats, and the stadium was designed so it could eventually accommodate a major league–sized crowd.[15]

The first sketch of the new ballpark was printed in the *Los Angeles Times* on January 12, 1925, under the headline "Not City Hall, New Angel Ballpark." The plans included a tower, looking to some like a pack of chewing gum standing on end. Dedicated to soldiers of World War I, it would become famous for the clock atop it with the twelve letters in the stadium's name, Wrigley Field, serving in place of numbers on the clock face.[16] Workmen began placing the first of 735 concrete piles for the grandstand on March 7, 1925.[17]

Ed Maier watched as construction began and, with his third attempt since 1916 to sell the Vernon Tigers thwarted by William Wrigley, realized that being shut out of Wrigley Field meant the Vernon Tigers were in danger of extinction. Maier tried to fight back, first threatening a lawsuit to restore his territorial rights and then announcing plans to expand the stadium in Vernon and play his home games there in 1926.[18]

But these were not the glory days of the Vernon Tigers. The franchise was rotting away just like Washington Park. Bill Essick's three-year contract as manager was up at the end of the season and he was ready to move on. In August, Maier agreed to let Essick out of his contract and replaced him with Rube Ellis, an old favorite of Angels fans.[19] No one put the blame for the team's fall on Essick; with Maier's on-again, off-again attempts to sell the franchise, it was clear the owner had not put sufficient effort or resources into forging a competitive roster.[20] Maier's hiring of Ellis seemed a somewhat pitiful attempt to trade on the memory of Angels fans in order to generate some interest in the moribund franchise, which sat in last place at the beginning of August with an embarrassing record of 43–75.

* * *

The building of Wrigley Field was entering the home stretch in August 1925. The steelwork, all 2,200 tons of it, was nearly complete. Work was progressing so rapidly that rather than waiting until 1926, it was decided the Angels would play the final three weeks of the 1925 season at the new stadium, which including land acquisition was estimated to have a final cost approaching $1.3 million.[21] William Wrigley was justifiably proud of his achievement, saying, "Our new park is being constructed for the fans of Los Angeles. They have been so loyal and appreciative that I am more than pleased to give them what they want."[22]

The final games at Washington Park featured not the Angels, but the Tigers, who swept a doubleheader from the Portland Beavers. Vernon's Charlie High hit the last home run at the old ballpark. Ed Bryan was the winning pitcher and also collected three hits in three at-bats. The crowd stood after the last out as a lone bugler played "Taps."[23]

Wrigley Field opened two days later, on September 29. Print ads for the new stadium trumpeted it as "Baseball's Finest Home!" and boasted, "Here is the finest and most modern ball park in the United States. In structural beauty it is not exceeded by the Polo Grounds or the Yankee Stadium in New York City."[24] The new ballpark lived up to the hype, receiving rave reviews for its tower, wonderful panoramas of the city from the upper grandstand, the red brick outfield wall, and excellent sightlines from every seat in the park. Harry Williams called Wrigley Field "unquestionably the last word in baseball architecture and construction."[25]

The Angels won the first game at their new home, defeating the pennant-bound San Francisco Seals, 10–8, before eighteen thousand fans. Los Angeles took a seven-run lead in the second inning and held on to win. Jigger Statz hit for the cycle, San Francisco's Paul Waner hit the first home run, and teammates Smead Jolley and Bert Ellison also homered. William Wrigley was pleased; Los Angeles may not have had a big league team, but there was no question it had a big league baseball facility.[26]

* * *

Bill Lane remained in charge of the Salt Lake franchise, which was disappointing news to the many Bees fans who had anticipated that new ownership would bring a new stadium, a revived franchise and an end to the annual rumors of the team moving to a new city.[27] Despite their antipathy toward Bill Lane, Bees fans would enjoy a memorable 1925 season because of a young Italian shortstop from California. Thanks to the world's longest baseball schedule, Tony Lazzeri—whose name was often spelled "Lazerre" or "La Zerre" in the press—turned in one of the greatest hitting performances in baseball history. In the process, he obliterated the sport's established slugging records.

Growing up in the Potrero section of San Francisco, Lazzeri had been destined to a life in the iron works alongside his father until his talent on the baseball diamond was discovered.[28] Originally signed off the Oakland sandlots in 1922, Lazzeri was extremely skinny with long arms and could throw a baseball as far as anyone. He spent two years in the lower minors, almost quitting at one point, but by 1924 had blossomed into a power hitter, blasting a combined forty-four home runs for Salt Lake City and Lincoln of the Western League. Lazzeri was embraced by the small Italian community in Salt Lake City—and practically adopted by a local restaurateur named Cesare Rinetti, who made sure the young star had plenty of authentic Italian food to keep him going. It was Rinetti who reportedly first shouted out to Lazzeri "Poosh 'em up Tony!" establishing a nickname that stuck to the future Hall of Famer for the rest of his career.[29] Bees fans began emptying their pockets of change with every Lazzeri home run, showering the youngster with coins as he crossed the plate.[30]

Lazzeri slugged his forty-third home run of the year on September 11, smashing a Willie

Ludolph pitch over the Washington Park scoreboard to tie Paul Strand's two-year-old league record.[31] He broke the mark the next day, swinging at the first ball thrown by Vernon's Clyde Barfoot.[32] He added three home runs in a doubleheader the day after that to run his total to forty-seven.[33]

Upon returning to Salt Lake City, Lazzeri slammed two more home runs off Oakland's Earl Kunz on September 15.[34] The next day, Oaks pitcher Hub Pruett, a little left-hander who had made a career out of dominating Babe Ruth, slowed down Lazzeri by walking him four times.[35] Home run number fifty came later in the week, in the first game of a doubleheader against the Oaks, a game won by the Bees, 18–0.[36]

Lazzeri kept slugging and "pooshed" his total to fifty-six — thirty-nine of which had come at home. Only three shy of Babe Ruth's two-year-old professional record of fifty-nine home runs with sixteen games remaining, Lazzeri's pace slowed as the Bees ended their season on the road; seven games passed before he hit two home runs in the second game of a doubleheader on October 11 in Seattle. The second shot, his fifty-eighth home run of the year, was an inside-the-park blast that rolled to the flagpole in center field nearly five hundred feet away.[37]

It took Lazzeri six more days to tie Ruth's mark, with number fifty-nine coming at the expense of Sacra-

Tony Lazzeri, the first man to hit sixty home runs in a season, pictured with Salt Lake City in 1925 (National Baseball Hall of Fame Library, Cooperstown, N.Y.).

mento's Speed Martin, a shot that was clearly a home run from the instant it left Lazzeri's bat. Senators left fielder Merlin Kopp never moved as the ball sailed far beyond the fence; Martin waited for Lazzeri at home plate so he could be the first to congratulate him.[38] But Lazzeri had only two games to break the record, the doubleheader against the Senators on the final day.

Lazzeri was moved to the leadoff spot to maximize his number of at-bats but managed only a double in five trips to the plate in the morning game. He also failed to homer his first two times up in the nightcap.

Finally, in the seventh inning of the last game of the season, Lazzeri hit a line shot that bounced past Sacramento center fielder Billy Cunningham, who by all accounts made little effort to cut it off. Lazzeri raced around the bases and Sacramento fans celebrated a new record set at Moreing Field — sixty home runs.[39]

But Lazzeri's was not the only historic feat to be achieved on the final day of the 1925 Pacific Coast League season. Several players were vying to become the league's first-ever .400 hitter over a full season. Salt Lake's Lefty O'Doul had led the PCL in hitting much of the year with an average well in excess of .400, vindicating those who for so long had urged him to give up pitching. During a series in mid–July against Vernon, O'Doul twice went six-for-six to raise his average to .422.[40] San Francisco's Paul Waner and Seattle's Frank Brazill were in close pursuit. O'Doul was still hitting .404 on September 7, with Waner at .397 and Brazill hitting .392. O'Doul then faded and was passed by the other two hitters. Waner, wielding his forty-ounce Reb Russell bat had collected six hits in seven at-bats to raise his batting average to exactly .400 entering the morning game of the season-ending doubleheader against Oakland. Amid conflicting reports as to whether he was indeed at or below the mark, Waner decided to play in the morning game at Recreation Park. He singled twice, stole a base, and drove in two runs, pushing his average to .401. Finally satisfied, he took the afternoon off.[41] Frank Brazill finished second at .395.[42]

* * *

When Charlie Graham purchased the San Francisco Seals in 1918, a team left virtually bankrupt following years of financial problems endured by Cal Ewing and Henry Berry, he promised to revive the game in San Francisco. And revive it he had, with the help of a pair of shrewd partners in Sacramento newspaper sports editor George Putnam and San Francisco dentist Charles "Doc" Strub.

Putnam was an affable man comfortable in any gathering. He had countless friends and loved nothing more than sitting down to a meal and swapping stories late into the night. An excellent public relations man — his chief responsibility with the Seals — Putnam's enthusiasm was contagious. He promoted a winter league in 1921 that featured numerous major league stars, and he also had a hand in persuading Ty Cobb, Babe Ruth and Lou Gehrig to barnstorm in California.

A great judge of talent, Putnam was also unmercifully successful in negotiating sales of players to the major leagues. Quick to realize that big league teams would be willing to pay high prices for talent in exchange for a tax write-off, Putnam was chiefly responsible for the sales of Willie Kamm and Jimmy O'Connell.[43]

The other partner, Doc Strub, was an entrepreneur at his core. One of the first dentists to use advertising to attract business, he had played baseball at Santa Clara under Graham and was later captain of the baseball team at the University of California. When Graham and Putnam were a bit short of the cash needed to acquire the Seals, Strub was brought in to bridge the gap. Outspoken and sure of himself, Strub was always the visionary. During the Depression he would boldly partner with film director Hal Roach to build Santa Anita racetrack, which became one of the most important venues in the country and world famous for staging the first one-hundred-thousand-dollar stakes horse race. Strub was also super-stitious; he once sat on the bench with Seals players when the team ended a losing streak and continued to do so when the team kept winning. Not one to laugh at himself, he cringed at a rumor that he was wearing the same clothes during the streak, protesting, "Why, I change my shirt and collar every day."[44]

A decade earlier, the McCredies had established that teams could make money by discovering and developing talent for sale to the major leagues. The Seals took a quantum leap in that business strategy during the 1920s. Strub described how the team evaluated athletes:

> We handled baseball players like a trainer handles race horses.... We tested them for speed and for throwing. We'd take each player and walk around the block with him and get him to talking to see whether he could think. We stripped him down and looked him over physically, just as a trainer looks over a horse. If his thighs were too big, we knew he couldn't run. If his rear stuck out too far, we knew he would be out of balance. If he didn't measure up in every way, we passed him up.[45]

By the mid–1920s, it was estimated that the Seals had collected a half-million dollars selling players to major league teams by demanding their price for a brace of men who would become stars.[46] As a result, Graham, Putnam and Strub earned the collective nickname "Murder, Mayhem & Manslaughter, Incorporated."

After falling short in 1924, the Seals resumed their destruction of Pacific Coast League competition in 1925 with one of the greatest teams in minor league history, adding to the titles they had captured in 1922 and 1923. They accomplished this with a roster that had remained remarkably stable at its core during that four-year period.

The infield, with the exception of Willie Kamm in 1922, was unchanged during that time. First baseman-manager Bert Ellison had driven in 468 runs over the previous three seasons and was presented a watch from the partners in appreciation of his efforts.[47] Thirty-two-year-old second baseman Pete Kilduff, who had joined the Seals in 1922 from Brooklyn after five years in the major leagues, was considered the best at the position for San Francisco since the days of Kid Mohler. He was also credited with helping develop young shortstop Hal Rhyne into one of the most coveted prospects in baseball.

Rhyne was still emerging as a hitter at age twenty-five but was already smooth and spectacular in the field, adept at making accurate throws on the run as well as ranging far to his right and making throws across his body. Experts considered him the best shortstop in the PCL and a sure major leaguer.[48]

Veteran third baseman Eddie Mulligan rounded out the infield. Acquired from the Chicago White Sox as part of the deal that sent Willie Kamm to Chicago after the 1922 season, the thirty-year-old was coming off his best season.

The star talent of the team, along with Rhyne, was twenty-two-year-old Paul Waner, whose father had been a star semi-pro player in Illinois before the turn of the century. The Waners moved to Oklahoma City to establish a farm and Paul learned to

The first man to hit .400 over a full Pacific Coast League season in 1925, Paul Waner was sold to the Pittsburgh Pirates the next year and began a Hall of Fame career (David Eskenazi Collection).

hit using old baseballs and, when those were unavailable, the ends of corn cobs. "I have never batted a curve ball thrown by any pitcher that was as hard to hit as the cobs the boys used to throw at me down on the farm," said Waner in a 1926 interview.[49]

Waner developed into a bona fide star in 1925 with his .401 batting average and league-leading seventy-five doubles. Eddie Mulligan, a teammate of Waner in both San Francisco and Pittsburgh, called the outfielder the best hitter he ever saw, and also the least superstitious about the bats he used. Because of Waner's success, his nineteen-year-old brother, Lloyd — a right-handed thrower and a left-handed hitter who almost exactly copied his older brother's batting stance — was also signed by the Seals, although at the time there was less certainty of his potential. Both brothers would eventually be enshrined in the Baseball Hall of Fame.

The Seals outfield included Gene Valla, who was adept at hitting to all fields as well as dragging chop bunts and beating them out for base hits. However, he hit with his foot in the bucket — habitually falling away from the plate as he swung — and that tendency and his lack of power were the main reasons he never played in the majors even while consistently hitting higher than .330 in the Pacific Coast League.

Frank "Turkeyfoot" Brower was a thirty-two-year-old veteran who had been waived out of the major leagues after five seasons with Washington and Cleveland. A left-handed pull hitter whose stroke was tailor-made for the short right-field dimensions of Recreation Park, Brower hit thirty-six home runs and drove in 163 runs for the Seals in 1925 — a good return on the $7,500 the Seals paid to acquire him.[50]

Smead Jolley, who joined the Seals late in the 1925 season, was a strapping young outfielder acquired from Corsicana in the Texas Association. He was an immediate sensation for San Francisco; in thirty-eight games, the twenty-three-year-old converted pitcher hit twelve home runs and batted .447. His weakness would also be noted early — the scouting report in *The Sporting News* stated that "Jolley is far from a good outfielder."[51] But he was not being paid for his glove.

Off-season hunting buddies Sam Agnew and Archie Yelle had shouldered the bulk of the catching for San Francisco since 1920. They knew each other so well they would switch off catching duties without having to say a word. The pitching staff they handled had been remarkably stable as well. Oliver Mitchell, a tall, thin left-hander that sportswriter Ed Hughes said could throw his curveball through a knothole, was in his fourth season with the Seals, having won twenty-four games in 1922 and twenty-eight in 1924.[52] Fastball pitcher Bob Geary, a traffic cop in Cincinnati in the offseason, was also in his fourth year with the team. Doug McWeeny was one of four twenty-game winners for the Seals in 1925, along with Geary, Mitchell and Guy Williams. Thirty-seven-year-old Jeff Pfeffer, a right-handed pitcher who had won 158 games during his thirteen-year major league career, mostly with Brooklyn, won fifteen games.

After winning three pennants in four years, Graham, Putnam and Strub felt it was time to break up the team and cash in. Paul Waner and Hal Rhyne were sent to Pittsburgh and immediately placed in the starting lineup of the defending world champions. In return, the Seals received one hundred thousand dollars and three players.[53] The Seals would fall to last place in 1926, but they would not stay there long.

* * *

The end of the 1925 season also marked the end of both the Vernon Tigers and the Salt Lake City Bees. Many players looked forward to the trek to Utah, thanks to Pat Goggin, a Salt Lake City ice house owner whose free home-brewed beer was the stuff of legend among the athletes. But PCL owners continued to resent the long and expensive trip.[54] William Wrigley, among those repeatedly insisting that the league needed to abandon Utah, had promised Bill Lane that he could be a co-tenant in the Angels new stadium if he would move his franchise to Southern California.[55] Lane was ready to take Wrigley up on his offer.

Wrigley also continued to push for a second team in San Francisco, hoping another club in the league's most lucrative market would translate into more money for everybody.[56] He wielded considerable influence on the matter, thanks to his virtual control over the fate of the Vernon Tigers due to the Angels' exclusive territorial rights to Los Angeles. This made Ed Maier's team virtually worthless in Southern California.

As Wrigley prepared to host the annual minor league winter meeting on Catalina, Maier made a last-ditch attempt to hold on in Vernon for another year, reviving his plan to renovate Maier Park and expand its seating capacity to twelve thousand in anticipation that the team would play there full-time. Business manager Howard Lorenz announced that the inner fences would be moved back to eliminate short home runs, with the left-field fence being placed 360 feet from home plate and the barrier in right field measuring five feet further than that.[57]

Maier also announced the signing of Walter McCredie to a three-year contract as manager.[58] McCredie had spent three years scouting for the Detroit Tigers and Maier thought his connections would help him field a competitive team. But Maier's stubbornness in the face of William Wrigley's intransigence was not enough to ensure the viability of the Vernon franchise. Maier understood that his inability to use Wrigley Field left him without any realistic options.

On New Year's Eve, William Wrigley revealed that he was brokering a deal with San Francisco banker Herbert Fleishhacker, who was representing individuals interested in purchasing the Vernon Tigers from Ed Maier and moving them to San Francisco.[59] When the transaction was finalized a week and a half later, the lead investor was revealed to be shipping magnate Stanley Dollar.[60]

Ed Maier had finally sold his team, and this time it was for good.[61] But as Maier accepted his lifetime Pacific Coast League pass from Harry Williams and faded into history, another name thought to be long gone resurfaced in connection with the franchise: the new president of the Tigers was William McCarthy.[62] Included in Maier's valedictory was a statement about the ex–PCL president's involvement with his old team: "I am very happy to see my Tigers in the hands of a real gentleman and a square fellow like my friend Bill McCarthy."[63]

It must have made Ed Maier quite pleased to leave William McCarthy behind as a final jab at William Wrigley.

* * *

With the Vernon Tigers out of the way, Bill Lane was free to move his team to Los Angeles and choose Hollywood as the city his team would represent. Although the franchise would play home games exclusively at Wrigley Field, Lane wanted the team to have its own identity and he felt that the film capital of the world would fill the bill. Team president and ex–PCL star Spider Baum handled the details of the move, including the establishment of team offices at Wrigley Field. Joe Patrick announced the Angels would assist Lane by donating to him half of their lucrative exhibition schedule.[64]

Prior to spring training, Lane strengthened his team with one of the best trades he would ever make, acquiring spitball pitcher Frank Shellenback from Sacramento in exchange for Rudy Kallio.[65] Shellenback, who had to rely on his spitter because of the elbow problem that had cost him most of the 1922 season, would spend the rest of his playing career with the franchise, winning 211 games during thirteen seasons.

With a pair of contending teams and a new stadium the envy of many major league franchises, a record crowd was expected in Los Angeles for both teams' 1926 debuts. Opening Day for the Angels was delayed four days because of bad weather. The predicted crowd did not materialize, but ten thousand fans were on hand when Hollywood opened its season against the Angels at Wrigley Field the following Tuesday.

The Angels quickly took command of the 1926 pennant race, thanks to a three-week road trip in May that included a thirteen-game winning streak. By then they were already four games ahead of the rest of the league and on their way to a winning margin of ten-and-a-half games.

The San Francisco teams were generating far less excitement than their Southern California counterparts. The 1926 season began as anything but a smashing success for Ed Maier's old team, now called the Missions. Walter McCredie was in poor health and resigned as manager in May with the team in seventh place.[66]

The Missions would rally to finish third, but there was no rallying by the rebuilding Seals, who had sold their best players to the major leagues. The defeats began weighing heavily on player-manager Ellison, compounded by a personal streak of bad luck that included a broken wrist in June. A couple of days after his return to the lineup, Oakland's Jake Caveney hit a ground ball that took a bad hop and smacked Ellison in the eye.[67] Ellison decided he did not want the pressures of managing anymore, resigning in favor of Nick Williams, an old friend of both Doc Strub and Charlie Graham.[68]

* * *

Alarmed at the rapidly escalating cost of acquiring minor league talent, major league owners tried once again to persuade the high minors to accept the draft for the 1927 season. The American Association, the International League and the Pacific Coast League responded by offering to let players go for $10,000, but the majors voted to keep the purchase price at $7,500.[69] The Pacific Coast League directors then rejected the draft proposition by a 6–2 vote at their annual league meeting.

In February 1927 Bill Lane unloaded Lefty O'Doul to the Seals for $7,500, a move the left-handed slugger and San Francisco native welcomed.[70] O'Doul had not gotten along with Hollywood manager Oscar Vitt, landing in his doghouse when he hit into a double play after being signaled to bunt. Vitt felt that the fun-loving O'Doul's insubordination was causing dissension in the clubhouse and at one point placed the colorful outfielder on waivers.[71] The decision was made to give O'Doul another chance, and the slugger responded with a game-winning grand slam against the Missions.[72] But O'Doul and Vitt never warmed to each other and Bill Lane sent the slugger packing. O'Doul was extremely popular in his hometown and relished the prospect of taking aim at the short right-field fence at Recreation Park for an entire year. He also wanted to make Lane regret letting him go.

During spring training, it appeared as if the Seals would have no better luck than in 1926, when injuries had contributed to a continual shuffling of the lineup. Outfielder Earl Averill was driving several of his teammates back to Boyes Springs when he collided with another automobile outside Sonoma. Oliver Mitchell was found wandering down the road, dazed and bleeding profusely from a scalp wound. He lost consciousness shortly after being found, and further examination revealed a shoulder injury that was thought could cost him the season. Luckily, the injury was not as serious as first believed and Mitchell was back in uniform by the end of training camp.[73]

Although little was expected of the Seals, the 1927 season looked to be a good one for their cross-bay rivals in Oakland, who had finished second to the Angels in 1926. The Oaks' double-play combination of Lyn Lary and Jimmie Reese was attracting the attention of major league scouts. The twenty-one-year-old Lary was a natural, with big league range and a batting eye lacking only experience to make him a major league player. Twenty-six-year-old Reese was an excellent fielder who had come a long way since Sam Crawford used to look after him on road trips when he was an Angels batboy. But Cal Ewing was not about to sell his team's middle infielders quite yet, sure that they would only improve and ignite a bidding war to the benefit of the Oaks. Ewing thought so much of his star infielders that he had them insured against death or incapacitation for one hundred thousand dollars each.[74]

* * *

Third baseman Frank Brazill once said, "I would rather play for Wade [Red] Killefer than any man I know in baseball."[75] For his part, Killefer said of Brazill, "Two seasons is as long as a manager can have Brazill on a club. He'll drive you crazy."[76]

A gifted offensive player, like many minor league hitting stars Brazill was somewhat challenged defensively. But no one out-hustled Frank Brazill on a baseball diamond. He gave everything he had and expected no less of others. His penchant for writing poetry belied his terrific temper, which he often aimed at teammates. Accordingly, he wore out his welcome in many clubhouses during his career. Atlanta Crackers president Charlie Frank once called Brazill a "baseball Bolshevik" and said he had to get rid of him before he wrecked the team.[77]

Originally signed by the Brooklyn Dodgers, Brazill was a reserve for the Philadelphia Athletics in 1921 and 1922 before Connie Mack traded him to Portland. Brazill played second base for the Beavers, filling the hole resulting from Commissioner Landis' suspension of Duke Kenworthy in the wake of the Bill Klepper fiasco.[78] An instant fan favorite at Portland, which won fourteen of seventeen games after his arrival, Brazill hit .318 in 131 games, including thirteen home runs.

In 1924 he once again replaced Kenworthy, this time as player-manager when the Duke resigned in midseason. The assignment made the twenty-five-year-old Brazill the youngest manager at the Class AA level.[79] He also matured into a truly dangerous slugger, pounding thirty-six home runs with 148 runs batted in and a batting average of .351. Nevertheless, Brazill asked to be traded to Seattle after the season and was accommodated, sent along with catcher Tom Daly to the Indians in exchange for outfielder Ray Rohwer.[80] Even though dealt at his request, Brazill was insulted that another player was thrown into the trade by Portland. Knowing how competitive Brazill was, Portland sportswriter L.H. Gregory predicted that when Brazill made his first return visit to Vaughn Street Park, he would hit three home runs during the series. Unhappy that Gregory had put him on the spot, Brazill nevertheless made the writer appear prophetic when he not only hit three home runs in the series, he hit them in the very first game.[81]

After a season with the Indians in which he flirted with the .400 mark before ending the year at .395, Brazill tore up Red Killefer's 1926 contract offer and mailed the pieces back to him. Joe Patrick decided to acquire Brazill for the Angels, offering Seattle $10,000.[82] Brazill settled in at third base for Los Angeles and was the leading slugger on the 1926 pennant-winners. Brazill's second season in Los Angeles went less smoothly.

* * *

On April 15, the Oakland Oaks defeated the Angels thanks to a disputed home run in the ninth inning against Los Angeles. The Angels led, 5–4, with two out in the top of the ninth and the Oaks had two runners on base. Wilbur Cooper hit a fly ball down the left-field line that Art Jahn ran over to catch. However, Jahn stumbled over the foul line — a white wooden plank in the ground — and the ball ricocheted off of him and into the stands. Umpire Tom Crooke ruled it a fair ball, and by the time Jahn could retrieve it, all three Oaks runners had circled the bases to give Oakland a 7–5 lead.

Crooke's call that Jahn was in fair territory instead of foul ground when the ball hit him caused the Angels to scream that the arbiter's surname was entirely appropriate in light of his ruling. The resulting argument grew so heated that three Los Angeles players — Brazill, Ed Hemingway and Johnny Mitchell — were sent to early showers.[83] Brazill argued so long and loud that Harry Williams fined him fifty dollars and suspended him indefinitely.[84]

Brazill was allowed back in the lineup three days later. During that game, umpire Mal Eason ruled that a grounder appearing to bounce in foul territory was a fair ball, another call that went against the Angels. When Los Angeles manager Marty Krug confronted Eason about his ruling, the umpire refused to answer. Krug reacted by grabbing Eason and shaking him while cushions and even a glass bottle came flying out of the stands onto the field.[85]

The Angels and Sacramento were tied the next day, 2–2, in the fourth inning when the Senators' Frank McGee tried to steal third base. Brazill fielded the throw from the catcher ahead of McGee's arrival, but Eason ruled the third baseman had failed to apply the tag. Brazill went berserk, hitting the umpire in the head at least four times before wrestling him to the ground and punching him several more times in the face. Brazill was booed by his own fans as he left the field following his ejection.[86] For the second time in less than a week, Frank Brazill was indefinitely suspended. Calling the assault "an affront to a great American sport which is supposed to stand for fair play and a high standard of sportsmanship," Harry Williams said, "I doubt very much if Brazill will get back into the game this season." Williams immediately imposed a two-hundred-fifty-dollar fine.[87]

On May 6, Williams announced that Brazill would return to the Angels after another week of suspension but remain on "probation."[88] PCL umpires were outraged, arguing that Brazill's actions warranted a full-season suspension. They petitioned Commissioner Landis and National Association president Mike Sexton, imploring them to investigate the attacks on Eason "for the good of the game and the protection of umpires' lives."[89] Landis and Sexton agreed to review the incident.[90]

Soon after, Sexton was at Wrigley Field when Mal Eason was involved in another altercation that brought cushions flying onto the field and sent Marty Krug and Johnny Mitchell to the showers.[91] On June 1, Landis reinstated Brazill, but vowed any player assaulting an umpire in the future would be sidelined for a minimum of ninety days.[92]

Harry Williams fired Mal Eason a few weeks later and the umpire in turn filed suit against Krug, Brazill and the Angels, asking $85,000 damages. He claimed the attacks had cost him his reputation and his profession.[93] Eason was eventually awarded $650 in the case against Brazill and then settled his claim against Krug out of court.[94]

* * *

On May 1, the Oakland Oaks had a record of 20–14 and were one game ahead of Seattle in a tightly packed league; fourth-place San Francisco was only two games off the pace. A month later, the Oaks' lead was up to three and a half games over Sacramento. Oakland's margin remained steady until the last week of July when, with a record of 70–51, the Oaks took seven of eight games against the Missions, a series highlighted by a triple play started by Lyn Lary in the second game of the Sunday doubleheader, which the Oaks swept by scores of 14–4 and 6–0.[95] At about the same time, a rumor surfaced that Lary had been sold to the Chicago White Sox, but New York Yankees scout Bill Essick was not about to let the Oakland star go to an American League rival. He quickly signed both Lary and Jimmie Reese for future delivery to the Yankees. The White Sox instead signed Portland shortstop Billy Cissell in a deal said to be worth an incredible $123,000 to the Beavers.[96]

Oakland won twenty-seven of thirty-eight games through the end of August to put the 1927 pennant race away and claim their first title in fifteen years. Along with Lary and Reese, one of the major reasons for the Oaks' success was their twenty-eight-year-old star outfielder, Russell "Buzz" Arlett, who at 6'2" and two hundred fifty pounds was an "Oak among Oaks" as it were.

A former spitball pitcher, Arlett had won as many as twenty-nine games for Oakland before an arm injury brought about his conversion to the outfield in 1924. A rare switch-hitting power hitter, Casey Stengel would later say, "Next to Mantle, [Arlett] could ride a ball harder from both sides of the plate than any man that ever lived."[97]

Arlett quickly became one of the league's most feared sluggers, driving in 140 runs or more for three straight seasons from 1924 through 1926. But his temper surfaced from time to time and he could be lackadaisical in the field, leading to rumors that he often sulked. He was not a good judge of fly balls and generally would catch only what was hit directly at him. This made him much more valuable to the Oaks than to major league teams and Arlett remained in the PCL, growing increasingly frustrated. Louie Guisto, a teammate of Arlett's for much of his career, felt the slugger's morale had been damaged because so many players of lesser talent were promoted to the majors while he was passed by. In Guisto's opinion, the slugger would shine if he could get out of the Pacific Coast League.[98] But even after helping lead Oakland to a PCL championship, Buzz Arlett's chance remained a few years away.

* * *

Radio was becoming wildly popular, and in 1927 two important developments accelerated growth in the fledgling industry. First, radio manufacturers reached agreement with the Radio Corporation of America (RCA) to use company patents that were essential in mass production of radio sets. Second was the development of the alternating current radio tube, which made it possible to manufacture radios that could be plugged into a standard electrical outlet.[99]

Mass broadcasting to the general public was on the horizon and sports were to be a major beneficiary of this new technology. Baseball had been broadcast on radio since 1921, and the New York Yankees had aired the World Series for several years, more or less in the same play-by-play fashion as today. However, most baseball coverage consisted of a simple recitation of wire accounts sent by telegraph to the local station, providing only the actual details of the game without commentary.

KHJ in Los Angeles broadcast play-by-play results of the World Series in 1925 to great fanfare, relaying results from three thousand miles away almost as they happened.[100] By 1927 KPO radio in San Francisco was using a direct line from Recreation Park to provide play-by-play details of every game. In Oakland and Seattle, game accounts and scores were provided nearly every day except Sunday.[101] William Wrigley, who had a direct telegraph wire into his home on Catalina Island so he could keep abreast of his Chicago Cubs, took notice of radio's potential to promote the last-place Los Angeles Angels.[102] Hoping broadcasts would drum up interest in an otherwise uninteresting team, Wrigley announced that KHJ would cover the Angels every day.[103]

There would be lively debate about radio in the PCL over the next few seasons — Bill

Lane for one remained skeptical — but there was no turning back. At the league meeting following the 1928 season, a resolution was defeated that would have banned radio from the ballparks.[104] Though yet in its infancy, radio would soon become as inseparable from baseball as newspapers were.

Ironically, at the same time radio was becoming established, a new invention was being developed on the second floor of a warehouse at 202 Green Street in San Francisco, near Telegraph Hill. This new all-electric technology would further revolutionize broadcasting and the world of sports. In January 1927, Philo T. Farnsworth, the twenty-year-old son of an Idaho farmer, met with Crocker Bank vice president James J. Fagan and pitched his idea. Fagan, whose son would later own the San Francisco Seals, was able to convince W.W. Crocker, president of the bank, to invest in it. Nine months later, Farnsworth completed the first successful demonstration of his new technology at the Green Street warehouse. On that day in San Francisco, modern television was born.

* * *

The Seattle Indians had not been able to capitalize on their success of 1924, and the team had to continually sell off its best talent — to the consternation of other PCL owners and Indians fans. On Christmas Eve 1927, Red Killefer and Charles Lockard bowed to the inevitable and sold the franchise to Bill Klepper for $300,000. The transaction gave Klepper ninety percent ownership and brought him full-circle to the franchise he had helped establish after World War I.[105]

Klepper's arrival meant Red Killefer was out at Seattle, but it did not take long for him to land a new job. However, his destination proved a surprise — replacing Harry Hooper as manager of the Missions. Red Killefer would be working for William McCarthy only four years after playing a pivotal role in McCarthy's ouster as president of the Pacific Coast League."[106] McCarthy, who had gone through several managers in short order, signed Killefer to a three-year contract that was the richest in PCL history. Killefer was also reunited with Frank Brazill, who had been acquired from the Angels.[107]

Predictably, Brazill did not last long with the Missions. First placed on waivers after playing poorly because of what he claimed was a bad arm, McCarthy and Killefer countered with their appraisal that Brazill's problems were "mental" issues.[108] Those comments spurred Brazill to return to the playing field, but the team released him in June with the explanation that he had a bad knee.[109]

Despite losing league MVP Lefty O'Doul to the New York Giants through the draft, Recreation Park's other tenant, the San Francisco Seals, had completed its rebuilding phase and prepared for another run at a pennant. Roy Johnson, a reserve in 1927, replaced O'Doul and joined Earl Averill and Smead Jolley in a truly formidable offensive alignment. Eddie Mulligan had been sold to Pittsburgh, so Babe Pinelli, returning to the PCL after six seasons with the Cincinnati Reds, alternated with youngster Frankie Crosetti at third base.[110] Hal Rhyne was back from the Pirates after two seasons, and the Seals added veteran pitchers Elmer Jacobs and Dutch Ruether from the Chicago Cubs and the New York Yankees.

Smead Jolley was the real star of the 1928 Seals. In his third full season with San Francisco, the twenty-six-year-old left-handed slugger had a rifle arm and he used it to his advantage in Recreation Park's short right field, often throwing out runners at first base who either turned too far or came down the baseline too slowly. However, Jolley was terrible with grounders and hopeless at judging fly balls. Former Washington Senators coach Al Schacht said that Jolley ran pigeon-toed, with a little hop in his step that made his efforts seem even more ludicrous. More than one reporter likened Jolley's attempts at catching balls to a child chasing soap bubbles. Despite the criticism, Jolley was comfortable in his own skin, confident of himself and what he was—a country hardball player. Always good-natured about his misadventures in the outfield, he sometimes joked in his Arkansas drawl about there being a "bad sky out there today." Jolley's managers, who lost years off their lives watching him play, were not always as good-natured; Seals manager Nick Williams habitually referred to Jolley as "that bum out in right."[111]

But there was no deriding Smead Jolley's hitting; he struck fear into opposing pitchers. Frank Shellenback said of Jolley, "He could hit anybody, anywhere, anytime." Jolley held his bat at the bottom of the handle and wrapped it around his ear, swinging it like a buggy whip. His bat was always in motion as he waited for the pitch—often right up to the point when the pitcher released the ball. Fastballs, curves, changeups, lefthanders, right-handers, it did not matter. An instinctive hitter, Jolley loved high, inside pitches and seldom used the same

Frank Shellenback said of Smead Jolley, "He could hit anybody, anywhere, anytime." Jolley's manager in San Francisco, Nick Williams, cringed at Jolley's defensive shortcomings, calling him "that bum out in right." Jolley batted .305 lifetime in four major league seasons and .367 in the minor leagues, with 336 home runs and more than three thousand hits (San Francisco History Center, San Francisco Library).

approach at the plate in consecutive at-bats. Once asked for advice about the correct batting stance, Jolley replied, "Son, when you're up there at the plate, never be superstitious."[112] Smead Jolley was unorthodox, but there was no questioning the results. In 1927, he had missed hitting .400 by just three points while driving in 163 runs and tying Lefty O'Doul for the team lead with thirty-three home runs. That was just a warm-up for 1928.

* * *

The Sacramento Senators had never won a Pacific Coast League title. Always considered one of the league's weak sisters because of their market size, the Senators were allowed several concessions, including a slightly higher share of revenue from ticket sales. The Senators also were always allowed to open the season at home.

The only significant change to Sacramento's roster in 1928 was veteran first baseman Earl Sheely, who had been released to the Senators by the Chicago White Sox.[113] After missing a few weeks because of a broken finger, he was again one of the best hitters in the Pacific Coast League. The split-season format had been reinstituted by the league directors, and San Francisco won the first-half championship. Thanks to a healthy Sheely, Sacramento was challenging San Francisco for the second-half title.

Encouraged by a rare opportunity to win, the Senators broke with tradition and spent money on veterans to improve their pitching staff, adding not only Pudgy Gould, but also Doc Crandall. This gave Sacramento three legal spitball pitchers — Gould, Crandall and Ray Keating.[114] Gould, who had pitched extremely well for the champion Oaks in 1927, won eleven games for the Senators, most of them in the second half of the season. Keating, enjoying his best season in the PCL, finished second to the Seals' Dutch Ruether in wins. The three veteran pitchers would prove vital to Sacramento, which managed to finish in a tie with San Francisco for the second-half title.

The first half of the 1928 season had been very successful for the PCL; Harry Williams reported that the league had drawn more than 1.1 million admissions, a twenty percent increase over the previous year.[115] The tightness of the second-half race only added to the league's financial success. The Senators defeated the Seals in a special best-of-three-games series to determine the second-half champion, with Doc Crandall, John McGraw's ancient "Doctor of the Pitching Emergency," saving the win for Pudgy Gould in the deciding contest. Sacramento's victory put them into a playoff between the same teams for the 1928 Pacific Coast League pennant.[116]

In the first game of the championship series, San Francisco pounded Ray Keating for a 12–5 victory. Sacramento evened the series the next day behind two home runs by Ray Rohwer, one of which led to an inexcusable outburst from Elmer Jacobs, San Francisco's losing pitcher.

Jacobs was pitching to Rohwer in the fourth inning with the bases loaded and began fuming when umpire Henry Fanning called balls on two pitches Jacobs thought were strikes. Rohwer hit the next pitch for a grand slam. Jacobs fumed as the Sacramento slugger rounded the bases. Fanning, who had only one arm, tossed a new baseball to Jacobs and stood to the side of the plate, waiting for Rohwer to finish his home run trot. Suddenly, Jacobs took the baseball and fired it at Fanning as hard as he could, striking the umpire in the knee. Fanning fell to the ground and began writhing in agony. The umpire had to be carried off the field and was unable to return for the remainder of the series. Jacobs was ejected, but Harry Williams declined to suspend him, instead only fining him a portion of his playoff share, an action that seemed remarkable in light of Commissioner Landis' edict the previous year in the Frank Brazill incident.[117]

The series was eventually won by San Francisco in six games; it was an offensive show-case, with the Seals hitting .379 and Sacramento batting .350. Smead Jolley, who batted a record .404 during the regular season and drove in 188 runs, led all players with a .517 average. Teammates Earl Averill and Gus Suhr hit .483 and .458, respectively. There was little doubt that the Seals built by Murder, Mayhem and Manslaughter, Incorporated, had to be considered the Pacific Coast League's team of the decade.

* * *

William Wrigley increasingly viewed himself as the financial engine driving the Pacific Coast League. As a result, he felt he had the right to run his franchise without interference from the league. Wrigley grew increasingly obstinate, engaging in several battles with Bill Lane and the other league directors. The main source of these conflicts involved women; that is, letting women attend games without paying.

Back in 1926, Wrigley announced that all women would be admitted free of charge to every Angels game. However, at the league meeting the next winter, PCL owners voted to outlaw the practice and Wrigley grudgingly discontinued it. When attendance decreased the next season, Wrigley reinstated the policy with the explanation that he needed to build a following and utilize forward thinking, contrasting his outlook with "the rest of the club owners, who have a lot of two-by-four ball parks decorated with signs and props to keep them from falling to pieces."[118] Visiting teams were given a share of the gate calculated on what would have been collected from women had they paid their way into the ballpark. Wrigley felt his largesse should quiet any criticism about "Ladies Day" since he was assuming the financial obligation.

Wrigley also meant for his policy to cover the other team using Wrigley Field as its home stadium; he insisted that Bill Lane implement the same practice for the Hollywood Sheiks, which were drawing twice the crowds the Angels were.[119] Lane refused. Joe Patrick and William Wrigley responded by inviting Lane to leave Wrigley Field. But the Sheiks were not the Vernon Tigers of 1925, teetering on the brink of insolvency and forced to capitulate to the wishes of the gum magnate. Lane stood firm. His franchise had value. Soon, San Diego was being mentioned as a possible destination for Lane in 1929, and another group of businessmen based in Phoenix, Arizona, formed a group to explore the possibility of the Sheiks moving there.[120]

In late August 1928, Wrigley and Lane met to discuss the situation. Compromise plans were exchanged and they agreed to meet again.[121] In October, it was announced that Lane would pay twenty thousand dollars annually for the use of Wrigley Field as the Sheiks' home. The Sheiks would cover their own stadium costs (utilities, grounds keeping, clubhouse expenses, etc.) rather than splitting them with the Angels, as in the past. Wrigley retained all concession revenue. Women would be admitted free to all games played by either the Angels or the Sheiks at Wrigley Field, and Wrigley would make the payment to visiting teams on behalf of both Hollywood and Los Angeles. Finally, the Sheiks would not be allowed to host any exhibition games at Wrigley Field.[122] With that, it seemed the great "Ladies Day" war was over.

In the meantime, another battle was brewing. Harry Williams was up for re-election as league president and, as he had been warned five years earlier, some of those who had once been his closest friends wanted to show him the door, including Bill Lane. A leap-year baby born in 1860 in Baton Rouge, Louisiana, Lane was the very definition of a self-made man. Gruff and blunt, he was a mining engineer by trade, graduating from the Colorado School of Mines in 1883. Lane's mining interests had taken him all over the world. He had trekked to the Klondike during the gold rush of the 1890s, and also studied law and was admitted to the Utah bar, although he never practiced except on his own behalf. Lane's philosophy was to attack until he emerged victorious. He also never forgot an enemy. Lane was an insatiable fan of pulp fiction, especially detective and mystery novels, and there were numerous stories, many exaggerated—but some true—about his carrying guns into league meetings.

Lane had a bad heart but was vigorous nonetheless. At age sixty-eight he did not use glasses, even for reading, and was as active as anyone in league affairs. Despite his hard-as-nails persona and lack of sentimentality (the source of his nicknames "Hard Rock" and "Hard Pan"), the confirmed bachelor had a sincere soft spot for orphaned boys that he hosted at his ballpark every year.[123] He hated losing and made every effort to win the pennant, but his teams generally finished in the middle of the pack. Having been part of the syndicate that purchased Harry Wolverton's moribund team after the 1914 season, Lane took control of the franchise three years later. But in the decade since, he had been unable to bring home a championship.

Lane had been a major force behind the ousting of William McCarthy on Catalina Island in November 1923. Five years later, he was one of the leading figures behind the movement to oust Harry Williams, who was being viewed as William Wrigley's tool.

Judge McCredie and William McCarthy were the declared candidates to unseat the league president.[124] Williams expressed surprise at his unpopularity, pointing to the unprecedented prosperity the league had enjoyed during his tenure. He insisted that "if a change was made, it will be due solely to politics and with not the slightest regard for results."[125] McCarthy's entry into the race actually improved Williams' chances to remain head of the league since at least half of the owners did not want to see the return of the PCL's former president. Bill Lane and Cal Ewing floated the name of former president Allan Baum as a compromise, but that proposal generated little enthusiasm and even less momentum.[126]

Williams failed to be nominated on the first ballot at the league meeting on November 12, five years to the day after his triumph at "the Battle of Avalon." Lew Moreing nominated McCarthy while Tom Turner offered McCredie's name. With the other six votes split evenly among the two camps, a deadlock resulted.

Lane finally nominated Williams on the ninth ballot but the vote remained evenly split, this time between the current and former league presidents. Faced with a stalemate, the owners adjourned the meeting and Williams remained head of the league for the time being, but without anything that could be construed as a vote of confidence.[127] League directors decided to take up the matter again in January.

When the owners reconvened on January 22, McCarthy received four votes on the first ballot, while Allan Baum, Judge McCredie, John Sullivan of Seattle and Williams each received one. At that point, Bill Klepper rose from his seat and suggested the deadlock be broken by unanimously electing Williams to a two-year term. The other owners agreed and Williams was re-elected.[128] Shortly after the owners returned to their homes, William Wrigley re-ignited the "Ladies Day" controversy, conveniently claiming to have discovered a loophole in the league constitution that allowed him to let women attend for free without covering the visitor's forty-percent share of the revenue, which had cost more than thirty thousand dollars the previous year. Wrigley also pointed out that the league constitution could only be changed at an annual meeting and the next one was not until November 1929. Therefore, he insisted he could do what he wanted during the coming season.[129]

The other owners howled in protest, with Portland's Tom Turner and Seattle's Bill Klepper making a beeline for Harry Williams to demand he stop Wrigley. Williams agreed with them and forbade the Los Angeles owner from going through with his plan. Wrigley in turn said he would file a lawsuit, and in a fit of pique uncannily reminiscent of Jim Morley in his heyday, bellowed that no one would tell him what he could do with his property and that he was ready to close Wrigley Field, leaving Hollywood with no place to play, and would "let the Pacific Coast League go to hell."

Harry Williams pledged to hold his ground, even as he stated that Wrigley's action had brought the league to "its biggest crisis."[130] In early May, Oakland, Seattle, Hollywood, Portland and Sacramento voted to uphold Williams in the matter. Joe Patrick retorted, "As far as the Los Angeles club is concerned, that resolution will not affect our policy of admitting women free every day to Angel games at Wrigley Field. We will ignore the resolution and not send any answer to president Williams."

Patrick confirmed that Wrigley planned to sue and added that Wrigley Field might be closed. In that event, the Angels would play home games at either White Sox Park or Vernon, putting Bill Lane out in the cold and dropping the seating capacity in one of the league's most lucrative markets to around three thousand. "I imagine that will just about ruin the league, for instead of taking away from $7,000 to $10,000 checks, the visiting clubs will be able to take out only $1,000 for their local series," said Patrick.[131]

The matter was finally turned over to the National Association of Professional Baseball Leagues, which ruled in favor of Williams.[132] Wrigley grumbled but backed down. One of the more contentious fights in league history entered an uneasy truce.

The episode highlighted the barriers to successfully running the Pacific Coast League. At a time of unprecedented prosperity, team owners still could not get along. One had to wonder why Harry Williams, William McCarthy — or anyone else, for that matter — would seek the presidency of the league.

CHAPTER TEN

1929 to 1932: Let There Be Lights!

Bill Lane might not have been able to act as kingmaker in the Pacific Coast League like William Wrigley, but he *was* able to end Bill Rumler's eight-year exile from the PCL for his role in the 1919 pennant-fixing scandal.

The thirty-eight-year-old outfielder's suspension was finally lifted by Organized Baseball prior to the 1929 season, and Lane wasted no time signing one of his long-time favorites.[1] It was a satisfying moment for the Sheiks owner, tempered only by his disappointment that William McCarthy — who had resigned from the Missions in order to again pursue the PCL presidency — was no longer in the league. To Lane, it would have served as a measure of revenge; McCarthy's vow that Rumler would never again play in the Pacific Coast League still irritated the Sheiks owner.

Following his banishment along with Babe Borton and Harl Maggert, Rumler had remained active outside of Organized Baseball. He played and managed in Minot, North Dakota, in 1921 under the alias Bill Moore, although he made no effort to hide either his identity or the trouble that led him there. In an interview with the *Bismarck Tribune*, Rumler said he expected to be reinstated and again declared he had done nothing wrong. Minot proved a safe haven for another rocked by scandal; the team's ace pitcher, Jimmy Hightower, was none other than Casey Smith, the ex–San Francisco Seal released along with Tom Seaton in May 1920.[2]

After a year in Minot, Rumler moved to Hibbing, Minnesota, and after that to Canton, Ohio, where he played under his own name in a league that boasted several ex–major leaguers, including Dickie Kerr and Rip Hagerman. That was followed by several seasons in Kenosha, Wisconsin, in the independent Wisconsin-Illinois League.

When Rumler signed with Hollywood in 1929, it was expected he would be nothing more than a reserve outfielder and pinch-hitter. He immediately set out to disabuse that notion. Not long after reporting for spring training in San Diego, Rumler put on a batting practice display that demonstrated his eight-year absence had no effect on his batting stroke. He hit the two longest drives of the day, lining pitches off the top rail of the left-field bleachers.[3] The veteran outfielder made the Sheiks' final roster but saw limited action in the opening series against Sacramento, pinch-hitting against spitballers Pudgy Gould and Doc Crandall before sitting out the third game.[4]

Rumler was finally given a start in right field on March 29 and had three hits, including a home run in the third inning that cleared the scoreboard. Not coincidentally, Hollywood captured its first win of the season, erupting for twenty hits in a 15–4 rout.[5] Bill Rumler was in the lineup to stay; at the end of the first week his batting average was .444, tied for fifth best in the league.[6]

The Sheiks struggled, however, losing eleven of their first fifteen games before capturing the finale of a miserable series in Portland, played in conditions of nearly continuous rain. Rumler came away from the series with a sore shoulder that had to be placed in a cast, putting a temporary hold on his comeback.[7] Conditions in Seattle the next week were no better and the Sheiks faced more cancellations. After the series, Bill Lane chartered a plane to fly the team back to Portland so the players could catch a train that would reach San Francisco in time for the start of a series against the Seals.[8]

* * *

Although Bill Lane putting his team on an airplane seemed to be a more death-defying feat, it was the automobile that took its toll on the Pacific Coast League in 1929, with a series of tragic accidents marring the season. The year began with news that former Angels and Seals owner Henry Berry had been killed in a single-car accident while inspecting his oil wells near Taft, California. Hearing about the tragedy, Harry Williams wistfully recalled the rotund millionaire as being the most "picturesque character in the Coast League ... and I do not except my other dear friend, the late Hap Hogan."[9]

About a week after Berry's fatal accident, Portland outfielder Denny Williams was killed when an automobile driven by teammate Tony Rego was sideswiped on a curve near San Clemente, California, and flipped over an embankment, coming to rest against a boulder.[10] On March 31, less than a week after the death of Denny Williams, twenty-two-year-old Missions pitcher Clyde Nance was killed in a single-car accident just south of Merced, California.[11]

The strange string of tragedies continued into the regular season and beyond. Former Angels trainer Doc Finlay was fatally injured in June when the automobile in which he was a passenger plowed into a truck and trailer that had stalled in the roadway.[12] Just days after the league playoffs ended, Hollywood reserve outfielder Bill Albert was killed when the car he was driving collided with another automobile that was traveling on the wrong side of the street.[13]

In the most bizarre accident of all, Los Angeles catcher Gus Sandberg was fatally injured while assisting Angels manager Marty Krug, a long-time friend who had been visiting his home. Krug was leaving at five o'clock in the morning and discovered his gas tank was empty, so Sandberg volunteered to siphon fuel from his tank and fill Krug's. After doing so, Sandberg decided to see how much gas he had left in his tank and made the catastrophically unfortunate decision to check by lighting a match. The force of the resulting explosion blasted directly into Sandberg's face, inflicting first, second and third degree burns covering his head, neck and shoulders. He died two days later at California Lutheran Hospital in Los Angeles.[14]

* * *

After Red Killefer replaced William McCarthy as president of the Missions, he overhauled the team's roster. In mid–December 1928, he announced the acquisition of four key players: outfielders Walter "Cuckoo" Christensen and Pete Scott, catcher Fred Hofmann and pitcher Bert Cole.[15] He also landed veteran pitcher Dutch Ruether, fresh off a twenty-nine-win season for the Seals. Ruether had not been able to agree with Charlie Graham on a new contract, so he had purchased his freedom from San Francisco.[16]

The Missions pitching staff was solid, even after the tragic death of Clyde Nance. Besides Ruether and Cole, Killefer could call on former Stanford football star Ernie Nevers and veterans Herb McQuaid, Mert Nelson and Herm Pillette. Harry Krause was on the wrong side of forty but coming off a fifteen-win season and, as a bonus, was one of the best sign-stealers in the business.

But the true strength of San Francisco's "other" team was a powerful offensive lineup designed to take advantage of the cozy confines of Recreation Park. The Missions' middle infield of shortstop Gordon Slade and second baseman Mickey Finn, both holdovers from the old Vernon Tigers, was thought by Killefer to be ready for the big leagues, while the formidable heart of the batting order featured first baseman Jack Sherlock and outfielders Fuzzy Hufft and Ike Boone.

Sherlock, who had played for Red Killefer in Seattle, was a gangly first baseman said by *Los Angeles Times* columnist Bob Ray to be so loose-jointed "it looks as though he's going to fall apart when stretching for high or wide ones, (but he) makes the tough plays look easy."[17] Infielders could relax with Sherlock at first base because they knew he would catch whatever they threw. As a result, they made fewer wild throws.

The likeable Hufft was a squat, free-swinging left-handed-hitting outfielder who had also played for Killefer in Seattle. He signed with the Indians in 1926 after sending Killefer a short but accurate note saying, "I'm not much of a fielder, but I can certainly sock that apple." Hufft was also a free spirit, known to burst into song in the outfield and encourage those in the bleachers to join in.[18]

The Missions' other slugging star, Ike Boone, was a product of the University of Alabama and in his second stint with the Reds. The hulking left-handed batter had dominated every minor league he had played in, starting with his .403 batting average in 1920 in the Georgia State League. He first played for the Missions in 1926, a season that ended prematurely for him because of a broken jaw suffered during an attempt to break up a double play.[19] The Missions reacquired Boone in a July 1928 trade with Portland after the Beavers had received him as part of the Bill Cissell deal with the White Sox.[20]

The PCL decided to abandon the split-season format in 1929, but after the Mission Reds opened up a ten-game lead over second-place San Francisco in the loss column, some owners debated whether that had been a wise move. Concerned about sustaining fan interest, especially in those cities where teams had started the season slowly, Harry Williams began pushing for reinstatement of the split season.[21] Others, especially Bill Lane, echoed Williams' call, and the league directors voted unanimously to award the first-half championship to Killefer's Reds on July 1.[22] Three days later there were holiday fireworks, both literally and figuratively, thanks to a pair of outstanding hitting performances.

Oakland outfielder Roy Carlyle put on a memorable power display during his team's holiday doubleheader against the Missions, hitting a tremendous drive in the first game that nearly cleared the clubhouse in center field. The ball ricocheted off the fence and Carlyle tore around the bases for a two-run triple. In the fourth inning of the nightcap, Carlyle obliterated an Ernie Nevers pitch, sending the ball over two rooftops and into the rain gutter of a house on Park Street.[23] The blast was measured a couple of days later as having traveled an incredible 618 feet.

That same day, San Francisco Seals third baseman Babe Pinelli created holiday fireworks of his own by hitting three home runs in the second game of San Francisco's doubleheader against Seattle. Two of the home runs were grand slams. Pinelli went six-for-six in the game and drove in twelve runs as the Seals won, 22–10.[24]

The second half was off to a roaring start.

* * *

The biggest beneficiary of the split season in 1929 was Bill Lane, who was also its biggest proponent. His Hollywood Sheiks had done little more than reach the break-even mark in the first half of the 1929 season, finishing at 52–47. Lane was most happy with a "do-over."

At the same time Lane was trying to right his team's ship by adding veterans, Sacramento owner Lewis Moreing was trying to shed them to save money. Moreing began threatening to move his team to either Stockton or San Diego unless attendance improved. He also announced he would begin playing Thursday afternoon home games in Stockton—a possible first step to moving the team there.[25]

In early June, Moreing released thirty-six-year-old outfielder Emil "Irish" Meusel, who was attempting a comeback. A week and a half later, ten-year major league veteran Joe Harris, who was two years older than Meusel, was dropped even though he was one of the team's leading hitters.[26] On July 15, Moreing released expensive veterans Hank Severeid and Doc Crandall in another move calculated to save money.[27]

Bill Lane desperately wanted the last two victims of Moreing's youth movement but was unable to sign the forty-one-year-old Crandall, winner of 229 Pacific Coast League games, who decided to return to Los Angeles where he starred from 1916 through 1927.[28] Lane did land Severeid, a durable thirty-eight-year-old catcher whose reputation was built on his hitting and strong throwing arm. With seasons lasting nearly fifty games longer than any other circuit, it was essential that Pacific Coast League teams have two starting catchers. Although the Sheiks possessed an excellent first-stringer in Johnny Bassler, they needed another and Severeid fit the bill.[29]

Lane got the right veteran. Crandall was basically finished; he would win only one game for Los Angeles and retire at the end of the year. Meanwhile, the acquisition of Severeid had a major impact on the 1929 pennant race; it proved an especially great stroke of fortune when Johnny Bassler broke his thumb on a foul tip against Los Angeles on August 11. The injury was gruesome, with the bone protruding through the skin, and Bassler was sidelined several weeks.[30] Fortunately, catching nearly every day agreed with Severeid, and he went on a tear. Appearing in seventy-nine games for Hollywood, he hit nine home runs with a batting average of .414 in 263 at-bats.[31]

Hollywood battled Mission for the league lead throughout the second half, but at one point the frontrunners faced an unlikely challenger. Portland had finished last in the first half with a dismal 33–66 record. But the Ducks, as they were being called, were a different team after the season's restart; on August 27, they won their sixteenth straight game, scoring five runs in the ninth inning against Los Angeles with no one out to secure a 9–8 come-from-behind victory. Suddenly Portland was in first place by two games. The streak ended the next day and the Ducks cooled off, fading to a third place tie.[32]

The Sheiks held a one-game lead over the Missions for the 1929 second-half title going into the last day of the season. The first-half champion Reds had remained within striking distance thanks to Herm Pillette's no-hitter against last-place Seattle.[33] But the pennant race ended with a whimper instead of a bang. The Sheiks were swept by Portland behind pitcher Junk Walters, who had been cut by the San Francisco Seals earlier in the season because of issues about his weight; he won both games to keep Hollywood from clinching.[34] However, Mission could not take advantage. The Reds were embarrassed by lowly Seattle, which swept them despite entering the final day of the season with an abysmal second-half record of 26–75.[35]

Despite the manner in which the season ended, the playoff promised to be an exciting battle between two of the greatest offensive powerhouses in PCL history. The three main cogs for the Reds—Hufft, Sherlock and Boone—had impressive seasons. Boone enjoyed the greatest year of his great minor league career, a performance that came closest in PCL history to replicating Tony Lazzeri's 1925 season. Boone set a still-standing Organized

Baseball record with 553 total bases. He had 323 hits, forty-nine doubles, fifty-five home runs and an incredible 218 runs batted in, four shy of Lazzeri's record. Boone's .407 batting average set the PCL standard, while his number of base hits was just two shy of Paul Strand's all-time mark.

Like Mission, Hollywood was built around offense. First baseman Mickey Heath was the Sheiks' top slugger, with thirty-eight home runs, 156 runs batted in and a .349 batting average. The outfield included Elias Funk, who hit .384, and Cleo Carlyle, who batted .347. Even the team's best pitcher, Frank Shellenback, was frequently employed as a pinch-hitter. He hit twelve home runs and batted .322 while also winning twenty-six games.[36] The team's most popular player was Bill Rumler, who recovered from his shoulder injury to hit home runs in four straight games near the end of August and finish third in the league with a .386 batting average. A decade earlier Rumler had been embroiled in a conspiracy that involved these same teams — when they represented Vernon and Salt Lake City — to fix the 1919 pennant race. The teams and players had moved on but here was Rumler, ready for a shot at redemption.

It did not look good for the Sheiks early in the series as the Reds took the first two games at Recreation Park. But Hollywood stormed back in the third game thanks to Cleo Carlyle, who hit two home runs and a triple, and Frank Shellenback, who pitched a complete game and slammed two singles and a home run.[37]

The series then shifted to Wrigley Field. Mission carried a two-run lead into the eighth inning of the fourth game. Reds pitcher Herb McQuaid then suffered a streak of wildness, walking the first two batters in the bottom of the inning before getting two outs. McQuaid then fired a fastball up and in that caught Bill Rumler on the side of the head and sent him crumpling to the ground. Rumler was carried unconscious to the clubhouse, and though the injury was not life threatening, it appeared his comeback season was over.

McQuaid's wildness had loaded the bases, and shaken by what he had done to Rumler, he subsequently walked Cleo Carlyle to force in a run, making the score 3–2. Mert Nelson replaced McQuaid and recorded the final out of the inning.

Mission failed to score in the top of the ninth but remained one run ahead and only three outs from a commanding three-games-to-one lead in the series. After Nelson retired Hollywood's Johnny Bassler to lead off the ninth, Frank Shellenback pinch-hit for second baseman Mike Maloney and promptly smashed a home run into the houses across the street from Wrigley Field to tie the score. The Sheiks completed their come-from-behind victory in the tenth inning on Cleo Carlyle's run-scoring double, tying the series at two games apiece.[38]

With the momentum reversed, Hollywood took the fifth game of the series, 6–3, and then staged a five-run rally in the eighth inning of the sixth game to win the championship before a crowd of more than fifteen thousand at Wrigley Field. Frank Shellenback pitched a complete game in the series-clincher and hit his third home run of the playoff. One of the unlikely heroes in the pennant-winning contest was Bill Rumler, who was not supposed to play after the serious beaning he had suffered in the fourth game. Rumler brought the crowd to its feet with a pinch-hit line-drive single that drove in the first run of the decisive rally.[39]

Bill Lane finally had his first Pacific Coast League championship. Furthermore, Bill Rumler, whom Lane had defended all those years, had come through with a heroic clutch hit. It was a most appropriate "Hollywood ending."

* * *

The concept of baseball played at night was nothing new; barnstorming teams had done so for years. There had been experiments with temporary lighting beginning in the late 1800s, including an exhibition held at Athletic Park in Los Angeles in 1893.[40] In June 1927, two New England League teams played a seven-inning game at Lynn, Massachusetts, under temporary lights before several thousand people who were surprised at how well they could follow the action and noted that players seemed able to react quite well to the ball.

Lee Keyser, owner of the Des Moines Demons in the Western League, had attended a number of college and high school football games at night and was impressed with the quality of lighting at those events. Confident that a permanent set-up would work for baseball, he invested twenty thousand dollars to install 146 floodlights mounted atop a half-dozen ninety-foot-tall poles at the Demons' stadium and then announced that Des Moines would open its 1930 home season on May 2 at night against Wichita.[41] "If the game is successful ... I look for most of the minor leagues to follow the example of Des Moines and install floodlights for night baseball," said Keyser. "If it is unsuccessful, it will mean that sooner or later the minor league clubs will have to go out of business due to steady decrease in patronage."[42] Several major league executives made plans to attend the game and a national radio audience tuned in to the contest, which was carried by the National Broadcasting Company.[43]

Twelve thousand fans crowded into the stadium, and while the game was a less-than-artistic triumph — Des Moines jumped out to a 12–0 lead after three innings — the general consensus was that the quality of baseball was as good as it would have been during the day. Problems remained to be solved, including dark spots along the foul lines, and a fielder lost one pop foul in the lights, but Lee Keyser was undeterred. He addressed the national radio audience between the sixth and seventh innings and declared, "My reaction to night baseball is that it is glorious and wonderful. The players are happy, the crowd perfectly satisfied, and it means that baseball in the minor leagues will now live." The *Chicago Tribune* agreed with Keyser that night baseball might well be a "life saver" for the minor leagues.[44]

Continuing to struggle in Sacramento, Lew Moreing took notice. He quickly ordered lights and had them installed. On the night of June 4, 1930, at precisely 8:31 P.M., Moreing flipped a switch, generating a buzz from forty banks of lights, each carrying a trio of sixty-thousand-watt bulbs. The lights slowly grew brighter, illuminating the playing field as hundreds of people in their automobiles, surrounding the stadium to witness the spectacle, began honking their horns in celebration.[45]

Less than a week later, excitement pulsed through the capital city as the Oakland Oaks visited Sacramento for the first night game in Pacific Coast League history. It was a sweltering evening and as fans took their seats, fanning themselves with their scorecards, they could not help but notice the huge harvest moon, a vibrant orange globe floating just above the horizon. A contingent from Oakland was on hand with drums and accordions, as if to serenade the gigantic sphere in the sky. One unintended thrill during the game resulted from Oakland's Jack Fenton fouling a ball into a bank of lights, shattering some bulbs and sending sparks flying in a spectacular display.

It was quickly apparent, even to those skeptical about playing baseball at night, that lighting systems had advanced to the point where it was practical to do so. Fielders had little trouble seeing the ball and seemed to execute all plays, both easy and difficult. The Senators, at least, could see well enough to hit, especially after having practiced the night before — unlike the Oaks — and won the historic contest, 8–0, behind Ed Bryan.

An account of the game was carried on the front page of both major Sacramento newspapers. There was also play-by-play radio coverage beamed to cities as far north as Seattle. Moreing indicated that adjustments would be made, with additional lights installed to better illuminate the foul lines. He also announced that games would start at eight-thirty so both teams could get proper practice after twilight. Harry Williams was ecstatic, praising Lew Moreing for recognizing the potential for night baseball to draw large crowds that were impossible to achieve during weekday afternoons.[46]

"Think what it will mean to the clerk, the factory worker or the business man, who have been shut indoors all day, to be able to get out in the fresh air of a fine evening and enjoy an exciting game of baseball," said Williams. "I feel that the public and the Pacific Coast League is (sic) deeply indebted to Lewis Moreing for his courage in pioneering this departure on the coast."[47] Night baseball was instantly popular; Sacramento drew more fans in the first quarter of the 1930 season than in all of 1929. The franchise that Moreing had wanted to move to San Diego or Stockton was suddenly near the top of the league in attendance.[48]

Other Pacific Coast League owners took notice. Within days, William Wrigley announced he would install lights at Wrigley Field and the Angels would play their first night games in July.[49] Shortly after Wrigley's announcement, Tom Turner said that he too had arranged for lights and that Portland would begin night play as well.[50] Seattle and Oakland quickly followed suit. San Francisco and Mission were the only teams without immediate plans to inaugurate night baseball; with Recreation Park scheduled to be abandoned in 1931 in favor of a new $1.25 million stadium, neither franchise saw a reason to spend money wiring an obsolete facility.

* * *

The Brooklyn Dodgers had been scouting Oakland slugger Buzz Arlett during the summer of 1930 and were closing in on a deal with the Oaks that would finally fulfill Arlett's decade-long ambition to play in the major leagues. Arlett was out of the lineup one evening due to a chest cold but put on his uniform anyway to sit on the bench and support his teammates. In the midst of a sloppy game that lasted three hours, umpire Chet Chadbourne accused Arlett of heckling him over called balls and strikes. Arlett denied making the remarks but Chadbourne ordered him from the grounds anyway.[51]

Arlett was waiting for Chadbourne after the game and demanded an explanation. The discussion quickly escalated into a heated exchange and several players got between the two. Chadbourne, already agitated because of an argument about his call of a third strike to end the game, reached over another player's shoulder and swung his mask, connecting just above Arlett's left eye. The resulting gash bled profusely and the Oaks star had to be whisked to the emergency room where twelve stitches were required to close the wound.[52] Arlett was going to be out of the lineup for at least a couple of weeks. Harry Williams immediately suspended both combatants and boarded a train to Sacramento to personally investigate the matter.[53]

Williams first lifted Chadbourne's suspension, followed by Arlett's a week later. With that, Williams considered the matter closed.[54] Commissioner Landis felt otherwise. In light of the Brazill and Jacobs incidents, Landis was concerned that Arlett's punishment was not severe enough, and he immediately requested reports from both parties involved. The commissioner's action enraged Arlett's teammates, who were already angered by what they viewed as Williams' reluctance to hold Chadbourne culpable, and they responded by furnishing statements to Landis in Arlett's defense.

Even as the controversy raged, the Oaks assured everyone that the deal sending Arlett to Brooklyn was still on. Oakland vice president Cookie Devincenzi insisted that the perceived snag in negotiations had nothing to do with Arlett's injury, but rather the demand on the part of the Dodgers for a straight cash transaction instead of a combination of cash and players.[55] Three days later, Brooklyn announced the acquisition of Ike Boone, which came as a surprise to the Oaks and a devastating shock to Arlett, especially since the thirty-three-year-old Missions slugger had three previous stints in the major leagues and was no longer considered a prospect.[56]

After Landis completed his investigation, he decided against further punishment for Arlett. Chadbourne was fired. Arlett threatened to sue the Pacific Coast League for ten thousand dollars, claiming that Williams' mishandling of the situation had led to the investigation by Landis and that with the possibility of suspension hanging over his head, the Dodgers had signed Boone instead. It did

Buzz Arlett was one of the greatest minor league sluggers with 432 minor league home runs, all but seven at the highest level of the minors. He began as a spitball pitcher, winning as many as twenty-nine games in one season. Arlett was repeatedly frustrated by his failure to reach the major leagues because of his defense and reluctance by Oakland to sell him — he was past his thirtieth birthday when he received his only major league opportunity. When umpire Chet Chadbourne hit Arlett with a mask, it cost the slugger yet another opportunity to make it to the major leagues (National Baseball Hall of Fame Library, Cooperstown, New York).

not help, of course, that Chadbourne had injured Arlett in the attack.[57]

Arlett returned to the Oakland lineup, even taking the mound for the last two innings of the team's second-ever home night game.[58] He finally reached the majors in 1931, with the Philadelphia Phillies, but would last only one season there before returning to the minor leagues for good.[59] One of baseball's great minor league hitters, the blond, curly-haired switch-hitter would always be frustrated by his inability to play the prime years of his career in the major leagues. Instead, Buzz Arlett remains one of the more intriguing "what if" stories in baseball history.

* * *

Eager to see his team repeat as champion, Bill Lane added two big bats to the Hollywood lineup after the 1930 season started. The first was USC star athlete Jess Hill, who made his professional debut as a defensive replacement in the outfield during a game on June 4. Hill batted for the first time the next night, entering a game against Los Angeles in the seventh inning and bringing Sheiks fans to their feet by drilling the first pitch he saw for a home run.[60] He was soon playing regularly and hitting .390 by the end of his first month in a Hollywood uniform, second only to Ike Boone among hitters with more than one hundred at-bats.[61]

Two weeks after signing Hill, Lane purchased outfielder Dave Barbee from Seattle, an acquisition that impacted Hollywood's 1930 drive for the pennant in the same way as Hank Severeid's signing the year before.[62]

A native of Greensboro, North Carolina, Barbee had an easy-going personality and a southern drawl that fed a perception that he lacked the necessary fire to be a winner. Benched after falling out of favor with Seattle manager Ernie Johnson, Barbee was especially motivated when he arrived in Hollywood and met with Sheiks manager Oscar Vitt, who bluntly laid out his expectations.[63] The slugger responded, hitting ten home runs in his first nineteen games in a Hollywood uniform. Despite his lack of foot speed, Barbee played well in the sun field at Wrigley, repeatedly showing off his strong throwing arm. The team, in seventh place when Barbee was acquired, surged into contention with twenty-three wins in twenty-nine games, a streak that helped them rally to finish second in the first half, just behind Los Angeles.

Hollywood stayed hot in the second half, even as Barbee inevitably cooled off and yielded some of his playing time to Harry Green. Then on August 27, Bill Rumler broke his ankle trying to stretch a single into a double in the ninth inning of a game against Mission. The fracture was serious enough that the thirty-nine-year-old Rumler's Pacific Coast League career was over.[64] Barbee returned to the lineup and helped carry the Sheiks to the second-half title, hitting forty-one home runs in only 149 games.

There were other heroes, including pitchers Frank Shellenback and Jim Turner, who combined for a 40–16 record — with Shellenback winning his last thirteen decisions. Johnny Bassler, Hank Severeid and Jess Hill were among the league leaders in batting average. Second baseman Otis Brannan drove in 130 runs while first baseman Mickey Heath finished second on the team in home runs and set a record with twelve consecutive base hits against the Missions in early September.[65] But Dave Barbee was unquestionably a key factor for the Sheiks; lightning had struck twice for Bill Lane in the form of mid-season deals that had led to consecutive Pacific Coast League championships.

The Sheiks easily won the 1930 playoffs, defeating first-half champion Los Angeles in five games to capture their second straight Pacific Coast League pennant. The series was a slugfest, with Turner and Shellenback the only pitchers able to record complete games for either team. Dave Barbee continued his offensive onslaught with four home runs and eleven runs batted in during the series.

* * *

On March 13, 1931, the San Francisco Seals christened their new $1.25 million ballpark at Sixteenth and Bryant with an exhibition game against the Detroit Tigers.[66] Even though the facility was shared with the Missions, it was dubbed Seals Stadium. Seating nearly twenty thousand, it featured one of the largest playing surfaces in baseball, with the right-field fence located 385 feet from home plate. Home runs to left-center had to travel 375 feet and clear a wall fifteen feet high. It took gargantuan blasts of 415 feet to clear the right center field wall. The spacious stadium was a radical departure from the cozy confines of Recreation Park and the days of Smead Jolley playing line drives off the right-field fence and throwing out runners at first base.[67] The first regular season game was held on April 7, and Ty Cobb, a close friend of George Putnam, was on hand for the Opening Day automobile parade down Market Street. The Marine Band marched onto the field and led the crowd in "The Star Spangled Banner." Cobb swung and missed at the mayor's ceremonial first pitch, and more than twenty thousand fans watched the Seals crush Portland, 8–0, behind Sam Gibson.[68]

Despite its cold, unpainted concrete facade, Seals Stadium was impressive. The facility included a state-of-the-art public address system and its lighting was superior to that of any stadium in the United States — a total of 310 one-thousand-watt bulbs atop six 120-

foot-tall steel towers illuminated every part of the field. The lighting system paid immediate dividends as night baseball proved a boon to attendance. The team's first night game, on April 23 against Sacramento, was an unqualified success, with twelve thousand people attending on a Thursday evening. The *San Francisco Chronicle* raved that the game had been played "under perfect conditions."[69] One notable feature of San Francisco's peculiar weather was that winds from the ocean tended to die down in the early evening, usually before game time, and fans were able to watch night games at the new stadium in relative comfort.

George Putnam said he was receiving inquiries from several major league teams, including the Pittsburgh Pirates, about the stadium's lighting system and predicted the major leagues would turn to night baseball in the near future.[70] The Pacific Coast League now had facilities in its two largest cities that were the envy of nearly every city in America.

* * *

The Sacramento Senators were an early surprise in 1931, leading the PCL through the season's first twenty games, quite an accomplishment for a team many had picked to finish last. The team's infield featured Len Backer at second, slick-fielding Ray French at shortstop and Dolph Camilli, who had recovered from a severely broken ankle suffered in 1929, at first base. But misfortune struck Sacramento as Backer, who was hitting .355, suffered a fractured skull on a pitch from San Francisco's Bill Henderson on April 26, ending his season.[71] The team had already lost Jim McLaughlin with a broken finger, so the Senators moved twenty-one-year-old Stan Hack into the starting lineup at third base.

Hack became a favorite, a future star who fit Lew Moreing's vision of developing young players he could sell at a profit. Among Hack's new teammates were others that fit that mold, including Stan "Frenchy" Bordagaray, who joined the team in July, and twenty-year-old outfielder Frank Demaree, whose efforts to care for his deaf-mute parents made for a great human interest story.[72] Injuries and lack of depth ultimately doomed Sacramento, but the team's young, raw talent was impressive.

Portland was another early surprise and much of the credit went to legendary minor league manager Spencer Abbott, who was hired to run the team in 1931. Many thought the move had been forced upon Tom Turner by majority owner John Shibe. Whatever the reason, landing Abbott was considered a coup for Portland. Old school in the John McGraw tradition, Abbott had a reputation as an umpire baiter, and Harry Williams had been concerned enough to query several people about the veteran manager's tendencies. Williams said he was assured that most of Abbott's arguments with umpires were efforts to prevent his players from being ejected.[73] That is not to say Abbott was above engaging in theatrics when he felt it was warranted. If he disagreed with an umpire's call, it was not unusual for him to empty the entire contents of the dugout onto the field.[74]

Abbott was strict with players and meant for his words to be taken as gospel. He fined pitchers twenty-five dollars if they walked a batter who subsequently scored. Second baseman Johnny Monroe had a bad habit of breaking toward second base too early in double-play situations, leaving a hole for a batter to drive the ball through. Abbott said he would fine Monroe fifty dollars every time he left his position to cover before the pitch had crossed the plate.[75] Life was definitely different in Portland.

* * *

Frank Shellenback picked up where he had left off in 1930, winning his first five games in 1931 to extend his streak to nineteen straight, including his win in the playoffs in 1930. After losing, 2–0, to Phil Page in Seattle on May 3, Shellenback reeled off another fifteen wins in a row, giving him an incredible thirty-four victories in thirty-five decisions.[76] By early summer Hollywood was well in front of the rest of the league, with only Portland within striking distance. It was decided to split the season in half again. Harry Williams awarded the first-half title to the Sheiks and announced the season would start anew on July 7.[77]

The second half was dominated by the San Francisco Seals, who then swept Hollywood in four games to win the 1931 pennant, dashing Bill Lane's hopes for a third consecutive PCL championship. The Seals had lost Earl Sheely, who returned to the majors with the Boston Braves after hitting .403 for San Francisco in 1930, but were bolstered by three players acquired from the New York Yankees, along with seventy-five thousand dollars, for shortstop Frank Crosetti. The new Seals included pitcher Sam Gibson and former Hollywood third baseman Julian Wera.

Gibson, who credited Seals trainer Denny Carroll for ridding him of a sore arm, topped the PCL with twenty-eight wins and won the pitcher's Triple Crown, also leading the league in earned run average and strikeouts. Wera drove in more than one hundred runs. The third player acquired in the Crosetti deal, Bill Henderson, won eight of eleven decisions while pitching as a spot starter and reliever. Of course, this being another of the Murder, Mayhem and Manslaughter deals, the Seals also got to keep Crosetti for the year. He drove in 142 runs, second on the team to outfielder Henry "Prince" Oana, a Hawaiian who was not really a prince but played like one — at least in 1931.

But not all was sweetness and light in the Seals family. Rumors circulated about a fist-fight involving manager Nick Williams and trainer Denny Carroll aboard the train carrying the team back from Los Angeles the day after the Seals completed their playoff sweep. A few days later, the Seals announced Williams had resigned. Williams contradicted the team's official statement in a phone call to *San Francisco Chronicle* sportswriter Abe Kemp, telling Kemp that he had been fired because of his refusal to stop drinking. Shouting into the phone, Williams told Kemp, "I did not resign. I was fired. In case you do not understand me, I will spell it out for you. F-I-R-E-D."[78]

The Seals also dismissed Carroll, their legendary trainer, cutting ties after twenty-two years, even after Sam Gibson's success. Carroll almost immediately signed with the Detroit Tigers and would be credited with saving the careers of Charlie Gehringer, Schoolboy Rowe and Dick Bartell, among others.[79]

Nick Williams was replaced by a surprise choice, thirty-six-year-old Jake Caveney, an ex–Cincinnati Reds shortstop who, far from being a teetotaler, had not been above taking a swig offered from a hand extending a flask through the Booze Cage in old Recreation Park. But the veteran, who liked to cut the center out of his glove to get a better feel for the ball, served as a mentor to the team's younger players. The decision had been made. Nick Williams signed with the Portland Beavers as a coach and scout.[80]

* * *

Harry Williams' contract extension was up and there was — what else — a deadlock among league owners as to whether he should be replaced as league president. The PCL's annual meeting was held in Sacramento in early November 1931 and Williams had four votes: San Francisco, Sacramento, Los Angeles and Portland. Red Killefer had the support of three franchises: Mission, Seattle and Hollywood. Oakland spent two days casting its ballot for Cal Ewing. In the midst of the voting, Williams was informed his salary was being cut from $10,000 to $6,500. He promptly resigned. San Jose area newspaper publisher H.L. "Hy" Baggerly was elected to a three-year term on the next ballot, and Williams returned to the *Los Angeles Times*.[81]

Baggerly declared his advocacy for night baseball and free admission for women. Despite the dire financial conditions in the country and a resulting slump in PCL ticket sales, he expressed optimism about the future of the league, insisting, "I cannot see anything but success for the league over which I recently was elected to preside."[82]

* * *

Christmas came and went in 1931, and to all appearances everything seemed normal for William Wrigley. The Angels owner continued his frenetic pace and showed no signs of slowing down. Only closest family members knew the truth — that the multi-millionaire was less than a year removed from having suffered a major heart attack.

Immediately after the holidays, Wrigley began complaining about not feeling well. Upon finishing breakfast at his winter home in Phoenix on January 18, 1932, he began complaining of indigestion and suddenly passed out, the result of a blood clot that had formed in his brain.[83] Wrigley's personal physician, Dr. George Goodrich, was flown to Phoenix by chartered plane and traced the problem to his original cardiac episode.[84]

Although he rallied a bit at first, Wrigley was never fully coherent after falling ill, unable to say more than a word or two at a time. There was speculation about his absence from the public eye, but the seriousness of Wrigley's health problem remained a secret until he died at his Biltmore Estate on January 26.[85]

Tributes flowed from all corners of the baseball world. William Wrigley's body arrived in Southern California aboard a train from Phoenix and a funeral service was held at his mansion on South Orange Grove Avenue in Pasadena. His remains were then transported to a mausoleum to be stored until a burial place was prepared at Mount Ada on Catalina Island.[86] Wrigley's son, Philip K. Wrigley, was chosen as successor and vowed to carry on his father's policies. But Philip, or P.K. as he was often called, would not take the same interest in either the Cubs or Angels as his father had.[87] The Pacific Coast League had lost one of its major figures, one it could not replace.

* * *

The Depression was starting to eat away at the Pacific Coast League as memories of the league's glory days of the 1920s quickly faded. Hollywood's share of gate receipts for the opening weekend at Oakland in 1932 was only $2,600.[88] Hy Baggerly's optimism aside, the novelty of night baseball had worn off. In addition, horse racing, which admitted patrons for free, was contributing to the declining PCL attendance, especially in Northern California. The Oaks asked their players to take an across the board twenty-five percent pay cut, but rescinded the request when no other teams followed suit. They released several players instead. Team president A. Robert Miller said, "What the future holds for baseball is strictly something that cannot be foretold. Frankly I am sorry to admit that it looms dark and dismal."[89]

Rumors persisted that the Oaks were for sale, but they were not the only team in trouble. Hollywood's attendance was running half that of 1931, dropping precipitously after Dave Barbee was drafted by Pittsburgh and Hank Severeid was released to accept an offer to manage at Wichita Falls.[90] Both San Francisco teams announced an end to night games, citing declining attendance and an inability to compete with evening dog racing, which was attracting fifteen thousand people each night.[91]

Teams began using younger players who earned less and were easily sold to major league teams eager to acquire prospects. Sacramento's Lew Moreing continued embracing this philosophy, saying, "Using old ballplayers is strictly a losing proposition. Put the youngsters in there and develop them and you have a prospective sale to the majors, while with a veteran it's just a question of keeping him until he burns out."[92]

But this strategy caused controversy when it impacted the pennant race. In the middle of the 1932 season, prior to a key series against Los Angeles, Moreing sold Frank Demaree to the Chicago Cubs for immediate delivery rather than waiting until 1933. Harry Williams, writing in the *Los Angeles Times*, offered an obvious jab at his successor as league president when he cynically noted the Angels were the "little cousins" of the Cubs and that the deal made Demaree, one of Sacramento's best players, conveniently unavailable to play against Los Angeles.[93]

PCL teams selling the league's best talent was not going to help the effort to become a third major league. Although Hy Baggerly asserted that the Pacific Coast League was on a more solid financial footing than most other minor leagues and insisted it was not time to panic, he hinted there might have to be a return to twenty-five-cent baseball in order to draw larger crowds. Baggerly had already slashed his office staff and budget. League umpires had their salaries cut twenty percent and Baggerly voluntarily reduced his own pay. It may not have been time to panic, but it also was no time to celebrate.

* * *

Portland was the surprise of the PCL in 1932, a young team benefiting from the resurgence in the fortunes of the Philadelphia Athletics and the leadership of Spencer Abbott. The team responded to Abbott's old-school ways, winning sixteen of nineteen games in late May and early June to move within striking distance of first-place Hollywood.

Even though they had sent veteran Ed Coleman and his 183 runs batted in to Connie Mack after the 1931 season, the Beavers outfield remained their strength. Fast and powerful, twenty-six-year-old center fielder Bob Johnson would later drive in one hundred runs or more for seven straight seasons in Philadelphia. Twenty-two-year-old right fielder Lou Finney had already played briefly for the Athletics and would return in 1933 to begin a major league career that would last beyond World War II.

Twenty-three-year-old Fred Berger, whose brother Wally was a star for the Boston Braves, was in left. In his third season in the Pacific Coast League, the younger Berger showed off an impressive throwing arm, nailing six San Francisco Seals runners at the plate in one series.[94] The team's most highly regarded player was third baseman Mike "Pinky" Higgins, a twenty-three-year-old University of Texas product who would later be a three-time American League All-Star. Higgins improved greatly as a fielder during the 1932 season, although he was still weak on hard-hit grounders to his right. Tutored during spring training by Jimmie Foxx, Higgins led the Beavers in home runs and runs batted in and joined Finney as a Pacific Coast League All-Star selection.[95]

Utilizing younger talent was paying off for Tom Turner and his chief scout, the deposed manager of the Seals, Nick Williams. Together with manager Spencer Abbott, they helped Portland win its first pennant since 1914. Furthermore, the Beavers drew more than three hundred thousand fans. Abbott celebrated by pitching an inning and a third in the last game of the season and hitting a bloop single off Seattle's Junk Walters, who had played for the fifty-five-year-old Abbott the year before.[96]

The situation was not nearly as positive for the other team in the Northwest; the Seattle Indians were in complete disarray. Bill Klepper's team began 1932 with Ernie Johnson as manager and ended the year with first baseman George Burns in charge and Johnson filing a lawsuit.[97] The Indians also lost their home field — Dugdale Park burned down on July 5, hours after the San Francisco Seals swept them in a holiday doubleheader. The fire was discovered at one o'clock in the morning and completely destroyed the twenty-year-old stadium, claiming the team's home uniforms and equipment. Three nearby houses were severely damaged as twelve firefighting units desperately battled to keep the blaze from spreading.[98] The inferno originated in the wooden grandstand where a large oil drum was found sitting out in the open. A serial arsonist later claimed responsibility.

The University of Washington and the city of Fresno each offered their stadiums to the Indians for the rest of the season, but fans wanted the team to stay in town. Bill Klepper bowed to their wishes and arranged for the use of city-owned Civic Stadium, even though the playing surface — including the outfield — lacked grass. The city did agree to install lights for night baseball, but they were fixed to poles imbedded along the foul lines. Civic Stadium was obviously far from an ideal solution.[99]

* * *

Back in 1923, Los Angeles attorney William Himrod and Kiner Hamilton, vice-president of the Southern California Amateur Athletic Union, began discussing the impact hosting the Olympic Games would have on the city and the soon-to-be-constructed Los Angeles Coliseum. Before long, they had rallied politicians and businessmen to the cause.[100] William May Garland, president of the Community Development Association that had built the Coliseum, took charge of the campaign to bring the Olympics to Los Angeles. He traveled to Rome for the annual Olympic Committee Meeting and returned with an agreement that the City of Angels would host the Tenth Olympiad in 1932.[101]

Compared to previous hosts Athens, London, Stockholm and Paris — cities possessing hundreds and even thousands of years of history — Los Angeles was a controversial selection. It was geographically remote and had been of significant size for less than a half-century. There was serious concern whether athletes would travel there. Some felt the Games might as well have been staged in Australia or even Mars, for that matter. Undaunted, Garland forged ahead with the support of the president of the International Olympic Committee, Baron Pierre de Coubertin.

Despite the skepticism, the 1932 Olympic Games were considered a success, with numerous records set on a Coliseum track many ranked as the fastest in the world. More than five hundred thousand attended, a record for the event. Seventy thousand people were on hand at the Coliseum for the finish of the marathon.[102] The Games were also a public relations boon for Los Angeles, even as some Germans began deriding the event, insisting that any talk of Berlin hosting the next Olympiad, in 1936, was premature. The *Daily Preussische Zeitung*, the newspaper that served as an organ of Adolf Hitler's opposition party political machine, labeled the Olympics a "Jewish international enterprise" and editorialized, "If the Hitlerites will have anything to say there won't be any Olympiad in Berlin."[103] The posturing of German fascists aside, it was apparent that Los Angeles had arrived as a big league city, even if the baseball's major leagues did not officially recognize that fact by placing franchises there. It was only a matter of time.

* * *

On October 1, 1932, Mark Koenig sat in the Chicago Cubs dugout as his former teammate, Babe Ruth, hit what was forever after known as his "called shot." Ruth's famous moment during the 1932 World Series was rooted in Koenig's successful comeback with the PCL Missions earlier that year, leading to the former starting shortstop for the 1927 Yankees being acquired by the Cubs after their shortstop, Billy Jurges, was shot by a scorned woman. Koenig played a major role in the Cubs winning the pennant, but when the National League champions refused to allot Koenig a full World Series share, the Yankees branded them cheapskates and Ruth took revenge.[104]

A continent away, the fourth-place San Francisco Seals were playing the Missions to close out the 1932 Pacific Coast League season. A new face appeared in San Francisco's lineup, a seventeen-year-old shortstop whose older brother was playing outfield for the Seals. The new recruit did not smile much, as if self-consciously hiding bad teeth. He did not say much either.

On Saturday, the lanky teenager batted second in the lineup, behind Jerry Donovan and ahead of Art Garibaldi, and managed a triple in three at-bats against Ted Pillette as the Seals won, 4–3.[105] The two teams met the next day in a doubleheader to bring the season to a close, with the youngster playing in both games. After going hitless in the first game and committing an error, he had a double in two at-bats in the finale while driving in a pair of runs as the Seals pounded the Missions, 12–4.[106] Though seemingly insignificant at the time, the series was an important moment in baseball history. The young player would become a legend; within a year, the entire baseball world would know him, thanks to a spectacular, record-setting performance.

The young man's name was Joe DiMaggio.

CHAPTER ELEVEN

1933 to 1935: Joltin' Joe DiMaggio

The California Junior Chamber of Commerce, inspired by the success of the Olympics, felt the time was right to lay the groundwork for bringing major league baseball to the state. Harold P. Morgan, chairman of the chamber's Citizens Committee appointed to pursue major league baseball for the cities of San Francisco and Los Angeles, sent a letter to each of the sixteen major league owners, pointing out the increased practicality of airline travel and the explosive population growth in California. He asked them to consider moving their teams to one of the California cities.

"Your first reaction to such a proposal may be 'impossible! fantastic!'" read Morgan's letter. "That was the first reaction to the bid of Los Angeles for the games of the Tenth Olympiad years ago. Persistence and the belief that it was neither impossible nor fantastic won out, however, and their unparalleled success is now history."[1]

Morgan's assertion and the enthusiasm behind it were undeniable. Major league owners were certainly aware of the positive aspects of the weather, wealth and growth of the Pacific Coast, since their teams had been barnstorming there during the offseason for a half-century. But the major leagues were not ready to absorb Los Angeles and San Francisco. And on a tranquil day in March 1933 at Long Beach, California, the site of spring training for the Hollywood Sheiks, there was a reminder that even paradise had its faults.

Most of Hollywood's players were eating dinner in the oceanfront Robinson Hotel when a massive earthquake struck just before six o'clock on March 10.[2] Pitcher Vance Page was so unnerved by the shaking that he sought escape by jumping through a plate glass window, luckily cutting only his shoe. Oscar Vitt had just entered the hotel lobby when he heard the unmistakable rumble and the crashing of breaking glass. The Sheiks manager catapulted himself through a space where moments earlier the hotel's front window had been. As he dusted himself off, the brick façade of a building next door collapsed onto the sidewalk with a thundering crash and Vitt, along with dozens of others, made a frantic dash from the buildings to the beach.

Once at a safe distance, Vitt counted heads and quickly realized second baseman Otis Brannan was missing. Taking a couple of players with him, Vitt sprinted back into the hotel and found Brannan with his leg wedged between a restaurant booth and a door. After freeing their teammate, the group ran back to safety.[3]

Although no Sheiks player was seriously injured, the episode was unsettling. The 6.2 magnitude earthquake caused one hundred and twenty deaths and more than a thousand injuries. The Angels, training in Los Angeles, escaped unscathed save for pitcher Win Ballou, whose home suffered significant damage.[4] The Sheiks called off their exhibition game the next day against the Giants and announced they were moving to Sawtelle, in the western part of Los Angeles, where the Angels were training.[5]

For the moment, talk quieted about major league status for the West Coast.

* * *

The Great Depression was at full throttle. One of every four American workers was unemployed, and those still working were doing so for less pay. The economic catastrophe was decimating nearly every industry. Baseball was not immune; it was suffering at all levels. By the spring of 1933, five of the twelve high schools in Los Angeles were no longer fielding baseball teams.[6] Pacific Coast League attendance had plummeted from two-and-a-quarter million four years earlier to less than a million.[7] One ray of hope was a bill signed by the new president, Franklin Delano Roosevelt, allowing individual states to license the sale of beer containing no more than 3.2 percent alcohol content. Washington, Oregon and California all opted to allow sales, and PCL owners theorized that beer would provide a steady source of revenue.[8]

Meanwhile, Los Angeles manager Jack Lelivelt was optimistic about a youth movement he had undertaken a year earlier. The team had insured the right arm and both legs of twenty-year-old outfielder Tuck Stainback for seventy-five thousand dollars a week before trading him to the Chicago Cubs for pitcher Louis "Buck" Newsom, two other players and cash.[9] The Angels also kept Stainback for another year.

Newsom was expected to play an important role for Los Angeles. A likeable braggart who insisted his impersonations of *Amos & Andy* characters were superior to those of the show's popular stars, Newsom fancied himself a future radio personality and sometimes partnered with Oscar Reichow on broadcasts of Angels games. A willing worker, Newsom threw hard and never lost his cool, even during frequent fits of control problems. Instantly recognizable by his signature windup and habit of wiping sweat from his brow, he constantly hustled, always running as hard as he could to first base whenever he hit a ball. Newsom also drove fast — in April he earned a ticket for going fifty-five miles per hour in a fifteen-mile-per-hour zone.[10]

Newsom would serve as the PCL's answer to young St. Louis Cardinals star Dizzy Dean, attracting attention for outlandish remarks that left the public wondering what he would say next. Like Dean, Newsom backed up his boasts. During the broadcast of a game against Portland in June, he assured the radio audience that he would shut out the Beavers the next day. He did just that, allowing only three hits.[11] He also guaranteed he would win at least twenty games for the Angels.[12]

Newsom had plenty of help in the pitching rotation. Former USC football star and PCL veteran Fay Thomas was acquired from Brooklyn. A big man whose best pitch was an overhand forkball that he called "a sailer." Thomas had established strikeout records in the PCL that left many wondering why he had not been successful in the major leagues. Submarine pitcher Lee Roy Herrmann had won twenty-one games for the Angels despite being recalled by the Cubs in July. Hard-throwing Dick Ward, a former high school football star from Everett, Washington, had once dreamed of playing halfback for the Washington Huskies. By the end of the 1933 season many considered Ward the PCL's best pitching prospect thanks in part to veteran Win Ballou, who tutored the youngster on improving his curve to make his fastball that much more effective.[13]

The Angels were about to enjoy a great run of success.

* * *

Although Jake Caveney continued playing eighteen-year-old Joe DiMaggio at shortstop during spring training, the San Francisco manager recognized the teenager's future lay elsewhere than on the infield, especially since his wild throws were endangering patrons located behind first base. Caveney assigned veterans Jerry Donovan and Jimmy Zinn the task of tutoring the teenager in outfield play. They demonstrated the proper technique of sprinting to a spot and then turning to catch a fly ball rather than running while trying to keep an eye on the ball the entire way. Donovan and Zinn quickly realized there was little to teach — DiMaggio had a gift for playing the position.[14]

DiMaggio began the regular season on the bench, finally making his first appearance as a late-inning replacement during the third game.[15] A week later, he hit his first home run as a professional, over the left-field fence at Seals Stadium off Herm Pillette of the Missions.[16] The youngster, whose name was misspelled "DeMaggio" in newspapers, soon worked his way into the starting lineup, first as a center fielder and then in right field. Joe's development came at the expense of his brother, Vince, who was dropped by the Seals early in the season.[17]

Meanwhile, Portland right fielder George Blackerby was making a serious assault on the PCL-record forty-nine-game hitting streak of Jack Ness. On May 28, Blackerby extended his streak to thirty-six, hitting safely in both games of a doubleheader against the Seals. But he was stopped the next day by Dick Ward.[18]

May 28 also proved the beginning of an historic feat for Blackerby's San Francisco Seals right-field counterpart that day. Joe DiMaggio's double in the nightcap of the doubleheader was at first glance a seemingly insignificant base hit that did nothing more than put his batting average at an unimpressive .244. But that double was the beginning of a record-setting effort that would cause everyone to forget about Blackerby and transform eighteen-year-old Joe DiMaggio into one of the league's best known and most valuable commodities.[19] Over the next three weeks, the Seals outfielder collected forty-one hits in ninety at-bats against Seattle and Oakland pitching, quickly building his hitting streak to twenty-three games. On fourteen occasions, he had two or more hits. But DiMaggio would not be the only one to dim memories of George Blackerby's early-season performance. Incredibly, Blackerby's thirty-six-game hitting streak would not even be the league's second longest in 1933.

On June 11, Angels first baseman Jim Oglesby hit singles in both games of a doubleheader at Sacramento to begin a streak of his own.[20] DiMaggio and Oglesby then matched each other, day after day, week after week. When the Seals visited Wrigley Field at the end of June, DiMaggio's streak had eclipsed thirty games while Oglesby's had reached twenty.

Both men maintained their streaks in dramatic fashion while playing against each other on June 30. Oglesby had walked twice and grounded out once when he came to the plate for his final at-bat. As was his habit, the left-handed slugger spit on his bat for good luck, squeezing the handle in his hands to get a good, solid grip before settling into the batter's box. The ritual paid off as he blooped a single to right to keep his streak alive.

DiMaggio had also gone hitless in his first three at-bats that day. In the eighth inning the youngster hit a weak grounder to Carl Dittmar, whose throw, at least from the Angels' perspective, beat DiMaggio to first base. Umpire Hick Cady saw things differently and ruled DiMaggio safe, touching off an argument that brought much of the Angels bench onto the field in protest. Cady's ruling stood and DiMaggio's streak was at thirty-four games.[21]

On July 5, DiMaggio was attempting to stretch his streak to forty at Seals Stadium against Hollywood. He posed for a photograph before the game with his brother, Vince, who had signed with the Sheiks after his release by San Francisco, and Vince joked about making a catch to stop Joe's streak. But there was little joking when the teenager failed in his first three times up against Tom Sheehan. When DiMaggio came to the plate in the eighth inning, the streak was once again on the line.

Sheehan quickly rang up two quick strikes. Sheiks catcher Johnny Bassler then called for curveballs three straight times and DiMaggio unflinchingly took all three, working Sheehan to a full count. Bassler called for Sheehan to throw yet another curve out of the strike zone, knowing the Seals outfielder would have to either chase a bad pitch or take a base on balls. Either way, the streak would be over.

Sheehan called time. When Bassler walked out to the mound, Sheehan told him, "I'm as anxious to horse collar this kid as you, but I ain't gonna walk him in his last at-bat. These fans will swarm the field and hang me from the flagpole if I do."

Bassler returned to his position behind the plate, called for a fastball, and DiMaggio calmly smacked it for a double to extend the streak.[22] "I gotta hand it to Joe," said Sheehan. "He had the guts to lay off the curve and wait for a fastball." Later that week, DiMaggio ran the streak to forty-five with a single, double and triple off Sheehan.

DiMaggio tied Jack Ness' record on July 13 against Los Angeles with a bloop single off Fay Thomas in the second inning. He added a home run and another single for good measure. In the same game, Jim Oglesby ran his streak to thirty-five, thanks to a double in the ninth inning.[23]

The next night, before 7,500 shivering fans at Seals Stadium, DiMaggio was honored for tying Ness' record. San Francisco mayor Angelo Rossi presented the outfielder a watch that was specially engraved to mark the occasion. DiMaggio looked at the timepiece and whispered to team president Charlie Graham that his name had been misspelled — just as it had been in newspaper headlines all season long — as "DeMaggio."

DiMaggio was starting to be called "Deadpan Joe" in recognition that his face remained expressionless under pressure. He maintained the façade, not even sneaking a smile when he smacked a first-inning single off Buck Newsom to break Ness' mark and extend his streak to fifty games.[24] The only record ahead of him was Joe Wilhoit's unbelievable sixty-nine-game streak, set in 1919 with Wichita of the Western League.

Joe DiMaggio, far left, Vince DiMaggio, far right. Their parents are immediately to the right of Joe DiMaggio in the photograph. Dominic DiMaggio is near the middle, the only person other than a little girl who is not wearing a hat in the photograph (San Francisco History Center, San Francisco Public Library).

Oglesby kept pace with DiMaggio until July 23, when he was finally stopped by Oakland's Roy Joiner, who struck him out with the bases loaded in the tenth inning. The Angels first baseman had finally been held hitless after forty-four straight games.

Ordinarily, Oglesby's accomplishment would have brought him national notoriety. These were not normal circumstances.[25] The same day Oglesby's streak ended, DiMaggio ran his to an unbelievable sixty with singles in each game of a doubleheader against Sacramento. He was awarded infield hits in each game — his only successes all day — that some in attendance thought should have been scored as errors.[26]

In his next game two days later, it appeared that DiMaggio would finally be stopped. Clearly exhausted, he was retired easily his first four times up by Oakland pitcher Mike Salinsen. The Seals were the home team and led, 6–5, in the bottom of the eighth. With DiMaggio due up seventh in what were probably the team's final at-bats, it seemed unlikely he would have the chance to hit again. Certain he had witnessed the end of an epic achievement, Jake Caveney shook hands with the youngster and told him, "Never mind kid, you broke the [Pacific Coast League] record anyway, and it will take a good man to beat what you've done."

But an amazing thing happened — the Seals first three batters reached safely. Salinsen was replaced by Lou McEvoy, who surrendered two more hits. Augie Galan slapped yet another single, and suddenly Joe DiMaggio was walking to the plate. Seals fans jumped to their feet, imploring their hero to get a hit.

He did not disappoint them, smashing a line shot over second base for a two-run single. Jake Caveney broke into a wide grin and the Seals players stood at the edge of the dugout, applauding the young star whose streak now stood at an incredible sixty-one games. San Francisco plated eight runs in the inning to win the game by a score of 14–5. (DiMaggio was providing virtually all of the excitement for Seals fans — the victory improved seventh-place San Francisco's record to a still-ghastly 43–70.)

After the game, DiMaggio said, "Salinsen's stuff did not fool me but I could not meet the ball solidly. The heat at Sacramento last week got me down a bit and as I am not used to playing every day I guess I am a little tired."[27]

Caveney moved DiMaggio to the leadoff spot in the order the next day to get him an extra at-bat if needed, but Oaks pitcher Ed Walsh Jr. easily dispatched him his first four times up. In the ninth inning with the score tied, 3–3, the Seals had a runner on third base with one out. Walsh intentionally passed Jimmy Zinn, an excellent hitting pitcher, but declined to walk DiMaggio to load the bases as percentages would have dictated so as not to unfairly deprive the young star a final opportunity to extend his record. Billy Raimondi sat in the Oakland dugout and had mixed feelings about his fellow Italian. "We didn't want to see the streak end," admitted Raimondi. "He was bringing in people."[28]

But Walsh was not going to give in. After falling behind with curveballs, Walsh threw a fastball and DiMaggio swung, lifting a high fly ball to right field. It was obvious the ball would be caught and the crowd groaned in disappointment. However, the ball was hit deep enough to score the winning run. Although hitless on the day, DiMaggio had won the game with his fly ball out. The streak finally over, fans tumbled out of the stands, eager to slap their hero on the back as he rushed silently, head down, to the clubhouse.

DiMaggio owned a .405 average with 104 hits in 257 at-bats during the streak, including sixteen doubles, six triples and eleven home runs. He had one four-hit game and ten times had three hits. Tellingly, he had no extra-base hits during the last ten games of the streak.[29] Justifiably proud of his accomplishment, he was quoted in the *San Francisco*

Chronicle as saying he was glad the ordeal was over and admitted, "The strain was getting a bit tough."[30]

In a two-month span, eighteen-year-old unknown Joe DiMaggio had established himself as the brightest young star in the Pacific Coast League, if not all of baseball.

* * *

The baseball prodigy of the San Francisco Seals was not the only teenage sensation in the Pacific Coast League. The Los Angeles Angels had a nineteen-year-old slugging third baseman creating headlines of his own. Former Santa Barbara area high school star Gene Lillard had first joined the Angels in the spring of 1932 after being recommended to the team by western writer and baseball aficionado W.C. Tuttle. According to *The Sporting News*, Lillard arrived at training camp wearing shoes three sizes too large, with the toes rolled up so it appeared as if he was wearing footwear more suited to a silent film comedian than a top minor league baseball player. But the teenager impressed Jack Lelivelt with his powerful wrists, solid hitting stroke and explosive throwing arm.[31] Finally shod with proper-size cleats a few days later, Lillard caught everyone's attention. Farmed out to the lower minors at the beginning of the year to gain experience, he was back with the Angels before the end of the 1932 season when Lelivelt decided to go with younger players.

Joe DiMaggio was not the only teenage wunderkind in the Pacific Coast League. Former Santa Barbara High School star Gene Lillard would make his mark with the great 1933–1935 Los Angeles Angels teams (Ray Saraceni Collection).

Lillard proved to be an impressive hitter in 1933; he had already hit twenty-four home runs the day DiMaggio's hitting streak ended. He needed to improve defensively, especially on quickening his reactions to hard-hit balls to either side of him. The Angels prescribed handball, feeling it would force him to be up on his toes and better prepared to react at the hot corner.[32]

The Angels surged to the top of the standings thanks not only to Lillard, but also to a pitching staff so deep the team did not miss a beat even after the Cubs recalled Lee Roy Herrmann in the midst of the pennant race for the second straight year.[33] Buck Newsom had become practically invincible; he celebrated his birthday on August 11 by striking out a dozen Seattle batters, including six in a row at one point, in a 15–0 victory.[34] By Labor Day the pennant race had narrowed to Hollywood and Los Angeles, the Southern California rivals having leap-frogged over both Sacramento and Portland and into the top two spots in the standings by compiling identical 22–11 records during August. The teams' ace pitchers, Buck Newsom and Frank Shellenback, faced each other on September 6, attracting a record crowd of 24,695 to Wrigley Field, more than nine thousand of them women attending the free "Ladies Night." Newsom defeated Shellenback, 2–0, for his twenty-sixth win and eighth shutout of the year. The Angels and Sheiks were tied for first place with identical records of 95 wins and 64 losses.[35]

The series was considered important enough that the league office provided three umpires the next night as the Sheiks scored five runs in the ninth inning to defeat the Angels, 11–8.[36] But Los Angeles assumed control of the pennant race by sweeping a double-header on September 10, with Buck Newsom and Dick Ward stopping the Sheiks before a crowd of more than eighteen thousand. Newsom's win was his twenty-seventh of the season — far surpassing his early-season guarantee of twenty victories — and his second win in a week against Frank Shellenback, a fact that he was not about to let pass without comment. "It was just a breeze," he said. "I only wish I had to pitch against Hollywood all my life. I'd never lose." He then added, "There ain't nothin' going to keep me from winning my thirty this season."[37]

Los Angeles and Hollywood met again a week later, with the Angels' lead having stretched to four games. Newsom defeated the Sheiks, 5–3, on September 19 for his twenty-ninth win of the season — and his fourteenth in a row — to put the Angels five games in front with thirteen to play. Gene Lillard added his fortieth home run in that game, joining Wally Berger as the only players in franchise history to reach that mark.[38]

Newsom defeated Hollywood again four days later, ending the pennant race for all practical purposes. It was his fifteenth win in a row, thirtieth of the season, and eighth consecutive against the Sheiks. Gene Lillard, six weeks shy of his twentieth birthday, hit a grand slam to extend his team record for home runs to forty-two.[39]

The Angels clinched the pennant two days later with a 9–6 win against San Francisco. The players were so excited they borrowed the Seals' 1931 championship banner, carefully hiding the year, and posed for photographers.[40]

Newsom was named the league's Most Valuable Player by *The Sporting News*, ahead of Missions outfielder Oscar Eckhardt, whose .414 batting average broke Ike Boone's league record. Drafted by the St. Louis Browns, Newsom remained in Los Angeles during the winter and celebrated the birth of a baby girl soon after New Year's Day.[41] Then Newsom packed up his family, jumped in his car and headed to the major leagues to become one of the game's most celebrated and colorful personalities.

* * *

"I know I have peculiarities. Every manager I've played for has told me I'm the weirdest batsman in captivity."[42]

Oscar Eckhardt, who owned a career minor league batting average that even Ty Cobb would envy, was frustrated by his failure to attract attention from the big leagues. Conventional wisdom suggested Eckhardt was simply too unorthodox. Despite hitting left-handed, Eckhardt hit the ball to left field almost exclusively. Distinctive with his black baseball bat, red undershirt and a crouch so exaggerated that his back knee almost touched the ground when he swung, Eckhardt waited until the very last moment before lashing at pitches, consistently sending line drives whistling down the third-base line. Opponents deployed their defenses as if he were a right-handed pull hitter.

Eckhardt's other trademarks were aggressiveness and speed. He attacked the game with the attitude of the University of Texas football player he had once been, punctuating his often foolhardy base running with dramatic head-first slides that sent clouds of dirt flying in all directions. His outfield play was, to put it mildly, somewhat reckless — he generally got a good jump on balls hit to either side but had trouble going back on fly balls. His throwing arm was average at best.[43]

Eckhardt debuted in the PCL with Seattle in 1929 and won his first batting title two years later with a .369 average for the Missions. Despite his success, Eckhardt continued hearing dismissive comments about the numbers he was compiling in light of his unorthodox style. He became increasingly sarcastic when commenting on his critics.

"I know I have peculiarities. Every manager I've played for has told me I'm the weirdest batsman in captivity" — Oscar Eckhardt (David Eskenazi Collection).

"Someone who was an authority on the subject told me I have thirty definite weaknesses at the plate," he said. "They began at my toes, followed up my legs, carried on through my torso, branched off on each arm and then went up to my cap. Somehow, and not withstanding my thirty weaknesses, the safe hits kept rattling off my bat."[44]

Eckhardt went to spring training with Detroit a couple of times and briefly reached the majors in 1932 with the Boston Braves, but the Braves returned him to the PCL after using him in only eight games, all as a pinch-hitter. At first he refused to report but joined the Missions after being threatened with suspension.[45] Eckhardt subsequently fashioned a thirty-three-game hitting streak during which he did not hit a single home run and easily captured his second PCL batting crown.[46]

Maintaining an enormous lead in the batting race at the mid-point of the 1933 season, Eckhardt grew increasingly frustrated as his unorthodox style was repeatedly thrown back in his face. He began to talk about quitting: "I've had two trips to the majors but never played a full game of ball all the time I was in the big show. Anybody'll tell you I don't boast, but I know darn well I can hit as well as a lot of the fellows up there if only given the chance. If something doesn't happen this year I'm going to throw my bat away and go to coaching football. It's not how you hit 'em but how often and where. I don't see why I should be passed up because I'm no Pavlowa."[47]

Six weeks later, as if to demonstrate he could hit for power if he wanted, Eckhardt blasted a Willie Ludolph pitch over the back fence behind center field at Seals Stadium, just to the left of the scoreboard and into a car parked on Sixteenth Street. It was the first time a ball had been hit over that fence.[48] But Eckhardt was not drafted by a major league team even after completing the best season of his career in 1933 — hitting .414, driving in 143 runs and collecting 315 hits. Despite the rejection, Eckhardt decided not to follow through on his retirement threat and the Missions welcomed him back for another season. At one point Bill Lane, a great admirer of Eckhardt, inquired about his availability in exchange for Cleo Carlyle.

Missions president Joe Bearwald snorted, "(I) would not trade Eckhardt for the whole Hollywood outfield, let alone Carlyle."[49]

* * *

The National Association tasked its new promotional director, National Football League president Joe Carr, with reviving minor league baseball. In February 1934 he announced that between four and eight new leagues would be established, a significant goal when one considers there were only fourteen in operation at the time. As grim as the situation was, Carr took heart in the fact that the 1933 season had seen all minor leagues complete their seasons for the first time in two decades.[50] But Joe Carr faced a monumental task. Night baseball had been a great innovation, but it could not offset the impact of the Depression or the rise of horse racing and other gambling pursuits that held the promise, however remote, of the possibility of quick cash. The heady days of the 1920s were over and the members of the National Association were in the midst of a major crisis. Most teams were battling for survival — a fight they were finding increasingly hard to win. The Pacific Coast League was far from immune to these ills; several franchises were in severe distress, including Portland, where there had been whispers about financial trouble throughout 1933. Those rumors were confirmed when Spencer Abbott announced he was leaving as manager of the Beavers at the end of the season because of the franchise's fiscal instability. This enraged Tom Turner, who felt he had made concessions to Abbott only to be betrayed.[51]

Tired of criticism and what he saw as interference in the way he wanted to run the team, Turner bought out John Shibe and acquired controlling interest in the franchise.[52] To replace Abbott as a box office attraction, Turner called on the man most synonymous with Portland's baseball past, fifty-seven-year-old living legend Walter McCredie, asking him to make one more comeback. Turner announced the team would recall its glory days by returning to the distinctive dark blue road uniforms of McCredie's heyday. The old man could not have been more thrilled.

"I have accepted the offer of Mr. Turner with pleasure that it is hard for any other person to understand," said McCredie. "The Portland Beavers have always been my favorite team and, though I have seen hundreds of players pass from its ranks, I am certain that my coming tenure will be as pleasant as my association with these players."[53]

The Seattle Indians were in equal distress. The team had survived the 1933 season only by selling its best players, Fred Muller and Melo Almada (the latter becoming the first Mexican-born player to reach the major leagues), to the Boston Red Sox at mid-season.

Convinced the two non–California teams would drag down the rest of the league, Bill Lane proposed Portland and Seattle be dropped and that the PCL become a six-team organization.[54] But the teams in California were not immune to financial hardship. After using the Sacramento Senators as collateral for less-profitable ventures, including some connected to his late brother, Lew Moreing was out of cash and faced foreclosure from the banks. He owed one hundred sixty thousand dollars to three different lending institutions and the bill was coming due. Moreing traveled to San Francisco in mid–February 1934 in a futile effort to raise capital and was forced to relinquish the franchise. The banks turned to Senators manager Earl McNeely to act as temporary caretaker.[55] Twenty-four hours later, McNeely convinced the banks to let him take over the team in return for a small down payment.[56] The Sacramento franchise would remain afloat, but there was little money supporting it.

*　*　*

Bill Lane had high hopes for the 1934 season, thanks to the acquisition of shortstop Jimmy Levey, pitcher Wally Hebert and the legendary Smead Jolley from the St. Louis Browns in exchange for shortstop Alan Strange.[57] But the Sheiks owner suffered a serious heart attack on Opening Day in Oakland and was confined to bed, curtailing his involvement with the team for the year.[58] The seventy-four-year-old Lane would not be seen in public all season other than a few visits he made to the ballpark against doctor's orders.[59]

Hollywood also lost second baseman Otis Brannan, the team's best clutch hitter and the glue of the infield, who refused to report.[60] His absence left an opening that was filled mid-year by the youngest starting player in league history to that time, future Hall-of-Fame second baseman Bobby Doerr. Doerr, whose father was a semi-pro player and brother, Harold, was a catcher in the PCL, was only sixteen years old when he moved into the Sheiks starting lineup for the last two months of the 1934 season.[61] Despite his youth, Doerr had already played in fast semi-pro leagues in Los Angeles, starting two games at age twelve for a team run by George Stovall.[62]

The day Bobby Doerr's junior year of high school ended, his father and brother met him at the school entrance and asked if he wanted to sign with Hollywood. Offered a two-year contract and a guarantee he would not be sent to another team, Doerr remembered, "There was no question about it. They gave me two hundred dollars a month, which was big money then. We went down to Sears-Roebuck and bought a seven-dollar and fifty-cent Gladstone suitcase. They [Hollywood] were going to leave on Monday to go to Sacramento and so I remember going home that day ... and everybody was crying because I was signing so young."[63]

Not every player PCL teams pursued was in high school. Charlie Graham made an unusual offer to the New York Yankees, proposing to "rent" Babe Ruth and have him play for the San Francisco Seals in 1934. Ruth had been ill and Graham felt that the western climate might be attractive to the home run king. He offered to pay Ruth's thirty-five-thousand-dollar salary, which he knew would be easily recouped by an increase in ticket sales. According to Graham's plan, Ruth would return to the Yankees after the season, as if he had only been optioned to San Francisco.[64] Of course, the deal was never seriously considered but it would have been intriguing to see Babe Ruth and Joe DiMaggio in the same lineup, something that never happened in New York.

The 1934 season would not prove memorable for Ruth, whose diminished performance offered proof that the end of his career was near, or for DiMaggio. Following a doubleheader on May 20, DiMaggio stumbled while exiting an automobile and badly wrenched his knee.[65]

He was out of the starting lineup for a full month, although he did manage to remind the Angels how dangerous a hitter he was by hobbling to the plate and blasting a pinch-hit home run only six days after his injury. DiMaggio returned in late June but he was clearly not completely healed and reinjured himself on August 10, ending his season.[66] Attempts by the Seals to sell him to the major leagues came up empty, causing deep concern for Charlie Graham. He had counted on selling his best prospect in order to keep the team solvent. Instead, teams were scared away, worried the knee injury was permanent. The magic touch of "Murder, Mayhem and Manslaughter" was in question.

* * *

Tom Turner was growing impatient in Portland. Walter McCredie had far less energy than the Beavers owner had hoped—in fact, he was a very sick man—and Turner failed to concede the Beavers were short on talent. McCredie was able to use his Detroit contacts to acquire outfielder Bill Lawrence on option, and the Beavers manager declared the 6'4" Lawrence was already the best center fielder in the PCL, if not all of baseball.[67] But the veteran manager was too sick to actively participate once the season started, and Turner manned the coaching lines during McCredie's convalescence. Portland lost fifteen of its first twenty-one games, leading to rumors that Turner was going to ask George Burns to take McCredie's place.[68]

By early May, McCredie was finally able to put on a uniform and sit on the bench, but the team's play failed to improve. On May 16, with the team in last place with a record of 11–28, Turner traded outfielder Henry Oana to Atlanta in the Southern Association, where Spencer Abbott had landed, and asked waivers on every other player on the team.[69] Six days later, Turner met with McCredie and told him he needed to take a rest. McCredie instantly understood that Turner was telling him he was through as manager. *Oregonian* columnist L.H. Gregory witnessed the poignant scene and saw that the old man was crushed.[70]

A day in McCredie's honor was scheduled for July 30—essentially to assist the Portland baseball icon financially because of mounting medical bills resulting from his lengthy hospitalization. Amazingly, Walter McCredie had never been honored in Portland, and he was heartened by the plans. Unfortunately, his health deteriorated rapidly and he was soon in the hospital again. By mid–July it was clear he was dying. Unable to rally his failing body, McCredie hoped the day in his honor would help his wife.

As he slipped in and out of consciousness, McCredie requested that Irv Higginbotham, Vean Gregg and Gus Fisher serve as honorary pallbearers at his funeral. The *Oregonian* reported that in his final hours, McCredie returned to baseball: "Toward the end his mind wandered and he imagined that he was playing again. 'Hit it out!' they heard him say once, and 'Slide!' And at the very end, his final words, just a few minutes before he ceased to breathe, 'Let the game go on.'" McCredie died on July 29, the day before the exhibition game in his honor.[71]

Meanwhile, the Portland Beavers were going downhill as surely as Walter McCredie had. Finally able to run the team his way, Tom Turner ran it into the ground. The Beavers compiled an embarrassing 66–117 record and attendance fell to slightly more than fifty thousand—with one-quarter of those attending on Opening Day. At the end of the 1934 season, Turner sold the team to Portland drug store owner E.J. Schefter.[72]

* * *

The Los Angeles Angels had not been considered a shoo-in to repeat in 1934; many anticipated a three-team race between the Angels, Hollywood and San Francisco. The Angels had lost their top two starting pitchers, Buck Newsom and Dick Ward, to the major leagues. As if to highlight the peculiarities of putting together a competitive team in the minor leagues, Los Angeles was further impacted when San Francisco traded shortstop Augie Galan to the Chicago Cubs. To complete the trade, the Cubs sent two pitchers they had optioned to Los Angeles — Lee Roy Herrmann and Win Ballou — to San Francisco.[73] This meant the Angels had lost two of their best pitchers to a rival while receiving nothing in return.

The Angels still had Fay Thomas, who compiled a season as impressive as Buck Newsom's 1933 campaign, winning twenty-eight of thirty-two decisions. The rotation also included right-handers Whitey Campbell, Mike Meola and Lou Garland, a hard thrower who would adopt Thomas' wicked forkball and compile a 21–9 record.

The 1934 Los Angeles Angels may or may not have been the best team in the history of the Pacific Coast League — the talent level of the league was not as it had been during the previous decade — but they destroyed the competition. Only Jim Morley's 1903 Angels had approached the way the 1934 team lapped the field. The infield of Oglesby, Reese, Dittmar and Lillard remained intact from the prior year, as did two-thirds of the outfield; the only change was Frank Demaree, the ex–Sacramento outfielder, who replaced Tuck Stainback.[74]

Players set several records. Despite the newly adopted "dead ball," Demaree pounded opposing pitchers at a record pace, smashing twenty-seven home runs in the first eleven weeks of the season, eventually becoming the only man in league history to hit forty home runs and steal forty bases in the same season. Fay Thomas, who had won his last seven decisions in 1933, won his first fifteen in 1934 to set a league record for consecutive wins.[75] On May 19, with Los Angeles sporting a record of 36–11, the Chicago Cubs returned Dick Ward to the Angels. It was an embarrassment of riches for Angels manager Jack Lelivelt.

The face of the Angels in their most dominant season remained the team's thirty-six-year-old center fielder, Arnold "Jigger" Statz, whose professional career began when he went directly from Holy Cross to the major leagues to play for John McGraw and the New York Giants in 1919.

Statz was the Opening Day center fielder for the Giants in 1920, batting fifth in the order and collecting two hits, including a triple. But he was waived by New York in June and claimed by the Boston Red Sox.[76] Two weeks after his acquisition, the Red Sox gave Statz his choice of going to either Indianapolis or Los Angeles. He chose California and began his first stint with the Angels.[77] Statz spent the rest of 1920 and all of 1921 with Los Angeles, playing alongside veteran outfielders Rube Ellis and Sam Crawford. It was Ellis who convinced Statz to cut the center out of his glove in order to make a better pocket, a habit Statz maintained for the rest of his career.[78] He helped the Angels win the 1921 pennant and impressed William Wrigley, who brought the young outfielder back to the majors to play for the other team he owned, the Chicago Cubs.

Statz spent three seasons as a regular for the Cubs before returning to Los Angeles in June 1925 as partial payment for Charlie Root.[79] He hit for the cycle to help christen Wrigley Field and then led the Angels to the 1926 pennant, earning his third trip to the major leagues, with the Brooklyn Dodgers. By 1929, Statz was back with the Angels to stay and was undoubtedly the most popular player the team ever had. Many rank him the greatest defensive outfielder in Pacific Coast League history.

Like Walter Carlisle before him, Statz played extremely shallow and used his speed to run down balls that appeared to be hit over his head. Unlike Carlisle, he did not turn somersaults. He instead closely watched his pitcher and shifted his defensive position based on the type of pitch thrown and the tendency of the hitter. Statz played the last 134 games of the 1926 season without making an error and was the only PCL outfielder to ever record five hundred putouts in one year; by 1931 he had accomplished it three times.

An excellent athlete and a scratch golfer, Statz was fanatical about taking care of himself. Convinced that his legs were the key to a long career, Statz thought that keeping his weight down was vital to preserving his quickness. He usually ate only two meals a day and eschewed desserts — other than pastry baked by his wife.[80] Statz never picked up a golf club during the season but credited his diligence in playing in the offseason with keeping his legs in shape.[81] No one could argue with his success.

With Los Angeles convincingly capturing both halves of the schedule (a 66–18 record in the first half and a mark of 71–32 in the second half), attendance plummeted league-wide. It was proposed that the Angels play a post-season series of games against an all-star team of players from the other teams in the league. Fans selected the opponents through a contest sponsored by Coast League newspapers and the series began at Wrigley Field on October 3.

The All-Stars roster included a number of familiar faces, including Ox Eckhardt, Sam Gibson, Herm Pillette, Smead Jolley, Johnny Bassler, Mike Hunt, Louie Almada and Babe Dahlgren. Joe DiMaggio did not participate because of his injured knee. It would not have mattered had he played; the Angels crushed the All-Stars in six games.

There was no doubt about the best team in the Pacific Coast League in 1934. Jack Lelivelt and the Los Angeles Angels had defeated the best the league had to offer.

* * *

After announcing his full-time return — and saying he took responsibility for Hollywood's poor showing — Bill Lane fired popular manager Oscar Vitt.[82] Vitt's replacement was another popular figure, pitcher Frank Shellenback, who as a playing manager helped cut costs. Although Shellenback was well liked, most fans were upset about Vitt's dismissal and many remarked that if Lane had been more involved with the franchise and given Vitt something to work with, there would have been no reason to make a change.[83] For his part, Shellenback spoke enthusiastically about his new job and, remaining only twenty-five victories short of three hundred in his Pacific Coast League career, promised to continue pitching.

"I don't plan on any radical changes from the way Oscar Vitt managed the club, but I do have a lot of my own ideas I want to try out," he said. "Ballplayers and children are much alike to handle. You have to be firm with them now and then to keep them in line, but you can't be too bossy with them and expect results." Shellenback also promised that the Sheiks would continue to be a "hustling club."[84]

When Shellenback arrived for spring training in March 1935, he discovered several of his Hollywood Sheiks wearing Chicago Cubs uniforms. It turned out the players were to perform as extras in the Joe E. Brown film, *Alibi Ike*, which had been largely inspired by Ring Lardner's retelling of stories related by PCL legend Ping Bodie. Even Johnny Bassler, who *never* arrived on the first day of training camp, was present and ready to go. Of course, Shellenback was not completely surprised by the turn of events — he was the film's technical director.[85]

* * *

In November 1934, a team of major league baseball stars, including Babe Ruth, Lou Gehrig and Jimmie Foxx, embarked on a playing tour of Japan.[86] The series of games was an enormous success and as a follow-up to the American visit, New York Giants outfielder Lefty O'Doul encouraged Japan's first professional team, the Tokyo Giants, to undertake a six-month tour of the United States and Canada in 1935.[87] That tour was also a financial and public relations success.

The Tokyo team that barnstormed across North America featured Japan's best players, including a pair of teenage pitching sensations, Eiji Sawamura and Russian-born Victor Starfin. The team played more than one hundred games in the United States and Canada during an itinerary that lasted through June.[88]

Lefty O'Doul had arranged the trip to Japan and remained a favorite both in the Far East and in his hometown of San Francisco. Since leaving the Seals after the 1927 season, O'Doul had won two National League batting titles, just missed beating out Rogers Hornsby for the National League Most Valuable Player Award in 1929, and had become one of the most popular players in New York. But as the 1935 season approached, the thirty-eight-year-old O'Doul realized he was nearing the end as a player. He approached Bill Terry, manager of the Giants, and asked for his release so he could accept an offer from Charlie Graham to manage the San Francisco Seals. The request was granted and O'Doul signed a three-year contract with San Francisco.[89] Over the next seventeen years, Lefty O'Doul and the San Francisco Seals would become inseparable in the minds of Pacific Coast League fans.

The team O'Doul was going to manage was not that much different than the 1934 edition, although the Seals had lost twenty-seven-game winner Lee Roy Herrmann, who was taken in the draft by the Cincinnati Reds.[90] There was also question about the condition of the team's star right fielder, Joe DiMaggio, who had been limited during the 1934 season by his knee injury.

Yankees scout Bill Essick was sure DiMaggio's knee would be fine. Along with Northern California scout Joe Devine, he had already convinced the New York Yankees to acquire DiMaggio, with the outfielder remaining in San Francisco for one more season. New York sent two players to the Seals immediately, pitcher Floyd Newkirk and outfielder Ted Norbert, and promised three more if DiMaggio proved as healthy as Essick said he was.[91] It was a good deal for the Seals, but there was no question DiMaggio's knee injury had knocked tens of thousands of dollars off his value and Charlie Graham needed every dollar he could get. It was a far cry from the deals the Seals had engineered to collect hundreds of thousands of dollars in the 1920s.

Meanwhile, the Hollywood Sheiks had a rough start to their season, beginning when catcher Johnny Bassler collapsed from an abdominal hemorrhage and nearly died in the dugout during an exhibition game against Chicago. Bassler was said by doctors to have lost half of his blood before he was stabilized.[92] Bill Lane made it clear that if Bassler could not play, he would still have a role on the team as a coach.[93] A photograph of Bassler appeared in the *Los Angeles Times* the next day, showing him propped up in bed smiling while holding a copy of his favorite newspaper's sports page.[94]

Lane's young middle infield combination was looking more and more like the salvation of the team. Still only seventeen years old, second baseman Bobby Doerr was a great hitter and a defensive whiz beyond his years, smoothly turning the double play as if he had been doing it for longer than he had been alive. Eddie Collins, considered the greatest second baseman of them all, journeyed to the Coast in July to personally inspect Doerr on behalf of the Boston Red Sox.[95]

Twenty-one-year-old shortstop George Myatt was another major league prospect. Like

Ernie Sulik, Mike Hunt and Joe DiMaggio (left to right) with the San Francisco Seals in 1934. Despite the outfielder's knee injury, the New York Yankees gambled that DiMaggio would be their next great star (San Francisco History Center, San Francisco Public Library).

Doerr, he had grown up playing for George Stovall in Long Beach, and the fiery ex–big leaguer could not help gushing over his protégés. "They're better right now than [Lyn] Lary and [Jimmie] Reese were when they broke in," Stovall said. "Nobody thought they'd hit like they are, and maybe they won't keep it up, but how are you going to prove they can't continue? They'll both go to the majors as sure as I'm sitting here."[96]

* * *

Los Angeles easily won the 1935 first-half championship and the Angels seemed poised to dominate the PCL for the third year in a row. But the second half started out a lot tighter than the first. On the morning of August 12, fans opened the sports page at the breakfast table to see that only two-and-a-half games separated the first-place Missions and Seals and the sixth-place Oakland Oaks.

San Francisco was led by a resurgent Joe DiMaggio, who flirted with the .400 mark most of the season and fashioned a twenty-seven-game hitting streak beginning in late June that sparked memories of 1933.[97] More importantly, he showed no lingering effects from his knee problems of the year before. Lefty O'Doul openly bragged about his young star and predicted he would be one of the all-time greats.

New York Yankees management felt much better about what had seemed to be a risky investment a year earlier. On August 15, the Seals moved DiMaggio from right field to center at the request of the Yankees, who wanted him to gain experience at the position he was expected to play for them.[98] At that point, the Seals were in a virtual tie with their co-tenants, the surprising Missions, who had finished last in the first half. Ox Eckhardt continued compiling his gaudy offensive statistics, carrying a .423 batting average into early August. First-half champion Los Angeles was struggling, but third baseman Gene Lillard was making a serious run at Tony Lazzeri's PCL home run record, hitting his forty-second on August 11. Three weeks later, Lillard had forty-seven home runs and was purchased by the Chicago Cubs for delivery in 1936.[99]

On September 4, the Seals finally opened up a two-game lead over the Missions thanks to a dramatic two-run pinch-hit home run by Lefty O'Doul that lifted them past Hollywood.[100] O'Doul again had a key hit a week later, a two-run single that sparked a four-run ninth-inning rally to defeat Oakland, putting the Seals five games up in the loss column over Portland and the Missions.[101] The Seals clinched the second-half title against the Angels on September 29 and then defeated Los Angeles in the playoffs.[102] Just as in 1931, when the Seals stopped Hollywood from winning its third straight PCL pennant, San Francisco had denied the Angels' attempt to accomplish the same feat.

* * *

The final day of the 1935 season was noteworthy for both milestones and antics. Gene Lillard hit his fifty-sixth home run in the first game of a doubleheader against Sacramento, breaking a tie with Ike Boone for the second-most home runs ever hit in a Pacific Coast League season.[103] Playing in twenty-seven fewer games than Tony Lazzeri in 1925, Lillard fell only four home runs short of the league record.

The Hollywood Sheiks and Mission Reds played their final games of the season at Wrigley Field, splitting a doubleheader highlighted by the appearance of Joe E. Brown, who served as master of ceremonies. Brown's foster son, former UCLA football star Mike Frankovich, was a catcher for the Missions and had six hits in nine at-bats during the doubleheader. When Frankovich hit a home run in the second game, Brown, who was "umpiring," playfully slapped him on the cheek as he rounded the bases.[104]

W.C. Tuttle's son pitched for the Sheiks in the nightcap while songwriter Harry Ruby played the final four innings of the game at second base. When Ruby stepped to the plate with two out in the ninth, Joe E. Brown took the mound for the Missions and struck him out to end the game and the season.[105] Although no one realized it at the time, Brown's dispatching of Ruby marked the end of the Hollywood Sheiks.

The league batting title went down to the final day of the season. Oscar Eckhardt sat out the second game against Hollywood to protect his .399 batting average and waited to see if it would be enough to hold off Joe DiMaggio for his fourth PCL batting championship. The Seals were hosting Seattle in another farcical doubleheader; DiMaggio bunted twice for hits in the first game when Seattle third baseman Dick Gyselman insisted on playing deep on the grass, and then hit a lazy fly ball that Bill Lawrence let fall for a double. DiMaggio was embarrassed by the display. Between games he tried to persuade the official scorer to call Lawrence's lack of effort an error, pleading, "I don't want to leave this league under any cloud."

But the ruling stood. In the second game, DiMaggio made sure that none of his hits were in doubt, slamming a pair of home runs and a double to give him a final batting average of .398, one point lower than Eckhardt.

The season concluded with Seals pitcher Walter Mails sending his outfielders to the dugout with two out in the final inning. After getting two strikes on the next hitter, Mails had his infielders walk off the playing field as well, leaving him alone on the diamond with his catcher. Mails then threw the third strike past the batter to end the game. As the *San Francisco Chronicle* put it, "It was probably a frame act, but it was a good one."[106]

* * *

After agreeing to contract terms with the Yankees in mid–February, Joe DiMaggio jumped into a car along with Frank Crosetti and Tony Lazzeri for the cross-country drive from San Francisco to his first spring training as a New York Yankee.[107] Surprisingly, Oscar Eckhardt was headed to the major leagues as well.

At age thirty-four, Eckhardt was invited to spring training in 1936 with Casey Stengel's Brooklyn Dodgers and was an early sensation. He even uncharacteristically pulled some pitches to right field, including a long drive over the right-field fence at Clearwater, Florida.[108] But Eckhardt was relegated to a reserve role once the season began, as even the legendarily unorthodox Stengel could not see playing the odd athlete on a seventh-place team going nowhere. Stengel tried to explain to Eckhardt that, unlike DiMaggio, he did not hit the ball hard enough to be successful in the major leagues.

"A lot of your hits out there with the Missions are just another put-out up here," Stengel told the outfielder, "because the fielders are faster, cover more ground and nip the runner by a foot on what would have been a safe hit out there."[109] Eckhardt did hit a home run off New York Giants pitcher Harry Gumbert, but after compiling a batting average of .182 in sixteen games, he was optioned to Indianapolis in the American Association.[110]

Two of the greatest stars to ever play in the Pacific Coast League were gone, but there was still plenty of talent in the league — and a new star to rival Joe DiMaggio was about to arrive on the scene.

CHAPTER TWELVE

1936 to 1937: Bill Lane Leaves Hollywood and Finds a Star

A weary Hy Baggerly had concluded that fulfilling his long-time desire to visit South America sounded more exciting, and far less risky, than remaining president of the Pacific Coast League. On November 5, 1935, he submitted his resignation, effective at the league meeting that would be held nine days later. Bill Lane snidely remarked that Baggerly had merely beaten the owners to the punch.[1]

The league president's announcement initiated a mad scramble as everyone from umpire George Hildebrand and Los Angeles newspaperman Jack James to former league presidents Harry Williams and Cal Ewing were rumored as possible successors. Predictably, when the owners met they could not agree on a replacement for Baggerly. Bill Lane was selected to act as interim president, and the directors tabled the matter.

But the league had problems that could not wait. The most pressing concern involved Earl McNeely's faltering effort to save Sacramento; he had been forced to sell players whose contracts had been used as collateral to keep the franchise afloat.[2] At seven o'clock on the morning of December 12, the phone rang in McNeely's home. Bill Killefer of the St. Louis Cardinals was at the other end of the line and he told McNeely, "If you can get us the franchise, the St. Louis Cardinals will take over the Sacramento team. We must know by 12 o'clock noon or the deal is off. I have the permission of Branch Rickey to make this transaction."[3]

McNeely arranged to have the franchise turned over to the Cardinals for five thousand dollars.[4] Of course, the Senators had almost no players and their finances were somewhat entangled with various banks, but conventional wisdom was that Cardinals president Branch Rickey would utilize his vast farm system to field a competitive team. Arrangements were made to lease Moreing Field for five years to the Cardinals.[5]

With the Sacramento situation apparently resolved, owners refocused their efforts at finding a new league president. Missions president Joe Bearwald had announced that Herbert Fleishhacker was selling the franchise to a group of businessmen who planned to move the team to San Diego. Bearwald then planned to resign his position in order to campaign for the presidency.[6] But Bearwald was too late on both counts.

Bill Lane had already arranged to relocate his Hollywood Sheiks to San Diego. At the same time, one of Lane's friends had already secured the votes for the league presidency; on December 16, Wilbur C. Tuttle was elected president of the Pacific Coast League.[7] The son of a frontier sheriff, Tuttle had gained fame and fortune during the previous two decades as an author of western novels, a number of which had been adapted for motion pictures.

The nearly bald Tuttle was a constant presence at Wrigley Field, instantly recognizable in his cowboy hat and striped western shirts. He would fancy himself as the Pacific Coast League's no-nonsense sheriff, demanding discipline from owners, umpires and players and dispensing his own particular brand of justice.[8]

* * *

Baseball had been played in San Diego as far back as 1871 when the first clubs — the Young Americans, Old San Diego and Lone Stars — were formed. The first organized game was staged on May 27 when the New San Diego Baseball Club played against the Extempore team of Old Town. It was not a particularly competitive contest since the team from Old Town had only seven players. The first proper game was played on July 4, when the Lone Star team defeated Old San Diego by a score of 51–8.[9] But the game was slow to take root in what was then best characterized as a sleepy border town. The most celebrated game during the early years of San Diego baseball, a fifteen-inning, 1–0 pitcher's duel in March 1901 between Dummy Taylor and Oscar Jones, is still considered a landmark in local baseball history.[10]

Bill Lane had always kept his eye on San Diego and in January 1936 decided the time was right. He met with a group dedicated to bringing the PCL to the city and announced a tentative agreement to relocate the Sheiks on the condition that a suitable ballpark would be constructed there.[11]

President Tuttle insisted that Lane would need support of three-fourths of the league directors in order to move his team, but Lane declared he would move to San Diego whether he got the votes or not. "If the other club owners were able to stop me from moving, who'd pay the rent at Wrigley Field? Not me," he said.[12] The next day, Tuttle announced that league directors had approved the franchise shift, although he would not divulge the vote. A new ballpark was to be built on the waterfront as a Works Progress Administration Project.[13] Joe Bearwald, cut off from his preferred destination, had no choice but to officially declare that the Missions would remain in San Francisco, at least for the 1936 season.[14]

Frank Shellenback continued as manager of the former Sheiks and insisted he would add to his league record for wins by a pitcher, which stood at two hundred eighty-nine and counting. Determined to reach the three-hundred-win mark, Shellenback had already pitched more than four thousand innings in the PCL. When asked if he thought about quitting to become a full-time bench manager, Shellenback insisted he had never felt better and said, "They'll have to knock me off that mound when I finally quit — and it'll take a lot of base hits to do it."[15]

* * *

Convinced that a vast wealth of untapped talent existed in California, St. Louis' Branch Rickey made a grand announcement that the Cardinals would fill out the Sacramento roster by holding a tryout camp for the purpose of finding talented, home-grown players.

President Tuttle said, "Rickey has my blessings and I hope he succeeds, but frankly, it's hard for me to make out whether he is being forced into this experiment by necessity or believes the scheme will work."[16] It didn't. By mid–February the team's roster consisted of only nine players, and that included four assigned on option from the Cardinals' Rochester farm team.[17] Rickey traveled to Sacramento in early March and visited the stadium, holding court for some young prospects playing an informal game. Before long, the Cardinals executive had shed his jacket and was on the field, running drills and dispensing individual instruction.[18]

The Cardinals may have stabilized the franchise financially, but Rickey had to admit in a speech the next day that Sacramento would not contend in its first year.[19] "The Pacific Coast League constitution requires that each club have at least fifteen players who have had Class A, or better, experience," said a greatly displeased Tuttle. "And unless Rickey lives up to this rule at Sacramento his franchise will be forfeited. At present, Sacramento has a flock of rookies at Riverside training camp who could not beat a Class D team." Tuttle went on to declare, "I do not propose to sit idly by and let Branch Rickey prostitute Pacific Coast League baseball."

Ignoring the fact that no one else was willing to step in and assume the debts of the franchise, Tuttle gave Rickey a week to strengthen the team or lose it. Rickey refused to take the bait and insisted on patience. His aide, Charles Kelchner, took a less tactful approach, calling Tuttle "a rookie president trying to make the grade in professional baseball."

Tuttle retorted, "I'll admit that, but there's nothing in the league rules that prevent a rookie from being president. The rules say a club can't have rookie players."[20]

* * *

Beginning his second year in charge, Portland Beavers president E.J. Schefter thought it time to remake the Portland roster. Soon, he had the oldest team in the league, with a dozen players age thirty or older. One of those veterans was a sore-armed submarine pitcher who had written every Pacific Coast League team in the offseason in a last-ditch effort to forestall retirement.

Ad Liska had adopted his unique underhand style while pitching for Minneapolis in 1928, making it a staple of his repertoire because of arm problems.[21] After mastering the delivery, Liska won twenty games and lost only four for the Millers and was purchased by the Washington Senators for an amount said to be the most paid by Clark Griffith since his acquisition of Earl McNeely.[22]

Ad Liska wrote to every Pacific Coast league team in 1936 in the hope of salvaging his career. Only the Portland Beavers responded. Liska would pitch fourteen seasons for the Beavers, winning 198 games and two PCL pennants (Ray Saraceni Collection).

Liska pitched for Washington in 1929 and 1930 but missed almost all of 1931 when his arm problems returned. Ineffective after his recovery, by 1936 Liska was preparing to begin corporate training with C & H Sugar in Hawaii and decided to take one last shot at keeping his pitching career alive. He wrote letters to all eight Pacific Coast League teams, reasoning that if he did not make a team at least he could cover the cost of a train trip to the West Coast. Only Portland responded. Liska stopped in Oregon, prepared to fly on to Hawaii if he was not signed. The Beavers decided to extend Liska's baseball career and he instantly became one of the anchors of the pitching staff.[23]

Liska's knuckles almost scraped the mound when he threw; veteran PCL pitcher Frank Dasso recalled, "He'd [Liska] throw the resin bag down alongside his foot and throw the ball right out of that bag."[24] Whenever the San Francisco Seals played against Liska, Lefty O'Doul would offer young players ten dollars if they hit a fly ball the first time they faced him.[25] John Leovich, a catcher for Portland in the early 1940s, marveled at Liska's control: "I could have caught him in a rocking chair." He added, "The minute I threw the ball back to him, I'd better be ready because he was ready to fire it back."[26]

Liska quickly became a favorite of the workers who watched him from the windows of the metal foundry beyond the right-field fence at Vaughn Street Park. They made a special iron baseball for him that he used for warming up the same way batters used weighted bats.[27] The foundry also proved a home field advantage. Lilio Marcucci remembered, "Sometimes when they had the furnaces going, the smoke would blow onto the field and they'd have to call time and see if they could get rid of it."[28]

Whenever Ad Liska took the mound for the Beavers during his fourteen seasons with them, he was motivated by other PCL teams not having even bothered to answer his letter in the spring of 1936. He said, "I thought of that every time I went out there."[29]

* * *

On March 28, 1936, Bill Lane's brand-new San Diego Padres opened at Wrigley Field, their home the previous year as the Hollywood Sheiks. The Padres had an enthusiastic rooting section since many of the Hollywood faithful came to say goodbye to what had been their team. San Diego shortstop George Myatt lined the first pitch of the game for a single off Los Angeles starter Fay Thomas to ignite a two-run first inning, but Thomas and the Angels eventually won the game, 7–5. The hitting star in a losing cause was Padres first baseman Ray Jacobs, a long-time former Angels player who drove in four runs with a double and two singles. He also had the most telling blow of the game, a line drive off Thomas' pitching hand, causing a wound that required three stitches and knocked the veteran pitcher out of action for a month.[30]

Lane's new stadium — creatively named after him — was hurriedly completed. When the Padres arrived at their new home, it was still lacking a roof over the grandstand and had a backstop located only thirty-one-and-a-half feet behind home plate. The facility impressed few observers in any way other than the speed at which it was constructed. Some of the bleachers were left over from the motorcycle race track that had occupied the site. The infield was the worst in the league, composed of "sandy dust" so loose that players left holes behind when they ran on it.[31] San Diego sportswriter Earl Keller quipped, "Lane Field was falling apart the day it was finished."[32]

More than ten thousand fans attended San Diego's home opener and the Padres scored five runs in the third inning to drive Seattle pitcher Dick Barrett to the showers. Herm Pillette made the runs stand up as San Diego won, 6–2. Pillette even drove in the Padres' final run with a single in the seventh inning.[33]

Aerial view of Lane Field, San Diego. Coronado Island is in the distance (San Diego Hall of Champions).

Manager Frank Shellenback took the mound the next day against Seattle, wearing the same glove he had used for every game he had pitched since 1924, and picked up his 290th career Pacific Coast League win by a score of 10–5. He also collected two of the team's seventeen hits against four Indians pitchers.[34] But back and leg injuries hampered Shellenback as the season wore on, and after pulling himself out of a July 4 doubleheader, he began to accept that he was not going to achieve his long-time goal of reaching three hundred wins in the PCL.[35] He turned his focus more and more to managing.

San Diego fans quickly demonstrated that they fit the rough-and-tumble Pacific Coast League. Several of them cornered President Tuttle after a game against Seattle and demanded that he remove umpire Jack Powell, who had ruled that a line drive hit by Padres outfielder Cedric Durst was a foul ball. Durst's teammates drove small stakes into the ground in fair territory, encircling the indentation they claimed had been caused by the ball. During a series against Portland the next week, fans showered the playing field with cushions and bottles, again in protest of a ruling by Powell, who had called Durst out on a close play at first base. It took thirty minutes to clear the field. That night, police provided a protective escort for Powell and fellow umpire Bill Engeln as they went to the train station for their next series.[36]

Bill Lane was incensed by the resulting press coverage, especially that of *Los Angeles Examiner* reporter Bob Hunter, who wrote that Padres fans attacked a policeman and threatened Tuttle during the melee. Hunter also reported that Portland players had wielded baseball bats to keep the crowd from storming the field.[37] The *Examiner* was banned from Lane Field and the newspaper, which featured daily coverage of the Padres because of its large circulation in San Diego, made plans to circumvent the ban by erecting a pole outside the stadium with a platform atop it from which Hunter would report on the games.[38] Lane calmed down and the pole was never put in place.[39]

In late June, it was announced that Lane Field would be properly completed while the Padres were on the road. A roof would be put over the grandstand and a press box constructed, delighting reporters who had to sit among the spectators, to the irritation of both parties, during the first three months of the season.[40] Energized by the positive reception of the team by the city of San Diego, Lane uncharacteristically embraced innovations he had previously rejected. He installed lights and began testing them in anticipation of introducing night baseball later in the summer.[41] He also devised all manner of creative promotions to entice fans to the ballpark. In August, George Myatt, one of the league's fastest men and author of the team's first base hit, accomplished another first when he was married at home plate at Lane Field before a crowd of nine thousand.[42] Halfway through the season, Lane noted that the Padres had already drawn more fans than the Sheiks had during all of 1935 at Wrigley Field.[43]

Another coup for Lane was the signing in June of a local drawing card: a half–Hispanic high school pitcher who had recently graduated from San Diego's Herbert Hoover High School. It had not been easy to land the youngster; Lane had to outbid both the New York Yankees and St. Louis Cardinals for his services.[44] The Padres announced that the future star would not pitch for San Diego but would instead be moved to the outfield because of his hitting ability.[45]

When he first joined the team, the teenager stood in front of the mirror in the Padres clubhouse, practicing different batting stances and checking out his swing, behavior that drew laughter from his new teammates.[46] The painfully skinny kid, a splinter at 6'3" tall and 147 pounds, paid no mind. Frank Shellenback was throwing batting practice one day as the youngster stood quietly off to the side, watching. When one of the veterans started to take his turn in the batting cage, Shellenback waved him away and pointing to the youngster shouted, "Let the kid get in and hit a few!" Bobby Doerr was standing nearby and heard the grumbling of the veterans, who resented that their time was going to be taken up by the scrawny teenager. Then they saw what he could do with a bat. "He hit about seven balls out, and two were out of the *ballpark*," remembered Doerr. "He hit *shots*. The guys said, 'Good night! Who's *this* guy?'"[47]

Lane's find made his debut on June 27, pinch-hitting for pitcher Jack Hile. With that, Theodore Samuel "Ted" Williams began his professional baseball career.[48]

* * *

There was no question that the San Francisco Seals had lost a major talent with the sale of Joe DiMaggio to the New York Yankees. But Lefty O'Doul still had a star outfielder in Joe Marty, who was judged by many to be nearly as good a prospect as DiMaggio. In later years, Lefty O'Doul would claim that Marty had more natural talent than the Yankees superstar.[49]

The twenty-one-year-old was discovered in Sacramento by George Putnam and possessed all the physical tools a ballplayer needed — power, speed and a strong throwing arm. But he lacked the burning desire to take his game to the next level. As an American Legion baseball star, Marty had to be picked up at his house for each game or the coach would not be sure he would show up.[50] Sacramento sportswriter Bill Conlin said that an eighteen-year-old Marty was scouted by Lew Moreing and the Senators owner decided not to sign him after noticing that when Marty was not due to bat, he would walk over and plop himself under a shade tree instead of coming to the bench. According to Conlin, Moreing said, "If the kid is that lazy, I don't want him on my club."[51]

After Marty won the PCL batting title in 1936, he was sold to the Chicago Cubs and discovered liquor. He roomed with pitcher Tex Carleton, who asked him, "Kid, what do you drink on the coast?"

Marty replied, "I'm a beer drinker."

Carleton said, "Kid, you gotta quit. That beer is bad for you. It'll slow you down. You should drink scotch."

Marty told Bill Conlin, "I took the big leaguer's advice and I've been drinking it ever since."[52]

* * *

Even though manager Max Bishop was dismissed in May over his refusal to play second base, the Portland Beavers captured the 1936 pennant in one of the closest races in league history and then easily dispatched Seattle and Oakland in the playoffs, losing only one game. There was grumbling that Portland had violated league rules by having too many veterans on the roster but Bill Sweeney, who had taken over for Bishop as manager, laughed at the notion that Portland would have to forfeit its title.[53]

One surprise at the end of the season was the resignation of Los Angeles Angels manager Jack Lelivelt. Even though the team had finished out of the playoffs, the Angels had been beset by injuries and it was thought that Lelivelt's position was secure. But Angels president Dave Fleming was unhappy, insisting that Lelivelt had been given carte blanche to secure players he needed to turn the team around.[54] Lelivelt, who had stated in June he would probably quit, responded by saying that he wanted to take a break from managing. *Los Angeles Times* sportswriter Bob Ray surmised that the resignation might not have been entirely voluntarily and pointed to the rumors of discord between Lelivelt and Fleming.[55]

Whatever the cause of Lelivelt's withdrawal from the Los Angeles baseball scene, one of the league's most successful managers was no longer with the Angels. He accepted an offer to scout for the Chicago Cubs, the other team owned by P.K. Wrigley.

Another popular figure left the PCL in December 1936 when Joe Marty was sold to the Chicago Cubs in a deal Charlie Graham said "kept the sheriff from the door."[56] Marty's replacement in center field was a brand-new face with an old, familiar name. Dominic DiMaggio was a slight, frail-looking twenty-year-old who wore glasses and weighed less than one hundred and sixty pounds. His physique was nothing like that of his brothers, but when he hit the ball it was clear he was a DiMaggio. Dominic's signing was marked with a special ceremony that included his being carted into Seals Stadium in a wheelbarrow pushed by his brother, Joe.[57]

Lefty O'Doul immediately began working with the younger DiMaggio to eliminate a bad habit he had developed on the San Francisco sandlots. "He was, very definitely, the one person who helped me to be the hitter that I was," recalled DiMaggio. "I used to lunge. My body would go forward into the ball. I thought I would get more power that way. I was wrong. I had to keep my body back."[58]

DiMaggio, who played shortstop during his amateur days, was converted to the outfield, just as his brother Joe had been. O'Doul turned the youngster into a pull hitter — something that DiMaggio later changed when he went to Boston and realized that his line drive stroke was not a good match for Fenway Park's Green Monster.

During the summer of 1937, the elder Dominic DiMaggio, fisherman father of the young man playing center field for the San Francisco Seals, swelled with pride as he spoke of his three baseball-playing sons. Two years retired from fishing, the patriarch of the DiMaggio baseball dynasty would pore over box scores every morning, looking to see how Joe and Vince were doing in the major leagues. Then he went to Seals Stadium in the afternoon to watch his youngest son. For the edification of those unable to attend the game, each evening the sixty-five-year-old re-enacted plays made by the younger Dominic at Seals Stadium earlier that day.[59] No prouder father of three sons could be found anywhere.

* * *

Cal Ewing had remained in touch with baseball following his resignation as a director of the Oakland Oaks. He attended as many games as he could, sitting in the front row of the director's box in back of home plate at Oaks Park, or behind third base at Seals Stadium with friend Eddie Carey. He attended baseball's winter meetings every year and was honored at a dinner in Oakland where he was photographed with former PCL presidents Hy Baggerly, William McCarthy, Allan Baum and Thomas Graham. Ewing was getting older, yet his love for the game was undiminished.

Ewing's health began to fail after his wife was fatally injured in the explosion of a gas stove at their home in 1935. A year later he suffered a serious stroke and was confined to bed. For the first time in decades he did not attend the winter meetings. On January 18, 1937, the seventy-year-old Ewing sat in bed talking to his daughters, now fully grown with families of their own, and his thoughts turned to his old friend Mike Sexton, the former National Association president who had died the day before. The old man and his daughters talked into the early evening until he grew tired. Ready to go to sleep, Ewing kissed his daughters good night and turned out the light. He never woke up.

The next day, the daughters spoke of their father and paged through the scrapbook they had kept since he first took them to his games. Telegrams and tributes flowed from across the country. Charlie Graham, reminding everyone how Ewing had saved the PCL after the San Francisco earthquake, spoke of how strange it would be looking over at Ewing's old spot at Oaks Park and not seeing him there. On Opening Day in Oakland, after the playing of "The Star Spangled Banner," Ewing was remembered with a full minute of silence. After bowed heads were raised, the umpire yelled, "Play ball!" and action began, just as Cal Ewing would have wanted.[60]

* * *

Despite his run-ins with various Pacific Coast League factions, Wilbur "Two-Gun" Tuttle was re-elected in November to a three-year term, presumably because the owners realized they would never find anyone else willing to take the job for only $4,500 a year. In reaction to the news, league secretary Frank Herman decided he'd had enough of the colorful western novelist and resigned.[61] Tuttle named former league president Harry Williams as Herman's replacement.[62]

Sacramento was turning things around in its second season under Cardinals ownership and veterans were spearheading the charge from incompetence to contention. Thirty-six-year-old outfielder Nick Cullop, who already had more than three hundred career home runs in the minor leagues, hit the ball as hard as anyone, scaring pitchers and infielders alike. He and twenty-nine-year-old third baseman Art Garibaldi led a potent Solons offensive lineup. Branch Rickey had held up his part of the bargain in making sure Sacramento had a contender—and fans were beginning to hope that at long last they had a team that would win a Pacific Coast League pennant.

The team's most significant acquisition was actually an old face: twenty-nine-year-old pitcher Tony Freitas. Having grown up in Mill Valley, north of San Francisco, Freitas used to watch the Seals play in Recreation Park and always made sure to be at the train station to see Smead Jolley whenever the slugger visited Freitas' hometown.[63]

The left-hander had made his debut with Sacramento in 1929 thanks to a recommendation from a cab driver who knew Senators manager Bud Ryan. A pitcher who relied on control and savvy ("I never did have what they call a good fastball, so I had to rely on the three Cs — control, change-ups and curveballs"), Freitas remained with the Senators until he was sold to the Philadelphia Athletics during the 1932 season, shortly after throwing a no-hitter against Oakland on his twenty-fourth birthday.[64] Freitas won his first six decisions for Connie Mack and finished the season with a 12–5 record.[65] He played briefly for Portland in 1933 and then returned to the majors with the Cincinnati Reds. He enjoyed his best major league moment against Dizzy Dean and the St. Louis Cardinals, engaging in a pitcher's duel with Dean for seventeen innings before the Cardinals finally prevailed in the eighteenth.[66] Although he'd had a taste of the big leagues, Freitas was far from disappointed about returning to the PCL: "I think that everybody that came back to the Coast League always said, 'This is the place I want to finish my career.' Everybody liked it out here. The big leaguers would say, 'If you can't play in the big leagues, this is the place to play.'"[67] Freitas' normal routine included pitching batting practice every other day during spring training while also running and playing pepper; he stopped pitching batting practice once the season started. A competitor whose winning attitude would carry Sacramento to numerous victories over the years — the 1937 season would mark the first of six consecutive twenty-win seasons for him — Freitas had a simple philosophy: "Every time I went out on that mound, I went out there for one reason. That was to win. (The opposition) changed my mind a few times, but they didn't change my attitude."[68]

By mid–June, the Solons were hanging onto first place by two games. Although manager Bill Killefer worried about his team's lack of depth should injuries strike, the Solons kept pace with the leaders as the summer wore on. But Sacramento lost seven straight games to Los Angeles at the end of July and the Solons were suddenly three-and-a-half games behind San Diego. Despite the slump, the Solons slid no further.

On August 19, the Solons were to host the first-place San Diego Padres in a key game. That afternoon, Bill Killefer received a phone call from umpire Jack Powell, who asked if he could borrow fifty dollars to stave off some unspecified trouble. The Solons manager went to Powell's hotel and handed him the money in person, both to see that it was indeed Powell who had called him and that the umpire was all right. Satisfied, Killefer returned to the stadium to prepare for that night's game.

But Powell, a stubborn man with more than three decades in the game and easily the most respected umpire in the league, was not all right. When he arrived at the stadium that evening, it was apparent why he had wanted the fifty dollars. Jack Powell had never been known as a drinking man, but on this night he was drunk and had an attitude.

Sacramento Union sports editor Steve George, a friend of Powell's, witnessed the umpire's arrival at the ballpark at seven-thirty. When Powell saw George, he exclaimed, "The great Powell is retiring, Steve. I'm through. I'm going to give you a great story some day. Steve, this is the last of Umpire Powell." Steve George spent the next fifteen minutes, along with the other umpires, trying to talk the drunken Powell out of going onto the field. Powell brushed aside any suggestion of that. "My duty is out there on that field," he said. "When I quit, I quit. I'm not running out."

Powell staggered out of the dressing room several minutes late and began arguing with everyone he came in contact with. Once the game started he made a farce of it, calling Sacramento's Lou Vezilich out on a steal attempt even as the ball clearly rolled away from Padres shortstop Joe Berkowitz. Solons president Phil Bartelme finally ordered the police to escort Powell from the grounds. Powell resisted, and it took three officers to finally subdue him as fans were treated to the unique spectacle of an umpire being handcuffed on the baseball diamond and hauled away to be booked for being drunk in public.[69] After being processed, Powell was bailed out by San Diego second baseman Jimmie Reese. Steve George castigated Powell, pointedly asking, "You've made it tough on your friends, Jack. What made you do it?"

The umpire offered no explanation for his actions. He said only, "Write as you have always written, Steve. Just as you see it and on the up and up.... I know what you will write will be the truth. Anyway, I went out in a blaze of glory, didn't I?"[70] Wilbur Tuttle fired Powell the next morning although he would later make a comeback and become chief of PCL umpires.[71]

Sacramento continued winning after the Powell incident while the Padres faltered. After sweeping a doubleheader on September 6 against Oakland, the Solons were four-and-a-half games ahead. Three days later the lead was up to six games and they were never headed, finishing four games ahead of San Francisco. The Padres faded to third place, one game behind the Seals.

* * *

Ted Williams had exceeded expectations in 1936, hitting .271 in just over one hundred at-bats for San Diego. During the day, Williams worked with veteran Cedric Durst on his outfield play. After games, he would take extra baseballs home so boys in his neighborhood could throw batting practice to him.[72] Frank Shellenback praised Williams' defense and insisted that he would have hit over .300 in his rookie season had he been with the team all year.[73] Recognizing that Williams was not only extremely talented but also extremely intense, the Padres manager asked veteran pitcher Herm Pillette to room with the youngster on the road.[74]

Ted Williams. "He hit about seven balls out and two were out of the ballpark. He hit shots. The guys said, 'Good night! Who's this guy?'" — Bobby Doerr (San Diego Hall of Champions).

Williams was not yet nineteen years old as the 1937 season began, but Shellenback was soon writing the teenager's name into the lineup as the left fielder nearly every day. On June 22, Williams won a game at Lane Field against Portland with a two-run inside-the-park home run in the eighth inning off Bill Posedel. The ball traveled nearly 460 feet to straight-away center field before Beavers outfielders Moose Clabaugh and Nino Bongiovanni could track it down. He also made a spectacular one-handed leaping catch for the final out of the game.[75] Three weeks later, Williams hit two home runs in another game at Lane Field, against the Missions, and repeated the feat on September 1 with a pair of homers off San Francisco's Sam Gibson, with the second clearing the street behind the stadium.[76]

Even crafty veteran Ad Liska found pitching to Williams a challenge. When the two faced each other in a game on August 25, Liska decided to go right at the youngster, who responded with two screaming line drives along the first-base line, just foul. After working the count full, Liska challenged Williams twice more, with the same result. He finally gave in and walked him.[77]

Williams finished third in the league in home runs in 1937 despite playing in only 138 of 178 games. "The kid's a natural," marveled Shellenback. "I can't see how Williams can miss being a big league star during the next ten years."[78]

Lefty O'Doul also raved about the skinny outfielder and tried to convince Charlie Graham to acquire him for San Francisco. But Bill Lane was well aware of what he had. He sold Williams to the Boston Red Sox at the end of the season, where he joined ex–Padre Bobby Doerr in the Red Sox organization. Williams initially believed the news that he had been sold was a joke, but he was ecstatic after learning it was true. While it was hoped that

Frank Shellenback taking charge of his San Diego Padres during spring training in 1937. Ted Williams can be seen poking his head in, second from the right in the bottom row (David Eskenazi Collection).

Williams would spend one more season in San Diego, the Red Sox decided to send him to Minneapolis instead.[79]

* * *

Seattle pitcher Dick Barrett entered the final week of the 1937 season with seventeen wins. Team president Bill Klepper had guaranteed Barrett a two-hundred-fifty-dollar bonus if he won twenty, something Klepper had thought unlikely since the pitcher spent spring training with Cincinnati and had not made his first start for Seattle until May.

The Indians were hosting Sacramento to close out the year and Barrett won the first game of the series. He then sat. And sat. And continued to sit. Barrett remained on the bench even though everyone wanted to see him get twenty wins and the bonus; everyone, that is, except Bill Klepper. Barrett finally pitched again in the first game of the doubleheader on the final day of the season, earning his nineteenth win by scattering four hits in a 4–1 victory. Barrett's teammates lobbied manager Johnny Bassler to pitch the veteran in the second game — not that Bassler really needed convincing. Learning of this, Klepper visited Bassler in the clubhouse between games and ordered him to pitch Marion Oppelt in the nightcap, insisting that the bonus should be for games that meant something, not for wins after Sacramento had already clinched first place. Bassler shouted back, "I'm running this ball club and Barrett is going to pitch!"[80]

Klepper stalked out of the clubhouse, muttering that the decision was "going to cost" Bassler. Witnessing the spectacle, the Seattle players rallied around their manager and ace pitcher and vowed to win the game.[81] Hal Spindel, who caught both games, said, "and did we all fight to put [Barrett] over."[82] Seattle was ahead, 11–0, by the third inning and Barrett, whose foot had been badly bruised in the first game on a line smash through the box, coasted to his twentieth victory of the season.[83]

Meanwhile, the reason for Klepper's tightfisted attitude became apparent when federal treasury agents, state police and city officials descended on the box office to collect thousands of dollars owed for state and federal taxes. A half-dozen government agents began pounding on the box office doors, threatening to break them down. Stadium manager Bill Coyle, a city employee and former star college quarterback, realized the Indians had not yet paid the stadium rent and grabbed whatever money he could. Scurrying out the door, he shouted over his shoulder, "The city's got the rent money; now you fellows can fight over the rest!"[84]

The team was in obvious disarray. *Seattle Post-Intelligencer* sportswriter Royal Brougham reported that team director Lloyd Nelson had paid the back salaries of players in exchange for the contracts of four Seattle players. Brougham also said that Klepper had tangled with one of his players and left the clubhouse with a black eye.[85]

The next day Klepper fired Bassler for insubordination. Team vice president John Savage announced that Bassler would also be fined five hundred dollars, but the other team directors overruled him. Bassler was out as manager, but he was not fined.[86]

* * *

Although Sacramento had finished the regular season in first place, under the Shaughnessy Plan adopted by the Pacific Coast League, that meant nothing. The top four teams in the league advanced to a post-season playoff. To capture the 1937 pennant, the Solons had to win two series, beginning with San Diego as an opponent. Unfortunately, Sacramento was swept in the first series by the Padres, who in turn swept the Portland Beavers in four games — winning eight straight playoff games to capture their first PCL pennant in San Diego.[87] (The second-place San Francisco Seals were swept by Portland in the first round of the playoffs, but Charlie Graham was impressed with his team's effort and announced that Lefty O'Doul would be named manager of the Seals for life. It would eventually mean Graham's life, not O'Doul's.)[88]

Despite finishing in first place after one hundred and seventy-eight games, one bad week cost the Solons their first PCL pennant, extending nearly three decades of frustration. In recognition of the unfairness of the situation, league directors decided that beginning in 1938 the winner of the regular season would be declared league champion, while the winner of the Shaughnessy Playoff would take home what would be called the Governor's Cup and a cash prize. It was a great idea, but it came a little too late for the 1937 Sacramento Solons.

* * *

After the debacle on the final day of the 1937 season, the Seattle Indians directors finally had enough of Bill Klepper. Shirley Parker, a former University of Washington quarterback and organizer of the Western International League, offered to purchase majority ownership amid rumors that Klepper, in a fit of spite, had traveled to Los Angeles to sell his interest to a group that would move the team to Hollywood. Klepper worked successfully to thwart Parker, who withdrew his offer because of the chaos surrounding the team.[89] There were a number of rumors about who would take over the franchise, but most were simply that and nothing more. Four times team directors postponed meetings that were to settle the financial status of the franchise. Bill Klepper was finally instructed by the team's directors to attend the minor league meetings in Chicago in early December. Former Gonzaga athletic director Bill Mulligan, who was said to be representing a mystery buyer for the Seattle franchise, accompanied Klepper on the trip. "Mr. X," as the buyer was called, was reportedly offering to advance funds to erase the team's debts and build a new stadium.[90] "Mr. X" would prove to be more than a rumor; he was a brewery magnate named Emil Sick.

CHAPTER THIRTEEN

1938 to 1941: A New Wizard
for the Emerald City

In December 1937, Emil Sick announced he was purchasing the Seattle Indians—although it might be more accurate to say he was rescuing them. The Indians had only one first-division finish in the previous ten years, and Sick declared he wanted to establish a winning baseball team in the Pacific Northwest. To help accomplish that goal, the Rainier Brewery owner announced that his old friend, New York Yankees owner Jacob Ruppert, would provide assistance by steering talent to Seattle.[1]

Emil Sick was one of the most respected businessmen in the Pacific Northwest and both willing and able to transform the franchise into a first-class organization. According to Frank Finch of the *Los Angeles Times*, Sick had "a bankroll that would clog one of those spillways in Hoover Dam."[2]

Sick announced that Seattle's new manager would be Jack Lelivelt and the choice was a popular one. Lelivelt signed a three-year contract and was assured there would be no interference from the front office.[3] Sick also promised to build a new ballpark for the team, which he was re-christening "Rainiers" in honor of his brewery.[4] He retired the team's debts and began construction on the new ballpark, to be called Sick's Stadium, at the site of old Dugdale Field. Because of the late change in ownership, the Rainiers had only sixteen players on the roster when Sick bought them and the core of the team would not look much different than the 1937 version except for first baseman Len Gabrielson, on option from the Yankees, and two local high school stars, outfielder Edo Vanni and pitcher Fred Hutchinson. But along with Jack Lelivelt, they would transform the team's fortunes; for two decades Seattle had been a drain on the league. Thanks to Emil Sick, the Rainiers were to become a cornerstone of the PCL and one of the most successful franchises in all of baseball.

* * *

Although the situation in Seattle had been straightened out, the last team in the PCL without its own stadium — the Missions — finally confirmed what had been an open secret. Herbert Fleishhacker was moving the franchise from San Francisco to Hollywood. Nationally renowned advertising executive Don Francisco was hired as team president and Fleishhacker was confident the ad man's background and expertise was exactly what was needed to make a success of the second PCL team to call Hollywood home.[5] There were also rumors that the appointment of Francisco was tied to an effort to lure an existing major league baseball team to Los Angeles.

Plans were announced to convert Gilmore Stadium, owned by oilman Earl Gilmore and used primarily for football and midget car racing, into a home for the team, which had been rechristened the Stars.[6] However, as spring training approached, Don Francisco deemed it woefully inadequate. Convinced that money to remodel Gilmore Stadium would be better spent on a new facility, Francisco announced he would search for a suitable site in Hollywood. In the meantime, he asked that the Angels allow the Stars to play at Wrigley Field for the 1938 season, a request that raised some eyebrows since approval for moving the Missions had been predicated in part on a promise that the team would not play there.[7]

Francisco assured the league that the Wrigley Field arrangement would be temporary. Details were hammered out with a decidedly unenthusiastic Angels president Dave Fleming, and the Stars settled into the Angels home for 1938.[8]

Early in their existence, the Hollywood Stars were party to an altercation that proved ironic, even by Pacific Coast League standards. On May 22, they hosted Sacramento at Wrigley Field on "Brotherly Love Day," because the managers of the opposing teams were Red Killefer and his brother Bill. Bill's Solons won the first game of the doubleheader and were leading the nightcap when Stars pitcher Wayne Osborne demonstrated his contempt for the decisions of umpire Cicero Falls by flipping his glove in the air in disgust. Falls immediately ejected Osborne.

Red Killefer reacted by storming onto the field and launching a stream of invectives at Falls. Osborne refused to vacate the premises, and Falls warned Killefer that if he did not bring in a new pitcher the game would be forfeited to Sacramento, which would also result in an automatic one-thousand-dollar fine for Hollywood. Killefer ignored the warning, and the umpire instructed the stadium announcer to inform fans that the game was being forfeited.

The crowd reaction was especially ugly, with beer cans and cushions thrown at Falls as he left the field. A group of sailors attempted to storm the umpire's dressing room and numerous fights broke out among those remaining in the stands. Police had to be summoned in order to safely extract the umpires.[9]

Wilbur Tuttle backed Falls and levied the one-thousand-dollar fine on the team, plus another one-hundred-dollar fine for Red Killefer. The Stars were playing mediocre ball, in sixth place at the beginning of June, and Herbert Fleishhacker's team was no more solid financially than it had been in San Francisco. A one-thousand-dollar fine was a cause for angst. Fleishhacker decided it was necessary to cut expenses. On June 1, he dropped expensive veterans Walter "Boom-Boom" Beck, Gordon Slade and Smead Jolley.[10] Jolley quickly found new employment, moving across the field from the Stars dugout to the Oakland clubhouse and finishing the season with the Oaks.[11] That same day, Lee Roy Herrmann lasted only two innings against Oakland. After the game, he too was released.[12]

Not all of the league's older players were having a rough time. On May 29, the San Francisco Seals were trailing, 7–3, in the ninth inning of the first game of a doubleheader in Seattle. Manager Lefty O'Doul decided to shake his team's lethargy by grabbing a bat to pinch-hit against Dick Barrett. O'Doul promptly homered, as did the next man up, Dom DiMaggio. Before the inning was over, the Seals had hit four home runs and rallied to win the game.

In the nightcap, the Seals were again trailing, this time by one run in the sixth inning, and O'Doul decided to see if he could duplicate his pinch-hitting magic of the first game. Incredibly, he again hit a home run, tying the score, and the Seals went on to win the game. Lefty O'Doul had become the first player in PCL history to hit pinch-hit home runs in both games of a doubleheader.[13]

* * *

By mid-summer, the Seattle Rainiers were starting to click both on the field and at the turnstiles. The team had already drawn nearly a quarter-million fans and was on pace to easily top four hundred thousand for the year.[14] Teenage pitching sensation Fred Hutchinson was the toast of the town and the team's top drawing card. He also drew a large following on the road and Jack Lelivelt was criticized whenever he saved him for a home game in Seattle. The former local high school star with the gigantic hands — as a high school freshman he could hold a basketball in each hand, palms down — had a record of 17–5 and there was no doubt he was bound for the major leagues. Lefty O'Doul said of Hutchinson, "He's absolutely the smartest pitcher for his age that I ever saw."[15]

A grim-faced competitor who might throw his glove to the ground and scream at teammates when their mistakes cost him, Hutchinson did not possess the most impressive fastball or breaking pitch, but the pitches he threw were effective and he knew how to use them. He came straight over the top with a delivery devoid of bad habits, thanks to the instruction of his coach at both Franklin High School and in American Legion, Ralph "Pop" Reed. Knocked out of his first start after facing only six batters, Hutchinson lasted until the seventh in his second appearance and then told Jack Lelivelt, "I'll finish a game for you one of these days, and win it too."[16] Hutchinson was popular with teammates, who bristled at those saying his fastball was not effective enough for him to be successful in the major leagues.[17] Rainiers catcher Hal Spindel countered that Hutchinson threw harder than most people thought and could always reach back for a little extra when the situation called for it.[18]

The Rainiers were entertaining, thanks to a pitching rotation that besides Hutchinson included popular veterans Dick Barrett, Paul Gregory and Hal Turpin. The team also had a new venue in which to play. Sick's Stadium opened on June 15 with Dick Barrett on the mound as the Rainiers hosted Portland. After nearly six years in Civic Stadium, playing in the new ballpark must have seemed as if something out of *Field of Dreams*, with players wondering if they had died and gone to heaven.

Built at a cost of one hundred and fifty thousand dollars, Sick's Stadium was the only ballpark in the PCL with equidistant left- and right-field fences, negating

Fred Hutchinson. "He's absolutely the smartest pitcher for his age that I ever saw" — Lefty O'Doul (David Eskenazi Collection).

some of the effectiveness of the team's star sluggers, Mike Hunt and Fred Muller, who had long taken advantage of the 290-foot left-field fence at Civic Stadium. Sick brought in forty-year-old sod to provide the best playing surface possible.[19] Hillis Layne, who played for Seattle in the late 1940s, remembered the stadium for its green foliage and noted that when standing at home plate he could see Mount Rainier and it appeared as if he could reach out and touch it. Layne declared, "It's one of the prettiest sights that I've seen."[20] There was also a small rise above the left-field fence that afforded a view into the stadium; it was not long before the area became known as "Tightwad Hill" in honor of those who populated it each evening to watch the Rainiers without having to purchase a ticket.

The team responded to its new surroundings. Fred Hutchinson celebrated his nineteenth birthday on August 12 with his nineteenth win of the season, 3–2, against San Francisco before the largest crowd ever to attend a game in Seattle.[21] Five days later he shut out Sacramento, 9–0, striking out twelve batters and winning his twentieth game. He also had three hits in as many at-bats, driving in four runs with two singles and a two-run home run.[22] Although the win only served to move the fifth-place Rainiers within one-half game of fourth place San Diego, it marked the beginning of a streak that saw Seattle win an incredible twenty-seven of thirty games, including fourteen in a row.[23] By mid–September, the Rainiers were only two games behind first-place Los Angeles.

But Jack Lelivelt could not catch his old team. Although the Angels had no twenty-game winners, compared to two for Seattle (Hutchinson and Paul Gregory), Los Angeles had a deep staff in 1938 that included veterans Fay Thomas, Ray Prim, Jack Salveson, Joe Berry and Dutch Lieber. Gene Lillard had returned as a pitcher rather than a third baseman, and was the team's top winner with sixteen victories before breaking his left ankle tripping over a base in a game against Hollywood.[24] The Angels even signed "the Mississippi Mudcat," Guy Bush, the former Chicago Cubs star and winner of 176 major league games who was granted his free agency by the St. Louis Cardinals in May when he refused assignment to the minor leagues.[25] Bush was given a five-thousand-dollar bonus to come to Los Angeles and he won eight of thirteen decisions, including a key complete-game victory over Oakland on September 14 that kept the Angels two games ahead of the Rainiers.[26] Los Angeles clinched the pennant two days later with a doubleheader sweep of Oakland.

But it was Sacramento, not Los Angeles, that won the 1938 Shaughnessy playoffs and the Governor's Cup that went with it, a major surprise considering the misfortune that seemed to dog the Solons all year.

First, the roof above the grandstand in Sacramento collapsed in February during a terrible windstorm.[27] A month later, Commissioner Landis freed one hundred players in the St. Louis Cardinals farm system and fined several of the teams involved, including Sacramento, for illegally hiding players through secret working agreements that allowed the Cardinals to control more than one franchise in a league.[28]

Shortly after "Brotherly Love Day," manager Bill Killefer was hospitalized with jaundice and missed much of the season. Coach Doc Crandall ran the team in his absence and the Solons played well, winning twenty-nine of their first thirty-eight games under his charge.[29] In June, outfielder Buster Adams broke his ankle sliding home on an inside-the-park grand slam home run.[30] On July 1, the Solons lost seventeen-game winner Cotton Pippen for the remainder of the season because of a sore arm.[31] Nick Cullop was beaned and missed considerable time as well.[32] In September, it was announced the Solons would get famous football star Sammy Baugh, who was playing as a shortstop in the Cardinals farm system. However, Washington Redskins owner George Preston Marshall's contract with Baugh allowed him to ban the athlete from playing any other sport. Marshall chose to exercise the clause, depriving Sacramento of a potential drawing card.[33]

The Solons overcame these obstacles. However, because the team had not been awarded the pennant the previous year when they lost the playoffs after winning the regular season, the rules had changed to once again recognize the regular-season champions as the league's pennant winners. As a result, the Sacramento Solons were still in search of their first PCL championship.[34]

With Seattle also falling short, Emil Sick followed the advice of Jack Lelivelt and sent star pitcher Fred Hutchinson, who had won twenty-five games, to the Detroit Tigers in exchange for cash and four players, including veteran outfielder JoJo White and first baseman George Archie.[35] It was further evidence that the Pacific Coast League seemed unwilling or unable to retain its best players, even with an owner and a franchise that was well financed. The return on cashing out talent was simply too great.

* * *

Bill Lane had been ill for much of the 1938 season and was feeling the weight of his seventy-six years. The gruff Padres owner had not appeared at Lane Field since Dick Ward's epic performance against the Angels on August 30, when the veteran right-hander pitched a no-hitter for twelve and two-thirds innings. Eddie Mayo's bloop single broke up Ward's no-hitter, but the Padres pitcher eventually defeated Los Angeles, 1–0, in sixteen innings. The only other hit he allowed was a solid single by Charlie English in the sixteenth.[36] San Diego finished the 1938 season in fifth place, a half-game out of the playoffs. Although Frank Shellenback was dissatisfied with that result, he felt he had done the best he could, considering that his relationship with Lane had become strained by the owner's insistence that he follow orders all season to bunt and play for one run — interfering with his preferred strategy. In addition, Lane had sold many of the team's best players, including Ted Williams, George Myatt, Vince DiMaggio and Bobby Doerr, which enriched the team's coffers but diluted its talent.

Ignoring his own role in the Padres' second-division finish, Bill Lane was unhappy and growing impatient. While he could be quite generous, as demonstrated by his good deeds over the years to assist orphans, Lane could also be shockingly cold and insensitive, as Frank Shellenback was about to discover. On October 2, the Padres owner directed team vice president Spider Baum to drive to Frank Shellenback's home and hand him an envelope. Shellenback opened it and read the brief note inside: "Frank Shellenback released unconditionally. W.H. Lane."[37]

With that terse missive, one of the franchise's longest relationships was severed. Shellenback's thirteen years in the organization, including the last four as manager, ended without explanation in much the same manner as had the tenure of his predecessor, Oscar Vitt. There was no press release, and it was left to Shellenback to inform the *San Diego Union* of his own dismissal. Lane left his sick bed to announce that Cedric Durst, the team's most popular player, would replace Shellenback as manager in 1939.[38]

Five days later one of the team's directors, Major Charles Lott, was visiting Lane, who was sitting in bed smoking a cigar and listening to the final game of the World Series.[39] Suddenly, the cigar fell from Lane's hand. Lott looked over and realized the owner of the San Diego Padres was dead.[40]

Lane's funeral was held in San Diego on October 12 at St. Didacus Catholic Church. Pallbearers included Cedric Durst, Herm Pillette, Dick Ward, Bill Starr, Howard Craghead, Les Cook, Spencer Harris and Ernie Holman.[41] The content of Lane's will, drawn in 1936, contained several surprises. Lane had not been a lifelong bachelor as presumed. It turned out that he had an ex-wife living in Spokane, Washington, who was left a stipend of one hundred dollars a month.[42] Baum, who had been Lane's trusted right-hand man for fourteen years, was named Padres president in the document but the will also directed that all of Lane's assets be converted to cash "at the first favorable opportunity," an indication that the team would have to be sold.[43]

Yet another surprise involved Lane's caretaker of the last several years, thirty-eight-year-old Florence Eastwood, who Lane called "my friend." She was awarded five thousand dollars cash, an automobile and all household and personal effects. The will further stipulated that upon the death of Lane's former wife, Miss Eastwood was to inherit the remainder of the estate, including the San Diego Padres.[44]

* * *

Don Francisco left the Hollywood franchise during the 1938 season for the presidency of Lord and Thomas Advertising in New York. Herbert Fleishhacker was unable to work out financing for a stadium in Francisco's absence and surrendered to the inevitable after the season ended by selling the Hollywood Stars to a syndicate headed by Bob Cobb, president of the Brown Derby restaurants, and attorney Victor Ford Collins, who had succeeded Francisco as president of the Stars.[45] Red Killefer was retained as manager, ex–Angels executive Oscar Reichow was named business manager, and Collins announced that the team would build a stadium in Hollywood.[46]

Like Emil Sick, Bob Cobb had a vision of making his franchise an organization of the first rank. A former cowboy who grew up in Montana, Cobb moved to Los Angeles as a young man to seek his fortune, working as a bank messenger before deciding to try the restaurant business. After working for others, he was persuaded by Gloria Swanson's ex-husband, Herbert Somborn, to invest in the first Brown Derby restaurant in 1926, followed by a second a year later at Hollywood and Vine and a third in Beverly Hills. After Somborn died in 1934, Cobb became company president.[47]

Both Cobb and Collins felt the key to energizing support behind their team was to enlist as many prominent Hollywood figures as they could. Cobb was especially excited by the potential. "The Coast League has been fast asleep," he explained. "It has permitted the majors to come in and steal our material. We are moving toward something. Perhaps — now don't laugh — it is major league ball. We will see big league ball in Hollywood within our time. When the majors come out our way, they will find Hollywood a few steps ahead of them in many things."[48]

Cobb and Collins needed to get a stadium built and fast. This meant a ballpark of wood construction, which caused some concern, but Cobb assured everyone the stadium would be fireproofed. Even with a rush on construction, the new ballpark, to be located on property owned by Earl Gilmore across the street from Gilmore Stadium, would not be ready before early May. Unwilling to continue as host to an unwelcome guest, Dave Fleming hiked the rent for Wrigley Field to an unaffordable level. The Stars responded by arranging to play their first home series in 1939 at Gilmore Stadium, the venue they had previously rejected. The facility had no dugouts and a right-field fence so short that balls hit into the first few rows of the bleachers were ground-rule doubles.[49] The Stars' permanent home, to be named Gilmore Field, would be completed by the time the team returned from a three-week road trip.[50]

Bob Cobb wanted to field an entertaining team, but his roster was old and short on talent. Realizing he was without a first baseman or a real drawing card, Cobb asked ex–big league star Babe Herman to leave his turkey ranch in Glendale and fill both roles for the Stars. Herman, owner of a .324 lifetime major league batting average, arrived in Cobb's office and put his feet up on the new owner's desk, lighting a cigar as he quickly rejected an offer of $7,500. Cobb tried to hold firm but Herman remained equally unmovable until the day before the start of the season. As Cobb explained, "He (Herman) knew he was talking to novices. We called him ... and told him he had won."[51]

Herman was in the Opening Day lineup, wearing one of the Stars' new blue uniforms with the ugly white back pockets, and brought twelve thousand people to their feet by hitting a three-run home run on the very first pitch he saw. Herman also doubled and was walked twice intentionally as the Stars won a 10–9 slugfest against the Angels.[52]

Gilmore Field opened for business on May 2 with the Stars hosting Seattle. Bob Cobb's wife, actress Gail Patrick, threw the first pitch to Joe E. Brown with thirteen-year-old actress Jane Withers at bat. The motion picture illuminati were out in force as a Hollywood team played for the first time in its own stadium. Louise Brooks and Harold Lloyd were there, along with Rudy Vallee, who filmed the proceedings with his sixteen-millimeter camera. Jack Benny, Gary Cooper, Buster Keaton, Maxie Rosenbloom and Ralph Bellamy also attended. Celebrities purchasing season tickets had their names engraved on a plaque and affixed to their seats, testimony to their status.

The new stadium was a hit with the public. Cobb understood that the Hollywood elite were accustomed to the best in life and he aimed to provide them a first-class experience. He upgraded concessions. He added two extra ladies' restrooms. He recruited the prettiest cigarette girls he could find, selecting fourteen out of more than five hundred applicants, and put them in flattering uniforms. Vendors were dressed in white shirts and bowties and their uniforms were cleaned every day. Courtesy was the rule; the entire crew went through a dress rehearsal before each game.

Sportswriter Bob Hunter was impressed with Gilmore Field and thought it a wonderful place to watch a baseball game. But he could not escape a feeling of uneasiness every night as he sat in the Gilmore Field press box. Despite the assurances of Hollywood management that the stadium was safe, the veteran reporter would always remember his experience at the ballpark during its construction.

"I went by just to check it out ... and the workmen there said, 'This wood is all fire-proofed now.' I was concerned about the structure and they said it was going to be all right. So I took some of the wood home — they said to take a little if I wanted — so I put it in the back of my car ... for my fireplace.

"It burned *real* good. The best firewood I ever had."[53]

* * *

On May 27, Art Cohn of the *Oakland Tribune* wrote a column based on a rant by Hollywood infielder Bill Cissell that had taken place in an Oakland bar owned by ex–PCL player Jack Fenton. Cissell, the former $123,000 acquisition of the Chicago White Sox, insisted that league president Tuttle knew nothing about baseball and that George Hilde-brand should be hired to replace him. He also called Coast League owners greedy and interested only in collecting money to the detriment of the game on the field, the quality of which he said had fallen below that of other Class AA leagues — and even below the Texas League. Finally, Cissell delivered the biggest blow of all; he intimated that Tuttle was not that great a writer.[54]

Never described as a man with thick skin, Tuttle immediately announced Cissell was being suspended indefinitely. Judge W.G. Bramham of the National Association threatened

Cissell with a lifetime ban if Cohn's quotes of the infielder in his column were accurate. Cissell protested his innocence and declared, "I wouldn't know Cohn if I met him right now."[55]

Cohn insisted that he and Cissell had spoken for an hour. He said the ballplayer knew exactly who he was and furthermore agreed with everything that had been said.[56] After cooling off, Tuttle backed off the suspension, instead fining Cissell two hundred dollars.[57]

That was not the end of Cissell's trouble; Red Killefer suspended the infielder in July after he went on a drinking binge in Portland.[58] While there had never been any question of Cissell's hustle on the diamond, he was known as a drinking man, and alcohol was clearly the root of his overly candid nature. After he returned to the lineup, Cissell swore off drinking and would play well for the Stars through the 1940 season.[59] Unfortunately, he eventually began drinking again and would be dead within ten years.[60]

Other players encountered trouble not of their own making, as occasionally the zeal to generate publicity outstripped reason and logic. In a "What were they thinking?" moment, the San Francisco Seals lost their starting catcher due to an ill-advised stunt in August to promote the team and the World's Fair being held on San Francisco's Treasure Island, a manmade landmass constructed specifically for the international exposition. Everyone involved was extremely fortunate that the catcher, Joe Sprinz, was not killed during the promotional event gone wrong.

The idea sprouted from the fertile mind of Walter Mails, who had retired as a player and was acting as head of publicity for the Seals. The plan was to drop a baseball eight hundred feet from the *Volunteer*, one of the blimps owned by the Goodyear Tire and Rubber Company, to Seals players stationed within a special area. The intention was to replicate the feat of an Ohio state senator who caught a ball dropped from the Terminal Tower in Cleveland, Ohio, at a distance of just over seven hundred and fifty feet. Mails reasoned that the extra fifty feet would allow one of the Seals to break the record. Temporary bleachers were erected well away from the target area for the safety of the estimated 1,200 spectators. No such precautions were taken on behalf of the players.

The first few attempts went astray. One ball crashed into the bleachers — somehow without injuring anyone — and another buried itself deep into the turf. Seeing this, an alarmed Lefty O'Doul screamed that the stunt was "too dangerous" and tried calling it off. Unfortunately, before he could do so, World War I bombing ace A.T. Sewell dropped one last ball from the blimp.

Joe Sprinz drew a bead on the sphere and settled under it, even as it accelerated to one-hundred-and-fifty miles per hour during its descent — a speed he had unfortunately misjudged. As Sprinz staggered, trying to keep aligned with the projectile, it ricocheted off his glove and slammed into his face, breaking his jaw and several teeth. It was speculated that had Sprinz failed to get his glove on the ball and been struck in the head, the blow would have killed him. As it was, he missed the rest of the season.[61]

* * *

The Los Angeles Angels lost their first two games of the 1939 season and then threatened to make a shambles of the pennant race thanks to a record-tying nineteen straight wins, a streak finally halted by San Diego on April 22.[62]

Although they had stopped the red-hot Angels, things were not starting out well for the San Diego Padres. After selling many of their best players and facing an uncertain future following Bill Lane's death, the Padres seemed to languish. It did not help that the team was rocked by the tragic loss of its best pitcher during spring training. Jim Chaplin, winner of forty-three games over the previous two years, died when the car in which he was a passenger struck a stalled automobile south of San Diego late at night.[63]

The unsettled nature of the team extended to the front office where in mid-season Florence Eastwood, along with Joseph Truxaw and fellow director Phil Purcell, led a successful move to oust Spider Baum as team president. The only explanation provided was a disagreement over the scheduling of night baseball.[64] Baum's dismissal created a howl of protest among San Diego fans but the team's directors were not swayed by public sentiment. Charles Lott assumed Baum's position on a temporary basis.

By mid–July it was apparent the Pacific Coast League pennant race once again was going to come down to a battle between Seattle and Los Angeles. Both teams split their doubleheaders on July 16 — Seattle with Hollywood and Los Angeles with San Diego. Jigger Statz shocked everyone by hitting two home runs in the first inning of the first game of the Angels doubleheader against the Padres.[65] The Angels remained one-half game ahead of the Rainiers.

Five days later the Angels were swept in a doubleheader by Sacramento, losing the second game, 4–1, to Carl Hubbell's brother, John, before a crowd of twenty-one thousand on Radio Appreciation Night.[66] Meanwhile, Seattle defeated Oakland to move three full games ahead of Los Angeles for first place. By August 23, the Rainiers had opened up a ten-game lead.[67]

From there, the Rainiers coasted to the pennant, easily clinching the Pacific Coast League title on September 12 with Hal Turpin defeating Los Angeles, 4–3, before the home crowd at Sick's Stadium. It was Turpin's twenty-third win of the year and Seattle's first pennant in fifteen seasons.[68] Emil Sick rewarded the players with fourteen-karat gold rings featuring small diamonds representing the four bases and a larger diamond in the middle signifying the pitcher's mound. Surrounding the bigger diamond were the words "Pacific Coast League Champions." And that they were, both on the field and at the turnstiles. Emil Sick's franchise had outdrawn seven major league teams while setting a new minor league attendance record of more than a half million.[69]

With Fred Hutchinson in Detroit, Hal Turpin and Dick Barrett carried the Rainiers pitching staff. Turpin was a thirty-four-year-old junk-ball pitcher whose career in the PCL dated to 1927. The key to his success involved his ability to control both his fastball and curve while also mixing in an effective knuckleball. Turpin constantly worried aloud about his age and whether he could coax one more year out of his arm. He would never play in the major leagues, but if it bothered him, he did not say so.

Moon-faced Dick Barrett was a roly-poly 5'9" right-hander whose physique and ever-present smile earned him the nickname "Kewpie" from *Seattle Post-Intelligencer* sportswriter Royal Brougham.[70] A fiery competitor who constantly challenged his teammates to bear down, Barrett's enthusiasm was infectious and, as L.H. Gregory of the *Oregonian* put it, the veteran pitcher "could make a deaf-and-dumb infielder start talking." When Barrett first joined the Rainiers, his windup included turning to face second base before completing his follow-through. He had since eliminated that habit and now wasted nothing in his pitching motion.[71] Barrett had excellent pickoff moves to both first and second base and worked quickly, nibbling the corners to set up his best pitch, a curveball, often working deep into the count on batters. He relied on his fastball and curve, rarely throwing anything other than variations of those two pitches.

Turpin had four straight twenty-win seasons for the Rainiers while Barrett did the same seven times in eight years. They would both pitch into their forties and combine to win more than four hundred games in the Pacific Coast League.

Seattle Rainiers owner Emil Sick (left) and manager Jack Lelivelt raising the pennant at Sick's Stadium (David Eskenazi Collection).

* * *

Wilbur Tuttle was re-elected president for another three-year term after the 1939 season and Harry Williams was retained as league secretary-treasurer for the same time period.[72] In the offseason, more Pacific Coast League stars graduated to the majors as the owners continued to sell their most valuable talent. The St. Louis Browns acquired Alan Strange from the PCL for the second time, while Sacramento pitcher Tom Seats was drafted by the Detroit Tigers. The Pacific Coast League's Most Valuable Player, San Francisco's Dominic DiMaggio, joined his brothers in the major leagues when he and teammate Larry Powell were sent to the Boston Red Sox.[73] The Seals would miss the younger DiMaggio, who Lefty O'Doul predicted would "be a sensation" in Boston. For his part, DiMaggio called his promotion to the major leagues the greatest thing that had ever happened to him and said he felt sure he would do well.[74]

New stars would emerge. Twenty-four-year-old Angels outfielder Lou Novikoff had taken the Los Angeles baseball scene by storm during the latter stages of the 1939 season. Nicknamed "the Mad Russian," Novikoff's natural ability as a hitter was amazing, especially considering how late he had come to the game. Novikoff's older brother had been a semi-pro player in Los Angeles and used to throw to him but Lou, afraid of the ball, always stepped away from the pitch as he swung. His brother eventually gave up on him. Novikoff turned to softball and was so gifted that at age thirteen he was already pitching for the best local teams. Two years later he was playing for a team in Bakersfield. From there he was hired to play for Torrance, pitching them to the championship of the National Softball League.

He attracted the attention of Joe Rodgers, who convinced Novikoff to pitch for a team he ran in Huntington Beach. It was soon apparent Novikoff could go no further in softball. Rodgers told him he was wasting his talent and should start playing baseball, so he attended a tryout with the Los Angeles Angels and signed with them in 1937.[75] Novikoff was sent to Ponca City, Oklahoma, where he tore up the league even while recovering from a broken ankle suffered before the season started. He led his league in hitting the next year as well, playing for Moline, Illinois. That performance earned him a spot on the Angels' Opening Day roster in 1939.

Relegated to pinch-hitting duties, Novikoff was optioned to Milwaukee of the American Association, subject to twenty-four-hour recall. After about two weeks he was brought back to Los Angeles and then sent to Tulsa, Oklahoma, where he hit .368 in 110 games and was leading the Texas League in batting average.[76]

Recalled by the Angels in August, Novikoff proved almost impossible to stop. After playing a combined thirty-six games in his two stints for the Angels in 1939, Novikoff hit an otherworldly .452 with eight home runs and thirty-seven runs batted in. He hit one ball so hard in Seattle, the pitcher victimized by it claimed "it looked like the fence ran in to meet the ball and then ducked under it."[77] Thanks to his performance in Tulsa and Los Angeles, *The Sporting News* named Novikoff the outstanding minor league player for 1939.[78] He was just warming up.

With his distinctive Russian accent and genial personality, Novikoff was colorful and unorthodox, as was his wife, who yelled at the top of her lungs every time he came to bat, "Strike that big bum out!" When Novikoff asked his wife why she did that, she replied, "I have fun doing it and what do you care, anyhow? I know none of those pitchers can strike you out." Novikoff conceded that when he heard his wife yelling at him, he bore down more at the plate.[79]

A classic "bad ball" hitter, Novikoff had particular success against Portland. Beavers ace Ad Liska noted that Dick Barrett had little trouble with the slugger and asked for the secret. Barrett replied, "You throw the ball belt high on the inside corner. Then on the next pitch, you throw it inside a little bit more and on the next one a little more." Liska followed Barrett's advice the next time he faced Novikoff and retired him easily. Then Liska decided to tempt fate: "His last time up, I thought, 'I wonder if I could get him out on an outside pitch?'" Liska threw a ball several inches out of the strike zone. "He took that ball and lined it off the right-field wall," Liska recalled. "I went to him after the game and said, 'How did you know I was going to give you that outside pitch?' He said, 'I figured that you were gonna get smart at some point.'"[80]

Novikoff won the Pacific Coast League Triple Crown in 1940, hitting forty-one home runs and driving in one hundred and seventy-one runs with a .363 batting average. The Chicago Cubs purchased him, along with second baseman Lou Stringer, for a reported one hundred and fifty thousand dollars.[81]

Despite Novikoff's super-human performance, Seattle drubbed the competition for the second year in a row. Jack Lelivelt's crew finished nine-and-a-half games ahead of second-place Los Angeles. To top it off, the Rainiers finally won the Governor's Cup in 1940 after losing in the first round the previous two years, capturing both series in five games, first defeating Oakland and then Los Angeles.

* * *

A favorite of fans and players alike, actress Gail Patrick was one of the biggest boosters of her husband's Hollywood Stars. During the 1939 season she gave every player a lucky rabbit's foot. When the team's luck turned sour, she gathered them all up and threw them into San Francisco Bay.[82] It now seemed that her luck had turned sour as well. In October 1940, the Hollywood Stars family was torn apart when Patrick filed for divorce from Bob Cobb after less than four years of marriage. She shrewdly asked her spouse's business partner, Victor Ford Collins, to act as her attorney.[83]

The Pacific Coast League family was also shaken by the death of several major figures after the 1940 season ended.

The first was legendary trainer Shine Scott, who died of a heart attack in October. Scott had joined the original Vernon Tigers in 1909 and remained with the team through its moves to San Francisco and Hollywood. In 1939, the old trainer was in failing health and the Stars granted a pension to the African American son of slaves.[84]

Two days before Christmas 1940 it was announced that Jim Morley had passed away at his home on Griffith Park Drive.[85] Morley had remained active in the Los Angeles sports scene until his death. After leaving the Angels for the second time following the 1919 season, he resumed his entrepreneurial pursuits but had remained a fixture at Opening Day for the Angels every year. In 1936, he and George Van Derbeck, owner of the 1892 Angels, were honored guests at an old-timers game sponsored at Wrigley Field by the Association of Professional Baseball Players of America.[86] Morley was buried at Forest Lawn in Glendale the day after Christmas. His old shortstop, Jimmy Toman, attended the funeral, as did George Stovall and Harry Williams.[87]

The most shocking and unexpected loss of all came in January 1941. Jack Lelivelt was attending a Harlem Globetrotters basketball game at Civic Auditorium in Seattle on January 20, along with Rainiers vice president Roscoe "Torchy" Torrance. The two had dined at Torrance's home earlier in the evening and Lelivelt was in excellent spirits. Basking in the glow of his second straight PCL pennant, Lelivelt laughed with the rest of the crowd at Ted Strong's sleight of hand with a basketball and Sonny Boswell's sharpshooting and comic play. Lelivelt spotted *Seattle Sports-Intelligencer* reporter Royal Brougham and talked about his three-acre property in the San Fernando Valley, near Los Angeles. He assured Brougham, "I have a fine, big turkey with your name on it." He also spoke enthusiastically to Brougham about the coming season and how healthy he felt.

Torrance and Lelivelt were walking outside the arena after the game when Lelivelt suddenly felt a sharp and severe pain in his chest. Torrance rushed Lelivelt to the hospital, but the Rainiers manager succumbed to a heart attack about twenty minutes after arriving. The headline in the *Seattle Post-Intelligencer* the next day screamed "JACK LELIVELT DROPS DEAD."[88]

Lelivelt's funeral was scheduled for Los Angeles, with Rainiers official Bill Mulligan accompanying the body on the train from the Pacific Northwest. Pallbearers included Frank Demaree, Truck Hannah, Jigger Statz and popular Los Angeles sports columnist Bob Ray.[89]

A couple of weeks later, the thirty-seven-year-old Ray was diagnosed with cancer and underwent an operation. The prognosis was not good, and fans and players rallied around the popular assistant sports editor of the *Los Angeles Times* and his young family. A benefit game, featuring teams of major league and PCL stars, was held in Ray's honor on March 9,

1941. Dizzy Dean took the loss for the major leaguers in a game that featured forty-nine players in the box score. Ray surprised everyone by attending, arriving at the ballpark via ambulance. He even visited the Brown Derby after the game.[90]

At first, Ray insisted to everyone that he would beat his illness. He rallied and doctors allowed him to return to his job to cover the PCL for the *Los Angeles Times* during the early part of the 1941 season. But the cancer returned with ferocity and he was confined to his home, forced to continue his column from his bed. Ray was eventually admitted to the hospital in early July and died two months later.[91]

* * *

One little-noticed item in the *New York Times* in January 1941 was a report about a Congressional inquiry spurred by Iowa Senator Guy Mark Gillette. The Democratic lawmaker, a veteran of both the Spanish-American War and the World War, was extremely concerned about the activities of the Japanese, especially on the West Coast.

He said he had received letters from members of a Hawaii-based group, the Sino-Korean People's League, which was warning of nefarious Japanese activities. The organization told Gillette that Japan had completed a census of all Japanese living in Hawaii and had begun drafting them into the Imperial Army through the consulates on the islands and the Pacific Coast. Gillette called for an investigation and said he was alarmed by the potential of American citizens collaborating with the enemy. Saying the matter "deserves serious attention," Gillette declared, "It could be especially serious when we remember that Pearl Harbor, Hawaii, is the base for our Pacific fleet."[92]

* * *

There was a stampede among those wanting to succeed Jack Lelivelt as manager of the most successful minor league franchise in the country. By the end of January there were more than a dozen applicants, both formal and informal, including Rogers Hornsby, Willie Kamm, Paul Waner, Grover Cleveland Alexander, Earl Sheely, Lyn Lary and Mickey Heath. The manager of Babe Ruth's baseball school in Florida said the Sultan of Swat was interested.[93] Babe Herman applied, while at the same time lamenting his image as a "screwball."[94]

Bill Skiff, the director of the New York Yankees minor league system and a former catcher for Lelivelt with the Los Angeles Angels, arrived in Seattle and met with Emil Sick for a half-hour. Comfortable with Skiff's background and ties to the Yankees, the Rainiers' owner quickly signed him to a two-year contract as Lelivelt's successor.[95] Babe Ruth called Emil Sick the next evening, directly expressing interest in the manager's job with Seattle. After being told that Skiff had already been hired, Ruth replied, "Well, okay ... I just thought I had better ask."[96]

Although Seattle did not hire a big-name manager, Sacramento did, courtesy of Branch Rickey and the parent St. Louis Cardinals, who assigned "Gas House Gang" star Pepper Martin to lead the Solons. The four-time National League All-Star became a player-manager at age thirty-six. "I gave everything I had while I served as a player and I'll do the same as manager," he said, signing a two-year contract for the same amount he had earned the previous year, plus a tractor for use on his farm in Oklahoma.[97]

Martin drove to spring training in mid–February with his wife and children and three dogs. "I am starting a new career. I was in the big leagues as a player and had considerable success. I want to eventually go back to the majors as a manager. I think I can do it, and I know I will hustle hard to make good in Sacramento." Declaring he would give West Coast fans Gas House Gang baseball, Martin seemed ready to wake up the Pacific Coast League."[98]

Pepper Martin *did* wake up the PCL. Sacramento won twenty-three of its first thirty contests, opening up a six-game lead. On May 8 against Oakland, Buddy Blattner stole four bases, including thefts of second, third and home in the same inning.[99] Martin and his team was also proving to be a box office draw, both at home and on the road. The team was playing so well that Martin put himself on the bench.

By mid–June, the Solons were an incredible thirteen games ahead of second-place San Diego, with Seattle in third. The team honored its manager with a special evening in July. Before a crowd of more than fourteen thousand, a choked up Martin accepted gifts, including a rifle, a hunting dog, a rooster and hens, and a 1941 Chrysler New Yorker.[100]

While Sacramento was flying high, the two-time defending champion Rainiers were struggling. Outfielder Edo Vanni broke his leg and was lost for the season. JoJo White was also injured. Al Niemiec lost a ball in the lights that hit him squarely in the face and he too missed several games.[101] The Rainiers attempted to plug their outfield gap with veteran Earl Averill, a native of nearby Snohomish, Washington. The ex–San Francisco Seals and Cleveland Indians star had flirted with the Rainiers in the spring before signing with the Boston Braves. Following his release by Boston at the end of April, he agreed to contract terms with Seattle and came home to play.[102] The Rainiers were doing whatever they could to remain afloat.

* * *

The Los Angeles Angels' attempt to end Seattle's two-year reign as league champion suffered a major blow because of two high-profile suspensions. Sinkerball specialist Julio Bonetti, a twenty-eight-year-old native of Italy, was popular among fans and well known for his extreme sensitivity about being prematurely bald; he was almost never seen without a hat. Bonetti made his mark by winning twenty games in his first season with Los Angeles in 1939 despite a series of injuries that included being hit on the hand by line drives twice in one game, spraining an ankle, suffering a spike wound while covering first base, and problems with his tonsils that were removed after the season.[103] He set a PCL record by not allowing a base on balls for sixty-four consecutive innings.[104] He defeated Oakland, 1–0, in a nine-inning game, throwing just sixty-six pitches and driving in the only run of the contest.[105]

Sold to the Chicago Cubs in 1940, he pitched in only one game before being sold back to the Angels.[106] Player-manager Jigger Statz was glad to have him back and Bonetti won fourteen games. Meanwhile, Commissioner Landis had become so concerned over reports of gambling at Wrigley Field that he assigned agents to investigate the situation during the last three weeks of the 1940 PCL season. The mayor of Los Angeles also had a detective looking into the charges, and he turned his notes over to the district attorney.[107]

Once the 1941 season began, fresh rumors surfaced and Angels president Dave Fleming decided to employ private investigators to check out the stories. Long-lens cameras were used to record suspicious activity. On May 7, one of Fleming's detectives observed Bonetti taking money from a racehorse owner named Albert "Frenchy" Reshaw outside the Coliseum Hotel in Los Angeles. Reshaw was observed that evening at Wrigley Field offering odds of 10 to 8 that Hollywood would beat Los Angeles, for whom Bonetti would be pitching. Bonetti left the contest trailing, 4–3, in a game Los Angeles eventually lost.[108]

The evidence was presented to the district attorney's office, which launched an investigation that stretched into June. Reshaw and Bonetti both attended a meeting that included investigators, a judge, and officials from both the team and the league. Reshaw did not volunteer any significant details about the transfer of cash during his interrogation but insisted

Bonetti was honest. He said that he might have given Bonetti some small bills to exchange at the bank for fifty-dollar bills.[109]

Bonetti's story changed several times over the course of his questioning. He claimed to be making change for Reshaw; when bank records failed to support that version of events, he then said he must have taken five or six fifty-dollar bills from Reshaw, who wanted him to change them for smaller denominations.[110] Bonetti met with investigators and league officials on June 25 and again on June 30, attempting to stick to a more coherent and consistent story. At one point, Fleming took Bonetti aside and asked if the money that had changed hands was related to betting on horseracing. Bonetti insisted his story about making change at the bank was the truth, but then he changed his story once more, saying that Reshaw had asked him to take money to another hotel and give it to a bookie in order to place a horseracing bet for him. Although the investigation failed to uncover any evidence that Bonetti had thrown games, his conflicting statements and ever-changing story led to his indefinite suspension on July 2.[111] Bonetti claimed he had been confused when confronted with the fact he was being investigated. He proclaimed his innocence and said, "I have always given my best efforts in baseball and never realized that placing some horserace bets for Reshaw would have any bearing on my career." Bonetti said he would appeal all the way to Commissioner Landis if necessary and hired an attorney to aid his effort to do so.[112]

Dave Fleming said, "I am very sorry for Julio, but very happy that all the evidence shows baseball's house is clean."[113] Fleming also reiterated his commitment to stamp out gamblers at Wrigley Field.

While Bonetti prepared to appeal his suspension, the Angels were playing against Hollywood at Gilmore Field in a doubleheader on July 13. In the first inning of the second game, Stars outfielder Frenchy Uhalt successfully stole third base. Angels third baseman Eddie Mayo, certain he had tagged Uhalt in time, went berserk, and he and manager Jigger Statz began screaming at umpire Ray Snyder, as documented by a photograph published in the *Los Angeles Times*.[114] Snyder ejected both.

A sullen Statz appeared at Mayo's front door the next day and handed the player a letter, informing the infielder that he had been suspended by the league for spitting in Snyder's face during the argument.[115] A stunned Mayo met with Wilbur Tuttle in his office in the Wrigley Field tower and was told there would be no final ruling on the matter until the league president received a response from a wire sent to William G. Bramham, president of the National Association. Two days later, Tuttle announced that Mayo was being suspended for a calendar year. Mayo, who was leading the PCL in home runs at the time, expressed shock at the ruling. "I do not believe I spat in Umpire Snyder's face," Mayo insisted. "I certainly did sputter at Snyder, but sputtering is not spitting."[116]

Phone calls and letters of protest immediately poured into the league office from those supporting Mayo's version of events and expressing outrage at the sentence. After reviewing the evidence, Angels president Dave Fleming leaped to Mayo's defense, pointing out that everyone else present denied the ballplayer had spat at Snyder. Hollywood manager Bill Sweeney and Stars outfielder Frenchy Uhalt, whose stolen base had precipitated the argument, were among those backing Mayo. They insisted the umpire must have been mistaken — that Mayo had probably just foamed at the mouth while screaming inches from Snyder's face.[117] There had been no mention of spitting in the game account. *Los Angeles Times* photographer Maurice Terrell, who snapped the photograph of Uhalt's steal attempt and also the argument itself, said he was only ten feet away during the shouting match and never saw Mayo spit.[118]

Like Bonetti, Mayo threatened to take the case all the way to Judge Landis, but unlike the pitcher, Mayo had Dave Fleming's backing. Ray Snyder weighed in by saying that while he had not changed his opinion about Mayo having spat in his face, he felt the penalty too harsh.[119] When asked whether he thought Mayo had spat deliberately or accidentally, Snyder replied, "I wouldn't know."[120]

The outrage over the suspension caught the attention of J.G. Taylor Spink, publisher of *The Sporting News*, who flew to Los Angeles to personally report on the story.[121] At William Bramham's insistence, Tuttle met with both Snyder and Mayo so that Tuttle could gather more evidence in what was widely viewed as an appeal.[122]

After listening to both Mayo and Snyder, Tuttle indicated he would send the transcripts to William Bramham. To the dismay of the Angels and their third baseman, Tuttle insisted he had no authority to change the ruling and was only gathering evidence for Bramham.[123] The transcript and the official notice of suspension were forwarded to Bramham, who then upheld the one-year penalty.[124] A shocked Mayo could not believe the news. "How could he do that?" said the ballplayer. "What did he say? What was his explanation? What did he base his ruling on? What did he say about all those affidavits?" Mayo added plaintively, "I was sure I would be reinstated."[125]

Fleming and Mayo decided to take up the matter with the executive committee of the National Association, which had agreed to hear Julio Bonetti's appeal at the same meeting. Mayo testified before the committee for an hour while neither Tuttle nor Snyder appeared. On September 4, after reviewing the evidence, the executive committee unanimously overturned Bramham's ruling and immediately reinstated Mayo, adding that there was no evidence to substantiate the claim that the player had spat on the umpire.[126] The committee took direct issue with both Tuttle and Bramham and their interpretation of the facts. Committee chairman George Trautman phoned Mayo, informed him of the decision, and advised him, "Next time, don't stand so close when you argue with umpires. Maybe you do foam a little." Mayo said he told Trautman, "Don't worry. I'll never argue again even if somebody hits a homer over the center-field fence and the ump calls it a foul ball."[127]

The jubilant ballplayer flew to Los Angeles and went through a quick workout in preparation for rejoining his teammates in Portland, where they were playing a series against the Beavers. He returned to the lineup on September 9 and tripled in two runs to help the Angels win the game.[128] Mayo made his return to Wrigley Field a week later and the fans showered him with gifts. He also received a check from Dave Fleming.[129]

Julio Bonetti was not as fortunate. The same committee unanimously upheld his indefinite suspension with little comment.[130] Bonetti enlisted in the army and after the war worked as a carpenter for his father. He was finally reinstated in 1949, his suspension lasting the same amount of time as Bill Rumler two decades earlier. But unlike Rumler, Julio Bonetti never played baseball again. He suffered a fatal heart attack less than three years after his reinstatement, only two weeks before his fortieth birthday.[131]

* * *

The Seattle Rainiers' chances for a third straight pennant seemed dead when they fell fifteen games behind Sacramento in mid-summer. But Bill Skiff's team caught fire at the same time that Pepper Martin's Solons slumped after their 50–19 start. On the first of September, Seattle moved to within three games of first place. Six days later, the Rainiers were a percentage point ahead of both Sacramento and San Diego.[132]

The Rainiers welcomed San Francisco to Sick's Stadium and it rained for two days. In order to complete the series, the teams had to play four doubleheaders in four days. Seattle rose to the occasion, winning six of the eight games. After sweeping a doubleheader on September 14, Seattle was four games up in the loss column over both San Diego and Sacramento with nine games to play.[133] The Rainiers traveled to Los Angeles to close out the season at Wrigley Field and on September 19 clinched their third straight pennant, something that had seemed impossible a couple of months earlier. Jack Lelivelt's widow was in attendance to proudly witness what would have been her husband's fifth Pacific Coast League title.[134]

The Rainiers then added their second consecutive Governor's Cup, winning a pair of tough seven-game Shaughnessy Series playoffs against Hollywood and Sacramento. Seattle was enjoying one of the best runs by a franchise in PCL history and it seemed as if nothing could stop them. Meanwhile, after three straight seasons as Seattle's main rival for the pennant, the Los Angeles Angels had finished a disappointing seventh in 1941, only one game out of last place. Manager Jigger Statz was on the hot seat. There had been extenuating circumstances, including the sale of Lou Novikoff and Lou Stringer, as well as the suspensions of Bonetti and Mayo and the resulting disruptions. But Dave Fleming was clear that he wanted no excuses in 1942. When Statz signed his contract in November to run the team for a third season, Fleming clearly laid out his expectations, saying in no uncertain terms that he would open the team's checkbook and expected his manager to deliver a pennant.[135]

* * *

Rosters were beginning to be altered by the draft — not that of the major leagues, but rather that of Uncle Sam. President Roosevelt had signed the Selective Service Act in September 1940, recognizing the country needed to be prepared even though it had not yet entered the war.[136] Portland was hit hardest by the draft boards, so much so that when first baseman Herman Reich received his notice in June 1941, he was allowed to finish the season even though he was quite willing to report at once. The delay was approved in recognition of the impact his absence would have on his team and the fact that immediate entry into a one-year training program would effectively cost Reich two seasons, which seemed unfair when compared to those in other professions.[137]

Despite the acceleration in the calling of draft-age players, the Depression was easing and those involved with the Pacific Coast League were not overly concerned. Even with the Angels' dismal record, league attendance had nearly matched that of 1940 and owners had realized about fifteen thousand dollars more in revenue. Sacramento's attendance nearly doubled, setting a franchise record thanks to Pepper Martin and his hustling Solons. San Diego, Portland and Hollywood also gained while Seattle nearly matched its record set in 1940.[138] It also appeared the Angels would be much better in 1942; they bought veteran Charlie Root from the Chicago Cubs shortly after the season ended.[139] Then the franchise was purchased by the Cubs, making the Angels a full-fledged Chicago farm team. (The franchise had been owned by the Santa Catalina Island Company, which was in turn owned by P.K. Wrigley. That company would retain title to Wrigley Field and rent the facility to the Angels.) Dave Fleming was forced out of the front office and replaced by former major league manager and umpire Clarence "Pants" Rowland and former Cubs general manager Charles "Boots" Weber.[140]

There was no question the Cubs taking over meant a prosperous and competitive team in Los Angeles that would benefit the entire league — if the major leagues did not complicate matters. St. Louis Browns owner Donald Barnes was prepared to drop a bombshell at the major league meetings in December; he intended to move his franchise to Los Angeles.

* * *

On Friday, December 5, 1941, Hank Greenberg turned in his equipment at Fort Custer, Michigan, and prepared to return to baseball, having completed his five-month hitch in the army. After receiving his ten-dollar paycheck, Greenberg was visited by Brigadier General Clyde Abraham, who told the Detroit slugger, "I was a baseball fan long before you began to play and I want to wish you a lot of luck from now on." A month shy of being thirty-one years old, Greenberg looked forward to the prime years of his career. Planning to spend the night in Detroit before traveling to his home in New York, Greenberg proclaimed, "Now I am able to be a ball player again."[141]

Meanwhile, Donald Barnes was preparing to depart for the major league meetings in Chicago, which were due to begin the next Tuesday. Five years earlier, Barnes had raised six hundred thousand dollars to purchase the St. Louis Browns and provide operating capital. Now he was facing a tough financial situation, having promised to deliver a winning team for long-suffering Browns fans, few as they were. Instead, under his watch the team had finished in last place twice and never higher than sixth. The operating capital was gone and Barnes was looking for a way out. He hoped to win approval to move the Browns to Los Angeles, a city of one and a half million people in one of the most prosperous metropolitan areas in the world.

Less than forty-eight hours later, the plans of both Hank Greenberg and Donald Barnes would take a most dramatic turn.

CHAPTER FOURTEEN

1942 to 1945: Gashouse Baseball and the Miracle of '42

At the major league meetings held the Tuesday following the attack on Pearl Harbor, Donald Barnes formally proposed moving the St. Louis Browns to Los Angeles—at the same time admitting the obstacles to doing so were overwhelming. American League owners unanimously rejected the plan without discussion.[1] Despite the bad timing for Barnes, *The Sporting News* editorialized that major league baseball for Los Angeles was inevitable, which, coming from baseball's best known and most conservative voice, was a significant statement. C. Taylor Spink predicted that Los Angeles would have a team in less than a decade.[2]

Meanwhile, Hank Greenberg re-enlisted only days after his discharge, sacrificing his $55,000 salary. "This doubtless means that I am finished with baseball and it would be silly for me to say I do not leave it without a pang," he said. "But all of us are confronted with a terrible task—the defense of our country and the fight of our lives."[3]

There was little doubt that Pacific Coast League owners would carry on with the 1942 season after President Roosevelt gave his blessing to baseball continuing. Harry Williams, speaking as league secretary, declared rather indelicately, "We went to the trouble of teaching the Japs baseball and we don't intend to let them obliterate it."[4]

Life went on. Wrigley Field was in use during spring training as the backdrop to a Lou Gehrig film biography, *The Pride of the Yankees*, starring Gary Cooper, Babe Ruth and Walter Brennan.[5] Despite sporadic Japanese attacks on the West Coast, the army approved night baseball for the Pacific Coast League in 1942, provided attendance averaged no more than five thousand and that lighting systems could be turned off quickly.[6] A curfew was enacted, and it contributed to the unusual cancellation of the second game of a doubleheader on July 16 between the Oaks and Beavers at Vaughn Street Park in Portland when a sinkhole threatened to swallow Portland center fielder Rupert Thompson as he jogged from his position to the dugout between innings. Oaks outfielder Emil Mailho ran out and jumped into the hole, which was deep enough to obscure him from view, save for his cap. Mailho waved to the crowd, which howled with laughter at the sight. It took fifteen minutes for groundskeeper Rocky Benevento and his crew to haul enough wheelbarrows of dirt to fill the hole to the satisfaction of the umpires. The game resumed, but only three innings could be completed before curfew took effect.[7]

The army eventually reversed its original decision and night baseball was eliminated, effective August 20.[8] The Los Angeles Angels marked their final night game on August 7 with a special ceremony. At the end of the seventh inning, the lights were turned out and 3,500 fans lit matches, casting an eerie glow as the hushed crowd listened to "Taps" and then sang the National Anthem.[9] The edict against night games would remain in effect through the 1943 season.

* * *

For a brief time in September, events a world away seemed as such, as the Sacramento Solons and Los Angeles Angels staged one the great pennant races in baseball history. The Solons had chased the Angels all season and were two games behind with seven to play — all against Los Angeles in Sacramento.

Solons manager Pepper Martin gauged the mood of his players as they headed home for the final series, having just played five doubleheaders in five days in Seattle. Following the collapse of 1941, misfortune had dogged the Solons most of the 1942 season and it seemed as if they were constantly struggling uphill.

Although bolstered by winter deals that netted them veteran catcher Ray Mueller and 1940 National League batting champion Debs Garms, the Solons lost outfielder Bill Shewey in late May when an errant throw by Oakland's Bill Rigney hit him in the eye.[10] First baseman Jack Sturdy was hampered by a bad shoulder, which robbed him of his ability to hit for power. Second baseman Gene Handley was twice disabled, first by a broken hand and then a severe knee injury that, after a couple of failed comebacks, appeared to end his season. Catcher Charles Marshall was pressed into service in the middle infield.[11]

In an attempt to change the team's luck, Handley, Garms and Steve Mesner shaved their heads before a game on June 11. At first, fortune seemed to have turned and the Solons moved into first place.[12] However, by late August, Sacramento had fallen eight games behind. The parent St. Louis Cardinals, in the midst of a heated pennant race with the Brooklyn Dodgers, were unable — and unwilling — to lend assistance The only player sent to the Solons was Rochester infielder and PCL veteran Gene Lillard, who had given up pitching to resume his career as an everyday player.[13] Somehow, the Solons closed the gap, with a furious rally that seemed to leave them with nothing left in the tank for the final push.

With the season entering its final week, Gene Handley approached Pepper Martin and lobbied to play despite his bad knee. Martin told him no. After Tony Freitas, making his fourth appearance — and third start — in seven days, lost the first game of the series against Los Angeles, Martin relented and put Handley in the lineup. It made no difference; the Angels battered five Solons pitchers and Sacramento was only one game from elimination.[14] The unlikely had become the nearly impossible. Trailing by four games, the Solons had to defeat Los Angeles five times in a row. Angels shortstop Billy Schuster had vowed not to shave until his team clinched the title, and the next day the Angels seemed poised to do exactly that, carrying a 4–1 lead into the eighth inning.

But the Solons rallied to tie the game, thanks to back-to-back home runs hit by Buster Adams and Ray Mueller. In the ninth, Steve Mesner bunted for a base hit with one out and took second on a single. Ray Mueller then hit a grounder to Billy Schuster, who tossed the ball to second baseman Roy Hughes for a force out. However, in trying to complete the double play, Hughes made a wild relay throw and Mesner scored the winning run for Sacramento.[15]

The Solons again staved off elimination on Friday as Debs Garms hit a grand slam in the first inning and Tony Freitas scattered eight hits to defeat the Angels, 10–2.[16] An animated home crowd of three thousand was on hand Saturday to root for their Solons. This time it was Los Angeles that rallied from behind, twice overcoming two-run deficits to send the game into extra innings tied at 4–4. Jess Flores had taken the mound for the Angels in the seventh inning and shut out Sacramento through the tenth. It appeared that Flores was going to be the hero; he slammed a double off the left-field fence in the top of the eleventh inning to give the Angels a 5–4 lead. Los Angeles was only three outs away from the pennant.

With one out and one on in the bottom of the eleventh, Pepper Martin asked Gene Lillard to pinch-hit. Martin's move paid off in a most dramatic way—Lillard promptly crushed Red Lynn's pitch for a game-winning, two-run walk-off home run, sending it screaming over the fence so quickly that Jigger Statz, playing because Barney Olsen had been hospitalized with an infection in his foot, could only stand in left field and watch the ball rocket overhead. Lillard was met by his teammates at home plate and carried from the field in triumph.[17]

The pennant was going to be decided in a doubleheader on the final day. A Solons sweep would enable them to capture their first Pacific Coast League championship, forcing an unprecedented collapse on the Angels while earning redemption for the disappointing finish in 1941.

More than eleven thousand fans crowded into Sacramento's ballpark on Sunday morning for the first game, but the mood was quickly dampened when the Angels scored three runs in the first and then stretched the lead to 5–0 in the top of the fourth. The Solons

When Pepper Martin was named player-manager of the Sacramento Solons in 1941, he declared he was going to bring "Gas House Baseball" to the Pacific Coast League. In his first season, the Solons started the year with a record of 50–19. In his second year, he led them to the title— The Miracle of '42 (David Eskenazi Collection).

struck back with two unearned runs in the bottom half of the inning, driving Ray Prim from the game, and might have scored twice more had Jigger Statz not made a spectacular leaping catch of Jack Sturdy's bid for a home run. But the Solons kept inching closer. In the seventh inning, Mel Serafini slammed a pinch-hit home run to make the score 5–3. Angels fans were growing nervous; they had a right to be.

Steve Mesner led off Sacramento's half of the eighth with an infield single and Buster Adams promptly followed with a two-run home run to tie the score. Jigger Statz brought in Jess Flores, and for the second time that week, Ray Mueller followed Adams' home run with one of his own. Suddenly, the Solons were ahead, 6–5.

The Angels were absolutely deflated. St. Mary's College student Stan Gilliam, who would later become a columnist for the *Sacramento Bee*, never forgot the sight of Jigger Statz in left field when Mueller swung. Gilliam said, "You could see him visibly sag when that ball went over his head."[18] The Solons added another run before the inning was over and the crowd responded with an ovation of such enthusiasm that the public address announcer was drowned out. The roar continued as Pepper Martin brought in Tony Freitas, who quickly retired the Angels in order in the ninth. Sacramento and Los Angeles were tied for first place.[19] One game would decide the championship.

But Pepper Martin was in a quandary. Both teams had used five pitchers in the first game and Martin knew his pitching staff was exhausted. The past few days had been exhilarating but had also exacted a physical toll on a battered team.

Between games, boxer Buddy Baer presented a wristwatch to Ray Mueller in honor of his being named the Solons' most valuable player. Meanwhile, Pepper Martin nervously paced in the clubhouse, desperate for a pitcher to step forward. Addressing the team, he asked, "Now who am I going to pitch? I don't have any pitchers left." Tony Freitas, who had pitched six times in twelve days, was sitting in front of his cubicle and locked eyes with his manager. Without hesitation the thirty-four-year-old veteran declared, "Hey, I'll take a crack at them. I'm still warm."[20]

Martin needn't have worried. The Solons were ahead, 5–0, by the third inning of the nightcap. It was basically over for Los Angeles. Unable to break through against Freitas, the Angels found themselves down to their final three outs, trailing, 5–1.

Freitas surrendered a pair of singles to lead off the ninth but then retired a now-bearded Billy Schuster on a pop-up. Jigger Statz, in the last regular-season at-bat of his illustrious career, fouled off two pitches before striking out. Pinch-hitter Glenn Stewart then hit a line shot to third base that Steve Mesner speared for the final out. Solons fans rushed the field to congratulate their heroes, littering the stadium with cushions, hats and scorecards.[21] Pepper Martin and his players had achieved what had seemed impossible.

Years later, Tony Freitas marveled, "Every string Pepper Martin pulled was the right one. And he pulled some dandies." Asked when he thought Sacramento had the pennant won, Freitas answered, "Sunday, after the last game."[22] Martin was hailed as a hero, and a photo showing him thrusting his fist in triumph was published in newspapers under the headline "Delivers." The final week of the season would be remembered in Sacramento as "The Miracle of '42."

Following the playoffs, forty-four-year-old Arnold "Jigger" Statz resigned as manager of the Angels and also retired as a player, ending his eighteen-year career with Los Angeles. Statz owned most PCL career records, playing in 2,790 games, collecting 3,356 hits, 597 doubles, 136 triples, and scoring 1,996 runs. In more than ten thousand at-bats for the Angels, Statz carried a lifetime batting average of .315.

Statz indicated he hoped to stay in the organization and admitted, "I was disappointed in not being able to bring home the bacon as I feel that the Angels should have won the pennant this year." Angels president Pants Rowland responded, "I have never met a man of such great character. They broke the mold after they made Jigger. I agree with Arnold — it was most unfortunate that Los Angeles missed the championship. It was just one of those things."[23]

It may have been "just one of those things" as Rowland put it, but he had no qualms in accepting Statz's resignation and replacing him with Bill Sweeney. It was a sad way for Jigger Statz to end a great career with the Los Angeles Angels. But the end had come, as it must for all who play the game.

* * *

As the 1942 season ended, it was unclear exactly how many minor leagues would continue to operate. Attendance in the Pacific Coast League was not bad, considering the ban on night baseball. The Angels drew almost 240,000, second in the minors only to Milwaukee in the American Association. The seventh-place Hollywood Stars drew a shade under 200,000.[24] But that was not the norm around the country. In the summer of 1941, an all-time high of forty-one minor leagues were operating in Organized Baseball. By the spring of 1943, that number had shrunk to nine.[25] Hundreds of players were in the armed forces — sixty-seven had enlisted from the PCL

The victim of the Miracle of '42, Jigger Statz retired after setting virtually every Pacific Coast League offensive record. In the PCL, Statz had 3,356 hits and scored 1,996 runs in 2,790 games (David Eskenazi Collection).

alone. The San Diego Padres had the most, twelve, followed by Hollywood, Portland and Seattle, each with eleven.[26]

The Pacific Coast League marched on, even without night baseball. The Portland Beavers received an infusion of cash when the franchise was purchased by Vancouver, British Columbia, hotel man and Lucky Lager brewery magnate George Norgan. A friendly rival of Emil Sick, Norgan was elected team president and immediately installed Bill Klepper as vice president and general manager. Norgan made no apologies for hiring Klepper and emphasized that the veteran PCL executive would be provided the financial resources to make the team competitive.[27]

At the same time, another major figure was leaving. In October 1942, Branch Rickey left the St. Louis Cardinals for a five-year contract as president and general manager of the Brooklyn Dodgers.[28] The move would prove an historic one for baseball and a boost for the Dodgers, but the Sacramento Solons would suffer. Cardinals owner and president Sam Breadon was not nearly the proponent of the farm system as Rickey. Pepper Martin was shifted to Rochester to manage the Cardinals' International League franchise. PCL Most Valuable Player Ray Mueller was sold to Cincinnati and Steve Mesner was drafted by the same team. Debs Garms and Buster Adams went to St. Louis. Tony Freitas joined the armed forces, along with a half-dozen other Solons.[29]

The result was a team even worse than the infamous 1936 edition. The Solons drew six thousand on Opening Day — and only twenty-five thousand during the rest of the season. Sacramento's fall from winning its first pennant to a record of 41–114 in 1943 ranks among the most dramatic reversals of fortune in PCL history. The Solons finished sixty-nine games behind first-place Los Angeles. Three pitchers lost twenty or more games, including John Pintar, who lost twenty-seven while winning only five.

The Solons were victims of a seven-inning perfect game by Oakland's Cotton Pippen.[30] They employed forty-three-year-old Paul Fitzke, a former University of Idaho star who was working as a junior high school teacher. Fitzke, whose major league career consisted of one game for the Cleveland Indians nineteen years earlier, was winless in eight decisions. During the last week of the season, Oaks catcher Wil Leonard was pressed into duty as a pitcher and shut out Sacramento on three hits in the nightcap of an Admission Day doubleheader. It was the first game Leonard had ever pitched in his life.[31] On the season's final day against Hollywood, the Solons allowed lumbering forty-year-old Babe Herman to hit an inside-the-park home run when outfielders Bill Ramsey and Gene Kavanaugh collided while chasing the ball. As if the Solons were not funny enough, in the same game the Stars' Johnny Dickshot called time in the midst of an intentional walk to change bats, eliciting gales of laughter from the crowd.[32]

* * *

There was suspicion all season that the shortage of raw materials was resulting in lower quality baseballs, which in turn was limiting home run totals; Oakland outfielder Emil Mailho likened the sensation of connecting with the ball to hitting a rock.[33] None of the starting infielders for Seattle hit a home run in 1943. No one on the San Diego Padres hit more than three. Gus Suhr had once hit 51 home runs in the PCL: He hit one in three years after his return to the San Francisco Seals in 1943. The "Dead Ball" era was back.

Despite the continual drain of manpower — two-thirds of the league's everyday starters in 1942 were not around in 1943 — and issues about poor playing equipment, the 1943 season featured some stellar performances. Al Brazle threw forty consecutive scoreless innings for Sacramento, and Johnny Dickshot hit in thirty-three consecutive games, starting on Opening Day.[34] The Los Angeles Angels played twenty-one straight games without a loss at one point, winning twenty and tying one and making a shambles of the pennant race.[35]

Only nine PCL players reached double figures in home runs; five of them played for the Angels. Los Angeles relied offensively on an outfield of Andy Pafko, John Ostrowski and Cecil Garriott, none of whom had previously played above Class B. Nonetheless, they were outstanding, with Pafko winning the Most Valuable Player award. Seven Angels pitchers won ten games or more, led by Red Lynn, who won twenty-one. Paul Gehrman had twenty wins and Ken Raffensberger, a future National League All-Star, won nineteen and had an earned run average of 2.14.

In July, the Angels signed fifteen-year-old Los Angeles High School catcher Billy Sarni.[36] Two weeks after joining the team, Sarni was pressed into service when the team's other receivers were injured. Sarni hit his first professional home run, "a towering circuit clout over the left-field wall" off San Diego pitcher Rex Dilbeck. The night after that, he went three for three against the Padres.[37]

Bill Sarni represented one end of the age spectrum in the PCL. There was plenty of gray hair in the league as well. Thirty-nine-year-old Fay Thomas, out of baseball in 1942, had a pair of short trials with Portland and Hollywood, dropping three decisions. Forty-four-year-old Charlie Root, in the second year of his return to the PCL after a seventeen-year major league career, won fifteen games for the Hollywood Stars. Sam Gibson was also forty-four and won six games with an earned run average of 2.45 for San Francisco. Joe Sprinz was forty-two but caught almost one hundred games. Harry Rosenberg, retired for more than a year and managing a trucking company, agreed to play for the Seals but only when they were home. He hit .362 in twenty-six games.[38] Forty-two-year-old Syl Johnson won eight games as a spot starter for Seattle while his forty-six-year-old teammate, Byron Speece, won thirteen. Forty-three-year-old Spencer Harris hit .276 as an outfielder for Portland. Forty-seven-year-old Herm Pillette was still an effective relief pitcher for Sacramento.

In all, there were eighteen players aged thirty-eight and older who saw significant playing time in the PCL in 1943.

* * *

The Oakland Oaks changed ownership at the end of the 1943 season, with Joe Blumenthal and Clarence "Brick" Laws purchasing majority ownership from Cookie Devincenzi.[39] The new brain trust began looking for a new manager. Early

FAY THOMAS
MOST VALUABLE LOS ANGELES
BASEBALL CLUB PLAYER · 1934
GAMES WON: 28   GAMES LOST: 4

All-time PCL great and star of the record-breaking 1934 Angels, Fay Thomas was among the many veterans who attempted comebacks during World War II (David Eskenazi Collection).

speculation centered on Babe Ruth, but the legendary slugger turned down the Oaks' offer of $15,000, reportedly standing firm on his demand for $25,000.[40]

A month earlier, former Brooklyn Dodgers first baseman Dolph Camilli had let it be known he was interested in being a player-manager. Only two seasons removed from a National League Most Valuable Player award, Camilli had been traded by the Dodgers to the New York Giants but refused to report.[41] He contacted the Oaks and the Oaks in turn contacted the Giants to see if a deal could be arranged.[42]

The Giants agreed to release Camilli in exchange for the first rights to Oaks shortstop Bill Rigney once he was discharged from military service; Rigney would join the Giants for a thirty-day tryout, after which if New York decided it did not want him, he would be returned to Oakland.[43] But Commissioner Landis would not approve the trade, objecting to the option. Landis said the Giants would have to purchase Rigney's contract outright.[44] Certain everything would work out, Camilli met with the Oakland Boosters and made plans for the 1944 season. He announced he would play first base and shift slugger Les Scarsella to the outfield.[45] As Camilli had thought, the deal was approved just before Christmas. He signed a two-year contract and officially took command of the Oaks.[46]

* * *

It was increasingly hard to ignore the lack of black faces on the playing fields of the Pacific Coast League, or in any other league for that matter. The closest blacks could come to participating in the white world of Organized Baseball was as good-luck charm mascots — the San Diego Padres employed such an individual as late as 1942.[47]

The war had intensified debate over integrating the sport. Labor unions took up the cause, arguing that America's enemies were using inequality as a propaganda tool. Opponents of the unions dismissed the criticism as the work of communist agitators.

In July 1942, Brooklyn Dodgers manager Leo Durocher ignited a firestorm when he was interviewed by the communist *Daily Worker*, a staunch advocate for integrating baseball, and said there were several Negro ballplayers he would sign if baseball allowed him to do so. An angry Commissioner Landis demanded an explanation and Durocher tried to claim he had been misquoted. Landis then made a public announcement: "There is no rule, formal or informal, or any understanding — unwritten, subterranean or sub-anything — against the hiring of Negro players by the teams of Organized Ball. I told Durocher that he could hire one Negro ball player, or 25 Negro ball players, just the same as whites."[48]

The commissioner's remarks inspired Pittsburgh Pirates president Bill Benswanger, who declared, "Colored men are American citizens with American rights. I know that there are many problems connected with the question but after all, somebody has to make the first move."[49] Benswanger asked black sportswriter Wendell Smith of the *Pittsburgh Courier* to suggest likely candidates for the Pirates to consider. Smith named Josh Gibson, Sam Bankhead, Willie Wells and Leon Day. But Benswanger then cryptically suggested the tryouts might not happen until after the season because the team's farm director was too busy.[50] December came and went and nothing happened.[51]

J.G. Taylor Spink weighed in on the issue in a *Sporting News* editorial, warning that integrating the sport would ruin the Negro Leagues and pointed to prominent black businessmen who agreed it was a bad idea. Spink also argued that integration could lead to riots if fans started hurling coarse insults at players, ignoring the fact that for years teams of blacks and whites had competed each winter without incident. Spink admitted other sports had been integrated but insisted that baseball was different.[52]

Satchel Paige also thought integration would not work. "You might as well be honest about it," he said. "There would be plenty of problems.... All the nice statements in the world from both sides aren't going to end Jim Crow."[53] Paige suggested the major leagues expand to include an all-black team.

There was renewed hope that something would change in 1943 when Los Angeles Angels president Pants Rowland announced he had been scouting Negro players during the winter and was giving a tryout to Nate Moreland, a young pitcher.[54] But again, nothing happened. In the spring of 1943, the Congress of Industrial Organizations, a labor group that would later merge with the American Federation of Labor to form the A.F.L.C.I.O., met with Negro League baseball stars Chet Brewer and Lou Dials and persuaded them to dare a Pacific Coast League team to sign them. Although there seemed to be initial interest on the part of Los Angeles and Oakland, again nothing happened. In May, the C.I.O. announced plans to picket Wrigley Field in Los Angeles, accusing PCL owners of cowardice and asking why Moreland, Brewer and Dials, who had played well against top-flight competition each winter, could not make the roster of a single Pacific Coast League team.[55]

During the major league winter baseball meetings following the 1943 season, a delegation including Paul Robeson and representatives from the National Negro Newspaper Publishers Association was allowed to address the issue of erasing the color line in baseball. Once again, Commissioner Landis insisted there was no such barrier and placed the burden squarely on the owners, declaring, "Each club is entirely free to employ Negro players to any extent it pleases and the matter is solely for each club's decision without any restrictions whatsoever."[56]

But Landis, who had repeatedly fought for the right of players to reach the top level of baseball without restriction, was not about to use his power to right this wrong. As the *New York Times* said in the same article, "Inasmuch as this (Landis' stating there were no restrictions on teams signing black players) appears to be all the delegation asked for in the first place, the matter probably will remain as it has been these many years. According to Landis there is no rule or agreement in baseball, written or verbal that prohibits a major or minor league team from engaging a Negro ball player. Whether this ever will be done is a matter still open to speculation."

A week after the meeting, the *Baltimore Afro American* spoke to several major league owners and, with Landis having figuratively put the ball in their court on the question of admitting blacks to the major leagues, asked if they had any plans to do so.

New York Yankees owner Ed Barrow replied, "If we find it necessary to hire colored, we will do it." Philadelphia Phillies president Bob Carpenter begged off responding to requests made by the black newspaper publisher contingent, insisting that because he was new to his position, he did not feel free to "make a definite statement." Washington Senators owner Clark Griffith spoke almost entirely off the record but was willing to say that Organized Baseball should help put the Negro Leagues on a solid foundation. Griffith also restated the position he had taken a year earlier that "colored players should have their own league and white players have theirs."[57]

* * *

Eager for a full-time president after eight years of turbulent cowboy-writer Wilbur Tuttle, the owners turned to Angels president Clarence "Pants" Rowland to direct the affairs of the Pacific Coast League. Rowland vowed to do what it took to help teams in financial trouble, "even if it comes to putting carnivals on the field."[58] He was also committed to pursuing major league status for the PCL.

Unlike predecessors Hy Baggerly and Wilbur Tuttle, Clarence Rowland was a man with important major league connections. The sixty-five-year-old Wisconsin native had been a minor league catcher and a minor and major league manager, winning the World Series with the Chicago White Sox in 1917. He was also a former American League umpire and a scout for the Chicago Cubs before assuming the presidency of the Los Angeles Angels in November 1941.[59] Rowland received a ten-year contract at $12,500 per year — more than three times what Tuttle was making — and his vow to help shaky teams was quickly put to the test. Sacramento, only twelve months after celebrating a great sports triumph, was once again in danger of losing its franchise.

In February 1944, Sam Breadon announced the St. Louis Cardinals were selling the Sacramento Solons to a group that would move the franchise to Tacoma, Washington. Emil Sick, eager for a rival in the Northwest, said he was confident the sale would be approved. Meanwhile, the Sacramento Chamber of Commerce complained that Breadon had not given them the opportunity to make a counter offer. Charlie Graham and Brick Laws agreed, immediately registering their opposition to the transfer.[60] Charles Lott added his voice to those voting against it. The Tacoma group reacted by making its first payment of ten thousand dollars — 20 percent of the purchase price — and characterized the actions of the Sacramento chamber as "unreasonable."[61]

League directors allowed the city of Sacramento a week to come up with the financing to purchase the team. Breadon said if the Tacoma deal fell through, he would offer the stadium, player contracts, equipment and the franchise to local interests for $110,000; without the stadium, the franchise could be had for $50,000. Sacramento civic leaders began to scurry, looking for a way to meet Breadon's offer.[62]

Breadon gave the Sacramento group until 10:00 A.M. on February 22 to come up with the money.[63] *Sacramento Union* sports editor Dick Edmonds and restaurant owner Yubi Separovich burned up the phone lines, calling every sports-minded person they could think of, and managed to raise $52,000 in forty-eight hours. The men then headed to Los Angeles, where the league directors had gathered to decide on the matter of moving the franchise. Long-time Tacoma baseball figure Roger Peck had in hand a certified check for $175,000 as evidence that his group had the resources to compete.

The train carrying Edmonds and Separovich was delayed by a snowstorm. Then the two men were switched onto a bus at Mojave, putting them a disheartening nine hours behind schedule. The other PCL owners, aware of their Herculean effort, waited for them to arrive and then pronounced themselves satisfied with the offer. The team would stay in Sacramento. Sam Breadon, impressed with the work done by Edmonds and Separovich, said, "For them, the price is cut to forty-thousand dollars."[64] The league attached a condition to its approval: The team had to average 125,000 in paid attendance for two straight years. If the Solons failed to do so the franchise would revert to the league.[65] Separovich, who as a boy had been a peanut vendor at Solons games, was named the team's business manager while former congressional candidate and gas station owner Joe O'Neil was elected team president. The new board of directors formed an association to sell stock and raise the money to purchase the ballpark from the Cardinals. Earl Sheely was named manager.[66]

Forty years after the city had turned down a deal offered by Mike Fisher, which ironically also involved moving a Sacramento team to Tacoma, the city had come through and saved its franchise.

* * *

Opening Day in 1944 was festive as usual in Hollywood; Jack Norworth, lyricist of the baseball song "Take Me Out to the Ball Game" was on hand to throw out the first pitch to sheriff Gene Biscailuz, who was behind the plate, with comedian Joe E. Brown at bat. Norworth, Brown and Biscailuz then joined with Babe Herman and actor George Tobias to sing Norworth's famous tune in what was jokingly called "a bit of barbershop disharmony."[67] Two days later, Hollywood ushered in the return of night baseball, the army having finally decided it was safe to resume the practice, and the Stars lost a three-hour marathon to Seattle, 14–8.[68]

Cold weather in Southern California depressed attendance for the opening games, but the crowds increased in the cities with new ownership. *Los Angeles Times* columnist Al Wolf claimed that when Brick Laws saw the number of fans lined up to get into Oaks Park on Opening Day, he turned to ex-owner Cookie Devincenzi and asked, "How long has this been going on?" Having suffered through multiple lean years, Devincenzi supposedly sighed and replied, "Not very long."[69]

Things were also going well in Sacramento under new manager Earl Sheely. The Solons had the Pacific Coast League's biggest crowd on Opening Day. At the halfway point of the season, the franchise had drawn 100,000, almost four times the number that had attended during all of 1943.[70]

* * *

Los Angeles took its second straight pennant in 1944, although not by as large a margin as in 1943. But there was no doubting the Angels had the most talent; only six batters hit ten or more home runs in the Pacific Coast League in 1944, and four of those played for Los Angeles. Ray Prim, the crafty veteran with the odd windup that included turning his back to the hitter during his delivery, won twenty-two games and walked only forty batters in 286 innings while compiling an excellent 1.70 earned run average. His ERA was second only to Sacramento's Clem Dreisewerd, whose control was even better with only twenty-one bases on balls in 252 innings.

Pitching again dominated the PCL, with the league boasting eight twenty-game winners. Besides Dreisewerd and Prim, the league's top performers included Portland's Marino Pieretti, who won twenty-six games, and Frank Dasso, who won twenty for the last-place San Diego Padres while leading the league in strikeouts with 253, the most in the PCL in nearly twenty years.

Hollywood's Frank Kelleher barely missed out on the Triple Crown, failing to win the batting title because of an average that was one-third of a point less than Oakland's Les Scarsella. Kelleher was playing for Hollywood only because he was due for induction into the armed forces and had received permission from the Cincinnati Reds to remain near his home while awaiting his draft notice.[71] Kelleher was the only player to hit more than twenty home runs and also the only one to drive in more than one hundred, but Scarsella won the Most Valuable Player award in a nod toward his versatility, an invaluable characteristic during times of war-ravaged rosters. Scarsella played first base and outfield for the Oaks, hitting .329 and driving in ninety-six runs. He also pitched, winning three games and compiling a 1.75 earned run average in sixty-seven innings.

* * *

The San Diego Padres changed hands in 1944 when they were finally sold by Florence Eastman, six years after she had inherited controlling interest from Bill Lane's estate. The new owners, Los Angeles businessmen Caesar Pastore, Vic Schulman, Harry Leddell and ex–Padres catcher Bill Starr, took control of the club immediately and announced that Starr would run it.[72] In an effort to kick-start interest among Padres fans, Pepper Martin was hired as manager.

Kenesaw Mountain Landis died in November 1944. As the search began for a successor, Pants Rowland stressed the need for the minor leagues to operate with greater autonomy than had been the case under baseball's first commissioner. Rowland was also confident baseball would continue despite the war and expressed optimism for the coming season. He said:

> Baseball naturally wants to cooperate to the fullest extent with the war effort. Baseball already has supplied more men to the armed services on a per capita basis than any other business in the country. Baseball has a job to do. Baseball has to offer relaxation for those who want it.... Baseball has to provide diversion for the thousands of servicemen hospitalized in this country. They tell me their morale picks up amazingly when they can listen to play-by-play broadcasts, read stories about their favorites and while away the long hours by keeping statistics and records for themselves.[73]

At the Pacific Coast League's annual meeting, a twenty-five-man roster was adopted and the regular-season and playoff reward pools were doubled.[74] As usual, there were rumors about possible sales of teams. One involved movie star Betty Grable and her bandleader husband, Harry James, buying the Sacramento Solons. That proved false, although James allowed that the couple was interested in purchasing a PCL franchise.[75]

Another rumor, involving the San Francisco Seals, proved true. At the beginning of the 1945 season the Seals got a new moneyman, Paul Fagan, whose family had long been involved with Crocker Bank in San Francisco. Fagan had at one time worked for the bank and later founded an import/export business in San Francisco. In 1929, he married Helene Irwin, daughter of a Hawaii sugar baron and the former wife of C. Templeton Crocker, grandson of Charles Crocker.[76] Fagan subsequently engaged in a series of investments in Hawaii, including the purchase of thousands of acres on Maui and Molokai. He established a cattle ranch and resort properties there and built a palatial estate near Diamond Head.

Dan Topping, a friend of Fagan, had purchased a share of the New York Yankees, which led Fagan to investigate the possibility of owning a team that he could relocate to Honolulu. Air travel was advancing rapidly as a preferred mode of transportation, but flights across the Pacific were still impractical, and another friend suggested Fagan look at buying a share of the San Francisco Seals.

Fagan walked into Charlie Graham's office and offered $250,000 for the late George Putnam's share of the team. Graham accepted. Fagan's infusion of cash meant the Seals were out of debt and in good financial stead for the first time since the beginning of the Depression. Both Graham and Doc Strub retained their ownership stake in the Seals but canceled tens of thousands of dollars owed to them by the franchise so Fagan would have some working capital.

Although lacking in baseball knowledge, Fagan wanted the Seals to operate as a first-class, major-league caliber franchise. "Baseball is the same as any other business," he said. "You have to meet your competition on equal footing. We are selling seats in a ballpark and we must give the fans a good show. That means a good club. And we must be in a position to meet any competition offered."[77] Fagan spoke of covering the stands at Seals Stadium, installing theatre seats for a more upscale experience, and adding steam heat to make patrons more comfortable during night games. He proposed building an ice rink at the stadium that could be open to the public during the winter.[78] He also showed his naiveté about the game, asking what it would cost to bring top major league stars such as Bob Feller and Ted Williams to the Seals.

For all his strengths—and faults—Paul Fagan had instantly rejuvenated one of the PCL's flagship franchises.

* * *

Just as Kenesaw Mountain Landis had been the only commissioner baseball had ever known, Franklin Delano Roosevelt was the only president anyone under sixteen years of age could remember. Everyone would recall where they were on April 12, 1945, when they heard about the president's death. The Pacific Coast League postponed games that were to be played that night but resumed the schedule the next day.[79] Attendance was dismal; only four hundred fans came out to Gilmore Field to see Hollywood play against Seattle. As a result, the PCL called off games to be played on the day of the president's funeral.[80]

The stops and starts of the schedule did not bother Seattle's Ted Norbert, who hit three home runs in the doubleheader on Sunday against Hollywood, giving him seven through the first sixteen games of the season.[81] Another stellar performance was that of Portland outfielder Frank Shone, whose thirty-nine-game hitting streak finally came to an end at Sick's Stadium on July 26 thanks to Seattle knuckleballer Joe Demoran.[82]

Meanwhile, Pepper Martin was not having a smooth time in San Diego. Having taken over a last-place team with new ownership and its top two pitchers from the year before—Frank Dasso and Rex Cecil—sent to the major leagues, the Padres roster was in a state of flux for much of the season.

At one point Martin engaged in an argument in an Oakland hotel lobby with his best pitcher, Vallie Eaves, which ended with the manager slapping Eaves in the face; some observers were of the opinion that the slap was more of a punch. Martin was frustrated with Eaves, who had already been suspended several times, because of his lackadaisical performance as a relief pitcher that afternoon. Martin was unapologetic about the incident: "He had it coming to him. He let me down during the game yesterday, besides upsetting the discipline of the club and setting a bad example for the rest of the players."[83]

With the war essentially over, it was time for some fun, and in late August it was announced that Hollywood manager Buck Fausett would take the mound against Pepper Martin. Both men vowed to continue pitching "until base hits or exhaustion cause them to retire."[84] Martin lasted only five innings but earned the victory, allowing two runs on six hits and leaving with a 6–2 lead. Fausett went the route, allowing six runs (only three were earned). The crowd of six thousand at Gilmore Field had a wonderful time.[85] With the surrender of Japan already announced and the official signing of peace treaties only a week away, the specter of boys dying overseas was no longer engulfing everything else in the consciousness of fans.

* * *

Bob Joyce was a thirty-year-old workhorse pitcher for the San Francisco Seals. Despite his inability to throw hard enough to break a pane of glass, he had been a twenty-game winner for the Seals for three straight years. Joyce missed spring training in 1945 because of his defense job as an electrician, but the lack of time in training camp seemed to make no difference as he once again reached the twenty-win mark—and then easily surpassed it, exceeding his previous career best. Featuring a slider that some suspected was made more effective by the addition of a foreign substance, Joyce responded to accusations with a shrug and a wry smile, often remarking, "Sometimes that slider does things and I don't know why."[86]

Whether or not he loaded his pitches is open to speculation—umpire Jack Powell for one insisted that Joyce did not use a spitter—but Joyce had excellent control of whatever he was throwing, working the corners with his curve and slider and then suddenly slipping his mediocre fastball past the hitter before the victim realized what was happening. By mid–August in 1945, Joyce had twenty-six wins and learned he was going back to the major leagues for the first time in seven years, having been traded to the New York Giants for five pitchers, effective at the end of the season.[87] On September 2, Joyce became the first thirty-game winner in the Pacific Coast League since Buck Newsom.[88] After earning almost exactly one-third of the Seals' ninety-six wins and hitting .321 with twenty runs batted in, Joyce was the lopsided choice as the PCL's Most Valuable Player.[89]

The Portland Beavers easily won the 1945 pennant, their first title in nine years, with a team not much different than the one that had finished second in 1944. But the San Francisco Seals triumphed in the playoffs for the third year in a row, thanks in large part to Joyce, who won four games — including three in the championship series against Seattle — bringing his total victories for the year to thirty-five.

Over the course of the season, Bob Joyce pitched thirty-five complete games and did not commit a balk or hit a batter all year. It was a remarkable performance from one of the most popular players in the league.

* * *

Jerry Angelich tried out as a pitcher with the Sacramento Senators in 1935. Although he did not make the team, he did pitch in an exhibition game at Moreing Field against the Tokyo Giants and their teenage pitching sensation, Eiji Sawamura, who had already achieved legendary status for his consecutive strikeouts of Charlie Gehringer, Lou Gehrig, Babe Ruth and Jimmie Foxx during a game in Japan a few months earlier. Angelich lost to Sawamura, 2–1, before a crowd of nearly five thousand.[90] He then defeated another future Japanese baseball legend, Victor Starfin, in a spring training game in Stockton.[91] Angelich was out of baseball and serving as an army aircraft gunner at Hickham Field, Pearl Harbor, on December 7, 1941, when he was killed during the Japanese raid.[92] He was one of several players with ties to the Pacific Coast League who made the ultimate sacrifice during World War II.

Henry "Marty" Martinez had once received a football scholarship to the University of Southern California. The twenty-eight-year-old Honolulu native played infield for Oakland and Seattle before joining Portland in 1942. He also played several years with Spokane in the Pacific Northwest League. Almost exactly three years after Angelich died, Martinez was killed in action at sea. His body was never recovered.[93]

Manuel "Nay" Hernandez, a reserve outfielder for the San Diego Padres, was killed in 1945 while serving as an infantryman in Germany following the Battle of the Bulge. First buried in Europe, his body was returned to the States in 1948 and re-interred in San Diego.[94]

Ernie Raimondi, an Oakland native and San Francisco Seals infielder whose brothers Al, Walt and Billy all played in the PCL, was fatally wounded at the European front in Italy on January 21, 1945, only six weeks after arriving. Raimondi also left behind a nine-month-old daughter, who he had seen only briefly before deployment.[95] In June 1947, Bayview Park at Wood Street in West Oakland, between Eighteenth and Twentieth streets, was renamed Ernie Raimondi Playground.[96] It remains in use for soccer, youth football and Little League baseball and also serves as the home diamond for the varsity baseball team of McClymonds High School, Raimondi's alma mater.

The first active professional baseball player to die in action also had ties to the Pacific Coast League, although he never played a regular-season game there.

Billy Hebert was an extremely likeable young man. He first caught the attention of Lefty O'Doul in 1936 after leaving Stockton High School to attend spring training with the Seals.[97] Too young to succeed at the highest level of the minor leagues, Hebert was cut by O'Doul early in training camp and signed with Ogden of the Pioneer League. By 1939, he was a fan favorite there. A hustling second baseman with a cocksure smile and the bill of his cap tugged slightly sideways, Hebert always looked a mess on the ball field. He was constantly wiping tobacco juice on his uniform pants, which when mixed with dirt and sweat gave him a very unkempt appearance. Fans barely recognized Hebert off the field, where he was always well dressed and immaculate.[98]

Hebert was invited to spring training by the Oakland Oaks in 1940 but was dropped before the season started and played that year for a semi-pro team in Stockton. The next year he joined the Merced Bears of the California League, batting .328 with twelve home runs. He was one of the team's most popular players and always noted for his hustle; team-mate Wally Westlake thought him to be a sure big league prospect.[99] Twenty-two years old, Hebert was one of five Bears recalled by the Oakland Oaks for the 1942 season. Instead, he enlisted in the navy three months before Pearl Harbor.[100]

Assigned to the Seabees, Hebert was repairing planes at Guadalcanal when he was killed on October 31, 1942.[101] *The Sporting News* said, "his memory will be cherished long in the annals of the game as the first to lay down his life so that both his country and the sport to which he dedicated himself might survive."[102]

In May 1943, a ceremony was held at Oak Park in Stockton to honor Hebert. A flagpole was erected to the ballplayer's memory, and Hebert's father, a metal smith from Berkeley, California, fabricated a bronze plaque that was installed at the base of the pole. Hebert's family was present for the dedication ceremony, which was followed by a game between two American Legion teams, one of which Hebert had captained in his teenage years.[103] After the war, a new baseball stadium in Stockton was named in Hebert's honor and served as the home field of the California League's Stockton Ports for a half-century. A real-life citizen of Ernest Thayer's immortal "Mudville" had achieved his immortality by making the ultimate sacrifice.[104]

* * *

Although not war-related, there was one final casualty during World War II. On July 20, 1945, Dick Edmonds died. Only thirty-one years old, the sports editor of the *Sacramento Union* had contracted viral pneumonia five weeks before his death. A year after rescuing the Pacific Coast League franchise for Sacramento, the man most responsible for saving the Solons was gone.[105] Moved by his untimely death, the citizens of Sacramento re-named the team's home field in honor of the sports editor without whom the team would have ceased to exist.

On September 9, 1945, the stadium was officially christened Edmonds Field in a ceremony held between games of a doubleheader against Oakland. The moment was especially poignant in light of the fact that Edmonds lay buried in a cemetery across the street from the ballpark that now bore his name. JoJo White, who received the team's Most Valuable Player award that same day, remarked, "This is one of the greatest honors of my life. I shall always remember it as having taken place on Dick Edmonds Day." To top off the occasion, the Solons swept the doubleheader from Oakland.[106]

Most appropriately, a milestone that would have meant a great deal to Edmonds had been achieved the day before. At a league meeting in Oakland, the Pacific Coast League announced that the local ownership of the Solons had met the criteria for retaining the team.[107] Required to draw at least 125,000 for two consecutive seasons, the Solons had achieved totals of nearly 200,000 in 1944 and more than 300,000 in 1945. The Sacramento Solons were finally, and officially, saved. It was a far cry from the sad situation Edmonds had faced when rescuing the franchise eighteen months earlier. There could not have been a finer tribute to the memory of Dick Edmonds.

CHAPTER FIFTEEN

1946 to 1948: Lefty, Casey and the Nine Old Men

Lefty O'Doul had been with the San Francisco Seals for eleven seasons and no manager in the Pacific Coast League was better compensated. When Paul Fagan came aboard, O'Doul's pay was increased to $39,000 per year, greater than most major league managers and more than three times what Dolph Camilli was paid by Oakland.[1]

Popular and colorful, O'Doul was a showman on and off the field and the press loved him. Somewhat superstitious, his rituals were more habit than a reflection of his thinking they had an effect on the outcome of an at-bat or a game. At a time when useful instruction at the professional level was rare, O'Doul actually favored teaching the game more than managing it. Dom DiMaggio developed into an excellent hitter under O'Doul's tutelage and considered him the greatest hitting instructor in baseball history.[2] It did not matter to O'Doul whether a player was property of the Seals or not. When pitcher Frank Dasso was on loan to San Francisco from the Cincinnati Reds, O'Doul worked with him on his mechanics as if he belonged to the Seals. "He was teaching all the time," said Dasso. "He was not out for O'Doul. Most managers are saying, 'You win or I'm out.' O'Doul never did that. O'Doul never worried whether he was going to be manager or not. And hell, he lasted longer than any of them."[3]

Bobby Doerr noted that opposing players would also approach him: "We used to go over ... and ask him things. I was having a little trouble dipping [on my swing]. I wasn't pivoting my hips. I just couldn't figure it out. I remember him telling me, 'Just think of your head, your shoulders and your hips being three spools and that they're turning instead of dipping.' That made a big impression on me."[4]

When not on the golf course — an activity that would become a bone of contention over the years — O'Doul loitered in hotel lobbies, wearing his trademark green suit and swapping stories with reporters.[5] He mingled just as easily with movie stars as with baseball men. And no one was allowed to buy him anything in San Francisco; it was Lefty O'Doul's town, and if you were visiting, everything was on him.

Standing in the third-base coach's box, waving a red bandanna to rally fans (who responded by bringing their own handkerchiefs and waving them in unison with the Seals manager), O'Doul seemed as much a part of Seals Stadium as the concrete façade or the San Francisco skyline. He was most definitely a "player's manager" with a strong sense of each member of his team. O'Doul lived by the credo that if a player wanted to play, he would take care of himself— no one could do it for him. He explained to Larry Jansen, "If you want to play, you don't need any rules."[6] Neill Sheridan said, "As long as you hustled, you never had any problem with Lefty."[7]

Although the San Francisco Seals had won the last three Governor's Cups, they had not captured a PCL pennant since O'Doul's first season as manager in 1935. Money was tight and the Seals had neither aggressively pursued talent nor held onto what they had. Things would be different for Lefty O'Doul and the Seals in 1946. Paul Fagan's wealth injected life into the franchise, which because of the war, the death of George Putnam, the aging of Charlie Graham and Doc Strub's increasing lack of active interest, had become focused more on survival than winning.

Meanwhile, the Oakland Oaks were seeking their seventh manager since Lefty O'Doul had taken the reins of the Seals. Dolph Camilli resigned from the Oaks in the middle of the 1945 season in a dispute over whether he should be playing more. Blaming his inactivity on a sore foot, Camilli remained on the bench and played teenage prospect Vic Picetti instead. Local favorite Billy Raimondi finished the 1945 season as manager but was clearly not the long-term solution — nor did he want to be.[8] It was time for a change. A theatre man, Brick Laws recognized the value of having an attractive name on the marquee and vowed to find one.

It was not long before Laws had his man: one of the best-known characters in baseball. On October 17, 1945, Laws announced that Charles Dillon "Casey" Stengel had signed a one-year contract for $12,000 to manage the Oaks.[9]

There was no question that Stengel fit Brick Laws' criteria; he was colorful and drew fans to the ballpark, although many, including Lefty O'Doul, were of the opinion that the fifty-five-year-old was more clown than manager. Indeed, Stengel was less famous for his baseball acumen than for stories of releasing a live sparrow from under his cap, perfecting his sliding technique by practicing as he came on and off the field between innings, thumbing his nose at the Yankees when he hit two home runs against them in the World Series, or his tortured method of storytelling.

But Stengel insisted he was going to win this time or else while hoping to parlay a term in Oakland into a return to the major leagues. Not that Stengel was going to change all *that* much. *Los Angeles Examiner* reporter Bob Hunter recalled that whenever the Oaks visited Southern California, Stengel held court in all-night bull sessions with reporters after a game.

"It was always a must to wind up at the fifth floor (in the tower) at Wrigley Field or in the press room at Hollywood, or in Bob Cobb's room and sit down with him. Many times he'd stay there until eight or nine o'clock in the morning just talking baseball."[10]

The Bay Area teams were revitalized in 1946 and both attracted crowds as never before. The Oaks and Seals played a series against each other beginning July 30 that drew 114,000 — the first time in PCL history that any series had played host to more than 100,000 patrons. San Francisco took five of the seven games and moved within easy striking distance of the minor league attendance record of 517,657, set in 1939 by the Seattle Rainiers. The Oaks were not far behind.

* * *

On April 24, 1945, a United States Senator from Kentucky, Albert "Happy" Chandler, was named the new Commissioner of Baseball.[11] The selection of Chandler was significant in that he was not Kenesaw Mountain Landis and therefore would not stand in the way of progress. Six months later, Jackie Robinson agreed to play for the Montreal Royals, the top farm club of the Brooklyn Dodgers, becoming the first African American in the twentieth century to sign a contract to play in the regular season for a team in Organized Baseball.[12] Congressman Adam Clayton Powell proclaimed, "This is a definite step toward winning the peace and now that this gentleman is in the International League, the other leagues will not be able to furnish any alibis."[13]

But other leagues did continue to stall, the Pacific Coast League included. The number of ballplayers returning from the war and the lack of any urgency to desegregate the game created an opportunity for Mexican multimillionaire Jorge Pasquel and his brothers, who had grand visions of jumping ahead of the PCL to achieve major league status for the Mexican League. Their effort was ultimately unsuccessful and the Mexican League would eventually join Organized Baseball but not before mounting the most serious challenge to the reserve clause since the Federal League.[14]

Frustrated by the lack of action on the part of Pacific Coast League owners to cross the color line, a group met in Oakland to form a Negro version of the PCL. Teams in the West Coast Negro Baseball League included the Seattle Steelheads (formerly the Harlem Globetrotters baseball team, not to be confused with the basketball team, which was also owned by Abe Saperstein), Portland Roses (operated by Olympic track star Jesse Owens), Oakland Larks, San Francisco Sea Lions, Fresno Tigers and Los Angeles White Sox.[15] Saperstein served as league president and Owens vice president.

California Governor Earl Warren threw out the first ball in San Francisco as more than five thousand fans attended the opener between the Sea Lions and Los Angeles.[16] The Oakland Larks, who opened in Fresno, were expected to be the front-runners thanks to a deep pitching staff that included Negro League veteran Marion "Sugar" Cain and Lionel Wilson, who later became mayor of Oakland.[17] But attendance was mediocre from the beginning; the second-best attended game was in Seattle, where 2,500 witnessed the Steelheads' home opener at Sick's Stadium on June 1.[18] In Portland, Jesse Owens tried to stimulate interest by staging an exhibition of his running skills between games of a doubleheader at Vaughn Street Park.[19]

The league struggled. The Fresno franchise shifted to San Diego a week after the season began.[20] The transplanted Tigers drew less than one thousand fans for their first game, a 15–3 loss to Los Angeles, as they surrendered seven runs in the first inning and committed an appalling nine errors.[21] The next day, the Tigers split a doubleheader with San Francisco in front of two thousand fans, with one of the games highlighted by a magnificent catch by Jesse Alexander, the Sea Lions one-armed outfielder.[22]

Attendance dwindled further as summer wore on. By August, the league was history. Some teams, including the Oakland Larks, continued as barnstorming squads, but the league itself permanently disbanded.

* * *

The Selective Service Act was adopted in an effort to protect servicemen so they would have employment upon returning home from the war. The law required they be reemployed in their former positions for one year. Organized Baseball never signed on, instead setting its own rule that returning ballplayers would be afforded a spot in training camp and a place on the roster for the first two weeks of the season, as a tryout of sorts to ensure they could still play.[23] After that, there were no guarantees.

In the spring of 1946, after three years as an athletic instructor at the Naval Pre-Flight School in California, Al Niemiec reported to the Seattle Rainiers to reclaim his spot as the team's second baseman, a position he had held from 1940 through 1942. Although Niemiec made the team out of spring training, it was apparent that the thirty-five-year-old infielder had slowed down. On April 21, he and first baseman Len Gabrielson were handed their releases.[24] Niemiec responded by contacting his draft board and arguing that under the

Selective Service Act he had a right to remain on the Rainiers roster for one year. The draft board agreed and ordered the team to reinstate him. Seattle vice president Torchy Torrance argued that the team had done more than enough for Niemiec and declared the Rainiers would appeal. Niemiec signed with Providence in the New England League but continued his legal battle with Seattle.[25]

Meanwhile, Rainiers manager Bill Skiff was under intense pressure. Team directors had offered Skiff, already the longest-tenured manager in franchise history, a contract extension through the 1947 season. But hang-ups over minor details prevented the contract from being executed and Skiff was growing increasingly frustrated. The Rainiers started slowly in 1946 and the roster became a revolving door. Ted Norbert, the PCL's leading home run hitter in 1945, was released the same day Skiff sold former Phillies catcher Bob Finley and veteran infielder Heine Heltzel to the Texas League.[26]

Skiff wrote a letter to Rainiers business manager Bill Mulligan in early May expressing annoyance at what he termed the incompetence of umpiring in the PCL and warned he would "not tolerate it any longer without a protest." In the same missive, Skiff betrayed his anger over the questioning of his expense account. In that letter, which was copied to Torchy Torrance, Skiff said the reason for each expense was noted on the checks and pointedly added, "It is necessary to get information to complete deals without a scouting system, and I know the record of these last five years on deals I have made certainly covers the small expense."[27]

Skiff became more combative over the next three weeks as the team continued to struggle, mired in seventh place with a record of 23–36 going into a Memorial Day doubleheader against Oakland. The Rainiers won the holiday opener but were trailing in the nightcap when umpire Monte Heard ruled a Seattle player out on a close play at home. Skiff snapped. He rocketed out of the dugout and kicked dirt over home plate. For good measure, he also covered Heard's shoes. After ejecting Skiff, Heard bent over to clean off the plate and in the process presented an inviting target for the furious manager. Almost as a reflex, Skiff lifted his knee and booted Heard in the posterior.[28]

The next day, Pants Rowland announced a fifty-dollar fine for Skiff, accompanied by an indefinite suspension. There were loud calls coming from many quarters for Skiff to be fired, led by influential *Seattle Post-Intelligencer* columnist Royal Brougham.[29] Emil Sick met with team directors in a special session on June 11 and a list of potential replacements was developed, including Jimmie Dykes and Babe Ruth, although Ruth was almost as quickly rejected because he would prove "too hard to handle" and "had dubious value as a long-term drawing card."

Skiff ultimately agreed to step down as part of a settlement that included a clause requiring him to remain available as a witness in the Niemiec case.[30] JoJo White, star outfielder of Seattle's championship teams from 1939 to 1941, was acquired from Sacramento in exchange for outfielder Bill Ramsey and installed as player-manager.[31]

During the Niemiec hearing, Skiff was subjected to the indignity of having his judgment of Niemiec's ability called into question since "he had been unable to hold his job" with Seattle. Niemiec won the case and the Rainiers were ordered to pay him the difference between his salary in Seattle and what he was making in the New England League.[32] The ruling was seen as a serious challenge to the reserve clause, and the Rainiers enlisted the help of Commissioner Chandler as they appealed the decision. Niemiec eventually settled for a little less than three thousand dollars; he was also hired by Sick to work as a salesman for his brewery.[33]

* * *

The 1946 San Francisco Seals were not without challenges as injuries proved to be a serious problem. Third baseman Ray Perry broke his ankle in April, a gruesome injury that not only ended his season but was thought by many to be career-ending.[34] Ex–New York Giants star pitcher Cliff Melton won seventeen games, but only two came after he injured a ligament in his elbow in July. Melton was winless between July 21 and September 15. In addition, the team did not have much offensive firepower. But they did have two young stars that enjoyed breakout seasons. Four years earlier, Charlie Graham had practically begged the New York Yankees to buy these two top prospects to keep him solvent. The Yankees refused.[35] Thanks to Paul Fagan's money, Graham could hold onto his two future major league all-stars, first baseman Ferris Fain and pitcher Larry Jansen.

Fain was the son of a former Kentucky Derby jockey who died when Ferris was a child. Extremely competitive and prone to outbursts of temper, Fain led the Seals with eleven home runs in 1946 and was gaining a reputation as one of the best fielding first basemen in baseball history thanks to an aggressive style many compared to Hal Chase.[36]

When Fain originally joined the team prior to the war, he struggled offensively. Lefty O'Doul continually watched Fain stagger about and curse during batting practice until he finally could stand it no longer and shouted, "Stop it! Stop it! Ye gods, what swinging!" He told Fain, "Your heart is in the right place, but your keester is three blocks away."[37] Heeding O'Doul's counsel, Fain batted .301 in 1946 and eventually captured two American League batting titles and played on five AL All-Star teams.

Jansen was a right-handed pitcher from Oregon, returning to the Seals after missing nearly three full seasons because he had to work on a dairy farm as part of the war effort.[38] Jansen delivered his pitches with an unusual grip, holding the bottom of the ball with only the knuckle of his thumb. It was a technique recommended by Jansen's American Legion coach, who told him the grip would produce better movement on his curveball. But it was the slider taught to him by San Francisco coach Larry Woodall that caused his career to take off.

Having honed his slider by pitching semi-pro ball on weekends, Jansen served notice early in the 1946 season that he was developing into a star. By mid–June he had a 15–3 record with an incredible 1.14 earned run average and was on his way to winning thirty games for the Seals and a contract with the New York Giants.[39]

* * *

The 1946 season started well for Casey Stengel in Oakland. Twenty-five-year-old Bryan Stephens, returning to baseball after three seasons in the military, pitched two extra-inning shutouts in April: an eleven inning, 1–0, win over Tony Freitas and Sacramento on April 13 and a twelve-inning win by the same score against Los Angeles on April 30. He even singled to drive in the only run to defeat the Angels.[40]

Two months later, Stengel signed veteran outfielder Brooks Holder following his release by Hollywood. Holder hit three home runs in a game against Seattle on June 28, making him the first to accomplish the feat in the PCL since Steve Mesner in 1937.[41] Les Scarsella had never hit more than fourteen home runs in a season; in 1946 he was leading the league from the start of the year and had twenty-two by the beginning of July.

But Oakland's luck began to turn sour. Stephens developed a sore arm and would win only ten games.[42] Scarsella was hampered by a hernia; he attempted to play through it with a specially fitted support but finally had to submit to surgery, ending his season in late July.[43] (Scarsella returned for the playoffs but was not able to appear in any more regular-season games.) Veteran pitcher Cotton Pippen was similarly afflicted, but his injury was not as debilitating as Scarsella's and he pitched through the pain.[44] The Oaks were rocked by tragedy in late June when several young prospects they had assigned to Spokane in the Western International League, including nineteen-year-old Vic Picetti, were killed in the crash of a bus transporting that team to a game in Bremerton, Washington.[45] On July 8, the Oaks played in Spokane against the Seattle Rainiers to raise money for the families of the nine players that had died. Fifty thousand dollars was raised, including $2,500 from Spokane native Bing Crosby, who bought a block of tickets to be distributed to servicemen.[46]

The Oaks continued fighting but were eliminated on the next-to-last day of the season, giving the Seals their first pennant in eleven years. The intense battle between the geographic rivals reignited interest, proving a boon for both franchises as each drew more than 600,000 fans, with San Francisco attracting a minor league record 670,563, a mark that would stand for nearly forty years.[47] To top it off, in the first round of the Governor's Cup series against Hollywood, Larry Jansen shut out the Stars in the opening game, then pitched seven-and-two-thirds innings of relief and hit a home run to win the clincher that sent them to the championship series.[48] In the finals, San Francisco defeated Stengel's Oaks in six games, giving O'Doul and his Seals their fourth consecutive post-season playoff championship.

Never had the Pacific Coast League enjoyed the level of box office success that it had in 1946. More than 3.7 million fans bought tickets, led by the Seals' record. According to *The Sporting News*, every Pacific Coast League team made a profit.[49]

Seeing this success, Paul Fagan continued lobbying hard for the PCL to pursue big league status, especially after Los Angeles and San Francisco became major league sports cities in the winter of 1946. The Cleveland Rams, defending champions of the National Football League, were relocated to the City of Angels by grocery store millionaire Dan Reeves.[50] The move was made to combat the new All-American Football Conference, which had recently placed a team, to be called the 49ers, in San Francisco.

During a conversation with San Francisco sportswriter Dan Daniel in Lefty O'Doul's bar on Powell Street, Fagan vowed to continue polishing the major league image he wanted the Seals to project. He installed the first glass backstop to give fans behind home plate an unobstructed view.[51] He also painted over the tacky advertisement signs on the outfield walls at Seals Stadium, explaining, "I believe that we should have nothing in a ball park you would not find in a theater. Why mar the place with advertisements?"

Fagan supplied electric razors in the clubhouse so every player would take the field clean shaven. He made sure a washing machine was available so players would wear clean socks each day. He provided free medical services for players and their families. He flew the team to Hawaii for spring training. He paid salaries comparable to those of major league teams and awarded the players on the championship team expensive diamond rings.[52] Lefty O'Doul, listening to the interview, enthusiastically interjected, "In fact, we are major league!"[53]

* * *

Veteran Portland pitcher Jack Salveson was one of the most popular stars of the PCL, and he had a long history in the sport. His uncle had pitched for the Beavers in 1914, and as a ten-year-old Salveson had served as batboy for Babe Ruth's team in the Halloween 1924 game at Brea against Walter Johnson's Elks squad.[54] In 1932, determined to meet New York Giants shortstop Travis Jackson, an eighteen-year-old Salveson barged into the Giants' spring training camp at Wrigley Field in Los Angeles and came away with a contract and the distinction of being the last rookie ever signed by John McGraw.[55]

Salveson roomed with Lefty O'Doul in New York and it must have paid dividends; he proved to be a good hitter, knocking out three home runs in only seventy-seven major league at-bats and another seventeen during his career in the PCL. Salveson won only nine games in the majors but found a home in the Pacific Coast League, eventually winning more than 200 games there.

"I love baseball," he declared. "To me it is more than a means of earning a good living. It is fun, a game, a joyful experience."[56] The 6'1", two-hundred-pound right-hander was nicknamed "the Barber" because of his reputation as a talker; he even hosted a sports radio show for a time. He was also famous for working fast with minimum effort. Lefty O'Doul called him "the Great Conservationist." Hot dog and peanut vendors simply swore under their breath when he pitched, calculating the money he was costing them by completing games in well under two hours. Irv Noren, a teammate of Salveson's when both played for Hollywood, said, "When you're playing the outfield, you gotta be ready. He got rid of the ball. He didn't mess around with rubbing up the ball or standing to the side of the mound." Salveson eschewed screwballs, sliders and knucklers, which he declared a waste of time. "I don't monkey around with those.... I have two grips, one for a fastball and another for a curve. It's as simple as all that."[57]

Jack Salveson won 204 games in the Pacific Coast League while pitching for six different teams. In 1947, he pitched and won two of the greatest games in PCL history (Ray Saraceni Collection).

In 1947, thirty-three-year-old Jack Salveson turned in a pair of the greatest pitching performances in Pacific Coast League history. The first came on May 7, when he pitched a twenty-inning shutout to defeat Sacramento, 1–0, allowing only eight hits — seven singles and a double. He threw only 171 pitches, an average of less than seventy-seven per nine innings. During one nine-inning stretch, he threw only fifty-four pitches.[58]

Three months later, Salveson was again pitching against Sacramento in an extra-inning game. In the top of the tenth, he hit a home run to put the Beavers ahead, 3–2. However, the Solons managed to tie the game in the bottom of the inning. Undaunted, Salveson homered again in his next at-bat and won the game.[59]

Jack Salveson was not the only veteran pitcher enjoying success in the PCL. Ten years after signing with Portland in a last-ditch attempt to keep his career alive, Ad Liska pitched a seven-inning no-hit game against Hollywood, becoming the first to throw a no-hit shutout at Vaughn Street Park since Ferdinand Henkle in 1911.[60]

Tommy Bridges joined Portland in 1947 after having pitched a total of thirty-two innings over the previous three years. The forty-year-old Bridges was a three-time twenty-game winner and six-time American League All-Star but had never thrown a no-hitter.[61] On April 20, Bridges faced the minimum twenty-seven batters in no-hitting the San Francisco Seals in Portland, allowing only one base runner, who was subsequently erased by a double play.[62]

In 1948, it was Dick Barrett's turn. On May 16, the forty-one-year-old right-hander pitched a seven-inning perfect game against Sacramento and, as in the case of Bridges, it was the first no-hitter of his long career.[63] Said to be "slicing the edge of the plate as thin as restaurant cheese," Barrett became nervous only in the top of the seventh, which he called "the longest inning of my life." After the game he confessed, "I was afraid I'd slip one down the middle and someone would break up my first no-hitter."[64] For Barrett, it marked the culmination of several recent highlights of his career that included becoming the PCL's all-time strikeout king and winning his 200th PCL game.[65]

Life in the PCL definitely seemed to begin at forty — at least for pitchers.

* * *

The Los Angeles Angels appeared ready to dominate the Pacific Coast League in 1947, opening up a big lead in mid-summer. But Lefty O'Doul's Seals were not about to surrender easily, erasing a seven-and-a-half-game deficit to put themselves in position to clinch the pennant in their final game of the season, against San Diego.

In that final game, the Seals had the bases loaded in the seventh inning with two out and the score tied, 3–3. Weak-hitting Roy Nicely worked the count to three and one. At that point, Lefty O'Doul had Dino Restelli attempt a steal of home. From his vantage point in the third base coach's box, O'Doul was sure Restelli was safe on two counts — first on the tag, which by all accounts was not even close, and also because the pitch was clearly ball four, which would have meant Restelli automatically scored.

But umpire Phil Mazzeo ruled otherwise. O'Doul came tearing out of the dugout with the rest of the team close behind. When he learned that Restelli had not only been called out, but that the pitch had been called a strike, O'Doul pretended to faint and fell over home plate. Mazzeo ejected both O'Doul and Restelli.[66]

Instead of a one-run lead, the game remained tied. Darkness descended and the lights were turned on at Lane Field. The Padres quickly put runners on first and second with no one out in the bottom of the ninth. Max West then belted Al Lien's first pitch for a three-run home run, his forty-third of the year, to end the game.[67]

Lefty O'Doul fumed in the clubhouse, convinced he had been robbed by Mazzeo's call, but there was nothing he could do about it; the Seals and Angels had ended the regular season tied for first place. The 1947 pennant race was going to come down to one sudden-death playoff game.

The Angels hosted the contest at Wrigley Field, sending Seals nemesis Cliff Chambers to the mound on only one day's rest. O'Doul's choice was ex–USC and New York Giants pitcher Jack Brewer. The capacity crowd was augmented by a mob of non-paying customers who parked themselves on the roof of a house across the street, beyond the left-field fence.

As expected, the game was a pitcher's duel. Three times the Seals had potential rallies snuffed out by double plays, and the game remained scoreless through seven innings.

In the bottom of the eighth, Cecil Garriott worked the count to three and two before drawing a base on balls. Billy Schuster followed by executing a perfect hit and run through the infield and Garriott took third. Jack Brewer then hit Ed Sauer with a pitch to load the bases.

The next batter was Clarence Maddern. Maddern lifted Brewer's first pitch high in the air and toward the house populated by the freeloading Angels rooters. The fans on the roof leaped in jubilation as the ball cleared the fence to give the Angels a 4–0 lead. Larry Barton added a solo home run before the inning ended and Chambers coasted to a shutout, his twenty-fourth win of the season. The Angels had won the 1947 pennant.[68]

"That was the greatest game I pitched in my life — with all the money on the line and one day's rest," declared Chambers more than sixty years later. He rated it a bigger thrill than the no-hitter he later threw as a member of the Pittsburgh Pirates against the Boston Braves.[69]

* * *

In November 1947, Chicago American Giants catcher John Ritchey was signed by the San Diego Padres, making him the first black player in the PCL. Fresh off a Negro American League batting title in his first season as a professional, Ritchey was thrilled to sign with the Padres and return to the city where he had played Little League, high school and college baseball. Ritchey was photographed wearing a San Diego Padres cardigan and shaking the hand of Padres owner Bill Starr, who declared, "We are not crusading for any cause. Ritchey was signed because of his ability to hit the ball."[70]

Starr was always looking for ways to expand his team's fan base — he once signed three Mexican League stars in an attempt to build a following among those living just across the international border — and he was sure signing Ritchey was good business. He added, "We believe we have signed one of the best prospects in the country." The twenty-five-year-old catcher simply said that he was "happy at the opportunity to play in the Coast League — especially in San Diego."[71]

Not everyone was happy, however. Some PCL players felt opening the game to those previously barred threatened their livelihood. Bill Conlin remembered receiving a phone call from a worried Sacramento Solons ballplayer after Jackie Robinson's signing. The player told Conlin, "Don't you realize down the line there's gonna be two of them on every team in baseball and that'll be two jobs taken away from us white guys?"[72]

But progress would not be halted. On March 30, 1948, John Ritchey pinch-hit in the ninth inning for the San Diego Padres. Ritchey received "a nice round of applause" before grounding out to second base.[73] The next night, Ritchey again pinch-hit in the ninth inning and singled sharply off the leg of Los Angeles pitcher Fred Schmidt, establishing another

The color line is broken in the Pacific Coast League, November 23, 1947. San Diego Padres owner Bill Starr (left) and Johnny Ritchey. Starr said, "We are not crusading for any cause. Ritchey was signed because of his ability to hit the ball." Starr would also warn hotel owners that he would not tolerate Ritchey having to find accommodations separate from his teammates (David Eskenazi Collection).

historic first in the PCL.[74] Ritchey got his first start behind the plate on April 1, catching Jess Flores in a slugfest won by the Padres.[75]

Ritchey collected seven hits in his first eleven at-bats for San Diego and was soon excelling as a pinch-hitter, with eight hits in his first seventeen attempts in that role, including two in one inning against Portland on May 15.[76] History had been made. The Pacific Coast League was finally, and irreversibly, integrated.

* * *

After drawing a record four million fans in 1947, with five teams topping a half-million in attendance, Pacific Coast League directors met in February 1948 and dropped their threat to go outlaw in pursuit of major league status. Instead, the league would attempt to become a third major league within the confines of Organized Baseball.

But Charlie Graham, a veteran of wars with Organized Baseball, was certain the action of the owners meant the dream of the Pacific Coast League becoming a third major league was over. When Paul Fagan arrived on the scene, Graham had an ally in his cause to defy the majors and go independent. Graham was now convinced they were fooling themselves. He had been present when the PCL was formed as an outlaw in 1903, and again in 1909 when Ban Johnson had tried talking sense into Cy Moreing and the outlaws of the California State League.

Graham was keenly aware that Johnson had engaged in a similar struggle with Organized Baseball when he formed the American League as a rival to the National. There was never any other choice but to take the fight to the game's establishment. As Johnson put it, "If we had waited for the National League to do something for us, we would have remained a minor league forever."[77]

* * *

Former Milwaukee Brewers owner Oscar Salenger purchased controlling interest in the Sacramento Solons prior to the 1948 season.[78] The short, stocky Chicago attorney, who resembled a cross between Oscar Levant and Peter Lorre, had a reputation for antics. As a result, Charlie Graham and Paul Fagan convinced Brick Laws to join the Seals in voting against the newcomer. However, no one else was persuaded to do so, making the league vote 6–2 in Salenger's favor.[79]

Chain-smoking his beloved cigars, Salenger held a press conference and proceeded to allay fears he would move the team, saying it was he who would move — to Sacramento — where he hoped the dry climate would benefit his asthmatic son. Salenger also pledged to strengthen the team's working agreement with the Pittsburgh Pirates. One of his first actions was to send catcher Ed FitzGerald, the team's best prospect, to Pittsburgh. This caused friction between Salenger and his holdover partner, Yubi Separovich, who had a deal worked out to send FitzGerald to the Boston Red Sox for outfielder Neill Sheridan.[80] Sheridan went to Seattle instead and the Rainiers immediately won seventeen of their first twenty-one games.[81]

Meanwhile, Salenger chose Opening Day against the Seals to retaliate against Charlie Graham for his opposition at the league meetings. He assigned the Seals to the old, decrepit home locker room while the Solons dressed in the newly refurbished visitor's clubhouse. The overflow crowd of more than thirteen thousand resulted in some fans having to stand in the outfield. With the Solons fielding a lineup of nine right-handed hitters, Salenger decided to place all of the fans in left and center field, leaving right field empty to Sacramento's advantage.

Lefty O'Doul protested and umpire Jack Powell ordered the Solons to spread the crowd evenly. When they refused, Powell told O'Doul there was nothing he could do — the home team had the right to set the ground rules. O'Doul notified Powell he was filing a protest, putting him in the unusual situation of having done so before the season had even started. The Seals won anyway. After the game, Charlie Graham admitted that O'Doul had no grounds to protest but he termed Salenger's move "poor sportsmanship" and added, "(I hope) Salenger won't take to donning a uniform and clowning along the coaching lines as he has done in Milwaukee."[82]

Meanwhile, there was news in Portland, where a fire the previous September had burned down the foundry outside Vaughn Street Park and taken the right-field fence with it. Balls would burst through the brittle wooden outfield fences. Groundskeeper Rocky Benevento scurried about extinguishing the frequent small fires resulting from carelessly tossed cigarettes while fans cried, "Let it burn, Rocky!" The rickety old stadium had been condemned over the winter as a fire hazard but the fire marshal relented on his order after Beavers general manager Bill Mulligan reached a compromise by installing a sprinkler system and other safety measures at a cost of nearly fifty thousand dollars.

More importantly, Mulligan announced the Beavers planned to build a new facility that he hoped would be ready for 1950, an announcement that probably saved the Beavers from becoming a road team with a condemned stadium in 1948.[83] However, two months into the 1948 season, a terrible flood on the Columbia River caused a dike to burst, inundating the Portland suburb of Vanport. Five Beavers players were among the eighteen thousand residents who lost their homes in the disaster. Outfielder Mayo Smith's wife and daughter had to be rescued from the rooftop of their home.[84] Duane Pillette's wife barely made it out alive when she lost the keys to their car while scrambling for family belongings.[85] Mulligan's proposed stadium site became a home for the refugees, delaying the project indefinitely.

* * *

The 1948 season marked Casey Stengel's third year as manager of the Oakland Oaks and he still had nothing to show for it. At age fifty-eight, the window of opportunity for a return to the major leagues was closing. After losing Les Scarsella to a broken hand in April, Stengel seemed determined to make the already-veteran Oaks even older.

Cookie Lavagetto, fresh off his pinch-hitting heroics for the Brooklyn Dodgers in the 1947 World Series, was signed to a two-year contract — a rarity in the minor leagues — early that month.[86] Returning to the Oaks fifteen years after breaking into pro baseball with the team, Lavagetto worked diligently with Stengel's prize pupil, Billy Martin, teaching the twenty-year-old techniques to speed up his pivot at second base.[87] Oakland also added a link to their 1927 pennant-winning team with the purchase of forty-year-old Ernie Lombardi, who was returning to the Pacific Coast League after closing out his big league career as a two-time batting champion, an eight-time all-star and the National League's Most Valuable Player in 1938. The legendary catcher lived only six blocks from Oaks Park but had started the 1948 season with Sacramento. He was acquired two weeks after Stengel watched him blast a 578-foot home run off Lloyd Hittle that rocketed over a sixty-foot tall light tower 340 feet from home plate.[88] "I will tell you one thing," said Stengel. "If we've got the winning run on base and I send in Lombardi as a pinch-hitter and the other infield plays in to save the run, I'll delay the game until I can call an ambulance because the big fellow is apt to kill somebody with a line drive."[89]

The aging of the team's roster (twenty-one players thirty or older saw action for the Oaks in 1948) led to their being called "the Nine Old Men," a nickname that had been bestowed on the Supreme Court by Franklin Delano Roosevelt. In late July, Oakland was in first place, ahead of three other tightly bunched teams: Los Angeles, San Francisco (which had been hurt by the loss of leading hitter Gene Woodling for several weeks after he tore ligaments in his ankle), and San Diego.[90] But the Oaks played poorly in a series against Hollywood and dropped back to third place. The week included several memorable fights, including a pitched battle on the first of August when Billy Martin was tagged out by Hollywood second baseman Lou Stringer on a steal attempt. Martin retaliated by stepping on Stringer's hand, which sparked an all-out brawl that included the sight of Casey Stengel lying flat on the ground at one point during the melee.[91] The stage was set for another wild finish for the Pacific Coast League pennant.

* * *

Sluggers dominated the Pacific Coast League in 1948. Nick Etten hit 43 home runs and drove in 155 for the Oakland Oaks, Cliff Aberson hit 34 home runs in only 389 at-bats for Los Angeles, and Mickey Rocco drove in 149 runs for San Francisco. But two power hitters caught the attention of PCL fans more than the others: Hollywood's Gus Zernial and San Diego's Jack Graham.

A strapping Texan dubbed "Ozark Ike" by Hollywood announcer and former PCL star Fred Haney, Zernial was still developing as a ballplayer. He would frequently lose fly balls in the sun until Stars teammate Al Libke mentioned to him that he was wearing his baseball cap too far back on his head, leaving the bill pointing straight up rather than over his eyes.[92] As a hitter, Zernial could pound the ball far and deep, but when he was due to bat and the team needed a single, Stars manager Jimmy Dykes would cover his eyes and say to no one in particular, "Tell me if he strikes out or pops up."[93]

Zernial slammed two homers on Opening Day against Seattle.[94] He tied a league record with four consecutive home runs over two games against San Diego in May.[95] Two weeks later he hit a pair of home runs in one inning against Sacramento at Edmonds Field.[96] Zernial hit 40 home runs with 145 runs batted in and a .322 batting average for Hollywood in 1948.

As great as Zernial was, he had to take a backseat to San Diego's Jack Graham. The son of former major league utility man Peaches Graham had spent the 1946 season with the New York Giants, hitting fourteen home runs in one hundred games along with an unsatisfactory .219 batting average. He rebounded in 1947 with Jersey City in the International League, setting a team record for home runs in a season.

The Giants traded Graham to San Diego in a deal that sent Jack Harshman to New York, angering Charlie Graham and the San Francisco Seals, who thought they should have received the slugger as part of the Larry Jansen trade.[97] The transaction definitely worked in Graham's favor; he was a dead fastball hitter with a swing made for Lane Field. Padres manager Rip Collins predicted Graham would better the forty-three home runs hit in 1947 by Max West, the man he was replacing in the lineup.[98]

A pull hitter who saw the "Boudreau Shift" employed against him when the Padres opened the 1948 season against Los Angeles, Graham hit fourteen home runs in the Padres first twenty-seven games.[99] It was not long before fans perched atop box cars at the Santa Fe depot across the street from Lane Field to watch him play.[100]

Casey Stengel was less impressed and bragged that he knew how to stop Graham. In Graham's first visit to Oaks Park on June 2, the slugger answered Stengel's challenge with three home runs to lead the Padres to an 11–0 win.[101] Graham broke West's one-year-old team record for home runs by swatting his forty-fourth on July 18, curling a Damon Hayes pitch just inside the right-field foul pole in the first game of a doubleheader.[102] With more than seventy games left in the season, Graham needed only sixteen more home runs to break Tony Lazzeri's league record of sixty, and the Padres were only one game behind first-place Oakland.

But then San Diego dropped seven straight games. On July 25, the Padres played a doubleheader in Los Angeles against the Angels. Graham tried to rally the team in the first game of the twin bill, hitting his forty-sixth home run off Don Carlsen, but it was not enough and the Padres suffered their eighth straight defeat, 7–6, in ten innings.

Red Adams pitched for Los Angeles in the nightcap. He was one of the few pitchers against whom Graham had not hit well; when he came to the plate against Adams in the third inning, Graham was hitless in eight at-bats against him for the year. As Adams stared in for the sign, he noticed that Graham had opened his stance a little bit and was in a deeper crouch.

The pitcher had success pitching in on Graham's hands and thought the slugger, a good low-ball hitter, was trying to negate the advantage Adams had. Determined not to give in, Adams refused to change his tactics. "Once in awhile I'd throw a ball that would sail," remembered Adams. "I got a little farther in, a little farther up than I intended to, and the ball took off." The ball struck Graham behind the right ear and bounced back toward Adams, who thought it had hit Graham's bat. He fielded the ball and then saw Graham collapse in a heap.[103]

Instantly recognizing the severity of the injury, players from both teams rushed to render aid and Graham's mother vaulted from the stands to check on her son.[104] Graham was helped to his feet and tried walking to the dugout but collapsed and was taken to the hospital, where it was determined he had a fractured skull.

Adams visited Graham and the slugger laughingly chided Adams about the fact that he had not had a hit off him all year. Graham also assured Adams that he knew the pitch was not intentional. Hospitalized for a week and a half, Graham was out of the lineup for several weeks and hit only two more home runs for a final total of forty-eight. Rip Collins was fired as manager a week after Graham's injury and was replaced by Jim Brillheart.[105] Things only got worse. The Padres finished in seventh place, losing fifty-seven of their last seventy-six games.

Jack Graham was on pace in 1948 to shatter the Pacific Coast League record for home runs in a season when he was severely injured by a pitch from Red Adams (David Eskenazi Collection).

* * *

Although the men running the Sacramento Solons, Oscar Salenger and Yubi Separovich, were constantly at odds, they managed to unveil plans to build a new ballpark in Sacramento. Salenger felt that Edmonds Field had outlived its usefulness and claimed the team was forced to spend upwards of $30,000 per year on repairs to the stadium. The proposal for the new facility involved locating a twenty-acre site in the city, selling the Edmonds Field site, and raising an additional half-million dollars by marketing five thousand season tickets on a ten-year plan. It seemed a prudent idea. The wooden ballpark was notoriously flammable — Solons catcher Lilio Marcucci claimed the ground crew routinely extinguished one or two fires each night because of smoldering cigarettes dropped by careless hands.[106] At 1:00 A.M. on July 9, 1948, a fire in the grandstand was spotted by a passing policeman. Luckily, it was caught in time and the damage was confined to a few seats behind the Solons dugout.[107]

Two nights later, Sacramento fire battalion chief Peter Mangan finished his root beer at a drug store on Sixteenth and Broadway and began walking to his car to go home. He suddenly caught sight of something out of the corner of his eye in the direction of the ballpark. Turning, Mangan saw an angry red glow over the center of the stadium and instantly realized that Edmonds Field was on fire.

Racing to the stadium, Mangan grabbed a one-inch garden hose and tried fighting the blaze as best he could. "Suddenly the press box and the whole of the seats in front of it exploded into flames," said Mangan. "They cracked so loud they hurt my ears. I never ran so fast in my life, for I knew then the ball park was a goner and I would be if I stayed there one second too long."[108] Within half an hour, embers had ignited the remaining wood structures and three nearby homes.[109] Sixteen-year-old Cuno Barragan, who lived only a half-dozen blocks from the stadium, rushed to the ballpark with some of his friends; they could not believe what they were seeing.[110]

The ballpark was quickly consumed in a fire so hot that flames erupted out of the collapsed debris several times the next day. The ferocity of the blaze was blamed on the open space under the roof of the ballpark, which acted as a draw for the flames, similar to a flue in a chimney. The first and third base sides then burned almost simultaneously, racing out to the bleachers. In the end, only a small portion of the left-field bleachers and the light poles remained. Most of the team's uniforms and equipment was lost. It was determined that the blaze originated in the rear of the press box and the fire department blamed the inferno on a carelessly tossed cigarette.

However, some pointed to the fire two days earlier and whispered that the source of the conflagration was a more sinister one — a rumor that still makes the rounds to this day. It was said that Oscar Salenger accused Yubi Separovich of setting the fire to collect on the insurance; only a couple of weeks before the fires of July 9 and 11, Salenger had increased the coverage on the grandstand at Edmonds Field from $50,000 to $235,000.[111] The cause of the fire was always an open joke among Solons players and front office personnel but there was never any proof of arson.[112]

Sacramento became a road team for the remainder of the 1948 season, and Salenger and Separovich sold the Solons to four men, including former Oaks owner Cookie Devincenzi.[113] Insurance covered $197,000 in losses and Devincenzi announced himself "highly satisfied" with the settlement.[114]

While Sacramento struggled with the loss of its ballpark, the San Francisco Seals and the Pacific Coast League struggled with the loss of one of the league's giant figures. On August 29, 1948, Charlie Graham died.

Although Graham's son, Charles Jr., had assumed the duties of general manager of the Seals, the elder Graham remained an active advisor to the team and was also serving as president of the Association of Professional Baseball Players of America, which assisted ballplayers in need. Five days before his death, Graham was stricken with food poisoning. At first he seemed to recover, but the seventy-year-old head of the Seals developed pneumonia and lapsed into a coma on Friday, August 27.[115] Placed into an oxygen tent, he died shortly after four o'clock on Sunday morning.[116]

Later that day, the flags at Seals Stadium flew at half staff and a crowd of slightly more than seven thousand stood for a moment of silence before the start of a doubleheader between the Seals and Sacramento in the ballpark Charlie Graham had built. A fifty-year career in baseball was at an end. The Pacific Coast League had lost its most respected voice.

* * *

Casey Stengel kept adding to his roster: many felt he was doing so by manipulating the disabled list and "optioning" players to give him two or three extra bodies he could call on a moment's notice. The Oaks signed pitcher Jim Tobin, a thirty-five-year-old right-hander who had not pitched in nearly two years. Tobin debuted in relief of Will Hafey in the first inning on August 22 against the Angels, pitching five and two-thirds scoreless innings. He returned three days later, picking up for Charley Gassaway with one out in the first inning and completing the game to pick up a 10–6 victory over Seattle.[117] Catcher Billy Raimondi was lost for the year when he broke his wrist on September 17 in a game against San Diego. Gene Lillard, released early in the season by the Oaks, was re-signed for the final week to back up Ernie Lombardi.[118]

The Oaks continued winning on "Ernie Lombardi Day," when the slowest runner in baseball brought fans to their feet in disbelief by stealing a base, his first in five years.[119] By the end of the Sunday doubleheader, the Oaks were only a game and a half behind the Seals and in the midst of a hot streak that would result in their winning better than seventy-five percent of their remaining games.

In late September, the Oaks settled a five-week-old controversy with the Seals by replaying the final inning of a game against San Francisco from August 14. The Oaks had won the game, 4–3, scoring two runs in the ninth inning for a come-from-behind win. But controversy erupted when umpire Ziggy Sears caught Oaks reliever Ralph Buxton defacing the ball with what appeared to be pine tar. Sears forced Buxton to change his glove and the ball but did not throw him out of the game.[120] Lefty O'Doul officially protested, arguing that Buxton should have been ejected. The protest was upheld and the inning was replayed on September 21.[121] Before resumption of the game, a suitcase labeled "Oaks Pitching Tools" appeared at home plate beside a can of pine tar along with several rusty files and hacksaw blades. In the end it did not matter, as the Seals were retired in order and the initial result from five weeks earlier stood. Billy Martin ended up in possession of the tool box after the game and remarked, "Maybe I can sell these files to a second-hand dealer, unless the Seals want to borrow them in the playoffs." Ralph Buxton was forever after nicknamed "Pine Tar."[122]

Momentum was clearly in favor of the Oaks as they played their final series of the season against Sacramento. Solons manager Joe Orengo was doing everything he could to beat Casey Stengel, who according to conventional wisdom would be hired by a major league team if the Oaks won the PCL pennant. A rumor also circulated that if the Oaks failed to win, Stengel would be hired by Cookie Devincenzi to manage Sacramento.

Orengo entered the elevator at the Leamington Hotel and encountered Stengel, who eyed him suspiciously as the door closed. Finally turning to the Solons manager, Stengel sarcastically snarled, "What are you doing, trying to win? Don't you know if you beat me, I'll have your job in Sacramento next year?"[123]

A sell-out crowd of twelve thousand watched as the Oaks used four pitchers against Sacramento to win, 10–8, clinching the title on the final day of the season. Ralph Buxton and Jim Tobin pitched stellar relief to save the game; Tobin retired the Solons one-two-three in the ninth inning, erasing the final batter on a ground ball he fielded before running over to touch first base. Cookie Lavagetto and Ernie Lombardi had key hits to keep rallies going. Buxton added a key hit in the ninth, and for the first time in more than two decades the Oaks were Pacific Coast League champions.[124]

After the game, excited players willingly posed for photograph after photograph. A jubilant Casey Stengel stood next to Brick Laws while Ernie Lombardi hugged the team's batboy in celebration. Lombardi announced he was retiring and declared, "It sure is a grand way to hang up your spikes."[125] Stengel was clearly moved. "I want to pay tribute to all my players," he said. "They won the pennant for me. I'm proud of them all."

It was the first pennant at any level of professional baseball for several of the team's veterans, including Dario Lodigiani, Billy Raimondi and Brooks Holder. A parade through downtown Oakland and a city-wide celebration was planned for Stengel and his "Nine Old Men."[126] As an encore, the Oaks also swept through the playoffs, defeating Los Angeles in six games and Seattle in five. Oakland players split the $30,000 pot that went with the Governor's Cup.[127]

Casey Stengel was hired by the New York Yankees, beginning a managerial stint that would earn him a place in the Baseball Hall of Fame. Despite his landing the Yankees job, it was not universally accepted that Stengel had been the reason for the Oaks success. Although Stengel's platoon system had proved effective, Bill Conlin asserted that the Oaks won the pennant largely because Brick Laws provided whatever players the manager wanted. Conlin was convinced that the team's manipulation of the disabled list, which allowed the Oaks to have nearly thirty players at their immediate disposal, was the real reason for Oakland's pennant.[128]

But none of that mattered. Stengel had his pennant and was ready to reap the reward. And he would owe his Hall of Fame plaque in no small part to Brick Laws and his three-year stint in Oakland, without which it is doubtful he would have ever returned to the majors as a manager.

The Pacific Coast League had never been more powerful or popular, with attendance figures nearly double that of its previous golden era during the 1920s. Unfortunately, the seeds of the league's destruction were already sown. It would take a few more years for that to become apparent, but the signs were there.

CHAPTER SIXTEEN

1949 to 1951: The Golden Boy and the Natural

In March 1949, the Sacramento Solons christened a new concrete and steel baseball stadium at Riverside and Broadway with an exhibition against the Pittsburgh Pirates attended by nearly ten thousand people.[1] A couple of weeks later additional bleachers had to be secured from the State Fairgrounds and Sacramento High School to accommodate more than twelve thousand people on Opening Day — the second largest crowd in team history.[2] By then ownership of the Solons had changed hands again, with Ed Sparks and George Klumpp, president and vice president of the Sacramento Baseball Association, purchasing the shares of the Solons owned by Cookie Devincenzi.[3] The Solons also had a new manager (their fourth in four years) in former Detroit Tigers manager Del Baker, who had won an American League pennant with the Tigers in 1940.

But the real headline of the 1949 season concerned two men who unquestionably generated the most interest among the league's fans. One was known as "the Golden Boy" and the other today is often called "the Natural," and their popularity highlighted a fundamental problem of the Pacific Coast League. Despite their instant notoriety, both would be in the major leagues within months.

"The Golden Boy" was Jackie Jensen, whose major league career after his stint in the PCL would include an American League Most Valuable Player award, a Gold Glove and three All-Star appearances. An All-American baseball and football star at the University of California, where he had led the Golden Bears to the first College World Series baseball title in 1947, the twenty-two-year-old Jensen was one of the country's most celebrated college athletes and a genuinely gifted, if still undeniably raw, "five-tool" baseball star with the ability to field, run, throw, hit and hit with power.

Jensen was aggressively pursued by the Pittsburgh Pirates, who employed entertainer Bing Crosby, part-owner of the team, to lead a campaign to convince Jensen of the wisdom in accepting Pittsburgh's offer of a three-year contract instead of signing with the New York Yankees.[4] But both teams wanted Jensen to finish his college baseball career, and he was determined to turn professional immediately.[5] An opportunity to do so suddenly presented itself.

The son of Oakland Oaks owner Brick Laws was good friends with the college star and on May 26, Jensen shocked the sports world by transferring his well-known "36" from a University of California football jersey to an Oakland Oaks baseball uniform. To celebrate the three-year contract that made him the highest paid player in minor league history, Jensen bought a brand-new, cream-colored Cadillac with red leather upholstery. He also signed a

Jackie Jensen (right) pictured with another young Oakland Oaks star, Billy Martin. Jensen was called "The Golden Boy" thanks to his movie-star good looks and football stardom at the University of California. His signing a multi-year contract with Oakland shook up the baseball establishment (National Baseball Hall of Fame Library, Cooperstown, N.Y.).

seven-year deal with a talent agent tasked with the development of motion picture opportunities and commercial endorsements.[6]

The contract with Oakland, worth a reported eighty thousand dollars, alarmed big league executives, who were unaccustomed to being outbid by a minor league team. They worried that Jensen's contract signaled a seismic shift in the relationship between the majors and the Pacific Coast League, which had repeatedly threatened revolt. But the Oaks had no intention of Jensen fulfilling the three-year obligation. Instead, the plan was for him to play in 1949 and then be sold to the highest bidder prior to the October 15 draft deadline.[7]

As talented as he was, Jackie Jensen's play was inconsistent. He appeared in his first game the night he signed his contract and was hitless in two at-bats against Seattle.[8] He followed that with three hits in his first start the next night.[9] A week later, a crowd of more than twenty-two thousand came to see Jensen play at Seals Stadium and he lost the game by dropping a fly ball in the ninth inning.[10] Three weeks into his professional career, Jensen's batting average hovered near .200. "Get it right — Jensen has great natural ability," said Oakland's new manager, Charlie Dressen, "but he still has an awful lot to learn. On the football field the quarterback called Jensen's signal and he took the ball and ran. But he's all by himself out there in left field and he has to make his own decisions. Only experience will give him the knack of throwing to the right base, playing the batters and making up his mind what to do in a split second."[11]

As Dressen said, Jackie Jensen had a long way to go to become a bona fide star, but the Oaks would not regret signing him. He played in 106 straight games after joining Oakland and there were times when the charismatic outfielder with movie-star looks proved himself a "Golden Boy," such as the time he hit two home runs the same day he announced his engagement to beautiful Olympic diver Zoe Ann Olsen.[12]

The league's other exciting newcomer, Luke Easter, was a prodigious slugger who had spent his prime years outside of Organized Baseball because of the color of his skin. He quickly became the PCL's top drawing card — possibly the greatest the league ever had. No one who saw Luke Easter play would ever forget him.

Said to be age twenty-seven, it was apparent even to the untrained eye that Easter was seven years older than that. He exploded onto the scene as if he were the title character stepping out of Bernard Malamud's novel *The Natural*, a sensational talent who had not signed a professional contract until his thirtieth birthday had passed.

Easter played semi-pro ball in his native St. Louis until he was sidelined by injuries sustained in a car accident in 1941. He then worked in defense jobs during the war. In 1946, Easter signed a contract with the Negro League Cincinnati Crescents and became the first man to hit a home run into the center-field bleachers at the Polo Grounds. He played for the legendary Homestead Grays in 1947 and 1948 before Bill Veeck acquired him for the Cleveland Indians and optioned him to San Diego.[13]

Standing 6'4" and weighing two hundred-thirty pounds, Luke Easter could hit a baseball the proverbial country mile. He put all he had into every swing of the bat, emitting a thunderous grunt that sent shudders through pitchers, who prayed he would not smash a line shot back at their face. Easter had power to all fields and, unlike Jackie Jensen, was a sensational player from his first day in spring training.

On March 10, the big first baseman slammed a pair of triples off Seattle pitchers Guy Fletcher and Rugger Ardizoia that Rainiers manager JoJo White claimed were the hardest hit balls he had ever seen. Ardizoia claimed Fletcher had ducked when Easter swung, only to see the ball carry to the fence on the fly.[14] By the middle of spring training, Easter was hitting .474 with four home runs in thirty-eight at-bats.[15] Fans arrived in droves simply to watch him take batting practice.

Easter did have a weakness — his Achilles heel as it were. He had painful corns all over his feet and also had a bad knee, exacerbated by an injury suffered during spring training. As a result, he was unable to play any position other than first base. But those shortcomings failed to bring comfort to pitchers, who quickly learned to fear him. Tommy Byrne, who pitched against Easter in both the American League and the PCL, said, "He would grunt louder when he swung at a ball than most people in the stands would yell at a ball game. You could make a mistake to him and he would hit it so far, you wanted to make sure he pulled the ball because if he hit it back through the box, he could hurt you."[16] Cal McLish agreed that it was imperative to pitch Easter inside. "I used to worry about him hitting the ball back through the box," he said. "That's how strong he was. He liked to get those big, long arms and big, long bat out over the plate. I mean, he was *dangerous*, especially in those [Pacific Coast League] ballparks."[17]

A full three years after Jackie Robinson's debut with the Montreal Royals, the vast majority of teams still did not have a black player. As a result, African Americans in Organized Baseball, including Easter, carried the weight of additional responsibility both on and off the field. The NAACP worked with ballplayers to develop strategies meant to ensure against incidents that might bring an excuse to reintroduce the color barrier. When Bill Conlin asked Easter for an interview on his first trip to Sacramento in 1949, the writer suggested they meet in the hotel lobby. Easter insisted the interview be held in his hotel room; he had been instructed to stay out of the hotel lobby and the dining room and make every attempt to remain as inconspicuous as possible.

Easter was also to avoid fights at all cost. Conlin recalled that when Joe Marty collided with Easter on a close play at first base, "Luke not only picked Marty off the ground, he dusted off his pants. Marty (started laughing) at the idea of an enemy player dusting off his uniform; here again was this instruction that Luke had to be gentle and not arouse any animosity."

Easter had to confront fear

Luke Easter, "the Natural." Pitchers feared him hitting balls back through the box. The good-natured slugger did not sign his first professional contract until he was past the age of thirty (David Eskenazi Collection).

and resentment among some white players, rooted in the reality that blacks were coming into the league and would be taking some of their jobs. That resentment often manifested itself in negative ways. When Conlin interviewed Easter, the Padres had recently arrived in Sacramento from Portland and the columnist asked the slugger who the best Beavers pitcher was.

"Well," said Easter, "Mister Tommy Bridges."

Puzzled, Conlin asked, "Why do you like Bridges?"

Easter replied, "He's the only one who doesn't throw at my head."[18]

* * *

No San Francisco Seals player was more popular than Joe Brovia, the left-handed slugging outfielder labeled the "the Davenport Destroyer" in honor of his hometown, located just outside of Santa Cruz, California. Brovia first signed with the Seals in 1939 as a pitcher. But when he took a bat in his hands and started launching shots into the olive grove at

Boyes Springs, Lefty O'Doul told the youngster to toss away his toe plate. O'Doul purchased the seventeen-year-old a new pair of spikes and sent him to El Paso, where he hit .383 in his first season as a professional.

Brovia had a distinctive presence at the plate, grinding the bat handle in his hands and pulling his cap down over his eyes as if to block out the pitcher to better focus on the ball. He held his hands belt-high with the bat pointing straight up, a stance that left him vulnerable to fouling pitches off his instep. Looking at him, it seemed impossible that Brovia could hit a good fastball, yet it was nearly impossible to get one past him. Despite his reputation as an aggressive hitter, Brovia was not a wild swinger. Only once did he strike out more than fifty times in a season and he twice led the Pacific Coast League in drawing bases on balls. In 1953 he struck out only thirty-two times in 165 games.

As dangerous as Brovia was with fastballs, if a pitcher chose to throw him a curve, he had better put it in the right spot. In April 1947, Seattle's Sig Jakucki hung one chest-high and Brovia crushed it for one of the longest home runs ever hit in Seals Stadium; the ball bounced out of the ballpark and into the parking lot.[19]

Brovia hated when pitchers got the better of him, especially southpaws. Bill Conlin remembered that Brovia had particular trouble with left-hander Glenn Elliott. "He'd get Joe out and Joe would go back to the bench and he'd yell at Elliott. He'd call him every name in the book. I remember, 'You four-eyed syphilitic son of a bitch!'"[20] Angels pitcher Eddie Chandler once knocked Brovia down with a pitch. After picking himself up, Brovia brushed the dust from his uniform and remarked, "If that guy wasn't so good to hit, I'd go out and get him." The slugger lined the next pitch off the scoreboard.[21]

Brovia was a hitter — that is all he wanted to do — which drove Lefty O'Doul to distraction. "He'd see Brovia out there with a bat in his hands," remembered Larry Jansen, "and he'd holler out to him, 'Joe, we know you can hit. Put that bat down. I want to see you in the outfield, that's where I want to see you!'"[22] Brovia owned a tattered glove with the pocket cut out that was given to him by Brooks Holder. When the rules changed to prohibit leaving gloves on the field between innings, Brovia frequently kicked his all the way from the dugout to his outfield position after a tough at-bat.[23]

That did not sit well with Paul Fagan, who was particular about the appearance and behavior of his players. He and Brovia had clashed on several occasions; Fagan was disgusted by players spitting or blowing their noses while on the field and ordered every player to carry a handkerchief. Brovia refused. There was also the matter of how Brovia wore his baseball pants, with the leg pulled low in the style of Ted Williams, leaving almost no sock showing. Brovia said, "Fagan used to tell me, 'You got to bring [the pant leg] up closer to the knee.' I said, 'I'm not bringing them up around the knee.'"[24]

A holdout in the spring of 1949, when Brovia finally agreed to report he received the shock of his life — the Seals were selling him to Portland. Recently hired radio announcer and public relations man Don Klein was handed as his first assignment the task of informing the press about Brovia's departure. "O'Doul was upset about it," remembered Klein. "Brovia was a hero to the fans. I had to tell the writers and they didn't believe me. They thought I was kidding. And I said, 'No, it's true. He's been traded to Portland.'"[25]

Dumping Brovia after he had hit .322 in 1948, despite missing several weeks because of an appendectomy and a broken hand, puzzled everyone who followed the team.[26] *San Francisco Examiner* columnist Curley Grieve responded, "Any time a .322 hitter doesn't fit in your plans, it's time to change the plans."[27] Even though it was Fagan who had banished Joe Brovia, fans held Lefty O'Doul responsible, reasoning that he could have prevented

Brovia's transfer if he had wanted to.[28] Fagan would never earn Brovia's forgiveness — not that he ever sought it — and the resulting rift between Brovia and O'Doul lasted several years. It is not an exaggeration to say that along with Charlie Graham's death, the unceremonious departure of the popular Italian slugger proved the beginning of the decline in the Seals' popularity.

Brovia's first opportunity to exact revenge against Fagan and O'Doul came in San Francisco on Opening Night in 1949. The Seals had been heavily criticized in the press throughout spring training, with O'Doul receiving most of the vitriol.[29] Seals fans cheered their former favorite and unfurled banners deriding O'Doul as "Marble Head." Brovia enjoyed one of the most satisfying days of his career, banging out three hits as the crowd jeered the home team, and especially Lefty O'Doul.[30]

The next night, Brovia injured his back crashing into the wall at Seals Stadium. After playing the rest of the week and batting .500 for the series, x-rays revealed he had fractured a vertebra in his neck.[31] Sidelined for six weeks, Brovia found other ways to get back at his former team. Sacramento right-hander Frank Dasso was getting hit hard by the Seals every time he faced them, even when he felt he had his best stuff. Dasso happened to cross paths with Brovia and the outfielder told him, "(The Seals) know everything you're throwing. If you're going to throw a fastball, you go up and over your head. If you're going to throw a curve, you stop right in front of your eyes."

Dasso could not wait to face the Seals again so he could confuse them by changing his patterns. "I *begged* to start against San Francisco," he said.

Dasso's wish was granted and he responded with a complete-game victory. "That was the night I hit (a home run)," remembered Dasso, "and the bat I was using was (a) Lefty O'Doul (model). I carried it around the bases when I hit that ball and when I went around third base ... I held the bat up — and one finger."[32]

* * *

The San Diego Padres Opening Day starting lineup featured three black players — Luke Easter, catcher Johnny Ritchey and shortstop Artie Wilson. It was the first time any PCL team had fielded a lineup including more than one African American. But the Padres would lose Wilson to a rival only a few weeks into the season on a technicality. During the winter Bill Veeck had flown to Mayaguez, Puerto Rico, where Wilson was player-manager of a winter league team, and signed him to a Cleveland contract. The problem was that the New York Yankees had already reached agreement with the Black Barons to acquire him.[33] Veeck ignored that fact and sent Wilson to San Diego. The Yankees appealed to Commissioner Chandler and he ruled in New York's favor.[34] A week later the Padres were forced to watch Wilson pack his gear and join the rival Oakland Oaks. After being awarded the infielder, the Yankees sold him to San Diego's competitor rather than keeping him.[35] Oakland manager Charlie Dressen was delighted. "I haven't had a shortstop or a lead-off man all year. (Wilson will) go into the lineup as soon as he gets here."[36]

That would not be the only change for the Oaks. After three years of the fun-loving and player-friendly Casey Stengel, Oakland players and press were in for a period of adjustment. As the Oaks unfurled their 1948 championship banner, Charlie Dressen began dismantling the "Nine Old Men," trading away two of the most popular players to ever wear an Oakland uniform. Billy Raimondi was sent to Sacramento while second baseman Dario Lodigiani was traded to San Francisco along with outfielder Brooks Holder. The trading of Raimondi, a member the Oaks since 1932, came during a homestand against the Solons, making Oakland fans further inflamed by seeing their favorite in an enemy uniform for the rest of the week. They lit into Dressen with gusto.[37] Despite the outcry, Dressen insisted the moves were for the best and Brick Laws agreed. They felt the only way to win another pennant was to assemble a younger roster, accomplished in part by acquiring Artie Wilson and signing Jackie Jensen.[38]

Dressen worried that he had another delicate issue to deal with—finding Wilson a roommate; the Oaks were only the second PCL team to integrate, and white and black players did not room together on the road. That problem was solved when second baseman Billy Martin volunteered to be Wilson's roommate.[39] The two formed an excellent double-play combination and contributed offensively as well. The left-handed-hitting Wilson had little power, having lost part of his right thumb as a teenager. Unable to consistently pull fastballs, he adjusted by hitting almost exclusively to left field, like Ox Eckhardt, and had an amazing ability to put the ball beyond the reach of infielders. Wilson spent the summer at or near the top of the league in batting average.

Meanwhile, Dressen worked hard with Martin on his hitting, insisting that the young infielder choke up on the bat. He placed adhesive tape two inches from the handle on all of Martin's bats as a reminder. It helped, and the second baseman drove in ninety-two runs and hit a solid .286.[40]

Bill Veeck tried to make up with the fans and management of the Padres for his faux pas with Artie Wilson. In mid–May, he optioned Cuban prospect Orestes "Minnie" Minoso to San Diego.[41] Minoso took over left field for San Diego, making the already-formidable Padres lineup more intimidating by adding an element of badly needed speed to the heart of the batting order. Minoso amazed everyone by scoring from first base on a single in his home debut.[42] By the middle of June, both Max West and Luke Easter had hit more than twenty home runs. Minoso also demonstrated his power and competitiveness. Picking himself up after being knocked down by Seals pitcher Al Lien with two out in the bottom of the ninth of a game on July 28, Minoso slugged the next pitch for a game-winning walk-off home run to defeat the Seals, 6–5.[43]

The Padres quickly became the league's top draw despite their position in the middle of the league standings. More than twenty-three thousand attended a May 15 doubleheader at Wrigley Field between the Angels and Padres, with the near-record crowd entirely attributable to Luke Easter, who played despite being hampered by his increasingly chronic bad knee.[44] Another near-record crowd of more than twenty-three thousand—with more than one-third consisting of African Americans—squeezed into Seals Stadium a week later to see baseball's newest sensation. *Life* magazine sent a photographer in preparation for a profile of Easter.[45] Seals fans booed whenever a San Francisco pitcher threw a bad pitch to the big slugger and they flooded onto the field after the game to get his autograph.[46]

At the beginning of July, San Diego received promising infielder Al Rosen from Cleveland; like Minnie Minoso, Rosen was subject to twenty-four-hour recall.[47] Unfortunately, at almost the same time, the Padres were forced to bid farewell to Luke Easter, who was ordered by the Indians to Cleveland to undergo surgery on what had finally been diagnosed as a fractured kneecap.[48] The Indians insisted that Easter would return to San Diego to complete the 1949 season after he finished healing, but Padres fans were sure he was gone for good. Indeed, after his recovery, Easter remained in Cleveland and appeared in twenty-one games for the Indians.

Even with the loss of Easter, the Padres were one of the best offensive teams in league history. Outfielder Allie Clark replaced Easter in San Diego and hit two home runs in his first game with the Padres and eleven during his month with the team.[49] Max West hit forty-eight homers, equaling Jack Graham's team record from the previous year, and drove in 166 runs while setting a PCL record by drawing 201 bases on balls. Minnie Minoso impressed everyone by combining his tremendous speed with power, hitting twenty-two home runs in 137 games. Al Rosen played well, hitting fourteen home runs in only 273 at-bats while splitting time between first and third base. But mediocre pitching doomed San Diego to a fourth-place finish.

* * *

The Hollywood Stars could no longer afford to be uninteresting in a town that by its nature was anything but. When Bob Cobb purchased what was left of the moribund franchise from Herbert Fleischhacker, he saw it as his civic duty to rescue it. The community responded, even throwing a party for the team when it finished last in 1945. But with increasing competition to draw fans, Cobb felt the time had come to put a contender on the field. The Stars negotiated a working agreement with the Brooklyn Dodgers and looked to the broadcast booth for a fiery and unconventional manager with a long history in the PCL — Fred Haney. The Stars thrived under Haney in 1949, emerging as frontrunners all summer, building a ten-game lead by early July thanks to a pitching staff led by half-Cherokee knuckleballer Willard Ramsdell, thirty-seven-year-old Gordon Maltzberger and George "Pinky" Woods, who would tie for the league lead in wins. Thirty-five-year-old Jack Salveson, who kept his own strict pitch count, won twelve games and had the second-best earned run average on the staff, behind only Ramsdell.

Bespectacled third baseman Jim Baxes, with his size fourteen feet, was the star of the infield. A converted middle infielder who played spectacularly at the hot corner, Baxes was one of three men who drove in more than one hundred runs for the Stars. Veterans Chuck Stevens, Gene Handley and Johnny O'Neil filled out the remainder of the infield. Irv Noren, who like Baxes was Dodgers property, made his PCL debut by hitting .330 while driving in 130 runs, and was sold by Brooklyn to the Washington Senators for $60,000.[50] He was joined in the outfield by the team's second-best RBI man, Herb Gorman, and veteran Frank Kelleher, an intimidating low-ball hitter and legend in the PCL. The team added depth in mid-season by signing veteran JoJo White after he resigned as manager of the Seattle Rainiers.[51]

Cobb's box seat was near the Hollywood bat rack and in close games he was known to remark to the next Stars batter, "You know ... I'm really nervous."[52] He needn't have been. Hollywood clinched the 1949 pennant with a 7–4 win over Seattle on September 22 and fans stormed the field, throwing confetti and carrying Fred Haney on their shoulders. A banner proclaiming the Stars champions of the Pacific Coast League was raised on the flagpole to mark the first outright league championship for the franchise since 1920, when the team took the field as the Vernon Tigers. An ebullient Haney declared, "This is the greatest thrill of my life."[53]

Meanwhile, although Brick Laws and Charlie Dressen fell short of their goal to win another pennant in Oakland, they were able to cash in after the season with the sale of Jackie Jensen — who hit .261 and drove in seventy-seven runs — and Billy Martin to the New York Yankees for eighty thousand dollars and four players.[54] With that, "the Golden Boy" and "the Natural" had both exited the PCL. Jensen's signing with Oakland, far from signaling a change in philosophy on the part of the Pacific Coast League, proved no more than a quick blip on a radar screen. On the other hand, the appearance and disappearance of Irv Noren, Al Rosen and Luke Easter, under contract to major league teams, was increasingly becoming the norm.

* * *

In addition to the Joe Brovia debacle, Lefty O'Doul faced other setbacks during the 1949 season. Shortstop Roy Nicely suffered recurring bouts with ulcers. Cliff Melton had his foot broken by a line drive early in the season and spent several weeks in a cast; he would win only five games. Outfielder Dino Restelli, who had grown up across the street from the DiMaggio family in San Francisco, was traded to the Pittsburgh Pirates during the season in exchange for pitcher Hal Gregg, sent to the Seals on option, and outfielder Culley Rikard.[55] Gregg had a sore arm and lasted all of six games, five of them losses, before quitting for the season. Rikard drove in only fifteen runs the rest the year and was gone by 1950.

Restelli was a sensation in Pittsburgh, praised as the second coming of Babe Ruth after blasting seven home runs in his first twelve games and a dozen in his first few weeks with the Pirates.[56] When grilled by angry Seals fans about Restelli's success, Lefty O'Doul said, "Yeah, wait until he gets around the circuit once. They'll start throwing curve balls at him and that'll be it."[57] O'Doul was right — Restelli stopped hitting home runs and was back in the PCL the next season.

Eager to put the 1949 season behind them, O'Doul and the Seals embarked on a tour of Japan that winter, the first for the San Francisco manager in fifteen years. To his astonishment, O'Doul discovered he was not only remembered by the Japanese, he was considered a hero thanks to his efforts in helping establish professional baseball there. It was a welcome contrast to the deteriorating situation for O'Doul in his hometown. The Seals arrived in Tokyo on October 12 and were greeted at the airport by a bevy of actresses tossing flowers in their path. During the parade through downtown, the team was showered with confetti.[58] People lined the road for five miles and the turnout was said to be greater than any experienced by Emperor Hirohito.[59]

The Seals defeated the Japan All-Stars, 2–1, at Osaka on October 23 before eighty thousand people.[60] A week later the Seals were in Tokyo for their last appearance on the tour, against a team of Japanese college all-stars. Fifty thousand jammed into Korakuen Stadium on what was declared "Lefty O'Doul Day." The fifty-two-year-old O'Doul was so enthused he pitched the first three innings of the game, surrendering two runs in the third. The Seals finally won, 4–2, in thirteen innings.

Emperor Hirohito invited O'Doul, Charlie Graham Jr. and Paul Fagan to meet with him at the Imperial Palace. After congratulating the men on the tour's success, the Emperor turned to O'Doul and said, "It is a great honor to meet the greatest manager in baseball." A beaming O'Doul, granted an audience with the emperor for the first time on this, his fifth tour of Japan, replied, "I've waited a long time for this day."[61]

* * *

When Paul Fagan returned from Japan with the Seals, he decided to make another appeal to Doc Strub, the last living member of the troika that had purchased the San Francisco franchise in 1918. Strub still owned one-third interest, which he had retained despite not having played an active role with the Seals since the mid–1930s, the point at which he began to spend much of his time running the Los Angeles Turf Club.[62] Fagan was accustomed to Strub laughing him off but this time, to his amazement, the offer was accepted. As Fagan put it, "I gave Dr. Strub my figure and he took it. There was no haggling." With that, the final remnant of what Cubs scout Jack Doyle had dubbed "Murder, Mayhem and Manslaughter, Inc." was no more.[63]

Oakland's Brick Laws said, "I believe acquisition of the controlling interest of the Seals by Paul Fagan is a good thing for the Coast League. It is an asset to have a man as interested

Lefty O'Doul returned to Japan and was thrilled to find he was not forgotten. Here he is shown pinch-hitting during one of the games. During the trip, O'Doul was granted an audience with Emperor Hirohito, who declared he was in the presence of baseball's greatest manager. O'Doul replied, "I've waited a long time for this day" (San Francisco History Center, San Francisco Public Library).

in baseball as he is participating in league affairs and I believe we would all be better off if we paid more attention to his progressive ideas."[64]

Progressive — maybe. But of all the things he could have picked as his first significant action as majority owner, Paul Fagan used his new power to ban the sale of peanuts at Seals Stadium. Arguing that sweeping up peanut shells cost the Seals $20,000 every season, Fagan calculated that he spent five cents per bag to have the fans throw the shells on the floor. He could not be persuaded that doing so was good business. When pressed further about the wisdom of such a move, Fagan insisted, "No, they need to go. They create a nuisance. They gather in little piles and get windblown to all corners of the stadium. It's not that I really dislike the things. Enjoy munching them myself. But, I'm careful not to crush them into little atoms and cause a mess."[65]

Almost immediately, independent vendors prepared to sell peanuts outside the stadium, confident of making a killing. Fans were reportedly buying every peanut in San Francisco with plans of taking them into Seals Stadium and grinding them up in protest.[66] The outcry in newspapers, the radio and on the street was such that Fagan had to lift his ban within twenty-four hours of his proclamation or risk becoming a national laughingstock.[67] Even Fagan's gardener thought it was a bad move. "I had no idea this thing would cause such a furor," said Fagan. "I never dreamed this would prove a story of nationwide interest. And I never thought I would be kayoed by a peanut. I have found out the public wants peanuts. The public shall have peanuts, large, fresh roasted ones."[68] On Opening Day, Fagan gave every fan a free bag.[69]

Despite the embarrassment of "the Great Peanut Incident," Fagan was also responsible for a number of positive changes that stamped his identity on the franchise. Seals Stadium was one of the cleanest parks anywhere, with restrooms the envy of many five-star hotels. Security made sure if someone was getting out of line, they did not bother other patrons for long. Fagan guaranteed that complaints were responded to promptly. If a female fan snagged her hose on one of the stadium seats, she received a new pair. If someone got paint on their trousers, they were replaced.

He established a sporting goods shop at the stadium where fans could buy bats, gloves and balls, as well as Seals caps. He allowed fans to reserve tickets by phone and held them until the last out of the game, trusting that most people were honest. He claimed that fans rarely took advantage.[70]

Fagan was on the same page with Brick Laws when it came to the draft, joining him in calling for an end to the practice. Laws was particularly upset about losing pitcher Milo Candini, standing by helplessly as the Philadelphia Phillies drafted him for $10,000. "If the Phils are a major league outfit," said Laws, "why is it necessary for them to draft a player from our roster? If they wanted Candini, why didn't they ask me about him? I would never stand in the way of a player's advancement. We could have made a deal that would have been better for all parties concerned, including Candini."[71]

Fagan again declared that the only cure for the problem was for the Pacific Coast League to operate as a third major league. Noting the failure of minor league football and hockey, Fagan feared the PCL was next and pointed to what he called weak ownership of several franchises, with Los Angeles operating as a de facto Cubs farm team and Hollywood beholden to the Brooklyn Dodgers for their survival. In addition, Sacramento had signed a two-year agreement with the Chicago White Sox while Cleveland Indians president Hank Greenberg joined the board of directors of the San Diego Padres, strengthening the already-close ties between the Padres and Cleveland.[72]

Television was another bone of contention. Attendance in Los Angeles and Hollywood was beginning to decline precipitously and visiting teams were alarmed by the corresponding drop in their forty percent share of the gate receipts. Brick Laws was especially critical of decisions by the Stars and Angels to televise every game of their home series. Joe Wilmot of the *San Francisco Chronicle* noted the resulting small size of the crowds and said, "Evidently the only people who came out to watch were the poor souls who didn't own a television set — and brother, that isn't many." Brick Laws insisted he was going to push for home teams to keep all gate receipts so visitors would not suffer and said that he would continue to broadcast only two games a week. "Let Hollywood and Los Angeles keep the few bucks they take in at the gate," he said, "and we'll keep all we can make here in Oakland."[73] Unfortunately for the Pacific Coast League, neither the major leagues nor television were giving in or going away.

* * *

Hollywood manager Fred Haney had read a story penned by *Los Angeles Times* columnist Braven Dyer about advances in equipment and lighter uniforms worn in other sports, which inspired Haney to adopt soccer-style shorts as part of the standard baseball uniform. He and coach Gene Handley tried them out and discovered they could slide in them without hurting themselves — or so they claimed. They unveiled the new uniforms in the Hollywood clubhouse, along with a team of tailors to make the players look their best. "We had guys on that ballclub that didn't have real good bodies," admitted Chuck Stevens.[74]

On April Fool's Day 1950, the Hollywood Stars trotted onto Gilmore Field wearing the new shorts, eliciting a mixture of shock and amusement from the home crowd. With his beer belly and knobby knees, Jack Salveson was clearly the most ill-suited to the new look and his appearance led to the perception it was an act. Haney insisted it was no joke and claimed the new uniforms would translate into increased speed and comfort for his players. When asked about the reaction of female fans to the uniforms, Haney quipped, "A little sex appeal might be just what baseball needs."

Portland manager Bill Sweeney was not about to let a golden opportunity pass. Donning an apron and a woman's wig and pulling a puppy on a leash while carrying a bouquet of flowers, Sweeney walked up to Haney before the game and planted a kiss on his cheek. He handed the bouquet to Haney, who turned the flowers over to a shocked umpire Jack Powell.[75]

Undeterred, Haney presented the uniforms to Brooklyn Dodgers president Branch Rickey, who was reportedly intrigued by the idea and talked about spreading the concept to other minor league teams in the Dodgers farm system. Haney said if the experiment proved successful, the team would wear the shorts whenever weather permitted.

Many purists were less than impressed, including Portland writer L.H. Gregory, a staunch traditionalist who thought Haney was making a mockery of the game and insisted that if the Stars kept wearing the new uniforms, he would call them the "Hollywood Bloomer Girls." Haney responded, "I don't care what you call us, just so you keep mentioning our club."[76]

* * *

Time was marching on. Portland's Ad Liska retired after the 1949 season, having lost much of his effectiveness after foolishly throwing occasional overhand pitches in 1948. The resulting arm injury from his silliness cost him two months of action.[77] Liska won only four games in 1949 — all of them against second-place Oakland — and retired two wins short of two hundred for his Pacific Coast League career. One of Liska's last games was a classic pitcher's duel at Lane Field on September 16, 1949, against the equally ancient Dick Barrett. Both men pitched shutouts for nine innings, with Liska losing in the tenth after surrendering a pinch-hit grand slam home run to Harvey Storey.[78]

Sacramento's Tony Freitas had his PCL career come to an end when he was released on May 13, 1950.[79] The little left-hander had lasted sixteen seasons in the Pacific Coast League, winning 228 games, with all but four of them coming for Sacramento. Claiming that he never regretted spending most of his career on the Coast rather than in the major leagues, Freitas said, "It was nice pitching in my backyard. I loved playing, period."[80] The Solons honored Freitas a week later, presenting him with a number of gifts and retiring his iconic number 17. Addressing a crowd of 4,500, Freitas said simply, "Words cannot express the way I feel and someday I hope to come back home."[81]

Even with Freitas and Liska gone, the Pacific Coast League, long a haven for veterans, was not suffering from a paucity of older players. Dick Barrett, Cookie Lavagetto, Brooks Holder, Frank Kelleher, Joe Marty, Billy Raimondi, Cliff Melton, Denny Galehouse, Jack Salveson, Jack Graham, Max West, Lou Tost and Buster Adams were among those well into

Bill Sweeney (left) could not resist donning an apron and a woman's wig and handing a bouquet to Hollywood manager Fred Haney when the Stars first unveiled their shorts on April Fool's Day, 1950 (David Eskenazi Collection).

their thirties and forties. The San Diego Padres discovered that twenty-eight-year-old pitcher Roy Welmaker was actually thirty-six.[82]

In addition, an amazing number of major leaguers continued their careers — some quite briefly — in the PCL in 1950. Forty-year-old Bill Dietrich pitched a couple of games for the Oaks after having been out of the game for a year. He was joined in Oakland by big league veteran Augie Galan, former bonus baby Dick Wakefield, fourteen-year big league pitcher Clyde Shoun, and a forty-year-old grandfather, ten-time National League All-Star Billy Herman. Sore-armed Schoolboy Rowe attempted a comeback with San Diego. His Padres teammate, making a return to the PCL after thirteen seasons, was thirty-six-year-old catcher Mike Tresh, who celebrated with the first grand slam home run of his professional career on May 31.[83] Infielder Johnny Berardino was the highest paid player in the league when he was optioned by Cleveland to San Diego. When it was clear that playing shortstop did not suit the veteran, he was transferred to Sacramento and shifted to second base.[84] There, Berardino joined Bill Bevens, Clem Dreisewerd and forty-year-old, fifteen-year big league veteran Harry Gumbert. Pitcher Kirby Higbe, infielder Lonny Frey and catcher Jeff Heath were in Seattle, pitcher Bob Muncrief and first baseman Stan Spence played for Los Angeles, and Johnny Lindell was with Hollywood. Some of the expensive veterans, like Muncrief, Lindell, Galan and Shoun, enjoyed success, but most had short tenures in the league.

The big names, and their big salaries, were not helping attendance, which was running ten percent behind 1949. Surveys of television viewing revealed the number of fans watching games for free on the new medium was well into six figures; the Hollywood Stars learned that the broadcast rights they had sold for $20,000 to KLAC had earned the television station ten times that amount.[85]

While growing in popularity, television had not yet overtaken radio as the medium of choice for fans unable to attend games in person. Home games were generally carried live while many road games were recreated from wire accounts sent from the ballpark back to the radio station. Land lines were expensive and teams rarely broadcast road games live unless a key series was being played.

Fans often could not tell the difference between live radio and re-creations. Don Klein, the San Francisco Seals announcer, broadcast only from Seals Stadium, Oaks Park and Edmonds Field and did re-creations of the other games. He was experienced in the practice, having gotten his start in Hawaii when he performed that chore for Seals games at the behest of Paul Fagan. As a result of Klein's broadcasts and the Seals training in Hawaii, the team generated a strong following on the islands. Klein used to pepper his broadcasts with fake public address announcements asking a "fan" along the left-field line to remove a jacket from the railing or publicizing that tickets were going on sale.

One of the most popular announcers in the Pacific Coast League was Seattle's Leo Lassen. Broadcasting Rainiers games beginning in the 1930s, Lassen was thought by many to be a superior broadcaster to many major league announcers, especially in his knowledge of the game. His distinctive nasal voice kept him from becoming a national broadcast figure, but his influence was undeniable. Don Klein pointed out that five of the league's announcers owed their desire to become broadcasters to Lassen: himself, Rollie Truitt at Portland, Bud Foster at Oakland, Tony Koester at Sacramento and Al Schuss at San Diego. They had all grown up listening to Lassen in Seattle. But the fans' love affair with radio, and live baseball, was clearly cooling in favor of a flickering screen.

* * *

Many were surprised when Charlie Dressen, whose contract consisted of only a handshake, returned for a second season in Oakland in 1950. He continued tinkering with the roster, keeping Cookie Lavagetto at third base and adding veterans Billy Herman and Augie Galan to add some infield depth. Jackie Jensen and Mel Duezabou were replaced in the outfield by Earl Rapp and George Metkovich, who combined for 286 runs batted in. Interestingly enough, as evidence of the crazy world that was Pacific Coast League baseball, Rapp and Metkovich were teammates only because they had been traded for each other.[86] Ex–American League pitcher Al Gettel finished second in the league in wins with twenty-three and four other Oaks pitchers won at least sixteen games. It was a successful formula, and in late August 1950, the Oaks were threatening to run away from their closest pursuers, San Diego and Hollywood.

San Diego once again boasted a scary lineup. Jack Graham was back after a season with the St. Louis Browns and for the first time was paired in the Padres' lineup with Max West. Minnie Minoso was stationed at third base so he could play every day. A new addition was Cleveland farmhand Harry Simpson, a former Negro League outfielder who had led the Eastern League in home runs and runs batted in. Featuring a batting style Eddie Gottlieb compared to Ted Williams, Simpson would also lead the PCL in runs batted in as well as total bases in 1950.[87] The four hitters in the heart of San Diego's batting order would each drive in more than 100 runs.

San Diego kept chasing Oakland, winning twenty-five of thirty-two games in August to move within five games of first. Minoso was a particular thorn in the side of the Oaks, hitting three home runs against them on September 26, the second time that season he had victimized Oakland in that manner.[88] But the Padres could not prevent Oakland from capturing its second championship in three years, a pennant that earned Charlie Dressen another shot at the majors, with the Brooklyn Dodgers, and a rendezvous with Bobby Thomson on the wrong side of baseball history.

* * *

Despite his attempts at creating a big league atmosphere in San Francisco, Paul Fagan watched his team play mediocre baseball in 1950, finishing at exactly .500. There were occasional bright spots. Stanford University star Dave Melton hit a home run on the first pitch he saw as a professional, off Jack Salveson, but he lacked experience and was soon farmed out to Yakima.[89] Another rare highlight came when Al Lien pitched a seventeen-inning complete-game shutout of the Hollywood Stars on September 10. Gordon Maltzberger matched Lien for the first fourteen innings before giving way first to Pinky Woods and then Art Schallock, who took the loss. Jackie Tobin got the key hit for the Seals in the seventeenth, a double off Schallock. After a daring dash to score on Harry Eastwood's sacrifice fly, Tobin joked, "I hit Schallock's curve because I didn't want to miss the first race at Bay Meadows tomorrow. We might have been here all night."[90]

Fagan bought out Charlie Graham Jr. near the end of the season and became sole owner of the San Francisco Seals only nine months after buying out Doc Strub to become majority owner of the franchise. Lefty O'Doul was to continue as manager and Joe Orengo was named general manager. Fagan believed that major league status was not only possible, he felt sure it could be achieved in short order. But the Seals owner would discover the path to what he wanted was less certain than he had hoped.

Fagan's bank executive father had played a role in financing the invention of television. Now Fagan was realizing the medium was killing attendance. Despite the longer two-hundred-game schedule, PCL attendance declined another 600,000, to slightly more than three million in 1950. As the 1951 season approached, only Seattle and Los Angeles had reached agreement to televise. The Angels planned to broadcast night games, picking up the contests in progress at nine o'clock except on Fridays, when they would be pre-empted for wrestling. Day games would be covered in their entirety. Hollywood wanted to televise but insisted on $150,000 against a guaranteed attendance of 400,000. The northern teams protested, worried about their share of the gate decreasing in cities that televised games. But the Angels and Stars were committed and there was no turning back. No other teams were interested in televising their games. Oakland, San Francisco and San Diego decided against continuing and the cities of Sacramento and Portland did not yet have television stations.[91]

The twenty-five percent decline in attendance forced the league to abandon its 200-game schedule in favor of a more modest 168-game slate. The PCL discarded the traditional week-long series and also announced to its players that they should expect salary cuts.

* * *

Lefty O'Doul was hoping to tap into a wealth of international talent by inviting two Japanese stars to spring training with the Seals: Tetsuji Kawakami, a first baseman nicknamed the "Lou Gehrig of Japan" and third baseman Tomio Fujimura. Also joining the Seals was pitcher Shigeru Sugishita, who O'Doul admitted "probably isn't up to PCL standards," and outfielder Makoto Kozuru. According to general manager Joe Orengo, the four men were not in training camp to make the final roster but would join the Seals at training camp in Modesto and play in some exhibition games.[92]

During spring training, O'Doul became weary of Paul Fagan's increasingly odd ideas. The Seals owner was impressed with outfielder Bob Thurman's smile and told O'Doul that Thurman should be moved from the outfield to first base so fans could see him better. When O'Doul protested that Thurman was an outfielder and not a first baseman, Fagan shrugged and told the Seals manager, "Teach him to play first base."[93] O'Doul was able to resist Fagan's demand, but the Seals owner was becoming more and more critical. Don Klein remembered that O'Doul's passion for the links was a particular source of friction between the two men, with Fagan warning his manager, "I don't want to hear any more about you playing golf."[94]

Meanwhile, in Southern California, a spring training incident served as the catalyst for one of the great celebrity romances of all time. The Hollywood branch of the Kiwanis Club staged its twelfth annual benefit game for crippled children at Gilmore Field in March 1951, with the Hollywood Stars playing a team of major league all-stars.

Chicago White Sox outfielder Gus Zernial, still immensely popular among Hollywood fans who remembered his two-year stint with the Stars, was one of the members of the All-Stars. A few days before the game, Zernial was asked to pose in a publicity photo arm-in-arm with twenty-five-year-old actress Marilyn Monroe, who had been chosen as the All-Star team's mascot for the game.[95] Twentieth Century–Fox decided to enlist Zernial in another publicity photo with Monroe, which was set up to appear as if he was teaching her how to bat. The New York Yankees were playing exhibition games in California, and Joe DiMaggio reportedly saw the provocative photograph and asked Zernial about Monroe. Zernial gave DiMaggio the phone number of Monroe's agent and the rest was history.[96]

* * *

The Sacramento Solons attempted to upgrade their image in 1951. Shortly after the 1950 season ended, the Solons got a new manager, Cleveland Indians star second baseman Joe Gordon, and a new general manager and owner, Eddie Mulligan, who bought out Ed Sparks, George Klumpp and Harry Devine. Mulligan became the first true baseball man in charge of the franchise since the days of Earl McNeely.[97]

The addition of Gordon, returning home after a stellar career in the major leagues that led to his induction into the Baseball Hall of Fame in 2009, and Bob Boyd, an outstanding young first baseman optioned by the Chicago White Sox, energized Solons fans. Boyd had some problems defensively but swung the bat with authority, hitting for the cycle against Oakland on April 26.[98]

It looked as if Mulligan's effort to bring a contender to Sacramento would bear fruit. Boyd and player-manager Gordon, who would shatter most Solons offensive records in a season many regarded as one of the best ever turned in by a player in the PCL, helped Sacramento to a surprisingly strong start. Mulligan even gave Gordon one of his old bats and the veteran hit eleven home runs with it before breaking it while fouling off a pitch.[99] Veteran Joe Marty drove in sixty-five runs in his first seventy games. On May 16, before an excited Edmonds Field crowd of more than ten thousand, Marty hit a three-run home run off Portland's Marino Pieretti to put the Solons in first place.[100]

But the Solons soon faded into familiar territory, deep in the second division. Bob Boyd remained a bright spot, hitting .342 and leading the league in stolen bases. But Marty dislocated his thumb and drove in only sixteen runs over the final three months of the season. Joe Gordon cooled off in the second half of the year and the team sputtered. Despite the disappointing conclusion to the year, Sacramento managed to increase its attendance by eleven thousand over 1950, impressive considering the shorter schedule that included sixteen fewer home games than the previous year.

Bob Boyd was not the only new face to make an impression in the Pacific Coast League in 1951. The latest in a line of African American stars to play for San Diego, hard-throwing pitcher Sam "Toothpick" Jones became an instant sensation. On option from the Cleveland Indians, Jones had not played baseball until entering the army in 1943. After his discharge, he joined the Negro American League Cleveland Buckeyes as an infielder/catcher, but soon was converted to pitcher by Quincy Troupe, who had former Kansas City Monarchs star Chet Brewer teach him a curveball. Jones, who rarely showed emotion on the mound, received his nickname because he constantly chewed on toothpicks while pitching, the remnants of which were invariably scattered about the mound. He was an extremely hard thrower who led the league in strikeouts with 246, the second most in the PCL in a quarter-century, behind only Frank Dasso's 253 in 1944.

Pacific Coast League teams looked for ways to stimulate attendance: African Americans continued to be drawing cards, and the Hollywood Stars became the seventh PCL team to integrate after acquiring Roy Welmaker from San Diego, leaving Seattle as the lone holdout. The Stars dragged out their shorts when the weather warmed up. San Diego got a boost when 1950 American League Rookie of the Year Walt Dropo slumped in Boston and the Red Sox sent him to the Padres to get straightened out; he spent a little over a month with San Diego before being recalled. Charlie Dressen had returned to the major leagues to manage the Brooklyn Dodgers, and Brick Laws replaced him with former New York Giants star Mel Ott. On the same day that Artie Wilson was optioned to Oakland by the New York Giants to make room for a young outfielder named Willie Mays (who Wilson had mentored when both were playing for the Birmingham Black Barons), Ott challenged Lefty O'Doul to a hitting contest as part of what developed into a series of matches between PCL managers during the season.

In mid-season, the New York Yankees signed seventeen-year-old pitcher Ed Cereghino to a lucrative bonus contract and assigned him to play for his hometown San Francisco Seals. Cereghino, one of the last players signed by Yankees scout Joe Devine, had pitched seven no-hitters and eighteen one-hitters in high school and drew a large crowd for his first game at Seals Stadium. He lost his debut but won a week later at home against Seattle, even though Rainiers manager Rogers Hornsby needled him throughout the game and dismissed his pitching talent afterward.[101]

The Hollywood Stars dragged out their shorts in an attempt to stimulate attendance in 1951. Here, Chuck Stevens is at first base, receiving a throw to double off Los Angeles Angels base runner Leon Brinkopf during a game in August 1951 (courtesy of University of Southern California, on behalf of the USC Libraries Special Collections).

Sacramento tried out Jack Pickart, a heralded twenty-one-year-old right-handed pitcher from St. Mary's, and he threw a one-hitter in his professional debut against San Diego, defeating Sam Jones, 2–0, on August 6.[102] But Pickart proved a flash in the pan, winning only sixteen games as a professional. Youngsters were less and less the lifeblood of the Pacific Coast League.

* * *

Baseball legend Rogers Hornsby, fresh off a Texas League pennant as part of his attempt to make a comeback as a manager, was hired by Seattle to replace Paul Richards for the 1951 season. Even at fifty-five years old, Hornsby could still impress with the bat during pre-game warm-ups and hoped a successful stint with Seattle would earn him a sixth chance to be a major league manager; his most recent, with the lowly St. Louis Browns, had ended in 1937 and time was running out. Hornsby was firm — many would say inflexible and negative — and valued hustle over everything else. Jim Rivera said if a player hit .240 but hustled, he always had a job with Rogers Hornsby.[103] A loner who never smoked or drank (he even eschewed drinking coffee), Hornsby's life revolved around his own narrow interests.

Hornsby forbade his players from fraternizing with the opposition and required pitchers who were knocked out of the box to remain on the bench until the end of the game. He had no use for anything other than baseball, with the exception of horse racing, and could always be found in the hotel lobby, eating an ice cream bar or chewing gum while perusing the racing form for the most promising odds. He was often spectacularly insensitive; he publicly labeled pitcher Vern Kindsfather, a twelve-game winner in 1950, as weak and useless and notified him of his release by placing a note in his locker.[104] (Kindsfather would return to Seattle after Hornsby left and win twenty-one games with a 2.40 earned run average in 1952.)

The 1951 Rainiers moved into first place on June 16 and never relinquished the top spot. Despite the loss of Jim Wilson, traded to the Boston Braves after winning twenty-four games in 1950, Seattle boasted excellent defense, a deep pitching staff, and a roster of players that got along famously and hustled for Hornsby, even if they did not particularly like him. The Rainiers' pitching staff included Marv Grissom, one of two twenty-game winners in the PCL in 1951 (Oakland's Bill Ayers was the other), and Hal "Skinny" Brown, who had been drafted by the Chicago White Sox but was returned to Seattle in May. Brown mixed in a knuckleball with outstanding control of his other pitches and won sixteen of twenty-two decisions. Former Detroit Tigers pitcher Paul Calvert was plagued by blisters and won only six games, but one of those was a no-hitter on May 27. The Rainiers also signed long-time Red Sox pitcher Earl Johnson after his release in June by the Detroit Tigers and he won eight of eleven decisions.[105]

The Chicago White Sox provided several players, including Brown and infielders Rocky Krsnich and Gordon Goldsberry, which infuriated the management of the Sacramento Solons, who insisted they were supposed to have first rights to White Sox players being optioned to the PCL.[106] Thirty-five-year-old Walt Judnich joined Jim Rivera and Al Lyons in the Rainiers outfield. Lyons doubled as a pitcher; after throwing a shutout early in the season he developed a sore arm and refused to pitch for awhile but eventually returned to double duty, winning eight games while hitting twenty home runs and batting a solid .286.

Charley Schanz pitched a seven-hitter to defeat Oakland on September 5 to clinch the pennant for the Rainiers, their first in a decade. It was the first complete game Schanz had pitched in three months. Emil Sick donated the next evening's gate receipts to the players because the bonus pool was expected to shrink from $40,000 in 1950 to $25,000 in 1951. The evening raised more than $7,000.[107]

Jim Rivera was clearly the star of Hornsby's team, leading the PCL in batting average, hits, total bases, doubles and triples. In addition, he was second in the league to Bob Boyd in stolen bases and third in runs batted in, behind Joe Gordon and Joe Brovia. The Puerto Rican outfielder from New York City had originally aspired to a career in prize fighting but began playing baseball in the military and discovered he had a talent for it. Drafted by the Rainiers from Pensacola of the Southeastern League at the insistence of Hornsby, who had seen the outfielder playing winter ball, Rivera's hustle and head-first slides into bases would later earn him the nickname "Jungle Jim." Not always a favorite of either teammates or opponents, Rivera was nonetheless a favorite of Hornsby's and the feeling was mutual. Hornsby would later famously say of Rivera that he was the only player he would pay to see play.

Rivera won the PCL's Most Valuable Player award, which brought with it a trophy from the league and a check for $1,500 from Emil Sick. Rogers Hornsby said, "Rivera contributed more than anyone else to the success of our club. I don't know where we would have finished without him."[108] The outfielder took Sick's check, purchased a Buick Dynaflow and drove it across country to his home in New York City.[109]

Seattle's pennant earned Rogers Hornsby another major league managing job, with the St. Louis Browns, and he took Jim Rivera with him. Rivera would have a solid ten-year major league career and returned to Seattle to play in the early 1960s. Meanwhile, Hornsby would prove a poor match for Bill Veeck's antics and his second stint with the Browns ended fifty-one games into the 1952 season. That was followed by one-and-a-half seasons with the Cincinnati Reds. Hornsby would end his career as a coach for the expansion New York Mets before suffering a fatal heart attack in January 1963.[110]

* * *

Pacific Coast League owners were growing increasingly restless, especially about the draft and the lack of progress toward becoming a third major league. It was not helping that the franchises in the league's two largest cities were floundering. When it became clear that Happy Chandler was not going to be re-elected commissioner, PCL owners held special meetings and rumors flew that they planned to press for major league status.[111] On July 27, the directors voted on a motion made by Damon Miller, representing the Seals on behalf of Paul Fagan, for the PCL to go outlaw.

Oakland, Portland and Sacramento joined San Francisco, but the three Southern California franchises and Seattle voted no, effectively killing the plan on a tie vote. Those against the measure said they wanted to give the major leagues time to respond to a proposal to allow players to sign individual agreements exempting them from being drafted by the majors.[112] Paul Fagan reacted to the deadlock by threatening to quit the league. He began spending more and more of his time in Hawaii.

The Seals got off to a terrible start in 1951, losing their first thirteen games and never recovering. At the beginning of July, only eleven of the thirty-six players that had attended spring training with the Seals were still on the team. Fagan's prize player, Bob Thurman, was hospitalized for a month with yellow jaundice.[113] Chet Johnson, a twenty-two-game winner in 1950, started the season 3–11 and was sent to Oakland. The Seals suffered the indignity of being shut out on August 3 by Hollywood's Bob Chesnes, back in the PCL after three years with Pittsburgh and suffering from a sore arm that had limited him to just eleven innings up to that point in the year. Chesnes had thrown twenty-three complete games, winning twenty-two, for the Seals in 1947 but had somehow failed to throw a shutout. Lefty O'Doul reminded him of that fact, repeatedly yelling, "You never threw a shutout for me, Bob! You never threw a shutout for me!"

As Chesnes grabbed Joe Grace's bouncer with two out in the ninth, he yelled back at O'Doul, "I dood it, skipper!" and threw to first for the final out.[114]

Increasingly impatient at the lack of progress toward attaining major league status and with his own team settling into the cellar, Paul Fagan seemed serious about walking away from the PCL. "I'm not being unreasonable about this, please believe me," he said. "I'm just convinced that San Francisco deserves baseball of the highest caliber, and that is impossible to acquire with the draft annually taking our best players and forcing us to sell others or suffer great financial loss."[115] Fagan asked Damon Miller to meet with him in Hawaii to determine the next move.[116]

Meanwhile, congressional hearings were held in Washington, D.C., during the summer of 1951 to determine whether major league baseball was an illegal monopoly. One debate centered on the contention that new cities had been prevented from joining the major leagues for the past half-century. Damon Miller testified that if allowed to the PCL could attain major league parity, but that the major leagues had "brushed off" the league at every turn. Several congressmen pointedly agreed with Miller's argument and the PCL's plight was repeatedly referenced to buttress the notion that the major leagues were unfairly advantaged. Miller said it would be "financially impossible" for the Seals to continue operating under the current draft rules. He also said the PCL could never compete with the majors if its teams always had to sell their best talent or risk losing good players to the majors for a paltry $10,000 at a time when "bonus babies" were signing for ten times that amount.[117]

With even P.K. Wrigley opining that "someone has to break up the baseball monopoly," PCL directors implemented a plan to offer contracts to players including a clause that allowed them to exempt themselves from being drafted by major league teams; contracts containing that provision were generally made more lucrative for the player.[118] The first Pacific Coast League player to announce his willingness to take advantage of the new agreement was Angels first baseman Chuck Connors, who wanted to remain in Los Angeles to pursue an acting career.[119]

The new contracts failed to persuade Paul Fagan. The Seals had finished in the cellar in 1951 and had not posted a winning season since Charlie Graham died. "Everything is first class in San Francisco except for baseball," complained Fagan. "You can't operate a minor league in a great town like that."[120] If a buyer could be found, Fagan said he would sell the team while retaining title to Seals Stadium. He offered to rent the stadium to the buyer of the franchise for $60,000 a year.[121] If a buyer could not be found, he said he would fold the team. As the season ended, Lefty O'Doul, general manager Joe Orengo and team secretary Damon Miller were told by Fagan that their jobs no longer existed. Only a groundskeeper would remain.[122] O'Doul, who still hoped to remain with the Seals, held court on September 9 at the Fairmont Hotel as hundreds of friends and fans gathered to honor San Francisco's favorite baseball son. California Governor Earl Warren traveled from Sacramento for the event and Japanese newspaperman Saturo Suzuki was there, finalizing details related to O'Doul's next tour of Japan, set to begin in October.

An obviously touched O'Doul listened to several speakers extol his virtues before rising to address the crowd. "Baseball is my life," he said, "and I'm going to stay in it. My mother and father were born in San Francisco, and lived their lives in San Francisco. Even when I was in the big leagues I couldn't wait for the season to end so I could return to San Francisco. This is my home and I expect to stay here."[123]

San Francisco real estate man Louis Lurie, whose son would later buy the San Francisco Giants, said he was interested in making an offer to acquire the team.[124] Rogers Hornsby reportedly huddled with Gene Autry to discuss a partnership.[125] There was talk that Lefty O'Doul might buy the team or become manager of the Boston Red Sox.[126] It was also rumored that Brooklyn Dodgers manager Charlie Dressen might become the Seals manager.[127] Another rumor had Fagan shutting the Seals out of their stadium by leasing the facility to an existing major league team willing to relocate to San Francisco.[128]

It was clear that the once-proud flagship franchise of the Pacific Coast League was falling apart. And what's more, with the league focused on fighting the major leagues, the other directors seemed to have lost sight of the need for strong ownership to accomplish what they were proposing to do, whatever that was. The lack of unanimity was crippling. The Seals had finished in last place — an old team in complete disarray. Competing with television, horse racing, the increased exposure of major league baseball to West Coast fans, and constant rumors about the majors coming west, there was probably little anyone could do anyway. It was only a matter of time for all of them.

In the meantime, the Pacific Coast League would make one last noisy effort to gain the recognition that it had desired for so long. And the major leagues would throw the Pacific Coast League one last bone. The result would be called "Open Classification."

CHAPTER SEVENTEEN

1952 to 1954: Hooray for Hollywood

As the Pacific Coast League began its fiftieth season, owners took stock of what had been another brutal year financially. Although Seattle had led all of minor league baseball in attendance with 465,727, the turnstile count in the PCL had dropped by another third in 1951, the fourth consecutive season of decline. Hollywood had dropped by 150,000. Oakland's count was 300,000 less than the year before, and Brick Laws faced additional financial pressure because of the impact television had on his movie theatre chain. San Francisco, with Paul Fagan seemingly prepared to abandon the franchise, drew fewer than 200,000 fans in 1951, including three crowds of less than five hundred during the team's final homestand. It was the Seals' lowest attendance figure since 1936, when Charlie Graham's sale of Joe Marty had kept the franchise afloat.

It was decided to return to week-long series, a tradition that had been abandoned the year before. It was also hoped that the PCL's new "Open Classification" designation would prove the cure for the league's ills. But the conditions for the Pacific Coast League to move beyond its new designation and become a bona fide major league were daunting.

The new baseball commissioner, Ford Frick, headed a five-man council that insisted on all eight PCL teams agreeing to every condition it set, thereby preventing cities such as Los Angeles and San Francisco from qualifying on their own. (However, those cities were eligible to join the major leagues through the shifting of existing major league franchises, leaving open the possibility of a windfall for major league owners while easing the pressure brought to bear by congressmen from states such as California, Texas, Wisconsin and Maryland, whose constituents hoped to someday see major league baseball where they lived.)

In order to earn recognition as a major league, the cities representing the PCL were required to have an aggregate population of fifteen million. The league's paid attendance had to average 3.5 million over three years. The PCL also had to adhere to the major league minimum salary structure, a condition it already met. All league stadiums had to boast a minimum capacity of twenty-five thousand and the league had to resolve internal territorial provisions and financial obligations; in the PCL's case, Hollywood had been granted a twenty-year exemption to play within the territory of the Los Angeles Angels. In exchange, the Stars paid the Angels five cents from each ticket sold. It was an arrangement set to expire after the 1957 season. Another condition was the requirement that the Pacific Coast League set aside two million dollars to establish a pension fund.

Frick's committee made a couple of concessions to the Pacific Coast League. No major league team could move to a PCL city without permission from the other teams in the league. This required the other franchises be compensated in order to gain their acquiescence.

Additionally, PCL players were not subject to the draft until they had played five years in the league.[1]

The Pacific Coast League adopted some new rules, including a provision that its teams would no longer accept players on option from the major leagues, beginning in 1953. At that point, major league teams would be prohibited from playing exhibition games against each other in PCL territory during spring training. But those were minor protections. The conditions mandated by Frick's committee made it almost impossible for the Pacific Coast League to achieve its goal unless it dropped some of its weaker members in favor of teams representing such cities as Houston or Dallas.[2]

Other existing protections began to erode. In October 1951, major league owners repealed Rule 1(D) of the Major–Minor League Agreement, which restricted the broadcasting of major league games into minor league markets when the minor league team was at home.[3]

Then in January 1952 the Pittsburgh Pirates, under new general manager Branch Rickey, announced the purchase of sixteen percent interest in the Hollywood Stars, eliciting a reaction from PCL owners somewhat akin to that produced by whacking a beehive with a stick.[4] In a late January meeting, Pacific Coast League owners announced their opposition to the sale of Hollywood stock to the Pirates and directed Pants Rowland to draft a protest to Ford Frick.[5] However, since there was no rule against what Bob Cobb and Victor Ford Collins had done, the purchase was ultimately approved. Unable to prevent the deal between the Pirates and Stars, the other owners vowed a similar sale would never again happen.[6]

* * *

Paul Fagan decided to hold onto the San Francisco Seals but stuck to his decision to fire Lefty O'Doul.[7] Informed during his trip to Japan that he was officially dismissed, O'Doul told the press: "It's no fun getting released. But I'm not the first manager to get fired. And, I won't be the last."[8] Despite being outwardly philosophical in the beginning, once reality sunk in and he realized he was no longer associated with the team and the city he had loved all his life, O'Doul grew bitter, telling reporters, "What does that guy expect of a man? I've sent players up to the majors for big dough during every one of my seventeen years as manager of the Seals. I worked under restriction, protected Fagan, and took the rap. He'll regret it."[9]

Like Joe Brovia, Lefty O'Doul was leaving San Francisco reluctantly and with no love lost for Paul Fagan. O'Doul was not unemployed for long; ten days after he became available he was named manager of the San Diego Padres. Tommy Heath, who had been managing the New York Giants farm team at Minneapolis, took over the Seals.

The signing of O'Doul by San Diego was somewhat of a surprise since it was common knowledge Padres owner Bill Starr held the same opinion as Paul Fagan that the veteran manager had become less committed to baseball than to golf. But if Starr was not a fan of O'Doul, he knew hiring him was good business. Starr offered an arrangement similar to the agreements O'Doul had in San Francisco, with incentives for attendance and team performance that could earn him up to twenty-five thousand dollars.

It was quickly apparent that Lefty O'Doul and the San Diego baseball community would prove to be a good marriage. Sluggers Jack Graham, Max West and Luke Easter were gone and fans had become disinterested in the team, which had finished sixth in 1951. The hiring of O'Doul got people talking about the Padres again. O'Doul understood and exploited his hold on the public by hosting a local television show on Saturday mornings. As had long been his custom, he talked to fans before games, much to the consternation of Pants Rowland, who felt it unprofessional and fired off an official letter of warning.[10] That merely added to O'Doul's popularity; Lane Field vendors were soon selling replicas of the manager's famous red bandana for twenty-five cents.

* * *

Just as he had in 1936 with Sacramento, Branch Rickey claimed to have only the best of intentions and said he was hurt by the negative reaction to his second foray in the PCL. Putting his "hurt feelings" aside, Rickey did not want a repeat of his first season with Sacramento and stocked the Hollywood team with talent, including speedy outfielder Tom Saffell and baseball's first $100,000 bonus baby, pitcher Paul Pettit.

Few prospects had signed with as much fanfare as Pettit, who was returning from the far-flung reaches of the Pirates farm system to his home in Southern California, lacking confidence and with a sore arm. Fred Haney approached the pitcher and asked, "Have you ever been fined for any team you've played for?" When Pettit replied he had not, Haney told him, "Well, you'll be fined $100 on this club every time I catch you listening to anyone who is telling you how to pitch. I saw you pitch as a youngster in high school and I know you can pitch winning ball in any league if only you pitch that way."[11]

Pettit won his debut for the Stars, 5–3, against Seattle at Gilmore Field, and while only two thousand were on hand for his first start, Pettit's star power was reflected in the half-million television sets tuned into the contest.[12]

The Stars continued benefiting from their new relationship with Pittsburgh. In late April, twenty-three-year-old outfielder Gus Bell, who hit sixteen home runs and batted .278 in 1951 for the Pirates, was demoted to Hollywood because of a supposed lackadaisical attitude and an insistence on having his family travel with him on road trips. Both Branch Rickey and Pirates manager Bill Meyer had lectured Bell but he had not responded to their satisfaction. Shrugging off his punishment, Bell hit a game-winning home run off Jack Salveson less than twenty-four hours after his arrival in Hollywood. Bell's exile lasted seventeen games, at which point he was recalled by Pittsburgh and replaced by outfielder Ted Beard.[13]

The team's most popular player, a man who would become a legend in the PCL, did not come from the Pirates. Carlos Bernier was drafted by Hollywood from the Florida International League for $3,500 thanks to Bill Burwell, an old roommate of Fred Haney. Burwell had been impressed by the fleet Puerto Rican outfielder and told Haney that Bernier would be a bargain.[14] Bernier had a lot of talent — many thought his career should have been more distinguished, but that his temperament and love of night life held him back. Paul Pettit roomed with the outfielder and said Bernier was somewhat near-sighted, which caused him problems in picking up the ball out of the pitcher's hand as quickly as he should, especially against right-handers.[15]

Bernier first caught the attention of Stars fans on April 3, the day after his wife gave birth to a daughter, when he threw out Seattle base runner Al Lyons twice in one game.[16] A week later, he hit a home run to win a game in the eighteenth inning against Los Angeles, ending an Angels seven-game winning streak.[17] Bernier received a watch as the Stars' player of the week after stealing six bases in a series against Sacramento, and a ritual quickly developed every time he reached first base. In anticipation of Bernier's next steal attempt, fans at Gilmore Field began shouting, "There he goes!" A major weapon in the Stars' offensive arsenal, Bernier quickly earned the nickname "Comet."[18]

After a slow start at the plate, Bernier fashioned a thirteen-game hitting streak that raised his batting average close to the .300 mark. He also continued taking advantage of base stealing skills honed in the lower minors, where he had pilfered eighty-nine bases with Bristol of the Colonial League in 1949, followed by ninety-four steals for the same team the next year. With Fred Haney as Bernier's tutor, some speculated that he had a chance to break one of the PCL's oldest records. Haney, a great base stealer himself, declared, "I couldn't break the PCL record set by Jimmy Johnson (sic) at 124 in 1915, but I'd like to see Carlos do it."[19]

* * *

The Los Angeles Angels 1952 home season started with Zsa Zsa Gabor throwing out the first ball and it was said that she "panicked the customers ... her effort went for a strike ... but across third base." Grover Cleveland Alexander's widow was also in attendance; the story of her late husband's life had recently been filmed at Wrigley Field. *The Winning Team* starred Ronald Reagan and Doris Day and featured several PCL players in bit roles, including George Metkovich, Jerry Priddy, Peanuts Lowery, Irv Noren, Gene Mauch and Al Zarilla.[20] Like all other Los Angeles home games, the opener was televised locally.[21]

Three hundred miles to the north, the San Francisco Seals opener was highlighted by the return of Lefty O'Doul; it was clear he had not been forgotten in his hometown. More than twelve thousand fans showed up at Seals Stadium following a parade through the streets in honor of the team's ex-manager.[22] O'Doul arrived at the ballpark at six o'clock sharp, something unheard of for him in recent years, and he spent an hour going over the Seals' lineup with his team. He seemed uncharacteristically stoic during warm-ups and did not even acknowledge the cheers when he took his familiar post in the third base coach's box. O'Doul loosened up as the game progressed, blowing kisses to his admirers behind the Padres dugout between innings. He was ejected by Cece Carlucci when he came to Guy Fletcher's defense in an argument over calls on balls and strikes but continued managing the game from the clubhouse via messages couriered to coach Jimmie Reese.[23] The Padres lost, 6–2, but that would prove the exception; to O'Doul's delight, the Padres won twenty-one of the twenty-eight games they played against the Seals in 1952.

But defeating the Seals on a regular basis did nothing to dissipate O'Doul's distaste for Paul Fagan. The Padres visited Oakland in May and O'Doul decided to play golf at one of his favorite courses one morning. He had a good day, shooting a 72. That night, the Padres defeated the Oaks and O'Doul shouted to reporters, "Why don't you tell Paul Fagan that I can still play golf and win games?"[24]

O'Doul had the Padres playing well at the season's outset; in mid–May, San Diego was in first place with a 28–15 record. Meanwhile, defending champion Seattle had a new manager to replace Rogers Hornsby — PCL veteran Bill Sweeney, who had resigned from Portland at the end of the 1951 season because of health issues.[25] The Rainiers also had to replace Jim Rivera and much of their pitching staff. Artie Wilson was purchased from the New York Giants, which served to weaken rival Oakland, where the infielder had played on option in 1951.[26] Seattle's new agreement with the Chicago White Sox resulted in several of their players being assigned to the Rainiers, including Bob Boyd, who had played for Sacramento in 1951.[27] The arrival of Boyd and Wilson meant the Seattle Rainiers were finally integrated, the last PCL team to do so.

The 1952 season featured a number of memorable milestones and record-breaking performances. San Diego's Jack Salveson became the eleventh pitcher to win 200 games in the Pacific Coast League with a 6–1 win over Oakland.[28] In early April, Sacramento's Jess Flores came within one out of a no-hitter for the second time in his PCL career, giving up a hit and then the tying run before finally defeating Portland, 2–1, in ten innings.[29] Less than two weeks later, Flores and San Francisco's Elmer Singleton engaged in one of the great pitcher's duels in baseball history.

Lefty O'Doul signals from the dugout during a game. Trainer Les "Doc" Cook looks on. After leaving San Francisco, O'Doul loved nothing more than to beat his former team (San Francisco History Center, San Francisco Public Library).

The Seals were hosting Sacramento on April 24 before a gathering of less than eight hundred people. Singleton, who had won his first three decisions of the year, was in command at the outset, retiring the first eighteen batters he faced. He walked Bob Dillinger to lead off the seventh and Dillinger was sacrificed to second. After issuing an intentional walk, Singleton got out of the inning by striking out Eddie Bockman and then fielding Al White's softly hit grounder and throwing him out at first. Singleton retired the side in order in both the eighth and ninth innings, still not having allowed a hit. But the Seals had been unable to score against Flores, so Singleton pressed on. He walked Bill Glynn in the tenth but Bob Thurman made a great catch of a line drive hit by Eddie Bockman and doubled Glynn off first. Singleton easily retired the next eight batters. Jess Flores likewise breezed through the Seals lineup.

Bill Glynn led off the thirteenth inning for Sacramento by hitting a line drive that brought the crowd to its feet, but Bob Thurman again made a great catch near the fence, leaving Singleton one out shy of Dick Ward's twelve-and-two-thirds no-hit innings in 1938. Eddie Bockman then ended Singleton's bid for immortality — or perhaps sealed it — by slicing a ground ball between short and third. The no-hitter was gone. Not only that, the game was still in the balance.

With Singleton's concentration broken, Al White singled Bockman to second, and John Ostrowski followed White's base hit with another shot through the left side of the infield to score Bockman with the first run plated by either team. Singleton escaped without further damage, but it was too late. Flores retired the Seals in the bottom of the inning and Singleton had lost a game in which he had thrown twelve and one-third innings of no-hit baseball.[30]

San Francisco Chronicle sportswriter Bob Stevens called it "a defeat that will probably never be forgotten."[31] Seals manager Tommy Heath considered it the best pitched game he had ever seen.[32] Singleton recalled Bockman's hit as barely reaching the outfield grass. He also remembered Ostrowski's hit that defeated him and good naturedly groused, "We'd played together on the [Chicago] Cubs and I'd taken him out to lunch that day. I should have fed him chicken bones."[33]

* * *

Oakland Oaks fans had plenty to be excited about. Hal Gregg, a veteran big league pitcher who had won only seven games over the previous four years, won his first eight starts for the Oaks in 1952, including a seven-inning no-hitter against Portland on May 1.[34] Gregg's success attracted the attention of the New York Giants, who sent $35,000 to Oakland, along with pitcher George Bamberger plus Ray Noble and Roger Bowman on option, to obtain him. The deal caused Laws to be branded a traitor by many; the trading of Oakland's hottest commodity in mid-season was a total about-face from his prior insistence that the league needed to keep its best talent in order to become a bona fide major league.

Although the Oaks traded away their best pitcher, and shortstop Eddie Lake was lost for nearly three months with a broken arm suffered on a tag play on June 7, the team continued winning. Former Philadelphia Athletics star Sam Chapman remained as competitive as ever at age thirty-six, running knees high on the base paths like the college football star he had once been and rattling outfield fences with his aggressive style of chasing fly balls. First baseman Tookie Gilbert hit thirty-one home runs. Al Gettel resumed his role as ace of the staff. Milo Candini and John Van Cuyk proved an excellent righty-lefty relief combination. The Oaks won fifteen of their first nineteen games after Ray Noble reported, while George Bamberger won eight of his first nine starts and Roger Bowman threw a no-hitter at Oaks Park on July 3 to defeat Hollywood.[35]

The Oaks won seven out of eight against Hollywood the week of Bowman's no-hitter and by mid–July had vaulted past the Stars and Padres into first place. The overachieving Padres remained within hailing distance but then dropped twenty-five of their next thirty-two games to fall out of contention while Oakland and Hollywood continued battling. When Johnny Lindell won his twentieth game in a replay of a protested contest against

Sacramento on August 18, the Stars and Oaks were tied for first place with identical records of 83–58.

Then Oakland had a bad series against Seattle in the third week of August, dropping a pair of extra-inning games and losing twice to Steve Nagy, giving the Rainiers left-hander a 6–1 record against them for the year. That allowed Hollywood to open up a three-and-a-half-game lead.

A week and a half after that, Hollywood swept a Labor Day doubleheader at Oakland to lengthen its lead to six-and-a-half games, a few days after Johnny Lindell's thirty-sixth birthday, which he celebrated after learning he had been named the league's Most Valuable Player.[36]

On September 6, the Stars signed thirty-eight-year-old Billy Schuster to a contract. The zany veteran — a long-time hated rival when he was with the Angels — had recently been fired as player-manager for Vancouver in the Western International League. He had not appeared in a game in two months, or in the Pacific Coast League for two years, but Fred Haney needed some infield insurance and felt Schuster would help.

That afternoon at Gilmore Field, the Stars were tied with Portland, 3–3, in the bottom of the ninth with two out and the bases loaded. Pitcher Joe Muir was due to hit but Haney called him back and told Schuster to pick up a bat. The crowd reacted slowly, as if not believing what they were seeing. As the *Los Angeles Times* put it, Shuster's appearance was as if a ghost was striding to the plate.

The veteran dug in and, trying to shake off the rust, managed to foul off Roy Welmaker's first pitch. Welmaker wound up and threw again. This time Schuster swung and connected, looping a lazy fly ball beyond the infield. Portland outfielder Mike McCormick raced in but could not reach the ball before it hit the ground. Johnny Lindell scored the winning run and the crowd cheered wildly for their former enemy.[37] The Stars clinched the pennant a week and a half later with a 6–3 win over Portland, capturing the flag with six games left.[38] Johnny Lindell won twenty-four games, earning him another shot in the major leagues, this time as a pitcher. Paul Pettit won nine of his first eleven decisions and finished second on the staff with fifteen wins. Although Carlos Bernier did not break Jimmy Johnston's PCL record, he did steal sixty-five bases and batted .301. Pettit and Bernier also earned promotions to the majors.

Mel Ott's disappointed Oaks managed to have some fun on the last day of the season. Piper Davis, who was presented with a $500 defense bond among other gifts to mark the end of a long season, played all nine positions in the first game of the penultimate doubleheader. Davis went hitless but pitched a perfect inning and Oakland defeated Sacramento, 3–1. Despite battling painful bone chips in his elbow, Milo Candini started the nightcap so he could pitch in his league record sixty-ninth game, topping the sixty-eight appearances by Portland's Irv Higginbotham in 1914. (Candini's bullpen partner, John Van Cuyk, had a busy year as well, pitching in sixty-one games.)

Sacramento pitcher Chet Johnson put on his comedy routine for Oaks fans by throwing his blooper pitch, using his two-armed windmill windup, hiding behind the mound in mock fright after Roy Nicely lined a pitch back through the box, and generally making sure the crowd had a good time. After the game, Brick Laws praised the job Mel Ott had done as manager but admitted the team could not continue paying $20,000 for a manager and $10,000 for a coach. It did not take a genius to figure out that money was tight and Mel Ott would not be coming back in 1953.[39]

It also did not take a genius to see the impact the Pittsburgh Pirates had on the Pacific

Coast League pennant race in 1952. Bolstered by an infusion of talent from a new major league partner, the Stars championship was a sign of things to come. Nothing could have been more foreign to the concept of Open Classification.

* * *

Fred Haney was rewarded for Hollywood's success, chosen to succeed Billy Meyer as manager of the Pittsburgh Pirates. He was replaced by Bobby Bragan, a veteran catcher and infamous umpire-baiter from the Texas League who recognized he had inherited a talented team from Haney, one that was very close knit and needed little coaching; he called it a "turn-key job."[40] Bragan ditched the infamous shorts, but the resulting void in sex appeal was amply filled by the team's pompom girl, Jayne Mansfield.

An excellent public speaker, straight shooter and teetotaler who banned beer in the clubhouse, Bragan would inspire some of the most riotous moments ever seen on a baseball field, becoming both a PCL legend and a thorn in the side of nearly every umpire in the league.[41] Hollywood began its championship defense in San Diego against Lefty O'Doul and the Padres. Branch Rickey was on hand and watched the Stars win four straight games after dropping the first two.[42]

Saturday's game would prove memorable because of Ted Beard, a 5'8", 165-pound left-handed-hitting outfielder who had never hit more than fourteen home runs in a season. Intense but notoriously quiet — Bobby Bragan joked that Beard's entire discourse during a season consisted of him saying hello in the spring and good-bye in the fall — Beard was capable of prodigious power displays despite his small stature. A veteran of several trials with the Pittsburgh Pirates, at the time he was the only man other than Babe Ruth and Mickey Mantle to have hit a home run that cleared the 135-foot high roof over the right-field stands at Forbes Field.[43]

Beard decided to switch to a lighter bat for the 1953 season — the one he generally used weighed forty-two ounces — and he shocked everyone by hitting four home runs in consecutive at-bats in a game at San Diego, only the eighth time the feat had been done in baseball history. All four blasts went over the right-field wall. Beard's first home run, off Theolic Smith, barely cleared the fence. The second, also off Smith, bounced onto the Pacific Coast Highway beyond Lane Field. Beard's third home run, hit off Bill Thomason, was similar to the first, hit on a high arc and barely landing beyond the fence. The fourth home run, also off Thomason, went down the right-field line and cleared the 335-foot barrier.

Beard came to the plate in the ninth inning with a chance to tie Pete Schneider's PCL record of five home runs. As the Lane Field faithful stood and cheered, Beard could not help but smile. He tipped his cap and settled into the batter's box to face left-hander Bob Schulte. After taking the first two deliveries for strikes, Beard was convinced Schulte was not going to waste a pitch and dug in. The Padres left-hander nodded his agreement with the sign from catcher Red Mathis and went into his windup. Beard tensed, readying himself for the pitch as everyone in the crowd held their breath. As Schulte released the ball, Beard was determined not to be cheated and made his decision, swinging with all his might. Mistiming Schulte's sweeping curveball, Beard swung through the pitch for strike three. A brief groan was heard from the crowd, followed quickly by a standing ovation as Beard walked slowly to the Stars dugout. After the game, Stars manager Bobby Bragan planted a kiss on the cheek of a grinning Beard for the benefit of newspaper photographers.[44]

Unfortunately, the day after Beard's four-home run barrage, his achievement was overshadowed by tragedy. Twenty-seven-year-old San Diego Padres outfielder Herb Gorman had not been feeling well but was insistent on making his first start of the season. Before

In April 1953, Ted Beard hit four home runs in one game. Later that month, he tied a Pacific Coast League record with twelve consecutive base hits. Beard is pictured here with the man whose base hit record he tied, former Hollywood Sheiks first baseman Mickey Heath (courtesy of University of Southern California, on behalf of the USC Special Collections).

the game, the first of an Easter Sunday doubleheader, Gorman confided to trainer Doc Cook that he was having chest pains but vehemently refused any suggestion that he sit out. Gorman seemed fine once the game started, doubling his first two times up and driving in a run. Between innings, Gorman mentioned to Lefty O'Doul that he had indigestion, but he was happy to be playing — there was no question about his remaining in the game.

But Herb Gorman did not realize how dire his condition was; a massive blot clot was blocking the coronary artery in his heart. After taking his position in left field to start the sixth inning, Gorman again felt ill. Doubled over in pain, he called time. Shortstop Buddy Peterson turned and immediately recognized that Gorman was in distress. Peterson ran to the outfielder and called for help.

Gorman was assisted from the field and as he neared the dugout, pulled away from those handling him and jumped a short retaining wall to enter the clubhouse. Once there, Gorman's condition quickly deteriorated. Doc Cook administered oxygen. A heart specialist who happened to be in the stands rendered first aid. Their efforts proved futile. Still wearing his baseball uniform, Herb Gorman was pronounced dead on arrival at Mercy Hospital. The second game of the doubleheader was cancelled and Lefty O'Doul announced that Gorman's uniform number 25 would be retired.[45]

* * *

Attendance continued to plummet in 1953 except in Los Angeles and Hollywood. Portland suffered through a stretch of bad weather, even by Oregon standards, and the poor attendance and resulting financial distress led owner George Norgan to announce that he had scuttled plans for a new ballpark there.[46] Against all odds, Vaughn Street Park continued as the Beavers' home.

With league attendance running another twenty percent behind the year before, the directors called an emergency meeting and there were whispers that as many as three teams might fold if the situation failed to improve. Frank Finch, writing in *The Sporting News*, called continued talk about the Pacific Coast League becoming a third major league "childish prattle" in the wake of weakening attendance figures.[47] Teams began talking about selling players, with Bill Starr suggesting, apparently with a straight face, that his trio of young talent, Tom Alston, Memo Luna and Dick Faber, might fetch as much as $250,000 from the major leagues.[48] The fact was, whether or not the previous summer's congressional hearings had provided the impetus, the weaker sisters in the two-team major league cities were beginning to move. The Boston Braves had relocated to Milwaukee, becoming the first major league team to shift to a new city in fifty years. The Philadelphia Athletics and St. Louis Browns would be next.

During the major league All-Star break in 1953, Yankees minority owner Del Webb told reporters that the majors should be looking at shifting franchises to Los Angeles and San Francisco. Seattle vice president Torchy Torrance responded by suggesting the PCL streamline to prevent the major leagues from invading by eliminating San Diego, Oakland and Sacramento in favor of Vancouver, Houston and Dallas.[49]

Unwilling to abandon dreams of major league status, PCL teams began to devise increasingly creative ways to separate fans from their televisions. The San Francisco Seals hosted a "We're with the Seals Day" on Memorial Day with Ty Cobb as an added attraction. They drew more than 16,000, the team's largest crowd in three years.

Sacramento tried to stimulate ticket sales by signing Rose Bowl football star Chuck Essegian in late June; Essegian had originally hoped to sign a contract with Oakland similar to the one given to Jackie Jensen.[50] A few weeks later, the Solons staged a race over a zigzag course between outfielder Neill Sheridan and an Arabian horse. Sheridan won the race by a tenth of a second and then belted two home runs in the nightcap of the doubleheader, one of which traveled more than six hundred feet, making it the second longest home run in PCL history.[51]

The San Diego Padres held a Western Day at Lane Field that featured Lefty O'Doul riding a horse to home plate for the pre-game meeting with the umpires. There were even Lefty O'Doul bandanas distributed to fans, who were treated to an hour-long ceremony featuring western music and square dancing.[52]

But it was becoming increasingly difficult to fill seats in the PCL. The league simply could not escape the fact that its rosters did not include talents such as Jackie Robinson, Mickey Mantle or Stan Musial, who thanks to television were appearing on a regular basis in living rooms from coast to coast.

* * *

Hollywood and Seattle continued battling for first place, with the Stars winning twelve of sixteen games to overtake the Rainiers for the first time on June 21. The Stars lost Joe Muir, who had a 5–2 record and a 2.33 earned run average, when he retired to become a Maryland state trooper.[53] But the Stars pitching staff did not miss a beat. Red Munger celebrated July 4 by throwing the first-ever no-hitter by a Hollywood Stars pitcher, defeating Sacramento, 1–0, in a seven-inning nightcap of a doubleheader. The no-hitter extended Hollywood's winning streak to six—all complete games by Stars pitchers—to open up a game-and-a-half lead.[54]

Bobby Bragan, who used antics rather than profanity to tweak umpires, honed his creativity. Before being ejected from one game, he wrote nasty messages in the coach's box and finally sent the team's sixteen-year-old batboy to coach third base. Umpire Ed Runge stopped the batboy before he reached the coach's box and told him, "Don't let Bragan make a fool of you." The batboy replied, "He's not. I'm enjoying this."[55]

Pants Rowland fined Bragan seventy-five dollars for his actions; Bragan planned to pay with one-dollar bills but thought better of it.[56] Two weeks later, Bragan was thrown out of a game after objecting to another call by Runge and responded by throwing every piece of his uniform onto the field, one by one, climaxed by a towel fluttering out of the dugout.[57] Pants Rowland ordered an indefinite suspension, which later turned out to be for four days, covering seven games.[58] Bragan's stunts aside, two weeks after Munger's no-hitter the Stars had opened up a five-game lead over Seattle.

* * *

There have been great sports rivalries: Yankees–Red Sox, Dodgers-Giants, Celtics-Lakers, Packers-Bears. But it would be hard to find a rivalry with greater intensity than that of the Los Angeles Angels and the Hollywood Stars.

Gene Mauch, who played for Los Angeles from 1954 through 1956, thought the rivalry between the Angels and Stars was equal to or greater than that of the Giants and Dodgers. "There were some historic, legendary battles," said Mauch. "(We were) never too far away (from fighting). Never. It was spirited."

Mauch quickly learned how seriously players and managers took the rivalry. The first time he played for Los Angeles against Hollywood in 1954, manager Bill Sweeney offered a new cashmere suit to the first player who got into a fight with the Stars. Mauch was the first to do so but it took until Friday, the fourth game of the series. When he attempted to collect on Sweeney's offer, the manager told him he had taken too long.

Mauch employed old-school tactics to slow down Carlos Bernier. He made sure he was always covering second base when Bernier attempted to steal or if he was the lead runner on a double play ground ball. "He'd come in *hard*," said Mauch. "Half the time I'd have a handful of dirt in my right hand as I went to cover the bag and I'd catch the ball and throw dirt in his face as I threw."[59]

On Sunday, August 2, 1953, fans of the Hollywood Stars and Los Angeles Angels gathered for what would be a memorable doubleheader. The Stars and Angels were about to stage what many rank as the most spectacular baseball fight ever. The genesis of the brawl was an incident on Friday night when the Angels' Fred Richards slid hard into Gene Handley at third base on a triple and both dugouts emptied. Richards and Handley were ejected. The Stars won in the ninth on Frank Kelleher's two-out pinch-hit single.[60]

Kelleher struck again on Saturday with a two-run pinch-hit home run in the eighth inning to give Hollywood a come-from-behind win. As *Los Angeles Times* sportswriter Al Wolf put it, this made Frank Kelleher a marked man on Sunday.[61]

As the teams gathered the next morning, the Stars sat comfortably in first place, five games ahead of Seattle and fourteen in front of the third-place Angels. Bobby Bragan decided to start Kelleher and he singled in a run in the first inning off Joe Hatten. When Kelleher came up in the fourth inning, Hatten threw two pitches at Kelleher's head and the slugger responded with a triple off the center-field fence. He later scored on a squeeze play that gave the Stars a 2–0 lead.

In the sixth, Hatten decided he'd had enough of Kelleher and drilled him squarely in the back. Kelleher stomped out to the mound and began swinging at Hatten. Fred Richards ran over from first base to jump into the fray and began striking Kelleher. Soon the infield was full of fighting ballplayers.

Kelleher was ejected for charging at Hatten and order was restored, but the fighting was far from over. Ted Beard was sent into the game to pinch-run for Kelleher. Later in the inning, Beard sprinted for third base and instead of sliding, he jumped feet first into the chest of Angels third baseman Murray Franklin, a former Hollywood Star who was making his debut in a Los Angeles uniform. Franklin forgot all about the ball and went after Beard. Soon there were at least six different fights going on. Players appeared from nowhere and everywhere. Angels pitcher Cal McLish was about to be blindsided by Hollywood's 6'4" shortstop Jack Phillips. McLish's teammate, outfielder Dick Smith, leveled Phillips with a perfectly timed rolling block that lifted Phillips off his feet, saving McLish from injury.[62] Chuck Stevens grabbed the first opponent he could find, not realizing until it was too late that he had corralled Bob Usher, whose arms were as big as Stevens' legs. Usher looked at Stevens and said, "Do you really want to fight?" When Stevens replied that he would rather not, the two stood to the side.[63] One of the most vicious fights ever seen on a baseball diamond, the brawl would become as famous as it was brutal thanks to photographs published in *Life* magazine.

Once the situation was under control, Beard and Franklin were ejected and every player not in the lineup was banished to the clubhouse. Between games of the doubleheader, Chuck Stevens sat in front of his locker and noticed several men in suits. "I got the red ass," remembered Stevens, "and I said, 'Who are these guys? Get them out of here!'" One of the men walked over to Stevens and opened his wallet.

"The guy said, 'I'm Lieutenant so and so with the LA Riot Squad,'" said Stevens. "I told him, 'Make yourself right at home.'"[64]

During the second game, police were stationed on the benches and the teams were warned by police chief Bill Parker that another fight would result in the end of play.[65] Five players drew fines from league president Pants Rowland, who declared, "Fist fights don't belong in baseball."[66] Bobby Bragan fanned the flames the next day by claiming umpire Cece Carlucci had admitted to him that he should have thrown both Hatten and Kelleher out of the game instead of only ejecting Kelleher.

Carlucci vehemently denied saying any such thing and said, "I will tell Bragan the same in person." In an interview, Kelleher seemed to indicate the entire incident was not that big a deal in his mind, saying, "I just couldn't let it continue."[67]

* * *

The Hollywood Stars captured their second straight PCL pennant in 1953 and their third in five years, never relinquishing first place after mid–July. George O'Donnell led the staff with twenty wins and was drafted by the Pittsburgh Pirates. Thirty-four-year-old ex–Pittsburgh pitcher Jim Walsh added sixteen wins against only nine losses. Thirty-nine-year-old Red Lynn closed out his PCL career with ten wins in fourteen decisions. The team did not have a .300 hitter, but Dale Long, a slugger optioned by Pittsburgh, led the league in both home runs and runs batted in.

Absent an exciting pennant race and the continued erosion of interest due to television, league attendance dropped another four hundred thousand in 1953, withering to 1.7 million — the league's lowest total since the height of World War II.[68] The Oakland Oaks drew only 135,000 and a fire destroyed a section of the box seats near third base during their last home series.[69] San Diego saw attendance drop forty percent from 1952. Portland had its smallest attendance since 1943. The Seals failed to draw 200,000 for the third straight year, and like the Oaks, had a fire at the stadium, this one destroying a concession stand behind first base on the last day of the season.[70]

The situation in San Francisco, one of the league's most important cities, was dragging down the entire league. Paul Fagan put Seals Stadium up for sale in July and predicted the Pacific Coast League would fold within a year. He dismantled the team's publicity department, declaring with a perverse sense of logic that the lack of attendance made it unnecessary.[71] Rumors swirled that Bing Crosby was interested in the franchise, but the entertainer contacted Pants Rowland shortly before a deadline Fagan had imposed for selling the Seals and told him that he had decided against making an offer.[72] At the same time, Crosby said he would love to be involved in a major league team moving to the city. Several San Francisco supervisors were said to be interested in sending a liaison to the American and National leagues to pursue such a possibility.[73]

In late September, Eddie Mulligan brokered a deal that resulted in Fagan selling the Seals to the league, bringing to an end his eight years as an owner. Seals general manager Damon Miller, who was put in charge of the team until another buyer could be found, proposed the creation of a corporation consisting of Seals employees to operate the franchise. The corporation would be headed by employees including himself, manager Tommy Heath and broadcaster Don Klein.[74]

Reaction to the proposal, and the end of Paul Fagan's involvement with the franchise, was almost universally positive. P.K. Wrigley felt the change assured stability while Bob Cobb expressed his happiness that San Francisco would remain in the league. Portland general manager Bill Garbarino called the news "better than a shot of Novocain" and Emil Sick declared he was "absolutely dee-lighted!"[75] Fagan retained ownership of Seals Stadium and agreed to rent the park to the league for five years at ten cents per admission plus the $33,000 annual tax bill.[76]

Excitement would prove short-lived, however, as league directors began to doubt the ability of the group to follow through on its plans, and soon the PCL was threatening to take the team from Miller's control. Reaction was swift; the directors were overwhelmed by supporters of Miller and the group, which was nicknamed "the Little Corporation," and they were allowed time to raise the $90,000 in debt that had been assumed by the league. Although they did not meet the deadline to raise the entire amount, enough progress was made that the league granted Miller's group a stay of execution. Earl LeMasters, president of Pacific National Bank in San Francisco, contributed a $50,000 indemnity bond to cover the stadium lease. A UHF television station, KSAN, agreed to pay $75,000 to broadcast weeknight games. The San Francisco Seals had been saved and it was nothing less than a miracle; the team's employees were paid for the first time in four months.[77]

At the same time, those dreaming of seeing a major league team in Los Angeles were dealt a blow when the St. Louis Browns, rumored several times over the last decade to be heading to Southern California, chose instead to move to Baltimore.[78] Del Webb had worked behind the scenes to deliver the Browns for Los Angeles, but the city had taken its chances for granted and lost out. "I did all I could, but nobody put up the dough," said Webb. "If the people in Los Angeles had worked hard and presented something definite, I think it would have been a different story."[79]

* * *

The league's umpiring staff was integrated in 1954 with the signing of Emmett Ashford, who employed a unique and colorful umpiring style cultivated in the lower minors. Bobby Bragan immediately tested Ashford. In the final exhibition game in Long Beach between the Angels and Stars, Bragan began arguing some of Ashford's calls on balls and strikes and finally lay flat on his back near home plate, remaining there for several minutes before finally leaving the diamond.[80] A photograph of Bragan reclining across home plate was published in *Life* magazine. The next time Ashford ejected Bragan, the Stars manager said, "That's the thanks I get for getting you in *Life* magazine." Ashford retorted, "I was the one who got *you* in *Life* magazine."[81]

The league entered the 1954 season with a shorter, 168-game schedule, down from 180 the year before. PCL owners had also agreed to rescind their self-imposed rules prohibiting working agreements with major league teams and acceptance of major league players on option. They also reinstated a post-season playoff.[82] There had been several managerial changes in the PCL. Brick Laws brought Charlie Dressen back after his winning a second straight National League pennant with Brooklyn brought nothing better than a one-year offer from the Dodgers.[83] Stan Hack was replaced at Los Angeles by Bill Sweeney, who had been fired by Seattle. The aging Sweeney would occasionally let Gene Mauch run the team.

Meanwhile, Bobby Bragan readied Hollywood for a run at a third straight pennant. Even though his team had sold Ted Beard to the San Francisco Seals at the beginning of the season — there were rumors that the two got into a fight over the winter, but Bragan denied that — the Stars received a boost when the Pittsburgh Pirates optioned Dale Long, Carlos Bernier, Jack Lohrke, Bob Hall, Paul Pettit and Andy Hansen to Hollywood.[84] George O'Donnell was gone and was replaced by Roger Bowman. Red Munger, Mel Queen and Jim Walsh were back on the pitching staff and joined by Lino Donoso, who had won sixty-one games in four seasons in the Mexican League. The Stars lost their first five games of the season but quickly recovered and opened a five-and-a-half-game lead over San Diego and Sacramento in late May.

The PCL had a reputation for adding high-profile veterans each year and 1954 was no exception. Besides Jerry Priddy, Tommy Byrne and Gene Bearden in Seattle, new old faces included Bob Elliott, Cliff Chambers and Bill Wight in San Diego, former Dodgers outfielder Gene Hermanski and long-time Tigers reliever Hal White in Oakland, and another former Dodger, Tommy Brown, with Los Angeles. Portland had tried to sign Satchel Paige during the spring but he declined.[85] Two veterans past their thirtieth birthdays, Al Gettel of Oakland and Bob Hall of Hollywood, engaged in a twenty-one-inning pitcher's duel on May 12, finally won by Gettel. Both men went the distance.[86] Tony Freitas returned to Sacramento as a coach and Marino Pieretti credited Freitas for his turnaround after a migraine-plagued 1953 season; Freitas took over as Solons manager later in the year after Gene Desautels resigned.

Tommy Byrne's comeback was one of the big stories in the league in 1954. At age thirty-four, Byrne was finally learning how to pitch after perfecting his slider and slow breaking pitches over the winter in Venezuela. The product of a broken home, Byrne grew up in Baltimore but even as a teenager was convinced he would one day pitch for the New York Yankees. And he did, making his debut with them in 1943. The left-hander loved to throw hitters off their stride by talking to them during their at-bats, often telling them exactly what pitch he was going to throw. "Hitting is timing," Byrne liked to say. "And pitching is untiming."[87]

Byrne was also frequently used as a pinch-hitter; two of his fourteen major league home runs were grand slams. After back-to-back fifteen-win seasons for New York in 1949 and 1950, Byrne bounced from the Yankees to the Browns, White Sox and Senators, winning only fifteen games while losing thirty between 1951 and 1953. After dropping six of seven decisions with Charleston of the American Association at the end of the 1953 season, Byrne appeared to have reached the end of the line when he arrived in the PCL. That would prove to be far from the case.

* * *

The San Diego Padres won twenty-one of thirty games in June and carried a ten-game winning streak into early July to vault into contention with a record of 57–38. The Padres then slumped slightly, falling four games behind. At that point, Lefty O'Doul received welcome news. One of the greatest drawing cards in Pacific Coast League history was returning after a five-year absence — Luke Easter was coming back to San Diego. Easter had been optioned to Ottawa of the International League at the beginning of the 1954 season and, after initially refusing to report, got into a heated argument with Ottawa manager Les Bell that by some accounts had the two coming to blows. Easter admitted he had grabbed Bell after being cursed at several times but denied there were any punches thrown.

Insisting he had been trying to get to San Diego for months, the first baseman flew all night from Cleveland in order to make it in time for a doubleheader at Lane Field against Portland.[88] Even though he was nearly forty years old, Easter quickly showed he retained his ability with the bat. In the first game of the doubleheader he had three hits, including a double high off the tire company sign in center field some 426 feet away. In the nightcap, he crushed a first-inning Bob Alexander pitch for a 490-foot home run that cleared the Pacific Coast Highway and caromed off the loading ramp at the Santa Fe depot on one bounce.[89] "The Natural" was back.

* * *

On August 20, 1938, Frank Shellenback threw the last legal spitter in Organized Baseball, to Los Angeles first baseman Rip Russell, as he mopped up in 9–0 loss.[90] That is far from saying that Shellenback threw the last spitball; although illegal, the pitch was alive and well, particularly in the Pacific Coast League.

Hitters hated the pitch as they had for a half-century, which is why pitchers kept throwing it. Jimmie Reese played when the spitter was legal: "It wasn't easy [hitting the spitball], I'll tell you that. There weren't too many [legal] spitball pitchers, thank God, or I'd have probably not hit for any average. Neither would have anybody else."[91]

Fielders were not fond of it either. When Bobby Doerr was breaking in at Hollywood in 1934, Shellenback was his teammate. The veteran pitcher used slippery elm, generally putting a wet spot on the ball about the size of a quarter. Doerr remembered, "The ball would be about as slick as can be. Every once and awhile, you'd hit that spot just right and throw a spitter over to first base."[92]

Throughout the 1940s and 1950s, a number of pitchers surreptitiously added the trick delivery to their repertoire, using it because it worked. The trick was to not use it too often, although some pitchers, like Ralph Buxton, were less subtle. Ed Cereghino said that Buxton wore a glove with the pocket cut out: "He'd have pine tar or honey every which way up there."[93]

Gene Bearden was a knuckleball pitcher but his best pitch was actually a spitter. Sportswriter Bill Conlin interviewed Bearden the night after Steve Bilko beat him with a home run and asked him, "Can that Bilko hit?" Giving the sportswriter a wink, Bearden replied,

"Look Conlin, he hit my best pitch last night. I had it just where I wanted it, low and on the outside, and that son of a bitch pulled it over the left-field fence."[94]

Most never admitted throwing the pitch but it was an open secret. Art Schallock remembered that Elmer Singleton had a crack between his upper teeth and spit through them while chewing Juicy Fruit gum.[95] Larry Jansen admired Singleton's sly way of loading the baseball: "The pitch before he was going to throw it, he would put spit on the back of his thumb. Then he'd go ahead and make that pitch. He'd get the ball back and it would be easy to get something off the back of his thumb — he would never go to his mouth or anything."[96] Told of Jansen's admiration of his spitball, Singleton laughed and said, "I had a good slider."[97]

Jansen also teased Oaks pitcher George Bamberger, once leaving a cup of water behind the mound and yelling to him, "Instead of going to the resin bag, just stick your finger in the cup. You won't have to go to your mouth!"[98]

Bamberger had by then reached the stage where his arm throbbed on every pitch. He openly admitted throwing the spitter, favoring slippery elm as his application of choice, and used the common knowledge that he threw it to his psychological advantage. In fact, he would often load up the ball in plain view, using methods passed down from a half-century before. "I used to chew pieces of (slippery elm) until the saliva was really, really slippery," he said. "So when you get a load on your fingers and you do it right in front of them, they say, 'Ah, the guy *can't* be cheating.'

"I did everything I could to stay in the game. All the other guys on the other teams knew it. And they'd be squawking about it (when) I wasn't even throwing it. I'd be throwing a screwball or slider ... now I had it in their minds so much that they're not looking for the other stuff. I made no bones about throwing it. But if I was going along and I really didn't need it, I wouldn't (throw it).

"If I got in a little bit of trouble or I was struggling a little bit, or my stuff wasn't good enough to get somebody out ... then I'd load it up. But even when I didn't use it, I was being accused. (It was) the same thing in the big leagues with Gaylord Perry when he was with Cleveland and I was [pitching coach] with Baltimore. Our guys accused him and I knew he wasn't throwing it. He'd be throwing some kind of breaking pitch ... and the guys were so psyched out. That's what I used to tell guys. Don't be scared to tell somebody what you're doing out there. You get it planted in their minds. Now you've got him thinking *more*."[99]

Often teammates "loaded" the ball up for the pitcher. Lilio Marcucci did it for Red Lynn when they played together in Portland.[100] Bill Conlin once asked Tony Freitas, who had a reputation for speeding and hunting out of season but was otherwise a straight-arrow who neither swore nor drank, if he ever threw a spitter. Aghast, Freitas exclaimed, "Oh goodness, no! Gracious no!"

Later Conlin told former Sacramento infielder Joe Orengo about his conversation with Freitas. Orengo replied, "Well, he's a goddamned liar. [Art] Garibaldi and I used to load the ball for him and in a tough situation we'd carry it in and hand him the spitball. And he'd throw it. He *wanted* it. If he had a couple of strikes on a good hitter like [Dom] Dallessandro, he wanted us to load the ball. I've carried many a loaded ball to Tony."[101]

* * *

Tommy Byrne's comeback proved an unqualified success and the veteran's determination to return to the major leagues intensified. Because of his ability with the bat, Byrne sometimes played first base or the outfield, often hitting fourth or fifth in the order. He hit seven home runs, including three in one week, and drove in 39 runs with a .295 batting average for the Rainiers in 1954. He also showed he was far from through as a pitcher, throwing twenty-four complete games. When Byrne defeated San Diego, 5–1, on a three-hitter on September 1 for his twentieth win, Rainiers general manager Dewey Soriano wired every major league club to let them know the left-hander was "available for immediate delivery."[102]

Meanwhile, the Hollywood Stars were in first place but experiencing their ups and downs. Mel Queen won eleven straight and then did not win another game for six weeks. Lino Donoso started out 15–5 before undergoing an emergency appendectomy on July 19, the day after Luke Easter rejoined the Padres.[103] But the Stars suffered their most serious blow when Carlos Bernier engaged in a violent confrontation with an umpire.

Plagued by a temper he blamed on headaches suffered since a beaning in 1948, Bernier had returned to Hollywood in 1954 following a season in Pittsburgh. The popular outfielder resumed his outstanding play of 1952, but seemed to feed off Bobby Bragan's antics in a negative way. Bragan and Bob Cobb had several conversations with Bernier about his temper and Bernier would always promise to do better.

On June 13, Bernier was involved in an altercation with Angels shortstop Bud Hardin. Already agitated at taunting he received from the Wrigley Field faithful earlier in the game, Bernier was tagged roughly by Hardin on a play at second base and reacted by kicking at the shortstop, trying to slash him with his spikes. Hardin took a swing at Bernier and the benches emptied. Both Hardin and Bernier were ejected, and as he left, Bernier began taunting the Angels from the dugout. Both men were fined fifty dollars and Bernier received a five-day suspension.[104]

Bernier continued his outstanding play after serving his time. In the second week of August he was leading the league in stolen bases, was fourth in batting average, and was playing his usual stellar defense.

The San Diego Padres visited Gilmore Field on August 11, trailing first-place Hollywood by three-and-a-half games. An argument erupted in the first inning when Luke Easter was called safe on a close play at first base. Hollywood players quietly fumed as the Padres quickly jumped to a big lead over the Stars, scoring four runs off Roger Bowman. Easter followed the next inning with a gargantuan three-run home run, a ball that cleared the twenty-foot-high fence in center field and sailed far out of the ballpark, making him the first to accomplish the feat twice.[105]

In the eighth inning of what had become a long, frustrating game for Hollywood, Carlos Bernier was retired on a called third strike. According to Irv Noren, Bernier never thought any he pitch he took was a strike, "whether it was right down the middle or not."[106] True to form, Bernier leapt into the face of home plate umpire Chris Valenti and they were soon nose to nose. Valenti had a less than masculine bearing and the best way to get under his skin was to call him "Sweetie."

Bernier told Valenti, "You missed that one, Sweetie." Valenti threw Bernier out of the game. Bernier reacted by slapping Valenti across the face.[107] The Stars outfielder was immediately sorry for what he had done. He apologized to Valenti after the game and awaited his punishment from the league office. Bobby Bragan tried defending Bernier, partially blaming the umpires for letting things get out of hand. But he had to concede, saying, "There is no justification, though, for what he did."[108]

The next day, Pants Rowland suspended Bernier for the rest of the season. Before leaving for his home in Puerto Rico, Bernier, who was the team's leading hitter with a .313

batting average, said, "I am not mad at anybody but myself. Mr. Rowland was good to me. I was afraid I might be barred for life."[109] Both Bobby Bragan and Bob Cobb said that Bernier would be welcomed back in 1955. The loss of Bernier and injuries to the Stars pitching staff gave the Padres an opportunity to once again close the gap.

San Diego was surging behind veterans Earl Rapp and Harry Elliott, the latter a great junk-ball hitter who led the PCL in batting average, total bases and outfield assists. Expected to star for the team, former National League MVP Bob Elliott was ineffective almost all year before catching fire the final week of the season. Luke Easter hit thirteen home runs in 198 at-bats. Pitcher Bill Wight, a veteran of five American League teams and renowned for having one of the best pick-off moves in the history of the game, led the league in winning percentage and earned run average.

San Diego defeated Los Angeles, 8–2, on September 10 to pull within a half-game of Hollywood, which had been rained out in Portland.[110] Four games remained on the schedule for the Stars and three for the Padres, and it appeared the two teams would continue their battle to the final day of the 1954 season, and perhaps beyond.

The Stars and Beavers played a doubleheader the next day that took seven hours to complete because of rain delays. The teams split, with Portland driving Hollywood starter Roger Bowman from the box in the first game before he could record an out. Bowman even made an error before heading to the showers as the Beavers won, 12–1. Hollywood came back to take the nightcap while San Diego shut out the Angels behind Lloyd Dickey's five-hitter.[111]

The teams went into their season-ending doubleheaders tied for first place. The Padres took on the Angels in Los Angeles. Hollywood was visiting Portland. Both teams lost the first game of their doubleheaders. At Wrigley Field, Cal McLish and Bill Wight dueled into the eleventh inning tied, 2–2. After McLish stopped San Diego in the top of the inning, Angels outfielder Tommy Brown drew a two-out walk off Wight and scored on Vic Marasco's double.

At the same time, the Stars fell to Portland, 1–0, as Beavers pitcher Dick Waibel threw his fifth shutout of the season to beat Lino Donoso. The Padres and Stars remained tied with one game left. Lefty O'Doul called on Al Lyons to pitch the nightcap against Los Angeles. Lyons, who had been a relief pitcher/outfielder since signing with San Diego after refusing to perform double duty for San Francisco earlier in the year, was making his first start for the Padres.[112] O'Doul's hunch paid off as Lyons scattered six hits en route to a 7–2 win that the Padres basically put away with a five-run fifth inning. O'Doul proudly posed for photographs with a tired Lyons after the game.[113]

In Portland, Roger Bowman was Bobby Bragan's choice to pitch the finale and the veteran was determined to make up for his dreadful performance two days earlier when he could not get a single batter out. He would more than make up for it.

Bragan caught the game and hit his first two home runs of the season. But Bowman did not need much help. Going into the bottom of the seventh, Bowman had not allowed a base runner. Bragan told the left-hander, "The first hit they get off you is going to have to be off your curveball."[114] Bowman retired the Beavers one-two-three, completing a seven-inning perfect game for a 10–0 win.[115] Bowman's second career PCL no-hitter meant there would be a one-game playoff between Hollywood and San Diego for the 1954 pennant — after 168 games, they had identical 101–67 records. O'Doul had been manager of the Seals the only other time this had happened, in 1947 when he lost to the Angels, and he was determined to bring the Padres their first Pacific Coast League regular-season championship.

The playoff was held at Lane Field on September 13. Bob Kerrigan volunteered to pitch for the Padres on one day's rest, telling Lefty O'Doul, "I don't throw hard enough to have a sore arm. I could go out there and throw all day if you want me to."[116] Bob Elliott, who had hit six home runs in the previous eight days, put the Padres ahead, 2–1, with a home run off Red Munger, also pitching on one day's rest, in the second inning. After the Stars tied the game, Harry Elliott singled in the go-ahead run for San Diego, followed by Bob Elliott's second home run of the day, a three-run shot off Mel Queen. Kerrigan easily handled Hollywood the rest of the way and the Padres captured their first PCL championship since winning the 1937 Shaughnessy Playoffs.

The crowd of more than eleven thousand rushed the field after the final out, lifting Kerrigan on their shoulders. Bob Elliott, who was replaced in the sixth inning by Milt Smith after he was hit in the back by a pitch, shouted above the din in the clubhouse, "This game was the top thrill in my life!"

When asked how it ranked with hitting two home runs in the 1948 World Series for the Boston Braves, the thirty-seven-year-old, who had lived in San Diego for many years, said, "Yes, that was something, too. But tonight I was playing before all my friends in my own town. That made it better, believe me." It would also prove to be the last regular season game of Elliott's career; he would hit a pinch-hit single in his only appearance in the post-season playoff and then retire as an active player.[117]

Scene of the city's celebration of the San Diego Padres' 1954 pennant at Horton Plaza downtown, a few blocks from Lane Field (San Diego Hall of Champions).

Bobby Bragan, his team suffering in silence after coming so close to a third straight pennant, told reporters, "I have no apologies for our club this year. The Stars did a great job. I just hope Hollywood clubs of the future play as well and fight as hard."[118]

The city of San Diego staged a parade for the Padres, with convertibles supplied by a local auto dealer carrying the players down Broadway. The procession ended with a big rally before thousands of people downtown at Horton Plaza. Lefty O'Doul seemed on top of the world.

However, despite the team's success, Padres president Bill Starr, who should have been the happiest person in the crowd, had become increasingly frustrated by the city's lack of progress toward a new stadium and was said to be interested in selling the team and devoting his time to developing shopping centers.[119]

The post-season playoffs were anticlimactic. Oakland swept San Francisco in three games after eliminating San Diego in the first round. The seven playoff games combined drew fewer than the number of fans attending the one-game regular season playoff between San Diego and Hollywood. It would be the last Shaughnessy series in the Pacific Coast League; the post-season playoff was finally abandoned for good. After eleven years, the league was also to have a new president. Pants Rowland was leaving the PCL to take a job in the major leagues.

CHAPTER EIGHTEEN

1955 to 1957: Stout Steve and the PCL's Last Great Team

After eleven years in charge, seventy-five-year-old Pants Rowland announced he was leaving the Pacific Coast League to become president of the Chicago Cubs.[1] Despite feeling there had been efforts to push him aside, Rowland publicly insisted that his departure was unrelated to any such attempts or any plan of major league baseball to invade PCL territory.[2] League directors replaced Rowland with Claire Goodwin, a twenty-year member of the California Athletic Commission some four decades removed from a stint as a Los Angeles Angels infielder. It was Goodwin who had ignited a controversy in 1914 by announcing he was jumping to the Federal League, incurring the wrath of Henry Berry toward the outlaw league.[3]

Goodwin faced serious challenges. Although the PCL was still the most popular minor league, attendance had dropped to less than half of what it had been seven years earlier.[4] Fans wanted major league baseball and it seemed to be only a matter of time before they would get it. San Francisco voters approved a five-million-dollar bond to replace Seals Stadium, provided a major league team committed to moving to the Bay Area.[5]

There was new ownership in Portland. George Norgan had been indicted on charges of income tax evasion related to alleged liquor profiteering during World War II, and as a result, he sold the team to Portland Baseball Inc., headed by lumberman Clay Brown.[6] Joe Ziegler, veteran general manager of Buffalo in the International League, was named to the same position with the Beavers.[7] Finally forced to abandon ramshackle Vaughn Street Park, the Beavers announced they were moving to Multnomah Stadium, closer to downtown, in time for the 1956 season. They signed a twenty-year lease, and the football and dog racing stadium was slated for renovation at the conclusion of the 1955 college football season.[8]

To counter falling turnstile counts, Goodwin declared that the PCL would speed up its games and promote a younger, more aggressive style of play. He instituted monthly prizes including a "Hustle Award" sponsored by Pepsi-Cola to the team displaying the most spirit each week. Seattle was the first recipient, taking the $1,500 that went with the honor.[9] The Rainiers continued to draw well, due in part to hometown favorite Fred Hutchinson, who replaced Jerry Priddy as manager.[10] General manager Dewey Soriano installed a punching bag in the clubhouse for the notoriously competitive Hutchinson's use. Soriano felt the bag, bearing an uncanny resemblance to an umpire, would allow his new manager a harmless way to work out his frustration.

The Rainiers featured a decidedly veteran look, made even more so by the acquisition of Elmer Singleton from San Francisco and the signing of Larry Jansen, deactivated by the

New York Giants during the 1954 season because of back problems that had plagued him for a couple of years.

Singleton, who three years earlier had lost a game despite not allowing a hit until the thirteenth inning, finally pitched a no-hitter on July 23 with a seven-inning effort against San Diego after having lost, 8–1, to the same team in his previous start. Singleton had his good "garbage," as he called his knuckler, curve and fastball, and was efficient as always, throwing only seventy-nine pitches. Center fielder Carmen Mauro caught the fly ball for the final out and the pitcher stood on the mound "momentarily dazed." As Singleton walked slowly toward the dugout, his teammates shook his hand and pounded him on the back. Mauro handed him the ball. After the heartbreak he suffered three years earlier, Singleton felt especially satisfied.[11]

Jansen was also effective and was asked to teach his slider to Rainiers pitchers, including hard-throwing right-hander Ryne Duren, which had to seem almost unfair to the league's hitters. Duren already intimidated batters with his fastball, made that much more frightening by his habit of peering from behind thick Coke bottle lens eyeglasses. Later, with the New York Yankees, Duren would throw his first warm-up pitch high against the backstop. To complete his routine, Duren would then squint as if to see whether the pitch had reached its intended target. Batters rarely dug in against him.[12]

* * *

Lefty O'Doul resigned as San Diego manager shortly after winning the 1954 pennant and Bill Starr was not sorry to see him go. There were rumors that O'Doul routinely arrived only minutes before game time and often left the task of running the team to coach Jimmie Reese. Cliff Chambers, who pitched for the Padres in 1954, said of O'Doul, "He'd come out to the ballpark and put his uniform on, rub his elbows a couple of times while we finished hitting, then he'd coach the game. Afterward, he didn't even take a shower. He never broke a sweat."[13]

Charlie Dressen had left the Oakland Oaks for a two-year contract to manage the Washington Senators, so Brick Laws hired O'Doul to succeed him.[14] Even though he had at one point been hung in effigy by Oaks fans, O'Doul was embraced even as he embraced a return to the Bay Area. He switched his uniform number to thirty-five, representing the year he first managed in the Pacific Coast League. *Oakland Tribune* sports editor Alan Ward said, "It is agreed by local baseball devotees that Laws couldn't have picked a better man to lead the Oaks during 1955."[15]

In another bold stroke, Laws traded for Joe Brovia, reuniting the outfielder and the manager for the first time since 1948. Brovia was excited to be working again for O'Doul and vowed to play harder than ever.[16] In his second exhibition game, in Brawley, California, Brovia blasted a home run against the San Francisco Seals that traveled nearly five hundred feet before bouncing onto the porch of a house across the street from the ballpark.[17] O'Doul said he thought that Brovia might hit forty home runs in the comfy confines of Oaks Park.[18]

O'Doul welcomed another colorful character to Brawley; wearing his cowboy boots and six-shooters, complete with holsters, two-time twenty-game winner Al Gettel arrived from his West Virginia home for his seventh season with the Oaks. Gettel's dream was to be a cowboy and star in a film with Rhonda Fleming. He never made it in the movies, but that never diminished his interest in acting the part. "He'd twirl those guns around," remembered teammate Bob Murphy. "He thought that was fabulous. Lefty used to get a big kick out of him ... but he was a helluva pitcher. When we played in Los Angeles or Hollywood, he would just go bonkers. He'd be out there at the studios every day. He'd have his cowboy suit on in the hotel. He was like a little kid."[19]

There were other roster changes for Oakland. Shortly after the season began, the Boston Red Sox optioned $60,000 bonus baby infielder Billy Consolo to Oakland specifically so he could work on his hitting mechanics with O'Doul. Consolo struck out three times in his first start, misfired twice while trying to complete double plays, and went hitless in five at-bats. O'Doul stuck with him.[20]

O'Doul also welcomed George Metkovich back to Oakland after four major league seasons, the last with the Milwaukee Braves. Metkovich celebrated his return with a streak of nine consecutive hits in April before he was stopped by Joe Hatten of the Angels. The next night he went three-for-three. Nineteen games into the season, the thirty-four-year-old Metkovich was third in the league in hitting.[21] Brick Laws was happy, certain he saw the potential for a third pennant-winner in eight seasons. Unfortunately, what he saw was a mirage.

* * *

Conventional wisdom had the Hollywood Stars avenging their loss of the 1954 pennant to San Diego. The community rallied behind its team; for the first time in franchise history, the city staged an Opening Day parade to the ballpark. Each Stars player rode in a convertible, accompanied by a movie starlet.[22] The team was much younger on Opening Day than the previous year, the roster averaging twenty-three years of age, a surprising full decade less than in 1954.[23] But the biggest shock came when Bobby Bragan was quoted as saying he thought the umpiring was improved.

In Los Angeles, Bill Sweeney resigned as manager on May 23 because of severe ulcers and was replaced by Bob Scheffing, a Chicago Cubs coach.[24] But before Sweeney exited, he witnessed one of the longest home runs in Pacific Coast League history, off the bat of first baseman Steve Bilko, a man destined to be one the league's greatest sluggers. The blast, measured after the game as having traveled 552 feet, came at Oaks Park during a game on May 4. Lilio Marcucci, working for the Oaks as a scout, was sitting in the team's business offices located at the left-field wall and claimed the ball was still rising as it went out of sight into the night sky. Marcucci declared, "I've played a lot of ball in my time, but I've never seen another hit to compare with that one."[25]

Bilko rarely pulled the ball, which did not hurt him in Wrigley Field. He could be pitched to — he was vulnerable to a good curveball and high, tight fastballs in on his hands — but his bat was unforgiving to pitchers making a mistake. He began hearing criticism from fans when he cooled off in May, at which point Bob Scheffing dropped him from the cleanup spot. Undaunted, Bilko homered in three straight games the first week of June. He was just warming up.[26]

Despite hustle awards, big names and monstrous home runs, attendance continued to plummet league-wide — Memorial Day contests drew twenty-five percent fewer fans than in 1954. The PCL's reserve fund, which had been established at $900,000, shrank to about $200,000.[27] In addition, the league was falling far short of Claire Goodwin's goal to field a younger, more energetic group of players. Once in awhile, a young player would make an impression, such as eighteen-year-old San Francisco Seals pitcher Lowell Creighton, who shut out San Diego on three hits in his professional debut.[28] But that was the exception. In spite of Goodwin's promises, old, expensive veterans were once again finding their way onto PCL rosters. Some played well; thirty-four-year-old Gene Bearden won his first eight decisions for San Francisco. Seattle signed former Reds star Ewell Blackwell after he was released by the Seals. When a series of injuries left Seattle short of pitching, he won several key games for the Rainiers.[29]

Hollywood began playing much better after thirty-seven-year-old Bobby Bragan started catching because of an injury to Bill Hall. Bragan continued his shenanigans, sending up eight pinch-hitters for one batter in a game on May 1—each of whom he called back immediately after they were announced; it was his way of retaliating for actions taken by an umpiring crew he felt had already made a farce of the contest.[30] Although the San Diego Padres were leading the league in early June, largely due to a fifteen-game winning streak, Hollywood won fourteen of seventeen to remain within hailing distance.[31]

Despite those winning streaks, Seattle would pass both teams, moving into first place on July 17 thanks to Elmer Singleton, at age thirty-seven enjoying the best year of his career, and a pair of thirty-four-year-old ex–major leaguers, infielder Vern Stephens and pitcher Lou Kretlow.[32] Kretlow, who had an unimpressive 23–38 major league record over nine seasons, won his first twelve games for Seattle, including four shutouts. Stephens was an eight-time American League All-Star who had been released by the Chicago White Sox. He hit four home runs in his first week and a half with the team, including a grand slam in his debut against Los Angeles. Stephens hit especially well when Kretlow pitched: In his first ten games behind the veteran, Stephens collected sixteen hits in thirty-three at-bats.[33] The PCL remained a league for graybeards, although one of its most popular veterans was finally going to leave for a shot at the big time.

* * *

Joe Brovia had enjoyed a long and successful career in the Pacific Coast League, but at age thirty-three was despairing of ever making it to the majors. His reputation as a poor outfielder had been cemented by an incident in 1951 when he was hit on the head by a fly ball off the bat of Sacramento's Joe Gordon. When Brovia began to chase after the ball, he discovered his pant leg was stuck in the fence. *Oregonian* sports editor L.H. Gregory wrote about the mishap and the story was widely disseminated, especially in *The Sporting News*.[34] That incident added to Brovia's reputation for indifference when it came to defense. Perceptions are hard to alter and he was becoming bitter. But in late June 1955, Joe Brovia received the surprise of his life.

The Oaks were in Seattle and Lefty O'Doul spotted Brovia, who was preparing for the game. Walking over to him, O'Doul causally asked the outfielder, "How would you like to go to the big leagues?" Brovia, thinking it was a joke, said, "Sure."

But Lefty O'Doul was not joking. After sixteen years, Joe Brovia was finally going to play in the major leagues, for the Cincinnati Reds.

"When O'Doul told me I was really sold to the Reds," said Brovia, "I couldn't pull myself together for a half an hour." Grabbing the first flight to Cincinnati, Brovia proudly donned a major league uniform for the first time and walked among some of his heroes, including the great slugger, Ted Kluszewski. Brovia declared, "When I put this uniform on, I was the happiest guy on two feet."[35]

It would be wonderful to say that Joe Brovia's tenure in Cincinnati resulted in a fairytale ending, but that unfortunately was not the case. His outbursts toward pitchers, which in the PCL were taken as a reflection of his competitive nature, seemed silly and childish in the major leagues, where they lacked the context of accomplishment. Brovia was hazed like a green rookie, not a respected power hitter. He collected only two base hits in eighteen at-bats, all as a pinch-hitter, and never felt he fit in except with roommate Gus Bell, who empathized with Brovia's situation.

"When I was told I was really sold to Cincinnati, I was the happiest guy on two feet"—Joe Brovia. Gus Bell, Ted Kluszewski, Wally Post and Joe Brovia (left to right), on the 1955 Cincinnati Reds (courtesy Cathy Brovia).

Unable to adjust to playing exclusively off the bench, Brovia grew increasingly angry and frustrated. He encountered Reds manager Birdie Tebbetts in a hotel elevator and began shouting at him, "Why don't you play me or send my ass out of here!" Tebbetts complied with the request; Brovia was immediately optioned back to Oakland. Years later he would lament, "I should have kept my damn mouth shut."[36]

Brovia tried salving his disappointment, returning to the Oaks lineup on August 9 and hitting a home run in the first game of a doubleheader. He then knocked out a pinch-hit single to drive in the winning run in the nightcap.[37] But he could not shake his bitterness over his short stint in the major leagues.

In an interview published in *The Sporting News* not long after his return to Oakland, Brovia said, "My pride is hurt. I'm a conscientious guy. When Cincinnati just gave me a short 'How do you do?' and the fast 'Good-bye' I began to hurt all over.

"I don't want to make anybody sore at me up there. They were nice to me, and you never know — maybe I'll get another chance to go up."[38]

He never did.[39]

* * *

The Hollywood Stars surged into first place on September 1, thanks to the pitching of Bob Garber, Joe Trimble and thirty-six-year-old George "Red" Munger. Munger would win twenty-three games and post a 1.85 earned run average, lowest in the PCL since Larry Jansen in 1946. Garber became a twenty-game winner the night after Munger did, and it was Trimble's shutout of the Angels, aided by two Carlos Bernier home runs before a crowd of 18,007 at Wrigley Field, that put the Stars into the league lead for the first time.[40]

But the Angels played spoiler the next week, defeating Hollywood in six of eight games. The series also served as a reminder of better times enjoyed by both franchises; the week featured three crowds in excess of fifteen thousand at Wrigley Field. Neighborhood residents charged fans $1.50 to park in their driveways and on their lawns.

While Hollywood struggled, Seattle reeled off six straight wins, vaulting the Rainiers past the fading Stars. That streak gave the Rainiers a two-game lead with four to play, a margin that would hold up as Seattle captured its first pennant since 1951.

With only two players reaching double figures in home runs (first baseman Bill Glynn led the team with thirteen), it was pitching and defense — along with constant maneuvering of the roster by Dewey Soriano and Fred Hutchinson — that had won the PCL pennant for Seattle. The 1955 Rainiers remain one of the most popular teams to ever represent the city, although that did not make them profitable. Despite more than doubling attendance to 342,000, the team posted a net loss of $48,000.[41]

* * *

The Oakland Oaks' lease at the stadium in Emeryville was ending and Brick Laws indicated he had no desire to return to the forty-two-year-old facility.[42] Bob Murphy joked that when the Oaks would lose a few games in a row, fans would become surly and start small fires. "Some guy asked me how many the place seated. I'd say, 'Well, we'd start out with about fourteen thousand seats each year, but they'd burn it down to twelve.'"[43] An old broken-down ballpark with a visiting clubhouse that featured only one overhead shower fixture, Oaks Park had reached the end of its useful life.

Despite Brick Laws' previous denials, rumors that the Oaks would move to Vancouver continued to circulate during the summer of 1955, growing in intensity as the Oaks fell from contention. One of those rumors was initiated by Padres owner Bill Starr during a newspaper interview. The timing of Starr's remarks was unfortunate, occurring the same day the Oaks sold long-time favorite Al Gettel to the St. Louis Cardinals.[44]

Starr had his own problems. The San Diego Harbor Commission was refusing to extend the lease on Lane Field past March 1956 and the city of San Diego was likewise refusing to construct a stadium in Balboa Park to replace it. As a result, Starr decided to sell the team to the Westgate-California Tuna Packing Company. The president of the company, a former elementary school principal named James Lane (no relation to former Padres owner Bill Lane), told reporters, "Our sole interest in buying the club is to assure that the Padres remain in San Diego and that everything possible will be done to continue to give fans of this city one of the top teams in the Pacific Coast League."[45]

It was not clear how much that mattered. In August 1955, Claire Goodwin commissioned a poll to determine what fans thought about the PCL. Readers of the major dailies on the Coast were asked about the state of the game and what fans wanted to see in the future. *Los Angeles Times* readers were asked why attendance was down. Of the two thousand responses, nearly a third cited the desire for major league baseball.[46] More than six hundred people answered the *San Francisco Chronicle* survey, with a slight majority preferring Pacific Coast League baseball to the major leagues. Most of those staying away from Seals Stadium said they did so because it was too cold.[47]

The league seemed to be in irreversible decline. Fans had a taste of major league baseball through television and seemed ready to embrace it. Portland manager Clay Hopper, a Southerner, was surveying the scene from the dugout one day. Noting the echoes reverberating off the empty seats, Hopper remarked to no one in particular, "This league is a dead peckerwood."[48]

* * *

After the San Diego Padres were sold, big league star Ralph Kiner was named the team's general manager.[49] Kiner, who was only thirty-three, had recently retired as an active player and continually denied rumors that he would play for the team.[50] He announced the franchise would explore building a new stadium in another part of the city and convinced the Harbor Commission to extend the lease on Lane Field for another year.[51] Kiner also said he would explore a working agreement with the Cleveland Indians or another major league team if a deal with Cleveland could not be arranged and retained Bob Elliott as manager.[52]

While the PCL teams in Southern California were facing serious financial challenges, baseball in the San Francisco Bay Area seemed all but dead by the end of 1955. San Francisco and Oakland had finished last in attendance, behind even Sacramento. The Seals, abandoned by Paul Fagan and taken over by the team's employees, had run out of money. With a bond passed by San Francisco voters to build a major league stadium, there was little enthusiasm for the dying Seals. Pacific Coast League owners met to discuss the future of the San Francisco franchise.[53] Unable to identify anyone willing to buy the team, "Little Corporation" president Damon Miller was given one final opportunity to try and save it.[54]

At the same time, Oaks president Brick Laws and PCL president Claire Goodwin were en route to Vancouver, British Columbia, to finalize plans to move the Oaks there, confirming one of the league's worst-kept secrets.[55] Two days later it was official. Lee Susman's cartoon in the *Oakland Tribune* featured a crying acorn and a Canadian Mounted Policeman riding off together into the sunset, confirming that PCL baseball in Oakland had come to an end after fifty-three seasons. The Oaks dropped a doubleheader in their final games at Emeryville. Less than three thousand fans were on hand.[56]

The decision to move had barely caused a ripple in the community. The truth was the fans of Oakland had left Brick Laws long before he had left them. Unless Damon Miller succeeded in his long-shot attempt to hang onto the San Francisco Seals, the Pacific Coast League faced the once unthinkable but suddenly very real possibility that it would have no teams in the Bay Area in 1956.

* * *

Damon Miller's attempt to rescue the San Francisco Seals was meeting resistance from the San Francisco Board of Supervisors, who viewed the Seals as an obstacle to bringing major league baseball to the city.[57] Rumors abounded that the American Association would seek to move its Toledo franchise to San Francisco, invading an obviously weakened Pacific Coast League's territory. Claire Goodwin raised an immediate objection.[58]

Cleveland Indians general manager Hank Greenberg offered to operate the Seals if the league would turn the team over to him at no cost. Greenberg said he would sign a three-year working agreement with the Cleveland Indians and deposit $150,000 of his own money in a San Francisco bank to use as working capital. He also was willing to use future profits to pay off the $200,000 debt that was sinking the franchise. If there were no profits, the debt would remain the league's responsibility. Greenberg made it clear that his eventual aim was to bring major league baseball to San Francisco.[59]

"The Little Corporation" tried closing a deal with Milwaukee that would make the Seals a Braves farm club but were turned down because the Braves did not want to operate the team in Seals Stadium. By that time, Greenberg had withdrawn his offer and the league was forced to take over the franchise.[60]

On November 28, the Boston Red Sox agreed to purchase the Seals. Red Sox president Joe Cronin, a San Francisco native, negotiated the purchase of the entire franchise for $150,000, far less than what Paul Fagan had paid for a one-third share of the team six years earlier. The Red Sox arranged to lease Seals Stadium from Fagan.[61] A few years earlier, the purchase of a minority interest in the Hollywood Stars by the Pittsburgh Pirates had created a firestorm that threatened to split the league. Now, the Red Sox's purchase of the franchise representing the PCL's second largest market was praised. Despite its "Open Classification," the Pacific Coast League was rapidly becoming just another farm system for the major leagues.

* * *

Claire Goodwin's one-year tenure as league president ended quietly. He was replaced by the original choice of PCL directors, league attorney Leslie O'Connor, the long-time aide to the late Commissioner Landis.[62] O'Connor was to preside over a league that had become international thanks to the new Vancouver Mounties. The Mounties opened the 1956 season in San Francisco, practicing in their home uniforms so they could avoid a customs charge for bringing new uniforms into Canada. After playing in Los Angeles and Sacramento, the Mounties opened their home season at Capilano Field on April 27 against San Francisco, losing 2–1. George Metkovich hit the team's first home run the next day and received a watch.[63]

Brick Laws was confident he had made the right decision in moving from California, even though Sunday baseball was still banned in Vancouver. But Laws discovered that Canadian sportswriters could be every bit as adversarial as those in the United States. He engaged in a feud with beat writer George Dobie that resulted in the virtual elimination of coverage of the Mounties in the *Vancouver Sun*. Dobie claimed the war began when he phoned Laws to ask when the team was going to acquire some new players. Dobie claimed Laws reacted with profanity. Laws denied cursing at Dobie, but the writer was granted reassignment and the paper did not replace him. The sports editor of the *Sun* then wrote an article questioning what Laws, an American, was doing in Canada.[64] Laws replied that public reaction was in his favor and that he was determined to make baseball a success in Vancouver. For several weeks, box scores and an unsigned game account appeared in the paper. Eventually, Dobie reappeared on the Mounties beat without comment.[65]

Meanwhile, the Los Angeles Angels unveiled new uniforms, designed by ex-outfielder Max West, who had established a sporting goods business in partnership with Angels president John Holland. The new uniforms featured a "waffle weave, three dimensional motif" with shadowed numbers to create the three-dimensional effect and a knitted weave allowing greater freedom of movement through the shoulders.[66] An IBM computer was unimpressed and predicted the Angels would finish fifth in 1956, with Seattle repeating as league champion.[67] Fans seemed equally unimpressed in the early going — only 376 were on hand to see Portland shut out the Angels on April 18.[68]

Nine days later, Portland made its debut in Multnomah Stadium, which after its remodeling became the largest ballpark in the PCL with a seating capacity of nearly twenty-nine thousand, more than twice that of Vaughn Street. Rocky Benevento and his crew uprooted the turf from the old ballpark and transplanted it to the new stadium.[69] The Beavers opened with their customary day-night doubleheader, against Sacramento. A total of 34,450 fans attended the two games, equaling one-fifth of the entire total drawn by the team in 1955. By Memorial Day, the Beavers had attracted more than 115,000 fans, compared to 36,000 at the same point the previous year. Portland was easily leading the league in attendance, selling more tickets than Los Angeles and Hollywood combined.[70] The ballpark itself drew mixed reviews. Despite a twenty-six-foot-high fence in left field, early indications were the ballpark would be home run friendly; thirteen were hit in the first four games, all into the left-field bleachers.[71]

Along with a couple of new ballparks, there were some exciting young players in the PCL in 1956, thanks largely to an infusion of talent optioned to the league by major league teams. San Francisco left-handed pitcher Ted Bowsfield elicited comparisons to Lefty Gomez among old-time Seals fans. Unfortunately, he broke his ankle sliding into a base and missed much of the season.[72] Bowsfield's teammates included outfielders Marty Keough and Albie Pearson and infielders Ken Aspromonte and Frank Malzone. Pitcher Jerry Casale would win nineteen games and also hit a 551-foot home run off Angels pitcher Marino Pieretti.[73]

Future Hall of Fame second baseman Bill Mazeroski played for Hollywood, as did knuckle-baller Bob Purkey, who would go on to star for the Cincinnati Reds. Still a teenager, Mazeroski would be called up by the Pittsburgh Pirates in mid–July, drawing raves from Pirates manager Bobby Bragan, who accurately predicted, "He's liable to be one of the greats."[74]

Former bonus baby pitcher Paul Pettit made a comeback as an outfielder–first baseman for the Stars and hit two home runs in the Opening Day doubleheader against Seattle.[75] Late in the season, the Cleveland Indians sent outfield prospect Rocky Colavito to San Diego. He hit twelve home runs in thirty-five games and also took a shot at the world's record for throwing a baseball, firing one over the center-field fence at Lane Field from home plate. Unfortunately, his longest measured distance of 435 feet fell eight feet short of the record, set by Chattanooga outfielder Don Grate in 1953.[76] Colavito would eventually play in six All-Star games and eclipse forty home runs three times in the American League. One of his Padres teammates was twenty-year-old outfielder Floyd Robinson, who would hit over .300 three times for the Chicago White Sox in the 1960s.

Twenty-one-year-old Charlie Beamon, distinctive with his gold front tooth, finished the 1955 season with Oakland after compiling an incredible 16–0 record for Stockton. He won thirteen games against only six losses for last-place Vancouver in 1956.[77]

Two of the brightest prospects in the PCL were hard-throwing pitchers — Dick Drott of Los Angeles and Ryne Duren, who had been moved from Seattle to Vancouver by the St. Louis Browns, to whom he was under contract. Drott struck out fourteen San Francisco Seals in six and one-third innings in a game in May, followed by fifteen strikeouts against Sacramento. He won thirteen games despite suffering a broken finger in August.[78] Duren, who had just missed a no-hitter against Los Angeles in 1955 thanks to a scorer's decision, struck out seventeen Angels in a game at Vancouver on June 27.[79] Duren got off to a slow start, losing six of his first seven decisions, but credited Lefty O'Doul with improving his control and he finished 11–11 for a last-place team.[80] Drott edged Duren by one strikeout for the season (in eight fewer innings) to lead the league. Both pitchers averaged more than eight strikeouts per nine innings but the two were not sharp every game.

They faced each other on May 31 at Wrigley Field and the result was an 18–13 slugfest, won by Vancouver. Steve Bilko hit two home runs off Duren — giving him twelve in an eleven-game span — and the right-hander was knocked out of the box in the fifth inning. Drott did not even survive the third. The game lasted so long that Vancouver's George Metkovich took off his spikes in the eighth inning and played the outfield in his socks because his feet hurt.[81]

* * *

Former big league infielder Eddie Joost was hired as player-manager of the San Francisco Seals in 1956, replacing Tommy Heath, who moved on to Sacramento. It was not going smoothly for Joost. On June 3, he watched his team squander a lead against Los Angeles and lose in eleven innings in the first game of a doubleheader. In the ninth inning of the nightcap, Seals batter Ken Aspromonte stepped out of the batter's box to argue a called strike by umpire Mel Steiner. "He was a tough guy and I had a little bit of a temper," recalled Aspromonte.[82]

Joost rushed out of the dugout and stopped Aspromonte when he tried to return to the batter's box. Steiner threatened to have the pitcher throw to the plate and call the next two pitches strikes. Joost screamed, "Go ahead, you'll call him out anyway!" Steiner then ordered Bob Thorpe to throw two pitches and the umpire followed through on his threat. Aspromonte was out. Seals fans showered the field with cushions. After the last out of the game the fans resumed their tantrum, firing everything they could find at the umpires while police escorted the arbiters to safety. Blamed for the unruly behavior of the fans, Joost was informed on his fortieth birthday that he was receiving a five-game suspension.[83]

Three weeks later, Steiner was umpiring at Seals Stadium and fans again threw cushions after he called a San Diego runner safe at the plate on a close play during what became a winning rally for the Padres. Joost was playing third base and, after recording the final out of the inning, took the ball and heaved it over the third-base stands. Dozens of fans stormed the field after the game and attacked Steiner, who began swinging his mask wildly in defense. Seals pitchers Max Surkont and Jerry Casale interceded and escorted Steiner to safety.[84]

The Seals were in San Diego on July 1 and Joost, playing a rare game at shortstop, committed the cardinal sin of mismanaging a visit to the mound. After talking over strategy with pitcher Bill Abernathie, Joost returned to his position and then came back for a final word of encouragement, forgetting that since he was also manager, his visit counted as a second trip to the mound; by rule Abernathie had to be replaced. Riverboat Smith was rushed in as a replacement and he promptly surrendered a grand slam on his first pitch, costing the Seals the ballgame.[85] "I just forgot the ruling," a pained Joost related afterward. "I messed it up."

A week after that, Joost learned he had received a ten-game suspension because of the second incident with Steiner. The Seals were tied for seventh place and the suspensions, coupled with the embarrassing loss to San Diego, convinced team president Jerry Donovan to make a change. He fired Joost and replaced him with Joe Gordon.[86]

* * *

There had been a number of great teams in the Pacific Coast League over the years, including the Portland Beavers of 1906 and 1910–1914, the San Francisco Seals of the 1920s, the Seattle Rainiers of 1939–1942 and the Hollywood Stars of the early 1950s. The Los Angeles Angels had several great teams, starting with Jim Morley's 1903 squad, led by Doc Newton, Cap Dillon, Gavvy Cravath, Joe Corbett and Dummy Hoy.

The 1934 Angels rank among the greatest in the history of the minor leagues, lapping the field and crushing an All-Star team of players from the rest of the PCL. Former team president Dave Fleming, who still reported each day to Wrigley Field at the famous tower where he oversaw Catalina Island operations for the Wrigley Company, was asked his opinion about which Angels team was superior. He said the 1938 team was the best he had seen. He also liked the 1939 team but allowed that either would be hard-pressed to defeat the 1934 squad.[87] The Angels had not won a pennant since the exciting playoff against the Seals in 1947.

The 1956 team, of which little had been expected, would end the franchise's dry spell and provide the PCL with its last great team. Gene Mauch unabashedly said of the 1956 Angels, "That was the best minor league team that was ever put together."[88] Six Angels hit twenty or more home runs. Four drove in more than one hundred runs. Outside of catcher Elvin Tappe, every regular hit better than .287. As a team, the Angels batted .297, the highest mark the league had seen in more than twenty years. They scored six runs per game (the highest in a quarter-century) and their 202 home runs were only two shy of the record set by Salt Lake in 1923. Mauch, in his third year as second baseman for the Angels, thought that Jim Bolger, who drove in 147 runs, was the best player on the team — even more valuable than Steve Bilko. "Bilko and I would clean up on the mediocre pitchers," he said. "Bolger would beat the good pitchers."[89] The Angels boasted one of the fastest outfields in league history, consisting of Bolger, Gale Wade and Bob Speake; in the cozy confines of Wrigley Field, it was almost impossible to get a ball between them. Wade, who was the best base runner on the team, kept a book on pitchers, noting which part of their body revealed that they were going home with the pitch.[90]

The pitching was solid as well. Dave Hillman won twenty-one games and Dick Drott averaged nearly a strikeout per inning. Gene Fodge won nineteen games and reliever Bob Anderson added twelve while breaking Milo Candini's record for appearances with seventy.

The Angels led the Seattle Rainiers by twelve and a half games on August 15. By then, Steve Bilko had hit forty-seven home runs and was making a serious run at Tony Lazzeri's record.[91] At that point, Angels president John Holland declared anyone wanting to acquire Bilko would have to offer at least $200,000.[92]

Growing up on the sandlots of Nanticoke, Pennsylvania, Bilko appeared in his first professional game at age sixteen, with Allentown of the Interstate League.[93] The barrel-chested, two-hundred-and-forty-pound first baseman was built like a tank, square from the shoulders down, and had the nickname "Humphrey" when he came to Los Angeles, bestowed by Eddie Stanky in honor of a character in the *Joe Palooka* comic strip. Ken Aspromonte remembered, "When you looked at the guy, you think, what a mean guy this must be! But he was just a sweet guy. He loved his beer. He'd always have a couple of six packs on ice. He was a happy guy."[94]

Bilko was already a veteran of several trials with the St. Louis Cardinals, winning a regular job in 1953 and hitting twenty-one home runs. He was sold to the Chicago Cubs during the 1954 season and backed up Dee Fondy at first base.[95] One of seven players sent by Pants Rowland to the Angels at the end of spring training in 1955, Bilko found a home.

He was an imposing figure at the plate, especially at cozy Wrigley Field, never cheating himself when he swung a bat.[96] Pitchers tried to entice him to hit something other than fastballs, although Bobby Bragan felt he could get him out with either a high fastball or a curveball.[97] He may have been a marginal major league hitter, but in the PCL Steve Bilko went on home run streaks like no one else. He led the league with thirty-seven home runs in 1955, earning him the Tony Lazzeri Memorial Trophy as home run champion. He was named the PCL's Most Valuable Player and also surprised some observers by playing a competent first base. Teammate Gale Wade observed that while Bilko did not cover a lot of ground, he did not make a lot of mistakes.[98] Bilko became known as "Stout Steve" and was so happy in Los Angeles that he signed a contract including a waiver exempting him from the major league draft.[99]

Bilko roared out of the gate in 1956 with a batting average of .500 through the team's first nineteen games, including seven home runs. He added seven more home runs in six days and twelve in an eleven-game homestand that ended on May 31. Steve Bilko had clearly become the face of the Los Angeles Angels. Even a mild bout with scarlet fever could not slow him down.[100] He was on pace to make league history, leading the league in eight offensive categories, and the Angels were making a shambles of the pennant race.

* * *

On August 4, 1956, Wrigley Field hosted an historic event when old-timers from the Los Angeles Angels and the San Francisco Seals squared off in a three-inning contest. The brainchild of Seals publicist and ex–pitching star Walter Mails, the exhibition attracted numerous players familiar to fans of the Pacific Coast League. Red Killefer and Truck Hannah agreed to act as co-managers of the old Angels. Those playing included Gene Lillard, Bill Schuster, Lou Novikoff, Fay Thomas, Jack Salveson and Max West.

The old-time Seals were managed by Willie Kamm and his lineup included Gus Suhr, Eddie Mulligan, Bob Joyce, Ted Jennings, Tom Seats, Sloppy Thurston, and even old Ping Bodie.[101] But what made the game especially significant was that the Seals' outfield would be occupied by the DiMaggio brothers, marking only the second time they had ever done so. Joe posed with brothers Dom and Vince before the game, all three wearing Seals uniforms and broad smiles.

The old-time Angels won the game, 3–2, but Vince hit a two-run home run, scoring Ping Bodie ahead of him, and Joe singled twice past Gene Lillard.[102] It was definitely a day to remember and a glimpse of fame that had its roots in the Pacific Coast League. But nostalgic events were becoming increasingly the most marketable feature of a PCL that was soon to be much different in character.

On the final day of the 1956 season, the Sacramento Solons played a doubleheader in Vancouver against Lefty O'Doul's last-place Mounties. Gene Bearden was pitching for the Solons when the fifty-nine-year-old O'Doul suddenly

Steve Bilko established himself as one of the greatest sluggers in the history of the Pacific Coast League, hitting 148 home runs in three seasons with the Angels and winning three straight Most Valuable Player awards (David Eskenazi Collection).

grabbed a bat and ambled to the plate. Seeing this, Sacramento manager Tommy Heath ordered the Solons outfielders to station themselves just behind the infield. O'Doul knocked a pitch into center field. By the time the ball was tracked down — with an effort charitably categorized as half-hearted — O'Doul had jogged to third base with a triple. (Fifty-one-year-old coach Eddie Taylor also hit a single for Vancouver but was picked off first base to end the game.)[103]

The Pacific Coast League pennant had long since been decided. The Los Angeles Angels finished sixteen games ahead of defending champion Seattle, winning 107 games while losing only 61, compiling the best winning percentage in the league since 1943. The Angels celebrated their pennant at the Cocoanut Grove in the Ambassador Hotel. John Holland allowed the players to invite their wives and everyone danced to the music of Freddy Martin and his orchestra. The party also featured a show by Nat King Cole.[104]

Meanwhile, there continued to be rumors that franchises were moving. Ralph Kiner angled for a new stadium in San Diego while at the same time combating speculation that the Padres were going to move to Phoenix. Kiner refused to take the bait but allowed there had been discussion of the possibility of moving the Padres if they did not get a new facility, calling it "a logical extension of our situation."[105]

* * *

In late January 1957, on the eve of his seventy-eighth birthday, the *Los Angeles Times* asked Pants Rowland his opinion on the latest rumors about major league baseball coming to Los Angeles. He replied, "I never expect to see the day when Los Angeles will be in either the American or National League. The only way we'll get major-league baseball out here is through a third major league!" Incredibly, Rowland insisted the opportunity for Los Angeles to land an existing major league franchise had passed because the Boston Braves, St. Louis Browns and Philadelphia Athletics had all moved during the previous four years. Noting he was present at the formation of the American League, Rowland said he envisioned a third league that would encompass teams in Dallas, Denver, Houston, Los Angeles, San Francisco, Seattle, Portland and perhaps Mexico City.[106] Rowland was very much alone in his opinion.

The *Times* profiled new Angels manager Gene Handley and the forty-year-old ex–PCL stolen base king waxed enthusiastic about the coming season despite his lack of familiarity with the roster he was being given. Handley predicted the Angels would best the Stars in the season series. When asked if the Angels had the nucleus to be a contender in 1957, he responded, "Steve Bilko is a good nucleus."[107]

Handley also looked forward to the arrival of former New York Giants great Monte Irvin, who had been sent to Los Angeles by the Cubs along with pitcher Jim Hughes in exchange for third baseman George Freese.[108] Irvin had hit fifteen home runs in 111 games for Chicago in 1956 and his swing was thought to be tailor-made for the short power alleys of Wrigley Field in Los Angeles.

But both the Angels and Gene Handley were in for a major surprise. On February 21, 1957, the Brooklyn Dodgers purchased the Los Angeles Angels and Wrigley Field for more than three million dollars. The transaction included the Chicago Cubs acquiring the Dodgers' Fort Worth franchise in the Texas League. The Dodgers were obviously serious about exploring the possibility of heading west.

Pacific Coast League owners seemed almost certain to approve the sale, with the main reluctance coming from the San Diego Padres, whose ownership had to consider its viability should a major league franchise locate only two hours to the north. Bob Cobb and the Stars indicated they would not stand in the way of the sale, although Cobb stated his opposition to the Dodgers moving to Los Angeles, saying it would destroy the Pacific Coast League.[109] The league unanimously approved the sale on March 2 after two other skeptical owners, Emil Sick of Seattle and Fred David of Sacramento, received assurances that the Dodgers had no intention of moving to Los Angeles.[110]

It also soon became clear that Gene Handley would not be managing the Angels in 1957 after all. The Dodgers named their hottest minor league manager, Clay Bryant, to take over. Handley decided to remain in the Cubs organization and replaced Bryant at Fort Worth.[111] Pants Rowland was out too, retained only for a transition period.

There was also a shake-up of the Angels roster. The Dodgers swapped the working agreement they had with Portland to the Cubs and took over in Los Angeles. Twenty-seven players switched teams as a result, although Los Angeles did keep Bilko, Gale Wade, Monte Irvin and Elvin Tappe. The Cubs retained their two prize pitching prospects, Bob Anderson and Dick Drott, and assigned them to Portland. As part of the deal, the Angels gained the PCL's top winning pitcher in 1956, Rene Valdes, as well as pitchers Ralph Mauriello and Larry Sherry, catcher John Roseboro, infielders Jim Baxes and Joe Macko, and outfielders Roy Hartsfield and Bob Borkowski. Most had played with various teams in the Dodgers farm system.[112]

Since the Cubs were undertaking yet another youth movement, Portland ended up with mostly young talent from the Angels rather than older, established players. A new season was to begin — one that would be almost entirely overshadowed by events off the field.

* * *

Prior to the 1957 season, Brick Laws sold the Vancouver Mounties to a group of local investors, headed by restaurateur Nat Bailey and former Portland owner George Norgan, who was able to be involved with the Canadian team without jeopardizing his freedom — provided he did not attend any road games.[113] The Mounties played their first game under new ownership at Wrigley Field against the Angels. Sam Crawford, nearly four decades removed from wearing an Angels uniform and newly elected to the Baseball Hall of Fame, took part in the opening ceremony along with Jigger Statz. PCL Triple Crown winner Steve Bilko was presented with *The Sporting News* award as the 1956 Minor League Player of the Year and then scored the season's first run for the Angels, ahead of Monte Irvin's home run in the fourth inning.

Bob Darnell pitched a complete game for the Angels and also hit a home run as Los Angeles won, 4–2, before a disappointing crowd of 3,554.[114] Interest picked up later in the week when the Angels and Stars played their first series of the year. Injuries had depleted the Stars lineup: Losses included outfielder Emil Panko, who broke his ankle at the end of training camp, and infielders Spook Jacobs and Dick Smith, sidelined after a horrific collision in San Diego.[115] But the rivalry still had drawing power. Hollywood had added its own rival to Steve Bilko in Dick Stuart, a Pittsburgh Pirates farmhand who had become nationally known in 1956 after smashing an incredible sixty-six home runs for Lincoln of the Western League.[116]

The brash, self-centered Stuart was a free swinger who seemed to either homer or strike out. He also confirmed Bobby Bragan's unremittingly harsh criticism of his defense; for example, in a game against San Diego he allowed a grounder to get between his legs in right field, only saving himself an error by chasing the ball down and throwing out the runner, who had tried to advance to second on the misplay.[117] Stuart failed to concentrate on defense, instead seeming preoccupied by his last strikeout or his last home run regardless of where he was on the field.

Unable to lay off high, inside fastballs, Stuart continued to strike out at an alarming rate. He also struck out at home; in April, his wife sued for divorce.[118] He suffered additional embarrassment when he lost a home run hitting contest to San Diego's Jim "Mudcat" Grant, a pitcher the Padres were trying to convert into an outfielder.[119] But Stuart also blasted a home run at Lane Field that traveled an estimated 500 feet, his third in three games. He hit five home runs in one week, leading San Diego general manager Ralph Kiner, a seven-time National League home run champion, to declare, "I've never seen a hitter with better power." Judging Stuart to be a more dangerous hitter than Steve Bilko, Kiner went on to predict that Stuart would hit fifty home runs.[120]

More than seven thousand fans arrived on April 16 for the first head-to-head meeting between Stuart and Bilko, with many still buzzing about Stuart's performance in the Stars' opening series against the Padres. Stuart effortlessly assumed the role of showman, boasting he would lead the PCL in home runs — a direct challenge to Bilko.

The highly anticipated showdown fizzled. Neither man hit a home run in that first game. Stuart struck out twice, giving him fourteen in his first twenty-seven at-bats of the season, a pattern that would continue throughout his career.[121] Two weeks later the teams met again and more than fifty thousand attended the series between the Stars and Angels, including fifteen thousand for the Sunday doubleheader on May 5.[122]

By that time, Stuart was not playing much. He had hit six home runs in seventy-two at-bats, but was batting only .236 with thirty-two strikeouts in twenty-three games. With Paul Pettit playing well, Stars manager Clyde King, tired of Stuart's act, shipped the slugger to Atlanta and replaced him with the pitcher-turned-outfielder. Stuart also failed to hit in Atlanta and was released by the Crackers in June. Pettit would drive in more than 100 runs for Hollywood in 1957, including ten in a September game against Seattle.[123] Meanwhile, Stuart finished the 1957 season back in Lincoln, where he had starred the year before. Stuart's power eventually got him to the major leagues, and he did prove to be a better major league hitter than Bilko, topping thirty home runs and one hundred runs batted in three times. But he never improved his fielding and earned the nickname "Dr. Strangeglove."

A few days after their second series against Hollywood, the Angels lost one of their drawing cards when Monte Irvin announced his retirement due to a back injury suffered in the second game of the season. After receiving treatment, Irvin was told by the Angels team physician that he had to quit before his disk problem became "real serious." Irvin heeded the advice, ending his career on May 10.[124]

At almost the same time, the Angels suffered another blow when Steve Bilko pulled a muscle in his shoulder while hitting a pop-up in a game against Portland, knocking him out of action for a week.[125] Soon after his return from that injury, he came down with the flu and missed three more games.[126] It seemed that neither Steve Bilko nor the Los Angeles Angels were going to repeat their magnificent 1956 seasons.

* * *

One of the PCL's best-known personalities became seriously ill in San Diego during the season's first week. Portland manager Bill Sweeney had always been a hard-drinking, hard-living man and his lifestyle was taking its toll. Despite coughing up blood for some time, Sweeney stubbornly refused treatment. During an April 16 game in San Diego, Sweeney began suffering intense pain but insisted on finishing his duties at the ballpark. Unfortunately, he had a perforated ulcer and collapsed after the game because of internal bleeding.

He was immediately rushed to Mercy Hospital in San Diego to undergo an emergency operation, but it was too late; Sweeney died early the morning of April 18, slightly more than twenty-four hours after leaving the playing field for the final time.[127] Flags at all league parks were ordered to be flown at half-staff.

Sweeney, who won three pennants in nineteen seasons in the PCL, was remembered as "Old Tomato Face" for his tendency to turn bright red when angry. An intense competitor who had once borrowed a gun from a night watchman and shot out the lights in the Gilmore Field press room after losing a doubleheader, Sweeney was praised as a genuinely good person on and off the field, even when riled up over losing a ballgame here and there.[128] Sweeney's pallbearers included Portland outfielder Luis Marquez as well as players Sam Calderone, Jack Littrell and *Oregonian* sports editor L.H. Gregory.[129]

* * *

Under new general manager Cedric Tallis and manager Charlie Metro, the Vancouver Mounties were the early leaders of the 1957 season, winning ten of twelve games to move into first place in late May, a streak highlighted by an eighteen-inning win over Seattle that included eleven innings of shutout relief by Charlie Beamon.[130] The surprising San Francisco Seals responded to the challenge, winning fourteen of eighteen to push one-half game ahead of Vancouver.

The Seals had lost the services of top pitching prospect Earl Wilson, who was supposed to be the team's Opening Day starter. Wilson was called up by his draft board shortly before the season began and opted to enlist in the U.S. Marines.[131] But relievers Bill Abernathie and Leo Kiely picked up the slack, with Abernathie throwing a one-hitter against Sacramento in his first start of the season on June 2.[132]

The Seals' thin staff had been made thinner because of financial challenges and decisions being made three thousand miles away in Boston. Duane Pillette was making a successful comeback from arm trouble, winning four of his first five decisions. However, the right-hander had a bonus clause in his contract if he was still on the roster in June. The Seals did not have the money to pay him and the Red Sox were about to send some young pitchers down after the cut-off date. San Francisco had already released Jim Konstanty, the former National League Most Valuable Player of the 1950 Philadelphia Phillies "Whiz Kids."[133] Money was tight; short-handed or not, the Seals released Pillette.

The pitcher called Lefty O'Doul, who after leaving Vancouver had signed with Seattle, and asked him, "Do you want a good right-handed pitcher?" O'Doul, who was not aware Pillette had been released, replied, "Who?" Pillette said, "Me."

O'Doul, who had seen Pillette pitch earlier in the season, enthusiastically signed the right-hander, who finished the season with a record of 16–8 and an earned run average slightly above three runs per game.[134]

The Seals continued to play well, even with their pitching shortage. They also managed to have some fun. One day they were rained out against the Padres and everyone was at the ballpark when the game was called. San Diego general manager Ralph Kiner was bored and approached Seals manager Joe Gordon.

"Kiner bet (Gordon) a case of whisky that he would not run around the bases and slide belly first into home plate," said Padres outfielder Bob Lennon. "It was all mud and he belly-flopped from about twenty feet out and slid across home plate. I guess Ralph Kiner thought Joe Gordon would never do that, but he did."[135]

But fans were less interested in what the Seals were doing than in events unfolding on the other side of the country. Rumors began to swirl that the New York Giants were coming to San Francisco. Those rumors gained credibility in May when a delegation from the Bay Area traveled to New York to meet with Walter O'Malley and Horace Stoneham, presidents of the Brooklyn Dodgers and New York Giants, respectively. Reports filtered back that the Giants were "sure" to move to San Francisco in 1958, playing in Seals Stadium for a year before moving into a 70,000-seat stadium at Hunter's Point. The story went that the Dodgers would come to Los Angeles and play in the Coliseum.[136]

Seattle owner Emil Sick reacted by saying he did not want to operate a franchise in what he called "a patchwork league," which he argued would result from the loss of San Francisco and Los Angeles. Sick said it was possible that the Rainiers might not play after the 1957 season and added, "I don't like the idea of being at the mercy of Walter O'Malley's whims."[137] Portland general manager Joe Zeigler countered by claiming he envisioned a Pacific Coast League that could be stronger in 1958, even without its two largest markets.[138]

The league called an emergency meeting on June 2. Instead of deciding to fight the major leagues, the owners asked that they receive help in locating replacement cities for San Francisco and Los Angeles. Although the owners did not discuss a figure for indemnification, they asked for a percentage of broadcast revenue from the Dodgers and Giants. Leslie O'Connor said, "We think part of that money belongs to us."[139]

A formal announcement of the Giants' intentions came on August 19, with an eight-to-one vote by the Giants' board of directors in favor of moving the team to California. The agreement included the city of San Francisco receiving the receipts from the parking concession at the new stadium, and there was talk that pay–TV was part of the deal. A forty-five-thousand-seat stadium, to be called Bay View Stadium, was to be built at a cost of ten to twelve million dollars, financed in part by the five-million-dollar bond passed by San Francisco voters in 1954. While it was being constructed, the Giants would lease Seals Stadium from Paul Fagan.

Emil Sick complained that no one had yet talked to the Coast League owners about damages to their investment caused by the move. He moaned, "There will be no Coast League left."[140]

* * *

The long, intense rivalry between Los Angeles and Hollywood was about to come to an end. All that remained was to stage one last brawl for old time's sake. The teams met at Gilmore Field on August 24 with Tommy Lasorda on the mound for the Angels. After surrendering a long home run to Hollywood relief pitcher Fred Waters, an incensed Lasorda threw high and tight to the next batter, Spook Jacobs, who bunted the next pitch down the first-base line. An angry Lasorda ran toward the first-base line. Making no effort to field the ball, he threw a block at Jacobs that would have made an offensive tackle proud, sending the Stars base runner sprawling in the dirt.

Jacobs, never one to back down from anybody, charged at Lasorda and the benches emptied. Jacobs then began swinging wildly at anything that moved, spending most of his time battling Los Angeles second baseman Sparky Anderson. Anderson's teammate, shortstop Bobby Dolan, swung at Jacobs and the two of them started another fight. Still another round of fisticuffs was staged near first base by rival catchers Earl Battey and Pete Naton. During the melee, fans were treated to the unusual sight of Gale Wade and Carlos Bernier acting as peacemakers. Steve Bilko was left alone.[141] Order was finally restored and no one was ejected. It was the final Angels-Stars brawl.

Two days later, the Angels and Stars played against each other for the last time. The teams split the traditional Sunday doubleheader, with Hollywood taking the opener behind

Bennie Daniels and Los Angeles winning the nightcap thanks to Steve Bilko, who had recovered from his early-season maladies and hit two home runs, running his total to forty-nine on the season. The PCL's most celebrated rivalry ended when Carlos Bernier hit into a game-ending double play.[142] The day after the final Angels-Stars game, Bilko hit a home run in Vancouver off Erv Palica to become the first man in Pacific Coast League history to hit fifty home runs in consecutive seasons.[143]

September 1957 was marked by a series of good-byes. On the fifth, the Stars played their last game at Gilmore Field, which was slated to become a parking lot for CBS Studios. Hugh Pepper, an ex–Pittsburgh Pirates pitcher who had won only four of eleven decisions for the Stars, was given the honor of pitching Hollywood's final home game, versus San Francisco.

Ab England, president of the Hollywood Chamber of Commerce, led Stars fans in a standing ovation for team president Bob Cobb, and Paul Pettit hit what would be the last home run at Gilmore Field. Meanwhile, by the sixth inning Pepper had collected his third hit in three at-bats — three more than the Seals had as a team.

Pepper held a 6–0 lead in the ninth inning and still had not allowed a hit. After retiring the first two batters, the only man standing between Hugh Pepper and immortality was Ed Sadowski; no one could say the Gilmore Field finale lacked drama. Stars fans stood in unison hoping to witness history but their festive mood was quickly deflated; Sadowski lined the first pitch past second baseman Spook Jacobs for a single. Pepper retired the next batter and Hollywood's tenure at Gilmore Field ended. Stars fans predictably rained boos on Sadowski but Pepper was philosophical, saying the pitch Sadowski hit was a fastball down the middle "with good stuff on it."[144]

Another good-bye was said at Lane Field, which the Padres were finally escaping after more than two decades for a new home in Mission Valley. They lost both games of a doubleheader against San Francisco on September 8.[145]

A week later, on the eve of the Los Angeles City Council vote on a resolution to approve negotiations with the Brooklyn Dodgers to move to Los Angeles, the Angels were swept in a doubleheader against San Diego. Both games were delayed by bomb threats called in to the Wrigley Field switchboard.[146] Steve Bilko, who was named the league's Most Valuable Player for the third straight year, finished the 1957 season with fifty-six home runs, capping a three-year run during which he had hit one hundred and forty-eight home runs in less than five hundred games, creating an unparalleled statistical history.[147] With that, the Angels became a memory; fifty-seven seasons after Jim Morley had founded them, they were to be supplanted by a major league team.

That same day it was San Francisco's turn to say good-bye, although Seals Stadium was to continue in use for two more years as a host to major league baseball. The Seals had already clinched the 1957 pennant, having won 101 games. Relievers Leo Kiely and Bob Abernathie won thirty-four games between them — making only ten starts while appearing in a combined 104 games. Kiely led the PCL in wins with an incredible twenty-one victories, while Abernathie finished with a record of 13–2. Ken Aspromonte won the batting title while Frank Kellert and Bill Renna both drove in more than one hundred runs. Other players who would go on to significant major league careers included outfielders Marty Keough and Albie Pearson.

More than fifteen thousand fans came to see their Seals for the last time. The first game of the doubleheader against Sacramento was played straight up and the Solons won on Len Neal's home run with two out in the ninth. The Seals' final game after fifty-five years as a franchise in the PCL — the team's sixtieth season if one traces the team back to the 1898 rebirth of the California League — was a joke contest enjoyed by all who were there. Seals manager Joe Gordon started the nightcap at second base even though he had not appeared in a game in five years and was not on the active roster. He shuttled in and out of the lineup and even pitched at one point. When umpire Chris Pelekoudas called a ball on one of his pitches, Gordon rushed to the plate to argue and then donned the umpire's chest protector, switching places with Pelekoudas, who threw a pitch.

The Solons sat down on the field when Gordon came to bat and fans vaulted onto the field for his autograph. No one was turned away. Gordon poked a couple of hits but the Solons won the game, clinching seventh place for Sacramento. Tommy Heath announced, "I'm the happiest man in the world to finish so high."

The ball that was used to record the final out was gathered up and shipped to Cooperstown for posterity. Pacific Coast League baseball in San Francisco was over.[148]

CHAPTER NINETEEN

Endings and Beginnings

The day after the 1957 Pacific Coast League season came to an end, the Los Angeles City Council approved a resolution authorizing final negotiations to bring the Brooklyn Dodgers to Los Angeles. Although Walter O'Malley had purchased Wrigley Field several months earlier, he made it clear he did not plan to have the Dodgers play there. Instead, he proposed that the city sell him property in Chavez Ravine, near Griffith Park in the north of the city, where he would build his own stadium without use of public funds.[1]

At almost the same time, the newly minted San Francisco Giants confirmed they would play the 1958 season in Seals Stadium. San Francisco mayor George Christopher negotiated a deal with Paul Fagan allowing the Giants to lease the stadium for $125,000 a year.[2] Giants star outfielder Willie Mays had a much more difficult time trying to purchase a house in the Bay Area. After submitting an offer on a home in the exclusive St. Francis Wood community, he was told that a restrictive covenant forbade the sale of the home to an African American. Mayor Christopher was outraged and invited Mays to stay at his home until things could be worked out. Public outcry led to Mays being allowed to purchase the home, but it was a reminder that discrimination and bigotry were not confined to the Deep South.[3]

In December 1957 the Pacific Coast League agreed to a $900,000 settlement that cleared the final hurdle for the Dodgers and Giants to take Los Angeles and San Francisco as their territory. The settlement money was divided equally among the six remaining teams, to be paid over three years.[4] The PCL dissolved the Angels and Seals franchises, replacing them with teams in Spokane and Phoenix, which became farm teams for the transplanted major league franchises.[5] Bob Cobb announced he was selling the Hollywood Stars and that they would move to Salt Lake City.[6] Sixty-year-old Lefty O'Doul, after twenty-nine seasons of wearing PCL uniforms, announced he was retiring from baseball.[7] Clearly, the Pacific Coast League as it had existed for nearly six decades was no more.

Meanwhile, Walter O'Malley was facing obstacles in his effort to build a permanent home for the Dodgers at Chavez Ravine. Vociferous opposition to the plan led to fears that O'Malley might reverse course and remain in Brooklyn.[8] Even Bob Cobb decried the way the Dodgers were being treated, likening the situation to inviting a relative to live in your home and then saying, "Sorry, you stay in the parlor. I'm not sure I even have a room for you. What's more, you've got to pay the mortgage on the house!"[9]

O'Malley denied having any second thoughts and investigated the possibility of using the Coliseum, which could handle large crowds but was difficult to layout for baseball. However, after the Coliseum Commission failed on a 4–4 vote to invite the Dodgers there, O'Malley began eyeing the Rose Bowl.[10] An expansion of Wrigley Field was also considered;

Ford Frick thought it was a terrible idea and further insulted Los Angeles baseball fans by calling their revered ballpark "a cow pasture."[11]

The Dodgers eventually rejected the idea of converting the Rose Bowl and with time running out, announced in mid–January that they planned to play at Wrigley Field. The Dodgers preferred destination remained the Coliseum, but the Coliseum Commission was reluctant to provide the facility, even on a temporary basis. Mayor Ken Poulson chastised Los Angeles County Supervisor Burton Chace, serving as president of the commission, sending him a letter that read in part, "we are the laughingstock of the country for the way the Los Angeles Dodgers are being kicked around."[12] Four days later, the Dodgers reached agreement to rent the Coliseum for two years while O'Malley pursued his own stadium.[13] Wrigley Field went dark and all was finally in place.

* * *

Old Doc Strub, the former San Francisco Seals owner and builder of Santa Anita, was the subject of a major profile in the *Los Angeles Times* on March 16, 1958. Strub had spearheaded a number of projects during his life and his influence was felt from coast to coast. A director of New York's Metropolitan Opera, he invited the company to perform in Los Angeles and saw the community as a natural for first-run Broadway-style events. At age seventy-three, Strub was brimming with ideas and had recently seen his latest come to fruition — Pacific Ocean Park, a ten-million-dollar amusement park at Santa Monica Beach that was intended to compete with three-year-old Disneyland.[14]

"It's time that Los Angeles became the great city it can be," said Strub. He then wistfully added that completion of the effort to do so would probably fall to a younger man.[15] A few days later, Strub suffered a stroke and his condition quickly deteriorated.[16] He died on March 28, less than two weeks after the article appeared.[17]

* * *

The first regular season major league game on the West Coast was played at Seals Stadium in San Francisco on April 15, 1958. More than twenty-three thousand fans sat in "whispering winds and under nursery blue skies" as Dodgers center fielder Gino Cimoli stepped to the plate to face Giants pitcher Ruben Gomez. Cimoli struck out.

San Francisco's Jim Davenport drove in the first run with a bases-loaded sacrifice fly. Shortstop Daryl Spencer and rookie Orlando Cepeda, son of famed Puerto Rican star Pedro Cepeda, homered for the Giants. Gomez shut out the Dodgers on six hits as the Giants won, 8–0. One of baseball's oldest rivalries was officially transplanted to the opposite site of the continent.[18]

Three days later, the teams traveled to Los Angeles to play a series there. The Giants and Dodgers paraded through downtown, tossing toy baseballs to the crowd. When fans arrived at the ballpark they were treated to a startling sight — Duke Snider, Pee Wee Reese, Gil Hodges and Carl Furillo, the "Boys of Summer," cavorting in the familiar Dodger uniform but wearing caps that said "LA." It was enough to take a fan's breath away.

It was significant that the Dodgers were playing at the Coliseum, the stadium that had symbolized the city's coming of age on the world stage during the 1932 Olympic Games. Now Los Angeles was a major league baseball city. The Coliseum could hold more than 90,000 and everyone predicted that attendance records would fall, although looking at the layout of the field made it patently obvious why the stadium was never previously used for baseball. In an attempt to prevent cheap 250-foot home runs, a screen was installed above the left-field fence, reminiscent of the one at old Recreation Park. The players complained about the background for both hitting and tracking fly balls, but there was no complaint

Willie Mays stands outside Seals Stadium shortly after it was announced the New York Giants were moving to California (San Francisco History Center, San Francisco Public Library).

from fans. A record National League crowd of 78,672 gathered, including a raft of celebrities that would have made the Hollywood Stars proud in their heyday. Jimmy Stewart, Burt Lancaster, Jack Lemmon, Edward G. Robinson, Alfred Hitchcock, Gene Autry and Groucho Marx were just a few of the luminaries sighted in the stands. Danny Kaye was there, insisting that since he was from Brooklyn he was a *true* Dodgers fan. The Dodgers won their first home game and drew 167,209 for the three-game series against San Francisco, only fifty thousand fewer than the Angels had drawn for all of 1957. The opener set records for largest National League crowd, largest major league Opening Day crowd, largest major league crowd for a single game (non-doubleheader) in the regular season, and largest Opening Day crowd in Dodger history — more than double the previous record.[19]

A year later, Southern California witnessed its first World Series, as the Los Angeles Dodgers hosted the Chicago White Sox. Not only that, the Dodgers won the world championship. Instead of Bilko, Statz, Demaree and Novikoff, the local heroes of the franchise were named Koufax, Hodges, Snider and Drysdale. One had to wonder what Jim Morley would have thought had he been alive to see it. Fifty-four years after the Brooklyn Dodgers had stolen Cap Dillon from Los Angeles, the city of Los Angeles had stolen the Dodgers from Brooklyn.

Seals Stadium hosted Willie Mays and the San Francisco Giants for two seasons. Orlando Cepeda and Willie McCovey made their major league debuts during that period, each winning the Rookie of the Year Award in the National League. The former New York Giants drew nearly 1.3 million in their first year in San Francisco, twice what the Seals had drawn during their record-setting 1946 season and one million more than the PCL team had drawn in 1957. The Giants increased their attendance in 1959 by another 150,000 as they prepared to move to their new home on Candlestick Point.

The final game at the "Queen in Concrete" featured the Giants against the Dodgers on September 20, 1959. Duke Snider hit the last home run at the ballpark as Los Angeles won the game, 8–2, and Seals Stadium passed into history.[20]

* * *

Of course, the Pacific Coast League did not close shop in 1958. As previously mentioned, the Hollywood Stars went to Salt Lake City while Spokane and Phoenix replaced Los Angeles and San Francisco. The Padres remained in San Diego and christened their long-awaited new stadium in Mission Valley, which they named Westgate Park.[21] The day before the ballpark opened, the San Diego Chamber of Commerce sponsored a box lunch and nearly 1,200 showed up to look over the new facility.[22] The Padres opened the next day against Phoenix, the Giants farm club, with a day-night doubleheader that drew a total of more than eleven thousand fans. Despite major traffic snarls, the evening was considered a great success; termite-infested Lane Field was finally gone, replaced by a new, modern ballpark. Actor William Powell threw the first pitch to PCL president Leslie O'Connor and the Padres swept the doubleheader.[23]

Seattle, Portland and Sacramento remained where they were. The league's schedule was reduced to 154 games, but there were reminders of the league's glory days. George Bamberger set a PCL record with sixty-eight and two-thirds consecutive innings without surrendering a base on balls, besting the mark of sixty-four straight innings established by Julio Bonetti in 1939. Dick Stuart finally showed signs of fulfilling his promise, slugging thirty-one home runs in eighty games for Salt Lake City, evoking reminders of the days of Bill Lane's Bees. Future major league stars playing the PCL in 1958 included Maury Wills, Willie McCovey, Vada Pinson and Felipe Alou. There were also numerous faces familiar to long-time fans of the Pacific Coast League, including Larry Jansen, Elmer Singleton, Carlos Bernier, Bill Werle, Eddie Kazak, Eddie Basinski, Ray Orteig, Tom Saffell and Spider Jorgenson, among others. The league's Most Valuable Player in 1958 was Earl Averill, son of the Hall of Famer who had starred for the San Francisco Seals in the 1920s.

But the Pacific Coast League inevitably began to change. The Sacramento franchise shifted to Hawaii in 1961. The league expanded to ten teams in 1963 and then to twelve in 1964 when the American Association suspended operations. At that point, the PCL began encompassing foreign venues with strange names, such as Little Rock and Tulsa, cities one would never equate with the Pacific Coast.

A second major league team began playing in Los Angeles in 1961 when the American League, not wanting to be left off the West Coast gravy train, expanded to ten teams by adding franchises in Los Angeles and Washington, D.C. — the original Senators having moved to Minneapolis. Paying homage to the baseball roots of the region, the new Los Angeles team was called the Angels and played its first season at Wrigley Field. Roger Maris hit his fiftieth home run at Wrigley on his way to a major league record sixty-one home runs in 1961.[24] But Wrigley Field proved inadequate and the Angels moved in with the Dodgers at their new home at Chavez Ravine in 1962.

Wrigley Field hosted *Home Run Derby* in the early 1960s, a television program that involved major league hitters competing in a series of contests won by the player hitting the most home runs on a given number of pitches; it is now an annual event at the major league All-Star Game. But *Derby* proved only a temporary respite for the picturesque ballpark. Wrigley Field was torn down in 1969; today, Gilbert Lindsay Park sits on the site.[25]

Edmonds Field was demolished in 1964; its final event was an exhibition game between the Cleveland Indians and the San Francisco Giants. The ballpark made way for a shopping center, now anchored by a Target store. Gilmore Field made way for studios for CBS Television. Seals Stadium was torn down after the 1959 season; like Edmonds Field, it is occupied by a shopping center. Animated film giant Pixar Studios is located where Oaks Park once stood.

Sick's Stadium served as home of the ill-fated Seattle Pilots for their only season in the American League in 1969, before the expansion team was moved to Milwaukee by Bud Selig after being immortalized by Jim Bouton in his book, *Ball Four*. The ballpark was demolished in 1979, two years after the Seattle Mariners came into existence. The Mariners never played at Sick's, instead moving into a domed stadium, the Kingdome, that has also since been razed. A Lowe's store sits on the former Sick's site.

Vaughn Street Park was replaced by several industrial buildings. Nearby, a neighborhood of beautiful older homes occupies a rejuvenated area of Portland. Vaughn Street Park's successor, Multnomah Stadium, was renamed PGE Park. In 1969, it became the first outdoor baseball stadium in the country to install artificial turf. In 2011, PGE Park was converted to full-time use for major league soccer, and the latest incarnation of the Beavers moved to Tucson, Arizona, while awaiting a new stadium in Escondido, California.

San Diego's Lane Field is a parking lot, although there have been proposals to convert the property into an upscale residential development on the waterfront. The Santa Fe railway station, a frequent target of Luke Easter's mammoth home runs, is still there.

When Phoenix was replaced by Tacoma in 1960, Seals Stadium was in the midst of being demolished. Tacoma's new ballpark, Cheney Stadium, was the recipient of some of the seats and light standards. Fifty years later, they remained in use.

One by one, many of the old PCL cities joined the major leagues. Oakland welcomed back baseball after a twelve-season hiatus, adopting Connie Mack's Philadelphia Athletics by way of Kansas City in 1968. Joe DiMaggio returned to the Bay Area, wearing the Athletics green and gold as a coach for a time and serving as a team vice president for two years.

Seattle, as noted earlier, landed two expansion franchises, in 1969 and then again in 1977, when the Mariners were born.

San Diego retained the Padres designation when the city was brought into the National League in 1969, and the team played in a brand-new stadium further east from Westgate Park, in Mission Valley.[26] The ballpark, now called Qualcomm Stadium, also served as home to the Padres in their final PCL season in 1968.

Many of the old PCL beat reporters shifted seamlessly to coverage of the major leagues, but they soon realized it was not the same. Bill Conlin ran into Bob Stevens of the *San Francisco Chronicle* one day and asked him, "How's it going?" Stevens replied, "It was more fun in the Coast League. There, you used to have twenty-four good guys on a club and one asshole. Now, you have twenty-four assholes and one good guy."[27]

Although the Pacific Coast League underwent significant changes after 1957, veterans continued extending their careers in the PCL into the 1960s. Bob Lemon pitched for San Diego in 1958 and Satchel Paige did the same for Portland in 1962. Dick Stuart, Leon Wagner, Luis Tiant, Diego Segui, Jim Rivera and others appeared during the decade. But the days of the long-time minor league veteran or the major leaguer extending his career a few years by coming to the PCL were essentially over by the mid–1960s. The draft still existed, and remains in place today — it is called the Rule V draft — but it became less important with the advent of the amateur draft in 1965, which completely cut off the minor leagues from discovering and developing their own talent. The basic structure of the minor-major league relationship was forever altered and never again would a minor league like the PCL challenge the majors. Instead, the minor leagues became irreversibly dependent on the major leagues for survival.

* * *

In September 1962, Dodger Stadium hosted an old-timers game between former members of the Hollywood Stars and Los Angeles Angels. Lou Novikoff and Babe Herman were both there. So were Billy Schuster, Max West, Chuck Connors, Johnny Lindell, Red Lynn, Johnny Bassler and Jigger Statz. Chuck Stevens showed up, wearing the old shorts of the Hollywood Stars. Pants Rowland, Howard Lorenz and Fred Haney were on hand and Jack Powell, the old umpire, called balls and strikes as he always had, without an indicator. The Stars won, 11–3, and the only surprise was that no fights broke out. Powell did not even have to eject anyone from the grounds.[28]

But the ranks of the old-timers and the memory of what the Pacific Coast League had been were fading quickly and in equal measure. Paul Fagan spent most of his time in Hawaii after leaving the PCL, tending to his ranch and hotel on Maui. He suffered a fatal heart attack in his sleep a few days before Christmas 1960 during a visit to his mansion in Hillsborough, California.[29] Born the year of King Kalakaua's visit to San Francisco, like the King he died while on a trip to the Bay Area from his home in Hawaii. Fagan's funeral was held seventy years to the day following the King's appearance at the benefit baseball game held at Haight Street Grounds. A memorial cross sits on the famous Hana Highway on Maui and Fagan's brand, featuring the five point Hana Star, is still found on cattle grazing in the hills above the luxury hotel he used to own.

Ping Bodie moved to Hollywood after his playing days ended and worked as an electrician at movie studios for more than thirty years. He entertained everyone with his baseball stories and became fast friends with actor Charles Boyer. Bodie died from lung cancer in 1961.[30]

Johnny Ritchey, the Jackie Robinson of the Pacific Coast League, never reached the major leagues after his lonely season as the only African American in the PCL in 1948, but he did play seven solid seasons in the league, hitting .282. After closing out his career with a short stint in the Eastern League in 1956, Ritchey worked for the Continental Baking Company. He died in 2003, a few days after celebrating his eightieth birthday. A bronze bust of Ritchey was unveiled in 2005 at Petco Park, home of the current San Diego Padres, to honor his accomplishment.

Artie Wilson continued playing baseball until 1962, when he hung up his spikes for the last time after appearing in twenty-five games for the Portland Beavers. He topped two hundred hits five times in the Pacific Coast League and, although he never made it back to the major leagues, could derive satisfaction from the fact that Willie Mays often gave Wilson credit for his success. He continued mentoring young people and worked as a star salesman at a Portland car dealership well into his eighties. Artie Wilson died in 2010, three days after his ninetieth birthday, following his beloved Giants as they chased their first World Series title since 1954.[31]

W.C. Tuttle died in 1969, three weeks after Pants Rowland succumbed at age ninety-one in Chicago.[32] Claire Goodwin returned to Oakland after his one season as league president and died there on February 12, 1972.[33] Bob Cobb passed away in 1970, two weeks before he was to receive the Civic Award from the Baseball Writer's Association.[34] Phil Wrigley remained a favorite of Chicago fans despite his inability to deliver a World Series title in nearly a half-century as head of the Cubs prior to his death in 1977.[35] A staunch traditionalist, he never installed lights at Chicago's Wrigley Field.

Another long-time PCL figure, Jimmie Reese, served once more as interim manager of the San Diego Padres, in 1960, and then coached in the PCL for a number of years. Named conditioning coach of the American League Angels in the early 1970s, he reintroduced his legendary expertise in the art of fungo hitting to a new generation of ballplayers. Harry Elliott always remembered Reese taking a bat cut in half long-ways and using it to hit a baseball to a batter as if he were pitching to him.[36] Reese became very close to Nolan Ryan, who named his son after the old infielder. Jimmie Reese remained connected to the Angels until his death in 1994, seventy-seven years after Frank Chance hired him as batboy of the original Angels.

Joe Brovia severely injured his back in the 1970s and was laid up for several months; at one point he was told he would never walk again. Thanks to his wife, Brovia worked to regain his strength and fully recovered. He began answering fan mail, again at the urging of his wife, who insisted that he put aside his bitterness about his career. Brovia discovered he had not been forgotten by the legion of fans that had grown up watching him play. Inducted into the Pacific Coast League Hall of Fame, he was a member of a panel assembled at the Oakland Museum for a special exhibit and reunion of PCL players in 1994. Brovia died a few months later of cancer in Santa Cruz, California, at the age of seventy-two.

Steve Bilko returned to Los Angeles in 1958 after the Dodgers acquired him from Cincinnati at the trade deadline in exchange for Don Newcombe.[37] Bilko hit only .208 for Los Angeles and spent the 1959 season back in the PCL, playing for the Dodgers farm team in Spokane. That winter, he was drafted by Detroit and won the first base job but was benched when he went into a horrific slump.[38] Bilko was selected by the American League Los Angeles Angels in the 1961 expansion draft, making him the first to play for both Los Angeles major league teams while returning him to Wrigley Field, the scene of his greatest triumphs.[39]

The Angels won seventy games and finished eighth in their expansion season, with Bilko hitting twenty home runs and batting a respectable .279. But the Angels finished last in the American League in attendance and Wrigley Field was abandoned in favor of sharing the new stadium at Chavez Ravine with the Dodgers.

Fittingly, Bilko hit the last home run at Wrigley Field, a pinch-hit blast in the ninth inning off Cleveland pitcher Jim "Mudcat" Grant on the final day of the 1961 season.[40] He remained with Los Angeles in 1962, when the Angels surprised everyone by finishing third and doubling their attendance of the year before. But after hitting eight home runs in a limited role, Bilko came down with an infection in his leg in August and missed the rest of the season.[41] The Angels sent Bilko to the minors after the season, assigning him to Dallas–Fort Worth.[42] He asked to be traded and was accommodated with a transfer to Rochester in the International League, where he shared first base with Luke Easter.[43] Bilko retired following the 1963 season with more than three hundred minor league home runs, plus another seventy-six in the majors. He moved back to Wilkes-Barre, Pennsylvania, where he worked for a perfume company. He died in 1978.[44]

Former Angels slugger Lou Novikoff fell on hard times, having to retire from his job as a longshoreman because of emphysema. Friends held a benefit for him in 1966, which failed to bring him cheer. "It makes me feel ashamed," said Novikoff. "I am a man and this is what I have come to. All I have left now is my pride." Novikoff died in 1970.[45]

Jigger Statz scouted for the Chicago Cubs and briefly managed Visalia in the California League in the late 1940s. Always the golfer, Statz was occasionally lured to old-timers games, including one in 1969 in which he declared himself entirely satisfied to manage the team and stay off the playing field. Statz lived to the age of ninety and at his death in 1988 was remembered as the greatest Los Angeles Angel of all time.[46]

The league's all-time winning pitcher, Frank Shellenback, was a pitching coach for the St. Louis Browns, Detroit Tigers, Boston Red Sox and New York Giants after his career in the PCL. He was a key confidante of Leo Durocher when both were with the Giants and was known for his ability to steal signs from his spot in the first-base coach's box. Forever remembered as Ted Williams' first manager, Shellenback lived just long enough to see Williams manage his nephew, Jim Shellenback, a pitcher for the Washington Senators in 1969.[47]

After managing the Milwaukee Braves to two National League pennants and a World Series title in 1957, Fred Haney was selected by Gene Autry to be the first general manager of the expansion Los Angeles Angels. Haney remained in that post through the 1968 season and oversaw the team's move to Anaheim. In his later years, he was a consultant to the franchise. Haney had a reputation for spotting young talent, although he found the younger generation frustrating at times, as demonstrated by his public battles with Dean Chance and Bo Belinsky. Haney died of a heart attack at his home in Beverly Hills in November 1977. Former Angels manager Bill Rigney remarked, "If it weren't for Fred Haney, there'd be no Angels."[48]

Branch Rickey left the Pittsburgh Pirates and attempted to help create a third major league. Called the Continental League, it never got off the ground but did lead to expansion of the major leagues from sixteen to twenty teams in the early 1960s.[49] Rickey served as a consultant to the St. Louis Cardinals for two years and then, with his health failing, retired. He collapsed at a banquet held in November 1965 to mark his induction to the Missouri Hall of Fame and died three weeks later.[50] Forty years after Rickey's death, his grandson was serving as president of the Pacific Coast League.

Carlos Bernier remained in the Pacific Coast League, still lighting up cigars with his mother. He moved to Salt Lake City with what was left of the Hollywood Stars in 1958 and also played in Hawaii from 1961 through 1964, winning the PCL batting title with the Islanders in 1961 with a .351 average. Bernier completed his career with Reynosa in the Mexican League in 1965. In 2,287 minor league games, Bernier collected 2,374 hits, including 312 doubles, 129 triples and 212 home runs. He also stole 594 bases and had a .297 lifetime batting average. Bernier continued to play winter ball in Puerto Rico for many years, but post-baseball life was hard for "the Comet." In 1989, Bernier committed suicide by hanging himself in a garage.

After his half-season with San Diego in 1954, Luke Easter left the PCL and played nine years in the International League. He and Steve Bilko were teammates at Rochester in 1963; Easter hit six home runs in 188 at-bats while Bilko closed out his career with eight home runs in 261 at-bats. Easter served as a player-coach for the Red Wings the next year, collecting two hits in ten pinch-hit appearances at age forty-nine.

In March 1979, Easter was delivering a payroll to a bank located in a Cleveland, Ohio, suburb when he was approached by two men in the parking lot. The men demanded he turn over the money. Easter refused and was fatally shot in the chest with a sawed-off shotgun and a .38 caliber revolver.[51]

Emil Sick sold the Seattle Rainiers to the Boston Red Sox in September 1960 but remained active in Seattle civic affairs.[52] He served as a director of the Seattle World's Fair in 1962 — the remnants of which include Seattle Center and the Space Needle, along with the monorail that connects Seattle Center with downtown Seattle. He led a fundraising drive that led to the construction of Seattle's Museum of History and Industry. Sick lived in his ten-thousand-square-foot mansion on the shore of Lake Washington until his death in November 1964.[53]

Brick Laws died in 1971. He insisted that the 1950 Oaks were one of the greatest minor league teams in history. After leaving baseball, he partnered with Joe Blumenthal in a golf course. Summing up his days running the Oaks, Laws said, "I gave them big league names and home run hitters in a friendly little park and everybody had a ball."[54]

The man most identified with the old Pacific Coast League, Lefty O'Doul, resumed his life of celebrity in his hometown of San Francisco after resigning as manager of Seattle at the close of the 1957 season. O'Doul dedicated much of his time to his bar and restaurant, which still exists today near the famous St. Francis Hotel. O'Doul remained a hero in Japan

Lefty O'Doul's burial site at Cypress Lawn Cemetery in Colma, California, just outside San Francisco. "He was here at a good time and had a good time while he was here" (author's photograph).

and died of a heart attack in 1969, ironically on the anniversary of Pearl Harbor.[55] His headstone bears the inscription "The Man in the Green Suit ... He Was Here at a Good Time and Had a Good Time While He Was Here." There are continuing efforts to have O'Doul inducted into the Baseball Hall of Fame, as there should be.

* * *

Could the Pacific Coast League have ever survived as a third major league? The draft always made that problematical. Jim Morley was right when he argued in 1904 that the draft cost teams the ability to control their destiny and their best players. Morley never forgot that losing Cap Dillon, Doc Newton and Hal Chase for far below market value kept him from putting a great team on the field.

Not long after Morley's victimization at the hands of the major leagues, the McCredies decided to exploit the system rather than fight it and became extremely successful. But they were only able to keep their players for a year or two.

By the 1920s, when the PCL was arguably at its peak in terms of talent, teams continued selling off their best players because their value to the franchise was greater in monetary terms than as athletes. The Vernon Tigers tried to buck the trend by keeping Jakie May after his brilliant 1923 season, but his value plummeted when he had a bad season and the Tigers began a decline that led to their leaving Los Angeles.

Perhaps the Pacific Coast League could have succeeded as a third major league had it been willing to cross the color line in the 1920s, before the major leagues were ready. Rube Foster had successfully fielded African American winter league teams in California as early as 1913. If the PCL had done this along with keeping the impressive array of talent signed during that decade rather than selling it, they might have made it where others had failed. However, the league's wealthiest owners, William Wrigley at Los Angeles and John Shibe at Portland, were directly tied to the major leagues — a fact that cannot be ignored.

The quality of baseball was excellent, a notch above the other high minor leagues by all accounts largely because of the number of veteran ballplayers and an emphasis on winning rather than developing young players. But the right kind of owner was in short supply and those involved were too frequently at odds with one another. Other than perhaps Emil Sick and Paul Fagan, the other more independent owners were always far too undercapitalized to survive without selling their best talent. And there was never any real agreement on a strategy or even a consensus among owners to pursue major league status. Some thought it a necessity; others thought it either foolish or futile. Some thought they would make more money as an ivory hunter of sorts, simply finding and selling players to the major leagues. The major leagues did not have to divide and conquer; the PCL owners handled that chore for them. Had television taken another decade to develop as a medium, the Pacific Coast League might have built on the momentum of the late 1940s. But even as they set attendance records, PCL teams were selling off their best players.

It is worth noting that the Pacific Coast League was remarkably stable. Oakland, San Francisco, Portland and Los Angeles were all represented in the league for more than a half-century, and Seattle and Sacramento in excess of four decades. But the league did not have enough large cities to ultimately survive as a third major league. The fact that it was a regional league also worked against it. The PCL would have had to stretch to Colorado and Texas and beyond, invading other minor leagues, for that to have happened. More likely would have been the absorption by the majors of two to four teams through expansion, or as in the case of the Federal League, the taking over of a couple of weaker franchises, except moving them to the West Coast instead of keeping them where they were.

Although major league status never materialized, the Pacific Coast League does carry the distinction of being the only outlaw circuit other than the American League to directly challenge the majors and survive.

In reality the old Pacific Coast League has been absorbed by the major leagues in the past half-century. There are two teams in the San Francisco Bay Area, two in Los Angeles, one in San Diego and another in Seattle. Only Portland, Sacramento and Salt Lake City have been left out. The Pacific Coast League began with Henry Harris stealing the two largest cities of another league. The major leagues repeated the same strategy to bring the old Pacific Coast League to an end.

It was an ironic way for baseball's most prominent minor league to move into its next chapter. While still a top minor league, the Pacific Coast League that resulted from the invasion of the Dodgers and Giants was very different: Left behind was a treasure trove of memories and innovations, including routine air travel, broadcasting of games, widespread use of night baseball and the recognition that baseball was entertainment as well as a competitive endeavor. The PCL also left a legacy that included the development of some the greatest athletes to ever play the game. With most of its cities represented in today's major leagues, the Pacific Coast League was more than simply another minor league. It was truly "The Greatest Minor League."

Appendix

League Champions; Highest Batting Average, Season;
Most Home Runs, Season; Most Home Runs, Career;
Most RBIs, Season; Longest Hitting Streaks;
Most Wins, Pitcher, Season; Most Wins, Pitcher, Career;
No-Hitters; Unassisted Triple Plays; Most Wins, Manager, Career;
Replaced Managers; Spring Training Sites

Following are lists that include the highest single-season batting averages, home runs, runs batted in and pitching wins in the Pacific Coast League between 1903 and 1957. Also included are career leaders in home runs and pitching wins. Career leaders in batting average are not included because there are no established criteria for minimum games played or at-bats to determine the top career performers in that category. Career leaders in runs batted in are likewise omitted because that statistic was not consistently kept during the first years of the league.

League Champions

Year	Official Champion	First Half	Second Half	Playoff
1903	Los Angeles	N/A	N/A	N/A
1904	Tacoma (1)	Tacoma	Tacoma/LA	N/A
1905	Los Angeles	Tacoma	Los Angeles	Los Angeles
1906	Portland	N/A	N/A	N/A
1907	Los Angeles	N/A	N/A	N/A
1908	Los Angeles	N/A	N/A	N/A
1909	San Francisco	N/A	N/A	N/A
1910	Portland	N/A	N/A	N/A
1911	Portland	N/A	N/A	N/A
1912	Oakland	N/A	N/A	N/A
1913	Portland	N/A	N/A	N/A
1914	Portland	N/A	N/A	N/A
1915	San Francisco	N/A	N/A	N/A
1916	Los Angeles	N/A	N/A	N/A
1917	San Francisco	N/A	N/A	N/A
1918	Los Angeles (2)	Vernon	N/A	Los Angeles
1919	Vernon	N/A	N/A	N/A
1920	Vernon	N/A	N/A	N/A
1921	Los Angeles	N/A	N/A	N/A
1922	San Francisco	N/A	N/A	N/A
1923	San Francisco	N/A	N/A	N/A
1924	Seattle	N/A	N/A	N/A
1925	San Francisco	N/A	N/A	N/A

(League Champions *continued***)**

Year	Official Champion	First Half	Second Half	Playoff
1926	Los Angeles	N/A	N/A	N/A
1927	Oakland	N/A	N/A	N/A
1928	San Francisco	San Francisco	Sacramento (3)	San Francisco
1929	Hollywood	Mission	Hollywood	Hollywood
1930	Hollywood	Los Angeles	Hollywood	Hollywood
1931	San Francisco	Hollywood	San Francisco	San Francisco
1932	Portland	N/A	N/A	N/A
1933	Los Angeles	N/A	N/A	N/A
1934	Los Angeles	Los Angeles	Los Angeles	N/A
1935	San Francisco	Los Angeles	San Francisco	San Francisco
1936	Portland	N/A	N/A	Portland
1937	San Diego (4)	N/A	N/A	San Diego
1938	Los Angeles	N/A	N/A	Sacramento
1939	Seattle	N/A	N/A	Sacramento
1940	Seattle	N/A	N/A	Seattle
1941	Seattle	N/A	N/A	Seattle
1942	Sacramento	N/A	N/A	Seattle
1943	Los Angeles	N/A	N/A	San Francisco
1944	Los Angeles	N/A	N/A	San Francisco
1945	Portland	N/A	N/A	San Francisco
1946	San Francisco	N/A	N/A	San Francisco
1947	Los Angeles (5)	N/A	N/A	Los Angeles
1948	Oakland	N/A	N/A	Oakland
1949	Hollywood	N/A	N/A	Hollywood
1950	Oakland	N/A	N/A	N/A
1951	Seattle	N/A	N/A	Seattle
1952	Hollywood	N/A	N/A	N/A
1953	Hollywood	N/A	N/A	N/A
1954	San Diego (6)	N/A	N/A	Oakland
1955	Seattle	N/A	N/A	N/A
1956	Los Angeles	N/A	N/A	N/A
1957	San Francisco	N/A	N/A	N/A

(1) Tacoma and Los Angeles met in a post-season playoff that was not recognized by the league.

(2) Shortened season, top two teams met for playoff. Vernon finished first in the regular season, lost in playoff to Los Angeles. Angels officially declared champion in 1951.

(3) Sacramento and San Francisco tied for the second-half title. Sacramento won a best-of-three playoff to determine the second-half champion.

(4) Sacramento finished first in regular season. Shaughnessy playoff winner was recognized as league champion in 1936 and 1937.

(5) Los Angeles and San Francisco finished in a tie for first place. Los Angeles won a one-game playoff for regular season championship.

(6) San Diego and Hollywood finished in a tie for first place. San Diego won a one-game playoff for regular season championship.

Highest Batting Average, Season, 1903–1957 (minimum 400 AB)

Player	Team	Year	BA
Oscar Eckhardt	Mission	1933	.414
Ike Boone	Mission	1929	.407
Smead Jolley	San Francisco	1928	.404
Duffy Lewis	Salt Lake City	1921	.403
Earl Sheely	San Francisco	1930	.403
Paul Waner	San Francisco	1925	.401
Oscar Eckhardt	Mission	1935	.399

Player	Team	Year	BA
Joe DiMaggio	San Francisco	1935	.398
Smead Jolley	San Francisco	1927	.397
Frank Brazill	Seattle	1925	.395
Paul Strand	Salt Lake City	1923	.394
Duffy Lewis	Salt Lake City	1924	.392
Lefty O'Doul	Salt Lake City	1924	.392
Bill Bagwell	Portland	1926	.391
Smead Jolley	San Francisco	1929	.387
Bill Rumler	Hollywood	1929	.386
Gene Woodling	San Francisco	1948	.385
Paul Strand	Salt Lake City	1922	.384
Liz Funk	Hollywood	1929	.384
Harry Lumley	Seattle	1903	.383
Frank Demaree	Los Angeles	1934	.383
Buzz Arlett	Oakland	1926	.382
Babe Ellison	San Francisco	1924	.381
Earl Sheely	Sacramento	1928	.381
Gus Suhr	San Francisco	1929	.381
Ike Boone	Mission	1926	.380
Wes Schulmerich	Los Angeles	1930	.380
Fuzzy Hufft	Mission	1929	.379
Lefty O'Doul	San Francisco	1927	.378
Oscar Eckhardt	Mission	1934	.378
Ted Norbert	Portland	1942	.378
Lefty O'Doul	Salt Lake City	1925	.375
Buzz Arlett	Oakland	1929	.374
Smead Jolley	Hollywood	1935	.372
Earl Sheely	Salt Lake City	1920	.371
Fuzzy Hufft	Seattle/Mission	1928	.371
Oscar Eckhardt	Mission	1932	.371
Ernie Lombardi	Oakland	1930	.370

Most Home Runs, Season, 1903–1957

Player	Team	Year	HR
Tony Lazzeri	Salt Lake City	1925	60
Gene Lillard	Los Angeles	1935	56
Steve Bilko	Los Angeles	1957	56
Ike Boone	Mission	1929	55
Steve Bilko	Los Angeles	1956	55
Gus Suhr	San Francisco	1929	51
Jack Graham	San Diego	1948	48
Max West	San Diego	1949	48
Dave Barbee	Hollywood	1931	47
Elmer Smith	Portland	1926	46
Johnny Vergez	Oakland	1929	46
Smead Jolley	San Francisco	1928	45
Frank Demaree	Los Angeles	1934	45
Paul Strand	Salt Lake City	1923	43
Gene Lillard	Los Angeles	1933	43
Max West	San Diego	1947	43
Nick Etten	Oakland	1948	43
Joe Gordon	Sacramento	1951	43
Dave Barbee	Seattle/Hollywood	1930	41
Lou Novikoff	Los Angeles	1940	41
Ray Rohwer	Portland	1925	40

(Most Home Runs, Season *continued***)**

Player	Team	Year	HR
Elmer Smith	Portland	1927	40
Wally Berger	Los Angeles	1929	40
Gus Zernial	Hollywood	1948	40
Frank Kelleher	Hollywood	1950	40

Most Home Runs, Career (up to 1957)

Player	Teams	HR
Buzz Arlett	Oakland	251
Frank Kelleher	Oakland, Seattle, Hollywood	234
Max West	Sacramento, Mission, San Diego, Los Angeles	230
Smead Jolley	San Francisco, Hollywood, Oakland	217
Ted Norbert	San Francisco, Portland, Los Angeles, Seattle	205
Ray Jacobs	Los Angeles, Portland, Hollywood, San Diego	198
Fred Muller	Seattle, Portland	196
Ray Rohwer	Seattle, Portland, Sacramento	196
Mike Hunt	San Francisco, Mission, Seattle	177
Joe Brovia	San Francisco, Portland, Sacramento, Oakland	174
Gene Lillard	Los Angeles, San Francisco, Sacramento, Oakland	174
Earl Sheely	Salt Lake City, Sacramento, SF, LA, Port, Seattle	174
Fuzzy Hufft	Seattle, Mission, Oakland	166
Earl Rapp	Seattle, Oakland, San Diego, Portland	156
Steve Bilko*	Los Angeles	148
Frank Brazill	Portland, Seattle, Los Angeles, Mission	145
Buster Adams	Sacramento, San Diego, San Francisco	143
Johnny Vergez	Oakland, Sacramento	134
Jack Graham	San Diego, San Francisco	133
Wally Hood	Salt Lake City, Seattle, Los Angeles, Hollywood	132
Walt Judnich	Oakland, San Francisco, Seattle, Portland	127
Dave Barbee	Portland, Seattle, Hollywood	126

*—also hit twenty-six home runs for Spokane in 1959.

Most Runs Batted In, Season, 1903–1957

Player	Team	Year	RBI
Tony Lazzeri	Salt Lake City	1925	222
Ike Boone	Mission	1929	218
Lefty O'Doul	Salt Lake City	1925	191
Buzz Arlett	Oakland	1929	189
Babe Ellison	San Francisco	1924	188
Smead Jolley	San Francisco	1928	188
Paul Strand	Salt Lake City	1923	187
Fuzzy Hufft	Mission	1929	187
Wally Hood	Los Angeles	1924	184
Ed Coleman	Portland	1931	183
Earl Sheely	San Francisco	1930	180
Fuzzy Hufft	Mission	1930	178
Gus Suhr	San Francisco	1929	177
Earl Averill	San Francisco	1928	173
Frank Demaree	Los Angeles	1934	173
Lou Novikoff	Los Angeles	1940	171
Les Sheehan	Salt Lake City	1925	170
Joe DiMaggio	San Francisco	1933	169
Wally Berger	Los Angeles	1929	166

Player	Team	Year	RBI
Dave Barbee	Hollywood	1931	166
Max West	San Diego	1949	166
Johnny Vergez	Oakland	1929	165
Earl Webb	Los Angeles	1929	164
Steve Bilko	Los Angeles	1956	164
Frank Brower	San Francisco	1925	163
Smead Jolley	San Francisco	1927	163
Henry Oana	Portland	1933	163
Ted Norbert	San Francisco	1938	163
Henry Oana	San Francisco	1931	161

Longest Hitting Streaks, 1903–1957

Player	Team	Year	No.
Joe DiMaggio	San Francisco	1933	61
Jack Ness	Oakland	1915	49
Jim Oglesby	Los Angeles	1933	44
Nino Bongiovanni	Portland	1934	41
Frank Shone	Portland	1945	39
George Blackerby	Portland	1933	36
Paul Strand	Salt Lake City	1922	33
Oscar Eckhardt	Missions	1932	33
Johnny Dickshot	Hollywood	1943	33
Duffy Lewis	Salt Lake City	1921	32

Most Wins, Pitcher, Season, 1903–1957

Player	Team	Year	Wins
Doc Newton	Los Angeles	1904	39
Rube Vickers	Seattle	1906	39
Doc Newton	Los Angeles	1903	35
Jakie May	Vernon	1922	35
Jay Hughes	Seattle	1903	34
Bobby Keefe	Tacoma	1904	34
Elmer Califf	Portland	1906	34
Cack Henley	San Francisco	1910	34
Jim Buchanan	Oakland	1904	33
Lefty Williams	Salt Lake City	1915	33
Warren Hall	Los Angeles	1903	32
Orval Overall	Tacoma	1904	32
Jimmy Whalen	San Francisco	1904	32
Jimmy Whalen	San Francisco	1905	32
Roy Hitt	San Francisco	1906	32
Dolly Gray	Los Angeles	1907	32
Frank Browning	San Francisco	1909	32
Vean Gregg	Portland	1910	32
Oscar Jones	Seattle	1906	31
Cack Henley	San Francisco	1909	31
Bill Tozer	Los Angeles	1909	31
Jack Lively	Oakland	1910	31
Walter Moser	Oakland	1910	31
Irv Higginbotham	Portland	1914	31
Eric Erickson	San Francisco	1917	31
Bob Joyce	San Francisco	1945	31
Bobby Keefe	Tacoma	1905	30

(Most Wins, Pitcher, Season *continued*)

Player	Team	Year	Wins
Dolly Gray	Los Angeles	1905	30
Bill Steen	Portland	1911	30
Spider Baum	San Francisco	1915	30
Allan Sothoron	Portland	1916	30
Buck Newsom	Los Angeles	1933	30
Larry Jansen	San Francisco	1946	30
Ben Henderson	Portland	1906	29
Oscar Jones	San Francisco	1907	29
Bob Groom	Portland	1908	29
Alex Carson	Portland	1909	29
Specs Harkness	Portland	1909	29
Gene Krapp	Portland	1910	29
Jack Ryan	Los Angeles	1916	29
Paul Fittery	Salt Lake City	1916	29
Buzz Arlett	Oakland	1920	29
Bert Cole	Mission	1926	29
Dutch Ruether	San Francisco	1928	29
Jimmy Whalen	San Francisco	1903	28
Sea Lion Hall	Seattle	1904	28
Oscar Graham	Oakland	1905	28
Skeeter Fanning	San Francisco	1913	28
Harry Krause	Oakland	1917	28
Doc Crandall	Los Angeles	1919	28
Wheezer Dell	Vernon	1921	28
Oliver Mitchell	San Francisco	1924	28
Sam Gibson	San Francisco	1931	28
Fay Thomas	Los Angeles	1934	28

Most Wins, Pitcher, Career (up to 1957)

Player	Teams	Record
Frank Shellenback	Vernon, Sacramento, Hollywood, San Diego	295–178
Spider Baum	Los Angeles, Sacramento, Vernon, SF, SLC	262–236
Harry Krause	Oakland, Mission, Portland	249–220
Dick Barrett	Seattle, Portland, San Diego, Hollywood	234–168
Doc Crandall	Oakland, Los Angeles, Sacramento	230–151
Tony Freitas	Sacramento, Portland	228–175
Sam Gibson	San Francisco, Portland, Oakland	227–140
Herm Pillette	Portland, Mission, Hollywood, San Diego, Sac	226–235
Cack Henley	San Francisco, Venice, Vernon	215–171
Rudy Kallio	SF, Portland, SLC, Sacramento, Seattle	208–211
Jack Salveson	LA, Oakland, Portland, Sac, Hollywood, SD	204–166
Hal Turpin	San Francisco, Seattle, Portland, Sacramento	203–158
Roy Hitt	Oakland, Los Angeles, San Francisco, Vernon	202–147
Ad Liska	Portland	198–194
Howard Craghead	Oakland, Seattle, San Diego	182–179
Fay Thomas	Sacramento, Oak, Los Angeles, Port, Hollywood	179–136
Bill Prough	Oakland, Sacramento	175–192
Walter Mails	Portland, Seattle, Sacramento, SF, Oakland	173–171
Walt Leverenz	Los Angeles, Oakland, Salt Lake City, Portland	170–151
Elmer Jacobs	Seattle, Los Angeles, San Francisco	167–101
Ed Bryan	Vernon, Mission, Seattle, Sacramento, Portland	163–166
Willie Ludolph	San Francisco, Vernon, Mission, Oakland	156–129
Paul Fittery	Salt Lake City, Los Angeles, Sacramento	155–144

Player	Teams	Record
Win Ballou	Los Angeles, San Francisco	154–131
Red Adams*	Los Angeles, San Diego, Portland, Sacramento	153–137
Ray Prim	Los Angeles	150– 97

* Adams had a record of 0–1 in 1958 for Sacramento.

No-Hitters

Player, Team (Catcher)	Opponent (Place)	Date	Score
Doc Newton, Los Angeles (Bobby Eager/Heine Spies)	Oakland (Freeman's Park — Oakland)	11/8/1903	2–0
Frank Barber, San Francisco (Tom Leahy)	Oakland (Recreation Park I — San Francisco)	7/13/1904	1–0
Sea Lion Hall, Seattle (Ralph Frary)	Oakland (Idora Park — Oakland)	4/5/1905	6–0
Jimmy Whalen, San Francisco (Parke Wilson)	Seattle (Recreation Park Grounds — Seattle)	7/16/1905	2–0 (1)
Bobby Keefe, Tacoma (Charlie Graham)	Oakland (Cycler's Park — San Jose)	11/18/1905	3–0
Sea Lion Hall, Seattle (Cliff Blankenship)	Oakland (Recreation Park Grounds — Seattle)	5/12/1906	2–0
Eli Cates, Oakland (Jack Bliss)	Fresno (Idora Park — Oakland)	9/2/1906	7–0
Fred Brown, San Francisco (Jimmy Burke)	Oakland (Idora Park — Oakland)	10/13/1906	3–0
Bob Groom, Portland (Charley Moore)	Los Angeles (Vaughn Street Park — Portland)	6/16/1907	1–0
Eli Cates, Oakland (Jack Bliss)	Portland (Freeman's Park — Oakland)	6/25/1907	2–1
Elmer Koestner, Los Angeles (Jess Orndorff)	San Francisco (Recreation Park II — San Francisco)	4/16/1909	4–0
Jimmy Wiggs, Oakland (Carl Lewis)	San Francisco (Recreation Park II — San Francisco)	5/12/1909	3–0
Frank Browning, San Francisco (Claude Berry)	Sacramento (Oak Park — Sacramento)	7/5/1909	3–0
Alex Carson, Portland (Gus Fisher)	Los Angeles (Vaughn Street Park — Portland)	7/22/1909	1–0 (2)
Frank Miller, San Francisco (Claude Berry)	Vernon (Recreation Park II — San Francisco)	8/20/1910	3–1
Vean Gregg, Portland (Tommy Murray)	Los Angeles (Vaughn Street Park — Portland)	9/2/1910	2–0
Frank Arellanes, Sacramento (Mickey La Longe)	Vernon (Buffalo Park — Sacramento)	10/16/1910	0–2 (3)
Rube Suter, San Francisco (Claude Berry)	Oakland (Recreation Park II — San Francisco)	4/25/1911	1–0
Harry Ables, Oakland (Honus Mitze)	Los Angeles (Recreation Park II — San Francisco)	6/13/1911	2–1
Ferdinand Henkle, Portland (Walt Kuhn)	Sacramento (Vaughn Street Park — Portland)	7/5/1911	1–0
Red Toner, San Francisco (Walter Schmidt)	Portland (Recreation Park II — San Francisco)	5/21/1912	2–0
Bill Malarkey, Oakland (Honus Mitze)	San Francisco (Freeman's Park — Oakland)	6/30/1912	0–0 (4)
Jack Ryan, Los Angeles (Clarence Brooks)	Portland (Washington Park — Los Angeles)	5/18/1913	6–0
Roy Hitt, Venice (Happy Hogan)	San Francisco (Washington Park — Los Angeles)	7/19/1914	2–0

(No Hitters *continued*)

Player, Team (Catcher)	Opponent (Place)	Date	Score
Johnny Lush, Portland (George Yantz)	Venice (Vaughn Street Park — Portland)	9/20/1914	0–1
Rube Evans, Portland (Gus Fisher)	Oakland (Oaks Park — Oakland)	10/16/1914	3–0
Skeeter Fanning, San Francisco (Walter Schmidt)	Portland (Oaks Park — Oakland)	10/25/1914	7–0
Bill Piercy, Vernon (Tub Spencer)	Oakland (Washington Park — Los Angeles)	7/25/1915	3–0
Bill Prough, Oakland (Frank Elliott)	San Francisco (Oaks Park — Oakland)	6/4/1916	0–1 (5)
Skeeter Fanning, San Francisco (Lou Sepulveda)	Vernon (Maier Park — Vernon)	6/23/1916	4–1
Chief Johnson, Vernon (Honus Mitze)	Portland (Washington Park — Los Angeles)	4/15/1917	6–0
Suds Sutherland, Portland (Del Baker)	San Francisco (Recreation Park II — San Francisco)	7/25/1919	11–0
Cy Falkenberg, Oakland (Rowdy Elliott)	Seattle (Dugdale Park — Seattle)	8/19/1919	6–0
Wheezer Dell, Vernon (Truck Hannah)	Oakland (Washington Park — Los Angeles)	9/21/1922	1–0
Jim Scott, San Francisco (Archie Yelle)	Oakland (Oaks Park — Oakland)	4/14/1923	5–0
George Boehler, Oakland (Addison Read)	Sacramento (Oaks Park — Oakland)	5/28/1925	0–2 (6)
Claude Davenport, Mission (Rod Whitney)	Los Angeles (Wrigley Field — Los Angeles)	5/20/1928	4–0 (1)
Jack Knight, Portland (Eddie Ainsmith)	Oakland (Oaks Park — Oakland)	7/22/1928	5–0
Herm Pillette, Mission (Fred Hofmann)	Seattle (Recreation Park II — San Francisco)	10/5/1929	4–0
Jimmy Zinn, San Francisco (Alex Gaston)	Sacramento (Moreing Field — Sacramento)	5/14/1930	8–0
Willie Ludolph, Oakland (Addison Read)	Mission (Seals Stadium — San Francisco)	6/6/1931	4–0
Malcolm Moss, Los Angeles (Gilly Campbell)	Sacramento (Moreing Field — Sacramento)	6/12/1931	5–1
Tony Freitas, Sacramento (Larry Woodall)	Oakland (Moreing Field — Sacramento)	5/5/1932	2–0
Ed Walsh, Jr., Oakland (Pat Veltman)	San Francisco (Oaks Park — Oakland)	8/15/1933	5–0
Ernie Bonham, Oakland (Bill Baker)	Seattle (Civic Stadium — Seattle)	7/4/1937	2–0 (1)
Joe Berry, Los Angeles (Bob Collins)	Oakland (Oaks Park — Oakland)	7/10/1938	4–0 (1)
Dick Ward, San Diego (Shanty Hogan/Bill Starr)	Los Angeles (Lane Field — San Diego)	8/30/1938	1–0 (7)
Hal Turpin, Seattle (Bill Beard)	San Diego (Lane Field — San Diego)	4/12/1942	2–0
Cotton Pippen, Oakland (Wil Leonard)	Sacramento (Cardinal Field — Sacramento)	5/31/1943	10–0 (1) (8)
Jorge Comellas, Los Angeles (Don Grigg)	San Francisco (Seals Stadium — San Francisco)	5/7/1944	2–0
Manny Salvo, Oakland (Sam Fenech)	Sacramento (Oaks Park — Oakland)	7/19/1944	2–0

Player, Team (Catcher)	Opponent (Place)	Date	Score
Joe Demoran, Seattle (Bob Finley)	Los Angeles (Wrigley Field — Los Angeles)	4/4/1946	3–0
Ad Liska, Portland (Billy Holm)	Hollywood (Vaughn Street Park — Portland)	4/21/1946	1–0 (1)
Red Mann, Sacramento (Bill Conroy/Lilio Marcucci)	Seattle (Edmonds Field — Sacramento)	5/31/1946	6–0
Tommy Bridges, Portland (Eldon Muratore)	San Francisco (Vaughn Street Park — Portland)	4/20/1947	2–0
Dick Barrett, Seattle (Mickey Grasso)	Sacramento (Sick's Stadium — Seattle)	5/15/1948	2–0 (1) (8)
Paul Calvert, Seattle (Bud Sheely)	Sacramento (Sick's Stadium — Seattle)	5/27/1951	4–0
Warren Hacker, Los Angeles (Bob Dant)	Seattle (Sick's Stadium — Seattle)	9/7/1951	4–0
Elmer Singleton, San Francisco (Ray Orteig)	Sacramento (Seals Stadium — San Francisco)	4/24/1952	0–1 (9)
Hal Gregg, Oakland (Len Neal)	Portland (Oaks Park — Oakland)	5/1/1952	3–0 (1)
Roger Bowman, Oakland (Ray Noble)	Hollywood (Oaks Park — Oakland)	7/3/1952	5–0
Joe Hatten, Los Angeles (Al Evans)	San Diego (Lane Field — San Diego)	6/7/1953	6–0 (1)
Red Munger, Hollywood (Eddie Malone)	Sacramento (Gilmore Field — Hollywood)	7/4/1953	1–0 (1)
Jim Atkins, Oakland (Len Neal)	San Francisco (Seals Stadium — San Francisco)	8/25/1953	2–0 (1)
Bubba Church, Los Angeles (Johnny Pramesa)	Portland (Wrigley Field — Los Angeles)	8/3/1954	3–0
Bob Alexander, Portland (Joe Rossi)	Oakland (Vaughn Street Park — Portland)	8/17/1954	3–0 (1)
Roger Bowman, Hollywood (Bobby Bragan)	Portland (Vaughn Street Park — Portland)	9/12/1954	10–0 (1) (8)
George Piktuzis, Los Angeles (Elvin Tappe)	San Francisco (Seals Stadium — San Francisco)	7/21/1955	2–1
Elmer Singleton, Seattle (Joe Ginsberg)	San Diego (Sick's Stadium — Seattle)	7/24/1955	2–0 (1)
Chris Van Cuyk, Oakland (Bob Swift)	Los Angeles (Oaks Park — Oakland)	7/26/1955	2–0 (1)

(1) Seven-inning game, (2) Ten innings, (3) Eight innings, (4) Gave up one hit in tenth inning, (5) Pitched ten hitless innings, relieved after seventeen innings with a no-decision in which his team lost 1–0 in eighteen innings, (6) Gave up hit with one out in tenth inning, (7) Gave up hit with one out in thirteenth, won game in sixteen innings, (8) Perfect game, (9) Gave up hit with two out in thirteenth inning, lost game.

Unassisted Triple Plays

Player	Pos	Team	Opponent	Date
Larry Schlafly	2B	Portland	Seattle	6/21/1905
Walter Carlisle	OF	Vernon	Los Angeles	7/19/1911
Bill Rapps	1B	Portland	Oakland	9/14/1912
Bill Rodgers	2B	Portland	Salt Lake City	7/20/1916
Heine Sand	SS	Salt Lake City	Sacramento	7/4/1921
Bill Rhiel	2B	Portland	Seattle	9/21/1930

Most Wins, Manager, Career, 1903–1957

Manager	Teams	Record
Lefty O'Doul	San Francisco, SD, Oak, Vancouver, Seattle	2,094–1,970
Walter McCredie	Portland, Salt Lake City, Seattle, Mission	1,612–1,694
Red Killefer	Los Angeles, Mission, Seattle, Hollywood	1,487–1,338
Bill Sweeney	Portland, Seattle, Los Angeles, Hollywood	1,471–1,442
Frank "Cap" Dillon	Los Angeles	1,310–1,149
Oscar Vitt	Salt Lake City, Hollywood, Oakland, Portland	1,297–1,161
Jack Lelivelt	Los Angeles, Seattle	1,104–811
Danny Long	San Francisco	853–815
Buddy Ryan	Salt Lake City, Sacramento, Portland	789–850

Replaced Managers and Their Successors

Year, Team	Manager	Remark	Record
1903 — Portland	Sam Vigneaux	Fired Sept. 21	66–81
	Fred Ely		29–27
1904 — Seattle	Parke Wilson	Resigned Sept. 25	94–73
	Russ Hall		20–33
1904 — Portland	Fred Ely	Resigned May 18	11–33
	Dan Dugdale	Resigned Oct. 17	56–78
	Ike Butler		12–25
1905 — Oakland	Pete Lohman	Fired June 26	35–40
	George Van Haltren		68–79
1906 — Fresno	Mike Fisher	Fired Oct. 31	63–116
	Charlie Doyle		1–1
1909 — Oakland	George Van Haltren	Fired May 10	14–26
	Bill Reidy		74–99
1912 — Sacramento	Patsy O'Rourke	Resigned June 24	31–42
	Deacon Van Buren		42–79
1913 — Oakland	Honus Mitze	Resigned Sept. 26	79–101
	Gus Hetling	Interim	1–5
	Art Devlin		10–14
1914 — Oakland	Art Devlin	Fired June 7	25–37
	Tyler Christian		54–96
1915 — Venice/Vernon	Happy Hogan	Died May 17	17–24
	Dick Bayless	Interim	1–2
	Doc White		84–78
1915 — Oakland	Tyler Christian	Fired June 19	37–42
	Rowdy Elliott		56–71
1916 — Salt Lake City	Cliff Blankenship	Resigned Aug. 31	69–68
	Buddy Ryan		30–28
1916 — Oakland	Rowdy Elliott	Sold to Cubs July 28	42–72
	Del Howard		30–64
1917 — San Francisco	Harry Wolverton	Fired June 17	46–30
	Red Downs		73–63
1917 — Los Angeles	Frank Chance	Resigned July 3	43–44
	Red Killefer		73–50
1918 — San Francisco	Red Downs	Fired July 1	43–45
	Charlie Graham		8–6
1919 — Seattle	Bill Clymer	Resigned Aug. 16	38–70
	Charlie Mullen		24–38
1922 — Seattle	Walter McCredie	Fired June 27	34–48
	Jack Adams		56–59
1922 — Portland	Duke Kenworthy	Suspended Apr. 18	4–7
	Tom Turner	Resigned July 17	43–59

Year, Team	*Manager*	*Remark*	*Record*
	Al Demaree	Suspended Aug. 18	9–14
	Jim Middleton		31–32
1923 — San Francisco	Dots Miller	Resigned July 24	71–44
	Bert Ellison		53–33
1923 — Seattle	Harry Wolverton	Fired July 7	44–49
	Red Killefer		55–48
1924 — Portland	Duke Kenworthy	Resigned June 29	49–65
	Frank Brazill		39–45
1924 — Sacramento	Charlie Pick	Fired Sept. 22	75–97
	Buddy Ryan		13–15
1925 — Portland	Duffy Lewis	Resigned Sept. 4	72–80
	Truck Hannah		20–24
1925 — Vernon	Bill Essick	Resigned Aug. 1	43–75
	Rube Ellis		37–45
1926 — Mission	Walter McCredie	Resigned May 15	16–19
	Walter Schmidt	Fired Aug. 12	47–45
	Dennis Murphy	Interim	2–2
	Bill Leard		41–28
1926 — San Francisco	Bert Ellison	Resigned July 6	37–55
	Doc Strub	Interim	2–0
	Nick Williams		45–61
1927 — Mission	Bill Leard	Fired April 15	8–8
	Al Walters	Interim	8–9
	Harry Hooper		70–93
1928 — Portland	Ernie Johnson	Resigned June 25	35–50
	Bill Rodgers		44–62
1929 — Los Angeles	Marty Krug	Fired July 6	51–51
	Truck Hannah	Interim	6–3
	Jack Lelivelt		47–44
1931 — Mission	George Burns	Resigned July 1	42–44
	Joe Devine		42–59
1932 — Sacramento	Buddy Ryan	Resigned Aug. 4	56–69
	Earl McNeely		45–19
1932 — Seattle	Ernie Johnson	Fired May 31	24–35
	George Burns		66–60
1932 — Mission	Joe Devine	Fired May 12	8–29
	Fred Hoffman		63–88
1934 — Seattle	George Burns	Fired April 17	5–10
	Dutch Ruether		76–92
1934 — Portland	Walter McCredie	Fired May 21	13–32
	Tom Turner	Interim	21–37
	George Burns	Fired Sept. 14	25–34
	George Blackerby		7–14
1935 — Portland	Buddy Ryan	Resigned May 31	23–29
	Bill Cissell		64–57
1935 — Sacramento	Kettle Wirtz	Fired June 6	22–39
	Earl McNeely		53–61
1936 — Portland	Max Bishop	Fired May 11	21–19
	Bill Sweeney		75–60
1943 — San Diego	Cedric Durst	Resigned Aug. 9	50–66
	George Detore		20–19
1945 — Oakland	Dolph Camilli	Fired June 12	37–36
	Billy Raimondi		53–57
1946 — Hollywood	Buck Fausett	Resigned Aug. 7	66–65
	Jimmy Dykes		29–23
1946 — San Diego	Pepper Martin	Resigned Sept. 10	72–100

(Replaced Managers *continued*)

Year, Team	Manager	Remark	Record
	Jim Brillheart		6–8
1946 — Seattle	Bill Skiff	Fired June 12	26–46
	Eddie Taylor	Interim	1–1
	JoJo White		47–62
1948 — Hollywood	Jimmy Dykes	Resigned Aug. 28	65–88
	Lou Stringer	Sold to Red Sox	14–14
	Mule Haas		5–2
1948 — San Diego	Rip Collins	Fired Aug. 3	67–63
	Jimmie Reese	Interim	0–2
	Jim Brillheart		16–40
1949 — Seattle	JoJo White	Resigned July 13	56–54
	Bill Lawrence		39–39
1950 — Sacramento	Red Kress	Fired June 1	23–42
	Joe Marty		58–77
1954 — Sacramento	Gene Desautels	Resigned July 12	44–56
	Tony Freitas		29–38
1955 — Los Angeles	Bill Sweeney	Resigned May 22	25–23
	Jackie Warner	Interim	0–2
	Bob Scheffing		66–56
1956 — Seattle	Luke Sewell	Fired Aug. 14	73–57
	Bill Brenner		18–20
1956 — Portland	Tommy Holmes	Resigned July 11	44–49
	Bill Sweeney		42–33
1956 — San Francisco	Eddie Joost	Fired July 9	43–50
	Joe Gordon		34–38
1957 — San Diego	Bob Elliott	Fired May 16	17–18
	George Metkovich		72–61
1957 — Portland	Bill Sweeney	Died April 18	1–6
	Frank Carswell	Interim	1–7
	Bill Posedel		58–95

Spring Training Sites

The following are the spring training sites, arranged by city, for each team in the Pacific Coast League from 1903 through 1957. All spring training cities are in California unless otherwise noted.

Hollywood (1926–1935; 1938–1957)

Hollywood 1926; Santa Monica 1927–1928; San Diego 1929–1932; Signal Hill/Sawtelle 1933; Riverside 1934; Fullerton 1935; Santa Monica 1938; Lake Elsinore 1939; Santa Barbara 1940; Lake Elsinore 1941; Riverside 1942; Hollywood 1943; Ontario 1944–1947; Whittier 1948; San Fernando 1949–1952; Anaheim 1953–1957.

Los Angeles (1903–1957)

Los Angeles 1903–1906; Santa Monica 1907; Los Angeles 1908–1910; Murrieta Springs 1911; Los Angeles 1912–1913; Urbita Springs 1914; Los Angeles 1915; Lake Elsinore 1916; Los Angeles 1917–1919; Lake Elsinore 1920–1923; Long Beach 1924; Los Angeles 1925–1931; Pasadena 1932; Catalina 1933–1934; Santa Monica 1935; San Bernardino 1936; Ontario 1937–1942; Anaheim 1943–1945; Fullerton 1946–1955; Los Angeles 1956–1957.

Mission (1926–1937)

Stockton 1926–1931; Woodland 1932–1934; Marysville 1935; Monterey 1936–1937.

Oakland (1903–1955)

Fresno 1903; Hanford 1904; Oakland 1905; Bakersfield 1906; Santa Barbara 1907; San Diego 1908; Hayward 1909–1911; Livermore 1912–1913; Pleasanton 1914–1915; Boyes Springs 1916–1918; Oakland 1919–1920; Calistoga 1921–1928; Bakersfield 1929; Fresno 1930–1932; Calistoga 1933–1934; Modesto 1935–1938; Brawley 1939; Napa 1940–1943; San Bernardino 1944; Boyes Springs 1945–1947; San Fernando 1948; Glendale 1949; Mesa (AZ) 1950; Boyes Springs 1951–1952; Monterey 1953–1954; El Centro 1955.

Portland (1903–1917; 1919–1957)

San Jose 1903; Bakersfield 1904–1905; Stockton 1906; Salinas 1907; Santa Barbara 1908; San Luis Obispo 1909; Santa Maria 1910–1912; Visalia 1913; Santa Maria 1914; Fresno 1915; Sacramento 1916; Honolulu (HI) 1917; Crockett 1919; Ontario 1920; Santa Maria 1921; Pasadena 1922; Byron Hot Springs 1923; Stockton 1924; San Jose 1925–1927; Santa Ana 1928–1929; San Jose 1930–1933; Ventura 1934–1936; Fullerton 1937–1940; Santa Monica 1941; San Jose 1942–1946; Riverside 1947–1952; Glendale 1953–1957.

Sacramento (1903; 1909–1914; 1918–1957)

Stockton 1903; Sacramento 1909–1911; Marysville 1912–1914; Sacramento 1919–1920; Chico (Richardson Springs) 1921–1932; Sacramento 1932–1936; Riverside 1937–1940; Fullerton 1941–1942; Fullerton 1943; Sacramento 1944; Chico 1945–1946; Anaheim 1947–1950; Stockton 1951; Modesto 1952; Santa Cruz 1953–1954; Yuma (AZ) 1955; Pasadena 1956–1957.

Salt Lake City (1915–1925)

San Jose 1915; Modesto 1916; Porterville 1917–1918; Pittsburg 1919; Boyes Springs 1920–1921; Modesto 1922; Fresno 1923–1924; Long Beach 1925.

San Diego (1936–1957)

Fullerton 1936; San Diego 1937–1938; El Centro 1939–1942; San Diego 1943–1944; El Centro 1945–1946; San Bernardino 1947; Ontario 1948–1950; Yuma (AZ) 1951; Ontario 1952–1955; Palm Springs 1956; Ontario 1957.

San Francisco (1903–1957)

San Francisco 1903–1904; Visalia 1905–1906; Bakersfield 1907–1908; San Francisco 1909–1910; Modesto 1911; Paso Robles 1912; Boyes Springs 1913–1915; San Jose 1916; Sacramento 1917; Fresno 1918; San Jose 1919; Stockton 1920; Monterey 1921; Boyes Springs 1922–1924; Fresno 1925; Boyes Springs 1926–1927; Monterey 1928–1932; San Francisco 1933; Stockton 1934; Fresno 1935–1936; Hanford 1937–1938; Boyes Springs 1939–1942; San Francisco 1943–1945; Honolulu (HI) 1946–1947; Boyes Springs 1948–1949; El Centro 1950; Modesto 1951; San Francisco 1952; Riverside 1953; Monterey 1954; Brawley 1955; De Land (FL) 1956; Fullerton 1957.

Seattle (1903–1906; 1919–1957)

Ventura 1903; Sacramento 1904; Santa Barbara 1905–1906; Bakersfield 1919; Hanford 1920; Pomona 1921; Stockton 1922; San Jose 1923; San Bernardino 1924; Santa Maria 1925; Hermosa Beach 1926; Bakersfield 1927–1928; San Clemente 1929–1930; Woodland 1931; Santa Cruz 1932–1933; Santa Barbara 1934–1935; Santa Monica 1936–1937; El Centro 1938; Anaheim 1939; San Fernando 1940–1942; Lewiston (ID) 1943; Bakersfield 1944; San Fernando 1945–1946; Bakersfield 1947–1948; Wilmington 1949; Palm Springs 1950–1955; San Bernardino 1956–1957.

Tacoma/Fresno (1904–1906)

Fresno 1904–1906.

Vancouver (1956–1957)

Fullerton 1956; Riverside 1957.

Vernon/Venice (1909–1925)

Vernon 1909–1911; Los Angeles 1912; Venice 1913; Los Angeles 1914; San Diego 1915; Los Angeles 1916; Vernon 1917–1919; Los Angeles 1920; Venice 1921; Vernon 1922–1923; Los Angeles 1924; Vernon 1925.

Chapter Notes

Chapter One

1. *San Francisco Examiner*, December 5, 1890; *Los Angeles Times*, December 5, 1890.

2. *San Francisco Examiner*, December 19 and December 21, 1890; *Oakland Tribune*, December 19, 1890. The game attended by the King was organized to raise money for the purchase of Christmas toys for the poor and orphaned children of San Francisco. The "All-Californias" consisted of major league players from California while the "Picked Nine" was a group of locals mostly from the California State League. Charles Crocker, president of the Southern Pacific Railroad, was supposed to umpire but backed out at the last minute. He was replaced by local star Charles Sweeney and Boston third baseman Billy Nash, who just happened to be visiting for the holidays. Under a brilliant, cloudless clear-blue sky, the All-Californias, led by captain James Fogarty, marched onto the field wearing uniforms carrying the Hawaiian colors. Unfortunately, the King, who had been visiting Monterey, did not arrive until the bottom of the first inning and missed the opening pageantry. About four thousand people attended, paying twenty-five cents for general admission and fifty cents for a grandstand seat. The King remained through the seventh inning and expressed satisfaction with the event, saying, "If my coming here today will be the means of making even one poor orphan happy on Christmas Day, I shall feel more than repaid for coming." The All-Californias won the game, 12–8. The King, who was in the United States for secret treatment of an advanced case of Bright's Disease, died in San Francisco on January 20, 1891. His body was returned to Hawaii on the *Charleston* (*San Francisco Chronicle*, January 20 and January 21, 1891; *San Francisco Call*, January 21, 1891; *Washington Post*, January 21, 1891).

3. *Daily Alta California*, January 14, 1852. References to "base ball" go back to the mid–1700s and clearly the game evolved rather than being "invented" by any one individual. Cartwright and the Knickerbockers were credited with developing the rules for the modern game in 1845 after being forced out of their original playing venue at a vacant lot at Madison and 27th Street (*New York Times*, October 7, 1923).

4. Church, Seymour H., *Base Ball 1845–1871*, (1902). The Eagles were the first team formed in San Francisco, thanks to the influence of Boston native Martin Cosgriff, who brought regulation baseball equipment with him on his trip around the horn in 1858. Some credit a club formed in Sacramento in 1859 as the first actual baseball team.

5. *San Francisco Chronicle*, September 26, 1869; *Los Angeles Times*, August 18, 1911. George Wright of the Red Stockings impressed everyone by hitting three home runs in the first game against the Eagles, a 35–4 victory for the professionals from Cincinnati.

6. Natalie Vermilyea, *Kranks Delight: California Baseball 1858–1888*, March/April 1991 issue of *The Californians*. Vermilyea's article is an excellent summary of early baseball history in California. Also see *Always on Sunday* by John E. Spalding, the definitive source on California League baseball from the 1880s to the league's final collapse in 1915.

7. *New York Times*, October 26, 1887; *Los Angeles Times*, November 20, November 21 and November 25, 1887. Haight Street Grounds also served as the site of the first gridiron meeting, now called "the Big Game," between the University of California at Berkeley and Stanford University. The stadium was torn down in the mid–1890s and the lot converted to residential use (*San Francisco Call*, March 1 and April 18, 1895).

8. *Sacramento Bee*, October 24, 1887.

9. *San Francisco Call*, May 3, 1886.

10. *San Francisco Call*, May 10, 1886.

11. *The Sporting News*, May 31, 1886.

12. *Sacramento Bee*, October 24, 1887; *Sacramento Union*, October 24, 1887.

13. Piercy's entire major league career consisted of two games for the Chicago White Stockings in 1881. He made his first appearance on May 12 and had a rough debut, committing three errors at second base that led to a pair of unearned runs. He played his final game for Chicago six weeks later, this time at third base, and dropped a throw that led to a run (*Chicago Tribune*, May 13 and July 1, 1881).

14. *San Francisco Chronicle*, June 21 and July 5, 1880; *Washington Post*, May 16, 1880. Devlin and his three Louisville teammates had been banned from the National League for life in November 1877. The *San Francisco Chronicle* ignored this fact, saying only, "In 1878 he was secured by the St. Louis Browns, but through some misunderstanding, the contract with that club was never consummated." Devlin practiced with the team for ten days before he made his debut and was praised for his obvious talent and coolness under pressure. He had traveled to Chicago a few weeks earlier, pleading unsuccessfully with National League president William Hulbert for reinstatement. Devlin later became a policeman in Philadelphia and died there in October 1883 at age thirty-four from tuberculosis related to alcoholism (*New York Times*, November 3, 1877 and December 9, 1880; *Chicago Tribune*, April 18 and June 20, 1880).

15. *New York Times*, May 21, 1891.

16. *Los Angeles Times*, February 9, 1913.

17. *San Francisco Examiner*, May 14, 1883. Sweeney was pitching for a San Francisco team, the Niantics, against the Haverlys. After giving up eight runs in the third inning he was moved to second base and then refused to continue when the team took the field for the fifth inning. Under the rules of the time, the Niantics had to play with only eight players the rest of the game. They lost, 21–3.

18. An excellent catcher, the 5'6" Nava was behind the plate for virtually all of Sweeney's games in 1884, even while carrying a ridiculously low .095 batting average. Although

his first language was Italian, Nava is considered by some to be the first Hispanic player in the major leagues; he was dark-skinned and his mother was Mexican (*Boston Globe*, October 18, 1884; *Washington Post*, September 30, 1906).

19. *Boston Globe*, June 8, 1884. Sandy Nava was Sweeney's catcher for the record-setting game.

20. *Boston Globe*, July 23, 1884; *New York Times*, July 23, 1884. Providence was leading Philadelphia in the seventh inning, 6–2, when manager Frank Bancroft asked Sweeney to move to the outfield to save his arm. Apparently upset at having another pitcher replace him, Sweeney abandoned the field, forcing Providence to finish the game a man short, the same situation the Niantics faced the year before. Bancroft tracked Sweeney down in the clubhouse where he was putting on his street clothes. When ordered back to the field, Sweeney called his manager "an opprobrious name" and left the ballpark. After Sweeney's departure, Charles Radbourn pitched Providence to the National League pennant, winning an incredible fifty-nine games.

21. The Union Association was formed by St. Louis businessman Henry V. Lucas to compete with the National League and the American Association, the recognized major leagues of the time. (For background on the Union Association, see Harold and Dorothy Seymour's *Baseball—The Early Years*.)

22. *San Francisco Chronicle*, July 16, July 17, October 26, October 30, November 2 and November 10, 1894; *Los Angeles Times*, July 22, July 24 and September 21, 1894. Sweeney was bartending in a San Francisco saloon owned by the "King of Potrero Hill," Frank McManus, a feared gangster and ward politician in the notorious "Irish Hill" neighborhood of the city (located near the present-day western end of the Bay Bridge). McManus' brother, Con, initiated a fight with Sweeney at the saloon and the brawl ended with Sweeney shooting at Con McManus three times, "two taking effect." When informed that Con McManus had died, Sweeney reportedly "broke down and cried like a child." The reaction was most likely from fright — Frank McManus had tried to kill a previous assailant of his brother, rival gangster Jack Welch, while Welch lay in a hospital bed. McManus threatened to kill Sweeney and arrived outside the jail the next day, demanding to see the ex-ballplayer. When he was refused, McManus stuck his foot inside the jailhouse door and tried to force his way in. He was finally turned away. McManus then arranged for a funeral at St. Patrick's Church for his brother, but the priests refused to say high mass at the service. McManus, obviously a real piece of work, retaliated by throwing cobblestones through the church windows and threatening a priest's life. He was eventually apprehended for this crime while crossing Market Street with a ladder on his back, heading for the offices of the *San Francisco Examiner* where he planned to post a sign protesting the actions of the priests. When McManus finally appeared before the judge, no one was willing to testify against him and the case was dismissed. It was later charged that McManus tried to intimidate witnesses at Sweeney's trial but nothing came of that either. Despite testimony that Con McManus had been the aggressor in the fight, Sweeney was convicted of manslaughter. Sentenced to eight years in San Quentin Prison, Sweeney was released after three years for health reasons and died of tuberculosis in 1902 at age thirty-eight. King McManus was already dead by that time, a victim of congestive heart failure in 1896. One of the last events held at Haight Street Grounds was a benefit for Sweeney's wife shortly after he went to prison (*San Francisco Chronicle*, February 9, 1895, October 27, 1896, March 5, 1898 and April 5, 1902; *San Francisco Call*, April 5, 1902).

23. *Chicago Tribune*, September 25, 1896.

24. *Chicago Tribune*, October 16 and October 17, 1899; *San Francisco Chronicle*, April 17, 1900. Lange never acclimated to a life of domestic bliss. More at home with the boys at the club or on the road scouting for John McGraw, Lange would stay away from home as long as possible. He and Grace

divorced in 1915, but Lange became independently wealthy and was honored as an all-time baseball great at the time of his death in 1950 (*The Sporting News*, August 2, 1950).

25. *New York Times*, September 1, 1889.

26. *New York Times*, August 7, 1888.

27. *Los Angeles Times*, August 16, 1912.

28. *New York Times*, August 15, 1888. The *Times* said it "was most uproariously received."

29. *Los Angeles Times*, April 9, 1916. The film's climactic scene was shot in April 1916 at Washington Park, home of the Los Angeles Angels. One has to wonder how convincing the fifty-eight-year-old Hopper could have been as Mighty Casey on film.

30. *New York Times*, August 22, 1940; *Los Angeles Times*, August 22, 1940. Even after Thayer was identified as the author of "Casey," others claimed to have written it. The poem was credited in some early anthologies to Joseph Quinlan Murphy. In 1904, Frank J. Wilstach, a former press agent for DeWolf Hopper, insisted the poem had been created by his late friend, William Valentine, and was a parody of Thomas Babington Macaulay's *Horatius at the Bridge*. Valentine had been editor of the *Sioux City Tribune*, in which "Casey" was supposedly printed in 1882. Four years after Wilstach came forward, George Whitefield D'Vys began a campaign to claim authorship of the poem, which led to an investigation to settle the matter of the poem's creator once and for all. After completing his research, Columbia University Latin professor Harry Thurston Peck announced that Thayer was the author. DeWolf Hopper stated he had never doubted Thayer's claim. None of this dissuaded D'Vys, who continued to maintain he had written the poem and fought for the rights to it for the rest of his life. He also published a number of other Mudville stories. Thayer ignored D'Vys most of the time, although he was moved to protest in 1932 after reading yet another dispatch in which D'Vys claimed to have authored the verse. Thayer fired a missive to the *New York Times*, pointing out that D'Vys claimed to have sent the poem to the *New York Sporting Times* in 1886, where he said it had been published without attribution. Thayer noted that the periodical did not begin publication until 1888 — when it reprinted "Casey," crediting it to the *San Francisco Examiner* where, as Thayer stated, "it originally appeared over my initials in June, 1888." D'Vys went to his grave in 1941, nine months after Thayer, stubbornly insisting he had written baseball's most famous verse (*Los Angeles Times*, December 31, 1904; *Boston Globe*, May 8, 1908; *New York Times*, March 13, 1932, and June 1, 1941).

31. *Sacramento Union*, January 2, January 6 and January 7, 1892; *Los Angeles Times*, January 1, January 5 and January 7, 1892.

32. Maury Brown, *Early Portland Baseball History*, *Oregon Stadium Campaign*, 2010, <http://www.oregonstadiumcampaign.com/history_early.htm>. Harris had taken over at Portland after selling the San Francisco franchise for $2,200. Harris quit Portland and returned to California after the team's directors reinstated star player Tom Parrott, suspended by Harris for insubordination, over Harris's objection. Harris returned to California and ran the San Francisco franchise in 1891 (*San Francisco Chronicle*, July 4 and August 24, 1890).

33. *Seattle Post-Intelligencer*, May 24 and May 25, 1890.

34. *Fresno Daily Republican*, January 8, 1892; *Los Angeles Times*, February 1, 1892.

35. *Los Angeles Times*, September 10, 1892.

36. *Los Angeles Times*, August 24 and September 22, 1892.

37. *Los Angeles Times*, March 5, 1894.

38. *Washington Post*, August 12, 1893. McNabb was also said to be suffering from malaria (*Baltimore Sun*, August 12, 1893).

39. Skirt dancing was popular during vaudeville. The female dancer would perform ballet steps and acrobatic kicks in a skirt that would display just enough leg to keep the men in the audience interested.

40. William Rockwell, who had been a pitcher in his youth, re-married and moved to San Francisco where he became one of the managers of the *San Francisco Examiner* baseball tournament. Unfortunately, he did not live that much longer, succumbing to meningitis in August 1897 (*San Francisco Examiner*, August 5, 1897; *Los Angeles Times*, August 5, 1897; *Sporting Life*, August 14, 1897).

41. *New York Times*, March 1, 1894; *Pittsburgh Post-Gazette*, March 2, 1894; *Washington Post*, March 1, March 2 and March 3, 1894. Louise Rockwell claimed McNabb became angry when she said she was leaving him. He slugged her in the mouth and then accused her of being involved with Lou Gilliland. At that point, she said McNabb pulled out a gun, shot her and then shot himself in the mouth.

42. *Los Angeles Times*, October 29 and November 25, 1895; *San Francisco Chronicle*, November 19, 1895.

43. Chance eventually became player-manager of the great Cubs teams between 1906 and 1910. His parents, William Chance and Mary Russell, were married on a farm just outside Modesto, California, in September 1870. The family moved to Fresno in the middle of the decade and Frank was born there in 1876 (Dix, Mrs. Ray, *Early Records of Stanislaus County*, 1958).

44. *San Francisco Examiner*, December 6, 1897; *Oakland Tribune*, January 3, 1898.

45. *Los Angeles Times*, April 28, 1898; *Sporting Life*, May 7, 1898.

46. *Los Angeles Times*, October 2, 1899.

47. Russ Dille and David Eskenazi, *Daniel E. Dugdale, Baseball Pioneer, The Online Encyclopedia of Washington State History*, July 5, 2001 <http://www.historylink.org/essays/output.cfm?file_id=3431>.

48. *Los Angeles Times*, September 16, 1912.

49. *Los Angeles Times*, July 30, 1900.

Chapter Two

1. *Los Angeles Times*, January 13, 1901.

2. *Los Angeles Times*, June 30, 1927.

3. *Los Angeles Times*, March 27, 1910, March 6, 1912, January 15 and December 17, 1914.

4. *Los Angeles Times*, December 2, 1896. Morley was operating what is called, rather appropriately, a mangle — a machine used for squeezing water out of fabric and pressing it by means of heated rollers. He sued Crescent Laundry for twenty-five thousand dollars, arguing he had not been properly trained on the machine but was forced to operate it anyway. The injury was rarely mentioned; an article in 1914 about top billiard players referenced the amputation and a 1921 story about the Angels noted that Morley could not be drafted to officiate at a baseball game because it "was no job for a three-fingered umpire" (*Los Angeles Times*, January 15, 1914; June 1, 1921).

5. *Los Angeles Times*, April 5, 1936.

6. *Los Angeles Times*, January 1, 1900, August 2, 1925 and March 27, 1927.

7. *Los Angeles Times*, June 13, 1900.

8. *Los Angeles Times*, February 9 and August 25, 1900, and April 5, 1936.

9. *Los Angeles Times*, January 13, 1901. The players were banned for five years.

10. *Los Angeles Times*, April 1, 1901.

11. *San Francisco Call*, April 1, 1901; *San Francisco Chronicle*, April 1, 1901.

12. *Los Angeles Times*, April 6, 1901.

13. *Los Angeles Times*, April 22, 1922.

14. *Los Angeles Times*, August 27, September 6, September 7 and October 12, 1901.

15. *Los Angeles Times*, December 20, 1901.

16. Waddell struck out a single-season record 349 batters for the Philadelphia Athletics in 1904. That mark was not topped until Sandy Koufax struck out 382 in 1965.

17. *Los Angeles Times*, April 3, 1914.

18. One of Waddell's life-saving efforts took place in Lynn, Massachusetts, in February 1905 when he carried away an oil-burning stove that had been knocked over by a little boy walking through a store. With only a curtain he had grabbed to protect his hands, Waddell tossed the stove into the snow, preventing the store from burning to the ground. As was his customary pattern, Waddell was in trouble four days later. During a dispute with his father-in-law over past-due rent, Waddell struck the man with a flat iron and knocked out several of his teeth. When Waddell's mother-in-law tried to intervene, he smashed a chair over her, knocking her to the floor (*Boston Globe*, February 5, February 9, February 10 and February 11, 1905).

19. *Los Angeles Times*, March 28 and April 5, 1902. Waddell received a twenty-five-dollar fine.

20. As an example of his ability to swing the bat, Waddell had five hits in eight at-bats in a doubleheader against San Francisco on May 25. He hit a home run in the first game and added a home run and two doubles in the nightcap (*San Francisco Call*, May 26, 1902; *San Francisco Chronicle*, May 26, 1902).

21. *Los Angeles Times*, March 11 and April 16, 1902.

22. *Los Angeles Times*, June 20, 1902 and April 2, 1914.

23. Connie Mack was able to handle Waddell ... for a while. Rube had four straight magnificent seasons before Mack's influence began to fade and he was eventually dealt to St. Louis. The left-hander won 193 games in his major league career and was elected to the Baseball Hall of Fame in 1946. He died at age thirty-seven in 1914 of either pneumonia or tuberculosis — in either case exacerbated by his drinking — and was buried in San Antonio, Texas (*Los Angeles Times*, April 2, 1914).

24. *Los Angeles Times*, July 3, July 4 and July 7, 1902; *Detroit Free Press*, August 7, August 10 and October 7, 1902.

25. *San Francisco Chronicle*, January 14, 1903; *San Francisco Call*, January 11, January 13, January 14, January 15 and January 17, 1903; *Detroit Free Press*, January 14, January 15, January 17 and January 22, 1903; *Chicago Daily Tribune*, January 14, 1903. Mercer's death is one of baseball's enduring mysteries. On Saturday, January 10, he pitched at Recreation Park in San Francisco for a barnstorming team of major leaguers, losing, 4–2, to a squad that included Jack Chesbro as the opposing pitcher. On Monday, Mercer visited the racetrack in Oakland with other players and seemed in excellent spirits. He left his friends around six o'clock and two hours later walked out of his San Francisco hotel and checked into the Occidental, registering under the name George Murray. Late in the evening a bellboy walking down the hall outside Mercer's room noticed a strong odor of gas. When the room was entered, Mercer was stretched out on the bed, wearing his nightclothes. His coat and vest were over his head and a rubber tube was in his mouth with the other end connected to a gas jet that was wide open. A suicide note was left on the table, warning of the evils of women and gambling. Mercer also left notes to his mother and fiancée. He was treasurer for the barnstorming team and speculation centered on his heavy gambling and whether he might have lost a substantial portion of the team's bank account. First reports indicated a sizeable amount of money was missing; later it was claimed all funds were accounted for. Mercer's family argued he had been murdered, pointing to a recent attempt to steal money from him in Sacramento. It was also claimed that the letter to Mercer's mother mentioned two sisters when he had none. Some friends speculated his health was an issue; he had some "pulmonary" problems and was always worried about contracting tuberculosis like his brother. Others said Mercer's suicide had to do with his fiancée. More than three thousand people attended his funeral service in East Liverpool, Ohio, with another thousand standing outside in the rain and sleet. He was

buried with a floral bouquet from his fiancée. The barnstorming athletes agreed to stage a benefit game in San Francisco for Mercer's mother on January 18. Joe Corbett and Ham Iburg agreed to pitch and Bill Lange served as umpire. The event raised nearly $1,600. Corbett pitched a complete-game victory, which encouraged him to make a comeback with Los Angeles in 1903 after six years in retirement. Mercer's death was ruled a suicide by the coroner (*San Francisco Call*, January 19, 1903; *San Francisco Chronicle*, January 22, 1903).

26. Whalen was one of the more mild-mannered players in the league. Only 5'10" and one-hundred-fifty pounds, he won nearly three hundred games in his minor league career, playing in the California League, the Pacific Coast League, the Eastern League, and then with outlaws of the Tri-State and California State League before returning to the PCL. He was well liked by teammates, who loved encouraging his tendency to boast by telling him that other pitchers threw harder or had better breaking pitches. Whalen suffered a broken leg during spring training in 1911 with Tacoma in the Northwest League. When it became clear the injury threatened his career, the PCL set aside a percentage of gate receipts from games played on May 19 to assist him financially. Whalen made an unsuccessful comeback attempt with Vernon the next spring. After retiring, he was employed as a watchman on the grounds of the California State Capitol. Whalen died of kidney disease in Sacramento in 1915, a few months after his wife passed away and just two days after the death of Henry Harris, the man who had discovered "the Whale." Harris died of a heart attack in his sleep at his Hyde Street home in San Francisco on January 10, 1915 (*Los Angeles Times*, August 8, 1909, May 18 and June 23, 1911, January 13, 1915; *Sacramento Bee*, January 12, 1915; *San Francisco Chronicle*, January 11, 1915 and February 13, 1945; *Oakland Tribune*, September 2, 1914).

27. *San Francisco Chronicle*, March 13, 1902; *Chicago Tribune*, March 14, 1902; *San Francisco Call*, March 27, 1902. The thirty-five-year-old Shugart was available in part because he had been suspended for nearly a month of the 1901 American League season after his arrest following an attack on umpire John Haskell during a game. Ban Johnson had originally kicked Shugart out of the league permanently but changed his mind after a series of pleas by the ballplayer and Chicago owner Charles Comiskey. Shugart had been a shortstop most of his career but played second and third base for San Francisco (*Chicago Tribune*, August 22, August 23 and September 15, 1901).

28. *San Francisco Chronicle*, August 4, 1902; *The Sporting News*, May 31, 1902. Ironically, Shay had jumped from St. Paul to play for Shugart in San Francisco (*St. Paul Globe*, June 10 and June 11, 1902; *Sporting Life*, June 21, 1902).

29. Unfortunately, after the success of 1902, Lohman's life went into a downward spiral. His Oakland ball club fell back to last place the next year and then his arm went bad and he couldn't even throw the ball back to the pitcher. He continued to manage Oakland but his behavior became more erratic; in 1905 he was replaced by George Van Haltren. He caught a game for Fresno in the California State League but was soon reported to be "daffy" and unable to talk about anything other than baseball. He began wandering from home and would be found at the beach on his knees praying to God to take him and his wife and three-year-old son. At one point, he became convinced he had super-human powers. Lohman's wife was appointed guardian, but she was unable to control him. The final straw came in late May 1906 when Lohman accosted a visitor to his home, accusing the woman of stealing one hundred and sixty dollars. She locked herself in a room but Lohman broke down the door, dragged her to the top of the staircase and then lost his balance, sending both of them hurtling down the stairs. Lohman was arrested and committed to Patton State Hospital in San Bernardino following a hearing during which he thrashed wildly in restraints. Diagnosed with schizophrenia, Lohman spent the rest of his life — twenty-two years — in Patton Hospital (*Oakland Tribune*,

June 1, 1906; *Fresno Morning Republican*, September 23, 1905; *Los Angeles Times*, June 1 and June 2, 1906; *San Francisco Call*, June 2, 1906; George F. "Peter" Lohman's State of California Standard Certificate of Death).

30. *Sporting Life*, May 17, 1902; *Los Angeles Times*, June 2, October 15, November 3 and December 8, 1902. In the game in which he threw out three runners at home, Cristall was also at the front end of a relay to the shortstop that nailed a fourth runner at the plate.

31. *San Francisco Examiner*, November 20, 1913. Hildebrand was released by Brooklyn in early May and signed with the Philadelphia Athletics but never played for them. Instead, he went to Providence, where he met pitcher Frank Corridon. Hildebrand noticed that when Corridon wanted to get a better grip when throwing his changeup, he would spit on the baseball. Hildebrand asked Corridon what would happen if he applied more saliva and threw the ball harder. The result was a nasty downward break on the pitch. Corridon reportedly used it in one game but developed a sore arm and did not throw the pitch again. When Hildebrand moved on to Sacramento later in the year, he remembered the spitball and suggested it to Stricklett, who became the first to use it on a regular basis. For his part, in one interview, Stricklett claimed the pitch was actually discovered by Skel Roach, a one-game big league pitcher who also appeared in the Pacific Northwest League and the PCL. In that 1905 interview, Stricklett responded to those saying the spitball was a fad: "If a majority of pitchers learn to use it with the same effect I do the batsmen will be almost completely at our mercy" (*Brooklyn Daily Eagle*, May 1 and May 7, 1902; *Salt Lake Herald*, September 10, 1905; *The Sporting News*, March 23, 1955 and June 8, 1960).

32. *Los Angeles Times*, December 18, 1902.

33. *Oregonian*, July 11, 1902; *Los Angeles Times*, July 11, 1902; *San Francisco Chronicle*, July 11, 1902. Directors of the Seattle and Portland teams had already negotiated rates with the railroads prior to approaching the California League in the summer of 1902. The *Oregonian* indicated that news of the proposed defection had been common knowledge for several weeks.

34. *Oregonian*, December 22, 1902.

35. *Seattle Post-Intelligencer*, December 23, 1902.

36. *Los Angeles Times*, December 10, December 11 and December 12, 1902; *San Francisco Call*, December 11, 1902; *Seattle Post-Intelligencer*, December 27, 1902. Part of the issue Dugdale and the other Seattle directors had with Harris' proposal was that it left them taking all the risk in joining a new league headquartered more than eight hundred miles away. Joining the new league would doom the Pacific Northwest League, putting the Seattle directors in a difficult spot should the new Pacific Coast League fold.

37. *Seattle Post-Intelligencer*, December 23, December 28 and December 30, 1902; *Los Angeles Times*, December 24, 1902.

38. *Seattle Post-Intelligencer*, December 23, 1902; *Seattle Times*, December 24, 1902; *Los Angeles Times*, December 30, 1902.

39. *Seattle Times*, December 14, 1902.

40. *Los Angeles Times*, December 30, 1902. Bert is often mistakenly listed as league president in 1903. He did take more and more of the lead in league operations from fifty-five-year-old James T. Moran, who seemed to have little interest in involving himself with the PCL on a full-time basis. In the middle of the battle with the Pacific National League, Moran departed on a ten-week trip with his wife to visit relatives in his native New Haven, Connecticut, and make purchases for his clothing store. He finally returned in early July. Bert was named acting president late in the 1903 season and officially took over the office in 1904 (*Oakland Tribune*, July 6, 1903; *Los Angeles Times*, January 3, 1904).

41. *Los Angeles Times*, December 25, 1902.

42. *Washington Post*, December 26, 1902 and January 11, 1903.

43. *Brooklyn Daily Eagle*, December 1, 1902; *Los Angeles Times*, March 14, 1903 and August 19, 1904.

44. *Los Angeles Times*, November 15, 1903.

45. *Los Angeles Times*, March 14, 1901.

46. *Los Angeles Times*, January 23, 1903.

47. Hoy did not start playing baseball until in his mid-twenties. Early in his professional career he worked out a set of hand signals so the third-base coach could let him know whether a pitch had been called a ball or strike. It is often claimed Hoy is the reason hand signals by umpires were devised but there are no contemporary accounts supporting this, nor does it appear Hoy ever made the claim himself.

48. *Los Angeles Times*, January 4, 1903.

49. *Los Angeles Times*, February 20, 1903; *San Francisco Call*, February 20, 1903.

50. *Los Angeles Times*, January 4, 1903.

51. *San Francisco Chronicle*, March 7, 1903; *Los Angeles Times*, March 8 and March 9, 1903.

52. *Oregonian*, March 10, 1903.

53. *Los Angeles Times*, March 19, 1903.

54. *Seattle Post-Intelligencer*, April 30, 1903 and July 14, 1999. The location of the new ballpark was at Fifth and Mercer, near the present site of Seattle Center, Key Arena and the Space Needle.

55. *Sacramento Bee*, March 19, March 20 and March 21, 1903; *Los Angeles Times*, March 20, 1903. The players arrested were Win Cutter and Charlie "Demon" Doyle. Fisher charged they were advanced money and had therefore taken it under false pretenses. George Hildebrand was momentarily detained but then allowed to go on his way since he had not received any money from the Sacramento team owner. Fisher met with Cutter and Doyle the next day and convinced them to return and play for him in Sacramento. The city attorney then dismissed the case, remarking, "Peace has been patched up."

56. *Los Angeles Times*, March 21, 1903.

57. *Los Angeles Times*, September 13, 1903.

58. *Oakland Tribune*, May 21, 1903.

59. *Seattle Times*, October 26 and October 27, 1903; *Los Angeles Times*, October 26 and October 27, 1903; *The Sporting News*, November 7, 1903. Seattle was in last place with a record of 67–90 after losing to Oakland on September 30. The winning streak started with three in a row against Oakland followed by a tie when the next game against the Oaks was called due to darkness because a lacrosse match played before the baseball game went into overtime. Seattle then won five straight against Sacramento and six more in a row against San Francisco. After taking the first five against Los Angeles, Seattle's winning streak was finally ended at nineteen by the Looloos on October 26. Seattle was also awarded two games against Portland by forfeit from earlier in the season. The team peaked with a record of 91–91, moving into second place. Seattle eventually finished third with a final record of 98–100.

60. The twenty-nine-year-old Hughes compiled an 83–41 major league record prior to joining Seattle. Hughes first gained fame pitching for Sacramento-based Gilt Edge in 1897 when he defeated the two-time Temple Cup champion Baltimore Orioles, who were on a barnstorming tour. The Orioles signed him before leaving California. Hughes was an instant sensation, throwing a one-hitter in his major league debut. In his next start he threw a no-hitter. He led the National League in victories the next year, with a 28–6 record for Brooklyn. Hughes married a Sacramento girl and decided he did not want to play for Brooklyn in 1900. Local businessmen established a fund that enabled Sacramento to match the salary Hughes would have earned with Brooklyn and he remained in California that year. His holdout was a big story in the East, where Ned Hanlon constantly complained that Hughes would not respond to offers. After playing in Sacramento in 1900, he returned for two more seasons with Brooklyn, winning seventeen and fifteen games (*Sacramento Union*, November 25 and November 26, 1897; *San Francisco Chron-*

icle, November 26 and December 5, 1897; *Baltimore Sun*, April 19 and April 23, 1898; *Brooklyn Daily Eagle*, March 11, April 6 and April 10, 1900; *San Francisco Call*, April 14, 1900).

61. *Los Angeles Herald*, November 9, 1903. The Angels' massive lead helped them overcome injuries and personal problems. Cap Dillon, who married in mid–August, injured his knee and missed almost three weeks in September; catcher Heine Spies filled in for Dillon during his absence. (Spies was an excellent catcher, known for his ability to corral pop fouls; for years after he retired you could hear "Let Heine have it!" whenever there was a foul pop-up in Los Angeles.) Third baseman Jud Smith missed a lot of time with injuries as well. In mid–October, shortstop Jimmy Toman left the team to be at his terminally ill father's bedside in Philadelphia and missed the rest of the season (*Los Angeles Times*, September 16, September 21, October 18 and November 4, 1903).

62. *Los Angeles Times*, December 1, 1903. Portland stockholders sold the team for an amount equal to the twelve thousand dollars the franchise had lost in 1903 (*Los Angeles Times*, February 12, 1904).

63. *Sacramento Union*, October 26, 1903; *Los Angeles Times*, January 3, 1904. Fisher received permission to play the first and last months of the season in Fresno to escape the rainy springtime weather in Washington. Of course, the 1904 opener in Fresno was rained out. The next day, the Tigers wore their new uniforms, navy blue with "Tacoma" in white letters. The players also wore orange and black striped stockings. The Tigers defeated Portland, 2–1 (*Fresno Morning Republican*, March 25 and March 26, 1904).

64. *Los Angeles Times*, February 1, 1904.

65. *Los Angeles Times*, January 4, 1904.

66. *Los Angeles Times*, January 3 and January 4, 1904. Ned Hanlon, who was elected to the Baseball Hall of Fame in 1996, gained his fame as manager of the legendary Baltimore Orioles of the 1890s. It was there that he popularized "inside baseball" through use of the squeeze play and the "hit and run." John McGraw, Wilbert Robinson and Hughie Jennings played under Hanlon and later became Hall of Fame managers. Hanlon won three pennants for Baltimore and added two more for Brooklyn in 1899 and 1900. By 1904, Hanlon was more interested in making profits through the buying and selling of contracts, regularly claiming dozens of players and then selling them to anyone willing to meet his price.

67. *Los Angeles Times*, February 3, 1904; *The Sporting News*, March 5, 1904.

68. *Los Angeles Times*, October 1, 1903, December 30, 1903 and January 14, 1904; *St. Louis Post-Dispatch*, December 28, 1903 and January 13, 1904.

69. *Los Angeles Times*, February 10, February 20, February 24, February 25 and February 26, 1904. Morley claimed he had a contract signed by Dillon that was dated two weeks earlier than the one with Hanlon, but all he ever produced was an affidavit with the first baseman's signature. It should be noted that in the *Los Angeles Times* on September 2, 1903, it was announced that Dillon had signed with Los Angeles for 1904 after rejecting offers from other teams, including the Chicago Cubs. Brooklyn had persistently targeted Dillon after other teams had given up. Hanlon persuaded Dillon to wire his terms and Dillon did so but then changed his mind about leaving Los Angeles. Louis Castro was the first Latin American-born player to reach the major leagues, unless one counts Esteban "Steve" Bellan, a Cuban who played the 1871 and 1872 seasons in the National Association. Born in Medellín, Colombia, Castro served as a utility infielder for the American League champion Philadelphia Athletics in 1902 before joining Hanlon's minor league team in Baltimore the next year. A friend of Fred Ely, Castro jumped to the Portland Browns to play for him and act as team captain. Castro was a disappointment in the PCL and Dan Dugdale released him during his short tenure as Portland manager. (There is some controversy about Castro's Columbian heritage. His death certificate apparently lists his birthplace as New York, but earlier census

records say he was born in Medellin. Later research seems to show that Castro arrived in the United States aboard a ship in the 1880s, strengthening the claim that he was born in South America.) After leaving the PCL, Castro played in the American Association and the Southern Association. He was especially popular in the South, where he became known as "the Count" and was revered for his comic personality. He also worked as an undertaker in the offseason. There was a fourth player Hanlon disputed prior to the season. Former Cincinnati Reds pitcher Bill Dammann, who had been signed by Mike Fisher over the winter, was assigned to Spokane in a reconstituted Pacific Northwest League (*Los Angeles Times*, September 2 and December 17, 1903, January 12, March 1, March 23 and September 7, 1904; *Baltimore Sun*, February 17, 1904; *The Sporting News*, March 5, 1904; *Atlanta Constitution*, August 25, 1907; *Debating Louis Castro, Smithsonian. com*, September 1, 2007, 2010 <http://www.smithsonianmag. com/arts-culture/castro.html>).

70. *Los Angeles Times*, February 25, 1904. Morley later claimed that he resigned only so he could determine the depth of support he had from the team's stockholders. Since he held majority interest in the team, he did not have to worry about his resignation being accepted (*Los Angeles Times*, March 1, 1904).

71. *Los Angeles Times*, February 26, 1904.

72. *Los Angeles Times*, March 20, 1904.

73. *Bakersfield Californian*, March 12, 1904; *Los Angeles Times*, March 13, 1904.

74. *Oregonian*, March 22 and March 23, 1904.

75. *New York Times*, March 24, 1904; *Oakland Tribune*, March 25, 1904.

76. *Los Angeles Herald*, March 25, 1904; *Los Angeles Times*, March 25, 1904.

77. *Los Angeles Times*, March 25 and March 26, 1904. Dillon's departure had been choreographed the previous night as a compromise so umpire O'Connell would not have to defy either the league or the courts. Bert was still angry the next day, claiming as long as he was president of the Pacific Coast League, Dillon would never play for Los Angeles.

78. *Los Angeles Times*, March 25, 1904; *New York Times*, April 25, 1904; *The Sporting News*, May 14, 1904.

79. *Los Angeles Times*, March 17, 1904. Chase was playing second base for Santa Clara when Jim Morley first saw him. Santa Clara was playing against another college team at Chutes Park and Morley was serving as umpire. The *Los Angeles Times* called Chase "the fastest ever seen at an amateur game in Los Angeles." Morley signed him a week and a half later (*Los Angeles Times*, March 6, 1904).

80. *Los Angeles Times*, March 28, 1936.

81. *Los Angeles Times*, May 28, 1905; *San Francisco Call*, April 29, 1907.

82. *Los Angeles Times*, May 4, 1925.

83. *Los Angeles Times*, May 21, 1905. It was often said that Graham was totally responsible for Tacoma's success. In a 1906 interview, Fisher replied to his critics, saying, "Graham, while working for me, never signed up a ballplayer. I gave him full charge of the playing in the field, but to the other ends of the business I attended. I don't wish to throw any cold water on Graham. He was a great field captain, but I was always manager when it came to hiring, firing, buying or selling players" (*Fresno Morning Republican*, September 3 and September 10, 1906).

84. *San Francisco Chronicle*, August 1, August 4, August 6 and August 7, August 8 and August 15, 1904; *St. Louis Post-Dispatch*, August 1 and August 7, 1904; *Los Angeles Times*, August 21, 1904.

85. *San Francisco Call*, August 20, 1904; *San Francisco Chronicle*, August 19 and August 20, 1904.

86. *San Francisco Chronicle*, August 21, 1904.

87. *San Francisco Chronicle*, August 28, 1904. Corbett won thirteen games for San Francisco in 1904. Troubled by a sore arm, he pitched sparingly in 1905, splitting six decisions with

the Seals. By mid-season he was selling hats at a store he had established. He briefly threatened to sue after Brooklyn purchased him in September 1905 (*St. Louis Post-Dispatch*, July 9, 1905; *San Francisco Chronicle*, September 16, 1905).

88. *Los Angeles Times*, September 10, 1911 and May 28, 1922.

89. *Los Angeles Times*, January 17, 1905; *The Sporting News*, April 8, 1905.

90. *Los Angeles Times*, February 24, 1905.

91. *San Francisco Call*, October 1, 1904; *Los Angeles Times*, March 22, 1905.

92. *Los Angeles Times*, September 28 and October 2, 1904. Jim Morley argued that if the Pacific Coast League was going to honor the agreement, the draft price would have to be raised to at least $1,500 and teams should be protected against losing more than one player. PCL contracts did not contain a reserve clause, allowing league owners to argue that the drafting of players held no validity. Then they realized that the argument could work against them, since by the same logic PCL owners had no right to sell players.

93. *Los Angeles Times*, October 13, October 22 and October 23, 1904.

94. *Sporting Life*, October 29 and November 5, 1904.

95. *Washington Post*, September 28, 1904; *Los Angeles Times*, October 27, 1904. Jones won six of nine decisions for Los Angeles while Chance hit for a .274 average in seventy-three at-bats and stole eleven bases. When Chance played first base instead of catcher, Hal Chase generally shifted to second base or the outfield and Heine Spies caught. Mason had pitched early in the 1904 season for Washington before being turned over to Baltimore.

96. *Los Angeles Times*, November 24, 1904. Chance did not play again for Los Angeles since it was thought the team had been eliminated from pennant contention; Bert had not yet ruled on the protested game against Portland. When the umpire failed to show up the next day, Chance filled in as umpire and continued in that role for the last week of the season.

97. *Los Angeles Times*, November 29, 1904. Spider Baum, pitching for Los Angeles against Portland, tripled to drive in two runs but reached third base by taking a shortcut across the diamond, hoping the umpire would not notice. Umpire Jack McCarthy saw what Baum had done and called him out when the ball was returned to second base. McCarthy also ruled that the second run did not count, which was incorrect since both runners scored before Baum was called out and he was not retired on a force play. This would have left the game tied after nine innings. McCarthy admitted his mistake, which factored into Bert's ruling in favor of Los Angeles. Interestingly enough, the game account in the *Oregonian* does not mention the incident, only that Baum singled in a run (*Oregonian*, August 23, 1904).

98. *Los Angeles Times*, December 4, 1904.

99. *Los Angeles Times*, November 30, December 6, December 8, December 14 and December 15, 1904. The night before the series started, Fisher had a change of heart and said that Morley had convinced him the series between their teams was for the pennant, undoubtedly realizing that a series with nothing at stake would not draw well. The teams augmented their rosters. San Francisco outfielder George Hildebrand played for Los Angeles. Oscar Jones played for the Looloos but Frank Chance did not, nor did Warren Hall or Del Mason. Tacoma was without Truck Eagan, who had his arm broken by Chance on a stolen base attempt on November 5. San Francisco's Danny Shay replaced him in the Tigers lineup. Joe Corbett also pitched and played second base for the Tigers. The "forfeits" were pure theatrics as only Jim Morley could produce. On consecutive days, Morley had his team take the field and had his pitcher throw three pitches to catcher Bobby Eager, thereby "retiring" an imaginary batter. The Angels then left the field to celebrate their "victory." Morley claimed his team had won the series six games to five,

but no one paid much attention to the stunt (*Los Angeles Times*, November 6 and December 5, 1904).

100. *Los Angeles Times*, December 14, 1904.

101. *Oregonian*, December 15, 1904; *Los Angeles Times*, November 27 and December 16, 1904.

102. *Los Angeles Times*, February 15 and September 17, 1905. Because of the Lewis and Clark Exposition, Portland played its home games in 1905 at a ballpark located where PGE Park stands today rather than at Vaughn Street Park. McLean's major league career ended after he smashed a chair over the head of New York Giants coach Dick Kinsella. He was fatally shot through the heart six years later during an altercation in a Boston bar. Garvin was a heavy drinker who had several scrapes with the law, including shooting at a policeman in a Chicago saloon. He drank between innings and always carried a large knife on him, even when pitching. Garvin was not the only loose cannon in his household; his wife was declared insane on several occasions, the last time while Garvin was pitching for Seattle in 1906. He succumbed to tuberculosis in Fresno in June 1908 (*Chicago Tribune*, August 29, 1902; *Oakland Tribune*, September 29, 1906; *Los Angeles Times*, June 18, 1908; *St. Louis Post-Dispatch*, June 12, 1915; *New York Times*, June 12 and July 15, 1915; *Boston Globe*, March 25 and March 26, 1921).

103. *Los Angeles Times*, July 31, 1905. The games were played in forty-seven and fifty-three minutes.

104. *Seattle Times*, July 9, 1905. Shields held the strikeout record until 1971 when Burt Hooton tied the mark while pitching for Tacoma. (Sacramento's Fay Thomas also struck out nineteen batters, against Hollywood in 1930, but did it in thirteen innings.) A tough customer who never visited a doctor and preferred to pull out his own teeth with pliers rather than visit a dentist, Shields got into trouble in September 1905. He and catcher Cliff Blankenship were ordering at a lunch wagon in Seattle when an African American sailor sat beside them. A native of Tennessee, Shields objected to a black man sitting with him at the counter. He cursed the sailor and punched him, knocking him to the ground. When a policeman attempted to arrest Shields for assault he resisted and Blankenship came to his aid. Shields was finally knocked unconscious by the officers and dragged to jail. At first it was announced Shields had been fined one hundred dollars and suspended for the remainder of the 1905 season, but by early October he was again pitching for Seattle (*Seattle Times*, September 11 and September 12, 1905; *Sporting News*, September 9, 1953).

105. *Oregonian*, June 22, 1905. With Seattle runners taking off from first and second, Schlafly caught a low line drive, stepped on second to force the runner who had left that base and tagged the runner from first.

106. Whalen was chastised by the *San Francisco Call* for sulking in a 10–3 loss to Seattle on November 12, 1904. He responded by closing out the 1904 season in style, shutting out Portland twice and allowing only one run in two starts against Oakland to end the season. He began 1905 with shutouts of Seattle on March 30 and April 2, followed by shutouts against Portland on April 6 and April 9. The streak ended when he gave up five runs in the first inning against Tacoma on April 13 (*San Francisco Call*, November 13, 1904).

107. *San Francisco Chronicle*, November 19, 1905; *Los Angeles Times*, November 10 and November 23, 1905. Tozer's streak began with a scoreless inning against Seattle on October 28 and then two innings in relief of Dolly Gray on November 1. This was followed by shutouts of Portland on November 2, Tacoma on November 9 and November 12, and Seattle on November 18. The streak ended in the third inning of his next start, against Portland. Los Angeles shortstop Jimmy Toman made a throwing error that allowed Jake Atz to reach safely. Deacon Van Buren then stroked a double to score Atz and the streak was over. Tozer eventually won the game in eleven innings, shutting out Portland after the third.

108. Nagle appeared in thirteen games, pitching 110 in-

nings while allowing only twenty-three runs, an average of fewer than two per game. He added two more wins without a loss in the playoff against Tacoma.

109. *San Francisco Chronicle*, July 16, July 17 and July 18, 1905; *San Francisco Call*, July 16 and July 17, 1905; *Los Angeles Times*, July 17, July 28, August 3 and August 5, 1905. Mrs. Bert first told police that her husband heard a noise outside and was shot when he investigated. Then she claimed he came home drunk that night and was having paranoid delusions. Bert had been arrested for public drunkenness in 1900 but friends had tried to explain that as a misunderstanding, saying Bert was dazed after a fall from a buggy. Andrew Clunie claimed that Bert drank heavily because of a serious, undisclosed illness that was going to require surgery, a prospect that greatly frightened him. The family's subterfuge led to a number of rumors, including one that involved Mrs. Bert shooting her husband. She filed for divorce in June 1906, less than a year after the suicide attempt, on a charge of cruelty. Her claims included Bert's slow response in defending her against accusations she had shot him (*San Francisco Chronicle*, March 24, 1900; *San Francisco Call*, June 16, 1906).

110. *San Francisco Call*, August 25, 1905.

111. *Los Angeles Times*, August 31, 1905.

112. *Los Angeles Times*, August 31, 1905. Morley was required to reapply for the franchise, which he did, allowing league directors to claim that Morley had been chastened (*Los Angeles Times*, October 1, 1905).

113. *Los Angeles Times*, September 25, 1905.

114. Los Angeles easily defeated Tacoma in the post-season playoff series, five games to one. Just before that series, Morley and Fisher played first base when their teams faced each other in the nightcap of the season-ending doubleheader. Each collected a hit and made an error in a game called after five innings (*Los Angeles Times*, December 4, 1905).

115. *Los Angeles Times*, September 25, October 2 and October 7, 1905. There were rumors that the Tacoma franchise was going to be moved to Spokane (*Spokane Evening Chronicle*, November 15, 1904).

116. *San Jose Mercury*, November 18, 1905.

117. *San Jose Mercury*, November 19, 1905.

118. *Los Angeles Times*, October 1, 1905.

119. *Los Angeles Times*, October 14, 1905. Fisher, a notorious raconteur, told stories years later about how poor attendance was in both Tacoma and Fresno, where his team landed in 1906. He claimed that one day in Fresno there was only one fan in the stands. Fisher's account included the umpire looking at the stands and instead of saying "Ladies and Gentlemen," he stopped and instead announced, "Dear sir." It is often claimed that the record low for attendance at a PCL game is one, set November 8, 1905, in a contest between Oakland and Portland at Idora Park. However, the "record" seems to be related to Fisher's story — contemporary game accounts do not indicate that attendance was limited to a single individual, and later published versions of that record low attendance invariably include the umpire's "Dear Sir" remark from Fisher's account. The *San Francisco Examiner* did report that only one fan was in the grandstand on November 8, 1905, but did not state whether there were other fans elsewhere in the ballpark. Since official league records prior to 1906 were destroyed in the San Francisco Earthquake, it is probable that Fisher's exaggerated story is the source for this "record" (*San Francisco Examiner*, November 9, 1905; *San Francisco Chronicle*, June 7, 1943; *San Mateo Times*, June 7, 1943).

120. *Bakersfield Californian*, November 30, 1905.

Chapter Three

1. *Los Angeles Times*, December 20, 1905 and January 12, 1906.

2. *Los Angeles Times*, January 12 and January 24, 1906.

Fisher did receive a concession; the 1906 schedule included one series each against Portland, Seattle, and Oakland that his team would host at Chutes Park (*Los Angeles Times*, March 24, 1906).

3. *Los Angeles Times*, January 25, 1906.

4. *The Sporting News*, December 9, 1905; *Los Angeles Times*, January 12, 1906. The *San Francisco Examiner* had published articles critical of open gambling at Recreation Park and cautioned that turning a blind eye to the practice could easily corrupt the game. *The Sporting News*, reporting the results of the investigation, claimed that Seals pitcher Jimmy Whalen had refused an offer of four hundred dollars from gamblers to throw a game.

5. *Oakland Tribune*, January 9, 1906; *San Francisco Chronicle*, January 10, 1906; *San Francisco Call*, January 15, 1906; *Sporting Life*, February 3, 1906.

6. *Oakland Tribune*, March 6, 1906; *San Francisco Chronicle*, March 6, 1906.

7. *Los Angeles Times*, April 19, 1906.

8. *Los Angeles Times*, April 30, 1906.

9. United States Geological Service. By comparison, the rupture in the 1989 Loma Prieta Earthquake, along the same fault line, was only twenty-five miles long.

10. *Los Angeles Times*, July 22, 1906.

11. *The Sporting News*, May 5, 1906. The injured players were Pat Donohue and Jimmy McHale.

12. *Los Angeles Times*, April 22 and April 28, 1906.

13. The description of the fire breaks at Eighth and Harrison are included in a 1908 University of California master's thesis, "The Progress of the Fire in San Francisco April 18th–21st 1906 as Shown by an Analysis of Original Documents," by Lawrence J. Kennedy, which was based on papers from a committee appointed by Mayor Eugene Schmitz. A description is also in the official report of Ninth District Battalion Chief John J. Conlon. The ballpark is not mentioned in either report, but Conlon stated that he dynamited the northeast corner of Eighth and Harrison, across the street from the stadium, temporarily halting the march of the blaze in that direction. Despite this effort, the fire eventually jumped Eighth Street further north and then burned south all the way to Harrison, engulfing Recreation Park. *Sporting News* correspondent William J. Boradori witnessed the flames engulf the ballpark "like so much kindling wood" from his vantage point about two blocks away. The ballpark site is still clearly visible today, bounded by Harrison Street, Eighth Street, Ringold Street and Gordon Street. The property serves as the company garage for Gray Line of San Francisco and Coach USA Bus Lines (*The Sporting News*, May 26, 1906).

14. *Los Angeles Times*, April 24, 1906.

15. *Los Angeles Times*, April 28 and May 4, 1906; *Oakland Tribune*, June 15, 1906. Judge McCredie paid for the California teams to come north. Idora Park was the Oaks home field from 1904 through 1906. The team had played at what became known as Freeman's Park through 1903 and then returned there in 1907 (*Oakland Tribune*, April 13, 1904, March 20 and March 28, 1907; *Oregonian*, October 13, 1910).

16. *Los Angeles Times*, April 29, April 30, May 1, 1906. The 1905 season had been a financial nightmare. H.L. Baggerly, sports editor of the *San Francisco Bulletin*, provided the summary of the season in *Spalding's Official Base Ball Guide* and wrote, "There must be some retrenchment or Base Ball is doomed in this neck of the woods."

17. *Seattle Post-Intelligencer*, May 5, 1906; *Los Angeles Times*, May 5, 1906. Agnew had sent a telegram to J.H. Farrell, seeking permission to disband his team as Morley proposed to do. Despite Agnew's ultimate decision to remain in the PCL, rumors persisted that Seattle was going to quit or the franchise would not return in 1907. Eugene Bert traveled to Seattle in September to investigate reports that Agnew was going to shut down operations rather than make a southern trip. Bert threatened to confiscate the team's $1,500 guarantee and withhold its share of the relief money if it did not complete the schedule. Mike Fisher also claimed that Morley had contacted Fresno team president A.B. Evans about shutting down the PCL for the year, but Evans had refused to listen to him (*Fresno Morning Republican*, September 10 and September 15, 1906; *Los Angeles Times*, November 5, 1906).

18. *Los Angeles Herald*, May 17, May 18 and May 23, 1906.

19. *Los Angeles Herald*, May 22, 1906; *Los Angeles Times*, May 21 and May 22, 1906. The statement, signed by each Los Angeles player, read, "Your release is hereby granted you by the Los Angeles ball club for and in consideration of an agreement on your part to report to the Los Angeles Baseball Association prepared to play ball under said Los Angeles Baseball Association's management for the season of 1907."

20. *Los Angeles Times*, May 23, 1906.

21. *Los Angeles Herald*, May 23, 1906; *Los Angeles Times*, May 23 and May 25, 1906. Those joining Dillon included outfielders Curt Bernard, Gavvy Cravath (who brought the bat) and Rube Ellis, pitcher Fred Bergmann and infielder Mac McClelland.

22. *Los Angeles Times*, May 25, 1906; *Oakland Tribune*, October 24, 1929.

23. *Los Angeles Times*, June 24, 1906.

24. *Los Angeles Times*, July 4, 1906.

25. *Los Angeles Herald*, August 31, 1906; *Los Angeles Times*, August 31, 1906.

26. *Los Angeles Times*, June 6, 1901; *Bakersfield Californian*, March 14, 1929.

27. In his farewell to life in a Portland uniform during a doubleheader against Oakland on August 26, McLean went seven-for-seven, including six singles and a double that rolled under the outfield fence to score three runs (*Oregonian*, August 27, 1906).

28. *Oakland Tribune*, August 13, 1906; *Los Angeles Times*, August 13, 1906. It was a miracle that Dillon survived. Along with umpire George Hodson and players John Gochnaur and George Wheeler, Dillon was riding an electric trolley car on Telegraph Avenue, having left Idora Park following a game. The car made a stop at a powerhouse and then headed down the street at full speed in an attempt to make up lost time. The motorman failed to yield at a street crossing for a passenger train carrying two hundred people and the passenger train struck the street car in the center, throwing it off the tracks and dragging it fifty feet. The motorman claimed that his brakes failed. George Hodson was hurled through a window and suffered scalp wounds, George Wheeler was thrown from the car, and Dillon, who had been standing on the front platform, was tossed twenty feet and landed on his head, cutting him severely. Gochnaur emerged unscathed — just as he had in the San Francisco earthquake four months before.

29. *Oakland Tribune*, February 22, 1906. Schmidt also failed to win a game for Los Angeles. He pitched in only eight games combined for Fresno and Los Angeles and was winless in six decisions.

30. *Los Angeles Times*, August 19, 1906; *Fresno Morning Republican*, September 19, 1906. Hall was not particularly thrilled about going to Fresno. He asked for and received his release a couple of weeks later. Fisher also tried local talent, including Joaquin Robbins, who was billed as the great-grandson of an Indian chief, and a seven-foot-tall pitcher named Ed Blank. Blank lasted into the fourth inning in his only appearance while Robbins lasted only an inning (*Oakland Tribune*, September 3, 1906; *Fresno Morning Republican*, October 7, October 8, October 11 and October 15, 1906).

31. *Fresno Morning Republican*, November 2 and November 7, 1906. Team captain Charlie "Demon" Doyle replaced Fisher for the final four games of the season. Under Doyle, Fresno had a win, a loss and a tie. The last game of the season was rained out. Orval Overall, returning home from a National League season in which he had won sixteen games, played first base for Fresno in the tie game and was scheduled to pitch the game that was rained out (*Fresno Morning Republican*, November 5, 1906).

32. *Washington* Post, November 6, 1908; *New York Times*, July 19 and December 20, 1908. On November 3, 1908, Mike Fisher boarded a steamer bound for China on the first leg of a good-will exhibition tour with the first professional team to visit Japan, an all-star group of major and minor league players billed as the Reach All-Americans. Besides Fisher, whose toupee was said to be "poised especially for the occasion," those making the voyage included pitchers Bill Burns, Pat Flaherty and Jack Graney, catchers Jack Bliss and Nick Williams, infielders Babe Danzig, Jim Delahanty, Brick Devereaux and Harry McArdle, and outfielders Heine Heitmuller, George Hildebrand and Joe Curtis. Ty Cobb had originally agreed to go but changed his mind, using his wife's health as an excuse. Japanese players from Waseda University had previously traveled to the United States to play in 1905 and the University of Washington made a reciprocal trip three years later, but Fisher was the first to take professionals to Japan. When the Reach team traveled to the first game, against Waseda University, people lined the streets for three miles from the Imperial Hotel to the ballpark in Tokyo. The second game was against Keio University, considered the best team in Japan, and they gave Fisher's group all it could handle before losing, 2–0. The trip was a success; the only dicey moment came when it was decided to mix the teams. Jack Graney and Nick Williams acted as the battery for the Japanese team and a Japanese battery played for the All-American squad. At one point, Graney had control problems and walked four batters in a row. The Japanese fans thought Graney was pitching badly on purpose to give the Americans an advantage and many started leaving the stadium. The batteries were immediately switched back. The All-Americans won all seventeen games they played in Japan. They also played in China, the Philippines and Hawaii. Fisher stayed in touch with the game, organizing annual reunions of players from his favorite team, the 1904 Tacoma Tigers. The gatherings took place during the 1930s at Seals Stadium and were co-hosted by Charlie Graham, who was by then owner of the San Francisco Seals. Fisher was selected as the Pacific Coast League representative to the centennial celebration for baseball held in Cooperstown in 1939. He became wealthy after his baseball days, opening a chain of dancing emporiums in Seattle, Oakland and San Francisco. Fisher died in June 1943, a few days after his brother Moses; he was too ill to be told about his brother's death (*Detroit Free Press*, August 30, 1908; *Sporting Life*, October 31 and November 21, 1908 and January 2, 1909; *San Francisco Call*, November 4, 1908; *Los Angeles Times*, August 2, 1936; *San Francisco Chronicle*, June 7, 1943; *San Mateo Times*, June 7, 1943; *The Sporting News*, June 10, 1943).

33. *San Francisco Call*, January 29, 1907; *Los Angeles Times*, January 28, January 29 and January 30, 1907. Bert died only three years later. He was discovered two days before his forty-fourth birthday in a rented room on Fillmore Street in San Francisco. Emaciated and hemorrhaging due to the effects of alcoholism, the former PCL president was taken, semi-conscious, to the Central Emergency Hospital and placed in a detention cell. He died a week later (*San Francisco Call*, February 12 and February 19, 1910; *San Francisco Chronicle*, February 12, 1910).

34. *Los Angeles Times*, July 22 and December 8, 1906.

35. *Los Angeles Times*, January 17 and January 21, 1907; *Seattle Post-Intelligencer*, January 21, 1907.

36. *Fresno Morning Republican*, March 3, 1907; *Los Angeles Times*, March 3, 1907. Fresno was reimbursed for expenses accumulated in preparation for the 1907 season and each of the four remaining teams were allowed to draft one player from the Raisin Eaters roster. The league then assigned other players still under contract to Seattle and Fresno to other teams within the league (*Los Angeles Times*, March 6, 1907; *San Francisco Call*, March 31, 1907).

37. *Oakland Tribune*, October 24, 1929.

38. *Oakland Tribune*, January 22, 1937; *The Sporting News*, January 28, 1937.

39. *Oakland Tribune*, February 9, 1898 and January 20, 1937.

40. *San Francisco Chronicle*, March 24, 1907; *Oakland Tribune*, March 26, 1907.

41. *Los Angeles Times*, August 4, 1907.

42. *San Francisco Call*, March 29, March 31 and April 7, 1907.

43. *San Francisco Call*, August 19, 1907; *Oakland Tribune*, August 19, 1907. Carlisle's explosive production caught the eye of the Boston Red Sox, who purchased both him and Gavvy Cravath a couple of days later (*Los Angeles Times*, August 21, 1907).

44. *San Francisco Call*, May 8, 1907.

45. *Los Angeles Times*, April 7, 1957.

46. Although Dillon was an excellent judge of talent, he was famous for letting one great player get away. In 1905, he was persuaded to watch a lanky teenager pitch for a semi-pro team in Olinda, California. Afterward Dillon declared, "Well, he won't do yet. He telegraphs everything he throws." The pitcher was Walter Johnson. Dillon would hear about his negative appraisal of Johnson for the rest of his life (*Los Angeles Times*, September 21, 1913).

47. *Los Angeles Times*, October 17, 1909.

48. *Los Angeles Times*, May 20 and May 27, 1908.

49. There was considerable talent on some California State League rosters at the time. Sacramento's Harry Hooper went directly to the Boston Red Sox in 1909 and was joined there a year later by Alameda's Duffy Lewis to form, along with Tris Speaker, one of the greatest outfields in history. Pitcher Harry Krause went straight from the CSL to the Philadelphia Athletics and was a rookie phenomenon in 1909, winning his first eleven games and finishing 18–8 with a 1.39 earned run average. San Jose pitcher Frank Arellanes was sold to the Boston Red Sox late in 1908 and won sixteen games for them the next year. Ex-big leaguers on CSL rosters included Joe Nealon, Elmer Stricklett, Ham Iburg and Danny Shay. In early September 1908, Hal Chase, in the midst of a contract dispute with the New York Highlanders, showed up in Stockton and was put in the lineup. Frank Chance had connections with the Fresno franchise; he had even played there in 1905 after the National League season ended. There were a number of ex-Pacific Coast League stars in the CSL as well, including Brick Devereaux, Jimmy Shinn, Jimmy Whalen and Spider Baum.

50. *San Francisco Chronicle*, December 2, 1908.

51. *San Francisco Chronicle*, December 3, 1908. Ewing announced that several unacceptable demands were made, including the California State League's insistence on retaining all its players and using Recreation Park when the Seals were on the road. The PCL president said he was determined to place a team in Sacramento — the heart of the California State League's market — and take the fight to the outlaws. Cy Moreing evidently felt Ewing was bluffing. He mistakenly thought that Walter McCredie would not stand for another team being placed in California (*Oakland Tribune*, December 8, 1908).

52. *San Francisco Chronicle*, December 18, 1908.

53. *Stockton Evening Mail*, December 22 and December 23, 1908; *San Francisco Chronicle*, December 20 and December 22, 1908. Pulliam and Johnson came away equally frustrated as PCL officials. Johnson warned the California League owners that "they did not know what war was like." The *Stockton Evening Mail* countered by praising Moreing's stand and editorialized, "The fight was made for right and justice."

54. *Sacramento Union*, December 31, 1908.

55. *Sacramento Union*, January 2, 1909; *Los Angeles Times*, January 1 and January 3, 1909.

56. *Los Angeles Times*, January 22, 1909.

57. *Los Angeles Times*, January 15, January 16, January 22 and January 27, 1909. Fred Maier was a director of the company that operated Chutes Park; unfortunately, he would die a few days after the 1909 season began following an operation for appendicitis. The Tigers also drafted two players from each of the four established PCL teams. Sacramento was al-

lowed to keep its roster intact, including any outlaw players it managed to retain (*Los Angeles Times*, April 8 and April 12, 1909).

58. *Los Angeles Times*, January 7, 1909. This action was significant because higher classified leagues could draft not only players, but also territory from other minor leagues. Additionally, they could resolve their own internal disputes or submit them directly to the National Board of Arbitration, rather than having the Baseball Commission rule on their affairs.

59. *San Francisco Call*, January 8, January 21 and February 27, 1909; *Los Angeles Times*, February 24, 1909; *Oakland Tribune*, February 26, 1909. It was also said that the California State League would place a team in Los Angeles and install Hal Chase as manager.

60. *Stockton Daily Evening Record*, April 27, 1909.

61. *Oakland Tribune*, July 10, 1909.

62. *Stockton Daily Evening Record*, July 12, 1909; *New York Times*, November 9, 1909.

63. *San Francisco Chronicle*, June 9, 1909; *San Francisco Call*, June 9, 1909; *Oakland Tribune*, June 9, 1909. Henley and Oakland pitcher Jimmy Wiggs, a thirty-two-year-old veteran of major league trials with Cincinnati and Detroit, pitched the twenty-four-inning 1–0 game, one of the most remarkable contests in PCL history. The size of the crowd increased as the game continued and word spread about the epic pitcher's duel. The *Chronicle* called it the best baseball game ever played west of the Rockies. It was not the only pitching duel in the PCL that day — Sacramento's Jack Fitzgerald battled Portland's Jack Graney to a 1–1 tie in eighteen innings before that game was called due to darkness.

64. *San Francisco Call*, July 2, July 3, July 4, July 5, July 6 and July 7, 1909. The streak began on July 1 when the Seals held Sacramento scoreless for the final three innings of a 3–1 loss to Sacramento. Then the Seals won on shutouts by Frank Browning, Cack Henley, Ralph Willis, Ed Griffin and Browning again, on a no-hitter. The Seals streak extended to fifty-one innings before Oakland scored a run off Frank Eastley in the fourth inning of a game on July 6.

65. *Los Angeles Times*, October 10, 1909.

66. *Los Angeles Times*, August 29, 1909.

67. *Los Angeles Times*, July 27, 1909. Smith changed his mind and did not jump.

68. *Los Angeles Times*, September 6, 1909.

69. *Los Angeles Times*, September 28, 1909.

70. *Los Angeles Times*, October 28, November 17, November 20, November 22, November 24, and December 1, 1909 and January 5, January 6 and January 8, 1910.

71. *Los Angeles Times*, September 28, 1909.

72. *San Francisco Call*, November 16, 1909; *Los Angeles Times*, August 29, 1909.

Chapter Four

1. *Los Angeles Times*, November 11, 1913 and February 17, 1915; *The Sporting News*, August 9, 1934.

2. *Spokane Chronicle*, June 17 and July 7, 1909; *Washington Post*, January 17, 1911; *Boston Globe*, May 26, 1911.

3. *Oregonian*, July 5, 1910. In both games the only hits for Vernon came from their pitchers. Roy Willett singled off Bill Steen in the fifth inning of the first game while John Brackenridge singled off Gregg in the eighth inning of the nightcap.

4. *Oregonian*, July 10 and July 11, 1910.

5. *Oakland Tribune*, July 14, 1910.

6. *San Francisco Examiner*, September 19, 1910.

7. Bodie, who gave numerous explanations for the origin of his baseball name, was often said to be the inspiration for Ring Lardner's famous *You Know Me, Al* stories. However, Bodie insisted in a 1942 interview that the origin of the char-

acter had come from his own observations of pitcher Flame Delhi. Bodie said, "I put the finger on Flame as a fellow who constantly talked a good job of pitching and gave Ring a lot of boasts I had heard him make to other players and his fine wife, a little woman half Flame's size, who believed everything Flame told her." That is not to say Ping was shy about touting his ability. He supposedly once trained a parrot to say, "Ping made good," and had his seven-year-old son march up and down the aisles of the stadium proclaiming, "My daddy can out hit any man in baseball!" Bodie's lack of foot speed was legendary. After being thrown out trying to steal a base, New York sportswriter Bugs Baer famously said of Bodie, "He had larceny in his heart, but his feet were honest" (*New York Times*, May 26, 1914; *The Sporting News*, April 9, 1942 and December 27, 1961).

8. *Los Angeles Times*, September 10, 1910.

9. *San Francisco Call*, September 11, 1910; *Los Angeles Times*, September 11, 1910.

10. *San Francisco Chronicle*, September 14, 1910; *Los Angeles Times*, September 14, 1910.

11. *San Francisco Chronicle*, September 14, 1910.

12. *San Francisco Call*, September 18, 1910.

13. *San Francisco Chronicle*, September 18, 1910.

14. *San Francisco Chronicle*, September 20 and September 21, 1910; *Chicago Tribune*, November 9, 1906 and June 29, 1910; *New York Times*, July 13 and August 18, 1910; *Los Angeles Times*, September 14 and September 20, 1910. Walker pitched one game for the Cincinnati Reds on June 28, 1910, a blowout loss to the Cubs, surrendering two runs on four hits in three innings. On July 12 he signed with the New York Giants and was placed under the supervision of the notorious Bugs Raymond — a legendary drinker who himself was watched by private detectives because of his inclination toward mischief. With Raymond as his guide, the young pitcher predictably got into trouble. Walker disappeared on August 17 after learning he was suspected of assaulting a chambermaid at the Hotel Braddock in New York City. He was also accused of beating an elevator man who came to the woman's defense. Walker had not played for New York. He surfaced in Portland, Oregon, under the name Fred Mitchell and signed with the Seals on August 31. Not everyone believed the player was as mysterious as the Seals made him out to be. The *Oakland Tribune* called Mitchell "a bald fake to attract the suckers" (*Oakland Tribune*, September 25, 1910).

15. *San Francisco Call*, October 9, 1910; *San Francisco Chronicle*, October 9, 1910.

16. *San Francisco Call*, October 12, 1910; *San Francisco Chronicle*, October 12, 1910.

17. *Oregonian*, August 17, 1910; *Oakland Tribune*, August 17, 1910. In the second inning, Gregg struck out Don Cameron, Harry Wolverton and George Cutshaw on nine pitches.

18. *Los Angeles Times*, September 1 and September 3, 1910.

19. *Oregonian*, September 8, 1910; *San Francisco Call*, September 8, 1910.

20. *Oakland Tribune*, September 13, 1910; *San Francisco Call*, September 13, 1910. Gregg's fourth one-hitter was an eight-inning complete game; Portland was the visiting team and Oakland had already won the game after the top of the ninth. Harl Maggert led off the game for Oakland, beating out an infield grounder on "an exceedingly close play" for the Oaks' only hit.

21. *Los Angeles Times*, October 16 and October 17, 1910; *Oregonian*, October 17, 1910. Part of that streak included a doubleheader shutout of Sacramento by Vean Gregg on October 9. He defeated Herb Byram in both games, the second of which was called after five innings. The Angels finally ended the eighty-eight-inning shutout streak when Gregg walked the bases loaded and then surrendered a single that scored two runs (*Sacramento Union*, October 10, 1910).

22. *Oregonian*, October 2, October 3, October 9 and October 12, 1910; *Oakland Tribune*, October 2 and October 3, 1910; *Spokane Chronicle*, October 12, 1910; *San Francisco*

Chronicle, October 12, 1910; *The Sporting News*, October 20, 1910. Judge Graham had warned McCredie not to play Hetling but he did anyway. It was claimed Hetling had a contract with Spokane and was ineligible to play for Portland. McCredie denied that, saying Hetling had never been sold or released by the Beavers. It was clear Hetling was ineligible to play for one of the teams but that issue was not sorted out until after the season was over.

23. *Oregonian*, October 12 and October 13, 1910; *Oakland Tribune*, October 12, 1910. The *Oregonian* published two versions of league standings: one sans forfeits and another "as President Graham sees it."

24. *Oregonian*, October 13, 1910.

25. *Oregonian*, November 19, 1910; *Los Angeles Times*, November 20, 1910 and January 21, 1911; *Sporting Life*, January 28 and February 18, 1911.

26. *Oakland Tribune*, November 6, 1910; *Oregonian*, November 7, 1910.

27. The Tigers played twice a week at Vernon as well as on special holidays; the remaining home games were played at Washington Park.

28. *Los Angeles Times*, January 15, 1911. Among the players working on the new ballpark were Walter Carlisle, Elmer Thorsen, and Jimmy Wiggs.

29. *Los Angeles Times*, February 26 and March 3, 1911.

30. *Los Angeles Times*, August 28, 1910 and January 15, 1911.

31. *Los Angeles Times*, March 19, 1911.

32. *Los Angeles Times*, March 8, 1911.

33. *Los Angeles Times*, March 9, 1911.

34. *Los Angeles Times*, March 12, 1911.

35. *Los Angeles Times*, March 14, March 15, March 16, March 18, March 22, March 23, and March 27, 1911. Apparently Tozer, Pete Daley, Doc Finlay, newspaperman Lou Guernsey, horseracing enthusiast Florence Israel and a group of other hangers-on went to a dance hall. Returning to the hotel the evening of March 13, Israel decided to retire for the night while the other revelers chose to continue their party. After that things get a little murky. Awakened by the group when pebbles were thrown at his window, Israel claimed that he picked up a rifle and shot into the air in jest. Others insisted he fired down on the group until someone yelled, "Point that gun up; you'll shoot somebody." Other versions had Tozer retrieving a gun and shooting back at Israel but missing because someone hit the weapon as it was fired. Whatever transpired, Guernsey was wounded slightly in the foot and Tozer was shot twice, once in each shoulder. Doc Finlay quickly rushed Tozer to a hospital in Riverside where it was determined that the injuries were not life threatening. The same could not be said about the potential harm to Tozer's career; it was thought the wound to his pitching shoulder was particularly severe. It was decided to leave the bullets where they were. There was never a satisfactory explanation of the incident. Police were certain alcohol was a major factor and rumors surfaced about an argument involving a woman, but neither side was particularly cooperative, instead reaching agreement not to press charges. The case was dropped because none of the stories made any sense. Tozer returned to the mound on April 30, only six weeks after being wounded, and pitched like his old self in two starts. Then on May 9, Tozer entered a game against Oakland as a center fielder when a teammate had to leave the contest after being spiked. Batting in the eighth inning, Tozer was hit by a pitch that broke a bone just above his right wrist, knocking him out of action again for an extended period. While sidelined with the second injury, he was arrested, along with Doc Finlay, for public drunkenness on a Santa Monica beach at four o'clock in the morning, evidence that they had not learned their lesson about over-imbibing (*Los Angeles Times*, April 25, May 1, May 10 and May 23, 1911).

36. *Washington Post*, July 31, 1910 and June 4, 1911; *Los Angeles Times*, May 14, 1911.

37. *San Francisco Chronicle*, April 7, 1911.

38. *Sacramento Union*, September 11, 1911. Fitzgerald allowed only two hits over the final thirteen innings of the game, which was originally supposed to be the first of a doubleheader.

39. *Sacramento Union*, September 16, 1911. Baum shut out the Angels over the last eighteen innings and during one stretch allowed only one hit in eleven innings. The veteran pitcher had a hard year; in June, his two-year-old daughter was severely injured when she was struck on the head by a foul ball off of one of Baum's pitches. Then, a month after the twenty-one-inning game, Baum's twenty-two-year-old wife of four years died suddenly from blood poisoning (*Sacramento Bee*, June 15 and October 16, 1911).

40. The speed of Koestner's fastball was confirmed when he sent one crashing into the head of Sacramento's Jimmy Lewis on June 30. Lewis, whose nickname was "Hardhead," collapsed and was unconscious for five minutes, bleeding from both ears because of a fractured skull. Lewis was back in the lineup before the end of the season, but for quite some time wore a leather football helmet while batting (*Sacramento Union*, July 1, 1911; *Los Angeles Times*, July 1, 1911 and June 8, 1913).

41. *Oregonian*, July 7, 1911; *Los Angeles Times*, July 7, 1911. Henderson started the season pitching well, living up to his nickname, "the Ten Thousand Dollar Beauty." He bolted from the hospital once he learned Walter McCredie was going to suspend him.

42. *Los Angeles Times*, June 19 and June 20, 1911; *Oakland Tribune*, June 24, 1911; *Oregonian*, July 3, 1911 and July 6, 1911; *Sacramento Union*, July 6, 1911. Henkle's no-hitter was not without controversy. The game was played in Portland and in the third inning, the official scorer ruled a hit on a grounder fielded too slowly by Beavers first baseman Bill Rapps; the ruling was changed to an error a few innings later. Some accounts state that Henkle's no-hitter came in his first professional game; however, his debut was against Vernon on June 18, and he had also pitched for Seattle in the Northwest League the previous year. Henkle made two more appearances against the Tigers and then pitched on July 2 against Sacramento, surrendering eleven hits and four runs in three and one-third innings — just three days before no-hitting the same team. Articles of the time refer to Henkle's "professional debut." This was likely another way of saying that because of the no-hitter, he was no longer considered a "green busher." Henkle was a junk pitcher who threw mostly curves and changeups; he finished the year with a record of 4–4 for the Beavers.

43. *Los Angeles Times*, May 19, 1914.

44. *Los Angeles Herald*, July 20, 1911; *Los Angeles Times*, July 20, 1911.

45. *Los Angeles Times*, July 20, 1911. After Metzger rounded second and headed toward third, Happy Hogan yelled for Carlisle to throw the ball to first base but the outfielder decided instead to jog over and touch the bag himself. There is record of an earlier unassisted triple play by an outfielder, but it is disputed. On May 8, 1878, Providence National League center fielder Paul Hines was playing in a game against Boston. With runners on second and third and no one out, Hines caught a short pop fly that had drifted beyond the shortstop's reach. He then ran over to third base and touched the bag. This is where the controversy comes in. If both runners had passed third, as some accounts relate, then Hines would have had an unassisted triple play under the rules of the time. However, some accounts say the trailing runner was returning to second base and Hines threw the ball to second for the final out. Therefore, Hines' feat is usually not listed among the list of unassisted triple plays (*Boston Globe*, May 9, 1878).

46. *Los Angeles Times*, July 20, 1911. By 1915, fans were accusing Carlisle of executing his somersault catches purely for show. A hyper-sensitive individual, Carlisle's play began to suffer. Vernon owner Eddie Maier defended his star outfielder, insisting that he somersaulted to avoid injury and indeed, he

played more than two hundred games in four out of five years with the Tigers. The criticism continued and it gnawed at Carlisle. Portland acquired the outfielder in July 1915, but Walter McCredie's sarcastic manner was not a good match for Carlisle's personality and his performance continued to decline. At the beginning of September he was replaced in the lineup by newly acquired Billy Southworth, who homered in his first two games with the Beavers. On September 21, Carlisle was sent up as a pinch-hitter in the ninth inning of a tie game and struck out without swinging the bat, greatly displeasing McCredie, who had harsh words for him after the game. When McCredie needed a pinch-hitter the next day, he used pitcher Harry Krause. McCredie released Carlisle, who remarked, "I don't stand criticism any too well, anyway ... and when McCredie bawled me out the other day I resented it. I don't think I have had a square deal." Harry Williams said that few had thought Carlisle would last with McCredie, pointing out that the outfielder "withers under sarcasm." After leaving Portland, Carlisle spent three years in the Western League and then played sporadically after that (*Los Angeles Times*, May 19, 1914, September 22, September 27 and September 29, 1915; *Oregonian*, September 8, September 22, September 23 and September 26, 1915; *The Sporting News*, May 31, 1945).

47. *San Francisco Chronicle*, September 13, 1911.

48. *Oakland Tribune*, April 2, 1912.

49. *Oakland Tribune*, April 6, 1912.

50. *Los Angeles Times*, April 2, 1912. The experiment with uniform numbers lasted only one year — purists insisted if one could not recognize players by looking at them, they were not true fans. The Beavers did not have their numbers sewn on in time for the home opener, but attached them soon after (*Oregonian*, April 17, 1912).

51. Harry Ables hailed from Terrell, Texas, and was considered somewhat of a black sheep in a devout and wealthy Methodist family. Blessed with incredibly large hands — it was said his hand could completely span a baseball the way another man's might a billiard ball — Ables specialized in breaking off sharp curveballs. He played baseball against his family's wishes; his mother and sister prayed for him to lose whenever he pitched on a Sunday. Ables said he generally did not have much luck when he did so, leading him to reflect, "I'm not much of a Methodist, but this praying business has me guessing." Between pitching assignments he worked as a circus clown, an actor and a member of a cattle crew. Ables reached the major leagues with St. Louis in 1905 and Cleveland in 1909 but by his own admission was tempted too much by nightlife and was quickly sent back in the minors both times. Ables set the all-time Texas League single-season record for strikeouts in 1910, which led to a third shot at the major leagues, with the New York Yankees in 1911. That did not work out either and Ables was acquired by Oakland in May of that year, pitching three shutouts in his first four games with the Oaks and winning twenty-two games, including a no-hitter against Los Angeles. The Oaks built the highest mound in the league to better take advantage of Ables' curveball and in 1912 he was the PCL's best pitcher, winning twenty-five games and recording 303 strikeouts in 363 innings. After his career ended he returned to Texas, served as president of the San Antonio team in the Texas League from 1925–1928 and managed his father's lumberyard (*Los Angeles Times*, August 21, 1912 and July 10, 1913; *The Sporting News*, February 21, 1951).

52. *Oakland Tribune*, April 18, 1912. The winning streak came to an end the next day when the Angels beat the Oaks, 4–2, behind Bill Tozer (*Oakland Tribune*, April 19, 1912).

53. *Los Angeles Times*, August 23 and September 2, 1912.

54. *Los Angeles Times*, September 10, 1912.

55. *San Francisco Call*, November 15, 1903; *Los Angeles Times*, November 12, 1913.

56. Popular with teammates and fans alike, Heitmuller lasted a little more than a year and a half before being sold to

Baltimore during the 1910 season. Even so, when the Athletics split up the World Series money that autumn, Heitmuller received a check for five hundred dollars (*Baltimore Sun*, July 30 and November 3, 1910 and August 2, 1911; *Los Angeles Times*, September 8, 1912).

57. *Los Angeles Times*, October 9, 1912.

58. *Los Angeles Times*, July 7 and September 8, 1912. Heitmuller's choice of a thin-handled bat was unusual for the time, especially for a power hitter.

59. *Los Angeles Times*, August 7 and September 8, 1912.

60. *Los Angeles Times*, August 25, 1912; *Oakland Tribune*, August 25, 1912. When Heitmuller grabbed his bat to lead off the bottom of the ninth for Los Angeles, he vowed to "fix things up." Fans spilled onto the field, with dozens of them waiting at home plate while Heitmuller slowly circled the bases. The description of the crowd's reaction to Heitmuller's home run is an interesting example of early twentieth century sportswriting: "Strong men swooned. Women jabbed each other with hat pins in sheer joy. Invalids who had not walked for years rose up on their hind legs and jumped six feet in the air. Staid, dignified citizens got down on their hands and knees and tried to bite the iron knobs off the chairs. Possibly, some of them succeeded. Oh, it was some frenzy of joy."

61. *Los Angeles Times*, September 8, 1912.

62. *Los Angeles Times*, September 28, 1912.

63. *Los Angeles Times*, September 29, 1912.

64. *Los Angeles Times*, September 30 and October 9, 1912.

65. *Los Angeles Times*, October 9, 1912.

66. *Los Angeles Herald*, October 8, 1912. Heitmuller died at three o'clock in the morning on October 8.

67. *Los Angeles Times*, October 9 and November 13, 1912.

68. *Los Angeles Times*, October 9, 1912. Heitmuller's death was the second emotional blow to the team that season; in May, Andy Briswalter, a pitcher for the Angels from 1907 through 1910, died from tuberculosis at a Monrovia, California sanitarium at age twenty-four (*Sporting Life*, May 25, 1912).

69. *Los Angeles Times*, October 12, 1912. Games at Sacramento and San Francisco were cancelled out of respect for Heitmuller. A funeral was conducted in German at the Heitmuller home in San Francisco, followed by a service in English at St. Paul's German Church. Heitmuller was buried at Mt. Olivet Cemetery. Pallbearers included George Hildebrand, Harry McArdle, Harry Krause, Nick Williams and Doc Strub (*San Francisco Chronicle*, October 12, 1912; *Oakland Tribune*, October 12, 1912).

70. *Oakland Tribune*, September 11 and September 13, 1912. The *Tribune* asserted, "Mitze, in fact, is showing far more baseball ability than Sharpe ever dared show." The paper suggested that the Oaks should leave Mitze in charge for the rest of the season.

71. *Los Angeles Times*, September 23, 1912. Frick's roommate awoke in the early morning hours of September 17 to find the infielder pacing around their room at the Rosslyn Hotel in Los Angeles. Not sensing anything out of the ordinary, the teammate rolled over and went back to sleep. Later, Frick appeared in the lobby of the hotel where the desk clerk joked with him about being up so early. Frick smiled and walked out the front door with nothing but the striped brown suit and black derby hat he was wearing. He even left behind money he had on deposit at the hotel. The Oaks tried locating him for several days and finally had to leave Los Angeles without him. Frick had also disappeared in his previous stint in the PCL, with Seattle in 1905, which had acquired him from Oklahoma City of the Missouri Valley League. In that episode, Frick cleaned out his locker, checked out of his hotel, and returned to Oklahoma without a word to anyone (*San Francisco Chronicle*, August 19, 1905; *Sporting Life*, September 9, 1905).

72. *Los Angeles Times*, October 7, 1912.

73. *Los Angeles Times*, October 24, 1912; *Oakland Tribune*, October 24 and October 27, 1912.

74. *San Francisco Chronicle*, October 28, 1912; *Los Angeles Times*, October 28, 1912.

75. *San Francisco Examiner*, June 2, 1916. Malarkey had been one of the team's most consistent pitchers — his best game came on June 30 when he pitched a no-hit, no-run game for nine innings against San Francisco. Malarkey allowed a hit in the tenth and then the game was called due to a time limit with neither the Oaks nor the Seals scoring a run (*Oakland Tribune*, July 1, 1912).

76. *Oakland Tribune*, October 25, 1912; *Los Angeles Times*, October 25, 1912. The automobile, valued at $2,100, was presented to Hetling on the morning of the final Sunday doubleheader. Bill Lange drove the Chalmers to home plate and then paraded Hetling around the park (*Oakland Tribune*, October 27, 1912).

77. *San Francisco Chronicle*, October 28, 1912; *Oakland Tribune*, October 29, 1912. The Oakland players gave Sharpe a diamond cravat pin, presented to him by Honus Mitze, to show their appreciation.

78. *Oakland Tribune*, December 8 and December 9, 1912; *Los Angeles Times*, December 9, 1912.

79. *Oakland Tribune*, December 10, 1912; *Los Angeles Times*, December 10, 1912; *San Francisco Chronicle*, December 10, 1912.

80. *Los Angeles Times*, December 11, 1912.

81. *Oakland Tribune*, December 12 and December 17, 1912. Some of Walter's friends claimed his actions were a response to a rumor that Ewing planned to fire him and replace him with Leavitt.

82. *Oakland Tribune*, March 20, 1913; *Los Angeles Times*, December 8, 1913. Ables remained in the PCL for three more seasons, compiling losing records each year.

83. *Oakland Tribune*, March 29, 1913; *Los Angeles Times*, March 29, 1913. In early January, St. Louis Browns manager George Stovall visited Patterson, who was living in a tent in the middle of the Mojave Desert with his wife and toddler, trying in vain to recover his health. Stovall realized that Patterson, who was supposed to play for him in St. Louis in 1913, was a very sick man and came away convinced the outfielder would never play again. He took twenty-five dollars from his own pocket to start a fund to help Patterson and his family (*Los Angeles Times*, January 20, 1913).

84. *Oakland Tribune*, July 19 and September 17, 1913.

85. *San Francisco Chronicle*, June 2, 1916. George Stallings married Sharpe's widow eleven months later.

86. *Oakland Tribune*, November 21, 1912; *Los Angeles Times*, November 21, 1912.

87. *Los Angeles Times*, December 16, December 18 and December 25, 1912.

88. *Los Angeles Times*, August 14, 1912.

89. *Los Angeles Times*, December 18, 1912.

90. *Los Angeles Times*, January 26 and February 8, 1913 and December 20, 1914.

91. *Los Angeles Times*, February 2, March 14 and March 27, 1913.

92. *Los Angeles Times*, March 14, 1913. The Angels also played a handful of home games at Venice.

93. *Los Angeles Times*, March 18 and March 27, 1913.

94. *Los Angeles Times*, March 26, 1913. Road uniforms were navy blue with a white stripe.

95. *Los Angeles Times*, March 27, 1913.

96. *Los Angeles Times*, August 25, 1913.

97. *Los Angeles Times*, May 18 and May 23, 1915.

98. *Los Angeles Times*, March 28, 1936. Sportswriter Bill Henry claimed that Hogan's eyesight was so poor he had to turn and face the pitcher when he batted. There were those who insisted the rumors of Hogan's blindness were pure hogwash while others believed Hap was not only blind in one eye, but that the eye in question was made of glass.

99. *Los Angeles Times*, July 30, 1912.

100. Several years later, Hogan's brother was driving down the street in front of Graham's home and Graham's six-year-old son ran into the street and was struck by the car, killing him instantly (*Palo Alto Times*, May 8, 1922; *San Jose Mercury Herald*, May 8, 1922).

101. *Los Angeles Times*, July 20, 1914. Roy Hitt was a short, stocky left-hander whose expansive waistline and habit of snorting earned him the nickname "Rhino." An avid deep-sea fisherman, Hitt had the exclusive right to fish a particular sector of the Pacific Ocean, retaining the claim by working it three months a year. Hitt was also one of the PCL's great pitchers, becoming the second to win two hundred games in league play. He was a seven-time twenty-game winner with his best season coming in 1906 with San Francisco when he won thirty-two games. He played his only major league season in 1907 for the Cincinnati Reds. Hitt returned to the PCL to pitch for Vernon in 1909. Notoriously fond of hot dogs, easily devouring a half-dozen of them each day at the ballpark, it was joked that when the wind was just right, Hitt would catch a whiff of them and begin snorting wildly. Concerned about his pitcher's girth, Hogan reportedly threatened to put a "no hot dog" clause in Hitt's 1915 contract. Hitt threatened to jump to the Federal League and the clause was deleted. By 1916 Hitt was the last of the original Vernon Tigers. His career almost ended a couple of weeks into the season when his appendix turned gangrenous and he nearly died. He returned to pitch in a few games late in the year and then retired to take a job at Standard Oil (*Los Angeles Times, December 28, 1914, October 27, 1915, April 24, April 25, May 1 and August 9, 1916, January 11, 1917).

102. *Los Angeles Times*, May 12, 1914.

103. *Los Angeles Times*, September 24, 1911.

104. *Los Angeles Times*, July 10, 1913.

105. *Los Angeles Times*, October 17, 1913.

106. *Los Angeles Times*, January 16 and January 17, 1914.

107. *Los Angeles Times*, February 16, 1914.

108. *Los Angeles Times*, March 9, 1914. Kenworthy's jump was not for financial reasons. He was independently wealthy after being named one of fourteen heirs in the will of his uncle, a London industrialist, in 1913. Kenworthy's share was about four million dollars. As a result, William Kenworthy became known as "Duke" (*Los Angeles Times*, July 15, 1913).

109. *Oregonian*, January 17, 1914.

110. *Los Angeles Times*, May 8, 1914.

111. *San Francisco Examiner*, May 17, 1914; *San Francisco Chronicle*, May 17, 1914.

112. *Oakland Tribune*, May 17, 1914.

113. *Los Angeles Times*, June 17, 1914.

114. *Oakland Tribune*, July 16, 1914; *Los Angeles Times*, July 14, August 11, and September 16, 1914. At one point the Angels visited Ewing Field and only seventy-five people attended a Friday game. The next day, the Angels' share of gate receipts was forty-one dollars. Actor William Frawley, years after the fact, claimed that the Angels had once wanted umpire Bill Guthrie to call a game at Ewing Field because of the miserable conditions and when Guthrie refused, outfielder Pete Daley took some newspapers with him to center field and set them on fire to keep warm (*Los Angeles Times*, April 11, 1937).

115. *Los Angeles Times*, October 5, 1914.

116. *Sacramento Union*, September 4, 1914; *San Francisco Chronicle*, September 7, 1914; *Oakland Tribune*, September 2, September 7 and October 14, 1914; *Los Angeles Times*, September 4, September 7 and September 17, 1914. The "Missions" played at Ewing Field first, on September 6 for a morning game of a doubleheader against Portland. The afternoon game was played in Oakland. The idea had been for Oakland to have continuous baseball with the Missions playing a mirror home/road schedule of the Oaks. There had been rumors from the beginning that Wolverton would end up at Recreation Park; indeed, naming the team "Missions" fueled speculation since the stadium was located in the Mission District of San Francisco. Walter's lease was to take effect in March 1916 (*San Francisco Chronicle*, November 26, 1914).

117. *Los Angeles Times*, February 25 and July 17, 1914. Doc White had a long, successful career with the Chicago White Sox, setting a record with five straight shutouts during the 1904 season, pitching for the "Hitless Wonders" of 1906, and winning twenty-seven games in 1907. His shutout streak was finally topped by Don Drysdale in 1968. (White lived to see Drysdale break his record and sent a telegram during the streak telling the Dodgers pitcher that he was rooting for him.) White was thirty-five years old when he chose to sign with Venice instead of continuing with the White Sox; he had never before played in the minor leagues. White moved his wife and three children to an apartment across the street from Washington Park so they could watch him play. He even had a signal for his wife to let her know the game was almost over and she should start dinner (*Los Angeles Times*, March 4, 1914 and June 4, 1968).

118. *Los Angeles Times*, July 22, 1914. Orndorff had not played in the PCL since being hit in the head by Oakland's Jack Lively with a pitch in 1910. That injury left Orndorff unable to speak for a time (*Oakland Tribune*, June 6, 1910; *Los Angeles Times*, June 6 and June 7, 1910).

119. *Oregonian*, September 21, 1914; *Los Angeles Times*, October 7, 1914.

120. McGinnity's only win came on the next to the last day of the 1914 season. He shut out Los Angeles for six innings in the seven-inning nightcap of a doubleheader, carrying an 8–0 lead into the last inning when he weakened and was charged with seven runs before a reliever could bail him out. McGinnity's opponent, Tom Hughes, not only lost the game but lost out on a new Ford automobile that Angels owner Henry Berry promised to any Los Angeles pitcher who won twenty-five games for the year. The defeat, made excruciating by the furious rally that brought the Angels to within a run, left Hughes one win short. Teammate Jack Ryan also won twenty-four games. Incidentally, Cack Henley won the first game of the doubleheader for Venice, making him the first pitcher with two hundred career PCL victories, an achievement that went unnoticed at the time (*Los Angeles Times*, October 15 and October 25, 1914).

121. *Los Angeles Times*, June 1, 1913.

122. *Los Angeles Times*, July 5, 1914.

123. *Los Angeles Times*, June 12, 1914.

124. *Los Angeles Times*, December 28, 1914.

125. *San Francisco Chronicle*, October 29 and October 30, 1914; *Los Angeles Times*, October 29, October 30 and November 4, 1914.

126. *San Francisco Chronicle*, October 30, 1914; *Los Angeles Times*, October 30, 1914; *Oregonian*, November 6, 1914.

Chapter Five

1. *Oakland Tribune*, July 16, 1914; *San Francisco Chronicle*, October 27, 1914; *Sacramento Union*, September 29, 1914; *Los Angeles Times*, October 30, 1914.

2. *San Francisco Chronicle*, October 28, 1914; *Los Angeles Times*, October 29, 1914.

3. *San Francisco Chronicle*, October 28, 1914. Cities mentioned included Seattle, Salt Lake City, San Jose, Sacramento and San Diego.

4. *Los Angeles Times*, December 7, December 8 and December 9, 1914; *Salt Lake Evening Telegram*, December 8, 1914. San Diego had made several previous attempts to join the league. In 1912, a blue ribbon committee headed by the legendary Albert Spalding met with Allan Baum, Cal Ewing and Henry Berry to explore establishing a PCL team in San Diego, but investors backed out after learning the cost would be much greater than anticipated. The Panama-California Exposition of 1915 ran for two years and was a major success for San Diego. Created to mark the completion of the Panama Canal and highlight San Diego's importance in trade thanks

to the new waterway, it was intended as an international fair but was scaled back because of the Panama Pacific International Exposition and World's Fair being held the same year in San Francisco. The large park in the center of the city was renamed Balboa Park and many older buildings constructed for that event remain standing today. In March 1915, Eddie Collins led the Chicago White Sox in a three-game series against the Venice Tigers at the park to promote the fair (*San Diego Evening Tribune*, March 8, March 9, March 10 and March 11, 1915).

5. *Salt Lake Tribune*, November 18, 1914; *Salt Lake Evening Telegram*, November 18, 1914. Two thousand dollars for each visiting team was considered adequate to cover expenses as long as each team adhered to the salary limit.

6. *Los Angeles Times*, December 8 and December 17, 1914.

7. *Salt Lake Tribune*, December 18 and December 22, 1914; *Salt Lake Telegram*, December 22, 1914.

8. *Los Angeles Times*, December 1, December 2, December 3, December 6, 1914 and April 2, 1915.

9. *San Francisco Examiner*, December 2, 1914.

10. *San Francisco Chronicle*, December 2, 1914.

11. *Los Angeles Times*, December 2, 1914.

12. *Los Angeles Times*, November 27, 1914.

13. *Salt Lake Tribune*, December 24, 1914; *Los Angeles Times*, December 23 and December 24, 1914; *Oakland Tribune*, February 1, 1915.

14. *Los Angeles Times*, November 27, 1914.

15. *San Francisco Examiner*, December 31, 1914; *San Francisco Chronicle*, December 31, 1914.

16. Ewing Field, which Harry Williams said was located "[in] a spot chiefly famous for its large and apparently inexhaustible supply of wind," continued to host events. The Catholic archdiocese of San Francisco relieved Cal Ewing of responsibility for the lease in 1916 and then rented the stadium for numerous athletic events. There were spring training exhibitions held there for a couple of years after the Seals left. Otherwise, the stadium was used primarily for rugby, football, or as a practice field. It was St. Mary's home football field in the 1920s, and the first East-West Shrine Game was played there in 1925. Other football exhibitions by barnstorming gridiron greats, including Red Grange, Brick Muller and Ernie Nevers, were staged as well. A major fire in June 1926, originating from a carelessly discarded cigar, destroyed the grandstand and bleachers, as well as twelve buildings located across the street. Forty-mile-per-hour winds swept embers more than a mile away and burned an additional forty structures in a fire that the San Francisco fire chief deemed the most serious situation faced by the city since the 1906 earthquake. The field gradually fell into disrepair. It was used mostly for soccer and the occasional boxing match over the last decade of its existence and was torn down ahead of the World's Fair in 1939 because it had become an eyesore. It was replaced by residential development (*Oakland Tribune*, April 9, 1916; *San Francisco Examiner*, November 6, 1916 and June 6, 1926; *Modesto News-Herald*, June 6, 1926; *San Francisco Chronicle*, November 6, 1915 and June 18, 1938).

17. *San Francisco Chronicle*, January 4, 1915; *Detroit Free Press*, January 28, 1915.

18. *Oregonian*, April 20 and April 21, 1913. Heilmann played high school baseball as a shortstop at Sacred Heart in San Francisco. He went hitless in six at-bats for the Beavers in his two-game tryout, with three sacrifice hits and an RBI on a sacrifice fly. That August he was sold back to the Beavers in an unsuccessful attempt to hide him from the draft. McCredie would later say that the loss of Heilmann to Detroit had been a "sore point" with him (*San Francisco Call*, April 28, 1911; *Los Angeles Times*, August 3, 1913; *Detroit Free Press*, November 19, 1913; *Oregonian*, January 28, 1915).

19. *Los Angeles Times*, June 18, 1915. Wolverton was correct in preaching patience, but incorrect in his appraisal of Heilmann's defense. The youngster led PCL first basemen in errors despite playing less than one hundred games. He was never a

stellar defensive player in the major leagues either. But his hitting, which eventually included four American League batting titles — all with averages above .390, including a .403 mark in 1923 — led to his induction into the Baseball Hall of Fame in 1952.

20. *San Francisco Chronicle*, February 15, 1915; *San Francisco Examiner*, February 17, 1915.

21. *San Francisco Chronicle*, January 28, 1915. Fitzgerald was not only a good hitter, he was the fastest man in the PCL if not all of baseball. However, recurring arm problems hampered his career as an outfielder. Fitzgerald had originally come to the Coast to play for Oakland in the deal that allowed Harry Wolverton to leave the Oaks and manage the New York Yankees, but he was released by Bud Sharpe before the season because of his injured throwing arm (*Los Angeles Times*, September 20, 1912 and August 2, 1914).

22. At one point, Walter Schmidt declared he had been unfairly denied the chance to play in the majors for three years and would never play in San Francisco again. Berry made a trip to the Imperial Valley to convince Schmidt and Roy Corhan, who were playing winter baseball there, to change their minds and return to the Seals (*San Francisco Chronicle*, December 14 and December 16, 1914).

23. *Los Angeles Times*, December 20, 1914 and April 10, 1962.

24. *Los Angeles Times*, January 7, 1915.

25. *Salt Lake Tribune*, April 1 and April 5, 1915; *Los Angeles Times*, April 5, 1915.

26. *Los Angeles Times*, March 12, 1915. The Venice road uniforms were gray. The Angels also had new uniforms — blue on the road, white with blue trim at home.

27. *Los Angeles Times*, April 12 and April 21, 1915.

28. *Los Angeles Times*, April 23, 1915.

29. *Los Angeles Times*, November 17, 1914. The league had to pay Williams sixty dollars owed him by Sacramento. The player with the most unorthodox yet legitimate reason for reporting late to Salt Lake City was outfielder Buddy Ryan, who was arrested as he waited to board a train in Portland. He was taken into custody as a result of a complaint filed by his live-in girlfriend of ten years who had grown weary of the continual delay of their wedding. The two married that afternoon and authorities released Ryan so he could join his team at training camp in San Jose (Allan T. Baum correspondence; Dick Dobbins Collection on the Pacific Coast League, California Historical Society; *Salt Lake Tribune*, February 25, 1915).

30. *Salt Lake Tribune*, March 24, March 26, March 27, March 31, April 1 and April 2, 1915. Majestic Park, which had dimensions of 308 feet to left, 319 feet to right and 408 feet to center, was constructed on the southeast corner of a plot of land at State and South Nine streets in downtown Salt Lake City. Because of the muddy conditions and lack of time, only the infield was sod the first year. Grass was planted in the outfield the next year. It was located across the street from Walker's Field, where previous Salt Lake City professional teams had played. Walker's Field had larger dimensions than Majestic Park — 330 feet down the lines and 460 feet to center field. Majestic Park was renamed Bonneville Park prior to the 1917 season and stood until 1932 (Utah History Resource Center; *Salt Lake Tribune*, February 23, 1915).

31. *Salt Lake Tribune*, August 29, 1915; *Los Angeles Times*, September 29, 1915.

32. *Los Angeles Times*, May 30, 1915; *Salt Lake Tribune*, October 29, 1915.

33. *Los Angeles Times*, May 9, 1915.

34. *Los Angeles Times*, May 10 and May 17, 1915.

35. *Los Angeles Times*, May 16, 1915.

36. *Los Angeles Times*, May 17 and May 18, 1915.

37. *Los Angeles Times*, May 24, 1915; *San Francisco Chronicle*, May 24, 1915. White was named acting manager, with Hogan listed officially as manager until the end of the season.

38. *Los Angeles Times*, June 16, 1915. Hogan's assets consisted of ten shares of stock in the Tigers, worth one thousand dollars, and $300 salary due him (*San Francisco Chronicle*, May 27, 1915).

39. *Los Angeles Times*, June 26, 1915. Mike Fisher also held a benefit at one of his dance houses in San Francisco. Among those in attendance were Al Jolson, Bill Lange, Henry Berry and California Governor Hiram Johnson. A sad sidelight to Hogan's death involved his ashes. Cremated shortly after the funeral, his remains were placed in a $45 urn and stored at the Los Angeles Crematory Association, forgotten by all but the staff there. No space for his ashes was ever purchased or rented and the urn was kept in an obscure alcove. Harry Williams wrote about the situation in 1922, and although several people sent letters offering donations for a permanent place for Hogan's remains, there was never any serious effort undertaken to care for them (*San Francisco Chronicle*, June 28, 1915; *Los Angeles Times*, June 9 and July 27, 1922).

40. *Los Angeles Times*, July 12, 1915.

41. *Los Angeles Times*, December 20, 1914, July 26, 1915 and February 4, 1916.

42. *Oakland Tribune*, June 27, 1915.

43. This was considered the "modern" record. From April 22 through June 18, 1897, Willie Keeler had a forty-four-game hitting streak for Baltimore in the National League (*Baltimore Sun*, June 21, 1897).

44. *San Francisco Chronicle*, July 14, 1915; *Oakland Tribune*, July 14, 1915.

45. *Oakland Tribune*, July 15 and July 16, 1915.

46. *Oakland Tribune*, July 15 and July 23, 1915; *Los Angeles Times*, July 23, 1915. Ness failed to get a hit but drove in Oakland's only run with a sacrifice fly. He also walked and grounded out three times.

47. *The Sporting News*, December 23, 1915.

48. *San Francisco Examiner*, August 11, 1915; *Salt Lake Tribune*, August 19, 1915.

49. *San Francisco Chronicle*, February 23, 1915.

50. *San Francisco Examiner*, June 11, 1915; *San Francisco Chronicle*, June 15, 1915; *Los Angeles Times*, June 18, 1915. Wolverton was leaving a friend's house and stood in front of his automobile to crank the starter. Unfortunately, he was parked on a hill and had failed to set the brake. When Wolverton started cranking, the car rolled over him before smashing into a pole. Roy Corhan ran the team in Wolverton's absence but refused the title of acting manager out of respect for his boss.

51. *San Francisco Chronicle*, August 23, 1915; *Los Angeles Times*, August 17, 1915 and January 15, 1916. When Heilmann reported to Detroit in 1916, it still was not certain he was over his vertigo. There was also a question over who owed him his pay during his illness. Pointing out that they had not had benefit of Heilmann's services after July, the Seals argued that Detroit should pay him since he was under contract with them. Heilmann was concerned the dispute would result in his having to spend another season in San Francisco (*San Francisco Chronicle*, December 3 and December 21, 1915 and February 29, 1916).

52. *San Francisco Chronicle*, August 25, 1915.

53. *Detroit Free Press*, August 22, 1915; *San Francisco Chronicle*, August 27, 1915.

54. *Los Angeles Times*, September 16, 1915. A month later the Judge's nephew, Walter, complained, "This thing of bringing out broken-down major leaguers and paying them fancy salaries is bad business." McCredie later told the *Salt Lake Tribune* that he was more bothered by expenses assumed by the league, including the debts of the Sacramento franchise and interest payments on what he called "a useless park in Oakland" (*Salt Lake Tribune*, September 16, 1915; *Los Angeles Times*, October 13, 1915).

55. *Salt Lake Tribune*, September 30, October 5, October 6 and October 7, 1915.

56. *Chicago Tribune*, October 7, 1919. Williams and the White Sox lost the fifth game of the 1919 World Series, 5–0, to the Cincinnati Reds.

57. *San Francisco Chronicle*, November 3 and November 10, 1915.

58. *Salt Lake Tribune*, November 19, 1915.

59. *Salt Lake Tribune*, October 24, 1915.

60. *Oakland Tribune*, November 3, 1915.

61. *Los Angeles Times*, November 26, 1915.

62. *Los Angeles Times*, November 26, 1915.

63. *Chicago Tribune*, December 17, 1915; *Los Angeles Times*, December 17 and December 22, 1915; *Pittsburgh Press*, January 9, 1916.

64. *Chicago Tribune*, January 11, 1901.

65. *Los Angeles Times*, September 17 and September 22, 1912; *Chicago Tribune*, September 18, 1912. Orval Overall said Chance's problems actually stemmed from his first beaning while playing for Fresno as an amateur in the 1890s. Overall, who was then playing for a team in Visalia, said, "Along about the sixth inning the Visalia pitcher flung a high, fast inshoot (sic) and the ball hit Chance on the left side of the head back of the ear. He dropped to the ground as if shot. He was carried from the field unconscious and sent home to Fresno that night on the train. He did not really recover his senses for several days, and for sixteen years his hearing and speech have been affected by that blow."

66. *Los Angeles Times*, November 4 and December 30, 1915 and January 4, January 6 and January 7, 1916. Chance married his wife, Edith Pancake, in 1899. They had been high school sweethearts in Fresno, where they both grew up (*San Francisco Chronicle*, April 7, 1899).

67. *San Francisco Chronicle*, December 25, 1915, January 22, March 10, March 11 and April 7, 1916.

68. *San Francisco Examiner*, February 13, 1916; *San Francisco Chronicle*, February 22, 1914; *Los Angeles Times*, February 16, 1916. A father of nine children, "Brother Joe" had started engineering his fourth and final comeback in 1915. He began pitching in the San Francisco Municipal League and then made a start for Woodland against Oroville in the semi-professional Trolley League. He felt good enough about his performance to ask Seals manager Harry Wolverton for the chance to play again. Corbett made headlines in spring training with San Francisco not only for his comeback, but also for saving the life of a teenager who had attempted suicide by jumping into the ocean (*Woodland Daily Democrat*, August 28 and August 31, 1915; *San Francisco Examiner*, March 2, 1916).

69. *Los Angeles Times*, April 11, 1916.

70. *Los Angeles Times*, March 29, 1916.

71. *Los Angeles Times*, October 22, 1916.

72. *Los Angeles Times*, April 5, 1916; *Los Angeles Herald*, April 5, 1916.

73. *Los Angeles Times*, May 25, 1916.

74. *Oregonian*, April 20, 1916.

75. *Oregonian*, April 30, 1916; *Los Angeles Times*, April 30, 1916. Guisto was sold once it became clear that Portland was not going to contend for the pennant. After balking at first, Guisto reported to Cleveland and played as a reserve through the 1917 season before enlisting in the army for World War I. Gassed during action in the Argonne Forest and the Scheldt, Guisto played off and on with Cleveland through 1923 after his return from the war but claimed he could not tolerate the cold climate after his exposure to the chemical attack. Despite the power he displayed in the Pacific Coast League, Guisto never hit a home run in the major leagues and his lifetime batting average was only .196. He later played several more seasons in the PCL. He returned to St. Mary's as a baseball coach for a quarter-century before retiring in the 1950s. Guisto died in 1989 at age ninety-four. The baseball stadium at St. Mary's is named in his honor (*Los Angeles Times*, August 4, 1923; *The Sporting News*, November 6, 1989).

76. *Salt Lake Telegram*, July 21, 1916. Rodgers' triple play came against Salt Lake City; with Bees base runners Billy Orr and Buddy Ryan at first and second, Rodgers snared a line drive and tagged Orr as he ran toward second, then touched the bag before Ryan could return. Five years later Ryan and Orr were victimized *again* by an unassisted triple play. On July 4, 1921, the two were playing for Sacramento *against* Salt Lake City when Bees shortstop Heine Sand snagged a line drive and caught both men off base (*San Francisco Examiner*, October 26, 1916; *Sacramento Union*, July 5, 1921; *The Sporting News*, July 14, 1921; *Salt Lake Telegram*, July 5, 1921).

77. *San Francisco Examiner*, April 30 and May 2, 1916; *Oakland Tribune*, April 24, 1916; *Los Angeles Times*, April 24, 1916. Corbett, who claimed a "baseball age" of thirty-eight, made the Opening Day roster of the Seals but did not survive the final cut to eighteen players on May 1. He appeared in four games for San Francisco, splitting two decisions through guile and luck as much as anything else. His high point was a complete-game, four-hit victory over the Angels on April 23, despite walking eight batters. It was decided shortly after that game he would be released at the cut-down date. Corbett pitched once more, on what was called "Joe Corbett Day," at Recreation Park against Salt Lake City on April 29. He was allowed to stay on the mound as long as he wanted, pitching into the eighth inning while allowing ten hits and nine runs and walking nine batters. He also managed to get two hits in his three at-bats that day.

78. *San Francisco Examiner*, June 24, 1916; *San Francisco Chronicle*, June 24, 1916. The no-hitter was Fanning's second in the Pacific Coast League. *Examiner* reporter H.M. Walker thought Fanning had been the beneficiary of liberal scorekeeping, feeling that both errors charged to Seals third baseman Bob Jones could have been ruled base hits, but he agreed Fanning had pitched impressively. Fanning was multi-talented; for several years he handled the team's finances on road trips (*Oregonian*, January 17, 1914).

79. *San Francisco Examiner*, August 13, 1916.

80. *San Francisco Examiner*, May 18, 1916; *Los Angeles Times*, May 18, 1916.

81. *Oakland Tribune*, July 20, July 21, July 25 and July 30, 1916. Oaks player-manager Rowdy Elliott was sold to the Chicago Cubs to make room for Howard.

82. *Oakland Tribune*, December 21, 1916.

83. *Salt Lake Tribune*, September 1, September 2 and September 6, 1916.

84. *Salt Lake Tribune*, September 26, 1916; *Los Angeles Times*, September 19 and September 20, 1916.

85. *Los Angeles Times*, September 7, 1916. Davis, an ex-champion amateur boxer, was a gifted and aggressive athlete. While playing for Portland in 1915 he broke his leg in a home plate collision with Oakland catcher Rowdy Elliott. Oakland had originally acquired Davis in the hope that his leg would come around but it was slow to heal. (*Oakland Tribune*, January 12, 1916).

86. *St. Louis Post-Dispatch*, June 1, 1916; *Oakland Tribune*, June 5 and June 9, 1916.

87. *Oakland Tribune*, September 19, 1916; *Los Angeles Times*, September 20, 1916.

88. *Oakland Tribune*, October 22, 1916; *Los Angeles Times*, October 22, 1916. Earlier in the season, Prough turned in one of the greatest pitching performances in PCL history. On June 4, he and San Francisco's Spider Baum hooked up in an epic pitcher's duel, with Prough throwing a no-hitter through the first ten innings. After allowing an infield hit in the eleventh, Prough held the Seals hitless for three more innings. Pulled after the seventeenth inning of a scoreless game for a pinch-hitter because manager Rowdy Elliott mistakenly thought the game would be called at the end of the inning, Prough had allowed only four hits and one walk while striking out eleven. The Oaks finally won the game in the eighteenth inning on a walk, a sacrifice and a bad-hop single past the shortstop (*Oakland Tribune*, June 5, 1916).

89. *Los Angeles Times*, November 6, 1916.

90. *Los Angeles Times*, July 12 and July 14, 1916.

91. *Los Angeles Times*, January 23, 1917.

92. *Los Angeles Times*, August 30 and September 14, 1917.

Chapter Six

1. *Los Angeles Times*, January 19, 1917.
2. Infielder Lai Tin was the best athlete on the squad. He held the Hawaiian records for the one hundred-yard dash and the broad jump. During the team's first trip to the States, the *New York Times* said of him, "He grabbed hard bounders of the most puzzling variety just as handily as Jimmy Collins and Arthur Devlin used to grab them." Jimmy Callahan announced he was inviting Lai Tin to spring training in 1915 with the Chicago White Sox. However, Callahan was booted upstairs to the White Sox business office and Pants Rowland became manager. Lai Tin did not go to spring training with Chicago but later signed with the New York Giants, playing several seasons in the Eastern League under the name William "Buck" Lai (*New York Times*, May 23, 1912 and December 3, 1914; *Los Angeles Times*, December 6, 1914).
3. *Chicago Tribune*, September 24, 1912.
4. *Los Angeles Times*, December 15, 1914.
5. *Los Angeles Times*, December 14, 1914.
6. *Oregonian*, December 27, 1914. After umpire Jack Mc-Carthy visited Hawaii and assured McCredie that Akana "was not black at all," McCredie reconsidered and signed the Hawaiian with the intention of bringing him to spring training in Fresno. But Akana's fatal flaw was not his racial make-up. It was his weakness for pitches up and in; he could not hit them, but could not resist swinging at them either. A fast runner and a good outfielder, Akana did not hit well enough to overcome the problems McCredie knew he would have in trying to integrate the team. McCredie released him again shortly before spring training began (*Oregonian*, January 12 and January 14, 1915; *Oakland Tribune*, January 12, 1915).
7. Joy, born in Hawaii of mixed parentage, was signed by Cal Ewing for the 1907 season. Never shy about his ability, when Joy was asked by the Seals to recommend another pitcher, he wrote back that he was the only good pitcher in Hawaii. The *Hawaiian Gazette* predicted success: "If Barney can control his tongue and temper...." Leaving the islands for the first time in his life, Joy caused a sensation when he strode down Fillmore Street in San Francisco, a leather bat bag in hand sporting his initials in large black letters. A large man, it was thought Joy would be a power pitcher but he was not, relying instead on changeups and curveballs. He was also clumsy and a poor fielder; it was said he moved with the grace "of a sick hay wagon." He started the season well but after going around the league once he began losing as many as he won. Nevertheless, rumors circulated that major league teams were showing interest in him. Joe Cantillon of the Washington Senators supposedly offered five thousand dollars, but that is doubtful because had it been, the Seals would have snapped it up. Pittsburgh was also said to be interested. Boston of the National League finally drafted Joy for one thousand dollars near the end of the 1907 season, at which point the *Washington Post* printed rumors that Joy was a Negro. What was actually meant was that he was pure Hawaiian, which was categorized as Negro in the baseball world at the time. (This was still true in the 1930s when Charlie Graham advertised outfielder Henry Oana as a full-blooded Polynesian until he became a big league prospect. Oana was then said to be half-Hawaiian and half-Portuguese.) Boston team president George Dovey denied the report about Joy and said that the pitcher would receive every opportunity to make the team. Those who knew Joy best were skeptical of his chances for success. Cal Ewing, attending the winter baseball meetings, said Joy had not been good enough for the PCL and would not do well in Boston. Former Portland outfielder Tom Raftery, who had been acquired by the Boston Red Sox, was asked his opinion of Coast League players coming to the majors in 1908. He said that both Gavvy Cravath and Pat Donahue would do well but added, "I don't think very much of Barney Joy.... It might be that he was overworked when I saw him, but he certainly lacked the goods for a big league."

Joy never played for Boston, demanding four thousand dollars plus round-trip passage from Honolulu before he would report. The Braves refused and Joy remained on the team's suspended list until 1911. That September, Joy was granted reinstatement by the National Commission and was sold to Spokane for the 1912 season but again failed to report. There were rumors from time to time of his return to the States, but he never did (*Hawaiian Gazette*, October 5, 1906 and January 11, 1907; *San Francisco Examiner*, March 8, 1907; *Oakland Tribune*, January 29, 1907, March 1, 1909 and March 24, 1912; *Washington Post*, August 30, September 8 and November 16, 1907; *Boston Globe*, October 29 and November 22, 1907, February 13, 1908, September 6 and September 25, 1911; *The Sporting News*, January 18, 1934).

8. *Los Angeles Times*, April 10, 1916. Williams lived in Hawaii. An arm injury killed the $11,000 deal. Detroit took him for the draft price following the 1913 season (*Detroit Free Press*, January 21, 1914).
9. *Los Angeles Times*, February 16, 1915; *Oakland Tribune*, July 21 and July 27, 1917.
10. *The Sporting News*, December 16, 1943.
11. *Oakland Tribune*, April 2, April 22 and May 25, 1916.
12. *Oakland Tribune*, May 29, 1916; *San Francisco Examiner*, May 28 and May 29, 1916; *Los Angeles Times*, May 29, 1916. The son of a coal miner, Claxton was of French, Indian and African ancestry and was born on Vancouver Island in British Columbia in December 1892. In a 1964 interview, Claxton said he suspected a teammate had tipped off the Oaks that he was of mixed-race blood, which led to his release. Claxton had come from Oregon to Oakland in the spring of 1916 to pitch for the semi-pro Oak Leafs. He attracted the attention of the Oaks after striking out fifty-five batters in his first thirty-six innings against top competition, including the University of California. Claxton later pitched throughout the country for barnstorming teams and in various semi-professional leagues. Continuing to bill himself as a full-blooded Indian, Claxton pitched for the Cuban House of David team where he was a teammate of Luis Tiant, Sr. He also pitched in 1932 for the Washington Pilots of the East-West Colored League, the premier Negro baseball league. With the Pilots, he started and lost a game against the legendary Smokey Joe Williams, who was fifty-three years old at the time. Claxton moved to Tacoma, Washington, and played ball there into his fifties. He was elected to the Tacoma-Pierce County Sports Hall of Fame only months before his death on March 3, 1970 (*Chicago Defender*, March 26, 1932; *Baltimore Afro-American*, April 9, 1932; *Washington Post*, June 1, 1932; *Toronto Globe & Mail*, May 28, 2006).
13. *Los Angeles Times*, February 16, February 17, February 18, February 19, February 23, February 25 and February 26, 1917. Donaldson later became a scout for the Chicago White Sox, one of the first blacks to hold that position in the majors (*Chicago Tribune*, June 28, 1949; *Chicago Defender*, July 9, 1949).
14. *Los Angeles Times*, December 27, 1914.
15. *Los Angeles Times*, February 12, 1909.
16. *Los Angeles Times*, January 19, 1917.
17. *San Francisco Chronicle*, April 3 and April 4, 1917; *San Francisco Examiner*, April 3 and April 4, 1917. Recreation Park was torn down and completely rebuilt over the winter, featuring a new grandstand and an expanded playing field. The short porch in right field was moved back forty feet in an effort to keep power hitters honest. When the Chicago Cubs came to play an exhibition series against the Seals in March, the new stadium was not ready and the games were played at Ewing Field. Reporting on one contest, the *Chronicle* sportswriter dryly noted that "no one froze to death" (*The Sporting News*, February 15, 1917; *San Francisco Chronicle*, March 17, 1917).
18. *San Francisco Examiner*, June 13 and June 14, 1917; *Los Angeles Times*, June 13 and June 14, 1917.
19. *San Francisco Chronicle*, June 18, 1917; *Oakland Trib-*

une, June 18 and June 19, 1917. Smith was an excellent athlete, given a trial at shortstop for the Chicago Cubs during spring training in 1912. Murray was taunted for weeks about running away from Smith and decided to exact his revenge on the last day of the season. After the morning game of the season-ending doubleheader, Murray met Smith outside the San Francisco dressing room and challenged the Seals pitcher to fight. Smith responded that he did not want to, but Murray suddenly sucker-punched him in the jaw. Smith then pulled out a blackjack but was disarmed by other players. Grabbing a bat, Smith started swinging it, but that too was taken from him. Still suffering from the effects of Murray's first punch, the pitcher got the worst of the fight that ensued. Smith vowed to retaliate, claiming that he would stay in California all winter instead of going home so he could get back at Murray. Because the fight occurred on the last day of the season, there were no suspensions (*Chicago Tribune*, March 13 and March 17, 1912, and March 25, 1917; *San Francisco Chronicle*, October 29, 1917; *Oakland Tribune*, October 29, 1917).

20. *San Francisco Chronicle*, June 18, 1917; *San Francisco Examiner*, June 18, 1917; *Oakland Tribune*, June 18, 1917.

21. *Los Angeles Times*, June 19 and June 24, 1917.

22. *Chicago Tribune*, December 15, 1916; *Los Angeles Times*, December 17, 1916.

23. *Los Angeles Times*, July 3 and July 4, 1917.

24. *San Francisco Chronicle*, October 29, 1917.

25. The Angels were 73–50 under Killefer.

26. *Sacramento Bee*, December 21 and December 22, 1917; *The Sporting News*, December 27, 1917.

27. *San Francisco Chronicle*, February 24 and February 25, 1918; *Los Angeles Times*, February 25, 1918; *The Sporting News*, March 7, 1918.

28. *Los Angeles Times*, March 31, 1918. Crawford had lost his regular outfield job in Detroit during the 1916 season when Harry Heilmann was shifted from first base to right field; the change resulted in a precipitous drop in productivity for Crawford, who batted only .173 in 104 at-bats during the 1917 season. Crawford was in the final season of a Federal League-era contract that included his receiving a day in his honor. With a baby on the way, he decided to move to Los Angeles but spent the winter prior to the 1918 season hoping to land a major league berth so he could reach his goal of three thousand career hits. Johnny Powers met with Crawford several times throughout February and March while Crawford continued to hold out for a major league offer, but nothing materialized beyond false rumors involving the St. Louis Cardinals (*Washington Post*, July 29 and December 29, 1917; *Detroit Free Press*, August 26, 1917; *Los Angeles Times*, October 25, 1917, March 13 and March 19, 1918; *St. Louis Post-Dispatch*, March 3, 1918).

29. *Los Angeles Times*, April 3, 1918.

30. *Los Angeles Times*, April 8, 1918.

31. *Los Angeles Times*, April 22, 1918.

32. *Oakland Tribune*, May 23, 1918; *Los Angeles Times*, May 24, 1918; *Washington Post*, May 24, 1918.

33. *San Francisco Chronicle*, July 2, 1918; *Los Angeles Times*, July 2, 1918.

34. *San Francisco Chronicle*, July 2, 1918. Red Downs helped form the Association of Professional Ballplayers of America in 1924, which assisted ballplayers in need. During spring training in 1932, the New York Giants were staying at the Biltmore Hotel in Los Angeles and Downs visited some old friends on the team. On the way he stopped at the Everard Jewelry Store, which was located inside the Biltmore, and hatched a plan to rob it. Downs and an accomplice entered the store and, according to courtroom testimony, one of them held a gun to the manager's head while the other tied up the man and shoved a ball-gag into his mouth. Downs and his partner fled the scene with fifty-two thousand dollars in jewelry and cash. The accomplice was quickly caught and confessed. Downs was arrested two days later and also confessed. Looking at least a decade older than his forty-nine years, he

told detectives, "Liquor ... has put me out for the third time. First, it caused me to lose my place in the big leagues where I might, by this time, have been a successful manager. The second time it threw me out of the Coast League. And now it's got me into this jam." Downs received a sentence of five years to life at San Quentin (*Los Angeles Times*, March 20, March 29, April 6, May 21, June 3, June 4 and June 26, 1932).

35. *San Francisco Chronicle*, July 8, 1918; *Los Angeles Times*, July 7, 1918.

36. *Los Angeles Times*, July 11 and July 12, 1918.

37. *Los Angeles Times*, July 13, 1918. PCL record books continued listing Vernon as league champion until a league meeting in 1951 officially declared Los Angeles, the winner of the playoff, as champion of the 1918 season (*Los Angeles Times*, February 15, 1951).

38. *Los Angeles Times*, August 7, 1918.

39. *Los Angeles Times*, July 18 and July 19, 1918.

40. *Los Angeles Times*, July 23, 1918.

41. *Los Angeles Times*, July 27, 1918.

42. *San Francisco Chronicle*, July 21, 1918; *Los Angeles Times*, August 9, 1918.

43. *Los Angeles Times*, January 7, 1919; *Seattle Post-Intelligencer*, January 7 and January 8, 1919.

44. *Los Angeles Times*, January 29, 1919; *Seattle Post-Intelligencer*, January 30, 1919.

45. *Los Angeles Times*, March 4, 1919.

46. *Los Angeles Times*, January 16 and January 17, 1919.

47. *Los Angeles Times*, April 5, 1919. Among those present and making pledges were Fatty Arbuckle, Tom Darmody, Lou Anger, Jack Doyle, Sam Goldwyn, Sid Grauman, and Mack Sennett.

48. *Los Angeles Times*, April 26 and May 6, 1919.

49. *Los Angeles Times*, July 9, 1919.

50. *Los Angeles Times*, July 14 and July 15, 1919.

51. *Los Angeles Times*, July 17, 1919.

52. *Los Angeles Times*, July 29, 1919.

53. *Los Angeles Times*, September 25, September 26 and September 27, 1919.

54. *Los Angeles Times*, September 29, 1919.

55. *Los Angeles Times*, October 6, 1919.

56. *Los Angeles Times*, October 6, 1919. Although anticlimactic, the nightcap of the doubleheader was notable for the professional debut of Jimmie Reese, who played a few innings at second base and went hitless in his only at-bat. Reese said of that day: "I played four innings and of course it was the biggest thrill I'd ever had in my life." He had started his association with the Angels when Frank Chance was manager — Reese used to sneak into the ballpark and was always getting kicked out. Chance finally told management, "Leave him here. We'll make a batboy out of him." At the end of each week's home series, Chance would give Reese a baseball and a silver dollar. After Red Killefer became manager, he allowed Reese to make one road trip a year and assigned Sam Crawford to look after him. Reese signed a contract with the Angels at the beginning of the 1919 season to take effect on his eighteenth birthday, just five days before the game in which he played (Jimmie Reese, interview with the author, November 11, 1991).

57. *Los Angeles Times*, October 6, 1919.

58. *Los Angeles Times*, October 18, 1919. The series was so bitterly fought that legendary St. Paul manager Mike Kelley vowed to never play against Vernon again. Dell had failed to get out of the first inning of the eighth game, which St. Paul won to tie the series. He begged Tigers manager Bill Essick to let him pitch the deciding contest and delivered, allowing only one run and smashing a walk-off double to win the game in the bottom of the ninth.

59. *San Francisco Chronicle*, December 21, 1919.

Chapter Seven

1. *Oakland Tribune*, October 18, October 24, October 28, November 12, November 14 and November 15, 1905; *The Sporting News*, October 28, 1905. The thirty-two-year-old Schmidt had been successful in his only major league season, winning twenty-two games with Brooklyn in 1903. Hawbacker claimed to have overheard gamblers betting against Schmidt immediately before he fell apart in the game. Incensed, Hawbacker began yelling at Schmidt from the stands. His release immediately after the game was controversial; players on both teams involved in the contest, including Oaks captain George Van Haltren, vouched for him. Hawbacker was adamant, however, and *Oakland Tribune* sports editor Eddie Smith applauded him for his stance. Hawbacker later backed off somewhat, writing in a letter to Eugene Bert that Schmidt had simply not been pitching well. Schmidt almost immediately signed with the Oakland team in the California League and Smith said the pitcher was "the most popular man on the field. If he and Hawbacker were running for office in San Jose, Schmidt would be elected by a large majority." Smith had long been warning about gamblers. In a 1905 editorial he decried the open betting taking place and argued that it cast doubt on honest players as well as dishonest ones (*Oakland Tribune*, August 18, 1905).

2. *Oregonian*, July 20, 1910; *Oakland Tribune*, July 20, 1910; *San Francisco Call*, July 21, 1910; *Los Angeles Times*, July 21 and August 7, 1910; *San Francisco Chronicle*, February 26, 1911. Stories circulated that Portland gamblers had also approached Willis's teammate, Bill Harkins. Wolverton emphatically denied the accusation in the *Call*, saying, "In regard to the statement that the Portland gamblers approached certain of my pitchers, there is not a particle of truth to the rumor." Less than three weeks later, Willis, who had been acquired from San Francisco two months earlier, pitched one of the best games in PCL history: eighteen shutout innings against Portland in a game called because of darkness. Yet he never again played in the high minor leagues after 1910. Neither did Harkins (*San Francisco Chronicle*, June 14, 1910; *Oregonian*, August 7, 1910; *Oakland Tribune*, August 7, 1910).

3. *Los Angeles Times*, August 11, August 13 and August 28, 1912.

4. *Los Angeles Times*, May 24, 1914.

5. *San Francisco Examiner*, October 25 and October 26, 1919.

6. *Los Angeles Times*, January 6, 1920.

7. *Los Angeles Times*, January 28, 1920.

8. *Los Angeles Times*, February 24, 1920.

9. *Los Angeles Times*, February 28, 1920. John McGraw told *The Sporting News* that he had released Zimmerman for trying to bribe teammates Benny Kauff and Fred Toney to throw a game. He added that Chase had tried to bribe pitcher Rube Benton and he suspected Chase of throwing other games while playing for the Giants in 1919. McGraw unconditionally released pitcher Jean Dubuc to the minor leagues because he was constantly hanging around Black Sox conspirator Bill Burns. It was said that McGraw had confronted Dubuc during the 1919 World Series and that Roger Bresnahan had to step between the two to prevent fisticuffs. Despite this, Seattle president Bill Klepper indicated an interest in signing Chase for the 1920 season (*San Francisco Chronicle*, April 15, 1920; *The Sporting News*, November 11, 1920).

10. *San Francisco Chronicle*, May 8 and May 9, 1920; *San Francisco Call*, May 8 and May 9, 1920; *San Francisco Examiner*, May 8 and May 9, 1920. It was said that an unnamed Seals pitcher had been signaling gamblers during games in 1919. It was never revealed whether the pitcher involved was Seaton, Smith or someone else. There was criticism of the Seals for being so secretive. Warren Brown of the *San Francisco Call* asked, "If baseball is to be kept above suspicion, is this concealing of charges by the local club owners going to achieve that result?" Brown argued that Graham's actions would only lead to "ugly conjecture" and "scandalous rumors." In Seaton's last game for the Seals, on May 5 against Los Angeles, he threw a wild pitch in the second inning when Sam Crawford attempted to steal home. Before the inning was over, four runs had scored and Seaton was taken out of the game (*San Francisco Chronicle*, May 6, 1920).

11. It was alleged that Seaton had been in trouble with gamblers before, supposedly accepting a bribe to throw a game while pitching for a local team in Oxnard, California (*The Sporting News*, May 20, 1920).

12. *San Francisco Chronicle*, May 10, May 11 and May 12, 1920; *San Francisco Call*, May 10, 1920; *San Francisco Examiner*, May 10, 1920; *Oakland Tribune*, May 10, 1920; *Los Angeles Times*, May 11, 1920. McCarthy was walking to dinner with a young woman when Hurlburt approached him on Geary Street and asked to speak with him. Words were exchanged; Hurlburt claimed that McCarthy called him a liar—McCarthy denied that—and Hurlburt socked the PCL president in the jaw. Hurlburt, the part-owner of the Colonial Club on Powell Street, eventually paid a $100 fine (*San Francisco Chronicle*, August 8, 1920).

13. *Oakland Tribune*, May 13 and May 27, 1920. Hanford defied the order of the San Joaquin Valley League to release Seaton and the team was expelled from the league. The expulsion was rescinded when the team's directors finally agreed to let Seaton go. The outlaw leagues, especially those in Central California and the Utah-Idaho area, were causing problems for the Pacific Coast League during the 1920 season. They were able to offer outrageous salaries to athletes, who in turn had to play only once a week because the teams made most of their money through wagering on the results rather than gate receipts. Wheezer Dell left Vernon for an offer in Richmond, Utah, to work as an electrician and pitch on Sundays. He left with the team's permission, throwing a two-hit shutout in his last game for the Tigers on May 9. Dell was quoted as saying Essick assured him he could come back to Vernon if things did not work out. Also in May, Salt Lake City was hit by the defections of outfielder Duke Reilly and pitcher Nick Cullop; Reilly jumped to a league in Pennsylvania and was replaced in the lineup by Wally Hood, while Cullop signed with Wellsville, Utah, in the Cache Valley League. Bill Lane obtained a court injunction preventing Cullop from playing for Wellsville. Lane then filed suit against the directors of the Wellsville team, demanding ten thousand dollars in damages. Meanwhile, Wheezer Dell was said to be having a change of heart and wanted to return to Vernon. On May 22, Cullop and Dell were back with their old teams, less than two weeks after leaving the PCL, and pitched against each other in Salt Lake City. The outlaws continued siphoning off players anyway. In June, Portland pitchers Frank Juney and Lefty Schroeder jumped to the San Joaquin Valley League. Even though Salinas produced a telegram purportedly from Judge McCredie that gave Juney his unconditional release in exchange for five hundred dollars, he was eventually declared ineligible by Kenesaw Mountain Landis and remained outside of Organized Baseball until returning to Portland in 1923 (*Los Angeles Times*, February 28, May 10, May 11, May 13, May 15 and May 23, 1920 and February 27 and December 22, 1921; *The Sporting News*, May 20, 1920; *Ogden Standard-Examiner*, May 22, 1920; *Salinas Daily Index*, February 28, 1921).

14. *San Francisco Chronicle*, June 4, 1920. Casey Smith signed with Little Rock on May 20 and pitched in a couple of games for the Travelers. He was knocked out of the box in the third inning of a start against Mobile on May 21 and then pitched one scoreless inning of relief on May 29 against Birmingham. Southern Association president John Martin refused to approve Smith's contract when it reached his office because of complaints from team owners. Seaton was released by Hanford in the San Joaquin Valley League on May 26 after league directors threatened to kick the team out of the league for employing him. He also signed with Little Rock. Martin refused to approve Seaton's contract as well. Little Rock owner

Bob Allen sued on behalf of Smith and received an injunction on June 14 from federal judge John E. McCall. Smith continued to travel with Little Rock, throwing batting practice and hitting fly balls to outfielders. On June 17, both Seaton and Smith arrived at Ponce de Leon Park in Atlanta with the rest of their teammates. Crackers owner Charley Frank, who was not about to let a little thing like an injunction from a federal court stand in his way, announced his team would refuse to play against Little Rock as long as Smith and Seaton were with them. Several other owners backed Frank and after a two-day standoff, it was decided that Little Rock would play without the two pitchers. Several Little Rock players threatened to strike and one player did sit out. Little Rock manager Kid Elberfeld continued to back Seaton and Smith, saying, "Here, these two boys have been handed the rawest sort of a deal; have been let out by a Pacific League club for the good of the game, without being told why they were released; and they are as much at sea as anybody else to know just what they have done, or what people think they have done.... The strange thing about it is that their former manager on the coast who let them out has absolutely refused to tell why he fired them. Every effort to get details has failed. He ignores letters and telegrams." When Little Rock concluded its series with Atlanta and moved on to Memphis, the Travelers found the Chicks also refusing to play if Seaton and Smith were with the team. The two players continued to proclaim their innocence and when the team went to Mobile and faced another boycott, the Little Rock players tried to organize a strike among the league's players. However, the effort fizzled when players from the other teams refused to join. League owners met on June 20 and upheld President Martin's banishment of Seaton and Smith until they could prove they were clean. Atlanta's Charlie Frank declared that if the two were innocent, "I'd be the first man in the Southern League to welcome them to this circuit." He even pledged two hundred and fifty dollars to help fund an investigation into the charges. Martin appealed Judge McCall's injunction in the Court of Appeals, but the judge died on August 8 and the case languished for a couple of months. Suddenly, on November 29, Little Rock announced it was no longer interested in the two players and was abandoning the case. By this time both the larger PCL scandal and the Black Sox investigation were in full swing. The case was dismissed by the Circuit Court of Appeals on December 10. The court was located in Cincinnati, home of the Black Sox 1919 World Series opponent, probably one of the last places Bob Allen would have wanted to advocate the use of allegedly crooked ballplayers (*Oakland Tribune*, May 13 and May 27, 1920; *Atlanta Constitution*, May 20, May 22, May 29, May 30, May 31, June 2, June 3, June 11, June 15, June 17, June 18, June 19, June 21, June 22, July 24, November 30, December 10 and December 11, 1920).

15. *Los Angeles Times*, October 31, 1919.

16. *Los Angeles Times*, February 10 and April 16, 1920.

17. *Los Angeles Times*, January 27, 1920.

18. *New York Times*, December 15, 1920; *St. Louis Post-Dispatch*, December 20, 1920.

19. *Los Angeles Times*, December 8, 1920. Shellenback was sold to the Pacific Coast League just before the lists were created, which effectively froze him out of the major leagues as long as he relied on the spitter. Buzz Arlett was also allowed to use the spitter in the PCL, but he had converted to the outfield in the early 1920s and pitched only on rare occasions (*Chicago Tribune*, January 29, 1920).

20. *Los Angeles Times*, February 5, 1920.

21. *The Sporting News*, September 24, 1952.

22. *Los Angeles Times*, March 15, March 16 and March 31, 1918.

23. *Oakland Tribune*, August 22 and August 23, 1911; *Los Angeles Times*, August 23, 1911.

24. *San Francisco Chronicle*, July 2 and July 3, 1917.

25. *Los Angeles Times*, July 28, 1920.

26. *San Francisco Chronicle*, August 4, 1920.

27. *San Francisco Chronicle*, August 4, 1920.

28. *Salt Lake Telegram*, July 29, 1920; *Los Angeles Times*, July 29, 1920. The *Times* ran a feature about Maggert's amazing revival with Salt Lake City — ironically, on the same day his career ended.

29. *San Francisco Chronicle*, August 4, 1920; *The Sporting News*, August 19, 1920. Stroud's performance also seemed suspicious because of widely spread rumors that he had accepted $500 the previous fall to leave the Bees prior to the series against Vernon in Salt Lake City. Stroud left the team on September 19 and sat out the rest of the 1919 season in what was reported as a dispute over his 1920 contract. *The Sporting News* incorrectly mixed the two bribery stories together, claiming that Stroud had been offered $300 for pitching badly in 1919 — he did pitch badly in his last game in 1919, but that was against San Francisco, not Vernon. The $300 bribe offer came before and after the game on July 28, 1920, against Vernon. The rumored $500 bribe was for jumping the Bees and not pitching at all. Stroud denied receiving money either time. Los Angeles manager Red Killefer had accused Stroud of dishonesty, but later issued a written letter of apology (*San Francisco Chronicle*, September 15, 1919 and August 5, 1920; *Los Angeles Times*, August 14 and September 20, 1919; *The Sporting News*, August 26, 1920).

30. *Salt Lake Telegram*, July 30, 1920; *Los Angeles Times*, July 30, 1920.

31. *San Francisco Chronicle*, August 4, 1920.

32. *Los Angeles Times*, July 31, 1920; *Salt Lake Telegram*, July 31 and August 3, 1920.

33. *San Francisco Chronicle*, August 4, 1920; *Los Angeles Times*, August 4, 1920; *Salt Lake Telegram*, August 4, 1920.

34. *New York Times*, August 4 and August 5, 1920; *San Jose Mercury*, August 8, August 9 and August 12, 1920.

35. *Los Angeles Times*, August 4, 1920.

36. *Los Angeles Times*, August 7, 1920.

37. *Los Angeles Times*, August 12, 1920. A week later it was reported that Nate Raymond was hiring a taxi and peering through binoculars from behind the outfield fence in Seattle. Not only did Raymond know Rothstein, he was implicated although never charged in Rothstein's 1928 death. Raymond had been involved in a card game with Rothstein and other gamblers just weeks before Rothstein was shot. By all accounts, Rothstein owed Raymond more than two hundred thousand dollars. Raymond had not been paid. Rothstein died refusing to name his assailant (*New York Times*, November 6, 1928).

38. *Los Angeles Times*, August 12, 1920; *Oakland Tribune*, August 15, 1920; *San Francisco Chronicle*, August 15 and August 17, 1920. Other players mentioned made strong denials. Borton claimed that infielder Bob Fisher had paid off Portland's John Oldham, Jack Farmer, Art Koehler and Del Baker. Koehler said he had never taken a cent from Borton and warned that Borton had better stay as far away from him as possible. "I never talked to the fellow in my life off the ball field and so far as I know have never done anything that would cause him to want to get even with me. If anyone can find a flaw with my playing either last year or this that could cause suspicion, I shall give a whole lot more than the $100 I'm supposed to have received from Borton." Del Baker also denied receiving money from Borton. The Vernon first baseman also claimed that the Tigers helped Rumler win the batting title.

39. *San Francisco Chronicle*, August 13, 1920.

40. *Los Angeles Times*, August 13, 1920; *The Sporting News*, November 11, 1920.

41. *Los Angeles Times*, August 13, 1920.

42. *San Francisco Chronicle*, August 14, 1920; *Los Angeles Times*, August 14, 1920. Maggert claimed that Borton had approached him the previous fall when Vernon played Salt Lake City and asked who Maggert wanted to see win the pennant. Maggert said he told Borton that he did not care since he had friends on both contenders. Maggert said that Borton asked

him why "I didn't stick with the other fellows, saying, 'I have got Rumler, Dale and (Eddie) Mulligan.'" Maggert claimed he did not respond and was unaware he had money coming until Borton gave it to him. During the meeting with McCarthy, Maggert was asked, "Did you think the $500 was manna from heaven?" Maggert replied, "I don't know." Maggert did admit that Borton told him if anyone asked questions to say the money was payment for a gambling debt.

43. *Oakland Tribune*, August 16, 1920; *San Francisco Chronicle*, August 17, 1920.

44. *Los Angeles Times*, August 17, 1920. Rumler's affidavit stated that he and Borton made the safety bet on July 4, 1919, which he remembered because it was the day of the Jack Dempsey-Jess Willard heavyweight championship bout. At the close of the season, Rumler wrote Borton reminding him of the wager and Borton sent the $250. Rumler's teammate, catcher Butch Byler, stated that Rumler had told him about the agreement he had with Borton, essentially confirming the affidavit. Rumler did not confess to throwing games. The Salt Lake City club was in Los Angeles the week of July 4, playing against Vernon, and two games from the Salt Lake-Vernon series during that first week of July 1919 stand out; both were games pitched by Gene Dale. On July 2, Vernon won easily as Dale lasted only one and one-third innings, walking five batters, throwing a wild pitch and making an error. Butch Byler, who claimed he was aware of the bet between Rumler and Borton, also made a throwing error in the first inning. Three days later, Dale had almost perfect control, allowing only three bases on balls — all to Babe Borton. The game went to the twelfth inning when Byler and Maggert each bunted balls to Borton, who was too slow in fielding both of them, allowing runs to score on each play. Dale also lost three games to Vernon in Salt Lake City in September (*Los Angeles Times*, July 3, July 6, September 19, September 21 and September 25, 1919; *Salt Lake Telegram*, August 12, 1920; *Sports Collector's Digest*, September 3, 1993).

45. *Los Angeles Times*, August 18, 1920.

46. *Los Angeles Times*, August 18, 1920; *The Sporting News*, September 2, 1920.

47. *Madera Daily Tribune*, August 16 and August 19, 1920. Chase played first base and Maggert center field in a game against Chowchilla on August 15. Interestingly, Chowchilla lodged a protest against Chase playing, but not Maggert.

48. *Los Angeles Times*, August 21, 1920.

49. *Los Angeles Times*, August 31, 1920.

50. *Salt Lake Telegram*, August 26, 1920; *Los Angeles Times*, September 28, 1920. Even if Lane had been successful in the appeal, it was doubtful Rumler could have played again in 1920. On August 14, he badly injured his knee during a game against Sacramento (*Salt Lake Telegram*, August 15, 1920).

51. *Oakland Tribune*, September 30, 1920.

52. *Chicago Tribune*, September 23, 1920. New York Giants pitcher Rube Benton accused Herzog of offering him a bribe to throw a game the previous year. Herzog proclaimed his innocence but told what he knew about the Black Sox. Hendrix was supposed to pitch the game in question but Cubs manager Fred Mitchell got wind of the plot and substituted Grover Cleveland Alexander instead. Hendrix did not pitch again for the Cubs that season, although he continued to travel with them. Herzog and Hendrix were unofficially blacklisted after the season and never again played in the major leagues.

53. *Chicago Tribune*, September 29, 1920; *Los Angeles Times*, September 29, 1920. Jackson always denied the exchange with the kid ever happened, claiming it was made up by a Chicago reporter. He did tell reporters that he was afraid Swede Risberg might kill him for talking about the scandal, adding, "Swede's a hard guy." Eddie Cicotte was the next to emerge from the courthouse. He sobbed, "I was a fool."

54. Sleepy Bill Burns was a go-between for the gamblers and the players in the fixing of the 1919 World Series. Chase knew about the fix, bet on the series, and told others about it. Gedeon was also aware of what was going on and placed bets on Cincinnati.

55. *Salt Lake Telegram*, September 29 and September 30, 1920; *Oakland Tribune*, October 1, 1920; *Los Angeles Times*, October 1, 1920. Rumler was sitting in a San Francisco hotel, hoping to speak to league directors on his own behalf when the events in Chicago rendered his participation moot. During the directors meeting, San Francisco director Doc Strub threatened to pull the Seals out of the PCL if Rumler's suspension was lifted. Lane still tried to defend Rumler, saying that he was guilty of nothing more than a "mere indiscretion" and that he could not have been crooked since he led the league in hitting in 1919. Doc Strub leaped to his feet and charged that Rumler had only won the batting title because three players on the Oakland team had let him bunt for base hits on the last day of the season. The players in question were said by Strub to be catcher Honus Mitze, pitcher Buzz Arlett and Arlett's brother, Pop, who was playing third base. Mitze issued a lengthy denial, pointing out that Rumler was one of the hardest hitters in the game and anyone playing in close would be foolhardy to do so. Mitze said, "I remember each of the bunts very distinctly and honestly believe that Rumler crossed our gang up each time." The game account that day in the *Oakland Times* was especially critical of the Oaks, claiming that plays should have been made on at least two of the bunts. Cal Ewing became angry at Strub's accusations and challenged him to put his claims in writing. Strub replied that he had no solid proof but was quoting what had been reported in the newspapers. Lane asked if he could change his vote on the resolution to "no" and the meeting dissolved into a series of arguments (*Oakland Times*, October 6, 1919).

56. *Los Angeles Times*, October 14, October 15 and October 16, 1920; *Oakland Tribune*, October 18, 1920.

57. *Salt Lake Telegram*, October 21, 1920; *Los Angeles Times*, October 22, 1920.

58. *Los Angeles Times*, October 27, 1920.

59. *Los Angeles Times*, November 11, 1920.

60. *Los Angeles Times*, November 23, 1920.

61. *Los Angeles Times*, October 21 and October 23, 1920.

62. *Los Angeles Times*, December 11, 1920. Dale denied throwing games but refused any suggestion that he return and answer questions about the case. Dale's career did come to an end after the 1920 season, save for a single appearance with Newark of the International League in 1921, after which he disappeared as quickly as he had appeared (*San Francisco Chronicle*, August 17, 1920).

63. *Los Angeles Times*, December 12, 1920.

64. *Los Angeles Times*, December 14, 1920.

65. *Los Angeles Times*, December 15, 1920.

66. *Los Angeles Times*, December 18 and December 19, 1920. Another version of the story has Powers swinging and missing Cook, who slipped while ducking the punch and broke a bone in his ankle. Powers reportedly boasted for years afterward that he hit Cook so hard in the jaw that he broke his ankle (*Los Angeles Times*, January 14, 1944).

67. *Los Angeles Times*, January 7, 1921.

68. *Los Angeles Times*, December 24, 1920.

69. *Los Angeles Times*, December 25, 1920; *Salt Lake Telegram*, December 25, 1920. The judge said, "The action of the men, if they were guilty, was reprehensible, but there was no remedy along the lines of criminal prosecution."

70. *Los Angeles Times*, December 25, 1920. The words used by McCarthy were not dissimilar to those later used by Kenesaw Mountain Landis when he banned the Black Sox. The judge's ruling sent the prosecutors in the Black Sox case, who were due to go to court the next month, into a mad scramble.

71. *New York Times*, January 13, 1921.

72. *New York Times*, November 6–13, 1920; *The Sporting News*, November 11, 1920. The fifty-four-year-old Landis gained notoriety by fining Standard Oil twenty-nine million

dollars for being a monopoly. The *New York Times* called him "the most natural lawyer that ever lived." Even then he was known for his gray shock of hair and habit of shaking a bony finger while lecturing from the bench (*New York Times*, August 5 and August 11, 1907, and February 15, 1920).

73. *New York Times*, January 11 and January 12, 1921.

74. *Los Angeles Times*, January 12 and January 13, 1921. Or maybe he didn't. McMullin caused a flap when he appeared at a game in Washington Park in May 1921. He tried to speak to Salt Lake manager Gavvy Cravath, but Cravath turned his back to him. McMullin left the dugout and met with some of his old teammates in the clubhouse, but it was clear he was not welcome. McMullin, who was working as a carpenter, proclaimed his innocence in the Black Sox scandal. He was told he could save everyone a lot of embarrassment if he would stay away from the ballpark (*Los Angeles Times*, May 9, 1921).

75. *Los Angeles Times*, October 12, 1919.

76. *Detroit Free Press*, June 28, 1920.

77. *The Sporting News*, July 29 and August 19, 1920.

78. *San Francisco Chronicle*, May 24, July 2, July 3, and July 16, 1920. Corhan hurt his arm during the summer and rarely played during the second half of the season. Koerner was hit on the elbow in a game in May and his arm immediately swelled. He came back but did not hit well. Extremely sensitive to criticism, the day after the *Chronicle* noted Koerner's diminished hitting he said he was quitting and told Charlie Graham, "I've never played for a fairer manager than you." The Seals owner replied, "Well, that's a fine way to show your appreciation, leaving us in the lurch." The Seals traded Koerner to Seattle for Harry Wolter, who finished out the season with the Seals. Koerner never reported to Seattle. After the season, they were traded back for each other. Koerner continued to refuse to play while Wolter jumped to the semi-pro San Joaquin Valley League (*San Francisco Chronicle*, January 28, 1921).

79. *Los Angeles Times*, October 18, 1920. Sheely's home run came at Bonnefield Park during the nightcap of the season-ending doubleheader — a game called after four and a half innings because of rain.

80. *Salt Lake Telegram*, December 25, 1920.

81. *Los Angeles Times*, February 24 and February 25, 1921.

82. *Chicago Tribune*, November 25, December 1 and December 19, 1920 and January 27, 1921. Johnson was acquired to replace Swede Risberg. Then the Sox traded reserve first baseman Ted Jourdan and back-up catcher Byrd Lynn for Sheely. When it became clear that Buck Weaver would not be able to play in 1921, the White Sox acquired Mulligan in exchange for three players to be named later.

83. *Los Angeles Times*, November 22, 1920.

84. *Los Angeles Times*, August 26 and August 30, 1921.

85. *Salt Lake Telegram*, June 22 and July 5, 1921.

86. *Salt Lake Tribune*, July 29, 1921.

87. *Los Angeles Times*, August 12, 1921.

88. *San Francisco Chronicle*, July 31, 1921.

89. *Los Angeles Times*, September 4 and September 7, 1921.

Chapter Eight

1. *The Sporting News*, November 3, 1921; *Los Angeles Times*, March 12, 1922.

2. *Los Angeles Times*, March 9, 1922. Turner's hair turned white while he was a soldier in Europe during WWI.

3. *Seattle Post-Intelligencer*, December 9, 1921.

4. *The Sporting News*, May 4, 1922; *Washington Post*, December 8, 1922.

5. *The Sporting News*, May 4, 1922. McCredie told several people he had seen a check from Kenworthy representing payment for a share of the Portland franchise.

6. *Los Angeles Times*, April 25, 1922.

7. *Los Angeles Times*, May 29 and May 30, 1922.

8. *The Sporting News*, May 4, 1922; *Los Angeles Times*, July 16, 1922.

9. *San Francisco Chronicle*, July 21, 1922; *Oregonian*, February 20, 1944. Strand's streak began on June 21 and included eight doubleheaders. The Beavers made it two in a row the next day with a 22–5 thrashing of the Bees. During that game, Salt Lake City resorted to using center fielder Morrie Schick and shortstop Tony Lazzeri as pitchers; Lazzeri surrendered five runs in one inning plus (*San Francisco Chronicle*, July 22, 1922).

10. *Los Angeles Times*, August 2 and August 3, 1922.

11. *Los Angeles Times*, August 4, 1922; *The Sporting News*, July 8, 1959.

12. *Los Angeles Times*, March 7, 1922; *The Sporting News*, August 15, 1964.

13. *Los Angeles Times*, June 9, June 12 and June 26, 1922.

14. *Oakland Tribune*, May 31, August 9 and September 16, 1922.

15. *Oakland Tribune*, June 4, 1922.

16. *Oakland Tribune*, May 11 and September 16, 1922. Knight returned to the Oakland lineup in mid–July.

17. *Oakland Tribune*, September 16, 1922.

18. *Oakland Tribune*, February 11, March 6 and May 6, 1922; *San Francisco Chronicle*, February 12, 1922.

19. *Los Angeles Times*, February 25, March 16 and March 25, 1922. Crawford said that he had two to three years left as a player but that the Angels' offer involved a cut in pay far more than the $250 they publicly claimed. There were rumors that Crawford might play for Vernon, but the forty-two-year-old retired.

20. *Chicago Tribune*, January 19, 1922; *Los Angeles Times*, March 12, 1922.

21. *Los Angeles Times*, June 9, 1922.

22. *Los Angeles Times*, June 23, 1922.

23. *Sacramento Union*, May 8, 1922; *Los Angeles Times*, May 8, May 9 and July 21, 1922. The Senators had played Sunday morning home games in Stockton since 1920.

24. *Sacramento Union*, June 11, 1922.

25. *New York Times*, December 8 and December 16, 1921. O'Connell had been the subject of a bidding war among several teams, with the Giants finally winning out over the Yankees. New York quickly insured O'Connell for $75,000. When O'Connell signed his 1922 contract with San Francisco, he became the highest paid minor league player in history to that time (*San Francisco Chronicle*, February 19, 1922).

26. *San Francisco Examiner*, May 29 and May 30, 1922; *San Francisco Chronicle*, May 30, 1922. Kamm almost quit when he thought he was not going to receive a portion of the sale price. The White Sox purchased an insurance policy on Kamm, written by catcher Ray Schalk. That policy looked like it might come in handy when Kamm was beaned by Salt Lake City pitcher Elmer Myers in August and had to be helped from the field with "a lump as big as a hen's egg" behind his left ear. Luckily, he was not seriously injured (*San Francisco Chronicle*, August 11, 1922).

27. *Chicago Tribune*, May 30, 1922.

28. *Oakland Tribune*, October 12, 1922; *Los Angeles Times*, October 12, 1922.

29. *San Francisco Chronicle*, October 15, 1922; *Los Angeles Times*, October 15, 1922.

30. *Seattle Post-Intelligencer*, June 28, 1922.

31. *Oakland Tribune*, July 30, August 1, August 2, August 3 and August 6, 1922; *The Sporting News*, August 10, 1922.

32. *The Sporting News*, January 25, 1923.

33. *Los Angeles Times*, April 5, 1923.

34. *Seattle Post-Intelligencer*, March 20 and March 21, 1923; *Los Angeles Times*, March 20, 1923.

35. *Seattle Post-Intelligencer*, March 23 and March 24, 1923; *Los Angeles Times*, March 30, 1923.

36. *Los Angeles Times*, June 5, 1923.

37. *Los Angeles Times*, June 11, 1923.

38. *Los Angeles Times*, June 14 and September 5, 1923.

39. *Los Angeles Times*, June 14 and June 17, 1923.
40. *Los Angeles Times*, June 18, 1923. Wrigley held ninety percent of the stock of the Catalina Island Company.
41. *Los Angeles Times*, June 26 and June 28, 1923; *Oakland Tribune*, June 27, 1923.
42. *Seattle Post-Intelligencer*, July 8, 1923.
43. *Los Angeles Times*, March 21 and March 26, 1923; *Salt Lake Telegram*, April 1, 1923.
44. *Los Angeles Times*, June 1, 1941.
45. *Fresno Bee*, January 20, 1923.
46. *Los Angeles Times*, March 27, 1923.
47. *Los Angeles Times*, November 17, 1922.
48. *Los Angeles Times*, January 31 and March 7, 1923.
49. *Los Angeles Times*, July 12, 1923.
50. *Los Angeles Times*, May 1, May 2 and May 3, 1923.
51. *Salt Lake Tribune*, May 12, 1923; *Salt Lake Telegram*, May 12, 1923. One of the fastest men in the sport, Schneider once defeated Jigger Statz in a one hundred-yard footrace in Los Angeles. He pitched five seasons for the Cincinnati Reds, winning twenty games in 1917 before problems with the muscles in his shoulder forced him from the mound. After his shoulder recovered, he decided that he enjoyed the outfield more than pitching. An erratic hitter capable of impressive displays of power, Schneider hit a ball out of Washington Park that slammed into the old Chutes Park menagerie fence thirty feet beyond. Easily clearing the twenty-foot-high left-field fence, 375 feet from home plate, it was considered the longest ball ever hit there — Portland outfielder Biff Schaller never turned to watch the ball, simply putting his arms out in a gesture as if to say, "What can I do?" In the May 11, 1923, game against Salt Lake City, Schneider drove in fourteen runs and had twenty-two total bases. Two of his home runs were grand slams as the Tigers won by the incredible score of 35–11. Schneider just missed a sixth home run when he lined a double only inches below the top of the outfield fence. Despite this barrage, he hit only nineteen home runs all year. Schneider had an addiction to alcohol that led to a divorce from his wife in 1924 and his incarceration in 1935 after being convicted of manslaughter for killing a man in fight. Schneider had knocked down the victim three times in a bar; they seemed to make amends and left together. According to testimony, Schneider suddenly punched the man, who fell, striking his head on the pavement and fracturing his skull. Schneider was imprisoned at San Quentin where he tended the baseball field (*Los Angeles Times*, October 13, 1920, September 13, 1921, June 28, 1923, February 12, February 25 and March 27, 1924, February 21, May 17 and July 22, 1935).
52. *Los Angeles Times*, July 27, 1923. Mathewson's recovery was not as complete as the public was led to believe; he died at Saranac Lake two years later, during the 1925 World Series.
53. *San Francisco Examiner*, September 7, 1923; *New York Times*, September 7, 1923.
54. *New York Times*, September 11, 1923.
55. *The Sporting News*, October 11, 1923.
56. *Sacramento Union*, September 20 and September 21, 1923; *Los Angeles Times*, September 20, 1923.
57. *Los Angeles Times*, February 13, 1919.
58. *Los Angeles Times*, November 12, 1923.
59. Williams, Harry, "The Battle of Avalon" Chapter I, *Los Angeles Times*, December 7, 1931.
60. *Los Angeles Times*, November 13, 1923.
61. *Los Angeles Times*, November 13, 1923 and December 7, 1931. An angry William McCarthy characterized the meeting as "hoodlanism run riot" (*Salt Lake Telegram*, November 13, 1923).
62. "Minutes of the Meeting of the Directors of the Pacific Coast League, January 14, 1924," Dick Dobbins Collection on the Pacific Coast League, California Historical Society.
63. *Los Angeles Times*, November 13 and December 12, 1923. The board did censure William Wrigley for loaning Lockard and Killefer the funds to purchase the Seattle franchise, but the ruling carried no penalty.
64. Williams, Harry, "The Battle of Avalon" Chapter IV, *Los Angeles Times*, December 10, 1931.
65. *Los Angeles Times*, February 15, 1931.
66. *Los Angeles Times*, February 21, 1931.
67. *Los Angeles Times*, May 14, 1922.
68. *The Sporting News*, January 3, 1924.
69. *Boston Globe*, September 28, 1923; *Chicago Tribune*, October 27, 1923 and February 17, 1924; *Los Angeles Times*, September 16 and September 19, 1924. Chance never had any children. His wife, Edith, remained in Los Angeles for thirty years, dying of cancer in 1954 at her home in Beverly Hills. She was buried beside her husband (*Los Angeles Times*, February 23, 1954).
70. *New York Times*, October 2, 1924; *The Sporting News*, October 16 and October 30, 1924. The scandal dominated the sports headlines through the World Series. O'Connell provided details of offering the bribe to Sand and talking to other Giants about it after Sand turned him down. Sand testified that he told a teammate about the offer during the game but no one else. That night, feeling guilty about not having said anything, Sand woke Phillies manager Art Fletcher to tell him. He said that O'Connell had approached him when he was warming up with Philadelphia teammates Joe Oeschger and Johnny Couch and that O'Connell began talking about a team he was putting together to play in San Francisco during the winter. When Oeschger and Couch wandered away, O'Connell began asking Sand whether he preferred seeing the Giants or some other team win the pennant, a question that almost exactly mirrored the one Babe Borton had asked Harl Maggert back in 1919. When Sand said he did not care, O'Connell asked him if five hundred dollars would change his mind. O'Connell later said he had told Frank Frisch, Ross Youngs and George Kelly that Sand had refused the offer, and that it had been Dolan's suggestion. Dolan was quite evasive in his responses, while Frisch, Youngs and Kelly insisted they had not seen or heard anything unusual. O'Connell's testimony definitely seems like someone being left out alone on a limb, but it was one he put himself onto. O'Connell said, "Dolan is not telling the truth. I guess they figure I am to continue being the goat, and there doesn't seem anything much I can do." Landis released transcripts of the interviews in January 1925. A New York Grand Jury also heard testimony in January and February and placed the official blame on O'Connell while exonerating Frisch, Youngs and Kelly. The members of the panel did not feel there was enough evidence for bribery charges against Dolan but agreed he was very evasive in his answers to Landis and had therefore brought suspicion on himself. There had also been a dustup between Ban Johnson and Harry Williams after Johnson, following the revelations of the O'Connell-Sand incident, blamed the sorry episode on the Pacific Coast League, saying that gambling in the PCL was worse than anywhere else in the country. Williams replied that the gambling men behind most of the scandals had been from the East, and demanded that Johnson "should back up his reckless statements with names and facts, or cease his statements" (*Los Angeles Times*, October 8 and November 3, 1924; *New York Times*, January 11 and February 5, 1925).
71. *New York Times*, October 24, 1924.
72. *New York Times*, October 3, 1924.
73. *New York Times*, October 4, 1924.
74. *The Sporting News*, October 30, 1924. McNeely, who had played for Sacramento since 1921, was sent to the Washington Senators in exchange for thirty-five thousand dollars and three players in August 1924. When he reported to Washington, he had a shoulder injury, suffered while making a diving catch in a game against Portland on August 1. After claiming he had been dealt damaged goods and refusing to pay Sacramento, Washington owner Clark Griffith was ordered to close the deal by Commissioner Landis. Once McNeely healed he played well, hitting .330 in forty-three games. He also had the series-clinching hit in the 1924 World Series,

slapping a ground ball that bounded over the head of New York Giants third baseman Freddie Lindstrom to bring in the winning run and make Walter Johnson a world champion at last. Following the Series, McNeely was rewarded by Sacramento baseball fans with a banquet in his honor. The Moreing brothers gave him a brand-new 1925 Studebaker and the Senators' final game of the season was declared Earl McNeely Day (*Sacramento Union*, August 2, August 30, October 17, October 19 and October 20, 1924; *Washington Post*, August 9, August 28, August 29, August 31, 1924; *New York Times*, October 11, 1924).

75. *San Francisco Chronicle*, March 17, 1925. O'Connell played in semi-professional and outlaw leagues after his banishment. In 1931, he made plans to play for Lodi in the independent California State League. However, Judge Landis informed league president Al Earle that players in the league who were on the voluntarily retired list could become ineligible for reinstatement if they played with or against O'Connell. The league immediately dropped him (*New York Times*, March 24, 1926; *Lodi Sentinel*, March 21, 1931).

76. *Los Angeles Times*, August 22, 1924.

77. *San Francisco Chronicle*, August 23, 1924.

78. *Los Angeles Times*, April 15, 1924.

79. *Los Angeles Times*, April 23, 1924.

80. *Salt Lake Telegram*, December 12, 1923. In addition to winning his second straight Triple Crown in 1923, Strand set a still-standing record of 325 base hits in a season. A converted pitcher who had played for the Miracle Braves of 1914, Strand was sent to Philadelphia for $35,000 and three players, a deal made possible by the PCL's change in its stance on the major league draft. Strand was unsuccessful in Philadelphia and returned to the minors within months — and was regarded as one of the game's biggest rookie busts of all time (*Baseball Digest*, September 1951).

81. *Boston Globe*, February 3, 1924. Salt Lake manager Duffy Lewis was a teammate of O'Doul's in New York and had been one of those who continually tried to convince him to move to the outfield. O'Doul's sore arm gave Lewis the golden opportunity, and he declared, "O'Doul would be a major leaguer today if he had followed not only my advice, but the advice of others" (*Seattle Post-Intelligencer*, October 9, 1924).

82. *Los Angeles Times*, February 12, 1924. *New York Times* sportswriter John Kieran said of O'Doul as a pitcher, "(he was) the owner and operator of a magnificent curveball. It fooled every batter — once. But it never fooled any batter twice." O'Doul used to sit on the Yankees bench and flick peanut shells at Miller Huggins until the manager exploded in anger. O'Doul was sent to the Boston Red Sox, where he played for Frank Chance in 1923. On July 7, he pitched three innings against Cleveland and surrendered sixteen runs, with thirteen of those coming in one inning. O'Doul pitched for Salt Lake in 1924, winning seven games and losing nine with a ghastly 6.54 earned run average, but also played in the outfield, driving in 101 runs with an impressive .392 batting average. He became a full-time outfielder in 1925 (*Boston Globe*, July 8, 1923; *New York Times*, August 12, 1932; *San Francisco Examiner*, February 17, 1935).

83. *Los Angeles Times*, May 29, 1924.

84. *Los Angeles Times*, May 23, 1924.

85. *Los Angeles Times*, May 25, 1924.

86. *The Sporting News*, September 4, 1924.

87. *Los Angeles Times*, October 14, 1924.

88. *Los Angeles Times*, October 15, 1924.

89. *Seattle Post-Intelligencer*, October 19 and October 20, 1924 and October 29, 2003.

90. *Los Angeles Times*, October 19, 1924.

91. *Seattle Post-Intelligencer*, October 19, 1924.

92. *Seattle Post-Intelligencer*, October 20, 1924; *Los Angeles Times*, October 20, 1924; *The Sporting News*, October 23 and October 30, 1924.

93. *Washington Post*, October 9, 1924. The Yankees offered

Seattle thirty-five thousand dollars, which the Indians turned down because they were in the midst of a pennant race. Gregg was furious, afraid that he might not have another shot at the majors. During his next-to-last start of the regular season, Red Killefer shook Gregg's hand and told him, "You've been asking for a chance to go back into the big show and we are going to give it to you." The veteran pitched mostly in relief for Washington in 1925, splitting four decisions before he was farmed out to New Orleans in August. Gregg decided to make another comeback in 1927, signing a contract with the Missions of the PCL. Plagued by arm problems through spring training, he was released a week into the season without making an appearance. He signed with Sacramento in May and pitched in one game before going back to the Timber League, where he was still playing in the 1930s (*The Sporting News*, September 4 and October 23, 1924; *Seattle Post-Intelligencer*, October 9, 1924 and August 31, 1925; *Washington Post*, August 26 and November 29, 1925; *Atlanta Constitution*, March 29, 1926; *Oakland Tribune*, January 7 and April 11, 1927; *San Francisco Examiner*, February 17, 1927; *Sacramento Union*, May 18, 1927; *Los Angeles Times*, May 19, 1927).

94. *Los Angeles Times*, August 19, 1924; *The Sporting News*, September 4, 1924.

95. *Seattle Post-Intelligencer*, October 27 and October 30, 1924.

96. *Oregonian*, October 19 and October 22, 1924; *The Sporting News*, October 30, 1924. Roy Mack was named Portland's business manager (*Oregonian*, November 9, 1924).

Chapter Nine

1. *Santa Ana Register*, November 1, 1924.

2. *Los Angeles Times*, November 7, 1924.

3. *Washington Post*, October 28, 1924.

4. *Oakland Tribune*, October 29, 1924.

5. *Oakland Tribune*, November 5, November 11 and November 12, 1924.

6. *Washington Post*, November 18, 1924.

7. *Oakland Tribune*, November 17, 1924. Weiss paid five thousand dollars in exchange for an option to buy the team, with another twenty-five thousand dollars due at signing. The remainder of the purchase price was to be paid on January 2 (*Oakland Tribune*, November 23, 1924).

8. *Oakland Tribune*, November 23, 1924.

9. *Oakland Tribune*, November 25, 1924; *Nevada State Journal*, November 26, 1924.

10. *Los Angeles Times*, January 7, 1925.

11. *Los Angeles Times*, January 8, 1925.

12. *Los Angeles Times*, January 30, 1925. Johnson left no doubt that he laid the blame for his failure to purchase a team in the PCL squarely at the feet of Wrigley: "The chance to buy the Vernon club was good, but it seems William Wrigley wanted his friend, W.H. Lane of Salt Lake, to run it, and the deal fell through" (*New York Times*, February 10, 1925).

13. *Los Angeles Times*, January 31, 1925.

14. *Los Angeles Times*, May 7, 1928.

15. *Los Angeles Times*, December 19, 1924 and August 23, 1925.

16. *Los Angeles Times*, January 12, 1925.

17. *Los Angeles Times*, March 8, 1925.

18. *Long Beach Press*, August 31, 1924; *Los Angeles Times*, November 13, 1924, January 15 and March 9, 1925.

19. *Los Angeles Times*, August 2 and August 3, 1925.

20. *The Sporting News*, August 13, 1925.

21. *Los Angeles Times*, August 16, September 11 and September 20, 1925.

22. *Los Angeles Times*, August 17, 1925.

23. *Los Angeles Times*, September 28, 1925.

24. *Los Angeles Times*, September 27, 1925.

25. *Los Angeles Times*, October 4, 1925. Fans had to adjust

to the fact that foul balls frequently fell in the stands rather than going out of the park. With no seating at all beyond the left-field fence, home runs regularly bounced off the white apartment house across the street during the next three decades.

26. *Los Angeles Times*, September 30, 1925; *Los Angeles Examiner*, September 30, 1925. A final dedication ceremony was held the next January. Years later it was claimed by veteran groundskeeper James Fitzgerald — who later planned and maintained the Gilmore Field grounds — that Wrigley Field was laid out incorrectly. He said that the orientation of the field caused outfielders to constantly have to "blink the sun out of their eyes." Fitzgerald laid out Shibe Park in Philadelphia and his innovations included raising the pitcher's mound and creating a slope to the infield from the mound in all directions. He also pioneered the use of special clay mixtures for the infield. Fitzgerald worked the grounds for the Washington Senators from 1912 until moving to Los Angeles in 1923 (*Los Angeles Times*, January 16, 1926 and August 8, 1954; *The Sporting News*, December 19, 1956).

27. *Salt Lake Telegram*, January 9 and January 21, 1925; *The Sporting News*, January 22, 1925.

28. *San Francisco Chronicle*, December 5, 1940.

29. John Sillito, "'Our Tone': Tony Lazzeri's Baseball Career in Salt Lake City, 1922–1925." *Utah Historical Quarterly*, Fall 2004, page 348; *Los Angeles Times*, August 9, 1925.

30. *Los Angeles Times*, August 29, 1956. Former Salt Lake batboy Harry Guss, who was fifteen years old when Lazzeri had his sixty-home run season, was interviewed thirty years later and remembered that the young shortstop ran like a deer and was constantly eating peanuts during games.

31. *Salt Lake Telegram*, September 12, 1925; *Los Angeles Times*, September 12, 1925.

32. *Los Angeles Times*, September 13, 1925. Despite Lazzeri grabbing the headlines, Vernon won the game behind Clyde Barfoot's twenty-third win of the year. Barfoot pitched a ten-inning complete game, hit a home run — one of his six that year — and a double. He also executed a perfect squeeze bunt that scored the winning run. Barfoot won a league-leading twenty-six games for the last-place Tigers in 1925.

33. *Salt Lake Telegram*, September 14, 1925.

34. *Salt Lake Telegram*, September 16, 1925; *Oakland Tribune*, September 16, 1925.

35. *Salt Lake Telegram*, September 17, 1925; *Oakland Tribune*, September 17, 1925. Pruett's walking Lazzeri must have frustrated the young slugger — he made three errors at shortstop that game.

36. *Salt Lake Telegram*, September 20, 1925; *Oakland Tribune*, September 20, 1925.

37. *Seattle Post-Intelligencer*, October 12, 1925; *Los Angeles Times*, October 12, 1925.

38. *Sacramento Union*, October 18, 1925. A fan returned the ball to Lazzeri, who sent it to the Sacramento dugout and asked the entire Senators team to sign it.

39. *Sacramento Union*, October 19, 1925; *Sacramento Bee*, October 19, 1925; *Salt Lake Telegram*, October 19, 1925. The *Union* reported that Cunningham missed Lazzeri's fly ball while attempting a shoestring catch. The *Bee* merely stated that Lazzeri was "presented with the final four-base drive." Lazzeri also set still-standing records of 202 runs scored and 222 runs batted in for the season. His new world record for home runs lasted only one year; in 1926, John "Moose" Clabaugh hit sixty-two home runs for Tyler in the East Texas League. Clabaugh would later play in the PCL with Portland from 1934–1937 and in 1943.

40. *Salt Lake Telegram*, July 17 and July 19, 1925.

41. *San Francisco Chronicle*, October 19, 1925.

42. *Seattle Post-Intelligencer*, October 19, 1925. Brazill was hitting .397 going into the season-ending doubleheader against Seattle, and needed to go four-for-four in the first game or six-for-eight over both games to reach .400. He went two-for-seven. The *Post-Intelligencer* inaccurately reported

that Brazill's final batting average was .401 and Waner had finished at .400. In the first game of the doubleheader, Seattle pitcher Red Lucas played all nine positions, hitting a home run and flawlessly fielding five chances.

43. *Los Angeles Times*, May 17, 1936. *San Francisco Chronicle*, September 8, 1937; *San Francisco Examiner*, September 8, 1937.

44. *The Sporting News*, October 2, 1924.

45. *Los Angeles Times*, March 16, 1958.

46. *Los Angeles Times*, April 11, 1926.

47. The watch, one of Ellison's prized possessions, was stolen in Kobe, Japan, in 1933. Two years later, it was pawned in China. In 1946, the watch was found in a Vancouver, Washington, park by some boys who noticed the inscription. It was returned to Ellison and still ran perfectly (*The Sporting News*, July 3, 1946).

48. *The Sporting News*, April 26, 1923.

49. *Los Angeles Times*, December 19, 1926.

50. *The Sporting News*, April 2, 1925.

51. *The Sporting News*, December 31, 1925.

52. *The Sporting News*, June 19, 1924.

53. *San Francisco Examiner*, October 13, 1925; *Pittsburgh Press*, October 13, 1925.

54. *Los Angeles Times*, April 2, 1941. *Times* sportswriter Bob Ray said that any player who visited Goggin's icehouse was provided all the beer he could drink at no charge. Ray also said that the San Francisco Seals were by far the biggest drinkers in the league.

55. *Los Angeles Times*, August 16, 1925.

56. *Los Angeles Times*, August 16, 1925.

57. *Los Angeles Times*, December 5, 1925. Maier dubbed the Angels' new stadium "Wrigley's Folly."

58. *Los Angeles Times*, September 13, 1925; *The Sporting News*, December 3, 1925.

59. *San Francisco Examiner*, December 31, 1925.

60. *San Francisco Examiner*, January 9 and January 12, 1926; *Los Angeles Times*, December 31, 1925, January 9 and January 12, 1926; *Oakland Tribune*, January 9, 1926. Maier owned 4,498 of the 5,000 shares issued by the Vernon Tigers. As part of the deal, the Oakland Oaks received compensation for the league placing a second team in San Francisco. The Angels and Seals each gave Oakland $25,000 and the league added another $60,000 to be paid over six years from the league's holiday pool. Teams in the PCL divided gate receipts equally among themselves for games on Memorial Day, Independence Day and Labor Day ("Minutes of the Adjourned Meeting of the Directors of the Pacific Coast League, January 14, 1926," Dick Dobbins Collection on the Pacific Coast League, California Historical Society).

61. The Vernon Tigers quickly faded into memory. Ed Maier did not have an easy time of it after he left the PCL. His twelve-year-old son, Eddie Jr., died suddenly in June 1931 while attending military school after contracting a sinus infection. In March 1932, Maier's brewery was raided and the property was confiscated by Prohibition agents, who charged the company with selling "near-beer" of higher than the legally allowed alcohol content of one-half of one percent. In June of that year, a number of creditors filed an involuntary petition of bankruptcy against him. Maier's wife, Kathleen, died in a traffic accident in Los Angeles in March 1933. Two weeks before Christmas in 1943, Ed Maier died while trying to extinguish a fire in his beachfront bungalow in Malibu (*Los Angeles Times*, June 16, 1931, March 31, April 1 and June 14, 1932, March 25 and March 28, 1933, December 13 and December 15, 1943, and January 13, 1944).

62. *San Francisco Examiner*, January 9, 1926. One unidentified owner claimed he was almost inclined to stop the deal because of the thought of having to sit in league meetings with McCarthy.

63. *Los Angeles Times*, January 15, 1926. At the league meeting, Cal Ewing made a well-received speech about putting aside differences. Even Charles Lockard shook William

McCarthy's hand, welcoming him back to the PCL (*San Francisco Examiner*, January 12, 1926).

64. *Los Angeles Times*, January 25 and January 30, 1926.

65. *Sacramento Union*, February 16, 1926.

66. *San Francisco Chronicle*, May 16, 1926; *The Sporting News*, May 27, 1926. McCredie admitted that he had been ill for two months and could not stand up to the "exacting tasks of club manager." When originally hired, it had been noted by *The Sporting News* that McCredie had been ill all over the winter, had lost a lot of weight, and "...does not look well ... " (*The Sporting News*, December 3, 1925).

67. *San Francisco Examiner*, June 30, 1926; *Los Angeles Times*, July 1, 1926.

68. *San Francisco Examiner*, July 8, 1926; *The Sporting News*, July 15, 1926. Doc Strub spent over an hour trying to talk Ellison out of quitting. When Ellison met with reporters, he sat nervously strumming his fingers on the table and spoke of watching the slow death of Dots Miller. He said, "I am resigning because of my health." He went on to say, "Defeat is hard to take.... It's like a thousand little devils sticking you with a real hot brand, mocking you, taunting you, helpless to prevent it." Ellison returned briefly to the Seals in 1927 as a utility player, hitting one home run, a pinch-hit blast that tied a game against Oakland in the ninth inning. He was sold to Minneapolis soon after that. He served as player-manager for Dallas in the Texas League the next year before retiring for good at the age of thirty-one. Nick Williams had been a scout for the Seals over the previous three seasons while also managing in the Utah-Idaho League (*Los Angeles Times*, April 21 and April 23, 1927).

69. *Los Angeles Times*, January 19, 1927.

70. *San Francisco Chronicle*, February 4, 1927.

71. *Los Angeles Times*, May 16, 1926.

72. *Los Angeles Times*, May 23, 1926.

73. *Santa Rosa Press-Democrat*, February 19 and February 20, 1927.

74. *Oakland Tribune*, June 30, 1926. Reese claimed to be twenty, but that would have made him thirteen when he signed with the Angels in 1919. Obviously, a twenty-year-old infielder was more valuable to the major leagues than one who was twenty-six. The insurance policies, which were signed at the offices of the *Oakland Tribune* to prove it was not a publicity stunt, were written by ex-Pacific Coast League first baseman Phil Koerner. The Oaks sped up the process after Reese was hit in the chest by a line drive during practice before a doubleheader between Oakland and San Francisco on June 28.

75. *The Sporting News*, January 8, 1925.

76. *Los Angeles Times*, January 22, 1928.

77. *Atlanta Constitution*, April 11, 1920 and February 15, 1921. Brazill was not without the ability to charm fans. Early in the season while playing for Atlanta, he got into a heated argument with an umpire and was fined five dollars on the spot after using a few choice profanities. A fan almost immediately rose from his seat, opened his wallet, and handed Brazill the five dollars he'd lost, plus a little bonus in appreciation for the added entertainment and passion the young player had shown (*Atlanta Constitution*, May 11, 1920).

78. *The Sporting News*, June 15, 1922.

79. *The Sporting News*, August 28, 1924.

80. *The Sporting News*, January 8, 1925.

81. *Seattle Post-Intelligencer*, May 6, 1925; *Los Angeles Times*, April 7, 1942.

82. *The Sporting News*, April 15, 1926.

83. *Los Angeles Times*, April 16, 1927. Under the ground rules, the ball was live and Cooper was allowed to circle the bases while Jahn went into the stands to retrieve the baseball.

84. *Los Angeles Times*, April 17, 1927.

85. *Sacramento Union*, April 21, 1927; *Los Angeles Times*, April 21, 1927.

86. *Sacramento Union*, April 22, 1927; *Los Angeles Times*, April 22, 1927; *Los Angeles Examiner*, April 22, 1927.

87. *Los Angeles Examiner*, April 23, 1927; *Los Angeles Times*, April 23, 1927.

88. *Los Angeles Times*, May 7, 1927. The length of Brazill's suspension was especially surprising in light of Williams' nearly month-long suspension of Sacramento manager Bud Ryan a year earlier when Ryan knocked out umpire Roy Van Graflan with one punch during an argument. That added fuel to the argument that Williams was less likely to cross William Wrigley than other owners (*Los Angeles Times*, September 19 and September 26, 1926).

89. *Sacramento Union*, May 20, 1927.

90. *Los Angeles Times*, May 16, 1927.

91. *Los Angeles Times*, May 18, 1927.

92. *New York Times*, June 2, 1927.

93. *Los Angeles Times*, July 20, 1927. Eason sued Brazill for $50,000 and Krug for $35.000.

94. *Los Angeles Times*, May 22, May 23 and May 25, 1928. Umpire Fred Westervelt, Eason's partner during the assaults by Krug and Brazill, testified that Brazill had "poured the knuckles into Eason's ear." Brazill responded to the accusation that he had "brought the grandstand down on the umpire." The ballplayer said, "I never heard of any expression like that. It's a new one on me and I don't know what it means. But I know what you think it means." That elicited laughter from the spectators in the courtroom.

95. *Oakland Tribune*, August 1, 1927; *Los Angeles Times*, August 1, 1927.

96. *Oregonian*, November 6, 1927; *Los Angeles Times*, November 6, 1927. Cissell was in his first season as a professional. After buying his way out of the army, he borrowed a horse from his father, rode it to Des Moines, Iowa, and tried out for the Western League. Within two months, he had attracted the notice of Tom Turner at Portland, who paid $13,000 to acquire him. After six months with the Beavers, Cissell was property of the Chicago White Sox. The $123,000 amount, as in many of the larger PCL deals, was a derived figure rather than a literal one. The transaction involved $75,000 in cash and players Ike Boone and Bert Cole, who represented the balance of the published amount.

97. *New York Journal American*, October 23, 1957.

98. *The Sporting News*, June 11, 1931.

99. *Los Angeles Times*, September 4, 1927.

100. *Los Angeles Times*, October 8, 1925.

101. *Los Angeles Times*, May 17, 1927.

102. *Los Angeles Times*, July 28, 1927.

103. *Los Angeles Times*, August 31, 1927.

104. *Los Angeles Times*, November 13, 1928.

105. *Seattle Post-Intelligencer*, December 25, 1927.

106. That was not the only unusual move made by McCarthy while president of the Missions. In July 1926, he signed Hal Chase, Jr., the sixteen-year-old son of the man he had permanently banned from PCL ballparks six years before (*Oakland Tribune*, July 20, 1926).

107. *Los Angeles Times*, December 13, 1927.

108. *San Francisco Examiner*, April 15, 1928; *Los Angeles Times*, April 15, 1928.

109. *Los Angeles Times*, June 6, 1928. Brazill signed with Portland.

110. Crosetti also played some second base in an unusual platoon system. Sloppy Thurston both pitched and played first base. When Thurston was in the lineup at first base, Gus Suhr would play second. On days Thurston pitched, Suhr would move over to first base and Crosetti took Suhr's place at second.

111. *Sport Magazine*, June 1956.

112. *The Sporting News*, January 25, 1964. Red Adams was a teammate of Jolley late in his career and asked him whether he ever worried about being quick-pitched because he waited so late to get his bat in hitting position. Jolley, who hit .367 in his minor league career, replied, "That's just what I want 'em to do, Red Dog. They'd be diggin' themselves a big hole" (Red Adams, interview with the author, April 26, 2009).

113. *Sacramento Union*, January 21, 1928; *Chicago Tribune*, January 21, 1928.
114. *Los Angeles Times*, July 27, 1928.
115. *Los Angeles Times*, July 3, 1928.
116. *Los Angeles Times*, October 7, 1928; *Sacramento Union*, October 8, 1928.
117. *Sacramento Union*, October 12, 1928; *The Sporting News*, October 18, 1928. Fanning continued umpiring in the PCL until 1944, when he suffered a heart attack and collapsed during an argument with Oakland manager Dolph Camilli. Forced to retire from active duty, the next year he was hired to work the press gate at Wrigley Field. Fanning died in February 1955 (*Los Angeles Times*, February 28, 1955; *The Sporting News*, March 9, 1955).
118. *Los Angeles Times*, August 7, 1928.
119. *Los Angeles Times*, June 16, 1928. Hollywood drew 363,000 in 1928 versus 186,000 for the Angels.
120. *Los Angeles Times*, July 4, 1928.
121. *Los Angeles Times*, August 28, 1928.
122. *Los Angeles Times*, October 12, 1928.
123. *Los Angeles Times*, January 19, 1926. During his years at Salt Lake, Lane would usually pick out two boys and let them travel with the team for a couple of months. He continued the practice once he moved his team to California (*Los Angeles Times*, February 3, 1929).
124. *Los Angeles Times*, November 12, 1928.
125. *Los Angeles Times*, November 8, 1928.
126. *Los Angeles Times*, October 30, 1928.
127. *San Francisco Examiner*, November 12 and November 13, 1928; *Los Angeles Times*, November 13, 1928. Moreing and Turner were the two directors about whose votes there was the most speculation. Klepper, Lane and Ewing were firmly anti–McCarthy.
128. *Los Angeles Times*, January 22 and January 23, 1929.
129. *Los Angeles Times*, February 1 and February 2, 1929.
120. *Los Angeles Times*, February 22 and February 23, 1929.
131. *Los Angeles Times*, May 7, 1929.
132. *New York Times*, July 6, 1929.

Chapter Ten

1. *Los Angeles Times*, December 18, 1928.
2. *Bismarck Tribune*, June 13, 1921.
3. *San Diego Union*, February 20, 1929.
4. *Los Angeles Times*, March 27, March 28 and March 29, 1929.
5. *Sacramento Union*, March 30, 1929; *Los Angeles Times*, March 30, 1929.
6. *Los Angeles Times*, April 2, 1929.
7. *Los Angeles Times*, April 21, 1929; *The Sporting News*, May 2, 1929.
8. *Los Angeles Times*, April 20, 1929. A year earlier, on July 15, 1928, the Sheiks became the first professional team to fly when they chartered a plane from Seattle to Portland. The Sheiks were not the first baseball team to fly — that honor goes to the semi-pro Marysville Merchants, who on August 7, 1921, flew eighty miles from Gridley, California, to Woodland (*Woodland Daily Democrat*, August 8, 1921; *San Francisco Chronicle*, August 8 and August 9, 1921; *Los Angeles Times*, July 12 and July 16, 1928).
9. *Bakersfield Californian*, March 14 and March 15, 1929; *Los Angeles Times*, March 14, March 15 and March 17, 1929. According to witnesses, Berry was driving back to the highway when he came to a right-hand curve. However, instead of turning, he drove straight across the highway and hurtled into a ravine. Berry was pinned beneath the wreckage with a broken neck. It was unclear whether the car had a mechanical failure or if Berry had suffered a heart attack or blackout that led to the accident.

10. *Los Angeles Times*, March 24, 1929; *Santa Ana Daily Register*, March 25, 1929. The players were returning from an exhibition game played in San Diego when they were side-swiped near the San Diego-Orange County line. Williams was conscious after the accident but complained that he could not feel his arms or legs. The players flagged down a passing motorist who helped transport Williams to the hospital. His last words were "I'm all right. I'm still with you." He died a few minutes after arriving at the hospital. At the time of the accident, Williams' wife was in Mobile, Alabama, attending the funeral of her father. On Opening Day, flags at all PCL ballparks flew at half staff for Williams. A benefit game was played in April between Portland and Seattle to help Williams' wife and two-year-old daughter. Tom Turner, who had spent $6,500 to acquire the outfielder from the Pittsburgh Pirates over the winter, agreed to pay Williams' full 1929 salary to his widow (*Los Angeles Times*, March 26, March 28 and April 23, 1929).
11. *Merced Sun-Star*, April 1, 1929; *Modesto News-Herald*, April 2, 1929. Nance had a promising career ahead of him, having joined the Missions during the 1928 season after his release by Seattle and promptly winning nine straight games. He lost his first start of the season to Oakland, 6–1, two days before his accident. Nance was driving from San Francisco to his home in Fowler, California, where he planned to meet his wife before rejoining the team on its southern trip. According to a passenger in Nance's vehicle, the ballplayer was speeding and tried passing another car, but his tire left the roadway and made contact with some gravel, causing him to swerve. Nance overcorrected and the car careened into a ditch. He was pinned underneath the wreckage and suffered a fractured skull (*Oakland Tribune*, March 30, 1929).
12. *Los Angeles Times*, June 22 and June 23, 1929.
13. *Los Angeles Times*, October 15, 1929.
14. *Los Angeles Times*, February 3 and February 4, 1930.
15. *Los Angeles Times*, December 15, 1928.
16. *Los Angeles Times*, March 11, 1929.
17. *Los Angeles Times*, June 2, 1931.
18. *Los Angeles Times*, May 2, 1926; *San Francisco Sunday Examiner and Chronicle*, August 3, 1980.
19. *San Francisco Chronicle*, September 20 and September 21, 1926. Oakland second baseman Jimmie Reese hit Boone in the face with a throw while trying to complete the double play.
20. *Oregonian*, November 6, 1927; *San Francisco Chronicle*, July 21, 1928.
21. *Los Angeles Times*, April 16, 1929.
22. *Los Angeles Times*, June 29, July 1 and July 2, 1929.
23. *Oakland Tribune*, July 5, 1929.
24. *San Francisco Chronicle*, July 5, 1929.
25. *Sacramento Union*, July 6 and July 10, 1929; *Los Angeles Times*, April 28 and July 24, 1929; *Stockton Record*, July 30, 1929. Moreing was also coping with the April death of his brother, Charles.
26. *Sacramento Union* June 4 and June 15, 1929.
27. *Sacramento Union*, July 16, 1929.
28. *Los Angeles Times*, July 20, 1929.
29. *Los Angeles Times*, July 18, 1929.
30. *Los Angeles Times*, August 12 and August 13, 1929.
31. Severeid was hitting .289 with fifteen home runs when he was released by Sacramento.
32. *Los Angeles Times*, August 28, 1929.
33. *San Francisco Examiner*, October 6, 1929.
34. *Los Angeles Times*, October 7, 1929.
35. *San Francisco Chronicle*, October 7, 1929.
36. Shellenback hit seventy home runs during his Pacific Coast League career.
37. *San Francisco Chronicle*, October 11, 1929; *Los Angeles Times*, October 11, 1929.
38. *San Francisco Chronicle*, October 12, 1929; *Los Angeles Times*, October 12, 1929.
39. *Los Angeles Times*, October 14, 1929.

40. *Los Angeles Times*, July 3, 1893.

41. *The Sporting News*, April 17, 1930.

42. *Chicago Tribune*, April 29, 1930.

43. *New York Times*, April 26, 1930. Before the game could be played, a minor league team in Independence, Kansas, played a regular season game under temporary lights on April 28. The game staged by Des Moines was the first played under a permanent lighting system.

44. *Chicago Tribune*, May 3, 1930; *New York Times*, May 3, 1930. It was estimated that the evening inflated Keyser's electric bill by twenty-five dollars.

45. *Sacramento Union*, June 5, 1930. The *Union* said of Moreing, "Hail Lou Moreing, Sacramento's Joshua! Moreing didn't exactly command the sun to stand still, but he spent $10,000 and turned night into day at Moreing Field last night."

46. *Sacramento Bee*, June 11, 1930.

47. *Sacramento Bee*, June 10, 1930.

48. In July 1929, former Seals catcher Sam Agnew and his partner, Doc Atkins, offered to finance a stadium for Moreing if he would move his team to San Diego. Moreing visited San Diego to investigate the possibility the same day his team lost its tenth straight game to fall into a last-place tie with Seattle. Bill Lane, obviously wanting San Diego for himself, declared he would never approve Moreing shifting his franchise there (*San Diego Union*, June 6, 1929; *Sacramento Bee*, July 23 and July 24, 1929).

49. *Los Angeles Times*, June 21, 1930. The third night game at Wrigley Field was notable for the performance of Sacramento's Fay Thomas, who struck out seventeen Angels, including nine in the final three innings. Thomas later had nineteen strikeouts in a thirteen-inning night game on October 9 against Hollywood (*Sacramento Union*, July 25 and October 10, 1930; *Los Angeles Times*, July 25, 1930; *The Sporting News*, October 16, 1930).

50. *Los Angeles Times*, July 2, 1930.

51. *Sacramento Union*, June 13 and June 14, 1930.

52. *Oakland Tribune*, June 13 and August 2, 1930.

53. *Sacramento Union*, June 14, 1930.

54. *Los Angeles Times*, June 18 and June 21, 1930.

55. *Oakland Tribune*, June 27, 1930.

56. *Oakland Tribune*, July 1, 1930; *San Francisco Chronicle*, July 1, 1930. Even though he was hitting .447 as a follow-up to his monstrous 1929 season, with a league-leading twenty-one home runs in eighty-two games, Boone was considered by many to be washed up as far as the major leagues were concerned. Boone did have a spectacular debut with the Dodgers, making a leaping catch while falling over the outfield fence to prevent a home run and then slugging a homer himself. But he was soon back in the minors for good, where he compiled a .370 lifetime batting average (*New York Times*, July 7, 1930).

57. *Oakland Tribune*, August 2, 1930. Chadbourne served occasionally as a substitute in the PCL during the 1930s but never again umpired on a regular basis. He committed suicide in 1943 at his nephew's home in Los Angeles, leaving behind a note that read, "Sorry to do this, and sorry for everything else." The revolver he had used lay at his side (*Los Angeles Times*, June 22, 1943).

58. *Oakland Tribune*, August 7, 1930.

59. *The Sporting News*, February 5, 1931; *Oakland Tribune*, February 11, 1931. Arlett responded to his sale to the Phillies by playing handball and working out at the YMCA in Oakland, an unprecedented level of exertion for the slugger. He started off sensationally for the Phillies in 1931 but a hand injury slowed him and after that he was not hitting well enough to offset his stationary defense in the outfield. Although he hit eighteen home runs, second best on the team, and batted .313, by the end of the season Arlett was on the bench, sent there according to Philadelphia sportswriter Bill Dooly because of his lack of defensive skills. During his stint in Philadelphia he was the subject of a poem by sportswriter George Edward Phair:

Buzz Arlett weighs half a ton
He cannot field; he cannot run
But when he wields his trusty wood
The pellet leaves the neighborhood.

Arlett was traded to Baltimore of the International League and *twice* hit four home runs in a game for the Orioles during the 1932 season. On the second occasion he hit five home runs in a doubleheader, with four coming in the first game. Arlett never returned to the majors or the Pacific Coast League. Of his 432 minor league home runs, 251 came in the PCL, which still stands as the league's all-time career mark (*Baseball Magazine*, August 1931; *The Sporting News*, December 24, 1931; *Baltimore Sun*, June 2 and July 5, 1932).

60. *Los Angeles Times*, June 1, June 5 and June 6, 1930.

61. *Los Angeles Times*, July 2, 1930.

62. *Seattle Post-Intelligencer*, June 17, 1930; *Los Angeles Times*, June 17, 1930.

63. *Los Angeles Times*, January 4, July 6 and July 19, 1931.

64. *Los Angeles Times*, August 28 and August 29, 1930. Rumler was hitting .353 with eighty-two runs batted in at the time of his injury. He returned to Nebraska and was a player-manager for Lincoln in the Nebraska State League. After he quit playing, Rumler served in several public offices in Milford, Nebraska, including police chief, fire chief, justice of the peace and marshal (*The Sporting News*, June 11, 1966).

65. *Los Angeles Times*, September 3, September 4, September 5 and September 7, 1930.

66. *San Francisco Chronicle*, March 13 and March 14, 1931.

67. Charlie Silvera, who grew up in San Francisco and later played for both Portland in the PCL and the New York Yankees, remembered playing on the site of Recreation Park while attending Mission Dolores School in the late 1930s. At that time it was a bare patch of ground studded with a generous helping of rocks. San Francisco State University later constructed an athletic field on the site. It too was torn down, to make way for housing during World War II (Charlie Silvera, interview with the author, April 4, 2009).

68. *San Francisco Chronicle*, April 8, 1931. The steel flagpole in center field was a gift from Mike Fisher (*The Sporting News*, June 10, 1943).

69. *San Francisco Chronicle*, April 24, 1931.

70. *The Sporting News*, June 11, 1931.

71. *Sacramento Union*, April 27 and April 28, 1931. Backer suffered a linear fracture of the left temple and was rendered deaf in his left ear. The fracture went from his temple to the base of his skull.

72. *Los Angeles Times*, August 2, 1931. Demaree's father had also gone blind due to cataracts, but the ballplayer was able to pay for an operation and his father's sight was restored.

73. *Los Angeles Times*, April 5, 1932.

74. *Los Angeles Times*, May 12, 1931.

75. *Los Angeles Times*, May 18, 1932.

76. *Seattle Post-Intelligencer*, May 4, 1931.

77. *Los Angeles Times*, July 8, 1931.

78. *San Francisco Chronicle*, October 14, 1931; *The Sporting News*, October 29, 1931. Williams had bristled all year at rules designed to curtail his drinking, viewing the scrutiny as a lack of respect. He and Carroll had been feuding all year and had not spoken to each other in two months. Several Seals players witnessed the brawl between Williams and Carroll but made no effort to break up the fisticuffs. When Williams met with Graham, he was handed a letter of resignation to sign. Williams tore it into little pieces.

79. *San Francisco Chronicle*, January 7, 1932. Carroll learned about athletic training from Roger Cornell, who had trained heavyweight champion Jim Jeffries and was employed by the Seals. When Cornell accepted an offer from Portland in 1909, Jack Gleason tabbed the twenty-nine-year-old Carroll to take Cornell's place. Carroll held the position for more than two decades, refusing numerous offers from major league teams. After being let go by the Seals, Bill Lane recommended

Carroll to the Detroit Tigers. Carroll disdained surgery on throwing arms, except in the case of bone chips. He had what he called "seeing fingers," manipulating muscles and tendons by feel, augmenting the process with heat treatments. Carroll was credited with playing a key role in Detroit's pennants in 1934, 1935 and 1940 through his ability to bring dead arms to life. He retired to Boyes Springs, California, in 1941 but players continued visiting him each winter in the hope that he could revive their careers. Carroll died at Boyes Springs in 1957 (*The Sporting News*, October 3, 1940, January 16, 1941, April 15, 1953 and September 25, 1957).

80. *Los Angeles Times*, December 20, 1931.

81. *Los Angeles Times*, November 3, November 4 and December 6, 1931; "Minutes of the Adjourned Meeting of the Directors of the Pacific Coast League, November 2, 1931," Dick Dobbins Collection on the Pacific Coast League, California Historical Society.

82. *Los Angeles Times*, December 25, 1931.

83. *Los Angeles Times*, January 27, 1932.

84. *Chicago Tribune*, January 19, 1932.

85. *Los Angeles Times*, January 27, 1932.

86. *Los Angeles Times*, January 29, 1932. Wrigley was interred in the mausoleum on Catalina Island from February 1935 until World War II, when his body was moved to Forest Lawn in Glendale, California.

87. *Los Angeles Times*, January 28, 1932.

88. *Los Angeles Times*, April 12, 1932.

89. *Oakland Tribune*, May 7, 1932; *Los Angeles Times*, May 6 and May 13, 1932.

90. *Los Angeles Times*, October 1 and December 13, 1931. Barbee was claimed for $7,500.

91. *San Francisco Chronicle*, May 24, 1932.

92. *Los Angeles Times*, April 24, 1932.

93. *Sacramento Union*, July 19, 1932; *Los Angeles Times*, July 19, 1932.

94. *The Sporting News*, July 7, 1932.

95. *Los Angeles Times*, January 14, 1934.

96. *Los Angeles Times*, October 3, 1932.

97. *The Sporting News*, October 20, 1932.

98. *Seattle Post-Intelligencer*, July 5, 1932. The financial loss was estimated at seventy thousand dollars, with roughly one-third of that amount covered by insurance (*Seattle Post-Intelligencer*, July 6, 1932).

99. *Seattle Post-Intelligencer*, July 8 and July 9, 1932. A year earlier the city had spent nearly $80,000 upgrading the stadium for the purpose of bringing PCL baseball to the facility, but it was less than ideal, with the light poles in foul territory and a right field prone to having balls get stuck in bushes. Leo Lassen, the long-time Rainiers radio announcer became famous for his cry, "There's a fly ball ... it's over the outfielder's head and rolling toward the gooseberry bushes!" (*Los Angeles Times*, August 20, 1931; Don Klein, interview with the author, February 3, 2009).

100. *Los Angeles Times*, March 6, 1932.

101. *Los Angeles Times*, September 17, 1924.

102. *Time Magazine*, August 15, 1932.

103. *Los Angeles Times*, August 1, 1932.

104. Koenig considered himself the goat of the 1926 World Series, hitting only .125 and making four errors, including one on an easy double-play grounder in the fourth inning of the seventh game that opened the door for the winning runs for St. Louis. The Cardinals walked Babe Ruth four times in the game and Grover Cleveland Alexander struck out Tony Lazzeri with the bases loaded in one of the most famous moments in baseball history. He bounced back to hit .500 in the 1927 World Series against Pittsburgh and also played in the 1928 Series when the Yankees got revenge against the Cardinals. Koenig later portrayed himself in two classic baseball movies, *Pride of the Yankees*, the story of Lou Gehrig, starring Gary Cooper, and *The Babe Ruth Story*, starring William Bendix. Koenig first tried making a comeback as a pitcher — he was thought to have the strongest throwing arm in baseball.

The Missions used Koenig as a pitcher in four games during late May and early June 1932. He lost three times and had a no-decision. One story about Koenig's throwing arm that still circulates occasionally is that he was clocked by a machine at West Point as throwing somewhere in the neighborhood of 127 miles per hour. The day of the test, Koenig warmed up but it was discovered the machine was broken and he had to come back later that afternoon. "I think I threw a ball 96 miles an hour," he said later. "But some book has me throwing 127 miles an hour! Can you imagine 127 miles an hour? Gosh, you wouldn't be able to see it." Ironically, Koenig said his best pitch was a knuckleball, but for some reason he never tried using it. As far as the "Called Shot" is concerned, Koenig and Frank Crosetti, who was also there that day as a rookie for the Yankees, had different views on the subject. While Koenig gave Ruth the benefit of the doubt, Crosetti called it nonsense and said that Ruth told him the day after the famous home run, "If those writers want to say I pointed, let 'em. It doesn't matter to me." For his part, when Charlie Root, who gave up the home run to Ruth, was with Hollywood in the 1940s, he told reporter Bob Hunter, "That Babe Ruth pointing over the fence when he hit a home run off me in the World Series? Never happened. If he'd done that, I'd have buried him at home plate" (Bob Hunter, interview with the author, November 9, 1991; Frank Crosetti, interview with the author, September 3, 1991; Mark Koenig, interview with the author, October 21, 1991; *Chicago Tribune*, October 2, 1932; *New York Times*, October 2, 1932).

105. *San Francisco Chronicle*, October 2, 1932.

106. *San Francisco Chronicle*, October 3, 1932.

Chapter Eleven

1. *Los Angeles Times*, October 19, 1932.

2. *Los Angeles Times*, March 11 and March 12, 1933. Many of those killed or severely injured were attempting to escape from buildings as brick walls literally exploded onto the streets below. There was major damage to schools; eleven in Long Beach had to be razed. Future Hollywood and St. Louis Browns first baseman Chuck Stevens was in junior high school in Long Beach when the quake struck: "I had run in a track meet that day and was one of the last guys to leave the campus.... The shower area I had been in was completely demolished." Stevens said that until his senior year in high school, his classes were held in tents. There was speculation that had the earthquake struck during the school day, the loss of life would have been incredibly high. A month later, in response to the massive failure of public school buildings, the California Legislature passed the Field Act, mandating standards of construction and authorizing the state Division of Architecture to review and approve all building plans for public schools. No school built in California under the Field Act has ever failed in an earthquake (*Los Angeles Times*, March 15 and April 11, 1933; National Information Service for Earthquake Engineering; Chuck Stevens, interview with the author, December 11, 2010).

3. *The Sporting News*, March 23, 1933. Vitt later discovered the hotel room he had originally been given at check-in had partially collapsed. He had changed rooms after finding the first room too noisy.

4. *Los Angeles Times*, March 12, 1933. The Sheiks insisted they would not return to the hotel and instead stayed the night at the gun club near the baseball field in Long Beach.

5. *Los Angeles Times*, March 13, 1933. The Angels agreed to move their training headquarters to Catalina.

6. *Los Angeles Times*, January 19, 1933.

7. *Los Angeles Times*, February 1, 1933.

8. *New York Times*, March 23 and April 4, 1933.

9. *Los Angeles Times*, January 15, January 21, and March 28, 1933. Newsom would pitch more than twenty years in

the major leagues and become more widely known by the nickname "Bobo."

10. *Los Angeles Times*, April 14, 1933.
11. *Los Angeles Times*, June 3 and December 6, 1933.
12. *Los Angeles Times*, April 12, 1933.
13. *Los Angeles Times*, September 17, 1933.
14. Jim Zinn, Jr., interview with the author, November 19, 1991. Jimmy Zinn, Jr., son of Jimmy Zinn, remembered shagging flies along with DiMaggio, Donovan and his father that spring. Zinn Jr. played minor league baseball from 1947 through 1953, mostly in the Eastern League, Florida International League and the Interstate League.
15. *Los Angeles Times*, April 5, April 6 and April 7, 1933.
16. *San Francisco Chronicle*, April 17, 1933. Herm Pillette's brother, Ted, surrendered DiMaggio's first base hit as a professional the previous October (*San Francisco Chronicle*, October 2, 1932).
17. The brothers played a few games together in the Seals lineup before Vince was released; their most notable game together was on May 4 when they hit back-to-back home runs against Hollywood. Vince was signed by Hollywood in early July. Vince's release was reminiscent of an incident the year before in Seattle when Louie Almada brought his brother, Melo, with him to spring training and then lost his job to him. Louie Almada, one of the most popular players in Seattle baseball history, signed with the Missions. Melo Almada became the first Mexican-born player to appear in the major leagues when he was purchased by the Boston Red Sox late in 1933. The Almada brothers had both been high school stars in Los Angeles and Lou Almada had a tryout with the New York Giants as a pitcher in mid–1920s (*Seattle Post-Intelligencer*, April 15, 1932; *Los Angeles Times*, May 5, 1933; *The Sporting News*, July 13, 1933).
18. *San Francisco Examiner*, May 29, 1933; *Los Angeles Times*, May 29 and May 31, 1933.
19. *Los Angeles Times*, May 29, 1933.
20. *Los Angeles Times*, June 12, 1933.
21. *Los Angeles Times*, July 1 and July 19, 1933.
22. *San Francisco Examiner*, July 6, 1933.
23. *Los Angeles Times*, July 14, 1933.
24. *Los Angeles Times*, July 15, 1933.
25. *Oakland Tribune*, July 23 and July 24, 1933; *Los Angeles Times*, July 24, 1933. Oglesby extended his streak to forty-four games with a run-scoring double off Oakland's Lou McEvoy on July 22. Before Joiner stopped him, Oglesby had hit for a .384 average with eight home runs and forty-five runs batted in during the forty-four games. His feat is often overlooked even though it is the third longest in league history, and one of the select few in professional baseball to stretch for more than forty games. Oglesby would suffer misfortune when he finally got his chance in the major leagues, with the Philadelphia Athletics in 1936. He won the first base job, but in the second game of the season he had his hand accidentally stepped on by Red Sox infielder Oscar Melillo. Blood poisoning set in and Oglesby had to be hospitalized several times. He missed the rest of the year and never played in the majors again. He managed several minor league teams after the war and in 1955 was employed as a guard at Douglas Aircraft in Tulsa, Oklahoma. Despondent over health issues, the fifty-year-old committed suicide with a shotgun two weeks after being released from the hospital (*The Sporting News*, April 30, June 25 and December 31, 1936, and September 14, 1955).
26. *San Francisco Chronicle*, July 24, 1933; *Sacramento Bee*, July 24, 1933. Ed Bryan, who gave up the hit in the nightcap, insisted he could not argue with the official scorer, saying the plays could have been ruled either way. He said, "I've seen batters given hits on much easier chances. If the kid wasn't going after a record nobody would have said anything about those hits" (*Los Angeles Times*, July 26, 1933).
27. *San Francisco Chronicle*, July 26, 1933; *Oakland Tribune*, July 26 and July 27, 1933.

28. Billy Raimondi, interview with the author, March 21, 2009.
29. After the streak ended, DiMaggio hit in six more games in a row before going hitless in five at-bats against Sacramento's Laurie Vinci on August 2.
30. *San Francisco Chronicle*, July 27, 1933. Joe Wilhoit's widow, who was operating a luggage shop in Los Angeles, followed DiMaggio's streak and said she appreciated the attention it brought to her late husband's record feat. Wilhoit had died of cancer at age forty-four in 1930 (*Los Angeles Times*, July 27, 1933).
31. *The Sporting News*, April 14, 1932; *Los Angeles Times*, February 2, 1934.
32. *Los Angeles Times*, December 7, 1933.
33. *Los Angeles Times*, August 2, 1933.
34. *Los Angeles Times*, August 12, 1933.
35. *Los Angeles Times*, September 7, 1933.
36. *Los Angeles Times*, September 8, 1933.
37. *Los Angeles Times*, September 11, 1933.
38. *Los Angeles Times*, September 20, 1933.
39. *Los Angeles Times*, September 24, 1933. Lillard added a double and two singles in the 10–2 win.
40. *Los Angeles Times*, September 27, 1933; *San Francisco Examiner*, September 28, 1933.
41. *Los Angeles Times*, December 6, 1933 and January 7, 1934.
42. *New York World Telegram*, March 10, 1936.
43. *San Francisco Chronicle*, November 5, 1932. Yankees scout Joe Devine said that when Eckhardt smacked an extra-base hit, "he usually runs until he is out." Eckhardt also played a season at halfback for the New York Giants in the National Football League (Joe Devine, letter to E.G. Barrow, August 10, 1935, Dick Dobbins Collection on the Pacific Coast League, California Historical Society).
44. *Brooklyn Eagle*, March 10, 1936.
45. *San Francisco Chronicle*, May 16, 1932.
46. *San Francisco Chronicle*, July 3, 1932. Like DiMaggio, Eckhardt had his hitting streak stopped by Ed Walsh, Jr. He came closest to getting a hit in the seventh inning with a sharp ground ball right over second base. However, Oakland second baseman Ray Brubaker was playing directly behind the bag as part of the Oaks' defensive shift against Eckhardt.
47. *Los Angeles Times*, July 13, 1933. Anna Pavlowa, or Pavlova, was a famous Russian ballerina.
48. *San Francisco Chronicle*, August 30, 1933. A boy retrieved the ball and brought it to Eckhardt to have him sign it. When one of Eckhardt's teammates tried to buy the ball back after it was autographed, the young man replied that he would not take one hundred dollars for it.
49. *Los Angeles Times*, November 4, 1933.
50. *The Sporting News*, February 15, 1934.
51. *Los Angeles Times*, August 19, 1933; *The Sporting News*, September 7, 1933.
52. *Los Angeles Times*, December 21, 1933; *The Sporting News*, December 28, 1933 and February 1, 1934.
53. *Los Angeles Times*, September 28, 1933; *The Sporting News*, October 5, 1933.
54. *Los Angeles Times*, January 26, 1934.
55. *Sacramento Union*, January 30, February 14 and February 15, 1934; *Los Angeles Times*, January 30, 1934. The banks had assured Moreing that if he could come up with $125,000, they were willing to take a $35,000 loss. After losing the team, Moreing focused on his mining interests in the Mojave Desert. He died suddenly in 1935, leaving his widow destitute. The team held a benefit for her in June 1935 that raised more than two thousand dollars (*Sacramento Union*, June 17 and June 18, 1935).
56. *Sacramento Union*, February 15, 1934.
57. *Los Angeles Times*, December 14, 1933.
58. *Oakland Tribune*, April 4, 1934.
59. *Los Angeles Times*, August 7, 1934.
60. *Los Angeles Times*, March 21, 1934.

61. *Los Angeles Times*, August 17, 1934. Doerr was playing for an American Legion team when he signed with Hollywood. He was not the only sixteen-year-old in the PCL; his close friend, George McDonald, was signed a few days later. The Angels signed another teenage friend of Doerr's, third baseman Steve Mesner, out of Riis High School. He was farmed out to Ponca City, Oklahoma, where he hit .359 in 135 games. Mesner was widely expected to start for Los Angeles in 1935. The agreement was that Mesner could only stay with the team if he took at least two subjects in school. Oscar Reichow suggested English and mathematics. During spring training it was reported that Mesner was doing well with English, but the jury was out on his math grades (*Los Angeles Times*, March 11, 1934).

62. *Los Angeles Times*, May 2, 1935.

63. Bobby Doerr, interview with the author, August 20, 1991.

64. *New York Times*, February 14, 1934; *Oakland Tribune*, February 13, 1934. Charlie Graham said, "Our proposal, granting that the Babe does not fully recover his health, is that the New York Yankees, with the permission of the major leagues, send him to the Seals for the coming season. We appreciate Babe Ruth is still an outstanding big leaguer but the one year out here would rejuvenate him and prolong his major league career for many years." Although Ruth never played in the Pacific Coast League, his bat did. In the late 1940s, a Seals fan brought one of Ruth's bats to the Seals clubhouse. Dino Restelli and Neill Sheridan handled it and Sheridan decided to use it in a few games. "It was like swinging a telephone pole," remembered Sheridan. "I actually did get a hit. I got the bat around and hit the ball with it and it jumped off the bat. I think it was forty-two ounces" (Neill Sheridan, interview with the author, February 25, 2009).

65. *San Francisco Chronicle*, May 22, 1934.

66. *San Francisco Chronicle*, May 27, 1934; *Los Angeles Times*, August 12, 1934.

67. *Los Angeles Times*, April 3, 1934.

68. *Los Angeles Times*, April 27, 1934.

69. *Los Angeles Times*, May 16, 1934; *Atlanta Constitution*, May 16, 1934.

70. *Oregonian*, August 1, 1934.

71. *Oregonian*, July 30, 1934. McCredie's dramatic final hours as depicted in the *Oregonian* sound suspiciously like the last reported moments of Confederate General Stonewall Jackson's life, as related by Dr. Hunter McGuire, who was the medical director of Jackson's Confederate Corps. In McGuire's account, Jackson returns in his mind to the battlefield and calls out orders to A.P. Hill. McCredie's uncle, the Judge, died nine months later at age seventy-three (*Los Angeles Times*, May 11, 1935).

72. *Los Angeles Times*, December 8, 1934; *The Sporting News*, August 29, 1935. A rare highlight for the Beavers was a forty-one-game hitting streak by outfielder Nino Bongiovanni, who had been acquired by Portland after being released by Seattle in early May. The streak began in the second game of a doubleheader against Sacramento on August 5. He was finally stopped on September 16 by Hollywood's Jack Hile after hitting .390 for those six weeks. At the time, it was reported that Bongiovanni had hit in forty-three straight games; however, he is shown as hitless in box scores for games of both August 4 and the first game of the doubleheader on August 5 and there is no indication of scorer's changes for either game. Bongiovanni hit in twelve more games in a row before going hitless on the last day of the 1934 season. Like Jim Oglesby's streak, Bongiovanni's did not get much notice, perhaps because of the fact it happened only a year after Joe DiMaggio's amazing streak (*Los Angeles Times,* May 3 and September 17, 1934; *The Sporting News*, September 27, 1934).

73. Herrmann was so upset at his treatment by the Cubs that he refused to sign a contract with San Francisco unless the Seals agreed to never sell him back to Chicago (*Los Angeles Times*, March 6, 1934).

74. *Los Angeles Times*, December 8, 1935. Lillard brashly predicted he would hit fifty home runs in 1934. He was one year off, reaching that mark in 1935.

75. Thomas' streak came to an end on July 6 against Seattle when he lost, 12–9. The Indians scored three runs in the first and then knocked him out of the box with seven runs in the fifth inning (*The Sporting News*, July 19, 1934).

76. *New York Times*, April 15, 1920; *Boston Globe*, June 8 and June 9, 1920.

77. *Los Angeles Times*, June 22, 1920 and April 9, 1933.

78. *Los Angeles Mirror-News*, January 21, 1957. Statz said that Ellis told him that cutting the center out of the glove kept the ball from bouncing out of it. Statz also said that modern gloves were more pliable, making it unnecessary to cut the pocket.

79. *Los Angeles Times*, June 5, 1925.

80. *The Sporting News*, July 25, 1940.

81. *The Sporting News*, June 9, 1938.

82. *Los Angeles Times*, October 25 and October 28, 1934. One story is that Lane and Vitt had a falling out when Lane tried to cut his manager's salary from $10,000 to $7,500 before the start of the 1933 season. Vitt balked and Lane responded by offering $6,000, saying, "Take (it) or leave it."

83. *Los Angeles Times*, October 26, 1934.

84. *Los Angeles Times*, November 4, 1934.

85. *Los Angeles Times*, March 5, 1935.

86. *The Sporting News*, October 18, 1934.

87. *The Sporting News*, March 28, 1935.

88. It was during the American tour of Japan that Sawamura became a legend, losing a 1–0 pitcher's duel while striking out Charlie Gehringer, Babe Ruth, Lou Gehrig and Jimmie Foxx in succession. Lou Gehrig hit a home run to account for the game's only run. Sawamura was pitching for the Giants after having been kicked out of high school for playing professionally. The Japanese equivalent of the Cy Young Award is named in his honor. World War II shortened Sawamura's career and cost him his life; he was killed when the ship on which he was serving was sunk in the East China Sea.

89. *San Francisco Examiner*, February 17, 1935.

90. *Los Angeles Times*, October 3, 1934. The St. Louis Browns selected Fay Thomas in the same draft.

91. *San Francisco Chronicle*, November 22, 1934; *New York Times*, November 22, 1934.

92. *Los Angeles Times*, April 1, 1935.

93. *Los Angeles Times*, April 2, 1935.

94. *Los Angeles Times*, April 3, 1935.

95. *Los Angeles Times*, July 21, 1935.

96. *Los Angeles Times*, May 2, 1935.

97. *The Sporting News*, August 1, 1935.

98. *Los Angeles Times*, August 16, 1935. Joe Marty switched places with DiMaggio.

99. *Chicago Tribune*, September 5, 1935.

100. *Los Angeles Times*, September 5, 1935.

101. *San Francisco Examiner*, September 12, 1935.

102. *San Francisco Examiner*, September 30, 1935; *Los Angeles Times*, September 30, 1935.

103. *Los Angeles Times*, September 23, 1935.

104. Frankovich had been signed by the Missions shortly after his college football career ended. He was a star quarterback for the Bruins and also a catcher on the baseball team. In a 1935 scouting report, Joe Devine said, "Frankovich cannot do anything.... Don't know why (the Missions) carry him." His baseball career was essentially over by 1938 and he became a baseball broadcaster. After a brief acting career, Frankovich worked for Columbia Pictures in Europe. While there, he oversaw the production of films such as *The Bridge Over the River Kwai, Lawrence of Arabia, The Guns of Navarone*, and *Dr. Strangelove*. He was made vice president of production at Columbia Pictures and was responsible for *Guess Who's Coming to Dinner?, Cat Ballou, A Man for All Seasons, Funny Girl*, and *In Cold Blood*, among others. Becoming an independent producer, he made a number of films

including *Bob & Carol & Ted & Alice, Cactus Flower, Butterflies Are Free*, and *The Shootist*, which was the last feature film for both Frankovich and the film's star, John Wayne. Frankovich was presented the prestigious Jean Hersholt Humanitarian Award in 1984 by the Motion Picture Academy because of his work for underprivileged children (*Los Angeles Times*, January 4, 1935 and April 8, 1984; Joe Devine, letter to E.G. Barrow, August 10, 1935, Dick Dobbins Collection on the Pacific Coast League, California Historical Society).

105. *Los Angeles Times*, September 23, 1935.

106. *San Francisco Examiner*, September 23, 1935; *San Francisco Chronicle*, September 23, 1935.

107. *New York Times*, February 13 and February 21, 1936.

108. *New York Times*, March 8, 1936.

109. *Los Angeles Times*, August 24, 1936. Eckhardt spent the rest of career in the American Association, the Texas League and the Southern Association. His final career batting average in the minor leagues was .367. Eckhardt died following a heart attack in 1951 at age forty-nine (*The Sporting News*, May 2, 1951).

110. *New York Times*, April 16, 1936.

Chapter Twelve

1. *Los Angeles Times*, November 5, 1935.

2. *The Sporting News*, November 28, 1935. Sacramento had sold pitcher Art Herring and outfielder Henry Steinbacher to St. Paul of the American Association, Harry Rosenberg and Max West were sold to the Missions, and Johnny Frederick and Tom Flynn were sold to Portland. The Senators traded Paul Gregory and Lou Koupal to Seattle for catcher John Bottarini, who was then sold to Los Angeles. Manny Salvo went to San Diego. The team also lost pitcher Bill Hartwig, who had hidden a serious kidney ailment all year and died shortly after the 1935 season ended (*Woodland Democrat*, October 10, 1935; *Sacramento Union*, October 11, 1935).

3. *Sacramento Union*, December 13, 1935; *The Sporting News*, December 19, 1935.

4. *Sacramento Union*, December 13, 1935.

5. *The Sporting News*, December 19, 1935 and January 9, 1936. The stadium lease had to be approved by a Sacramento judge because the bank holding the lien against the ballpark, the California Trust and Savings Bank of San Francisco, had gone out of business. The superintendent in charge of liquidation of the bank's assets on behalf of the institution's depositors agreed to the arrangement and allowed the St. Louis Cardinals to pay a grand total of just under sixteen thousand dollars over the five-year term of the agreement. Judge Malcolm Glenn, when approving the deal, remarked, "The depositors of the defunct California Trust Bank will be virtually a Santa Claus to Organized Baseball for five years."

6. *Oakland Tribune*, December 16, 1935.

7. *Los Angeles Times*, December 15, December 16 and December 18, 1935.

8. *The Sporting News*, December 26, 1935.

9. *San Diego Union*, May 3, May 5, May 28 and July 6, 1871.

10. *San Diego Evening Tribune*, March 4, 1901.

11. *Los Angeles Times*, January 22, 1936.

12. *Los Angeles Times*, February 1, 1936.

13. *San Diego Union*, January 29, 1936.

14. *Los Angeles Times*, February 2, 1936.

15. *San Diego Evening Tribune*, March 29, 1936; *San Diego Union*, March 29, 1936; *Los Angeles Examiner*, April 9, 1936.

16. *The Sporting News*, January 16, 1936.

17. *The Sporting News*, February 27, 1936.

18. *Sacramento Union*, March 5, 1936. There was little that Branch Rickey enjoyed more than offering his opinion

and talking baseball. As *Los Angeles Examiner* reporter Bob Hunter put it, "If you said hello to him, he'd talk to you for half an hour" (Bob Hunter, interview with the author, November 9, 1991).

19. *Sacramento Union*, March 4, 1936.

20. *Sacramento Union*, March 12 and March 13, 1936; *Los Angeles Times*, March 12 and March 13, 1936; *The Sporting News*, March 19, 1936.

21. Ad Liska, interview with the author, October 7, 1991.

22. *Washington Post*, September 13, 1928.

23. *The Sporting News*, May 24, 1945; Ad Liska, interview with the author, October 7, 1991.

24. Frank Dasso, interview with the author, August 19, 1991. Liska said that infielder Ken Richardson used to scream at him, "Why don't you stand up and pitch like a man!" (*Baseball Digest*, February 1946).

25. Larry Jansen, interview with the author, December 29, 1991.

26. John Leovich, interview with the author, 1990.

27. *The Sporting News*, May 9, 1946. Liska was not the first to use a heavy ball for warming up. His teammate, Harry Carson, had used one at Portland the year before Liska joined the Beavers. Carson claimed that if it made sense for hitters to swing a heavy bat to make a wood bat feel lighter, the same should hold true for pitchers and baseballs. Ernie Bonham used one in the major leagues in the 1940s and said he had gotten the idea from Willie Ludolph, who used one when they had been teammates in Oakland in 1937. Sam Gibson of the Seals also used an iron baseball (*The Sporting News*, April 4, 1935 and July 23, 1942; Neill Sheridan, interview with the author, February 25, 2009).

28. Lilio Marcucci, interview with the author, June 5, 1995.

29. Ad Liska, interview with the author, October 7, 1991.

30. *San Diego Union*, March 29, 1936; *Los Angeles Times*, March 29, 1936. The move happened so fast that when Lane posed with the players for their team first photo, there were not enough San Diego uniforms to go around and three players had to wear Hollywood shirts (*Los Angeles Times*, February 22, 1936).

31. *Los Angeles Times*, June 4, 1936.

32. *San Diego Union-Tribune*, April 4, 2004.

33. *San Diego Tribune*, April 1, 1936.

34. *San Diego Union*, April 2, 1936.

35. *San Diego Union*, July 5, 1936; *Los Angeles Times*, July 5, July 8 and August 1, 1936.

36. *San Diego Union*, July 16, 1936.

37. *Los Angeles Examiner*, July 20, 1936; *San Diego Union*, July 20 and July 21, 1936.

38. *Los Angeles Examiner*, July 22, 1936; Bob Hunter, interview with the author, November 9, 1991.

39. Bob Hunter, interview with author, November 9, 1991.

40. *San Diego Evening Tribune*, June 27, 1936.

41. Not that Lane went all out to install the best system he could find; for years players complained that balls were often invisible against the night sky due to poor lighting (*Sacramento Union*, August 21, 1949).

42. *San Diego Union*, August 28, 1936. Myatt married a softball pitcher named Georgia Smith. Bobby Doerr was his best man and the bride's sister was maid of honor. Unfortunately, the marriage did not last; only four days before their second anniversary, and just a week after George Myatt's major league debut with the New York Giants, Georgia Myatt sued her husband for divorce (*New York Times*, August 24, 1938).

43. *Los Angeles Examiner*, July 22, 1936.

44. *San Diego Evening Tribune*, June 26, 1936; *San Diego Union*, June 27, 1936.

45. *San Diego Union*, June 28, 1936; *San Diego Evening Tribune*, June 27, 1936.

46. Jimmie Reese, interview with the author, November 11, 1991.

47. Bobby Doerr, interview with the author, August 20, 1991.

48. *San Diego Union*, June 28, 1936. Williams' mother was Mexican. It is rarely noted that Williams was the first Hispanic inductee into the Baseball Hall of Fame. He was also an original inductee into the Hispanic Heritage Baseball Museum Hall of Fame in 2002.

49. Bill Conlin, interview with the author, May 28, 1995. Sam Crawford, who was working as a PCL umpire, called Marty the best long-ball hitter to play in the league (*Los Angeles Times*, May 19, 1936).

50. Lilio Marcucci, interview with the author, June 5, 1995.

51. Bill Conlin, interview with the author, May 28, 1995.

52. Bill Conlin, interview with the author, May 28, 1995.

53. *Oregonian,* May 27, 1936; *Los Angeles Times*, May 13 and May 16, 1936; *The Sporting News*, October 8, 1936.

54. *Los Angeles Times*, June 2 and June 6, 1936.

55. *The Sporting News*, September 24, 1936.

56. Bill Conlin, interview with the author, May 28, 1995.

57. *Los Angeles Times*, March 2, 1937.

58. Dominic DiMaggio, interview with the author, January 10, 1992.

59. *Los Angeles Times*, June 2, 1937.

60. *Oakland Tribune*, January 19, January 20, January 21, January 22, January 24 and April 4, 1937; *New York Times*, January 19, 1937.

61. *Los Angeles Times*, November 10 and December 18, 1936.

62. *Los Angeles Times*, December 20, 1936.

63. Tony Freitas, interview with the author, August 2, 1991.

64. *Sacramento Bee*, May 6, 1932.

65. Tony Freitas, interview with the author, August 2, 1991.

66. *New York Times*, July 2, 1934. Freitas had three hits off Dean in seven at-bats.

67. Tony Freitas, interview with the author, August 2, 1991.

68. Tony Freitas, interview with the author, August 2, 1991.

69. *Sacramento Union*, August 20, 1937.

70. *Sacramento Union*, August 21, 1937.

71. *Los Angeles Times*, August 21, 1937; *The Sporting News*, August 26, 1937. Powell, who had umpired in the National League and had several run-ins with John McGraw, who he blamed for his not being in the majors, failed to appear in court the next day and forfeited the ten-dollar bail Reese had put up for him. Sam Crawford was hired as Powell's replacement (*The Sporting News*, August 14, 1971).

72. *The Sporting News*, March 20, 1965.

73. *The Sporting News*, November 26, 1936.

74. Duane Pillette, interview with the author, April 14, 2009.

75. *San Diego Union*, June 23, 1937; *Los Angeles Times*, June 23, 1937.

76. *San Diego Union*, July 14 and September 2, 1937.

77. *Los Angeles Times*, August 26, 1937.

78. *Los Angeles Times*, January 16, 1938.

79. *The Sporting News*, December 16, 1937. Doerr and Myatt had been sold to the Red Sox after the 1935 season for seventy-five thousand dollars (*Los Angeles Times*, November 23, 1935).

80. *Seattle Post-Intelligencer*, September 20, 1937.

81. *The Sporting News*, September 30, 1937.

82. *The Sporting News*, May 4, 1939.

83. *Seattle Post-Intelligencer*, September 20, 1937.

84. *Seattle Post-Intelligencer*, September 20, 1937; *The Sporting News*, September 30, 1937.

85. *Seattle Post-Intelligencer*, September 21, 1937; *The Sporting News*, October 21, 1937. *Los Angeles Times* reporter Bob Ray claimed it was Dick Barrett who gave Klepper his black eye (*Los Angeles Times*, November 11, 1937).

86. *Seattle Post-Intelligencer*, September 21, 1937.

87. *Sacramento Union*, September 25 and September 26, 1937; *San Diego Union*, September 26, 1937.

88. *San Francisco Examiner*, November 2, 1937.

89. *Seattle Post-Intelligencer*, September 27, September 28, September 29, September 30 and October 12, 1937; *The Sporting News*, October 7, 1937.

90. *The Sporting News*, December 2, 1937.

Chapter Thirteen

1. *Seattle Post-Intelligencer*, December 16, 1937.

2. *Los Angeles Times*, March 27, 1938.

3. *Seattle Post-Intelligencer*, December 17, 1937.

4. *Seattle Post-Intelligencer*, December 16, 1937; *The Sporting News*, December 16, 1937. Sick was born in Tacoma, Washington, and grew up working in his father's brewery in Alberta. Sick entered Stanford while his father kept the business alive during Prohibition by selling soft drinks and renting out his freezer space. Once Prohibition ended in the United States in 1933, the Sicks expanded their brewery to serve much of the Pacific Northwest and western Canada. In 1935, they purchased the right to brew Rainier Beer. The Rainier brand is now brewed by Pabst.

5. *Los Angeles Times*, November 16, 1937; *The Sporting News*, November 18, 1937. Although he had briefly been a director of the Los Angeles Angels in the 1920s, the forty-six-year-old Francisco admitted he knew little about baseball. He had not even known the team had finished in last place the year before. When apprised of that, he said, "Boy, that won't do for us in Hollywood. We'll have to have a winner to do business and that's what I'll try and get for the Hollywood fans" (*Los Angeles Times*, July 25, 1938).

6. *Los Angeles Times*, September 25 and December 19, 1937.

7. *Los Angeles Times*, January 15 and January 24, 1938.

8. *Los Angeles Times*, February 26 and February 27, 1938. There were also concerns because the franchise had no other officers or directors in place at the end of February other than Killefer and Francisco. Rumors continually circulated that Fleishhacker would be forced to sell the franchise.

9. *Los Angeles Times*, May 23 and May 24, 1938.

10. *Los Angeles Times*, June 2, 1938.

11. *Oakland Tribune*, June 6, 1938.

12. *Los Angeles Times*, June 3, 1938.

13. *San Francisco Chronicle*, May 30, 1938.

14. *The Sporting News*, August 4, 1938.

15. *Los Angeles Times*, September 5, 1938.

16. *The Sporting News*, May 26, 1938.

17. *Los Angeles Times*, August 31, 1938. Yankees scout Joe Devine was among those who were unimpressed with Hutchinson. Devine repeatedly questioned Hutchinson's fastball and curve, as well as his temperament, noting that during a playoff game he began "acting like a spoiled kid" after a bloop single drove in two runs against him (Joe Devine, letters to E.G. Barrow, June 22 and September 27, 1938, Dick Dobbins Collection on the Pacific Coast League, California Historical Society).

18. *The Sporting News*, May 4, 1939.

19. *Seattle Post-Intelligencer*, June 16, 1938; *The Sporting News*, February 10, 1938.

20. Hillis Layne, interview with the author, August 24, 1991.

21. *Seattle Post-Intelligencer*, August 13, 1938. Nervous in front of the large crowd, Hutchinson walked six batters and struck out only three.

22. *Seattle Post-Intelligencer*, August 18, 1938. In Hutchinson's next start, also against Sacramento, he again had three hits in three at-bats—a single and two doubles—and drove in three runs. He won the game, 8–2. For the season,

Hutchinson batted .313 and drove in twenty-three runs (*Los Angeles Times*, August 22, 1938).

23. *Seattle Post-Intelligencer*, September 16, 1938.

24. *Los Angeles Times*, August 10, 1938.

25. *Los Angeles Times*, May 10, 1938.

26. *Los Angeles Times*, September 15, 1938.

27. *Sacramento Bee*, February 10, 1938. The windstorm caused several million dollars of damage in Sacramento and killed three people.

28. *Sacramento Union*, March 24, 1938. The Solons were fined $588.

29. *Sacramento Union*, May 9 and June 23, 1938; *The Sporting News*, July 7, 1938.

30. *Sacramento Union*, June 25, 1938.

31. *The Sporting News*, September 1, 1938.

32. *Oakland Tribune*, June 23, 1938; *Los Angeles Times*, June 30, 1938.

33. *Sacramento Union*, September 11, 1938; *Washington Post*, October 2, 1938; *Los Angeles Times*, January 16 and January 23, 1939.

34. Sacramento finished third in the regular season, then defeated Los Angeles in five games and did the same to San Francisco to clinch the new Governor's Cup.

35. *Seattle Post-Intelligencer*, December 13, 1938.

36. *San Diego Union*, August 31, 1938. Ward had not been pitching well — his final record would be 9–12 with a 5.02 earned run average. He broke the old PCL record for hitless innings in a game, set by Portland's Alex Carson in 1909 and matched by Bill Prough in 1916. By coincidence, Carson, a retired San Diego police officer, was working as a ticket taker at Lane Field the night of Ward's epic performance. Ward's opponent that night, Ray Prim, also pitched the entire sixteen innings.

37. *San Diego Union*, October 3, 1938; *Los Angeles Times*, October 3, 1938.

38. *San Diego Union*, October 4 and October 5, 1938.

39. *Los Angeles Times*, October 10, 1938.

40. *San Diego Union*, October 10, 1938; *Los Angeles Times*, October 26, 1938.

41. *San Diego Union*, October 12 and October 13, 1938.

42. *San Diego Union*, October 18, 1938.

43. *The Sporting News*, October 20, 1938. Baum tried to explain away Lane's will by saying his old boss had been frustrated after losing one hundred thousand dollars over his last five years in Los Angeles and had not updated it after the franchise turned around financially following the move to San Diego (*San Diego Union*, October 19, 1938).

44. *Los Angeles Times*, October 18, 1938. Lane's brother and his nephews and a niece unsuccessfully challenged the will, charging that Lane had been dominated by Miss Eastwood thanks to a "strange attachment induced by unnatural flattery" (*Los Angeles Times*, April 28, 1939).

45. *Los Angeles Times*, December 9, 1938; *The Sporting News*, December 15, 1938; *Time Magazine*, August 1, 1938.

46. *Los Angeles Times*, January 10 and February 17, 1939.

47. *The Sporting News*, December 22, 1938. Cobb retained his cowboy ways — he was part of a roping club in Hollywood and performed in amateur rodeos once a month, along with Clark Gable and Harpo Marx.

48. *The Sporting News*, December 28, 1939.

49. *Los Angeles Times*, April 4, 1939.

50. *Los Angeles Times*, February 23, 1939.

51. *Los Angeles Times*, March 29 and March 31, 1939; *The Sporting News*, January 8, 1958. Herman had last appeared in the major leagues as a pinch-hitter for the Detroit Tigers in 1937. He played for Jersey City in the International League in 1938, hitting eighteen home runs with a batting average of .348.

52. *Los Angeles Times*, April 1 and April 2, 1939. Stars right-hander Rugger Ardizoia pitched the best game during Gilmore Stadium's brief tenure as a Pacific Coast League ballpark, defeating Portland, 6–1, while allowing only four hits.

Portland's only run scored on a home run by opposing pitcher Bill Radonits. The stadium was torn down in 1951 to make room for CBS Television City (*Los Angeles Times*, April 9, 1939 and December 30, 1950; Rugger Ardizoia, interview with the author, February 13, 2009).

53. Bob Hunter, interview with the author, November 9, 1991.

54. *Oakland Tribune*, May 27, 1939.

55. *Los Angeles Times*, June 3, 1939.

56. *Oakland Tribune*, June 5, 1939.

57. *Oakland Tribune*, June 6, 1939. Art Cohn got his start as a sports reporter in Long Beach, where he was covering a track meet at the time of the March 1933 earthquake. He became a columnist for the *Oakland Tribune* and seemed to take particular delight in Cissell's tirade. He wrote about it several times, including when Cissell returned to Oakland in 1940 and again on the occasion of Cissell reporting to the San Francisco Seals in 1941. During the war, Cohn was with General MacArthur during his first offensive and was on a ship in 1944 that was torpedoed by the Germans. He wrote a biography of Joe E. Lewis, *The Joker Is Wild*, and turned to screenwriting, with credits including *The Set Up*, *Stromboli*, *Tomorrow Is Another Day* and *Red Skies of Montana*. He was working on a biography of film producer Mike Todd, the husband of actress Elizabeth Taylor, when both men were killed in a private plane crash in New Mexico in March 1958. Ms. Taylor was supposed to accompany the group to New York for an awards dinner but backed out at the last minute because of a cold. The plane that claimed her husband's life was named Lucky Liz. Chillingly, Cohn was talking to friends about the Todd biography, titled *The Nine Lives of Mike Todd*, shortly before his death, and told them, "I've almost got it finished except for one thing. I haven't got an ending" (*Oakland Tribune*, May 6 and May 9, 1940, July 1, 1941; *Los Angeles Times*, March 23, 1958).

58. *Los Angeles Times*, July 20, 1939.

59. *Los Angeles Times*, April 23, 1940.

60. By the late 1940s, Cissell had dropped out of sight. After his wife's death he began drinking again and in January 1949 was discovered living in a dingy one-room apartment in Chicago near Comiskey Park in miserable conditions, emaciated, near death and penniless. His thirteen-year-old son, Gary, was living with him. Charles A. Comiskey, grandson of the man who had paid $75,000 and players worth another $48,000 to acquire Cissell more than two decades before, arranged to have the ex-Sox star admitted to a hospital under the care of the team doctor. Cissell responded to treatment, gaining fifteen pounds in the first three weeks he was being treated, but his heart finally gave out and he died in March, never leaving the hospital. He was forty-five years old (*Chicago Tribune*, January 18, February 6, March 8 and March 16, 1949).

61. *San Francisco Chronicle*, August 4, 1939.

62. *Los Angeles Times*, April 23, 1939.

63. *San Diego Union*, March 26, 1939. Chaplin had seemed indifferent during most of spring training at El Centro, clearly unenthusiastic about playing another year in the minor leagues. Although he had agreed to contract terms, he had not actually signed, preferring to wait to see if a major league team might offer him a job. With the season fast approaching, Spider Baum told Chaplin that he needed to sign his contract or face suspension. Chaplin finally began to train seriously and the day before his death asked manager Cedric Durst if another intra-squad game could be played so he could get an extra workout. Afterward, Chaplin drove to El Centro from San Diego to sign his contract. However, before reporting to the Padres offices, he decided to make a short trip to Tijuana with a woman named Alma Hamilton. The two were returning from Tijuana at four o'clock in the morning with Miss Hamilton driving. Ahead in the darkness, an automobile had stalled and the three men in that car were trying to push it off the highway when Hamilton and Chaplin came along.

Realizing there was going to be a collision, the three men jumped out of the way just in time and witnessed the terrible, grinding crash. Miss Hamilton never saw the stalled car. She suffered only minor injuries but Chaplin was thrown through the windshield and bled to death because of a severed jugular vein. Chaplin left a wife and two young children. When the coroner examined Chaplin's remains, he discovered a blood-stained Padres contract in the ballplayer's coat pocket. It was still unsigned (*San Diego Union*, March 25, 1939).

64. *San Diego Union*, July 26, 1939.

65. *Los Angeles Times*, July 17, 1939.

66. *Los Angeles Times*, July 22, 1939. Radio Appreciation Night was an annual contest among the Coast League cities to see which team could draw the biggest crowd to honor their radio announcers. The crowd at Wrigley Field was largest in the Pacific Coast League in six years.

67. *Los Angeles Times*, August 24, 1939.

68. *Seattle Post-Intelligencer*, September 13, 1939; *Los Angeles Times*, September 13, 1939.

69. *Los Angeles Times*, September 27, 1939; *The Sporting News*, October 19, 1939. The Rainiers drew 517,657 — a minor league record that would stand until 1946. Seattle outdrew St. Louis, Pittsburgh, Boston and Philadelphia in the National League and Washington, St. Louis and Philadelphia in the American League, both in total attendance and in average fans per game.

70. *Long Beach Press-Telegram*, August 8, 1947.

71. *Oregonian*, April 1, 1946.

72. *Los Angeles Times*, November 14, 1939.

73. *San Francisco Examiner*, November 13, 1939.

74. Dominic DiMaggio hit .360, scored 165 runs and had forty-eight doubles, eighteen triples, fourteen home runs and thirty-nine stolen bases in 1939. He also showed off a terrific throwing arm, best displayed on August 20 when he threw out four Hollywood runners in a doubleheader at Seals Stadium. Two were retired at third base and two at home. O'-Doul called DiMaggio, who also had five hits in six at-bats that day, "The greatest player in minor league baseball" (*San Francisco Examiner*, August 21, 1939; *The Sporting News*, August 31, 1939).

75. *Los Angeles Times*, December 17, 1939; *The Sporting News*, February 29, 1940.

76. *Los Angeles Times*, May 13 and May 16, 1939.

77. *Los Angeles Times*, August 22, 1939; *The Sporting News*, February 29, 1940.

78. *The Sporting News*, December 28, 1939.

79. *The Sporting News*, February 29, 1940.

80. Ad Liska, interview with the author, October 7, 1991. When asked how to pitch Lou Novikoff, Billy Raimondi said, "The harder you threw the ball, the harder he hit it" (Billy Raimondi, interview with the author, March 21, 2009).

81. *Los Angeles Times*, August 31, 1940.

82. *Los Angeles Times*, June 13, 1939. Pitcher Rugger Ardizoia kept his rabbit's foot because he was doing well. He still had it seventy years later (Rugger Ardizoia, interview with the author, February 13, 2009).

83. *Los Angeles Times*, October 29, 1940.

84. *Los Angeles Times*, October 8, 1940. Named William Harrison Garrison Scott, "Shine" was always positive, always upbeat, possessed a great sense of humor, and became a symbol of the franchise. When someone asked Shine Scott how things were with him, he would inevitably reply, "Boy, they're great. You know every time the sun comes up it's a new world." He moved with the Vernon Tigers when they became the Missions in 1926 and then returned to Southern California when the franchise shifted to Hollywood. In the Missions' last year in San Francisco, rookie pitcher Rugger Ardizoia would drive Scott on errands and remembered the old trainer being so large, his truck tilted to one side. Ardizoia also fondly remembered that Scott had friends in Seattle who would give him a half-dozen crabs whenever the Missions played there and that Scott would invite several players to partake in a crab feed. Scott lived less than nine months after leaving his job (*Los Angeles Times*, August 10, 1922, February 22, 1923, July 18, 1933, November 10, 1937 and January 26, 1940; Rugger Ardizoia, interview with the author, February 13, 2009).

85. *Los Angeles Times*, December 24, 1940.

86. *Los Angeles Times*, June 28, 1936.

87. *Los Angeles Times*, December 27, 1940.

88. *Seattle Post-Intelligencer*, January 21, 1941.

89. *Los Angeles Times*, January 23 and January 24, 1941.

90. *Los Angeles Times*, March 10 and March 11, 1941.

91. *Los Angeles Times*, September 9 and September 10, 1941. Ray had been a reporter at the *Los Angeles Times* since graduating from high school in 1922 and began his column, "The Sports X-Ray," in 1934. Despite being told that his chance of survival was slim, Ray firmly believed he would win the battle. He never mentioned his illness and his final column was a routine piece on the status of the Angels and Stars. More than a thousand people attended Ray's funeral on September 12 at the Little Church of the Flowers in Glendale (*Los Angeles Times*, June 10 and September 13, 1941).

92. *New York Times*, January 5, 1941. Gillette's warning has been used by conspiracy theorists asserting that the U.S. Government allowed the attack on Pearl Harbor.

93. *Los Angeles Times*, January 26, 1941.

94. *Los Angeles Times*, February 2, 1941.

95. *Los Angeles Times*, February 5, 1941.

96. *Los Angeles Times*, February 7, 1941.

97. *Sacramento Bee*, October 16, 1940; *Sacramento Union*, October 16, 1940.

98. *Sacramento Bee*, February 18, 1941.

99. *Oakland Tribune*, May 9, 1941; *Sacramento Union*, May 9, 1941.

100. *Sacramento Union*, July 12, 1941.

101. *Los Angeles Times*, May 13, 1941.

102. *Seattle Post-Intelligencer*, February 26 and May 15, 1941. Averill hit only .247 with one home run and seventeen runs batted in for the Rainiers. He retired after the season.

103. *Los Angeles Times*, October 27, 1939.

104. *Los Angeles Times*, September 2, 1939. Bonetti's streak ended when he walked Hollywood's Len Gabrielson with two outs in the ninth inning of a game against the Stars on September 1.

105. *Oakland Tribune*, August 11, 1939; *Los Angeles Times*, August 11, 1939; *Chicago Times*, January 4, 1940.

106. *Los Angeles Times*, April 27, 1940.

107. *Los Angeles Times*, November 18, 1940.

108. *Los Angeles Times*, May 8, 1941.

109. *The Sporting News*, July 10, 1941.

110. *The Sporting News*, July 10, 1941.

111. *Los Angeles Times*, July 3, 1941.

112. *Los Angeles Times*, July 5, July 8 and July 9, 1941.

113. *Los Angeles Times*, July 4, 1941.

114. *Los Angeles Times*, July 14, 1941.

115. *The Sporting News*, July 31, 1941.

116. *Los Angeles Times*, July 17 and July 18, 1941.

117. *Los Angeles Times*, July 21, 1941.

118. *The Sporting News*, July 24, 1941. Terrell was able to accurately estimate his distance because it matched the setting on his camera when the fight started.

119. *Los Angeles Times*, July 23, 1941.

120. *Los Angeles Times*, August 1, 1941.

121. *Los Angeles Times*, July 22, 1941.

122. *Los Angeles Times*, July 24, July 28 and July 31, 1941; *The Sporting News*, July 31, 1941.

123. *Los Angeles Times*, August 1, 1941; *The Sporting News*, August 7, 1941.

124. *Los Angeles Times*, August 2, August 6 and August 7, 1941. Bramham stated, "It is my opinion, and I so find, that player Mayo did spit into the face of umpire Ray Snyder as charged. That the player was angry cannot be taken into consideration. It is argued that the player has a good reputation. Everyone has a good reputation until he commits some act to

destroy it. The statement of Umpire Snyder, the conduct of the player when confronted by President Tuttle with the charge made by the umpire, his silence and failure to cross-examine Umpire Snyder when the opportunity was offered him, are facts which strongly support this finding against him. President Tuttle's decision suspending player Mayo for one year is sustained."

125. *Los Angeles Times*, August 6, 1941.

126. *Los Angeles Times*, September 5, 1941.

127. *Los Angeles Times*, September 7, 1941; *The Sporting News*, September 11, 1941.

128. *Los Angeles Times*, September 10, 1941; *Oregonian*, September 10, 1941.

129. *Los Angeles Times*, September 17, 1941. Mayo was still docked his pay for the eight weeks he was suspended (*Los Angeles Times*, February 15, 1942).

130. *The Sporting News*, September 11, 1941.

131. *The Sporting News*, April 13, 1949 and June 25, 1952; *Los Angeles Times*, June 19, 1952.

132. *Seattle Post-Intelligencer*, September 8, 1941.

133. *Seattle Post-Intelligencer*, September 15, 1941.

134. *Seattle Post-Intelligencer*, September 20, 1941; *Los Angeles Times*, September 20, 1941.

135. *Los Angeles Times*, November 4, 1941.

136. *Los Angeles Times*, September 17, 1940.

137. *Los Angeles Times*, September 21 and October 1, 1941.

138. *Los Angeles Times*, October 11, 1941.

139. *Los Angeles Times*, October 9, 1941.

140. *Los Angeles Times*, November 13, November 14, November 18, November 19 and November 27, 1941. The Santa Catalina Island Company owned all but 191 shares out of nearly 127,000 issued.

141. *New York Times*, December 6, 1941.

Chapter Fourteen

1. *The Sporting News*, December 18, 1941.

2. *The Sporting News*, December 18, 1941.

3. *The Sporting News*, December 18, 1941. Greenberg finally returned to the Tigers for the last half of the 1945 season, thirty-four years old and having lost four and a half years of his prime. He only played two more seasons.

4. *The Sporting News*, December 18, 1941. In mid–January, President Roosevelt responded to a letter from Commissioner Landis by saying that he felt baseball should continue operating during the war "in order to provide recreation for a hard-worked populace" (*New York Times*, January 17, 1942).

5. *Los Angeles Times*, February 20, 1942. Ballplayers appearing in the film included Lefty O'Doul, Bill Dickey, Bob Meusel and Jack Salveson, who had the honor of hitting Cooper, as Gehrig, in the head with a baseball made of cotton.

6. *Los Angeles Times*, March 25, 1942. The Japanese attacked a couple of oil tankers off the coast of California in December 1941 and a third two months later. In late February 1942, a Japanese submarine lobbed several shells at an oil refinery near Santa Barbara. While the attacks caused some panic, there were no casualties (*Santa Cruz Sentinel*, December 21, 1941; *Los Angeles Times*, December 22, 1941; *Time Magazine*, December 29, 1941; *Santa Barbara News Press*, February 24 and February 25, 1942; *San Francisco Chronicle*, March 3, 1942).

7. *Oakland Tribune*, July 17, 1942; *The Sporting News*, July 23, 1942; Billy Raimondi, interview with the author, March 21, 2009. Benevento explained that the cave-in was caused by rain washing away the ground around a drain in the outfield. Mailho's version of the event changed over time. He began saying that he had been in the outfield when the sinkhole opened. Later he claimed he had made a play on a ball when it happened (Emil Mailho, interview with the author, June 13, 1995; *Oakland Tribune*, August 13, 2006).

8. *Los Angeles Times*, August 5 and August 18, 1942; *The Sporting News*, August 13, 1942.

9. *Los Angeles Times*, August 8, 1942.

10. *Sacramento Bee*, May 29, 1942; *Sacramento Union*, December 4 and December 6, 1941.

11. *The Sporting News*, August 20, 1942.

12. *The Sporting News*, June 18, 1942. The three had to go without their hats at all times when off the playing field. Failure to comply would result in a twenty-five-dollar fine.

13. *The Sporting News*, August 20, 1942.

14. *Sacramento Bee*, September 16 and September 17, 1942; *Los Angeles Times*, September 16 and September 17, 1942. Gene Lillard, who Pepper Martin used on a hunch, was one of the five pitchers battered by Los Angeles.

15. *Sacramento Bee*, September 17 and September 18, 1942; *Los Angeles Times*, September 18, 1942.

16. *Sacramento Bee*, September 19, 1942.

17. *Los Angeles Times*, September 19 and September 20, 1942. Sacramento pitcher Bill Schmidt was an unsung hero of the game. Entering in relief of Kemp Wicker with the bases loaded and no one out, he allowed three runs — one earned — in ten innings.

18. Jim Van Vliet, "Miracle of '42," *Sacramento Bee*, September 20, 1992.

19. *Sacramento Union*, September 21, 1942.

20. Tony Frietas, interview with the author, August 2, 1991.

21. *Sacramento Union*, September 21, 1942; *Los Angeles Times*, September 21, 1942; *Modesto Bee*, September 21, 1942.

22. Tony Freitas, interview with the author, August 2, 1991.

23. *Los Angeles Times*, October 7, 1942.

24. *Los Angeles Times*, October 21, 1942.

25. *Los Angeles Times*, February 24, 1943.

26. *Los Angeles Times*, November 25, 1942.

27. *Oregonian*, November 11, 1942; *The Sporting News*, November 19, 1942.

28. *New York Times*, October 30, 1942.

29. *The Sporting News*, April 3, 1943.

30. *Oakland Tribune*, June 1, 1943. Pippen threw sixty-four pitches and struck out only one batter.

31. *Oakland Tribune*, September 10, 1943.

32. *Los Angeles Times*, September 6, 1943. The Solons had bright spots. Al Brazle earned eleven of the team's first twenty-seven victories and his streak of forty straight scoreless innings was only six short of Bill Tozer's league record. Seventeen-year-old infielder Nippy Jones was considered a future major leaguer. John Pintar and Clem Dreisewerd pitched one-hitters in a doubleheader against San Francisco; Gus Suhr collected the lone hit in both games (*Sacramento Union*, July 19, 1943).

33. Emil Mailho, interview with the author, June 13, 1995.

34. *Los Angeles Times*, May 23, 1943; *Sacramento Union*, July 3, 1943.

35. *Los Angeles Times*, May 20 and May 21, 1943.

36. *Los Angeles Times*, July 16, 1943.

37. *Los Angeles Times*, July 30 and July 31, 1943. Sarni would hit .229 for the Angels. He eventually played five years in the major leagues, mostly for the St. Louis Cardinals. His best season in the majors was in 1954, when he hit .300 with nine home runs and seventy runs batted in for St. Louis.

38. *The Sporting News*, August 5, 1943.

39. *Oakland Tribune*, September 18, 1943.

40. *Los Angeles Times*, September 18, 1943; *Oakland Tribune*, December 3, 1943.

41. *New York Times*, August 1, 1943.

42. *New York Times*, November 13, 1943; *The Sporting News*, November 18, 1943.

43. *Oakland Tribune*, December 3, 1943. Brick Laws was serious about his pursuit of Ruth. He met with Ruth's agent, Christy Walsh, and also visited with Ruth during the winter meetings.

44. *New York Times*, December 9, December 10 and December 11, 1943; *Oakland Tribune*, December 10, 1943.

45. *The Sporting News*, December 16, 1943.

46. *Oakland Tribune*, December 24, 1943.

47. *The Sporting News*, August 13, 1942. Bill Lane had hired Henry "Old Peg" McWilliams as the team's mascot when he opened Lane Field in 1937. McWilliams, whose age was unknown, continued to sit on the Padres' bench as a good luck charm until his death in August 1942.

48. *The Sporting News*, July 23, 1942.

49. *Los Angeles Times*, July 26, 1942.

50. *New York Times*, August 21, 1942.

51. *Washington Post*, December 4, 1942. A popular story, still often taken as gospel, is that Bill Veeck tried to buy the Philadelphia Phillies during the winter of 1942 and stock it with black ballplayers. It is claimed that his effort to do so was thwarted by Judge Landis. The veracity of this tale is doubtful.

52. *The Sporting News*, August 6, 1942.

53. *The Sporting News*, August 13, 1942.

54. *Baltimore Afro American*, December 12, 1942. Nate Moreland was a native of Pasadena who had played in Mexico and for the Baltimore Elite Giants. Well known in the Los Angeles area, he would have been a drawing card for the Angels; instead, he was managing a bowling alley.

55. *Chicago Defender*, May 15, 1943. Interviewed fifty years later by Tony Cooper in the *San Francisco Chronicle*, Lou Dials claimed that Pants Rowland had wanted Dials and Brewer to try out for the Angels but that P.K. Wrigley had vetoed the idea. Dials said that Oaks owner Cookie Devincenzi then indicated he would offer the two men a tryout but when they appeared at Oaks Park, Oakland manager Johnny Vergez turned them away, saying, "They'll crucify me — I'll quit before I do (allow blacks on the team.)" It would be another five years before the PCL integrated (*San Francisco Chronicle*, March 1, 1993).

56. *Baltimore Afro American*, December 4, 1943; *New York Times*, December 4, 1943.

57. *Baltimore Afro American*, December 11, 1943.

58. *Los Angeles Times*, January 18, 1944.

59. *Los Angeles Times*, November 19 and November 27, 1941.

60. *Sacramento Union*, February 14, 1944.

61. *Sacramento Union*, February 15, 1944.

62. *Sacramento Union*, February 16, 1944.

63. *Sacramento Union*, February 17 and February 20, 1944.

64. *Sacramento Union*, February 23, 1944; *Los Angeles Times*, February 24, 1944. Among the two hundred and ten stockholders in the Solons was a soldier stationed in North Africa. Private Robert Knezevich had played some semi-pro baseball and heard about the drive to save the team. He sent $100 and became part-owner of the franchise (*Los Angeles Times*, May 1, 1944).

65. The Cardinals had one other condition — they had to offer St. Louis the right to purchase one player after the war ended. In 1946, they bought pitcher Gerry Staley to fulfill the obligation (Bill Conlin, interview with the author, May 28, 1995).

66. *Sacramento Union*, February 27, 1944; *Los Angeles Times*, March 7, 1944.

67. *Los Angeles Times*, April 8 and April 9, 1944.

68. *Los Angeles Times*, April 11 and April 12, 1944.

69. *Los Angeles Times*, May 1, 1944.

70. *Los Angeles Times*, April 9, 1944; *The Sporting News*, July 27, 1944.

71. *The Sporting News*, May 25, 1944.

72. *San Diego Union*, September 29, 1944.

73. *Los Angeles Times*, January 10, 1945.

74. *Los Angeles Times*, January 17, 1945.

75. *Los Angeles Times*, April 23, 1945.

76. *Palo Alto Daily News*, February 24, 2007.

77. *The Sporting News*, April 12, 1945.

78. *San Francisco Chronicle*, May 26, 1945.

79. *Los Angeles Times*, April 13, 1945.

80. *Los Angeles Times*, April 14, 1945.

81. *Los Angeles Times*, April 16, 1945.

82. *Oregonian*, July 27, 1945. Shone's streak began on May 30 but had only reached thirty-nine because of a rib injury that had disabled him for two and a half weeks. A few weeks earlier, he had learned that his younger brother, Elmo, had been killed in action in Belgium. A versatile athlete, Shone signed after the 1946 season to play for the Sacramento Nuggets of the minor league Pacific Coast Football League. He played outfield again for Portland in 1946 before turning to pitching, which he had done sporadically during his career to that point. He won twenty-one games for Albuquerque in 1948 and pitched briefly for Oakland in 1949, losing four of five decisions. Shone returned to Albuquerque in late May and finished the season there with a record of 17–7. He died in an automobile accident in New Mexico in December, 1949 (*The Sporting News*, April 26 and July 26, 1945, October 2, 1946; *New York Times*, December 3, 1949).

83. *Los Angeles Times*, July 23 and July 24, 1945; *The Sporting News*, July 26, 1945.

84. *Los Angeles Times*, August 25, 1945.

85. *Los Angeles Times*, August 26, 1945.

86. *The Sporting News*, July 12, 1945.

87. *The Sporting News*, August 30, 1945. Joyce had pitched for the Philadelphia Athletics in 1939, winning three games and losing five in thirty appearances.

88. *San Francisco Chronicle*, September 3, 1945. It turned out that was not Joyce's thirtieth win of the season after all. In a situation that mirrored that of Buck Newsom in 1933, when he also was prematurely credited with thirty wins, Pants Rowland ruled that a win awarded earlier in the season to Joyce should not have been. Joyce had entered a game against Portland on May 25 as a relief pitcher in the bottom of the thirteenth inning after the Seals had already taken a 5–4 lead. He shut out the Beavers in the bottom of the inning and was erroneously credited with the victory. Joyce officially captured his thirty-first win on September 21 with a 5–4 win over Los Angeles (*Los Angeles Times*, May 26, September 12 and September 22, 1945; *San Francisco Examiner*, September 22, 1945; *The Sporting News*, September 27, 1945).

89. *The Sporting News*, October 18, 1945.

90. *Sacramento Union*, March 18, 1935. Angelich pitched eight innings in the loss.

91. *Stockton Daily Evening Record*, March 22, 1935. Starfin was of Russian parentage and eventually became the first pitcher in Japanese history to record three hundred career victories. He was not quite nineteen years old when he pitched against Angelich in 1935. Starfin was under house arrest during the war because he was not Japanese (*The Sporting News*, January 23, 1957).

92. *Los Angeles Times*, March 30, 1942. Angelich was on a list of eighty-seven additional casualties from December 7 that was released by the military some four months after Pearl Harbor.

93. *The Sporting News*, February 15, 1945.

94. *Los Angeles Times*, July 11, 1948.

95. *Oakland Tribune*, February 9 and February 20, 1945; *The Sporting News*, February 15, 1945; Billy Raimondi, interview with the author, March 21, 2009.

96. *Oakland Tribune*, June 29, 1947. Like Manuel Hernandez, Raimondi was first buried in Europe and then his body was returned to the United States in 1948 (*The Sporting News*, May 19, 1948).

97. *San Francisco Chronicle*, March 5, 1937.

98. *Stockton Daily Evening Record*, November 9, 1942; *Ogden Standard-Examiner*, November 11, 1942.

99. *Merced Sun–Star*, August 29, 1941; Wally Westlake, interview with the author, February 12, 2010.

100. *Merced Sun–Star*, September 5, 1941.

101. *Ogden Standard-Examiner*, December 9, 1942.

102. *The Sporting News*, November 19, 1942.

103. *Stockton Record*, May 29 and May 31, 1943.

104. There were others killed in accidents during the war while serving in the military. Former Oakland and Seattle pitcher Marcel Serventi was stationed at Fort Ord in 1941 when he died in a single car accident while returning to the base from Oakland on July 4, 1941. Former Sacramento infielder Jim Grilk was working as a civilian, organizing the military sports program at the Sacramento Army Air Base. He was in an automobile accident on July 13, 1942, near Woodland, California, and suffered a fractured skull and other injuries. Grilk never regained consciousness and died three days later. Hal Dobson, who briefly pitched for Sacramento early in the 1941 season, was stationed in Victorville for advanced flight training. On May 23, 1943, his plane collided with another over Silver Lake in California. Those in the other plane managed to make it safely back but Dobson and his crew were killed. Dobson had just married his high school sweetheart a month earlier (*Oakland Tribune*, July 6 and July 9, 1941; *The Sporting News*, July 23, 1942 and June 3, 1943; *Los Angeles Times*, May 24, 1943).

105. *Sacramento Union*, July 21, 1945.

106. *Sacramento Union*, September 10, 1945; *The Sporting News*, September 13, 1945.

107. *Oakland Tribune*, September 9, 1945; *Sacramento Union*, September 9, 1945.

Chapter Fifteen

1. Bill Conlin, interview with the author, May 28, 1995. O'Doul showed his contract to Conlin.

2. Dominic DiMaggio, interview with the author, January 10, 1992.

3. Frank Dasso, interview with the author, August 19, 1991.

4. Bobby Doerr, interview with the author, August 20, 1991.

5. Lilio Marcucci, interview with the author, June 5, 1995.

6. Larry Jansen, interview with the author, December 29, 1991.

7. Neill Sheridan, interview with the author, February 25, 2009.

8. *The Sporting News*, June 21, 1945; Billy Raimondi, interview with the author, March 21, 2009.

9. *Oakland Tribune*, October 17, 1945; *The Sporting News*, October 25, 1945.

10. Bob Hunter, interview with the author, November 9, 1991. Bill Conlin remembered Stengel, full of whiskey, reenacting a stolen base on the linoleum floor in the hotel lobby. Seattle infielder Hillis Layne remembered, "He told us stories all day, just one after another. Never take a breath hardly. And Mrs. Stengel would come, it must've been five-thirty, and she says, 'Case, are you going talk all day or are you going to go to the ballpark?' He said, 'Oh, I got coaches taking care of that.' And he kept on and *we* almost didn't get to the ballpark" (Bill Conlin, interview with the author, May 28, 1995; Hillis Layne, interview with the author, August 24, 1991).

11. *New York Times*, April 25, 1945.

12. *Montreal Gazette*, October 24, 1946; *New York Times*, October 26, 1945.

13. *New York Times*, October 25, 1945.

14. After the signing of several Negro League stars in the early 1940s, the Pasquel brothers targeted major leaguers after the end of World War II in yet another serious challenge to Organized Baseball's reserve clause. They signed eighteen major league players and even made headlines with some of their failures, including offers of three-year, $360,000 contracts to Ted Williams and Hank Greenberg, and five years

for $500,000 to Bob Feller. But the brothers quickly fell out with each other. Critics of the Pasquels questioned how they could afford the high salaries they were paying; in truth, the 1946 season was far from profitable. Still, Jorge Pasquel trudged to the United States and tried unsuccessfully to sign Roy Campanella. Two teams dropped out of the league prior to the 1947 season and two more threatened to fold. A salary limit was imposed and the star players were asked to take major cuts in pay. The 1948 season ended early because of financial problems and the Pasquels' dreams of major league status dwindled away. Pasquel pursued a lawsuit against former Brooklyn Dodger star Mickey Owen, who had jumped his contract in a pay dispute, and eventually won $35,000 on appeal in 1952. Three years later, Jorge Pasquel and five others died when Pasquel's private plane crashed 225 miles northwest of Mexico City in the San Luis Potosi Mountains. A month after Pasquel's death, the Mexican League opened its 1955 season as a new member of Organized Baseball (*Los Angeles Times*, April 2, 1946 and March 9, 1955; *The Sporting News*, January 22, March 5, March 19, 1947, February 4 and March 3, 1948, January 12, 1949 and April 13, 1955).

15. *Los Angeles Times*, May 7, 1946; *Seattle Post-Intelligencer*, May 31, 1946; *Oregonian*, June 4 and June 5, 1946.

16. *Chicago Defender*, May 25, 1946.

17. *Fresno Bee*, May 7, 1946; *Oakland Tribune*, May 12, 1946. The Tigers played at Italian Recreation Park in Fresno and lost what would be their only game to Oakland, 16–1, before moving to San Diego.

18. *Seattle Times*, June 2, 1946; *Seattle Post-Intelligencer*, June 2, 1946.

19. *Oregonian*, June 20, 1946.

20. *Fresno Bee*, May 22, 1946; *San Diego Union*, May 22, 1946.

21. *San Diego Union*, May 26, 1946.

22. *San Diego Union*, May 27, 1946.

23. *San Francisco Chronicle*, May 6, 1946.

24. *Los Angeles Times*, April 22, 1946.

25. *Los Angeles Times*, May 21, 1946; *The Sporting News*, June 5, 1946.

26. *Seattle Post-Intelligencer*, May 11, 1946.

27. Bill Skiff letter to Bill Mulligan, May 3, 1946, Washington State Historical Society.

28. *Oakland Tribune*, May 31, 1946; *Seattle Post-Intelligencer*, May 31 and June 4, 1946.

29. *Seattle Post-Intelligencer*, June 4 and June 11, 1946.

30. *Seattle Post-Intelligencer*, June 12, 1946; *The Sporting News*, June 26, 1946; "Minutes of the Special Board Meeting of the Seattle Rainiers Baseball Club, June 10, 1946"; Letter dated June 17, 1946 from Emil Sick to S.F. Chadwick, attorney for the Seattle Rainiers; Letter dated June 18, 1946 to Seattle Rainiers Baseball Club from S.F. Chadwick; Notice of Bill Skiff's resignation, dated June 19, 1946, Washington State Historical Society.

31. *Seattle Post-Intelligencer*, June 13, June 14 and June 16, 1946. White was paid $1,000 per month to serve as player-manager (Seattle Rainiers files, Washington State Historical Society).

32. *Los Angeles Times*, June 22, 1946; *The Sporting News*, June 26, 1946.

33. *Los Angeles Times*, July 2, 1946; *Alfred J. Niemiec vs. Seattle Rainiers Baseball Club, Inc.* Niemiec received $2,884.50, plus six percent interest, which amounted to just over twenty dollars. The Rainiers also settled with Len Gabrielson and two other players; John Yelovich was paid $1,000 and Larry Guay accepted $1,100. The San Francisco Seals were forced to pay two players, outfielders Henry Steinbacher and Wallace Carroll in back pay. Steinbacher received $5,184 and Carroll $3,334 in back pay ("Seattle Rainiers Baseball Club, Inc. Bonus Payments 1946," Washington State Historical Society).

34. *Oakland Tribune*, April 22, 1946. Paul Fagan continued to pay Perry his full salary. When the injury proved so severe

that Perry was out for a second season, Fagan hired him as a full-time scout. Perry eventually recovered and played several years in the lower minor leagues. He had four incredible seasons with Redding in the Far West League, including back-to-back .400 seasons in 1948 and 1949 and 170 runs driven in during the 1950 season. He drove in 100 or more runs eight times after his injury and won seven home run titles, all in the lower minor leagues. Fagan was known for his generosity with players. Neill Sheridan said that when his wife was having a baby, the Seals owner visited the hospital and gave the couple a portable radio and covered the hospital bill (*The Sporting News*, May 2, 1946 and May 7, 1947; Neill Sheridan, interview with the author, February 25, 2009).

35. Letter from Joe Devine to E.G. Barrow, December 30, 1941, Dick Dobbins Collection on the Pacific Coast League, California Historical Society. Graham had hoped to sell the two players for a combined $90,000 but offered them to the Yankees for $20,000 each, provided he could keep them another year.

36. *The Sporting News*, October 16, 1946.

37. *The Sporting News*, May 7, 1942.

38. *The Sporting News*, August 21, 1946; Larry Jansen, interview with the author, December 29, 1991.

39. *San Francisco Chronicle*, September 20, 1946.

40. *Oakland Tribune*, April 14 and May 1, 1946.

41. *Oakland Tribune*, June 29, 1946; *Los Angeles Times*, June 6, 1937.

42. *The Sporting News*, August 7, 1946.

43. *Oakland Tribune*, July 11, 1946; *The Sporting News*, August 14, 1946.

44. *The Sporting News*, August 21, 1946.

45. *Spokane Daily Chronicle*, June 25, 1946; *Los Angeles Times*, June 25 and June 26, 1946; *The Sporting News*, July 3 and July 10, 1946; *Sports Illustrated*, November 14, 1994. Immediately before the bus crashed through a guardrail and down a three-hundred-foot embankment, Gus Hallbourg remarked to teammate Bob Kinnaman, "This would be a hell of a place to go off the road." The cause of the crash was never determined. The driver, who survived the accident, claimed he was forced off the road by an oncoming vehicle but that was never confirmed. Pitcher Pete Barisoff was credited with saving teammate Irwin Konopka, who was trapped in the wreckage. Barisoff, who suffered minor injuries, died three years later in a house fire. Among the dead with ties to Oakland were Picetti, Kinnaman, Bob Paterson and Chris Hartje, who had joined the team only a few days earlier. One player, Jack Lohrke, was called off the bus at its last stop before the crash because he was being recalled by the San Diego Padres. Lohrke had also once escaped death when he was bumped from a transport plane that crashed, killing everyone aboard. A veteran of both D-Day and the Battle of the Bulge, Lohrke saw men to each side of him killed during combat in World War II. Although he never cared for the nickname, because of these events Lohrke would forever after be known as "Lucky" (*Los Angeles Times*, November 13, 1949; *USA Today*, April 30, 2009).

46. *Spokane Daily Chronicle*, July 9, 1946. Nine empty seats were set behind home plate with a placard placed on each bearing a deceased player's name. A total of $118,000 was raised and distributed to the surviving players and the families of those that died (*Oakland Tribune*, July 9, 1946; *Spokane Daily Chronicle*, December 20, 1946).

47. As impressive as the Seals new record was, they only outdrew two major league teams in 1946 — the Philadelphia Athletics and the St. Louis Browns — as opposed to the seven big league teams the Seattle Rainiers outdrew in 1939. The Louisville Redbirds of the American Association finally broke the Seals' record by drawing more than 800,000 in 1983.

48. *Los Angeles Times*, September 26 and September 30, 1946.

49. *The Sporting News*, October 2, 1946.

50. *Los Angeles Times*, January 13, 1946.

51. *The Sporting News*, February 26, 1947. To unveil the new backstop, Fagan had Bob Chesnes, his hardest throwing pitcher, fire baseballs at it from only a few feet away. The glass was unscratched. There were problems to be solved, however. Game sounds were deadened by the thick Plexiglas, so speakers were installed. Also, the glass would fog over on cold nights, so ushers had to use mops to clear the view for the spectators (*Pittsburgh Post-Gazette*, December 12, 1947).

52. Larry Jansen, interview with the author, December 29, 1991. Jansen said that Fagan promised the players rings after they won the pennant, and then said he would add a diamond to it if they won the playoffs. After the Seals won the two post-season series, Fagan kept his promise. Two of the rings, which went to Jansen and Ferris Fain, contained diamonds larger than the others.

53. *The Sporting News*, January 1, 1947.

54. *Historical Happenings — A Publication of the Brea Historical Society*, August 2003.

55. *The Sporting News*, March 18, 1943.

56. *Oakland Tribune*, September 12, 1942.

57. Irv Noren, interview with the author, February 15, 2010; *Oakland Tribune*, September 13, 1942.

58. *Sacramento Bee*, May 8, 1947; *Los Angeles Times*, May 8, 1947; *Long Beach Press-Telegram*, May 9, 1947; *The Sporting News*, May 14 and May 21, 1947.

59. *Sacramento Union*, August 9, 1947; *The Sporting News*, August 20, 1947.

60. *Oregonian*, April 22, 1946. Johnny Lush threw a no-hitter at Vaughn Street Park in 1914 against Venice but lost, 1–0.

61. Charlie Silvera caught for Portland in 1947 and 1948 and said the New York Yankees wanted to obtain Bridges, but he wanted to stay in Portland (Charlie Silvera, interview with the author, April 4, 2009).

62. *Los Angeles Times*, April 21, 1947; *New York Times*, May 6, 1947.

63. *Sacramento Union*, May 17, 1948; *Seattle Post-Intelligencer*, May 17, 1948.

64. *The Sporting News*, May 26, 1948.

65. *Sacramento Union*, April 7, 1948.

66. *San Francisco Chronicle*, September 29, 1947.

67. *San Francisco Chronicle*, September 29, 1947; *San Francisco Examiner*, September 29, 1947; *San Diego Union*, September 29, 1947.

68. *San Francisco Chronicle*, September 30, 1947; *Los Angeles Times*, September 28 and September 30, 1947.

69. Cliff Chambers, interview with the author, January 7, 2010.

70. *Chicago Defender*, December 6, 1947.

71. *San Diego Union*, November 23, 1947. Starr informed hotels in PCL cities of Ritchey's signing and suggested that there be no problems if the hotels wanted to keep the team's business. Nevertheless, Ritchey sometimes had to stay at different hotels than his teammates. He also had to room alone. Although racism in the West was not as pervasive as in the South, it was still there. In 1957, black players were still segregated in the living quarters at the San Diego spring training camp in Ontario, California (Jim "Mudcat" Grant, interview with the author, November 21, 2010; *The Sporting News*, April 14, 1948).

72. Bill Conlin, interview with the author, May 28, 1995. Joe Brovia recalled that Georgia native Johnny Rucker tried to circulate a petition to prevent blacks from playing in the PCL (*Sports Collector's Digest*, December 1, 1989).

73. *San Diego Union*, March 31, 1948; *Los Angeles Times*, March 31, 1948; *The Sporting News*, April 7, 1948.

74. *San Diego Union*, April 1, 1948.

75. *San Diego Union*, April 2, 1948.

76. *San Diego Union*, May 18, 1948.

77. Seymour, Harold, *Baseball: The Golden Age*, page 196.

78. *The Sporting News*, November 26, 1947.

79. *The Sporting News*, December 31, 1947. In 1946,

Salenger offered to purchase the Pittsburgh Pirates for slightly more than two million dollars (*Pittsburgh Post-Gazette*, July 3, 1946; *The Sporting News*, July 17, 1946).

80. *Sacramento Union*, November 16, 1947; *Sacramento Bee*, June 7, 1948.

81. *The Sporting News*, June 9, 1948.

82. *San Francisco Chronicle*, March 31, 1948; *San Diego Union*, March 31, 1948; *The Sporting News*, April 14, 1948.

83. *The Sporting News*, October 1, October 29, November 5, November 12 and December 3, 1947, January 14 and February 4, 1948; *Oregonian*, June 2, 1946. Clint Conatser claimed that in the 1950s, fires broke at nearly every game and firemen were always present (Clint Conatser, interview with the author, January 29, 2011).

84. *The Sporting News*, June 9, 1948; Charlie Silvera, interview with the author, April 4, 2009; Duane Pillette, interview with the author, April 14, 2009. The Beavers were playing in Seattle when they heard about the disaster. General Manager Bill Mulligan rushed to the site to search for the ballplayers' families. Those losing their homes and personal belongings included Smith, Jake Mooty, Duane Pillette, Frankie Zak and Fenton Mole (*The Sporting News*, August 18, 1948).

85. Duane Pillette, interview with the author, April 14, 2009.

86. *Oakland Tribune*, May 10, 1948; *Los Angeles Times*, May 11 and May 15, 1948; *The Sporting News*, May 26, 1948.

87. *The Sporting News*, June 9, 1948.

88. *Oakland Tribune*, May 5, 1948; *The Sporting News*, May 19, 1948; Lloyd Hittle, interview with the author, March 27, 2009. Lombardi hit another home run later that week that traveled almost as far. He had nearly retired in April when his wife was hospitalized and had to undergo a serious operation. He reconsidered after her recovery and rejoined the team in late April (*Sacramento Union*, April 28, 1948; *The Sporting News*, May 5, 1948; *Oakland Tribune*, May 10, 1948; *Hayward Review*, May 10, 1948).

89. *Oakland Tribune*, May 20, 1948.

90. *San Francisco Chronicle*, May 25, 1948.

91. *Oakland Tribune*, August 2, 1948. Martin gave his own account: "Stringer landed the first punch on my jaw, but it didn't even shake me. If this had been Phoenix (where Martin played the previous year), I would have gone to town, but I didn't want to do anything that might put me on the spot in the Coast League."

92. *The Sporting News*, June 1, 1949.

93. Rugger Ardizoia, interview with the author, February 13, 2009.

94. *Los Angeles Times*, March 31, 1948.

95. *San Diego Union*, May 19 and May 20, 1948.

96. *Sacramento Bee*, June 7, 1948; *Los Angeles Times*, June 7, 1948.

97. *New York Times*, April 7, 1948.

98. *Los Angeles Times*, April 1, 1948.

99. *San Diego Union*, April 1, 1948.

100. *The Sporting News*, July 28, 1948.

101. *Oakland Tribune*, June 2, 1948; *The Sporting News*, June 16, 1948.

102. *San Diego Union*, July 19, 1948.

103. Red Adams, interview with the author, April 26, 2009.

104. *San Diego Union-Tribune*, July 26, 1948; *Los Angeles Times*, July 26, 1948; Red Adams, interview with the author, April 26, 2009. Graham's career had been affected by a previous incident in Montreal in 1942 when he was hit in the cheek by a pitch that permanently impaired the vision in his right eye (*Montreal Gazette*, June 22, 1942; *San Diego Union*, August 5, 1948).

105. *San Diego Tribune*, August 4 and August 6, 1948.

106. Lilio Marcucci, interview with the author, June 5, 1995.

107. *Sacramento Union*, July 10 and July 13, 1948.

108. *Sacramento Union*, July 12 and July 13, 1948.

109. *Los Angeles Times*, July 13, 1948; *The Sporting News*, July 21, 1948.

110. Cuno Barragan, interview with the author, December 1, 2010. Barragan, who used to go to the ballpark each day in the seventh inning so he could get into the games for free, later became catcher for the Solons.

111. Salenger had given Separovich a four-week option to buy him out but was rebuffed. Salenger then announced that he would request that Separovich be fired (*The Sporting News*, July 14 and July 21, 1948).

112. Bill Conlin, interview with the author, May 28, 1995.

113. *The Sporting News*, July 21, 1948; *Sacramento Union*, July 16, 1948. Salenger retained four shares "for sentimental reasons" (*The Sporting News*, July 28, 1948; *Sacramento Union*, March 7, 1949).

114. *Sacramento Union*, August 18, 1948. The players were reimbursed for personal property and equipment lost in the fire (*Sacramento Union*, July 16, 1948).

115. *The Sporting News*, September 8, 1948.

116. *San Francisco Examiner*, August 30, 1948.

117. *Oakland Tribune*, August 23 and August 26, 1948; *The Sporting News*, September 8, 1948.

118. *Oakland Tribune*, September 18, 1948; *The Sporting News*, October 6, 1948.

119. *Oakland Tribune*, August 27, 1948; *The Sporting News*, September 8, 1948.

120. *Oakland Tribune*, August 15, 1948. Billy Raimondi was instructed by Casey Stengel to tell Buxton to throw nothing but screwballs. He was to add, "And if you throw anything else, tell them it is a screwball" (Billy Raimondi, interview with the author, March 21, 2009).

121. *Oakland Tribune*, August 27, 1948.

122. *Oakland Tribune*, September 22, 1948.

123. Bill Conlin, interview with the author, May 28, 1995.

124. *Los Angeles Times*, September 27, 1948.

125. *The Sporting News*, October 6, 1948. Lombardi operated a liquor store in San Leandro after retiring but became depressed and doctors recommended he be committed for a psychiatric evaluation. En route to the institution, Lombardi and his wife stopped at a friend's home. Lombardi excused himself and went into the bedroom. When Lombardi's wife checked on him a few minutes later, she found he had slashed his throat. Lombardi fought his wife and the ambulance attendants, screaming at them, "Leave me alone, I want to die!" In later years he worked in the press box for the San Francisco Giants until he was treated badly by one of the writers and quit. He dropped out of sight until he was discovered doing menial jobs at a gas station. Lombardi grew bitter about being repeatedly passed over for the Baseball Hall of Fame. In 1977 he claimed, "If they elected me now, I wouldn't even show up." The two-time National League batting champion died a few months later. He was elected to the Baseball Hall of Fame in 1986 (*Oakland Tribune*, December 21, 1950; *Los Angeles Times*, April 9 and April 10, 1953; *The Sporting News*, October 15, 1977).

126. *Oakland Tribune*, September 27 and September 28, 1948; *Oakland Post Enquirer*, September 27, 1948.

127. *Oakland Tribune*, October 11, 1948.

128. Bill Conlin, interview with the author, May 28, 1995.

Chapter Sixteen

1. *Sacramento Bee*, March 21, 1949. Only the left-field bleachers, some concrete ramps and the scoreboard remained from the old ballpark.

2. *The Sporting News*, April 13, 1949.

3. *Sacramento Bee*, February 15, 1949.

4. *Pittsburgh Post-Gazette*, May 27, 1949; *The Sporting News*, June 8, 1949.

5. *Oakland Tribune*, May 26, 1949.

6. *The Sporting News*, June 8, 1949.

7. *Los Angeles Times*, May 27, 1949; *Oakland Tribune*, June 3, 1949. Since Brick Laws was close friends with both Yankees part-owner Del Webb and Yankees manager Casey Stengel, some thought the Oaks had a secret agreement that would ensure Jensen would land in New York in 1950.

8. *Oakland Tribune*, May 27, 1949.

9. *Oakland Tribune*, May 28, 1949.

10. *Oakland Tribune*, June 4, 1949.

11. *Los Angeles Times*, July 2, 1949.

12. *Oakland Tribune*, June 5, 1949; *Los Angeles Times*, June 5, 1949. The fairytale romance between Olsen and Jensen did not last and Olsen obtained a divorce in Reno in 1963. The two reconciled and remarried the next year but divorced again not long after that (*Oakland Tribune*, October 14, 1949; *Los Angeles Times*, October 17, 1949, May 18, 1963 and July 13, 1964).

13. *The Sporting News*, March 30, 1949.

14. Rugger Ardizoia, interview with the author, February 13, 2009. Reno Cheso said he once played an exhibition game and Easter hit a line shot off the center-field wall at Seals Stadium that bounced back to him at second base (Reno Cheso, interview with the author, November 11, 2010).

15. *The Sporting News*, March 30, 1949.

16. Tommy Byrne, interview with the author, January 1, 1992.

17. Cal McLish, interview with the author, February 3, 1992. Jerry Streeter, who was a second baseman for Sacramento, said that Easter was extremely difficult to position against on defense because it did not matter where the pitcher threw a pitch. Easter was so strong that he could still hit the ball where he wanted (Jerry Streeter, interview with the author, January 22, 2011).

18. Bill Conlin, interview with the author, May 28, 1995.

19. *San Francisco Chronicle*, April 4, 1947.

20. Bill Conlin, interview with the author, May 28, 1995.

21. Cal McLish, interview with the author, February 3, 1992; Gene Mauch, interview with the author, March 11, 1992.

22. Larry Jansen, interview with the author, December 29, 1991.

23. *Sacramento Bee*, August 8, 1953. Despite his reputation, which was partially deserved, Brovia did lead PCL outfielders in assists in 1950 and in fielding percentage in 1952.

24. Joe Brovia, various interviews with the author, November 1989 and April 1990. There are other versions of this story that claim Pants Rowland was the one upset by Brovia's pant legs, but Brovia always said it was Fagan who objected.

25. *The Sporting News*, March 9, 1949; Don Klein, interview with the author, February 3, 2009.

26. *The Sporting News*, August 18 and September 8, 1948.

27. *The Sporting News*, February 22, 1950.

28. Don Klein, interview with the author, February 3, 2009.

29. *The Sporting News*, March 16, 1949.

30. *San Francisco Chronicle*, March 31, 1949; *Los Angeles Times*, April 2, 1949; *The Sporting News*, April 13, 1949. 3i*The Sporting News*, April 13, 1949.

32. Frank Dasso, interview with the author, August 19, 1991; *Sacramento Union*, May 25, 1949; *The Sporting News*, June 8, 1949. Dasso defeated the Seals, 3–2, and struck out seven batters in a complete-game victory. His home run traveled more than 410 feet.

33. *New York Times*, February 12, 1949.

34. *Oakland Tribune*, May 7, 1949; *San Diego Union*, May 10 and May 15, 1949; *New York Times*, May 14, 1949.

35. *San Diego Union*, May 18 and May 19, 1949.

36. *Oakland Tribune*, May 19, 1949.

37. *Oakland Tribune*, June 9, 1949. Billy Raimondi first played for the Oaks as property of the New York Yankees in 1932 and remained in Oakland through four seasons before he was traded to the Cincinnati Reds. After battling a sore arm for most of 1935, he over-extended himself playing winter ball and by the time he arrived in spring training with the Reds, he could not throw. He remained on the Cincinnati roster for the first three games of the 1936 season, rooming with Ernie Lombardi and failing to get any sleep for three nights thanks to the legendary snorer. Placed on the disabled list, Raimondi missed the rest of the year, never getting into a game. He was returned to the New York Yankees and sent to Oakland at his request. During spring training in Modesto in 1937, Oaks manager Billy Meyer urged Raimondi to progress slowly, allowing him to gain confidence and strengthen his arm. Soon, he was playing regularly. Yankees scout Joe Devine called Raimondi "very smart" and major league caliber behind the plate. But Raimondi was not a major league hitter and spent the next twelve years with Oakland. Famous for wearing glasses while catching and never taking off the mask when he chased foul balls, he played every position in the last game of the 1943 season and briefly managed the Oaks in 1945. He played with three of his brothers, Walt, Al and Ernie, on the Oaks at one time or another. He knew he was not Dressen's type of player and was not surprised by the trade — Dressen had also been Raimondi's manager at Cincinnati in 1936. Raimondi, who rarely had anything bad to say about anyone, was not fond of Dressen: "(Stengel) was great. He was real good to the players. He gave out extra money for meals. Dressen? No comparison. Dressen thought he was a great manager and the smartest man in baseball." During his first series against his former teammates, Raimondi three times successfully called for pitchouts (*Oakland Tribune*, September 12, 1943; *The Sporting News*, June 22 and June 29, 1949; Billy Raimondi, interview with the author, March 21, 2009; Joe Devine, letter to E.G. Barrow, August 10, 1935, Dick Dobbins Collection on the Pacific Coast League, California Historical Society.)

38. *The Sporting News*, June 22, 1949.

39. *San Francisco Chronicle*, March 1, 1993.

40. *The Sporting News*, September 21, 1949.

41. *Los Angeles Times*, May 19, 1949.

42. *The Sporting News*, June 8, 1949.

43. *The Sporting News*, August 10, 1949.

44. *Los Angeles Times*, May 16, 1949.

45. *The Sporting News*, June 1, 1949.

46. *The Sporting News*, June 1, 1949.

47. *Los Angeles Times*, July 3, 1949.

48. *The Sporting News*, July 6, 1949. Easter was also hitting .363.

49. *Los Angeles Times*, August 18, 1949.

50. *Los Angeles Times*, April 18 and June 5, 1949, March 15, 1952; *The Sporting News*, July 6, 1949; *Washington Post*, October 1, 1949. Lefty O'Doul said of Noren, "You can fool him on one pitch, and if you give him the same kind again, he'll knock it out of the park." He added, "And the only outfielder in the majors who is better is Dominic DiMaggio." Noren had a great rookie season in Washington in 1950, batting .295 and driving in 98 runs (*Washington Post*, December 6, 1949).

51. *Seattle Post-Intelligencer*, July 14, 1949; *Los Angeles Times*, July 19, 1949. White had been disturbed by rumors printed in the San Francisco newspapers that he was about to be fired. He decided to beat the team to the punch, phoning his resignation to general manager Earl Sheely on July 13. The Rainiers players considered striking to demonstrate their support for White, but he talked them out of it (Seattle Rainiers file, Washington State Historical Society; Neill Sheridan, interview with the author, February 25, 2009).

52. Chuck Stevens, interview with the author, December 11, 2010.

53. *Los Angeles Times*, September 23, 1949.

54. *Oakland Tribune*, October 13, 1949; *The Sporting News*, October 19, 1949. Jensen repeatedly failed to hit the cutoff man from the outfield, infuriating Casey Stengel, who tried

to convert him into a pitcher before trading him to the Washington Senators. The Senators in turn traded him to the Boston Red Sox in 1954. It was in Boston that Jensen became a star, driving in one hundred or more runs five times in six years and winning the American League Most Valuable Player Award in 1958. Jensen said of that period in his life, "I was operating in a dreamland where there were bubbles that would never burst. There was a money tree in my backyard. Why shouldn't I pluck off the dollars when I wanted to? Then all of a sudden, reality came by." Jensen developed a fear of flying that shortened his baseball career. He sat out the 1960 season, came back for one year, and then quit for good at the age of thirty-four (*New York Times*, February 23 and March 18, 1951, December 26, 1989; *Los Angeles Times*, March 28, 1969, May 4, 1974 and July 14, 1982; Art Schallock, interview with the author, February 12, 2010).

55. *The Sporting News*, May 19, 1948.

56. *Pittsburgh Post-Gazette*, July 10, 1949.

57. Don Klein, interview with the author, February 3, 2009.

58. *Los Angeles Times*, October 13, 1949.

59. *The Sporting News*, October 19, 1949. Reno Cheso remembered the Japanese treating players like royalty — bowing to them in stores and refusing to let them pay for items — especially after they had a good game. There was also twenty-four hour taxi service; each player's taxi had his uniform number on it (Reno Cheso, interview with the author, November 11, 2010).

60. *Los Angeles Times*, October 24, 1949.

61. *New York Times*, October 31, 1949.

62. *Los Angeles Times*, January 31, 1950.

63. *San Francisco Chronicle*, January 31, 1950; *The Sporting News*, February 8 and February 22, 1950.

64. *Oakland Tribune*, January 31, 1950.

65. *San Francisco Chronicle*, February 16, 1950.

66. *San Francisco Chronicle*, February 17, 1950.

67. *Los Angeles Herald-Express*, February 16, 1950.

68. *Los Angeles Times*, February 17, 1950.

69. *The Sporting News*, April 12, 1950.

70. *The Sporting News*, January 12, 1949 and March 1, 1950.

71. *Oakland Tribune*, February 3, 1950.

72. *Sacramento Union*, December 11, 1949; *San Diego Union*, January 31, 1950.

73. *San Francisco Chronicle*, May 17, 1950.

74. Chuck Stevens, interview with the author, December 11, 2010. Stevens loved the uniforms, which he felt helped players who had some speed. He noted that they were the first lightweight jerseys any of them had ever worn. Stevens said that when the Stars went on the road, they would let the home team know what days they would wear the shorts because they could always count on larger crowds when they publicized they would do so.

75. *Los Angeles Times*, April 2, 1950. The Stars won the game, 5–3, but did not record any stolen bases. Pitcher Art Schallock said that pitchers liked the shorts but hitters did not because of the danger inherent in running the bases and sliding (Art Schallock, interview with the author, February 12, 2010).

76. *The Sporting News*, April 12, 1950.

77. *The Sporting News*, May 19, May 26 and July 7, 1948. Charlie Silvera said that Liska was jawing good-naturedly at Frank Kelleher during a game and suddenly threw his next pitch with an overhand delivery, catching Kelleher looking with a fastball that could not have been traveling faster than seventy-five miles per hour. "Nobody'd seen him throw overhand," said Silvera. "He fell in love with that pitch and came up with a sore arm" (Charlie Silvera, interview with the author, April 4, 2009).

78. *San Diego Union*, September 17, 1949.

79. *Sacramento Bee*, May 14 and May 17, 1950.

80. Tony Freitas, interview with the author, August 2, 1991.

81. *Sacramento Bee*, May 24, 1950. There was speculation that Freitas might become a PCL umpire, but instead he signed with Modesto in the California League to continue his career as a pitcher. He won twenty games three times in four years before retiring following the 1953 season with the most wins for a left-hander in minor league history.

82. *The Sporting News*, May 10, 1950.

83. *The Sporting News*, June 14, 1950.

84. *The Sporting News*, July 12, 1950.

85. *The Sporting News*, October 11, 1950.

86. *Chicago Tribune*, June 11 and June 13, 1949.

87. *The Sporting News*, February 28, 1951.

88. *Oakland Tribune*, May 31, 1950; *San Mateo Daily Review*, September 27, 1950. Minoso also hit three home runs against the Oaks in the second game of a doubleheader on May 30.

89. *Los Angeles Times*, June 25, 1950.

90. *San Francisco Chronicle*, September 11, 1950; Art Schallock, interview with the author, February 12, 2010.

91. *Los Angeles Times*, January 5 and February 15, 1951.

92. *San Francisco Chronicle*, January 23, 1951; *Los Angeles Times*, January 23, 1951. Fujimura had hit forty-six home runs in 1950 for the Osaka Tigers while Kawakami had defeated Joe DiMaggio in a home run hitting contest over the winter. The players returned to Japan at the end of the month (*Modesto Bee*, March 6 and March 27, 1951).

93. Bill Conlin, interview with the author, May 28, 1995.

94. Don Klein, interview with the author, February 3, 2009.

95. *Los Angeles Times*, March 8, 1951.

96. There were numerous versions of this story related by Zernial and DiMaggio, as well as DiMaggio biographers. Some versions have Zernial dating Monroe and DiMaggio supposedly saying that Marilyn Monroe would never have dated "a busher" like Zernial.

97. *Sacramento Union*, October 18, October 19 and October 27, 1950.

98. *Sacramento Bee*, April 27, 1951. When Boyd went out for batting practice that night, he picked up a bat, looked it over and said, "This piece of wood has at least two hits in it." He had five hits that evening and tripled in his last at-bat.

99. *The Sporting News*, August 1, 1951. Bill Veeck purchased the St. Louis Browns about this time and mentioned Gordon as a prospective manager, but Gordon insisted he wanted to stay in Sacramento (*Los Angeles Times*, July 6, 1951).

100. *Sacramento Bee*, May 17, 1951.

101. Ed Cereghino, interview with the author, March 14, 2009. Lefty O'Doul was so angry at Hornsby's antics that he refused to pitch the teenager when the Seals visited Seattle the next time, depriving the Rainiers of a big box office draw. Cereghino insisted that he was not bothered by Hornsby, saying, "That was his M.O. He and Ty Cobb could have been brothers." Cereghino would win four of nine decisions for the Seals and then was invited to pitch in Japan during Lefty O'Doul's winter tour. While there, he witnessed first-hand Lefty O'Doul's popularity among the Japanese. "Lefty was a god there," remembered Cereghino. "And DiMaggio was not far behind." Unfortunately, the youngster would lose a game on the tour, the first time the Americans had ever been defeated by the Japanese. When Cereghino returned to the States, he received notice that there were three crates waiting for him. "I open them up and there was everything from Noritake china to jade ornaments, bolts of silk ... they (the Japanese) were so generous. I couldn't believe all this stuff." Cereghino went to spring training several times with the Yankees but never made it to the majors because of arm trouble.

102. *Sacramento Bee*, August 7, 1951. The game was a seven-inning contest and the only hit Pickart allowed was a double in the fifth by Jim Tabor.

103. Jim Rivera, interview with the author, January 8, 1992.

104. *Seattle Post-Intelligencer*, December 29, 2008.

105. *The Sporting News*, July 4, 1951.

106. *The Sporting News*, July 4, 1951. Brown was happy to return for a second season in Seattle, although he greatly preferred playing for Paul Richards, the Rainiers manager in 1950, over Hornsby. Brown spent most of his major and minor league career with Richards serving as either his manager or general manager and he thought Richards was by far the greatest influence on his fourteen-year major league career (Hal Brown, interview with the author, October 24, 2010).

107. *The Sporting News*, September 5 and September 12, 1951.

108. *The Sporting News*, September 12, 1951.

109. Jim Rivera, interview with the author, January 8, 1992.

110. *The Sporting News*, January 19, 1963.

111. *San Francisco Chronicle*, June 23, 1951.

112. *San Francisco Chronicle*, July 27, 1951; *Washington Post*, July 28, 1951.

113. *The Sporting News*, August 8 and August 15, 1951.

114. *The Sporting News*, August 15, 1951. Chesnes allowed only three hits, all singles, and did not walk a batter while striking out four. He came into the game with an earned run average of 8.74. He won only one other game that season and then suffered a scare when he suddenly had an attack that left him partially paralyzed, thought to be caused by an injection he had taken for his sore arm. Chesnes recovered but decided to retire. Cliff Chambers, who earned a degree in kinesiology from Washington State, was a teammate of Chesnes in Pittsburgh and thought the pitcher's arm problems might have been psychological: "Every once in awhile, he'd throw the ball real hard. If you had a bad arm, you couldn't do that." Chesnes umpired in the California League in 1953 and was to be promoted to the Pacific Coast League in 1954 but never responded to Pants Rowland's contract offer (*Los Angeles Times*, August 7, October 17, 1951 and February 24, 1952; *The Sporting News*, February 13, 1952, April 1, 1953 and April 28, 1954; Cliff Chambers, interview with the author, January 7, 2010; Eddie Bockman, interview with the author, January 23, 2010).

115. *San Francisco Chronicle*, July 28, 1951.

116. *San Francisco Chronicle*, July 29, 1951.

117. *New York Times*, August 2 and August 9, 1951; *Washington Post*, August 9, 1951; *Los Angeles Times*, August 9, 1951; *The Sporting News*, August 8 and August 15, 1951.

118. *Los Angeles Times*, August 30, 1951; *New York Times*, August 31, 1951.

119. *Los Angeles Times*, November 19, 1951.

120. *San Francisco Chronicle*, August 26, 1951.

121. *San Francisco Chronicle*, August 26, 1951.

122. *San Francisco Chronicle*, September 6, 1951; Don Klein, interview with the author, February 3, 2009.

123. *San Francisco Chronicle*, September 10, 1951.

124. *The Sporting News*, July 25, 1951.

125. *Los Angeles Times*, September 26, 1951. Emil Sick said he did not expect Hornsby to manage a second year in Seattle and thought it most likely he would either buy the Seals or return to the majors (*San Francisco Chronicle*, September 26, 1951).

126. *Los Angeles Times*, September 20, 1951.

127. *Los Angeles Times*, October 5, 1951.

128. *Los Angeles Times*, September 12, 1951; *San Francisco Chronicle*, September 19, 1951.

Chapter Seventeen

1. *Los Angeles Times*, January 1, January 17 and January 20, 1952 and January 7, 1953.

2. *Los Angeles Times*, November 29, 1951.

3. *New York Times*, October 9, 1951.

4. *Pittsburgh Post-Gazette*, January 18, 1952; *Los Angeles Times*, January 19, 1952.

5. *Los Angeles Times*, January 26 and January 29, 1952.

6. Clarence Rowland letter to Pacific Coast League Directors, February 4, 1952, and Rowland letter to PCL attorney Leslie O'Connor, February 6, 1952, Dick Dobbins Collection on the Pacific Coast League, California Historical Society; *Los Angeles Times*, February 19 and February 26, 1952.

7. *San Francisco Chronicle*, November 18, 1951. Ed Cereghino said that Fagan called O'Doul in Japan and said, "That's it." Earlier during the trip, O'Doul had told the players, "I don't know if I'll be going back to San Francisco, but I'll tell you one thing. I'll be in the Coast League somewhere" (Ed Cereghino, interview with the author, March 14, 2009).

8. *San Diego Union*, November 28, 1951.

9. *San Francisco Chronicle*, April 15, 1952.

10. *San Diego Union*, July 10, 1952.

11. *The Sporting News*, July 2, 1952. Paul Pettit was one of the most sought-after high school stars in baseball history. He pitched six no-hitters for Narbonne High School in Lomita, California, and already had an agent, motion picture producer and screenwriter Frederick Stephani, who was only two years removed from an Academy Award nomination for his contributions to the original screenplay for *It Happened on Fifth Avenue*. Stephani signed Pettit to an $82,000 contract and the Pirates beat out at least a half-dozen other teams for Pettit's services by adding another $18,000 to assume the contract Stephani had with the youngster. Stephani retained the rights to place Pettit in motion pictures. Pettit was assigned to New Orleans and his $100,000 was paid to him over a ten-year period. Pettit's father quit his job as a night watchman to manage his son and the family was able to move from a public housing project. But Pettit tried too hard to show his worthiness and had arm and knee problems while playing for four different teams, including a brief stint with Pittsburgh, and winning only two games. Soon after joining the Stars, he lamented, "Sometimes I wish I'd never heard of that $100,000—or at least that the public hadn't" (*Los Angeles Times*, January 23 and February 1, 1950 and April 16, 1952).

12. *Los Angeles Times*, April 5, 1952.

13. *Los Angeles Times*, April 23 and April 27, 1952; *Pittsburgh Post-Gazette*, April 22, April 23 and May 13, 1952. Branch Rickey felt Bell could be a superstar and was underachieving. He traded Bell to Cincinnati in 1953, where the outfielder became a four-time All-Star.

14. *San Francisco Call-Bulletin*, July 1, 1952.

15. Paul Pettit, interview with the author, December 6, 2010. Pettit also played with Bernier in Pittsburgh in 1953 and thought he would have been a good major league platoon player against left-handers.

16. *Los Angeles Times*, April 4, 1952.

17. *Los Angeles Times*, April 14, 1952.

18. *Los Angeles Times*, April 26, 1952.

19. *The Sporting News*, May 21, 1952. One of Bernier's biggest fans was Groucho Marx, who wrote to the *New York Times* declaring that the young base stealer was a player to watch once he went up to Pittsburgh. Marx then quipped, "If you can call that *up*" (*New York Times*, December 22, 1952).

20. *Los Angeles Times*, April 8 and April 9, 1952.

21. *Los Angeles Times*, February 6, 1952.

22. *The Sporting News*, April 23, 1952.

23. *San Francisco Chronicle*, April 16, 1952.

24. *The Sporting News*, June 4, 1952.

25. *Sacramento Bee*, September 17, 1951.

26. *New York Times*, December 11, 1951.

27. *Chicago Tribune*, March 21, 1952.

28. *San Diego Union*, May 26, 1952; *The Sporting News*, June 4, 1952.

29. *Sacramento Bee*, April 14, 1952. With two outs in the ninth, Flores walked Eddie Basinski. Portland shortstop Frankie Austin then golfed a low pitch into left-center field to end Flores' bid for a no-hitter. Flores also carried a no-hitter with two outs in the ninth inning while pitching for the

Angels in 1940; Marv Gudat of Oakland broke up that bid with a bloop single over second baseman Lou Stringer's head. Flores struck out twelve in that game. Flores was a tough-luck pitcher in 1952; despite an excellent 2.78 earned run average for Sacramento, he led the league in defeats with a 10–20 record. One of his losses came on May 9 versus San Diego on a strikeout; with two outs in the ninth and the score tied, 1–1, Dick Faber tried to squeeze bunt on a one-and-two pitch with Herb Gorman on third. Faber missed on the bunt attempt, but the ball eluded the Sacramento catcher and Gorman scored the winning run (*Los Angeles Times*, September 12, 1940; *The Sporting News*, May 21, 1952).

30. *Sacramento Bee*, April 25, 1952; *San Francisco Chronicle*, April 25, 1952 .

31. *San Francisco Chronicle*, April 25, 1952.

32. *The Sporting News*, May 7, 1952. Attendance was announced as 790.

33. Elmer Singleton, interview with the author, May 19, 1995. For his part, Eddie Bockman felt it was a clean hit. He claimed that Singleton cursed at him after he reached first base. The two had been roommates at Pittsburgh (Eddie Bockman, interview with the author, January 23, 2010).

34. *Oakland Tribune*, May 2, 1952; *Los Angeles Times*, May 8 and May 23, 1952; *The Sporting News*, May 14, 1952.

35. *Oakland Tribune*, July 4, 1952.

36. Lindell received the trophy before a game on September 8, and then won his twenty-third game of the year, defeating Seattle, 6–1 (*Los Angeles Times*, September 9, 1952).

37. *Los Angeles Times*, September 7, 1952.

38. *Los Angeles Times*, September 18, 1952.

39. *Oakland Tribune*, September 22, 1952.

40. Bobby Bragan, interview with the author, November 11, 1991.

41. *Los Angeles Times*, February 8 and June 23, 1953; *The Sporting News*, May 6, 1953.

42. *Los Angeles Times*, April 3, 1953.

43. *The Sporting News*, April 15, 1953. Beard's mammoth home run at Forbes Field came on July 16, 1950, against Bob Hall of the Boston Braves. The ball struck the top of the roof and then bounced out of the park (*Pittsburgh Post-Gazette*, July 17, 1950; Bobby Bragan, interview with the author, November 11, 1991).

44. *San Diego Union*, April 5, 1953; *Los Angeles Times*, April 5, 1953. Of Schneider's five home runs on May 11, 1923, only three were consecutive. Beard made another assault on the record book later that month, recording twelve straight hits to tie Mickey Heath's PCL record (*Los Angeles Times*, April 29 and May 2, 1953).

45. *San Diego Union*, April 6, 1953; *Los Angeles Times*, April 5, 1953; *The Sporting News*, April 15, 1953. Murray Franklin told Clint Conatser that Gorman died in Franklin's arms in the clubhouse (Clint Conatser, interview with the author, January 29, 2011).

46. *The Sporting News*, June 17, 1953.

47. *Los Angeles Times*, May 14, May 15 and June 4, 1953; *The Sporting News*, June 10, 1953.

48. *The Sporting News*, September 2, 1953.

49. *The Sporting News*, July 29, 1953.

50. *Sacramento Bee*, June 22, 1953.

51. *Sacramento Bee*, July 9, 1953; *San Francisco Chronicle*, July 9, 1953; *The Sporting News*, July 22, 1953. Sheridan's blast reportedly broke the window of a car parked more than six hundred feet from home plate. Solons officials later claimed the home run traveled 613.8 feet, less than five feet short of Roy Carlyle's blast in 1929. Sheridan, who preferred meeting the ball instead of overpowering it, said that Lefty O'Doul had always tried to persuade him to swing harder. "This one time ... I cranked up and the ball just happened to be where I was swinging. You don't feel the ball hit the bat. Everything was in sync. The next day, this fellow brought me the ball. He had been sitting on his porch, listening to the ballgame, and the ball went through the back window of

his car." Sheridan kept both the ball and the bat (Neill Sheridan, interview with the author, February 25, 2009).

52. *The Sporting News*, September 24, 1952.

53. *The Sporting News*, July 8, 1953.

54. *Los Angeles Times*, July 5, 1953. The streak ended at seven straight complete-game victories.

55. Bobby Bragan, interview with the author, November 11, 1991.

56. *Los Angeles Times*, July 1, 1953; *The Sporting News*, July 15, 1953.

57. *Los Angeles Times*, July 12, 1953. When Bragan was asked to name the best umpires he had seen, he surprisingly mentioned Runge first (Bobby Bragan, interview with the author, November 11, 1991).

58. *Los Angeles Times*, July 15, 1953.

59. Gene Mauch, interview with the author, March 11, 1992.

60. *Los Angeles Times*, August 1, 1953.

61. *Los Angeles Times*, August 2, 1953.

62. Cal McLish, interview with the author, February 3, 1992. Dick Smith is not to be confused with infielder Dick Smith, who played for Hollywood from 1954 through 1957.

63. Chuck Stevens, interview with the author, December 11, 2010.

64. Chuck Stevens, interview with the author, December 11, 2010.

65. *Los Angeles Times*, August 3, 1953; Lloyd Hittle, interview with the author, March 27, 2009.

66. *Los Angeles Times*, August 4, 1953. Kelleher was fined one hundred dollars while Beard and Franklin were fined fifty dollars.

67. *Los Angeles Times*, August 5, 1953.

68. *Los Angeles Times*, September 16, 1953.

69. *The Sporting News*, September 16, 1953.

70. *The Sporting News*, September 23, 1953.

71. *The Sporting News*, August 5, 1953.

72. *The Sporting News*, July 22, 1953.

73. *The Sporting News*, July 29, 1953.

74. *Sacramento Union*, September 25, 1953.

75. *San Francisco Chronicle*, September 20 and September 25, 1953.

76. *San Francisco Chronicle*, September 20, 1953; *Los Angeles Times*, September 25, 1953.

77. *San Francisco Chronicle*, December 3, December 11 and December 12, 1953; *San Francisco Seals 1954 Yearbook*. There were rumors Bill Veeck was interested in buying the Seals.

78. *Baltimore Sun*, September 30, 1953.

79. *Los Angeles Times*, September 30, 1953. The Pacific Coast League suffered a major blow to its dream of major league status six weeks later when the United States Supreme Court ruled, 7–2, to affirm Justice Oliver Wendell Holmes' 1922 ruling that baseball was not subject to anti-trust law. The ruling was less than two hundred words long (*The Sporting News*, November 18, 1953).

80. *Long Beach Press-Telegram*, April 5, 1954; *Los Angeles Times*, April 5, 1954; Bobby Bragan, interview with the author, November 11, 1991. When Bragan began arguing with Ashford, he ripped off his cap and threw it against the screen. The cap was brought back to Bragan, who slammed it at Ashford's feet. Ashford ejected Bragan, who then responded with his lying-down strike as the crowd booed him.

81. Bobby Bragan, interview with the author, November 11, 1991.

82. *Los Angeles Times*, October 31, 1953.

83. *New York Times*, October 15, 1953; *Oakland Tribune*, October 28, 1953. Dressen had wanted a three-year extension from Brooklyn and interpreted the failure to reach agreement as a lack of confidence (*The Sporting News*, June 2, 1954).

84. *Los Angeles Times*, April 7, 1954.

85. *The Sporting News*, August 25, 1954.

86. *Oakland Tribune*, May 13, 1954; *Los Angeles Times*, May 13 and May 14, 1954. Oakland's Jim Marshall clinched

the game at one o'clock in the morning with a grand slam. Bobby Bragan protested, arguing that it was already past curfew when Marshall hit his home run. The next night, Stars coach Gordon Maltzberger brought the starting lineups to home plate while wearing a dozen watches on each arm and an alarm clock hung around his neck. The umpires ignored the insult.

87. Tommy Byrne, interview with the author, January 1, 1992.

88. *San Diego Union*, July 18, 1954; *The Sporting News*, August 4, 1954.

89. *San Diego Union*, July 19, 1954.

90. *Los Angeles Times*, July 24, August 4 and August 21, 1938; *San Diego Union*, July 24, 1938.

91. Jimmie Reese, interview with the author, November 11, 1991.

92. Bobby Doerr, interview with the author, August 20, 1991.

93. Ed Cereghino, interview with the author, March 14, 2009.

94. Bill Conlin, interview with the author, May 28, 1995. Solons infielder Jerry Streeter was a teammate of Bearden and said the pitcher told him that he loaded the baseball with oil form the hair at the back of his head (Jerry Streeter, interview with the author, January 22, 2011).

95. Art Schallock, interview with the author, February 12, 2010.

96. Larry Jansen, interview with the author, December 29, 1991.

97. Elmer Singleton, interview with the author, May 19, 1995.

98. Larry Jansen, interview with the author, December 29, 1991.

99. George Bamberger, interview with the author, January 5, 1992.

100. Lilio Marcucci, interview with the author, June 5, 1995.

101. Bill Conlin, interview with the author, May 28, 1995.

102. *San Diego Union*, September 2, 1954; *The Sporting News*, September 15, 1954. The New York Yankees purchased Byrne on September 8 and he won three games for them during the stretch run of the pennant race. The next year, he won sixteen and lost five. He pitched two more seasons before retiring.

103. *Los Angeles Times*, July 20, 1954.

104. *Los Angeles Times*, June 15, 1954.

105. *Los Angeles Times*, August 12, 1954.

106. Irv Noren, interview with the author, February 15, 2010.

107. *Los Angeles Times*, August 12, August 13 and August 14, 1954; *The Sporting News*, August 18, 1954; Bobby Bragan, interview with the author, November 11, 1991.

108. *Los Angeles Times*, August 13, 1954.

109. *Los Angeles Times*, August 13, 1954.

110. *Los Angeles Times*, September 11, 1954.

111. *Los Angeles Times*, September 12, 1954.

112. *Los Angeles Times*, September 5 and September 17, 1954. After Lyons had refused to pitch for San Francisco, Tommy Heath released him. "You know, there are different ways of asking a man to do a thing," Lyons told *San Diego Union* columnist Jack Murphy. "I pitched for Hornsby and Sweeney because they asked it as a favor. And I pitched five innings for Heath when he put it the same way. But this time, he comes to me and says, 'Either you pitch or take your release.' I said, 'All right, Tom. Since you put it that way, give me my release.'" Lyons added, "Actually, they let me go because they couldn't afford to pay my salary as an outfielder. They're pressed for money. Heath has sold his house and gone heavily into debt and when we talked contract in the spring he wanted me to take less money than I was making when I first came into the league" (*San Diego Union*, September 2, 1954).

113. *Los Angeles Times*, September 13, 1954. Bobby Bragan always thought that the loss of Bernier cost Hollywood its third straight pennant (Bobby Bragan, interview with the author, November 11, 1991).

114. Bobby Bragan, interview with the author, November 11, 1991.

115. *Los Angeles Times*, September 13, 1954.

116. Harry Elliott, interview with the author, July 2, 2010.

117. *Los Angeles Times*, September 14, 1954.

118. *San Diego Union*, September 14, 1954; *Los Angeles Times*, September 14, 1954.

119. *The Sporting News*, August 11, 1954. Players received gold rings in honor of the championship, featuring crossed bats against a background of a baseball diamond with a real diamond in the center. Harry Elliott still wore his ring more than fifty years later, the only piece of jewelry he owned (Harry Elliott, interview with the author, July 2, 2010).

Chapter Eighteen

1. *Los Angeles Times*, November 13 and November 19, 1954.

2. *Los Angeles Times*, November 19, 1954.

3. *Los Angeles Times*, January 13, 1955 and February 16, 1914. See also Chapter 4.

4. *Los Angeles Times*, January 1, 1955.

5. *San Francisco Chronicle*, November 4, 1954.

6. *The Sporting News*, September 8, October 6 and October 27, 1954 and September 26, 1964. It was alleged that Norgan and his partners invested $1,000 in a whiskey distributorship during World War II, collecting a profit of more than $20 million without paying taxes by incorporating in other countries. Three of Norgan's partners in the scheme were found guilty in August 1955. Norgan remained beyond reach in Canada since the offense was not subject to extradition. He never again set foot in the United States (*New York Times*, May 12 and August 7, 1954, January 11 and August 23, 1955; *The Sporting News*, January 19, 1955).

7. *The Sporting News*, November 10, 1954.

8. *The Sporting News*, March 9, March 16 and August 24, 1955.

9. *Los Angeles Times*, March 30, 1955; *Seattle Post-Intelligencer*, May 11, 1955.

10. *Los Angeles Times*, October 17, 1954.

11. *Seattle Post-Intelligencer*, July 25, 1955; *San Diego Union*, July 25, 1955. Singleton's was one of three no-hitters in the Pacific Coast League within six days. Three days earlier, Angels left-hander George Piktuzis struck out nine batters in a 2–1 no-hitter against San Francisco. The Seals' only run scored on a sacrifice fly following a walk, a wild pitch and an infield out. Two days after Singleton, Oakland's Chris Van Cuyk pitched a seven-inning no-hitter to defeat Los Angeles, 2–0 (*Los Angeles Times*, July 22 and July 27, 1955; *Oakland Tribune*, July 27, 1955; *The Sporting News*, August 3, 1955).

12. Gene Mauch said that he once got too close as an on-deck hitter when Duren was pitching. Duren pointed to Mauch and yelled, "Get him the hell out of there!" When Mauch did not respond, Duren fired a baseball at him. Len Neal caught Duren in Vancouver. When asked about him, Neal laughed and said, "He *was* a little wild" (Gene Mauch, interview with the author, March 11, 1992; Len Neal, interview with the author, March 16, 2009).

13. Cliff Chambers, interview with the author, January 7, 2010.

14. *Washington Post*, September 28, 1954; *San Diego Union*, November 1, 1954; *Oakland Tribune*, November 4, 1954.

15. *Oakland Tribune*, December 3, 1954. More than two hundred fans welcomed O'Doul at a dinner held in his honor in January 1955 (*New York Times*, October 17, 1954; *Oakland Tribune*, January 11, 1955).

16. *Oakland Tribune*, March 7, 1955; *Sacramento Union*, April 18, 1955.

17. *Imperial Valley Press*, March 8, 1955; *Oakland Tribune*, March 7, 1955.

18. *The Sporting News*, March 16, 1955.

19. Bob Murphy, interview with the author, July 31, 1995. Harry Elliott roomed with Gettel in St. Louis and vividly remembers the pitcher standing in his underwear in front of a mirror, practicing his quick draw (Harry Elliott, interview with the author, July 2, 2010).

20. *Oakland Tribune*, April 20, 1955. Consolo's season in Oakland with O'Doul would be his best as a professional; he hit .276 with 14 home runs and 68 runs batted in.

21. *Oakland Tribune*, April 20 and April 21, 1955.

22. *Los Angeles Times*, April 13, 1955.

23. *The Sporting News*, May 4, 1955.

24. *Los Angeles Times*, May 24, 1955.

25. *Oakland Tribune*, May 5, 1955; *The Sporting News*, May 18, 1955.

26. *The Sporting News*, June 15, 1955. Albie Pearson, who played against Bilko in the PCL and with him in the American League, said that major leaguers were able to more consistently get fastballs in on his hands — a weakness the slugger had difficulty overcoming (Albie Pearson, interview with the author, January 18, 2011).

27. *The Sporting News*, June 8, 1955.

28. *San Mateo Times*, July 4, 1955; *The Sporting News*, July 13, 1955. Debuting at Seals Stadium with his family in attendance, Creighton pitched the seven-inning nightcap of a doubleheader. He almost waved to his parents after striking out Dick Sisler in the sixth inning but thought better of it, believing it "would be strictly bush." The Padres, who had not been shut out all season, insisted they were not impressed. Creighton thought that signing with San Francisco would give him a better shot at the big leagues in the long run. He not only did not make it to the majors, he never won another game as a professional.

29. *The Sporting News*, June 15, 1955.

30. *Los Angeles Times*, May 2, 1955.

31. The streak ended on May 28 when the Angels defeated San Diego in twelve innings. The Padres earlier had a ten-game winning streak (*San Diego Union*, May 29, 1955; *Los Angeles Times*, May 29, 1955).

32. *Seattle Post-Intelligencer*, July 18, 1955; *The Sporting News*, July 27, 1955.

33. *The Sporting News*, July 20 and August 31, 1955. Stephens had been released by the Chicago White Sox on June 30 while Kretlow was purchased from the Baltimore Orioles in early June. Stephens had been offered a spot in the White Sox farm system but decided to play for Seattle instead (*Baltimore Sun*, June 8, 1955; *Chicago Tribune*, July 1 and July 9, 1955).

34. *The Sporting News*, August 22 and August 29, 1951.

35. *Oakland Tribune*, June 29, 1955; *The Sporting News*, July 27, 1955.

36. Joe Brovia, interview with the author, 1990.

37. *Oakland Tribune*, August 7 and August 10, 1955.

38. *The Sporting News*, August 24, 1955.

39. Brovia's teammate, Don Ferrarese, claimed Brovia had a broken bone in his hand at the time he was sold to Cincinnati, but was keeping the injury quiet. Brovia remained property of Cincinnati and began the 1956 season with the Reds' International League affiliate in Buffalo. Released a couple of months into the season, he signed with San Jose of the California League and then spent 1957 in the Mexican League before retiring. He ended his minor league career with a .311 lifetime batting average, 214 home runs and 1,143 runs batted in (Don Ferrarese, interview with the author, November 23, 2010).

40. *Los Angeles Times*, September 2, 1955.

41. "Minutes from Seattle Rainiers Board of Directors Meeting, April 30, 1956," Seattle Rainiers file, Washington State Historical Society.

42. *The Sporting News*, August 3, 1955.

43. Bob Murphy, interview with the author, July 31, 1995.

44. *Oakland Tribune*, August 20, 1955.

45. *San Diego Union*, August 25, 1955.

46. *Los Angeles Times*, August 28, 1955. Other reasons cited were traffic and parking problems, high ticket prices, radio and television broadcasts and competing recreational interests. But the desire for major league baseball drew the highest response.

47. *San Francisco Chronicle*, September 11, 1955.

48. Red Adams, interview with the author, April 26, 2009.

49. *San Diego Union*, October 19, 1955.

50. *The Sporting News*, May 22, 1957.

51. *The Sporting News*, April 25, 1956.

52. *San Diego Union*, October 19, 1955; *Los Angeles Times*, November 21, 1955.

53. *San Francisco Chronicle*, September 11, 1955.

54. "Minutes of the Pacific Coast League Conference, September 12, 1955," Dick Dobbins Collection on the Pacific Coast League, California Historical Society. Miller and his partners were given ten days to come up with financing.

55. *Oakland Tribune*, September 13, 1955.

56. *Oakland Tribune*, September 4, September 5 and September 15, 1955. *Oakland Tribune* cartoonist Lee Susman had created the Acorn, which was happy in victory and sad in defeat, in 1946 when San Francisco sportswriter Abe Kemp challenged him to create a mascot akin to what the Vernon Tigers once had. Susman met the challenge and the Acorn was born. He also drew program covers for the San Francisco Seals and Sacramento Solons, as well as cartoons for the *Sacramento Union*. His Oaks logo would be revived when the American Basketball Association placed a team in Oakland. Susman also designed the logo for the ABA's Denver Rockets, (now the Nuggets) (*Oakland Tribune*, July 26, 2007; Lee Susman, interview with the author, February 26, 2009).

57. *Los Angeles Times*, October 6, 1955.

58. *Los Angeles Times*, October 7, 1955; *Milwaukee Journal*, October 8, 1955.

59. *San Francisco Chronicle*, October 21, 1955; *Washington Post*, October 21, 1955.

60. *Milwaukee Journal*, November 9, 1955; *San Francisco Chronicle*, November 11, 1955. The Braves indicated they would only operate the franchise if a new stadium was built to the south of San Francisco, in San Mateo County. County officials had said that a $3 million stadium could be ready by March of 1957, but that was not enough to keep the Braves interested.

61. *San Francisco Chronicle*, November 29, 1955; *Los Angeles Times*, November 29, 1955.

62. *Los Angeles Times*, November 18, 1955.

63. *The Sporting News*, May 9, 1956.

64. *The Sporting News*, May 23, 1956.

65. *The Sporting News*, July 27, 1956.

66. *Los Angeles Times*, March 27, 1956; *The Sporting News*, April 18, 1956.

67. *The Sporting News*, May 9, 1956.

68. *Los Angeles Times*, April 19, 1956.

69. *The Sporting News*, March 21, 1956. The Beavers also unveiled new uniforms, featuring a red undershirt with white stripes at the elbows. Opposing managers argued that the stripes were distracting to hitters and umpires forced Portland pitchers to change. General manager Joe Ziegler asked Leslie O'Connor for a ruling on the uniform and O'Connor deemed them legal. Sacramento Solons manager Tommy Heath responded by having polka dots sewed on his team's undershirts when they played against Portland. Umpire Chris Pelekoudas forced the Solons to change because the dots were not an integral part of the uniform. Leslie O'Connor ruled against the Solons and their polka dots at the same time he fined Sacramento manager Tommy Heath and coach Ferris Fain for smoking cigars in the dugout while defying an ejection (*Sacramento Bee*, April 28, 1956; *The Sporting News*, May 2, May 9

and May16, 1956; Letter from Leslie O'Connor to umpire Al Mutart, April 12, 1956, Dick Dobbins Collection on the Pacific Coast League, California Historical Society).

70. *The Sporting News*, June 13, 1956.

71. *The Sporting News*, May 9, 1956.

72. *The Sporting News*, April 25, 1956.

73. *The Sporting News*, June 13, 1956. Casale was a great hitter for a pitcher — he hit fifteen home runs in the minors and four more in 116 major league at-bats, including one of the longest ever hit at Fenway Park — but said of his blast at Seals Stadium, "To be honest, there was a strong wind blowing out that day." Casale claimed the Red Sox sent him to San Francisco because Joe Cronin wanted to ensure success for the franchise in its first season under the Red Sox and thought Italian ballplayers would be drawing cards for the large ethnic population in San Francisco (Jerry Casale, interview with the author, February 15, 2010).

74. *Los Angeles Times*, March 29, 1957.

75. *Los Angeles Times*, April 11, 1956.

76. *San Diego Union*, July 2, 1956. Colavito first made two attempts from the left-field foul pole, throwing across the outfield to right field, but crosswinds negated his effort. He then moved behind home plate for his final three throws, the longest of which cleared the wall and hit the scoreboard on one bounce. The Indianapolis Indians of the American Association were outraged by Colavito's assignment to San Diego; they had the first rights to any optioned Cleveland player (*The Sporting News*, June 27, 1956).

77. Beamon's aunt had been a housekeeper for Brick Laws for several years. He started and completed his fifteen starts for Stockton and added a win in relief. Beamon won his last two starts of the 1954 season and his first start for Oakland, giving him nineteen straight wins before he was finally defeated. Ernie Broglio was a teammate of Beamon's in both Stockton and Oakland and said the secret of Beamon's success was a nasty sinker. Broglio added, "He probably broke two or three bats a game" (*The Sporting News*, April 21, 1954 and July 20, 1955; Ernie Broglio, interview with the author, November 27, 2010).

78. *Los Angeles Times*, May 18 and August 1, 1956. Drott was given a $100 per month raise after his fifteen-strikeout game. Seals pitcher Jerry Casale was responsible for Drott's broken finger. It began when a fastball got away from Casale and sent Steve Bilko sprawling in the dirt. In the dugout, Gene Mauch began screaming, "You watch out! We're gonna get you, Dago!" Casale did not appreciate the language and began fuming. When Casale came to bat, Drott hit him with a fastball in the left arm, further angering the pitcher. When Drott came up the next time, Casale was ready. Shaking off a call for a curveball, Casale said, "I aimed the ball right for his mouth, hoping it would be open and go right down his throat." Drott turned to bunt and threw up his bat to protect his face. The ball struck his finger and broke it, nearly causing a riot (Jerry Casale, interview with the author, February 15, 2010; *The Sporting News*, May 30, 1956).

79. *Los Angeles Times*, June 28, 1956. Duren's near no-hitter came on May 15, 1955. In the first inning, Gene Mauch reached base when an infield throw drew the first baseman off the bag. Umpire Ceci Carlucci started to call Mauch out until he saw the ball carom off the first baseman's mitt. Scorer John Old ruled the play a base hit, even though Carlucci insisted that Mauch would have been out had the first baseman fielded the throw cleanly (*Los Angeles Times*, May 16, 1955).

80. Ryne Duren, conversation with the author, November 27, 2010. Duren credited O'Doul turning his career around. Albie Pearson, who played with Duren on the American League expansion Angels, said that O'Doul had a catcher with two gloves held outside of each side of the plate. Duren was told to hit one side or the other. The gloves were moved closer together until Duren could split the middle of the plate (Albie Pearson, interview with the author, January 18, 2011).

81. *Los Angeles Times*, June 1, 1956. *The Sporting News*, June

13, 1956. When the fact that Metkovich was playing without shoes was called to umpire Emmett Ashford's attention, he remarked that he wished he could do the same.

82. Ken Aspromonte, interview with the author, January 5, 2010.

83. *San Francisco Chronicle*, June 4, 1956; *The Sporting News*, June 20, 1956.

84. *San Francisco Chronicle*, June 25, 1956; *The Sporting News*, July 4, 1956.

85. *San Francisco Chronicle*, July 2, 1956; *San Diego Union*, July 2, 1956.

86. *San Francisco Chronicle*, July 10, 1956.

87. *Los Angeles Times*, June 12, 1952.

88. Gene Mauch, interview with the author, March 11, 1992.

89. Gene Mauch, interview with the author, March 11, 1992.

90. Wade later shared his base running theories and book on pitchers with Maury Wills when the two were teammates in Spokane in 1958. Wade thought Wills got more out his physical talent as a base stealer than anyone in history (Gale Wade, interview with the author, December 21, 2010).

91. *Los Angeles Times*, August 15, 1956.

92. *The Sporting News*, August 8, 1956.

93. *Los Angeles Times*, April 9, 1955.

94. Ken Aspromonte, interview with the author, January 5, 2010.

95. *Chicago Tribune*, May 1, 1954.

96. *Los Angeles Times*, March 26, 1955.

97. Bobby Bragan, interview with the author, November 11, 1991.

98. Gale Wade, interview with the author, December 21, 2010.

99. *Los Angeles Times*, September 16, 1955. Bilko received a $2,500 check from Pepsi and the Lazzeri Trophy, donated by Western Air Lines.

100. *The Sporting News*, June 20, 1956.

101. *Los Angeles Times*, August 4, 1956.

102. *Los Angeles Times*, August 5, 1956.

103. *Sacramento Bee*, September 17, 1956.

104. *The Sporting News*, September 26, 1956.

105. *San Diego Union*, October 29, 1956; *Los Angeles Times*, October 29, 1956.

106. *Los Angeles Times*, January 29, 1957.

107. *Los Angeles Times*, November 1, 1956.

108. *Los Angeles Times*, October 17, 1956.

109. *Los Angeles Times*, February 22, 1957.

110. *Los Angeles Times*, March 3, 1957.

111. *Los Angeles Times*, March 4, 1957.

112. *Los Angeles Times*, March 6, 1957.

113. *The Sporting News*, January 16, 1957.

114. *Los Angeles Times*, April 12, 1957.

115. *San Diego Union*, April 12, 1957; *Los Angeles Times*, April 10 and April 12, 1957. Panko, a promising outfielder in his first season with Hollywood, had hit thirty-three home runs for New Orleans in the Southern Association the year before. He would play in only eleven games for the Stars in 1957. Jacobs and Smith collided head-on while chasing a blooper into short center field. Jacobs was knocked unconscious and was thought to have suffered a skull fracture before it was determined he was not seriously injured. Smith had a broken jaw and missed several weeks.

116. The 1956 season was quite a year for home run hitters in professional baseball as several men, including Bilko, topped fifty home runs. Three topped sixty. Besides Stuart, the others with at least sixty home runs in the minor leagues were Ken Guettler, who hit sixty-two for Shreveport in the Texas League, and Frosty Kennedy, who smashed sixty home runs for Plainview in the Southwestern League.

117. *San Diego Union*, April 12, 1957.

118. *The Sporting News*, April 24, 1957. Paul Pettit said that after his hot start, Stuart started swinging at everything

and as a result struck out even more than usual. He felt that Stuart's divorce may have played a role in his performance (Paul Pettit, interview with the author, December 6, 2010).

119. *The Sporting News*, April 24, 1957. The twenty-one-year-old Grant had won forty games and lost only eight in his first two professional seasons in the lower minors. Nevertheless, Ralph Kiner saw him hit in spring training and was convinced he should play every day. Grant would not return to the mound full-time until the parent Cleveland Indians, having lost Herb Score to injury, insisted that he begin pitching again with the aim of developing him for the major league team. Grant did not win his first game until Memorial Day but then went on a tear, winning eighteen games against only seven defeats. He was later a two-time American League All-Star and won twenty-one games for the American League champion Minnesota Twins in 1965, becoming the first African American twenty-game winner in American League history. He won two games in the 1965 World Series and also hit a home run. Grant later became an advocate for the investment in baseball for inner-city youth with the aim of increasing participation of African Americans in the game. He also wrote a book profiling African American twenty-game winners (Jim "Mudcat" Grant, interview with the author, November 21, 2010; *The Sporting News*, April 3, 1957).

120. *San Diego Union*, April 12 and April 13, 1957. Stuart nearly hit another home run in his final at-bat. Padres pitcher Dolan Nichols threw a pitch up and in that sent Stuart sprawling. Stuart then hit the next pitch far over the left-field fence but foul by about fifteen feet. Nichols then struck Stuart out.

121. *Los Angeles Times*, April 16 and April 17, 1957. Neither Bilko nor Stuart homered in the other two games played in the series (*Los Angeles Times*, April 18, April 19 and April 20, 1957).

122. *Los Angeles Times*, May 6, 1957.

123. *Los Angeles Times*, September 13, 1957.

124. *Los Angeles Times*, May 11, 1957; *The Sporting News*, May 1 and May 15, 1957. Irvin was fitted with a brace at one point in a futile effort to ease his back pain. He appeared in four games with three hits in ten at-bats before retiring. The home run on Opening Day against Vancouver represented Irvin's only two runs batted in for the Angels (*Los Angeles Times*, April 17, 1957).

125. *Los Angeles Times*, May 13, 1957; *The Sporting News*, May 29, 1957.

126. *The Sporting News*, June 5, 1957.

127. *San Diego Union*, April 18, 1957.

128. *Los Angeles Times*, April 19 and April 20, 1957; *The Sporting News*, April 24, 1957.

129. *Los Angeles Times*, April 23, 1957.

130. *The Sporting News*, June 5, 1957.

131. *The Sporting News*, April 10, 1957.

132. *Los Angeles Times*, June 3, 1957.

133. *The Sporting News*, May 15, 1957.

134. Duane Pillette, interview with the author, April 14, 2009. O'Doul was collecting veterans as the season wore on. He signed Eddie Basinski, who had been released by Portland after a decade with the Beavers. Basinski was a legend in Portland; the bespectacled infielder was one of the best in the business with the glove. In addition, he was an accomplished violinist and had achieved fame for going directly from the sandlots of Buffalo, New York, to the major leagues without having played any high school, college or minor league baseball. Thirty-eight-year-old Red Munger joined the Rainiers after a year with the Pittsburgh Pirates. Bill Kennedy was one of the team's returning veterans and he was even better than he had been for the 1955 champions, winning nine of twelve decisions with an incredible 1.16 earned run average in 85 innings over fifty-one relief appearances. O'Doul was also reunited with Larry Jansen, who brought back a taste of the old days with a 7–0 shutout of San Francisco early in the season that included his hitting a home run, an event so shocking

to O'Doul that he "fainted" in the third base coach's box as Jansen rounded the bases (*San Francisco Chronicle*, April 21, 1957).

135. Bob Lennon, interview with the author, August 24, 1991.

136. *San Francisco Chronicle*, May 11, 1957.

137. *Seattle Post-Intelligencer*, June 8, 1957.

138. *Seattle Post-Intelligencer*, June 9, 1957.

139. *The Sporting News*, June 12, 1957. Emil Sick did not attend or send a representative to the meeting.

140. *San Francisco Chronicle*, August 20, 1957.

141. *Los Angeles Times*, August 25, 1957. Hugh Pepper, interview with the author, October 23, 2010.

142. *Los Angeles Times*, August 26, 1957.

143. *Los Angeles Times*, August 27, 1957.

144. *Los Angeles Times*, September 6, 1957; Hugh Pepper, interview with the author, October 23, 2010.

145. *San Diego Union*, September 8, 1957.

146. *Los Angeles Times*, September 16, 1957.

147. Bilko hit his fifty-fifth home run on September 6 and his fifty-sixth the next day, but did not hit a home run over the final eleven games of the year. That left him tied with Gene Lillard for the second most home runs in a PCL season. To put Bilko's accomplishment in perspective, during the 1956 and 1957 seasons when he was hitting fifty-five and fifty-six home runs, Portland's Luis Marquez had the second most in one season with thirty-one in 1957. Although Bilko slumped in September, one of his teammates, catcher Earl Battey, hit three home runs against Sacramento on September 8 despite a pulled shoulder muscle. All three home runs were solo shots and accounted for all of the Angels' runs (*Los Angeles Times*, September 7, September 8, September 9 and September 17, 1957).

148. *San Francisco Chronicle*, September 16, 1957.

Chapter Nineteen

1. *Los Angeles Times*, September 16 and September 17, 1957. At one point, Bob Cobb had proposed building a new stadium for the Hollywood Stars at Chavez Ravine. Three years earlier, it was estimated that expanding the seating capacity of Wrigley Field to fifty-two thousand would cost at least $7.5 million (*Los Angeles Times*, September 30, 1954).

2. *San Francisco Chronicle*, September 28, 1957. Fagan also received five percent of the net gate receipts after deducting admission taxes and the visiting team's share. The annual property tax, which amounted to approximately $36,000 per year, was paid by Fagan. The former Seals owner, who had always insisted San Francisco should have major league baseball, told Mayor Christopher, "I can't let you down."

3. *Los Angeles Times*, November 15, 1957. Mays had also put a deposit on a home five blocks away, but that had been returned with the dubious explanation that the house had been taken off the market.

4. *Seattle Post-Intelligencer*, December 3, 1957. The Pacific Coast League had originally asked for $1.5 million and the Dodgers and Giants countered with an offer of $600,000. The PCL lowered its demand to $1 million and the compromise of $900,000 was reached.

5. *Los Angeles Times*, December 3, 1957.

6. *Los Angeles Times*, December 6, 1957.

7. *San Francisco Chronicle*, December 11, 1957.

8. *Los Angeles Times*, December 6 and December 7, 1957.

9. *Los Angeles Times*, December 12, 1957. Cobb also accurately predicted that a second major league team would someday be placed in Los Angeles and play in Orange County, "probably in Anaheim."

10. *Los Angeles Times*, December 22, 1957.

11. *Los Angeles Times*, January 12, 1958.

12. *Los Angeles Times*, January 14, 1958.

13. *Los Angeles Times*, January 18, 1958.

14. Despite initial success, Pacific Ocean Park ultimately could not keep up with its Orange County neighbor. It closed after ten years in operation. The final episode of *The Fugitive* television series was filmed there shortly before the park closed.

15. *Los Angeles Times*, March 16, 1958.

16. *Los Angeles Times*, March 24 and March 25, 1958.

17. *Los Angeles Times*, March 29, 1958.

18. *San Francisco Chronicle*, April 16, 1958.

19. *Los Angeles Times*, April 18 and April 19, 1958.

20. *San Francisco Chronicle*, September 21, 1959.

21. Completed in time for the 1958 season, Westgate Park was the Padres' home for ten seasons until San Diego Stadium, later renamed Jack Murphy Stadium and then Qualcomm, was built in time for the 1968 season. The site of Westgate Park is now the upscale Fashion Valley Mall at the junction of Friars Road and Highway 163.

22. *San Diego Union*, April 29, 1958.

23. *San Diego Union*, April 30, 1958.

24. *Los Angeles Times*, August 23, 1961.

25. *Los Angeles Times*, January 24, February 15 and February 18, 1969. Wrigley Field became property of the Los Angeles Recreation Department and briefly served as a community recreation center in the summer of 1968 before finally succumbing to the wrecking ball (*Los Angeles Times*, July 4, 1968).

26. The Padres joined Montreal in the National League in 1969 for a fee of $10 million. Former Dodgers executive Buzzie Bavasi was named president of the franchise. Buffalo, Dallas and Milwaukee were also-rans (*Los Angeles Times*, May 28, 1968; *Montreal Gazette*, May 28, 1968).

27. Bill Conlin, interview with the author, May 28, 1995.

28. *Los Angeles Times*, September 12, 1962. Powell died in 1971. He was proudest of having a park in Lynwood, California, named in his honor (*Los Angeles Times*, July 27, 1971; *The Sporting News*, August 14, 1971).

29. *San Francisco Chronicle*, December 19, 1960; *The Sporting News*, December 28, 1960.

30. *Los Angeles Times*, December 19, 1961.

31. *Oregonian*, October 31, 2010.

32. *Chicago Tribune*, May 18, 1969; *Los Angeles Times*, June 8, 1969.

33. *Oakland Tribune*, February 17, 1972.

34. *Los Angeles Times*, March 23, 1970.

35. *Chicago Tribune*, April 13, 1977.

36. Harry Elliott, interview with the author, July 2, 2010.

37. *Los Angeles Times*, October 9, 1957 and June 16, 1958. Newcombe, only a year and a half removed from a twenty-seven-win season for the Dodgers, had a record of 0–6 with a 7.86 earned run average at the time of the trade. He finished his career in the PCL in 1961, winning nine and losing eight for Spokane.

38. *Time Magazine*, May 30, 1960. Bilko ended his season in Detroit with a .207 batting average.

39. *Los Angeles Times*, December 15, 1960. The Angels' first choice to manage the team was Casey Stengel, recently fired as manager of the New York Yankees. Stengel declined the offer and Bill Rigney was hired. The expansion team's decision to play in Wrigley Field was controversial; Bill Veeck thought the Angels faced financial ruin if they played there, predicting they would not draw 700,000. He was correct — they only drew 603,510 (*Los Angeles Times*, December 9, December 10 and December 14, 1960).

40. *Los Angeles Times*, October 2, 1961. Bilko's home run gave the Angels five players who hit twenty or more home runs that season. The others were Leon Wagner, Ken Hunt, Lee Thomas and Earl Averill.

41. *Los Angeles Times*, August 26, 1962. Doctors ordered Bilko to the sidelines as a precaution against his developing a blood clot in his leg.

42. *Los Angeles Times*, October 16, 1962.

43. *Los Angeles Times*, January 13, 1963.

44. *Los Angeles Times*, March 8, 1978.

45. *The Sporting News*, October 17, 1970.

46. *Los Angeles Times*, August 21, 1969; *The Sporting News*, May 2, 1988.

47. *The Sporting News*, August 16 and August 30, 1969.

48. *Los Angeles Times*, November 9 and November 10, 1977.

49. Cities to be represented were New York, Buffalo, Toronto, Minneapolis-St. Paul, Houston, Dallas-Fort Worth, Atlanta and Denver. Only Buffalo has not since been represented by a major league team.

50. *New York Times*, December 10, 1965. Rickey had been hospitalized prior to his appearance at the banquet and was supposed to return to the hospital afterward. He began making a speech, but then said, "I don't believe I'm going to be able to speak any longer," and collapsed. He never regained consciousness.

51. *New York Times*, March 30, 1979.

52. *Boston Globe*, September 17, 1960.

53. *Seattle Post-Intelligencer*, November 11, 1964.

54. *Oakland Tribune*, August 16, 1971.

55. *The Sporting News*, December 20, 1969.

Sources and Bibliography

Interviews

Red Adams, (2009) pitcher, 1942; 1944–1958
Rugger Ardizoia, (2009) pitcher, 1937; 1939–1940; 1946–1950
Ken Aspromonte, (2010) infielder, 1956–1957; 1963
George Bamberger, (1992) pitcher, 1950; 1952–1963
Cuno Barragan, (2010) catcher, 1957–1960; 1963
Bud Beasley, (1995) pitcher, 1944–1948
Eddie Bockman, (2010) infielder, 1951–1954
Bobby Bragan, (1991) manager/catcher, 1953–1955; 1959
Ernie Broglio, (2010) pitcher, 1953–1955
Joe Brovia, (1990) outfielder, 1941–1942; 1946–1955
Hal Brown, (2010) pitcher, 1950–1951; 1955
Tommy Byrne, (1992) pitcher, 1954
Jerry Casale, (2010) pitcher, 1956
Ed Cereghino, (2009) pitcher, 1951; 1955
Cliff Chambers, (2010) pitcher, 1942; 1946–1947; 1954
Reno Cheso, (2010) infielder, 1948–1950; 1952–1955
Clint Conatser, (2011) outfielder, 1947; 1950–1952
Bill Conlin, (1995) sportswriter, Sacramento
Frank Crosetti, (1991) infielder, 1928–1931
Frank Dasso, (1991) pitcher, 1940–1944; 1946–1950
Dominic DiMaggio, (1992) outfielder, 1937–1939
Bobby Doerr, (1991) infielder, 1934–1936
Ryne Duren, (2010) pitcher, 1955–1956
Harry Elliott, (2010) outfielder, 1954; 1956–1957
Don Ferrarese, (2010) pitcher, 1949; 1953–1955; 1957; 1960
Tony Freitas, (1991) pitcher, 1929–1933; 1937–1942; 1946–1950
Bill Glynn, (2010) infielder, 1952; 1955–1958
Jim "Mudcat" Grant, (2010) pitcher, 1957
Lloyd Hittle, (2009) pitcher, 1947–1949; 1951–1954
Bob Hunter, (1991) sportswriter, Los Angeles
Larry Jansen, (1991) pitcher, 1941–1942; 1945–1946; 1955–1960
Don Klein, (2009) broadcaster, front office, San Francisco
Mark Koenig, (1991) infielder, 1932; 1937
Hillis Layne, (1991) infielder, 1947–1950
Bob Lennon, (1991) outfielder, 1957
John Leovich, (1990) catcher, 1942
Ad Liska, (1992) pitcher, 1936–1949
Emil Mailho, (1995) outfielder, 1931–1935; 1942–1945

Lilio Marcucci, (1995) catcher/infielder, 1944–1946; 1951
Gene Mauch, (1992) infielder, 1954–1956
Cal McLish, (1992) pitcher, 1949–1950; 1952–1955
Bob Murphy, (1995) pitcher, 1953–1955
Len Neal, (2009) catcher, 1951–1961
Irv Noren, (2010) outfielder, 1949; 1962–1963
Albie Pearson, (2011) outfielder, 1956–1957
Hugh Pepper, (2010) pitcher, 1956–1957; 1959–1960; 1963
Paul Pettit, (2010) pitcher, infielder, outfielder, 1952; 1954–1960; 1962
Duane Pillette, (2009) pitcher, 1947–1948; 1955; 1957–1960
Billy Raimondi, (2009) catcher, 1932–1935; 1937–1953
Jimmie Reese, (1991) infielder, 1919–1920; 1924–1929; 1933–1938; 1940
Jim Rivera, (1992) outfielder, 1951; 1962–1963
Art Schallock, (2010) pitcher, 1949–1951; 1954; 1956
Carl Scheib, (2010) pitcher, 1954–1955
Neill Sheridan, (2009) outfielder, 1943; 1945–1951; 1953–1954
Charlie Silvera, (2009) catcher, 1947–1948; 1960
Elmer Singleton, (1995) pitcher, 1942; 1949–1956; 1958; 1960–1963
Chuck Stevens, (2010) infielder, 1948–1955; 1957
Jerry Streeter, (2011) infielder, 1954–1957
Gus Suhr, (1991) infielder, 1925–1929; 1943–1945
Lee Susman, (2009) cartoonist, Oakland
Lou Vezilich, (1995) outfielder, 1936–1937; 1939; 1944–1947
Gale Wade, (2010) outfielder, 1955–1959
Wally Westlake, (2010) outfielder, 1942; 1946; 1955–1956
Gus Zernial, (1991) outfielder, 1947–1948
Jimmy Zinn, Jr., (1991) minor leaguer, son of Jim Zinn, Sr.

Libraries

Bancroft Library, University of California, Berkeley
California Historical Society, North Hayes Research Library
California State Library, Sacramento

California State Library, West Sacramento
Lied Library, University of Nevada, Las Vegas
National Baseball Hall of Fame and Library
San Diego Hall of Champions
San Diego Public Library
San Diego State University Library
San Francisco Historical Society
San Francisco Public Library
Stanislaus County Library
Utah History Resource Center
Valley Library, Oregon State University
Washington State Historical Society

San Francisco Examiner
San Francisco Seals Yearbook, 1949 and 1954
San Jose Mercury-News
San Mateo Times
Santa Cruz Sentinel
Seattle Post-Intelligencer
Seattle Times
Spokane Evening Chronicle
Sporting Life
Stockton Evening Mail
Stockton Record
The Sporting News
Washington Post

Collections

David Eskenazi Collection
Dick Dobbins Collection on the Pacific Coast League
Frank Dasso, Scrapbook
Los Angeles Examiner Collection at the University of
    Southern California
National Baseball Hall of Fame Player Files
Ray Saraceni Collection
San Francisco Historical Photograph Collection
Seattle Rainiers File
The Sporting News Clipping & Transaction Card Files

Newspapers/Publications

Atlanta Journal-Constitution
Bakersfield Californian
Baltimore Afro-American
Baltimore Sun
Baseball Magazine
Boston Globe
Brooklyn Daily Eagle
Chicago Defender
Chicago Tribune
Detroit Free Press
Fresno Bee
Fresno Daily Republican
Los Angeles Herald
Los Angeles Times
Merced Sun–Star
Modesto Bee
New York Times
Oakland Times
Oakland Tribune
Orange County Register
Oregonian
Pittsburgh Post-Gazette
Reach-Spalding Baseball Guides 1903–1957
Sacramento Bee
Sacramento Union
St. Louis Post-Dispatch
Salt Lake City Telegram
Salt Lake City Tribune
San Diego Union-Tribune
San Francisco Call
San Francisco Chronicle

Books

Achorn, Edward. *Fifty-Nine in '84*. New York: Smith-
    sonian Books, 2010.
Armour, Mark, ed. *Rain Check; Baseball in the Pacific
    Northwest*. Cleveland, OH: Society for American
    Baseball Research, 2006.
Asinof, Eliot. *Eight Men Out*. New York: Holt Rine-
    hart and Winston, 1963.
Beverage, Richard. *The Angels: Los Angeles in the Pacific
    Coast League 1919–1957*. Placentia, CA: Deacon
    Press, 1981.
_____. *The Hollywood Stars, Baseball in Movieland,
    1926–1957*. Placentia, CA: Deacon Press, 1984.
Cramer, Richard Ben. *Joe DiMaggio, The Hero's Life*.
    New York: Simon & Schuster, 2000.
Crawford, Richard W., ed. *The Journal of San Diego
    History, Volume 41, Number 1*. Winter 1995. San
    Diego Historical Society.
Dawidoff, Nicholas. *The Catcher Was a Spy: The Mys-
    terious Life of Moe Berg*. New York: Vintage Books,
    1992.
Dewey, Donald, and Nicholas Acocella. *The Black
    Prince of Baseball: Hal Chase and the Mythology of
    the Game*. Wilmington, DE: Sports Media Publish-
    ing, 2004.
Dobbins, Dick. *The Grand Minor League: An Oral
    History of the Pacific Coast League*. Emeryville, CA:
    Woodford Press, 1999.
_____, and Jon Twitchell. *Nuggets on the Diamond*.
    San Francisco, CA: Woodford Press, 1994.
Fradkin, Philip. *The Great Earthquake and Firestorms
    of 1906: How San Francisco Nearly Destroyed Itself*.
    Berkeley: University of California Press, 2006.
Lange, Fred W. *History of Baseball in California and
    Pacific Coast Leagues 1847–1938*. Self-published,
    1938.
Leutzinger, Richard. *Lefty O'Doul: The Legend That
    Baseball Nearly Forgot*. Carmel, CA: Carmel Bay
    Publishing Group, 1997.
Macht, Norman L. *Connie Mack and the Early Years
    of Baseball*. Lincoln: University of Nebraska Press,
    2007.
Mackey, Scott R. *Barbary Baseball: The Pacific Coast
    League of the 1920s*. Jefferson, NC: McFarland, 1995.
Mulholland, Catherine. *William Mulholland and the*

Rise of Los Angeles. Berkeley: University of California Press, 2000.

O'Neal, Bill. *The Pacific Coast League, 1903–1988.* Austin, TX: Eakin Press, 1990.

Regalado, Samuel O. *Viva Baseball.* Champaign: University of Illinois Press, 1998.

Riley, James A. *The Biographical Encyclopedia of Negro League Baseball.* New York: Carroll & Graf, 1994.

Seymour, Harold, and Dorothy Seymour. *Baseball: The Early Years.* New York: Oxford University Press, 1960.

_____. *Baseball, The Golden Age.* New York: Oxford University Press, 1971.

Snelling, Dennis. *A Glimpse of Fame: Brilliant but Fleeting Major League Careers.* Jefferson, NC: McFarland, 1993.

_____. *The Pacific Coast League 1903–1957: A Statistical History.* Jefferson, NC: McFarland, 1995.

Society for American Baseball Research. *Minor League Baseball Stars, Volume I.* Manhattan, KS: Ag Press, 1984.

_____. *Minor League Baseball Stars, Volume II.* Manhattan, KS: Ag Press, 1985.

_____. *Minor League Baseball Stars, Volume III.* Cleveland, OH: SABR, 1992.

Spalding, John E. *Always on Sunday: The California Baseball League, 1886 to 1915.* Manhattan, KS: Ag Press, 1992.

_____. *Sacramento Senators and Solons: Baseball in California's Capital, 1886 to 1976.* Manhattan, KS: Ag Press, 1995.

Starr, Kevin. *America and the California Dream, 1850–1915.* New York: Oxford University Press, 1986.

Vitti, Jim. *Cubs on Catalina: A Scrapbook Full of Memories About a 30-Year Love Affair Between One of Baseball's Classic Teams and California's Most Fanciful Isle.* Bay City, CA: Settefrati Press, 2003.

Wilson, Nick C. *Early Latino Ballplayers in the United States.* Jefferson, NC: McFarland, 2005.

Articles

Beaumont, C.P. "A Training School for Baseball Stars." *Baseball Magazine,* 1916.

Brown, Gary. "Jigger Statz: A Study in Longevity." *Sunday Republican,* October 3, 1982.

Brown, Warren W. "Will There Be a Third Major League?" Baseball Magazine, April 1919.

Cattau, Daniel. "So, Maybe There Really Is Such a Thing as a Natural." *Smithsonian Magazine,* 1991.

Center, Bill. "Pitches in Time." *San Diego Union-Tribune,* April 4, 2004.

Clifton, Guy. "Foundation to Carry on Bud Beasley's Legacy of Helping Kids." *Reno Gazette-Journal,* May 17, 2005.

Cooper, Tony. "Breaking the PCL Color Barrier." *San Francisco Chronicle,* March 1, 1993.

Crowe, Jerry. "At This Game, the Baseball Players Didn't Pull Any Punches." *Los Angeles Times,* June 11, 2007.

Dasso, Frank. Undated autobiographical sketch.

Endsley, Dan. "West Coast Baseball: Too Big for Its Britches." *Harper's Magazine,* October 1946.

Erickson, Steve. "Fastball Gone, but Submarine Style Remains with Ad Liska." *Oregonian,* August 20, 1974.

Faber, Urban. "The Vanishing Spitball." *Baseball Magazine,* September 1922.

Fimrite, Ron. "O Lucky Man—A Twist of Fate Save Jack Lohrke from the Worst Tragedy in Minor League History." *Sports Illustrated,* November 14, 1994.

Garcia, Gilberto. "Beisboleros, Latin Americans and Baseball in the Northwest, 1914–1937." *Columbia, The Magazine of Northwest History,* Fall 2002.

Goates, Les. "Angel of Salt Lake Baseball Has Been Wrapped Up in Diamond Sport All His Life." *Deseret News,* April 24, 1948.

Graham, Frank, Jr. "The Great Mexican War of 1946." *Sports Illustrated,* September 19, 1966.

Graham, Thomas F. "Putting Over the Next Big League: How the Pacific Coast Has Developed the Fastest Minor League in the Country." *Sunset, The Pacific Monthly,* July 1914.

Graham, Tom. "Sunday Interview—Gladys Hansen." *San Francisco Chronicle,* April 14, 1996.

Gregory, L.H. "Beaver Bosses I Have Known." *Sunday Oregonian,* February 20, 1944.

Hawthorn, Tom. "Black Pitcher Threw World a Curve." *Toronto Globe and Mail,* May 29, 2006.

Herbert, Ian. "Debating Louis Castro: Was He the First Foreign-Born Hispanic in the Major Leagues?" *Smithsonian Magazine,* September 2007.

Hern, Gary. "Strand's Story of Record Flop." *Baseball Digest,* September 1951.

Herron, Gary. "Gene Handley Discusses Long Career." *Sports Collectors Digest,* October 12, 1990.

Hoe, S.H. "America Invaded by Oriental Foes." *Baseball Magazine,* March 1914.

Kelley, Brent. "Joe Brovia Talks About the PCL Days." *Sports Collectors Digest,* December 1, 1989.

Kernan, Kevin. "Down Memory Lane: Old Stadium Still Draws Smiles, Yearnings." *San Diego Union-Tribune,* June 9, 1996.

Kofoed, J.C. "The California Comet." *Baseball Magazine,* July 1917.

Lane, F.C. "The Most Remarkable Comeback on Record." *Baseball Magazine,* July 1917.

_____. "A Rising Menace to the Game." *Baseball Magazine,* August 1918.

Lemke, Bob. "Bad News Bees, Part I—Bees' Pitcher Stung Angels by Throwing Games." *Sports Collectors Digest,* September 3, 1993.

_____. "Bad News Bees, Part II—Caught Red-Handed Taking Bribe Money." *Sports Collectors Digest,* September 10, 1993.

_____. "Bad News Bees, Part III—Rumler's Story Mix of Eight Men Out, Natural." *Sports Collectors Digest,* September 17, 1993.

_____. "Black Sox Had Nothing on Babe Borton." *Sports Collectors Digest,* August 27, 1993.

_____. "Pirates Pawnee Pitcher Went 'Way of All Bad Injuns.'" *Sports Collectors Digest,* March 4, 1994.

Nack, William. "The Razor's Edge." *Sports Illustrated*, May 6, 1991.

Newhouse, Dave. "Lee Susman Was Clearly Drawn to Be a Bay Area 'Toon Legend.'" *Oakland Tribune*, July 26, 2007.

Norris, Frank. "San Diego Baseball: The Early Years." *The Journal of San Diego History*, Winter 1984.

Orr, Jack. "The Worst Fielder Anybody Ever Saw." *Sport Magazine*, June 1956.

Picini, Le. "The Pennant Race of 1929." *San Francisco Sunday Examiner and Chronicle*, August 3, 1980.

Raley, Dan. "From Reds to Ruth to Rainiers: City's History Has Its Hits, Misses." *Seattle Post-Intelligencer*, July 14, 1999.

_____. "The Life and Times of Royal Brougham." *Seattle Post-Intelligencer*, October 29, 2003.

Saul, Brian. "A New Look at the Big Game." *Historical Happenings, A Publication of the Brea Historical Society*, August 2003.

Schulian, John. "Of Stars and Angels." *Sports Illustrated*, June 21, 1993.

Silitto, John. "'Our Tone': Tony Lazzeri's Baseball Career in Salt Lake City, 1922–1925." *Utah Historical Quarterly*, Fall 2004.

Statz, Arnold "Jigger." "Coast League Was Better in My Time." *Los Angeles Mirror-News,* January 21, 1957.

Stump, Al. "Requiem for a Mad Russian." *Major League Baseball Annual*, 1961.

Svanevik, Michael, and Shirley Burgett. "Belle of the Peninsula." *Palo Alto Daily News,* July 7, 2007.

Van Vliet, Jim. "Miracle of '42." *Sacramento Bee*, September 20, 1992.

Vermilyea, Natalie. "Kranks Delight: California Baseball 1858–1888." *The Californian*, March/April 1991.

Walter, Bucky. "A Remembrance of Joltin' Joe Brovia." *San Francisco Sunday Examiner and Chronicle,* September 30, 1979.

Ward, John J. "Hollocher, the Wizard Shortstop." *Baseball Magazine*, October 1917.

Wells, Donald R. "The Wartime Seattle Rainiers." Presentation at SABR 36, 2006.

Williams, Jack. "John Ritchey, 80; 'Johnny Baseball' Was First Black in the PCL." *San Diego Union Tribune*, January 21, 2003.

Index

Numbers in **bold italics** indicate pages with photographs.